The Journals

Volume Two

ALSO BY JOHN FOWLES

FICTION

The Collector

The Aristos

The Magus

The French Lieutenant's Woman

The Ebony Tower

Daniel Martin

Mantissa

A Maggot

NONFICTION

Poems

Shipwreck

Islands

The Tree

The Enigma of Stonehenge

A Short History of Lyme Regis

Lyme Regis Camera

Wormholes

The Journals, Volume I

The Journals

Volume Two: 1966–1990

JOHN FOWLES

Edited and with an introduction
by Charles Drazin

Northwestern University Press

Evanston, Illinois

Northwestern University Press
www.nupress.northwestern.edu

Copyright © 2006 by JR Fowles Ltd. Introduction and notes
copyright © 2006 by Charles Drazin. Northwestern University
Press paperback edition published 2008 by arrangement
with Alfred A. Knopf, a division of Random House, Inc.

Printed in the United States of America

10 9 8 7 6 5 4 3 2 1

ISBN 978-0-8101-2515-5

Library of Congress Cataloging-in-Publication data

Fowles, John, 1926–2005.
  The journals / John Fowles ; edited and with an introduction by Charles Drazin.—Northwestern University Press
paperback ed.
    v. cm.
    Originally published: London : Jonathan Cape,
2003–2006.
    Includes index.
    Contents: v. 1. 1949–1965—v. 2. 1966–1990.
    ISBN 978-0-8101-2514-8 (v. 1 : alk. paper)—ISBN 978-
0-8101-2515-5 (v. 2 : alk. paper)
    1. Fowles, John, 1926–2005—Diaries. 2. Novelists,
English—20th century—Diaries. I. Drazin, Charles, 1960–
II. Title.
PR6056.O85Z466 2009
828'.91403—dc22
[B]
                                                2008031048

∞ The paper used in this publication meets the minimum
requirements of the American National Standard for
Information Sciences—Permanence of Paper for Printed
Library Materials, ANSI Z39.48-1992.

Editor's Acknowledgements

In the course of editing the two volumes of John Fowles's journals, I have often needed to consult John himself, his wife Sarah, his agent Anthony Sheil and his publisher Dan Franklin. I would like to thank them all for their unstinting support and encouragement.

Illustrations

1. John outside Belmont House, *c.* 1968
2. Elizabeth, John and Anna, Lyme Regis, 1966
3. Eileen Porter, Leonora Smith, Elizabeth Fowles, Anna Christy and Fred Porter, *c.* 1966
4. John in Lyme Regis high street
5. Ned Bradford and his wife, Pamela, on Cape Cod, *c.* 1967
6. Tom Maschler in his office at Jonathan Cape
7. Belmont House, Lyme Regis
8. John and Elizabeth at Belmont House
9. Anna Christy's wedding to Nick Homoky, July 1974, in the garden at Belmont: Nick Homoky, Roy Christy, John Fowles, Anna Christy, Boris Wiseman, Elizabeth Fowles, Ian Friend and Fred Porter
10. John Fowles, Malou Wiseman and Tom Wiseman on the beach at Lyme Regis, 1974
11. On the set of *The French Lieutenant's Woman*: Harold Pinter, John Fowles and Karel Reisz, 1980
12. At the BAFTAs, 1982: Jeremy Irons, Antonia Fraser, Elizabeth Fowles, John Fowles, Harold Pinter, Sinead Cusack
13. John in the garden at Belmont, 1995

All photographs are from the collection of John Fowles and are reproduced by permission. Photograph no. 1 is by Colin Graham for *Dorset – the county magazine*; nos. 4 and 8 are by Terry Spencer; no. 6 is by Mike Hill; no. 10 is by David Tringham; no. 11 is by Ray Roberts; no. 13 is by Basso Cannarsa.

For Sarah

Introduction

A diary is perhaps the most attempted of all literary genres. Most of us have kept one at one time or another, even if we have no further ambition to write. This universal quality perhaps accounts for why the genre defies easy categorization – there can be no common set of rules that all diary-keepers observe. To appreciate a diary's significance, it is worth reflecting a little on its illusory, deceptive nature, even if it is written with the unsparing honesty that John Fowles has shown in both this published volume and the previous one. A diary is commonly regarded as a place for candour, but the haphazard, shifting nature of diary-writing must none the less call for countless provisos and qualifications.

To take the most basic definition, a diary is recorded experience. But what of the gaps when experience goes unrecorded? Do they mean that passing time has offered nothing notable to record or, on the contrary, has been so full of experience as to deny the leisure to record? It is impossible to know for certain whether such gaps indicate a dull time or an exciting time.

Then a diary's purpose can be as varied as the number of people who keep one. It can be little more than a list of events, providing a basic orientation in the world and intended for no eyes other than those of the writer; equally, with a possible view to future discovery or publication, it can be a vehicle for self-justification or self-promotion – able as much to hide the truth as to reveal it.

Nor in any one case should we assume a consistent, fixed purpose, whether the diary in question is just a collection of crude notes or amounts to a polished memoir. All depends on the nature of both the first recording of experience and the subsequent revision. The seemingly simple, artless diary can be a lie – whether through calculation or self-delusion – and the highly contrived one as close to the truth as we are likely to get.

John Fowles has called the collection of fragments and different, often contradictory selves that comprise his journals 'disjoints'. Inevitably, these disjoints have taken on the colour of time and circumstance, as John's diary has passed through many different phases over the years. Exercise book in which to practice and hone the craft of writing; critique of books, plays and films; travelogue; confessional; notes of a passionate naturalist – the diary has been all these things.

This ever-changing quality is an essential characteristic. So too the fact that John uses his diary as the natural place for the spontaneous, unguarded impression. One of the great practical benefits of a diary is that it affords an arena in which you do not have to be correct or fair. It is a crucible of thoughts into which you can throw insights and prejudices alike. This freedom to think can facilitate observations of extraordinary perception but also of great foolishness. To preserve the spirit of the diary is to admit the validity of both. It is the home for the unreasonable self as much as the reasonable self – maybe even the means for the one to become the other.

Many selves make an appearance in these journals, but it is Fowles the writer who is finally the ringmaster. It is a self, which, in its quest to penetrate the surface of things, can make often merciless, uncompromising judgements, but it does so always with an egalitarian eye and as much at its own expense as at the expense of others. Ever probing and curious, the diarist refuses to accept things at face value, but goes on burrowing and questioning indefatigably. It is the same intellectual hunger that made John Fowles one of the most inventive novelists of his generation. Not content to accept established form or convention, always seeking new ways of telling, he was always first a writer, never a career author.

The writers who most matter are those who can best offer an insight into the human condition. As this second volume progresses, John comes increasingly to question his identity as an author in worldly terms, but he never falls short of this deeper purpose. The less he *feels* like an 'author', the more his true writer's self drives him on to articulate all the confusions of life. The voice that animates the diary finally belongs less to a noted literary figure than to a human being, remarkably free of vanity, who – through his very fallibility and frailty – is able to give touching resonance to life's inevitable ordeals.

This second volume provides the continuation of a narrative that began in Oxford a decade and a half previously. But to the extent that it consists of a necessarily pruned accumulation of spontaneous observations it differs from a more conventional narrative. As we resume the journey, it is worth remarking on the peculiar phenomenon of 'diary time', which can speed up or slow down according to the writer's degree of engagement with his journal. During the years of the first volume, John's diary played an intimate part in his development – a kind of engine room for thought and creativity – so that these crucial years of metamorphosis from undergraduate into successful author pass by at a leisurely pace. In this second volume, the relationship is through many years more casual and intermittent. Indeed, for three years between 1977 and 1980, John does not keep a diary at all. 'I don't know why, these last few weeks, I feel inclined to start again,' he writes when he picks up his pen again. It's impossible to give the definite answer that John is unable to find himself, but with hindsight we can at least speculate on the reasons for this resumption.

There is a tendency to respond to the moments of particular crisis and to capture the defining moments in his life – not the smoothly flowing years of professional achievement, but the disruptions and challenges. So in this second volume, for example, the first half of the 1980s zoom by, with such major highlights as the production of the successful film version of *The French Lieutenant's Woman* in 1981 or the publication of the novel *A Maggot* in 1985 receiving few entries, but then after John suffers a stroke in early 1988 the resulting turbulence seems to demand a deeper level of engagement. The 'diary time' switches down a gear to allow for a more intense focus.

Assuming a renewed importance, the diary operates not only as an aid with which to make sense of more difficult times, but also as his chief literary pursuit. The genius for narrative expresses itself not in a subsequent novel – although that novel is often mused over – but in chronicling the fortunes of himself and his wife Elizabeth. As they succumb to what John uses an ancient Greek word to describe, *keraunos* – the lightning of fate, the unanswerable – the diary can, in the latter wounded years, make rather grim reading, but the continuing narrative power, in spite of all that has been endured, offers a re-affirmation of a talent that remains true to what it is and has been.

Just as the first published volume of John's journals – distilled from the much longer original material – naturally took the form of a series of life stages, so this second volume seemed to call for a simple two-part structure, with the division provided by the break in the journals between 1977 and 1980. These years during which John kept no diary at all mark some kind of a sea-change. Passing through a hidden door, the John Fowles who resumes his diary in the autumn of 1980 is quite another self from the one who put it aside three years previously.

While the John Fowles of the first part, seemingly comfortable with his status as famous, bestselling author, is confident in his outlook and forthright in his often uncompromising judgements, the John Fowles of the second is gentler, less arrogant and more sceptical about literary achievement. The notion of 'John Fowles' – that strange creature who inhabits the spinners and dumpbins of the world's bookshops – slips into quotemarks, as he becomes increasingly aware of the gulf between the world's perception of him, and who he really is. He now lives in the shadow of the myth, doubt replacing the earlier certainty and self-assurance.

A dominant theme to emerge is the death or deconstruction of the successful author he appears to be. Yet at the same time another – in many ways more admirable – self is re-assembled out of the fragments. If this more reclusive figure seems to have turned his back firmly on the literary limelight, it's not because he feels any less devotion to the cause of literature, but on the contrary because he recognizes the truth of Emily Dickinson's observation that 'publication is not the business of poets', and because he knows that poetry is not only to be found in literature itself.

An equally dominant theme in this concluding volume of the journals is nature, which John has always recognized as by far the most profound influence in his life. Whatever misfortunes may overtake him in the latter stages of his journals, they are hugely offset by the contentment he has always found in the natural world. He has often written about the domain – the secluded, idyllic place that is out of time, beyond narrative, whose satisfactions lie not in any kind of doing but in simply being there. His own garden in Lyme, walks through the surrounding Dorset countryside, even watching the birds on the lake in Regent's Park during an otherwise reluctant visit to London – all are examples of this. As he travels through France, a day spent observing the flora and fauna is described as 'heaven'. On a holiday in Crete, a mountain meadow, rich in many different varieties of wild orchid, is the 'happy valley'. Even when his situation is at its most bleak, these domains provide far more than just a simple refuge: they are a source of lasting peace and fulfilment.

John continued to keep a diary long after the last page of this published volume. To this extent, the fact that it finishes where it does is arbitrary, but I believe that this ending does justice to the most insistent and haunting of all the stories that pull these disjoints together.

Charles Drazin
July 2005

Part One

Underhill Farm, Lyme Regis, 5 December 1965
The purity of the sun here: white, silver, gold. I have never been more conscious of it. And of how the sea changes in texture, colour, transparency – especially the first. If the waves run from the west they catch in the evening a kind of imperceptible brownish glaze on the westward slopes; the eastward are a glaucous grey-green. Very much the soft light in early aquatints.

Boredom with books, talk about ideas and books, trends and cultures, the intellectual life of our day; it is like a flood, a natural disaster. So many voices. Finally they blend into a universal scream.

Rats: they come round the back door at night and when we come out, blinded by the light, they cannon off walls and take all the wrong exits. I could have killed one the other night. But even a rat has a right to live.

Podge has been here.[1] He is anti-peace, anti-country, anti-nature, neurotic and disruptive, quirking out his endless questions, harping on sex, sexual freedom. His life seems a flailing fall, sometimes, a clutching at all around him. To arrest the fall, poor man; and to bring everything he clutches on down with him – it seems more that. He depresses us. And it rains, rains. The Aga oven goes out – and fire here is as precious as it was to primitive man. We feel desolate, and the moon glitters cruelly. On a hostile sea.

10 December
Finished the film treatment of *The Magus*, thank God.

The effect of leisure on sensibility. Most writers before this century had far more time to *see*; that is, they were steeped in objects to a degree we cannot imagine – the very word 'contemplate' is archaic now. Economic conditions have forced writers – and painters – to see (as well as create) far too briefly. Impressionism may have been born out of a boredom with academic art, but it must also have sprung from a need to create more quickly, to pack more into the time available: to put it absurdly, Impressionism was caused by a shortage of servants.

[1] 'Podge' is Fred Porter, JF's Marxist friend, whom he first met when they were both students at Oxford. See introduction to *The Journals*, volume 1, page xiii.

Dell have given $125,000 for the US paperback rights of *The Magus*. It drives Eliz into a mysterious evening of bad temper. In some way such good news always comes to her as a threat to security, to love – since love is a pact between inadequacies. The highest figure we hoped for was 60 or 70,000 . . . But of course I can't touch any of it. It really is meaningless. I still have to write begging letters to the bank to continue my £5,000 overdraft.

18 December

A terrible bitterness in Eliz these days. She seems determined to destroy our life here; not to settle in, not to make any compromises – everything must be perfect, and when it isn't she flies into a rage. Not to give me any tolerance at all if I disappear for an hour to the fields, if I spend a morning writing. Everything is futile, everything a waste of time . . . She hates the country, she hates the house, she hates me, she hates my life as a writer and of course she hates herself into the bargain. Living here has become rather like climbing a mountain with a corpse, a talking corpse, on one's back. Every so often there are compensations: views, moments of happiness. But then the corpse starts complaining, raging . . .

She seems to have entered a phase of her life where the masculine side is dominant. She's always talking of not being able to lead the life she wants, have the interests she wants, do the things she wants . . . But all these resentments are idealized. I can't get her to understand that she has no strong interests, no overwhelming desires and the basic trouble is not in the non-satisfaction of them, but in their non-existence; and that the solution to that predicament is love, not hatred. I never talk to her, I need her only as a cook, a valet, and so on . . . But even if that were true (as it must always be partly true, and I could as well say she needs me only as money-provider, coal-fetcher, admirer of her interior decoration, and so on), it still isn't a gross indignity, a failure. She has a violent antipathy to the notion of charity and service. The latest tempest is because I want to give Jonathan[1] five pounds for Christmas – I'm an ostentatious snob she tells me, I'm ridiculous. But I have earned over seventy thousand pounds this last fortnight. It doesn't seem much. I want to give little presents to Jane,[2] to a woman down the lane here; but no, her face stiffens, stiff like the faces of those people in medieval pictures descending into hell. They rarely look terrified; but stiffly, resentfully dropping into the lakes of fire.

If only equability, gentleness, calm helped. I realize now that they don't; if anything they make things worse and the more reason I show

[1] Born in August 1965, Jonathan is the son of JF's sister Hazel and her husband Daniel O'Sullivan.
[2] JF's cousin Jane Richards, who lived in Lyme.

the more anger I invite. She has cast herself as the implacably discontented, and so now my contentment (or the thin mask of it I wear) is the chief irritant. I think if I broke down and sobbed and said I couldn't go on she would be her old self. But I won't so deny both reason and love.

America, 3 January 1966
Night at a hotel by London Airport. The sound of the jets boiling up into the darkness. Going further than this world, and somehow this seems beautiful, this new power of voyage; though in reality it is uglier than any other way of travelling in the history of man.

4 January
To Boston. New England is sharp cold, but in a brilliant clear sunlight. At dusk it is a black and orange city, very arctic and attractive in colour, though a mess architecturally. Flowers from Ned Bradford,[1] whiskey from Julian,[2] we feel enveloped by the Roman generosity to favoured guests. Once again the Roman qualities of America overwhelm one: everything based on power, on mean gold rather than the golden mean. America is in a way the inability to think of gold metaphorically.

7 January
Formal lunch at the Union Club – old Arthur Thornhill,[3] who is cock-a-hoop after the huge Dell sale, made me a speech of welcome which tailed delightfully off into a sharp attack on the executives present: 'Joe, you want to get your men doing more legwork' . . . 'Bob, you haven't asked my opinion on those covers, but Mr Fowles is one of the family now and just let me say that I think they're all lousy and if that's the best we can do . . .' The others grin and bear it and I feel great affection for Yankees and Boston. He's faultlessly mean and we all love it.

Out in the afternoon to stay at Marshfield with the Bradfords. It sleets, the landscapes are dour as they are dour – kind, dour, reserved people. As always with them, and in this house, I feel very close to the deepest and most admirable qualities in America – qualities that are fundamentally English, but purer than we've kept them. We passed the Bradford house the next afternoon; Ned's ancestors came here in 1620. He has an Indian great-grandmother, but otherwise he remains English, three hundred

---

[1] JF's editor at Little, Brown, the publisher of his books in America.
[2] Julian Bach, JF's literary agent in America.
[3] Arthur H. Thornhill, senr. (1895–1970), was then chairman of Little, Brown. His son Arthur H. Thornhill, junr., had succeeded him as chief executive and president of the company in 1962.

and fifty years of blood on this England-facing seaboard, in this English climate . . . Standing on the beach at Cohasset the next morning, we watched huge rollers spuming in. Three centuries of standing there waiting for sails from the east. One could not emigrate to this part of America. It is too drenched in the past, in men too English to remain English in the face of colonial injustice.

9 January
Down to New York with Bob Fetridge.[1] All the public transport has stopped, which has hung up everything to do with the book. People can't think about books, all the news space goes to the strike. I feel a kind of absurd guilt. In this world a quick success – and a huge success – are all that matter. There are no halfway houses.

The *height* of New York, the feeling of an art form (the skyscraper) that has turned to madness. Sanity is that narrow space of sky at the end of each cross-street. Though the press is full of woe, there's very little sense, in midtown, of anything abnormal taking place. By London standards the 'grim and paralysing' traffic conditions seem almost easy. But the Americans live much further from chaos, dirt and disorder than we do. A civilization that has made a mania of being discreet and well-groomed (I have seen only two other beards since we arrived, and one of those was on an Orthodox Jew) has a thin wall between it and trouble. All cities are precarious; but none more than this.

10 January
Curious, the last time I was here, I noticed the skyscrapers. This time it is the cold blue columns of air at the end of each wall of windows. We buy *Time* – a savagely bad review. Don't worry, says everybody, no one reads *Time* for book reviews, they always mug the second novel, they're as sick as junkies . . . But it hurts. There is this recurrent simile – one is in a boxing-ring, but with one's hands tied. And the hazard of it all: a dozen men and women's chance mood, taste, temper. The analogy with the jury is false, since these are permanent jurors, and finally more interested in conviction than exculpation.

18 January
Party at Julian's. Barbara Tuchman was there, a quiet grey woman a little insipid and elsewhere, like all good writers, or good women writers, anyway.[2] Sidney Carroll, the man who wrote the script for that fine film

---

[1] Little, Brown's head of publicity.
[2] Barbara Tuchman (1912–1989) was a popular historian. She won the Pulitzer Prize for her book *The Guns of August* (1962), which chronicled the events that caused the First World War.

The Hustler; a pock-faced, bitter yet humane man. I liked him at once. A grotesque woman in her mid-forties in the most exiguous black dress I have ever seen.

The feeling here that the novel is a condemned form, has a few decades more of life and then will disappear – this is in spite of the huge prices paid for paperback and film rights. Quite what will take its place no one seems to know – or stops to imagine; nor does anyone appear to realize that there are countless things a novel can do that no other art form ever can. Other species are beginning to encroach and grow upon novel territory; but there is a lot of ground left. Eternally ground where it will grow, since human modes of apprehension and ability to analyse and fantasize constantly change.

For all that, fiction figures are down last year in both the US and Britain. And the look-out for the amateur novelist is poor. Little, Brown take about one in four or five hundred non-agency MSS. They receive some 1,400 MSS a year. With novels, they break even at about the 6,000 copies mark. Even with *The Magus* (the first three prints come to 37,500) the profit on the hardback edition will be minor compared to the sale to Literary Guild and Dell. In a way it is immaterial to them now whether the hardback edition sells or not.

The sexlessness of American women – there is a sort of compact well-groomed hardness about them, a sexiness learnt by recipe, an assertiveness that really asserts the opposite of what is intended: a queasy masculinity rather than an offered femininity. Of course men (and the whole society) must partly cause this: but it's distressing how few rebels there are. How so many women here assume their Americaneity.

No quietness, no tenderness.

Getting drunk with Arnold Ehrlich in the evening.[1] He is as good a New Yorker as Ned Bradford is a New Englander: salt and cynical, savage about America. I told him I wanted to write a book about America, and I needed a question that would also be a quest. He said: '"Who wants to think?"'

'Why is this a country where practically no one ever wants to think? Where everyone wants just to live and have fun? Why is this the only country in the world where you can go on retaining your most stupid national characteristics? Is that freedom – to be so stupid?'

It is a good question, and touches on what I feel more and more here: that the American way of life is a shorthand, a digest, a synopsis, a package tour . . . Not the real thing. I mean a driving past certain gates and interstices that to the American seem perhaps unimportant,

---

[1] Arnold Ehrlich (1923–1989) was a contributor to, and later editor of, the American trade magazine *Publishers Weekly*.

insignificant . . . but that lead to great fields, beautiful and fertile landscapes of experience.

Instant existing, like instant coffee. It's almost as good as real coffee
and easier to use. But it presupposes that quality is far less important
than consumption.

22 January
To Miami, to meet John and Jud.[1] Neat platters of houses, like trays with
canapés, float in the stagnant glaucous-green lagoons. The day is grey,
sultry, a warm bath after the astringent cold of New York. The palm-trees
stand limply, a little frightened, as if waiting for a typhoon. I think Miami
performs the incredible, and is actually an uglier town than Los Angeles.
I loathed it. Even the warm air seemed a product of machinery rather
than nature. We drove to Miami Beach, where a monstrous regiment of
huge hotels stand whitely against the stale Caribbean. To see the size and
vulgarity of these establishments, the Fontainebleau, the Eden Roc, the
Doral, is the only reason to go to the place: they are so vile, so nightmarish,
so (alas) American, that they cannot be missed. In a way it is a city of
the dead – all the people there are old, uninspired, industrial debris. In
the lifts the women of fifty and sixty stand like cattle. One has to push
them aside to get out. They drift round the lounges like somnambulists,
from meal to meal, from room to room, bound, chained, as the black
slaves were once chained in the slave ships, to a moronic routine in a
moronic world.

In a way it is a European city, a monument to the dream of countless
generations of underprivileged European peasants. They dreamt of an
aristocratic city like Venice, perhaps; and they translated it, when they
had the chance, into Miami.

Jud's current director calls it 'the painted toenail of America'. But it
needs some fouler apposition: the unwiped anus. All that is worst in the
country pours through it, and stands to be seen.

We sit in a hotel room going through the treatment I have done for
The Magus; my sense of reality fights John Kohn's sense of showmanship.
Everything with him is fuck and unfuck; he ruins all the details. Yet he
is good on that mysterious film god, Structure. I like him more. Under
the violence, the boyish love of athletics, of being a good Jewish father,
of being simple on one level and devious on another (business), lurks
a likeable man.

No primary producers. One never sees people gardening in the
States; or farming. No link with the soil. This emptiness between city
and city reproduces that other emptiness, that driving past the subtler

[1] John Kohn and Jud Kinberg, the American screenwriter/producers who had
produced the film version of JF's first novel *The Collector*.

gates of life; that oversimplification that ruins America artistically and intellectually.

No ink calligraphy. Everyone uses ballpoint pens.

24 January
Up to New York, and cold, and straight on to London.

Cold and wet and grey. A very English couple beside us at breakfast in the airport hotel. Mumbling cliché sentences to each other; little empty statements about nothing. Wife: 'Are you going to have another coffee?' Husband: 'Are you?' Wife: 'Um – no.' Husband: 'Oh, well I . . .' (trails into silence, then half a minute later) ' . . . I don't know, perhaps I will have another coffee.' Wife: 'Have it if you want to.' Husband: 'All right. Oh, waiter, I'll have another cup of coffee.' (The waiter pours it.) 'May as well.'

Nostalgia then for America; not because what the two said was silly – I knew a whole current of other things was being said: about their relationship, the concessions they made to each other, all through tone, pauses, not saying what they meant. But only a very old and decadent culture can produce such mysterious dialogue – mysterious and defeated. America lives, and England dies. The popularity of English art, English pop singers, English reviewers, English novelists like myself, in America today is as suspect as the Athenian 'cult' in ancient Rome. It is time-out from reality, not the reality. We entertain them, but we do not instruct or lead them in any sense.

We drive down – Eliz, brave girl, drives me down – through a grey damp day, streaks of snow on the Wiltshire hills, to Lyme Regis. The sadness, smallness, dampness of England; the little cars trying to be grown up – this feeble stretching out after Power, Technological Control, all that America has.

The house is cold, damp, sulking, minus its heart – the Aga cooker has been torn out and the old fireplace rebuilt. Eliz moans, cries every half hour, it is all so far from America, from central heating, comfort, the world at a button's end. But in a way the trip has confirmed for me our move here. It has rationalized what was largely instinctive, a feeling that the city and its increasingly Americanized culture ('culture' in the anthropological sense) is unpoetic, unreal, passing far too many unseen gates. I agreed in Miami to do the film script (and all it will entail) but I could agree only out of the life we lead here, the certainty that I have a place where I can shut out all the jet-life, the chase-after-success. I need the sea, the darkness at nights; in a way I even need the coldness, the damp, all the living problems this old bitch of a place poses. One must retreat at my age into what one is; stop running after the dream images; condense; protect what the age assaults or ignores.

31 January
Day after day of grey mist, grey drizzles out of the west. It is mild, but as damp as the tropics. The moss on the walls permanently beaded with winter dew.

And I stay in a grey mist over the book. No news for a week. It is like sending a rocket into space – losing contact with it. It is somewhere out there, someone must be reading it, it is being bought or not bought, on course or not on course for bestsellerdom. The strange thing is that no one writes – no letters from readers, either good or bad. The same thing happened with *The Collector*. So I am the rocket as well. The abysses between things.

Started on the script. Much more enjoyable than the treatment; and I think a good discipline – to be so forced to prune to essentials.

12 February
A big batch of late reviews from the States. Most of them are favourable. But more and more I know the pleasure is *in* the book – in the writing of it, above all . . . also in having it past, part of one. All the rest – the reviews good and bad, the money – clings, clogs, but finally goes, uneasy water off my back. The worst are the interviews. I am getting to the stage where I feel I never want to have another interview in my life. A boy called Nicholas Tresilian, fresh from Cambridge, came the other day. 'Are you a serious writer?' Then before I could answer: 'No, sorry, that's a silly question.' And terrible misrepresentations in some of the United States interviews. Pray God no one ever reads them for the truth.

14 February
A morning still as death, but a beautiful floating death, mist on the sea, first faint sunlight, a morning like a resurrection. I was at the bottom wall . . . Suddenly out of the light over the sea a faint soughing of wings, almost the whetting of a great scythe, louder and louder and moving westwards. For a few moments it seemed to fill the sky. I thought it must be some weird machine down on the Cobb but it moved over the sea well away from Lyme and down below me. Swans; and the sound magnified in some bizarre way. But the extraordinary thing is that I never saw them, though I had the Zeiss with me and visibility was good for at least two miles. Just the grey still sea and the huge winnowing wings.

16 February
Stormy days with Eliz – in contrast with the actual weather. She hates 'the silence, the space, the emptiness' – all the things I love, alas. Not that there is much emptiness here in springtime. The land gallops into

its summer. Then the house: it is 'bleak, a mess, a monstrosity'. I like the central heating noise, she hates it. She went to see the doctor at Uplyme, a nice old man, but he could give her only nice-old-man advice about outside interests and social work; this 'take up social work' is the modern equivalent of some Smilesian exhortation: Rise with a smile, Find your pleasure in duty – hopelessly inadequate. I trace most of her anxiety and hatred of this place and this life to the separation trauma we discovered in her dreams. All her positions are really based on the assumption that the future is hostile to the past. Things were always better *before*. Then she is obsessed by efficiency and order – a sort of idealism that comes from a broken education, a belief in never-never land where all machines work perfectly, all workmen are faultless, everything is planned to perfection.

Then she accuses me of never writing anything 'nice' about her here. But her personality is no longer very distinct in my mind from my own. It's an effort to write of her as 'her' – not quite, but almost as hard as it would be to write of myself as 'him'. 'He looked very handsome this morning', 'I loved him when he laughed', 'He cooked a lovely meal' – how can one say such things?

Love needs its theology. We need some phrase like the 'assumption of indivisibility', in the category of the trans-substantiation and the immaculate conception, in which people may or may not believe.

During one of her rows I told her that this place she hated so much was like living a poem. It is. A poem, a book of hours, a symposium of all the springs that ever were and will be. I wander round the fields in a sort of trance. Just as I feel physically so much healthier here, I feel a new (a revived) immediacy of impression. I had it when I was a schoolboy, but then it was clogged and clouded by all sorts of false notions about the importance of names, all the pseudo-scientific rubbish of twentieth-century adolescence. Though lines of poetry come, no poems come – in a way this is like Greece, it is too immediate, too constituted by poems of phenomenon, a constant flux of actual poetic events. The linnets that haunt the garden (because I am a bad gardener and the fescue is rampant) with their fine Stravinsky-like songs and their ancient Chinese harp flight calls; the first pale, huge violets on the big 'step' down to the sea; finding a bed of moschatel in the woods; the wonderful owls that haunt our nights; a flock of fifty oystercatchers, black, white, coral-red against a pearl-grey sea; the grey-black depths in a watching rabbit's eyes – these things are poems in their language, and in a way to write poems in mine about them is not creative, but merely a matter of translation.

22 April

Anna is with us.[1] She is assuming a certain problem aspect: a kind of demandingness that it isn't simple enough just to answer. Her insecurity is now used to extort privileges from Eliz – the main requirement being that Eliz should fulfil the role of the intelligent chum Anna seems to lack in London. She has there a series of lame ducks; while a meeting with Charlie Greenberg's academically clever daughter makes her prickle like a porcupine.[2] Eliz sides with her: 'Rebecca is a snobbish little prig,' and so on. Probably she is, but Anna's defence mechanism is not really the girls – it is flight. *Of course* she is not in any way to blame. Even if there was not her past, there is her present: the Victorian climate at Putney, where she seems to be half skivvy, half housemaid to the younger children. But she has to be understood – for her own good. Her need is to be disemotionalized: the one destructive quality Eliz and Roy share is a self-will that is highly emotional in derivation and effect and which she has inherited. Both she and Eliz have developed an animus against the Greenbergs, who are brash and brutal in emotional terms, but fundamentally an intelligent and enthusiastic family – and so extroverts who aggravate any insecurity in introversion. One senses in Anna a terrible and yet wistful love-hatred of the grammar-school stream, of extroverts, of people like myself who are not extroverts but are 'successful' introverts – enemies in her own camp, really. Eliz reproaches me for not being kinder to her, nicer to her, though I try to be these things without falling over into a false-jovial extrovert self – which Anna would spot as false at once. But it is fiendishly difficult to get far when I am cast as the adult the two sixteen-year-old chums escape from; the odd figure who fiddles about in the garden and the fields, who watches birds and collects flowers. The Greenbergs came to stay when she left and brought their younger daughter with them: a pert, knowing, precocious little creature, but free of that intense absorption in her own personal emotional problems. Eliz loathes her eagerness, her pertness, her constant questions and fey interruptions; and normally I probably would as well. But like her parents, she came as fresh air into an overheated room. Or not temperature, light; objects in sunlight and objects in the shadows.

[1] Elizabeth's then fifteen-year-old daughter, Anna Christy, was being brought up by her father Roy Christy, Elizabeth's first husband, and his new wife Judy (*née* Boydell).

[2] Charlie Greenberg was a Canadian architect who had been a friend of Roy Christy since the early 1950s, when they had taught together at the Kingston College of Art and Architecture.

25 April

In London, working on the script of *The Magus* with John Kohn. We stay in a filthy American tourists' hotel – the Washington – in Curzon Street. All the staff are foreign and bloody-minded, beaten into indifference. The weather is fine, temperatures in the seventies, our chests choke with the petrol-fumes, there are all our personal problems – I hate the city. Waking up at night, men screaming with rage at each other, a car being revved fiercely up and down the street below, wild drunken shouts. London *has* changed (I have changed too, but it is not all subjective) this last six months – it seems hellbent on pleasure, on going young, a city of the plain the night before God struck.

Eliz went mad the first day, and had her hair dyed a sort of Middle European red-brown and bought a dress that didn't suit her at all, that was a regression to the days at Heal's, a scramble back into her past that upset both of us. As if London alone was not enough.

The Magus comes out on May 2nd. A meeting with various literary editors at a lunch thrown by Cape; like being a horse *and* hearing the comments as he is led round the paddock. Not that they are anything but discreetly polite to my face; but I can hear behind their words. No one is further from a writer than a writer about writers; one's simplicity (given by the fact of creating), and their cynicism, their *tout vu, tout lu.*

Betsa Payne:[1] in trouble again, her life is empty, she won't go out. Perhaps agoraphobia is simply a metaphor for the inner emptiness. There is a facade of normality over their life and yet a bewildering paradoxality: that having near enough of everything should produce such stunted, unhappy life-forms. They are what we threaten to be; and though Eliz seems brisk and practical beside Betsa, there is an ominous element of identification: the next paratrooper to jump watching the one before plunge. Again the basic trouble seems to be this intense absorption in self: self seen as totally unconnected with external circumstance. A staring at self in a mirror – another metaphor for the Eliz–Betsa relationship. Neither will tolerate any outside interest, any energy that threatens to take their eyes away, to divert. Eliz says I am the most self-absorbed of all, but there is a distinction between living in a self-centred world and a self-absorbed one: the first interprets the world through the self, but can still live largely in external objects and aims, whereas the second literally absorbs and destroys all that is outside. I can get out of my own sloughs of despond by using the objects around me. But for the self-absorbed there are no objects around: all is self. It is like trying to lift oneself with one's own arms.

[1] The wife of Ronnie Payne, JF's friend from Bedford School and Oxford.

8 May
Reviews: two 'soli' in the *Times* and the *Observer*. A sour one from Angus Wilson, the hermaphroditic voice of the traditional (twentieth-century) English novel chastising the new. A totally expectable one – all vinegar – from Penelope Mortimer. Various sorts of in-between reviews; a few good. Cape will be gloomy. I don't really care now, reviews hurt far less than they should; and in a way it seems healthier, in a sick culture, to be rejected than approved.

All the pleasure is in the writing. This is true; but perhaps the other feeling I often have nowadays – that what I write must have meaning and value because I write it – is a falsehood engendered by this truth. Because *The Collector* was said to be good, I came to believe that it was good. Goodness or badness now seems far less material; *The Magus* is, and its being is its justification. Before I wrote; now I have a right to write. There is an obvious sense in which this feeling must be part of an arteriosclerosis syndrome; but a plant is also its soil. What is self-importance from one aspect is acceptance of fate, of one's specificity, from another.

17 May
Dan and Hazel with their boy Jonathan – Hazel and the baby stayed the week.

The baby is fine, an absolutely normal little homunculus with blue-grey eyes and an insatiable lust for new objects. I think the charm of a nine-month-old is less its innocence – of course it hasn't sinned yet; how could it? – than its normality, which is really a potentiality, a kind of blank-page, clean-canvas, I-may-become-anything quality.

28 May–1 June
Eliz in London, so I am on my own, in my landscape, the weather startlingly good for England, cloudless day after day, the roses running into bloom. I divagate and potter, not really liking all this fine weather – I love fine days, but fine periods give me the old Aegean depression, and the garden craves rain. Solitude is a sort of wife. In this century, and with my polarized mind, it's impossible to live happily in solitude. It has an evil effect on me, anyway: nothing curbs my imagination, which drifts and drifts and won't be confined in work – *The Orgiasts*.[1]

And the isolation in *The Magus*. No letter yet from an English reader, good or bad . . . Yet the book has been on the bestseller list for a month. The English reader is dead; not the English novel.

---

[1] An idea for a novel to be set in Turkey, which was inspired by JF's visit to the Cannes Film Festival in May 1965.

30 June

Colin Wilson. He wrote me a long letter the other day, mainly about *The Magus* and (by implication) to say how pleased he was to at last have a disciple in the wilderness.[1] Now letters fly between us, and books. I feel sympathy for him, his terrifying earnestness and obsessive need to publish (fourteen books in the last ten years), and in many ways for his attempt to create an optimistic existentialism. But he has a bewilderingly unclouded vanity as well. 'In fifteen years' time I shall be seen as the most influential thinker in Europe.' And (reflected glory): 'We are the only two major writers in this country.' This vanity, so transparently a defence mechanism he has borrowed from his heroes Shaw and Wells (and perhaps Nietzsche), I can stomach; but he shows alarming cannibalistic tendencies as well. Writers he doesn't like (almost anyone French) he dismisses in a sentence, and you with them for liking them. Cannibal theory was that if you ate your enemies, their spirits couldn't haunt you; and he does that to all the writers that he hates yet is haunted by. Sooner or later I shall have to inform him that I am not his dinner. I don't look forward to it. Being unkind to cannibals is dangerous . . .

25 July

Summer here seduces; runs out of hand as well, there are so many things to do in the garden, in the fields; so many invitations not to write, not to think. An invitation I should normally have turned down, to do a double profile on Vanessa Redgrave and a new universal sex-object, a Raquel Welch, came as a sort of temptation to get out in the world again. I don't feel so much that I need the experience of the outer world, but its humiliations. We live here in a detached, self-supporting, self-sufficient world. We see no one, the sun shines, the sea glistens, our birds and insects weave their summer world around us. It is beautiful, like being in a glass sphere whose diameter is the sea horizon, all seventy or eighty miles of it. The sense of enclosure is very small; yet finally one knows it.

The magazine that is commissioning the article is an insult in itself – the egregious *Cosmopolitan*. This morning they wrote saying they wanted 'the ordinary virile man's view' of the two girls. For 'virile' read 'sex-crazed'.

---

[1] The publication of *The Outsider* in 1956, when Wilson was only twenty-one, brought him huge success. But although he was briefly fêted as a leading figure in the 'Angry Young Men' generation, his subsequent prolific output of books was largely ignored. He left London in 1957 to live with his wife in Cornwall.

8 August

Our past has suddenly come viciously back to life. We should have known. First, Roy agreed to let us have Anna for all her summer holidays. Then we heard he was writing a book. Then he asked if we would mind reading it, and we went to Fulham to pick up Anna and get the typescript, and there were drinks, and a lunch, and bonhomie and little side-sentences about how much it meant to him to have this book published. Heinemann's have expressed interest, the opinion of a libel lawyer (Rubinstein again) got. We made nice noises, the past was past, the last thing we would do would be to stand in the way of a budding novelist . . .

On the way back here I sat in the back seat and read it. It is a kind of act of commination, poorly written and green with hatreds and revenges and envies. Events that did happen are misrepresented; but he evidently felt that we were not black enough yet, and so all sorts of faults from other people have been tacked on to us. It didn't anger me, but it's loathsome. It must be stopped. Only a man of not completely sound mind could have written it, let alone expected to publish it. He's up to his old tricks: putting people into unfair predicaments and then cursing them for not choosing as he wants. No wonder he once so loved the Jehovah of the Old Testament. Demand the impossible, then punish the failure.

And I feel sorry for him, too. There are two scenes he has invented – one in which he gives 'me' a thrashing and another, at the end of the book, where 'Elizabeth' comes crawling back to him, only to be sternly repulsed. I think the fact is that he still loves her – in some way she is Delicious Sin and Judy is Everyday Duty, and he can't exorcize her. If he really felt she was as bad as he makes her in his book, then he certainly wouldn't have fictionally punched me on the jaw for seducing her away from him – he'd have shaken my hand and thanked me. Somewhere deep down in his past there must have been a very ugly separation trauma.

I've written him a long letter. Now we wait for the dam to break.

18 August

A letter from Roy – only a note. He is 'bitterly disappointed' at our refusal and the way in which we chose to say it.

20 August

Anna is with us all this month. She has suddenly become nubile. Not a pretty girl in the contemporary fashionable sense of what counts as a pretty girl, but nowadays that is almost a refreshing change. Instead she has a sort of heavy, solid, peasant-girl charm – more German or Scandinavian than English or French; and the charm of her age, which is all consciousness of body, skin, shape, a kind of green sensuality exuded in every pose and movement and look. We get on a little better, though this business of my establishing a relationship with her is infinitely tentative – dozens of little steps forward and very nearly as many back. Meanwhile, in a tenuous, artificial sort of way the three of us enter the father/mother/only-daughter situation. Watching Anna lying on the grass the other day in a sort of innocently provocative – perhaps not a quite pure innocence – way, I suddenly saw the theme for a book. A kind of elongation into reality of the archetypal nature of this situation, which must become more and more fraught and significant in the context of our age and its obsession with pleasure and eternal youth. Tentative title: The Classicist.

Waiting for the others to pack up on the beach yesterday, I idly looked at a moraine of pebbles washed out by a stream coming down the cliff, and there suddenly was a fine sea-urchin test – only the fourth I have found, and in condition the most perfect. They are my favourite fossils here, with their beautiful axial symmetry and their delicate burred decoration. And suddenly seeing this theme as I looked at Anna the other day was very much the same: some themes come like that, so suddenly and unexpectedly, and with an immediate (long before one has worked out details) richness and potentiality. In a completely different way such a theme is like standing at some *rond-point* in a forest. One knows, before one has turned to see, that it is a *rond-point*, that it will give perspectives, evoke associations – that (if only one can find the skill) it will 'work'.

Unfortunately I am becoming overcrowded. The Turkish novel is half-finished and half-dropped; the Collioure one,[1] the same. There is the idea based on splitting myself in half, the 'pure' poet and the 'impure' novelist. The articles on Redgrave and Welch. Now this. I hate these stages in writing where one is also at a *rond-point*, but this time obliged to choose one vista only. When I wish I was six John Fowleses, instead of one.

Two weeks ago, when Eliz's mother was here: sitting down to table with her and Eliz and Anna. Like eating with the triple goddess.

26 August

Fox are going to take up the film option. Everyone said it was 'certain', but nothing is certain in that world. Quinn[2] is now the most likely choice for Conchis, Michael Caine for Nicholas, Maggie Smith for Alison.

Thirty-six thousand pounds richer, we went and picked the apples from the old tree in the orchard. I clambered about like a chimpanzee

[1] The idea for this unrealized novel originated in JF's experiences in the South of France during the summer of 1948, when he was staying in the Mediterranean port town of Collioure. See introduction to *The Journals*, volume 1, pages xiii–xiv.
[2] The film-star Anthony Quinn, who had two years previously appeared in the title role of *Zorba the Greek*.

– among the top branches, inviting fate to give me a thirty-six-foot fall in exchange for my ill-gotten gains. But fate is probably content to put her affairs into the hands of the taxmen; Boxall[1] calculates that if they got really nasty, I should receive exactly £3,600 of my money. We are trying for a six-year spread.

29 August

Eileen is with us.[2] She and Podge seem to live such separate lives that it is incomprehensible how they can still exist under the same roof. She is the easiest, quietest person to have with one: a beautifully Irish woman, for all her abolition of the accent from her voice. Of course she sees everything in a context of irony – where it isn't, she invents it. I think this Irish sense of irony (very different from, say, the French) is so attractive because it is fundamentally in tune with the universe, which is also full of irony. And even though Irish irony can sink at times into whimsy (in Eileen's case, into a sort of petulant contra-suggestibility – she defines her 'territory' by paradox, which is only one more way of banning logic) and into horrors like Roman Catholicism, it mirrors the basic reality of life much better than the empirical 'scientific' view. 'Face values' destroy; and humour saves.

6 September

Now Podge and Cathy[3] have come.

Cathy is grown into a sharply fastidious little creature, ears constantly pricked, or so I feel, for solecisms of thought and speech. What she has imbibed from both her parents is the basic notion that almost all other human beings are tasteless fools and unscrupulous hypocrites; one can only laugh at them. She is like a small space capsule from some other world, and rather alarming. I think the sad thing is that she has been taught to see art (especially writing) as a chief vehicle for tastelessness and hypocrisy. Otherwise I would have bet any money that she would become a writer; and a good one. Jane Austen, I think, would have been very like her.

7 September

A visit to the Loveridges for dinner at Bindon.[4] The house is very old,

---

[1] George Boxall, JF's accountant.
[2] i.e., Eileen Porter, wife of Podge Porter.
[3] The Porters' daughter.
[4] The Loveridges were John and Jean Loveridge, who lived at Bindon Manor near Axmouth. In 1954 John Loveridge had hired JF to teach at his family's language and secretarial college St Godric's in Hampstead, London. JF continued to work there until the publication of *The Collector* in 1963.

full of valuable antiques, all in excellent taste; and in it Jean and John go on living their absurd dream. I think one day he will start wearing doublet and hose and plumed hat and taking up Nicholas Hilliard stances.[1] When the ladies retired after dinner he held forth, some extraordinary rigmarole, all about how Elizabeth I had healed the breach between Protestants and Catholics and we needed to get back to her age, to her spirit.

10 September

We have converted the 'cottage' into a 'studio' – all wooden walls and new paint – but I haven't felt like writing for weeks. Or rather, seem to have so many other things to do. Podge and Cathy were here the other day. We discussed total freedom and its horrors, the chief of which is a sort of insidious apathy. It makes me feel like a clipper in the doldrums; and then exasperated, because the simile is so inexact. It is not that the winds are not there – I have lots to do, both in writing and round the garden – but that their total effect leaves me as unprogressing as if it was the doldrums. For five or six years now I shall earn £10,000 or more a year – even if I write no further books; and that brings the apathy of perfectionism. I must be in the mood, I must gestate endlessly, I must prepare and prepare and put off . . .

Podge says the horror is that of having no sense of social necessity, of being needed by other human beings. But that's rather like telling someone who's falling not to jump out of the window; my 'freedom' is now. The things he suggests – political activity, good works and the rest – would only set up new dissatisfactions in my case, since I'm not sure that the road I'm on isn't the best road for society (if society can make that demand) to require of me. As always his Marxist solutions seem hopelessly simplistic in face of reality. They may be right for peasant society, for unsophisticated man, at this stage of history. But I (and he) are already at another stage. What we are, the underprivileged will, if socialism institutes enough equality, become. *Nothing* political can solve this still rare dilemma of total economic and artistic freedom. In a sense I can understand how successful artists seem often to get progressively worse – to pander more to the cheaper aspects of their work just as they need to do so less. They've seen the gulf, the terrible face in the mirror, their free self: and the alternatives seem either to return to chains or to enter an eternal accidie.

---

[1] Nicholas Hilliard (1547–1619) was a portraitist who had painted some of the leading figures of the Elizabethan age, including Queen Elizabeth I, Sir Francis Drake and Sir Walter Raleigh.

11 September

We set off in two days' time for Paris, to see Hossein's[1] rehearsals of the play of *The Collector* he is presenting, then on down to Málaga to meet La Welch.[2] I don't want to leave – and nor, more surprisingly, does Eliz – but yet I feel the need to justify not wanting to leave . . . to go away and return.

15 September

Paris, to see the Hossein rehearsals of *The Collector*.

I haven't been there for fifteen years (except to pass through) and its staggering richness as a centre of civilization, its architectural beauty, came as a shock. On the way in from Orly we passed a bistrot – CAFÉ DES ARTS – and there it is, in one simple example. Where in England would one ever see a pub, except as some chi-chi gimmick in Chelsea, called The Arts? This is the glory of France – that even the humblest have an intrinsic respect for *style*. We English as a race care only for bulk – content.

At the Théâtre des Variétés to see Hossein rehearsing. He has ignored most of the notes I wrote on the adaptation. He isn't the sort of person to take much notice of inconsistencies. The spectacle's the thing. But he has power, a presence. The girl is a pretty, rather gentle little creature, very European (what did I write once? 'As inward as a silk-lined pocket') and remote from any English concept of Miranda. Obviously they hope to fill the theatre by the Grand Guignol, not by any intellectual content that may remain. I asked to what extent the play's popularity would depend on the pleasure it gave by confirming every good Frenchman's (not least Gaullist Frenchman's) view that England was an island of sexual perverts; but received only diplomatic answers. Hossein addressed me throughout as Fol – *Vous ne trouvez pas, Fol? . . . Maintenant, Fol, je veux vous montrer . . .*

To Málaga – a hot two hours in Madrid, and then a crowded flight down to Andalusia. The air is torrid. And the distressing shabbiness – the filth in the gutters, the peeling walls, the tired, fatalistic, obliterated people. I can't help thinking of the clean, pure whitewashed walls of Greece – the bright and totally *un*obliterated people there. Spain is a defeated country, in the way that countries are defeated outside the context of history – never mind what wars they have won or lost. In history Greece has been endlessly conquered, yet it is victorious. What is lacking here is that element of vitality the Greeks share with the Jews – a positive will to survive and to prosper.

[1] The actor and director Robert Hossein, who was producing a French stage version of *The Collector*. See *The Journals*, volume 1, page 629.

[2] The film-star Raquel Welch, who was in Spain shooting a film called *Fathom*.

20 September
Interviews with Pat Curtis, the mysterious Welch's putative husband,[1] and the girl herself. He came first, to the Miramar, a slim young man in pale blue jeans and shirt, buck teeth, brown eyes half assertive and half tentative; he has a characteristic way of listening with his mouth open, fly-catching. He answers questions simply, if not honestly – all for him is making money.

The girl is vaguely frightening – attractive in the way snakes are attractive. One takes a long look, but then steps back. One wouldn't want her as a pet. She is articulate, but banal in all ways except her ruthless ambition to project herself, to succeed as a personality. Like all movie-industry 'important' personages she seems ice-cold beneath the actressy warmth. I mean that the warmth seems no more natural than her make-up.

On location with the unit – they are shooting scenes on a yacht some ten miles from Nerja. Endless waiting about for the sun, for the shots to be set up, the 'brutes' to be set up, the cameras to be set up, the stars, the director . . . and all for a final thirty seconds or so of screen time. One hundred and forty people paid a minimum of £100 a week to waste time on an idiocy. . . . I feel Marxist and contemptuous. And soiled.

Guy Green, who is going to direct *The Magus*, flies in for a couple of days. He's a robin-eyed man of fifty or so, an ex-cameraman.[2] No real knowledge of art or life, one feels, but plenty of good sound technical knowledge – a good craftsman. He's obviously going to be on my side in most things – against John Kohn's Hollywood self. Best of all, I feel he is serious: that is, has standards he won't compromise.

27 September
Back to England, an aeroplane full of other English who had been holidaying in Torremolinos. Never more foreign or more repulsive. We were in the first-class, among the odious upper-class rich. Such greedy people; and so inhuman. I was glad to be home, in Dorset, wandering round Dorchester, then to the farm and the fruit and the vegetables and the same old sea. Ronnie and Betsa have been staying here while we are away.

30 September
Along the beach to Stanton St Gabriel. A peach-grey day, very dying yet mellow. We picked about for fossils. To me, much more enjoyable than any day in Spain. I simply don't want to travel any more.

---

[1] Then Raquel Welch's boyfriend and agent, Curtis would marry her in Paris in 1967.
[2] As a cinematographer, Green (1913–2005) had photographed several classic British films of the 1940s and 1950s, including David Lean's two Dickens adaptations, *Great Expectations* and *Oliver Twist*. He switched to direction in 1954 with the film *River Beat*.

20 October

Bad days with Eliz again, after a good summer. She goes into a sort of mute paralysis, like some animal trapped and now hopeless; the country, the isolation, the vast open spaces. This time she made me numb with rage. I often tell her to go away, but this time I wanted her to. She makes it impossible for me to work; to enjoy anything. In a way it's a lack of humour; to take everything so seriously. October is beautiful here, but she turns her back on it. Her parsimony distresses me, too; her hatred of spending money, which is part of her complex against freedom. It's as if routine is like cover to her, and in the open life we now lead she can only crouch, 'freeze', and hope to escape her destiny.

I'm writing a play – *Sensitivity*. The heroine will be a mixture of us both; and Betsa Payne, and Connie Farrer.[1]

30 October

Eliz has been away for ten days now. I live like a hermit, my closest companion the little blue tit that roosts under the canopy every night. The weather is very fine, cool but clear; the moon huge each night. It can't be good for me, I wear filthy old clothes, don't wash, eat bits of food at wrong hours, let the kitchen proliferate into piles of mess and dirty dishes, drift round the fields and let them become parts of me, like the wild life. Yet this last is a beautiful experience, in itself and because not many generations more will ever know it. Science and over-population must swamp nature; of course there will be reserves and naturalists still, but by 2066 no one will be able to have this strange symbiosis with nature. I live like Jefferies,[2] like John Clare. I can't celebrate it in words – not lack of words so much as the knowledge that I cannot surpass their words. I mean I become an element of nature myself. The other day two boys came, with guns, and asked me if they could shoot pigeons. I said no in a gentle series of explanations about why nature reserves existed and how lovely I knew, from my own past, it was to have a gun in one's hands, but . . . that great but. I was weak. I thought myself mean to stop their fun, and nearly said yes. But they were like two wild creatures too; and I outwitted them. If I'd said how dare you, get off my land, they'd have poached out of sheer and justified spite.

The old cock pheasant was in the strawberry bed when I went back

---

[1] Born Constance Morgenstern, Connie Farrer was the girlfriend and subsequently wife of JF's Oxford friend, Michael Farrer. See *The Journals*, volume 1, page 22.

[2] JF is thinking of the naturalist and writer Richard Jefferies (1848–1887). Ever since first reading the novel as a child, JF had strongly identified with Jefferies' *Bevis: The Story of a Boy* (1882). Based on Jefferies' own early life on his father's Wiltshire farm, the novel chronicled the boyhood adventures in the countryside of Bevis and his friend Mark.

in the garden, and flew off, showing no gratitude. Though my blue tit
does. We stare at each other at night, our eyes two or three feet apart,
and try to reach. He understands me (that I am always on the brink of
killing again) and I don't understand him.

But I am not really a happy solitary. I need to be two people, perhaps
three or four, if the truth were known. I can't miss Eliz as she is, but
I miss her all the time as she was. I live in two worlds, in one of which
I'm happy, 'related' as the Yanks say; in the other, social-marital, sour
as red blackberries, nothing fits, nothing goes, nothing works. Talk
after talk with Eliz in London over the telephone, listening to her
absorption in her misery over the flat in Pembridge Crescent, her
misery over Anna, her misery over her identity, who she is, do I love
her, does anyone love her, her isolation. The flat's unfurnished and
she sits in it and relives the events of fifteen years ago; and I haven't
any patience with her, with this chase after identity – or really, this is
it, this chase after the unattainable. Because she always wants something other than what she has. It's the age's sickness. I tried to write
a poem about it, but tore it up. Only the first line went. 'Wanting
more, wanting more, wanting more . . .' Wordsworth said it better, on
London Bridge.[1]

I know most men, most husbands, would run up to London and try
to pull her out of the quagmire she's got herself into. But my delusion
is that I am sane, and the rest of the world is mad. I pull her up to my
sanity, not let her drag me down into her madness.

5 November

Eliz returns. She looks haggard. Smiles contort her face, as they do a
Pierrot-le-fou's. All she says about London confirms (though I don't
think she quite intends it to) my worst fears and suspicions of it. Suzanne
Kinberg is undergoing a full analysis; Betsa P has been told she must
have one; Bert and Jane are lame-ducking a girl having an abortion;
their friend Daphne's parasite-cum-lover is having an affair with a young
girl, and Daphne has abandoned the house in Elm Row to the guilty
pair in one of those accesses of defend-the-cuckoo which is endemic to
their age. I don't sympathize. 'But where would she find another man
at her age?' says Eliz. And behind all these unhappy women is the same
horror: their loneliness, their unnecessity. The fault of our society has
been to emancipate women but to refuse to furnish (to train them for)
their freedom. They are to be equal to us; but the only equality offered
them is ours, the male definition (in social and career terms) of the

[1] JF is thinking of William Wordsworth's poem 'Composed on Westminster Bridge':
'Earth has not anything to show more fair: / Dull would he be of soul who could
pass by / A sight so touching in its majesty . . .'

concept. So the only ones who gain are the masculine type, the ones who can copy them. All that has happened to the true women is that they have been turned out, like so many cage birds, into a world where they cannot fend for themselves.

6 November
I'm going straight on with a second draft of *The Swallow and the Scythe*. Hearing Eliz talk about London, the unhappiness of women, is strange. As so often when I start writing I have the muse experience; the absurd feeling that life is arranging itself around me to illustrate what I already knew. I have written the play exactly as I first sketched it some months ago; and now here she is, and all the *galère* in London, to show I am right – not necessarily in execution, of course, but certainly in emotion . . . in the general drift.

9 November
Eliz is in gloom again, days of it. I can stand so much, then I revolt. She doesn't want my love, my sympathy, my understanding; but her will. She's aware of it; she calls it conflict. Last night it brought us to endless whisky, endless arguing, shouting, spent silence. I went to the end of the garden and stared out over the darkness of Lyme Bay. A gentle sea, my sea. And she is deep beneath it, two thousand fathoms out of love.

25 November–1 December
In London, in the Pembridge Crescent flat. Now Eliz hates that as well. No clearer symptom of her malaise than her hostility to London. Perhaps it is something quite simple. She has forgotten how to work. The flat is all right, all that we need, a place to sleep, to live a week or two if necessary. It is not only that she has the general architectural dream that haunts all visuals – gracious easy living; she wants gracious easy *compact* living. Some sort of huge room where everything goes on and I am never out of her sight or sound. We ended with a bitter row. She had read *The Scythe*, taken it all on herself. So that is banned, not to be gone on with except under the threat of her endless anger. She drives me now into a sort of silent rage that is new in my life.

Script 'conference' in London. Jud couldn't come. John K and Guy Green. The latter worries me a little, perhaps because I don't know yet how to manoeuvre him, as I do JK. Basically he retains his petit-bourgeois hatred of pretension, and it's plain he sees it rampant in *The Magus*. What struck me as curious is that this instinctive hatred, which he derives from his past, his being not middle class, his coming from below, starting as a cameraman, all that, is now married with exactly the same attitude fashionable among English intellectuals. At moments he seemed *poujadiste,*[1] at others, very highbrow. He wants, in fact, to present the film as a kind of dream that Nicholas has, because 'nobody's going to believe that people like Conchis exist'. To JK's horror (*Et tu, Brute*) I agreed. I couldn't tell GG that it was for different reasons from his: because I think the cinema is too realistic a medium to allow one to get away with what one can pass through the customs in a novel.

Coming back to Lyme. The relief of the clean air, the peace, the silence. It seems to me that people who live in London have now lost all touch with another half of existence. Cities turn their inhabitants in upon themselves, into a tight circle of prescribed conventions, fads, interests, methods of establishing superiority. I am sure this is an epoch when it is best to be out of London; just as there have been others – the sixteenth century, say, when it was best to have been in it. The city was an essential stage in civilization; and a return to the country may well be the next.

4 January 1967

We met Mike Caine just before Christmas. Dinner in the Terrazza. He is a thoroughly unlikeable young man, so set on, and in, his stardom that his cursory obeisances towards writers and proper artistic standards in the cinema become only the more offensive. My one hope is that still inside him – uneroded by his present fame (he's the current world No. 1 male box-office draw in his own and John Kohn's opinion, No. 2 in most other people's, after Sean Connery) – is a better self that can still get out through his mask of cheap irony. Of course he's good at poker-faced banter – that sort of thing. But he's got to give more than that.

Terry Stamp was here two days ago for the evening – he's shooting a Hardy film near Dorchester.[2] He has that Prince Hamlet aura still and his absurd vanity, certainly no less than his chum Caine's, but so much more lightly carried. His charm is really in the air of happy freedom he carries with him; a sort of eighteenth-century swagger.

15 January

Dinner with Twiggy, the latest idiocy in the fashion world. Impossible, really, to dislike her. Such innocence. One can no more blame her than a bird for pecking fruit-buds.

She describes how 'Duke Bedford' took her in his Rolls-Royce through Paris. Seeing flags in the Champs Elysées, she turns to him: ''Ere, 'ave you got a flag?'

---

[1] Reactionary, resistant to change. The word was coined after the post-war French politician Pierre Poujade.
[2] JF had got to know Stamp during the making of the film version of *The Collector* (see *The Journals*, volume 1, pages 589 ff.). Stamp was playing the role of Sergeant Troy in *Far from the Madding Crowd*, directed by John Schlesinger.

'Actually there is something that flutters over the house.'

Her mother seems the best part about her – a fine Cockney Mrs Malaprop. She calls *Paris Match* 'that Harry Patch'; and the egregious Vidal Sassoon 'Victor Baboon'.

I've written an article comparing her to Dubarry. A curious coincidence in dates; in two centuries' folly.

25 January
The French Lieutenant's Woman. I started this today. Not so much with a plot as a mood and a language I wanted to use. It was really just one visual idea: a woman standing at the end of the Cobb and staring mysteriously out to sea.

11 February
More trouble with the script. We are now split into two camps – Guy G and myself in one, John and Jud in the other – over the ending. They want it melodramatic and 'flamboyant', we want it quiet and emotional. Two days' fighting and arguing and losing tempers. Guy says very little. Jud goes wild with his vehemence; John and I have our separate parties of the centre. You cannot make good art like this. I know the film is doomed already at this level – never mind about the mess being made at lower ones.

22 February
A fossil sponge – only an inch across – in a ball of flint. I chipped it open. I suppose it is ninety million years old; yet the slightest touch on the miniature pockets of tawny branches crumbles them. So fragile; and yet so old.

16 May
In London for the 'testing' of the girls for the part of Lily. I want Jean Shrimpton, even though she can't act. The trouble in this film world is how little ability there is to visualize. People don't really see scenes as I (or any other novelist) do by nature. They read lines and descriptions of movements; I see events happening. More and more, ideas come to me through visual scenes analogous to stills or short cinematic sequences. At this stage of the film my importance dwindles before the director's and producers' – and it would be nice to think that this was just the wordman handing on the torch to the professional image-creators. What is so absurd, of course, is that they still don't begin to *see* the script one quarter as well as I do. More and more I feel the awful temptation to have a shot at directing myself. I could do the script and I could certainly direct performance as well as the only other two directors I have seen at work (Wyler and Green); and the technical knowledge

needed doesn't seem very great. If one could only gain the autonomy one has in a novel I should be very tempted.

We've seen Shrimpton several times recently.[1] The true reason she is hopeless for Lily is her innocence. She's really the least sophisticated person in the world, with the mentality of a bright, stable fourteen-year-old. A 'sweet' person. The cool looks she projects from magazine covers spring from nothing in her real self. She couldn't see us on Sunday because she'd found a chaffinch's nest on her father's farm and 'simply had' to take Terry down to show it to him . . . Such naturalness is bewitching, of course. She would be splendid in some gentle, tender, Edwardian part. I want her, still, for that face; after the test – she was better than I thought she would be, but not good enough to impress anyone else – I watched Eliz and her have lunch in her little house in Montpelier Place. Rather gawky in private, vaguely giraffe-like, almost aggressively shy and clumsy in her movements, as if she'd die rather than 'project' or move gracefully. Of course this nicely democratic intention is absolutely ruined by her marvellous face; the clumsiness becomes like Garbo's silence – the final charm.

What is really mad about the casting side of the movie business is the fact that a huge store of pretty and talented actresses (and their young male equivalents) is at hand – in the television studios. Watching Jean stumble through her scene, I couldn't help thinking of all those young women I see every week on the box who would have dazzled through it. But the cinema abhors competence.

20 May
The location in Crete is given up. Now it's to be Majorca. It isn't the boys' fault, really. The fascist coup in Greece – and the colonels' eagerness to get foreign money – makes the idea of spending three million dollars there unpleasant to all of us. In any case, the insurers won't pay out for production delays caused by political unrest.

A remark of McLuhan's (in this month's *Encounter*) to the effect that literature really has no ability to convey *all* the realities of words – that it's always a narrowing of the potential, a thin artifice compared to the full 'nature' of all language.[2] I am writing *The French Lieutenant's Woman* at the moment; and reading Mrs Gaskell's *Mary Barton* at the same time. Her dialogue is much more 'modern' than mine – full of contractions, and so on. Yet in order for me to convey the century that has passed since the time of my book I am right to invent dialogue much more

[1] At the time she was Terence Stamp's girlfriend.
[2] Marshall McLuhan (1911–1980) had become an influential commentator on modern media and culture after the successful publication of his book *Understanding Media* in 1964.

formal than the Victorians actually spoke. This gives the illusion better. In a sense an absolutely accurate Victorian dialogue would be *less* truthful than what I am doing. I don't know if McLuhan is attacking the novel for this 'perversion' of reality. If he is, I don't agree with him. But a novel is really a kind of metaphor, a poem about reality rather than a report of it. And even with novels far more overtly reality-reflecting than mine.

3–8 June
In London, doing the script properly with Guy Green. We have a sort of common ground, at last. He is that rare thing, a very slow thinker who is not a fool. Our 'conferences' are punctuated with silences that run into minutes; but at the end – I learnt to keep quiet during them, further ideas only confuse him – he generally comes up with something valid. I learn a great deal from him besides keeping quiet. That puritanical hatred of the word – Wyler had it too – which one must learn, to direct; hatred of the literary, of the unnecessary, line. He worries away like a terrier at what I mean, what the characters mean. Obvious things he doesn't see, very often; or pretends not to see; but I know he has to do this to find a way to film the scene for an audience that must include Japanese peasants, Chilean intellectuals, all the world that will pay the entrance price. He won't ever have poetry, with all its obscurity and perverse contempt for construction, one-to-one dialogue, on-the-nose trig-gers – all the Oscar-seeking *galère* of Hollywood movie tricks. I'd have liked a good furniture designer. Instead I have a carpenter; but I think he's a good one. In effect he's taking the script to bits and putting it together in a simpler way; and it's nice (healthily humiliating) to help him do it.

22 June
These last three weeks I have sweated in London as we have gone through a series of crises over the script. At one point it seemed Guy Green would get the sack: secret phonecalls were put through, 'feelers' for other directors. I turned myself into a sort of secretary of the script committee, trying to steer a course between, or among, my three masters. Nine times out of ten what is being disputed is really personal taste – and those three, alas, never heard of *De gustibus . . .*[1] Thus the endless dispute was really about each other's personality, though more or less politely disguised under production and directorial jargon and requirement. I don't think the script gets much better; we simply find compromises of the kind that hang like millstones round the neck of all community art.

[1] JF is thinking of the Cicero proverb, *De gustibus non disputandum est*: 'There is no accounting for taste.'

There are first of all the looming commercial pressures: the mass audience, the stars' egos. We have been constantly bedevilled by John and Jud's fear of alienating Mike Caine if he doesn't have a 'strong' last scene. The idea of presenting the Magus as a teacher and Nicholas as someone who needs teaching is anathema to them – it cuts Caine's balls off, in the jargon. So an element I loathe, of the Wild Western goodie finally gunning down the baddie, has had to be incorporated. Then there is Guy's phobia of pretension, which is really a confusion in him between the words *literate* and *literary*; and his general cultural ignorance, which is precisely what we don't need in this picture. There is John Kohn's sexual frustration. For him every scene has to end in a 'clinch' or a 'just about to screw'. And Jud is like a weathercock, disappearing every so often to see his psychiatrist and find out why he is haunted by a sense of failure – 'why I screw myself and my family trying to reach perfection' is the way he put it one evening. In fact I forgive him less than the others. He has the brain to see better what we ought not to be doing; but he has no consistency. One moment he's quibbling endlessly over a single line, the next he gives up and wants to jettison whole scenes.

The climate we work in is absurd. Fawning and overpraise in the morning, vitriolic abuse and anger in the afternoon. Perhaps this was always the curse of folk-art – the respect for others' opinion must inevitably become the tyranny of the majority, with the end-product a fatal averaging-down of whatever genius the individual has. I put it in two words one day, jotted it as they shouted at each other: *No Muses.*

John Kohn came in one morning with the truth about the Rolling Stones' drug case. The mysterious 'naked girl' was apparently Marianne Faithfull, and what she was really doing was lying with a Mars Bar stuck into her vagina. The young men were taking it in turns to have a nibble. Faithfull was one of the rejects when they tested three or four girls for Lily in *The Magus.* So a cascade of sick jokes: 'Jesus, what schmucks we've been, with all that free publicity . . .' and (every time we got stuck on the script) 'OK, we open on a close shot of a Mars Bar . . .'

8 August

The dog-days, and I have the usual summer cloud of accidie over me. I ought to feel guilty for being so lazy about writing anything new. I've turned down five magazine projects recently – or put them off, pleading the precise opposite of the truth: that I am too far sunk in *dolce far niente* to be interested. This last year's laziness is, I suppose, in part a reaction from *The Magus* – not only the writing of a long novel, but the awful trauma of getting it published and watching its fate. I dread that aspect more and more. Being published interests me a little less each year. I no more want to see myself in print now than a monk wants to do a vaudeville act.

I think last year the accidie was unpleasant; this year it is pleasant. Those three weeks in London enabled me to remember how rare the peace we have here – and my birds, my flowers, my land, I'm one with them. Also I feel rich in writing, even though I don't write – except *The French Lieutenant's Woman*, in infrequent chapters. I mean, I have novels planned until I'm fifty at least, if planned novels shall be what I need; and each day I see a little clearer what and how I must write.

Anna is with us again, a year more nubile, like a small brown Maillol – not only in shape, but in a sort of warmth, perhaps a forgiveness of us, that she diffuses around her.

6–20 September
To Palma, Eliz and I alone in the first-class compartment, over a magnificent sea of pink and cream baroque cloud. Palma at first sight (and every other sight) is so remote from Greece that we felt depressed when we arrived, though the hotel is an agreeably old-fashioned place overlooking the central bay.

It is architecturally a nicer town than Málaga, at any rate. A boom town, and so a kind of anomaly in Spain; an international town, and since Spain is what it is, an international fascists' town. Full of rich Belgians, French, Germans, obviously delighted to be in the doubly sunny climate. The town is run politically by Church and Falange and commercially by the Barcelona Jews – *les chouettes*, the owl-noses. Then it is also the Miami of Europe, the great cheap tourist centre.

It has a sort of energy-in-indolence; a city whose industry is pleasure. Sociologically, a very ugly town indeed.

The villa they have built for Conchis is very pleasant, though more filmsettish than Greek, and not particularly well sited, especially as a neighbouring landowner has had a road bulldozed across the overlooking hillside. He hoped to get money for stopping the work; and when the money was refused went ahead with it. Don Ashton (who designed the villa) showed us round. The two beaches were covered in tourist filth; more comes in on every tide. One forgets the cleanliness of Greece, those pure beaches.

The boredom of location shooting – orthodoxly made films like this require such an enormous amount of apparatus. Each small scene takes at least half an hour to set up; so much fiddling with the 'brutes' and the 'flags', so much shouting to 'lose' people in the backgrounds, and so little time spent on the actual acting. It's absurd, really; as if the frame mattered more than the painting.

Mike Caine on his first day of shooting. He brings a nice presence to what he does; a matter-of-factness the amateur always lacks. They made me play a little scene with him, so I am an authority now. It's not that I didn't know exactly what I ought to do; but doing it 'on camera' is something else.

Mike Caine said afterwards: 'You're always going to seem and sound artificial to yourself. It's finding the area where you can kid the audience into believing you're being natural.' He's very far from being a fool about his job; and his behaviour between takes, when he is endlessly bothered for autographs and snapshots, is exemplary.

Anna Karina arrives; a very pretty and vivacious creature, but there seems something a little *ben trovato* about it. The vivacity is like a good French scent; very seductive, but one wonders how much it costs. And her eyes are ice-cold, betraying her Scandinavian ancestry. Still, it's difficult to imagine her not stealing any scene she's in, and that's what we need.

A last drink with Guy. His son's supposed to go back to school, but he's infatuated with film-making and has cajoled his parents into letting him stay here as a kind of office-boy round the production. 'If he's going to go into the business he may as well start at the bottom,' says Guy. I wondered if that was the best way to become, finally, a director. 'It's experience,' Guy went on, 'the thing you need most is a lot of experience.' This gets near the centre of the inherent idiocy of the movie industry: that a good director needs technical experience more than general culture. As if all of art did not prove the contrary.

14 October
The French Lieutenant's Woman. I'm now about three-quarters of the way through and full of the usual doubts. That is, that I'm trying to do too much. Though it is enjoyable to write. Last thing at nights I'm reading Olivia Manning's *Balkan Trilogy*, which is very good, a kind of delicate feminine Waugh; beautifully sober and English and understated in style. No analysis of characters beyond what they say and do; the similes and metaphors discreet and excellent when they come: the vistas in Bucharest on a winter's day 'the colour of a bruise'. No overt irony. It is really a kind of *nouveau roman* and a perfect exemplar of the twentieth-century English novel in the manner of Forster. Half of me wishes I were writing like that. I am split between writing out of my Englishness and against it.

27 October
First draft of the novel finished.

28 October–7 November
In the new flat in Hampstead. It is bright, small, a pretty box, all new, since we are the first occupants, and about as far from the farm as it is

possible to imagine. But it's nice to be in the centre of Hampstead Village again,[1] with Edith Sitwell's just across the road and the old library; though flats have gone up on the site of the stables where we first lived here. Even in our fifteen years we have seen so much go; it is full of boutiques now and modish young people. But enough of the old faces – and places – remain. I'm glad we got to know Notting Hill Gate; but gladder that we've come back.

Bergman's *Persona*. With each film he becomes more clearly the best living director. This is a model of economy, as rigorous as a Bach fugue in its use of a very limited material. Two sets, one location, a minimum of furniture; the simplest cutting, the utmost restraint in camera angle. The effect is almost Japanese; yet it remains an intensely North European work of art. I'm sure he will one day be seen as the equivalent of Ibsen and Strindberg; and that if we are to have one day a genuine English cinema, we must base ourselves on his example.

Resnais's *La Guerre est finie*. Another good film.

8 November
The road to the farm is metalled. Sad to see the old flint track go, but it was becoming impossible to negotiate except in bottom gear.

9 December
Sudden snow and bitter cold. We hadn't even had a ground frost earlier this winter. The first time we have seen snow here. It is very pretty, especially as it is a *verglas* sort of snow and has rimed all the branches and tree trunks. Even the smallest twigs bear it; at the base, nearest the twig, ice – then snow on that, a beautifully gradated opacity from the twig up. The cold has caused an extraordinary migration: both on the 8th and the 9th birds were passing at a rate of fifty to a hundred a minute, all en route for Cornwall and southern Ireland: skylarks outnumbered everything else – an almost endless stream of them between ten and eleven o'clock this morning (the 9th). But also hundreds of song thrushes and redwings, many fieldfare, a few starlings (many more came towards sunset) and a number of blackbirds flying with the other thrushes. Out to sea, huge flocks of green plover. Both migrations seemed to reach a peak about eleven o'clock; towards evening, with the exception of the starlings, there were only a few stragglers. I haven't been able to work. I feel a strange identity with birds – that I have always felt, but living here has reinforced it – and I stood both mornings till I was frozen, with this strange flood of organisms pouring over the farm and the Undercliff.

[1] The flat was at 11 Hampstead High Street, just down the hill from Hampstead Underground station. John and Elizabeth had previously lived together in a number of different flats in the Hampstead area between 1954 and 1964.

I saw also in a bush seven cock bullfinches and a hen; they become noticeably tamer with the snow. They are after the spindleberries, mainly. And a fox who stood out before me, only a few yards away; the orange fur above like fire and the white fur beneath made whiter by the snow. This reflected light that snow gives is delicious; is best of all beneath the seagulls' wings – the most exquisite white in creation. The slope of thorns and ash-trees behind the farm is – a poor word, but the only one – fairylike at the moment. It belongs to myth; each branch iced and crystallized; such delicate complexity one is reduced to childhood when one looks up at it. And the sea has done the incredible and produced a new colour, a gunmetal grey-blue.

The crew is back in London, shooting finished in Majorca. They say Karina steals the picture. They've changed the ending yet again; but at least they have gone for simplicity. I feel no interest in it; a positive disinclination to get involved in it all again. We can't drive to London in this weather; so the problem is solved.

24 December
First violets in flower.

25 December
Christmas alone at the farm.

31 December
It seems generally agreed by the newspapers – but then, they're a part of the rottenness – that the state of 1967 has been putrid. All sorts of old national sins have come home to roost this year; the long incipient schizophrenia of Britain has bloomed – and no one likes the flowers. I earned over £21,000 this year; over £12,000 will go in tax. I suppose this would seem outrageous if I were a businessman. As it is, I am largely indifferent. I see no justice in any income over £10,000 or so, and I can't make myself an exception to that rule. I am giving the copyright of *The French Lieutenant's Woman* to a charitable trust, to benefit Hazel and Anna and other relations.

Britain is interesting to live in now. I feel very remote from it; and quite untouched about all the national woes. That's happening to a foreign country, not to me or mine. I think this attitude is very widespread. There's an absurd schism between what the newspapers and TV say we're thinking and what we are thinking. Basically, all we care about is, at its lowest factor, the amount of money we can screw out of contemporary life – that is, the amount of free time and pleasure we can get. There is conversely a total distrust of public expenditure – of public everything. Britain's opinion, Britain's role, Britain's destiny – who cares?

The world can get on perfectly well without us; and every time we inter-
fere (or even just try to be friendly, as with the Common Market) we
are snubbed and humiliated.[1] So the spirit is quietist. I think only a
catastrophe (or slow natural process) can shake us out of this lethargy.

A slump or a revolution – but the price of control is that even the
good that ill winds blow is averted.

6–23 January 1968

Eliz has been away. I meant to get on with the final stages of *The FLW*,
but a thriller story I have toyed with for some time suddenly seemed to
demand to be written. So I've written it, about 110,000 words, in seventeen days flat. I've gobbled down one meal a day, but otherwise worked
from nine to one or two the next morning. In a sense it's been a reaction from the third-person cerebrality of *The FLW*. Not meant to be
serious: just a headlong love-and-mystery story.

Title: *Somebody's Got to Do It.*

29 January

Eliz returns. Separation does us good, really. Her energy against the
present, my lethargy towards everything but the typewriter. I like living
alone. But hate sleeping alone.

17 February

To see Terry Stamp in his film set, one can hardly call it a flat, in the
Albany. His usual tense, slightly farouche self; as if he's both glad to see
you and wishes you would go. Although he's doing very well for himself
– Fellini wants him for his next big picture – he seems to me to have
lost touch with reality. Even further 'outside' society than I am. The
other day he met Edward Heath, who also lives in Albany. Heath asked
him to lunch. Terry harangued him for three hours: 'He could have
learnt a lot, but he just couldn't get the groove, didn't seem to hear
what I said.' Apparently Heath said that Wilson frightened him and hurt
him in the House. Terry's remedy was this: 'OK, you're sitting on the
Opposition Front Bench, old Wilson gets up. As soon as he starts
annoying you, you just think, This morning Harold got up at Number
Ten, he went downstairs to the kitchen, got out the best tea, warmed
the pot, did it all perfect, took it upstairs to the old woman, thinking,
Maybe this is it, this time, she'll open her arms and we'll have a lovely
screw. Instead of which the old bag just says, Oh gawd, and turns over
and goes to sleep again. You just think, It's not me he's trying to hurt,
it's his missus or whatever. All I got to do is work out what it is in Wilson's

---

[1] One of the more significant humiliations occurred in May 1967 when President
de Gaulle of France vetoed Britain's application to join the Common Market.

life that makes him have to hurt me. Then I can handle him.' I asked Terry if Heath appreciated his advice. 'He didn't understand,' said Terry. 'He's forgotten how to listen.'

We went on from Terry's down to see Roy, who recently decided he'd like to see me alone to talk about Anna. Though there wasn't much talk about Anna. He really wanted to tell me that at last he's getting a book published. I said, 'Well, let's forget all that business last year.' But he couldn't. What had affronted him was that I'd criticized the dialogue. The 'moral' issue he thought was quibbling: 'Look what Dostoevsky did to Turgenev – Turgenev didn't care.'[1] I said, 'But they didn't have an Anna between them.' Casting himself as Dostoevsky – he hasn't really changed his spots. Hutchinson liked his work, hadn't wanted a single change. 'I'm quite pleased, John, I feel it's quite a little literary work of art.' And so on.

All this was in the lounge of some horrid pub at the end of his road. He was very nervous, poor fellow. Both aggressive and trying not to be; so I put on my mildest face and voice and listened. As always it ended by his telling me we could be close friends, he liked me – could I like him? I said alas, I'm a born Trojan, I fear the Greeks, etc. But by dint of keeping him talking about his book (the title is *The Nightingales Are Sobbing*), we managed to end the evening quite well. The crux of the Anna situation seems to be that Judy is fed up with her and her moods and (probably) wants to get her out of the house. So now we are thinking of letting Anna do her pre-diploma year for art school down at Exeter.

21 February

Meeting with the barrister who is advising us on the discretionary trust: he seemed more amused than concerned at the hopelessness of the situation. We can't avoid capital gains tax; I must find the tax, which will amount to 30 per cent of the valuation, out of other income; so all depends on how low a valuation the Inland Revenue will swallow. This whole tax situation has become farcical. I cannot publish anything now for three years at least which will not be taxed at the highest rate: that is, over 90 per cent of my earnings will go to the ever-open maw. The only solution is to live abroad. I won't be forced out of England because of greed. So all I can do is to go on working for nothing.

[1] The two writers, who had previously been friends, fell out during a meeting in Baden-Baden in 1867. Dostoevsky owed Turgenev a long-overdue debt, but, instead of paying it back, used the occasion to harangue Turgenev for his book *Smoke*, accusing him of hating Russia and of being an atheist. When five years later Turgenev learned that Dostoevsky had written a caricature of him in his novel *The Devils*, he dismissed the matter as of no consequence. 'Let him have his fun . . . it would be simple libel, if Dostoevsky weren't insane – of which I don't have the slightest doubt.'

Working with the girl who is translating *The Magus* into French. She's quite bright, but exudes a distressing aura of tiredness and poverty. Several ludicrous mistranslations emerged. It's not only films that betray the books, but the fact that 90 per cent of all translating is done by Grub Street. They're grossly underpaid; and what results is not their fault.

25 February

We came back from London last night – late, when it was dark. I noticed vaguely that the dying elm at the bottom of Batch didn't seem to be there. But it was too dark to see well. I forgot about it. Then this morning – it's a Sunday – I went down the bottom of the garden, to find that the whole of the lower field, Batch, had subsided. Where the mushrooms grew is now a steep yellow cliff. The entire slope has sunk down in to a strange flat sort of tennis-court or tilting-ground. Huge cracks run right along the field to the hedge with the main ditch below the house – some forty yards from the garden wall. The bottom edge of Batch has also collapsed seaward. A unique experience – as if during our ten days in London God had decided to alter the whole landscape and set thousands of men to work on it.

It gave my heart a bad jolt, because I knew at once that we had lost the fifteen thousand pounds or so we have spent on buying the house and doing it up. It can never be sold for more than a knockdown price now. But coming as it does after all the stultifying discussions in London about how I can possibly keep any future money I earn, or even give it away, it seemed almost exhilarating . . . A kind of release. A challenge. Clearly now we've got to leave here – and the country. Within a couple of hours we'd decided that we must live in Paris. Eliz says we were too young to put down roots. It's partly that; and owning too much, not only in antiques and the greenhouse and the garden, but in attachment to solitude and nature.

The landslide is strangely beautiful in a chaos-creating sort of way: wild tilted tables of turf, naked faces of flint and greensand, like a golden dough, even the fences twisted flat as if the land hates fences and has at last got its revenge.

We spent most of the day trying to absorb the effects of all this. In a way I feel like leaving at once – handing over the whole mess to the professionals, the furniture storers, the auctioneers, the demolition men. And get on. It's the eternal packing and unpacking that I can't face.

26 February

It's fine weather, but an east wind, bitterly cold.

A curious thing: the badger that had made its sett at the foot of the slope which has collapsed is still there, as if nothing had happened.

Waking in the night and thinking that it was a bad dream: then remembering that it wasn't.

The consequence that worries me least is the loss of money: in some way I don't really fathom I hate the stuff. A surface part of me hated the loss we made at Highgate on the other house, but something deeper partly approved. The sums I earn don't help matters. I lose fifteen thousand pounds here; but I made more than that (on paper, of course, not in fact after tax) on the script work alone for *The Magus*. Money no longer has the reality for me it seems to have for other people. I noticed this during the discussions with Boxall and tax counsel. For them it is something to be earnest and respectful about; to me it is an irritation, something that gets in the way of more important things. So I throw it away wastefully.

Like losing a small fortune at roulette. Almost agreeable, since not many people have had the experience.

Another thing: I was becoming too English, too much of England. This attachment to an England of the past was morbid. My secret escape had become dreaming about six months in Persia, holidays in Japan, Peru, and a dozen other places. Not being able to travel had become a sort of pleasure, as constipation can become a pleasure.

27 February
How right I was to nickname it Nilmanet.[1]

2 March
Very strange, the seventh day running without either wind or rain, as if the land has had its wild night and is now enjoying peace and sleep. What will happen when it does rain, I try not to think. The cracks all over Batch are still creeping and widening and the bottom hedge, which has already fallen several feet, is really just perched on a slope of gault, the hard black clay that acts as the slippery table on which the greensand slips. Some of these gault 'tables' have been exposed where the topsoil has slipped away. Like oily black slides, treacherous beneath the golden greensand and brown loam strata.

We have put the farm into the hands of old Hulburd, Jane's father-in-law, and told him to sell it as fast as he can. He is briskly optimistic, though with glints of folly-rewarded in his eyes.

Boxall is against Paris. Yesterday we had an excitement for the Channel Islands. But the property prices are exorbitant and now we hear you have in any case to live there two years before you are allowed to buy a house. Boxall wants us to be on the move, resident nowhere, thus avoiding all tax liability. I like the idea, but it plunges Eliz into all her old fears. In

[1] 'Nothing remains.'

fact a weird sort of reversal has taken place: I am all eager to be up and away and she starts feeling she loves the dear old place after all.

A barn owl has suddenly appeared. It comes in daylight and flies about the yards, up round the studio, sits on the wall, watching me. The first I have seen here, so it seems more than a bird. An omen. We spent half an hour yesterday watching that white heart-shaped face, with the curious trickles of blood from the inner corners of the beautiful brown-black eyes down beside the beak (actually rust-red feathers). Really a very beautiful and gravely comic creature, and not in the least ominous. When it hawks, like a huge buff moth. The huge head, all symbolic weeping heart, is what makes it grotesque; and over those neat white trews.

I'm able now to know my reaction better, and it really remains one of relief. A feeling that Dorset was a dead end, though one I am very glad we explored. That such things ought to happen to writers. And it has been a kind of check on one's own stability, the value of one's real degree of philosophy – as opposed to what one labels oneself. I've called myself an existentialist, but always with a slightly untruthful feeling – something cerebral, intellectual, literary. And yet in this situation it has very definitely helped – at least so far – to accept reality. We are victims of two sets of circumstances over which we have no control: the landslip and the tax situation. But one's freedom isn't only in the choice of what future action to take, it's in the way one behaves now. Curiously, Voltaire – the Voltaire of *Candide* – has been constantly in my mind: almost like a pillar, a buttress, the one masterpiece of practical help in this situation. His paradox – that life is absurd, cruel and gay (and you can't dispense with any of the three adjectives, because the latter two define the nature of the first). What is really admirable about Candide (who was Voltaire himself) is how he always comes up smiling for more. I haven't read *Candide* for many years; and yet these last few days it has come back, very close, very pertinent, a very considerable consolation. I think it began with that first immediate reaction when I saw the collapsed field: a laugh. I suppose it was partly the reaction of shock. But it was funny, a very pure piece of humour, even though one was the victim.

Two other effects: writing becomes even more pleasurable. That doesn't subside. And – I think this is behind Eliz's volte-face – a fresh affection for all that is good about this place: the birds, the lights, the stirring of spring. Seeing it all for the last time – or, more precisely, *as if* for the last time.

5 March

Jud has returned from Hollywood from the showing of the rough cut to Zanuck and the other Twentieth Century moguls. He says they are delighted – which wouldn't mean much in my ears, if they hadn't also signed Guy Green for this summer's big picture and asked for the last scene (the happy ending in London) to be cut, as I've always wanted. Release 'in the fall'.

Clearing out the barns, a huge bonfire. At dusk I was back in the studio and a large black shape appeared on the bottom wall. It hopped off, stole through the garden, climbed up the fig-tree, shat on the wall, walked all along it, then leapt into the yard and came up the outside path below my window. I went out and puss-pussed it. But it ran off. A pure black cat. No one owns one round here. I've never seen it before. A little later the barn owl flew over.

7–9 March

In London to see the rough cut of *The Magus*. We saw it alone with Jud and Max, the cutting editor. A terrible feeling of disappointment, after the new hope I'd foolishly drawn from the Hollywood reaction. Quinn has done well, and the two girls quite well; but Caine is really excruciatingly bad, totally incredible as an English graduate, however proletarian in origin. Just Caine, the best-paid European film-star, drifting through a role he doesn't understand. He seems to have no notion of how to react, let alone act. Guy Green is to blame, of course – only Quinn has the ability to rise above the general ambiance of non-direction. No poetry, no mystery. And to make matters worse, they've cut it razor-sharp – the scenes skid and jump on so fast that there's no sense of space or even the briefest rest. The worst thing about Caine's failure is that it pervades the whole picture; the one part we couldn't afford to go wrong.

I saw it a second time two days later, reel by reel, and it didn't seem so bad, even though we'd seen a brilliant film (*Shakespeare Wallah*) in-between – a film that had everything we lack . . . Love, art, humanity. We agreed on a number of new cuts and restorations of footage and other changes.

That first was altogether a bad evening. Jud kept disappearing during the viewing to telephone Rome. We went to the Terrazza afterwards, at a table next to Zeffirelli and an assortment of stars . . . Richard Harris, Lynn Redgrave. Harris turned to say how much he'd loved *The Collector*. I could hardly speak to him. These celebrities, the whole vicious distortion that celebrity exerts on art.

I discovered yesterday how the landslip started. There was a big fall at the cliff over the beach. The whole ledge where the first wild strawberries always ripened has gone – the lias must have shifted forward and so started the commotion in the overlying gault and greensand. The cliff fall reaches thirty yards or more across the beach, blocking it at high tide.

Today – another angelic day, a ravishing spring blue (and still no rain) – I spent getting up all the old fence-posts and wire. I don't want any surveyor noticing what havoc has been wrought there. It's sad to see Batch, undoubtedly the oldest field here, a medieval field, and enormously rich in fungi, like all ancient pastures, so ravaged and rent. A whole microcosmos doomed.

15 March

The world falling apart economically: the London gold market and the Stock Exchange closed, an emergency bank holiday, a feeling of twenty-three evil, selfish Western years coming home to roost.[1] I feel some sympathy with the French, whom all the experts are blaming: their motives are basely political, of course. But the folly of keeping gold as the world's economic spine is so gross that one welcomes – in a way – anything that looks like dethroning it. Gold is a fundamentally inegalitarian metal: it goes with misers, hoarding, thinking of self instead of society. This last year has been rather like the landslip here: everywhere there is news of the Comintern splitting apart, of Russia and Russian-style Communism collapsing.[2] But it's been the least expected field that has subsided: the capitalist West.

After listening to all the gloom I went out last night into the garden, into a flawless spring night, a perfectly clear sky, a full moon, windless, the sea a great luminous sheen of honeyed silver: peace and solitude set on the world with the majesty of a late Beethoven adagio, with an authority so far beyond history, time, human folly, that it made me smile. The harmony in such moments is that such beauty exists and is seen: this forms a perfect interval, a chord which begins all and completes all in the one moment. Whether anything existed before, or will exist after, is irrelevant. All is justified now, now all is justified. I put it in poetic terms: but really it is the ultimate equation of science.

24 March

The unlikely Mr Steeds has offered £12,000, so I have to like him a little better. The land is still settling after the cataclysm. It's going to be a race between its subsiding and the completion date he offers – next September. We want another summer here; but I think it might be a very expensive one.

[1] The devaluation of the pound in November 1967 had led to a run on gold. While France withdrew from the international gold pool which had been intended to maintain a fixed price, Britain declared an emergency bank holiday on Friday 15 March 1968. The gold pool was officially disbanded and the London gold market remained closed for two weeks, reopening on 1 April.

[2] Most notably, in Czechoslovakia Alexander Dubcek had taken over as first secretary of the Communist Party on 5 January and, much to the alarm of the Soviet Union and the other Comintern countries, was introducing the series of liberal reforms that would become known as the 'Prague Spring'.

15 April

Jud here. I am going to do a script for him – well, not for him so much as for the idea (from a play by Ira Levin) he's got hold of: an attempt to found the Platonic Republic in a New England village.[1] I start on May 1st, by which time I must have *The French Lieutenant's Woman* cut and dried – cut especially.

Working on this last, a small spider stepped on to the page I was correcting – it turned out to be a rarity, *Scytodes thoracica* no less, a young one. Adults must be living in the workroom, as it is an indoor spider. *Scytodes* has the most ingenious of all arachnoid hunting systems. It captures its prey *retiarius* fashion, squirting a microscopic jet of 'glue' from its jaws and oscillating its head at the same time to produce a zigzag 'hose' effect. The victim is gullivered to the ground.

9 May

Three o'clock of a sunny afternoon, and a fox below the window. A very large one, and bold. It looked round, then went on its buoyant lope-walk along the sheds and down into the upper yard. No animal has quite such an air of vicious, savage independence about it; I think the more humorous aspects of the fox mythology – its tricks, its cunning – have something to do with the tail. Quite why such a long tail was thought necessary by evolution is a mystery; for it's certainly blinded man to the animal's nature.

12 May

I finish the first draft of the Ira Levin script. I started on April 29th. There's a lot to be done on it yet, but the back is broken.

1 June

The contract is signed for the sale of the farm. We move out on September 15th.

A pair of roe deer have taken up residence in the bottom field. They stand in the ferns, ears pricked if we go near. The ferns now reach just high enough to cover their heads, so they obviously think they're hidden, but the white ears stand above, quite ludicrously obvious on occasion. Even when they're lying down I can usually pick them out, so unmistakable is that bright caramel fur between the green inter-stices. The buck was very angry with us one evening and half-made across the field at us with a bark of rage. A frightening sound from so small an animal.

There must also have been a fox-earth in the gorse-thicket in Batch. The cubs lie outside in the sun in the evening.

[1] The Ira Levin play was called *Dr Cook's Garden.*

6 June

Assassination of Robert Kennedy. In the city and on the day *The Magus* was to be shown in public for the first time.[1] They cancelled the showing, of course. It seems to me a classic example – but then so was Oswald's story – of the effect of the nemo. I don't believe Sirhan can be explained by his reason: believing Kennedy was pro-Israel and so on. His motive was much more that of the nineteenth-century anarchists: to get his name into the history books, to do something about his nothingness. His only statement beyond yes or no in the first trial was apparently to tell the judge how to pronounce his name; just what one would expect. From now on, Sirhan survives, whatever happens to his body. Several women rushed to the police when it was announced that he might have had a female accomplice. All this happens in America, of course, because there the nemo can be most brilliantly defeated (by the successful) and most totally felt by the failures.

20–26 June

In London, to do a TV programme and discuss the Levin script with Jud. Two fruitful sessions with him – I realize so many past troubles must be laid at John Kohn's door. Perhaps there's some Jewish–Gentile balance Jud and I have struck, a sort of mutual understanding and toleration that neither of us would show, does show, to fellow-Jews or Gentiles. He's racially ashamed of John, basically; as I am of so much that is English.

23 July

Eliz has read *The FLW*; doesn't like the ending or the Carroll episode. I had doubts about them myself, so now I am changing them. Characters, thank heaven, are endlessly manipulatable at this stage in a manuscript.

30 July

We arrived some ten days ago at Charlie's mill to find Roy Christy and Judy there.[2] They came over the next day to have an evening with us – in pursuit of the great reconciliation. The evening ended at dawn the next morning; I think the most tedious ten hours I can recall. Roy still walks, and none too securely, the tightrope between a still resentful anger and a new persona he's clearly put on to cover – or perhaps

---

[1] Robert Kennedy was assassinated by a Palestinian Arab, Sirhan Sirhan, at the Ambassador Hotel, Los Angeles, on 5 June. Campaigning to be nominated the Presidential candidate for the Democratic Party, he was about to give a press conference after having won the California primary.

[2] The Christys' friend Charlie Greenberg had recently bought a country home at Farway in east Devon.

control – the old one. He's decided his literary forte is a mixture of comedy and more serious stuff. ('It's only what Shakespeare and Dickens did.' I like that 'only'.) And this is how he is now in private – sudden bouts of rather bellicose teasing and humour and then plunges into emotional seriousness. Beneath, the old monomania and egotism; I don't think there was ever a man so sublimely uninterested in everyone else around him. About two o'clock, after having drunk all we had offered, he came out with a proposal that I should send him a monthly cheque to pay for Anna's upkeep. And having come out with it he burst into tears. We all made comforting noises. Of course, of course . . . But hadn't we suggested it before? He was not to get upset . . . The hatred was over. It was such an astounding volte-face and swallowing of pride that there wasn't really much one could say. So we all sat in silence until he got over it and let us nurse him back into a good humour.

Now we have just seen him again in London – this time Anna was present, but after two hours of everyone being terribly nice he bolted for the pub. I went with him. We sat and had a beer. He got back on the old theme: how he hoped we would become good friends, close friends, we had so much in common . . . And as usual I jibbed. I think what liking he has for me is in the 'respectful' way I let him talk about himself and very seldom argue. He mistakes this for the possibility of communication. I said something about never having felt any need for close male friends, being a solitary, etc. And abruptly he is up in arms: 'Why do you always talk like that? Why do you pretend you can't get on with people?' I said, 'Because so many people have led me to believe it; I'm the conditioned dog.' We walked home in a grim silence. I ought to know by now; but his failure to understand that other people are different from him always makes him suppose that their difference (or mere declaration of independence) is a hostility.

I think it has become almost an argument for going abroad: the thought of many more such 'friendly' evenings nauseates me.

The film of *The Magus*. We went to see a showing – an audience of movie business friends of John and Jud. I thought there were distinct signs of a non-sale. It has turned out to be just about as vulgar as we feared. I suppose there is a certain slickness in the camera and cutting; but the music now added is repulsively banal. Caine's performance, in spite of all the cuts that have been made in it, remains wooden and hopelessly without depth. It's really the appalling hollowness and shallowness of the finished product that disgusts me. I am partly to blame – completely, where the script is just bad, and unconsciously, where I didn't foresee the danger of overwriting with someone like Guy Green. I understand better now why he wanted all literary lines cut: he simply doesn't know how to direct them. All the dialogue is spoken at snail's pace and every meaningful line is atrociously overstressed, both in delivery and in the killing pause that precedes it. I couldn't pretend, afterwards; which hurt Jud, the one person I don't want to hurt in all this.

Our future in the clouds again. Now there's an idea that I form a company and then get it taken over by Booker Bros. The final result, after five years, is that I get some 40 per cent of what I earn; as against the 20 per cent or so I should save on a straight tax assessment. The drawbacks are principally that if I join the Booker's set-up I join for five years; and that they take half of whatever is saved from tax.[1] It depends, says Tom Maschler[2] with his usual brutal clarity, whether you want to see your money going to swell a city company's profits or towards building a few roads and hospitals. That's oversimplifying, of course; but there's something in it. The alternative is exile, plainly with Malta top of the list, since the saving there is 95 per cent. We veer from day to day.

5 August
A pure white dove, alone, flying west over an iron-grey sea.

Hazel and Dan and the three children here.[3] They exhaust us; and make us feel guilty – the really atrocious amount of attention three small boy babies demand. Though Jonathan, three years old tomorrow, has the sort of wilful charm that can get away with murder; very instructive, the naked volition, mainly to smash, break, overturn, cover in water, in that small angelic face. Difficult to understand how the notion of the cherub arose; easy, rather. It arose from the experience of real children, by counterpole.

Interesting, too, that he was totally unafraid of the bullocks in the field, but flinched back at his first sight of a slow-worm curling round my fingers. I think this is purely the 'protective' influence of words: the bullocks he has classified as beneficial – 'moo-cows'. For the slow-worm he has no word and no previous pictorial experience. When I showed him how the slow-worm's tongue flickers out if you touch its nose, he wanted to kiss it.

14 August
Now it's Gozo, an allegedly unspoilt island near Malta. We've decided we'll go there when we've done the great retreat – to look, only.

18 August
And now it's not. Boxall thinks we should have to live there at least six months of each year; and there are snags in even this tax haven, it seems. We went yesterday to see a gaunt Victorian monstrosity of a manor, totally

---

[1] Booker was already operating such a tax-saving scheme with other successful British authors, notably Agatha Christie and Ian Fleming.
[2] JF's editor at his British publisher, Jonathan Cape.
[3] JF's sister Hazel had given birth to twins Simon and Tom in late 1967.

dilapidated, at Corscombe beyond Beaminster, then glanced at a house at Morecombelake, muttered again about Belmont House in Lyme, which we looked at six weeks ago – the most attractive house in the place, really, though the once fine garden has long been leased to the brambles and weeds. The asking price is absurd: £25,000. We could just about afford it. But it seems a weakness, to move away, yet stay so close. My instinctive desire to get away from Dorset, at least for a year or two, *is* right. More and more I hanker after a final something further west, in the South Hams or the Tamar valley – into Cornwall, perhaps. We change our minds each day, I think mainly because of the powerful hold this place exerts over us – has always exerted over me, though now it's Eliz who seems to feel it most (why did we ever sell, why did we not keep it till it fell, and so on). We shall never find a site like it again – neither in the landscape-of-peace sense, nor in the intricacy of the web of wild life that has the house so closely enmeshed. I can't write about it; it is an amputation and ought to be written about. But I can't write about it. Being stoic – that is, silent – is the only way of living through it without tears.

21 August
Hrabal, *A Close Watch on the Trains.*[1] A brilliant little work: as good, in its way, as Joyce's masterpiece in that genre (the long short story). I should like to attempt such a piece: the art is of showing a world through a narrow aperture. One does this either (Joyce and his funeral) by taking some single event and fully exploring it – more fully, in fact, than is possible in a novel proper – or (Hrabal, Voltaire) by condensing a novel to half or a third its length. In this latter method I think there is a parallel with watercolour painting: impressionism – with a small i – is inherent in the medium. Revision is in some way antipathetic; not impossible, as it is in a watercolour, but fatal if apparent. One has to get the technical pleasure of the *aquarelle*: first-time washes flawlessly placed. This pleasure Hrabal accomplishes beautifully.

25 August
The French Lieutenant's Woman.
   First draft completed October 1967.
   First revision 23 April 1968.

---

[1] Bohumil Hrabal's (1914–1997) tragic-comic novella (1965) follows the fortunes of a railway employee at a small station during the Nazi occupation of Czechoslovakia. The story ends with his heroic death when he blows up a train in an act of sabotage against the Germans. The film adaptation, *Closely Observed Trains*, directed by Jiri Menzel, won the Oscar for Best Foreign Film in 1967. In the wake of the film's international success, an English translation of the novella was published by Jonathan Cape in 1968.

Second revision 17 June 1968.

Third revision and new ending 25 August 1968.

I wasn't to know how apt my reading Hrabal was. We're now in the fifth day of the Czech crisis, and what I will call Hrabalism – David killing Goliath with humour rather than a slingshot – is very much in evidence.[1] In a way I am glad it's happened. The spectacle of girls chalking rude signs on the Russian tanks, the cascade of sparkling satire, is a great human step forward. The nicest shots out of Prague are of the bewildered Russian soldiers' faces. The whole thing indeed has been turned by the Czechs into a piece of satirical Czech literature – with Mrozek crossing from Poland and taking a hand.[2] In a way I feel sorry for the Russians; and credit is due for the way in which they have in general played their role – of the amiable, blundering, ridiculous 'heavy'.

What none of the fifty-one thousand commentators have explained to me is the real Russian motive in all this. There is first of all evidence that the occupation was planned long ago. It is certain they knew the odium they were inviting. They cannot, in the 'real' nuclear context, be very worried about the strategic loss (not that that was ever seriously in question) of Czechoslovakia. They must know that in doing it they are exacerbating their own internal discontent. I go back to my old theory of them as the chess-masters of the world. I look for evidence of the bold sacrifice in their intent. One excellent result for the Kremlin in the Czech intervention is immediately apparent: they put everyone's backs up and isolate their country, which allows them to carry on the old Stalinist line. Any drop in the tension of the Cold War is inimical to the economically underprivileged pole – to Russia. When the enemies disappear, so does the spirit of sacrifice. In its place comes the lust for consumer goods and all the rest of the fairground pleasures. I think they went into this deliberately hoping to create the situation they have.

30 August

Paramount are lukewarm about the script of *The Guardian*.[3] The theme 'is revealed too soon'; there is 'not enough suspense'. Which is like saying, Throttle down, but give me more power.

---

[1] Over the night of 20/21 August Warsaw Pact forces invaded Czechoslovakia. The leaders of the Prague Spring were whisked off to Moscow where, under duress, on 28 August they signed a memorandum agreeing to the presence of Soviet troops.

[2] Polish dramatist Slawomir Mrozek, who was actually living in Paris at the time, denounced the part that his country played in the Czech invasion in *Le Monde*.

[3] The working title for JF's screen adaptation of Ira Levin's play *Dr Cook's Garden*.

5 September
The FLW sent to Tom Maschler. With less trepidation than usual, though
I expect him not to like it as well as the first two. But I know it is more
or less what I intended.

6 September
Fine days, the hottest of the summer. The expectable feeling of sorrow,
now that the day is so close, irritation – because I think now we are
finally decided that we shan't go abroad – that we jumped so fast into
getting out. On the other hand we should never have been able to live
out our natural lives here. The slipping may delay ten years, but not
longer; and in a way the longer we stayed the worse it would have been.
And I have long felt the intense reluctance I have always had at leaving
this place even for only a day or two was not all love – was unhealthy.

7 September
I have offered £18,000 for Belmont House.
    The French Lieutenant's Woman is magnificent no less. Congratulations.
Letter follows. Love, Tom.
    That's a relief; after all. Though I suspect he says this to almost
everyone.

13 September
We settle at £20,000 for Belmont, subject to the usual things. Now we
lie awake at night dreading it, and live by day looking forward to it.
Partly it is because we have two financial philosophies: the old family
one, where to throw twenty thousand (plus the five or more that will
be needed to get the place habitable) down the same blue lias that
wrecked everything before is insane folly; and the other that really knows
the profit scale of values is remote from us. I have made so much money
these last few years that making money seems an absurd consideration
in a big decision. I think our nocturnal fears are really the old ant faces
reproaching the grasshopper – the puritans standing round and ready
to lynch the existentialist in us.

16–17 September
The great move out. It was done over two days by two patient old
men, who carefully wrapped everything and then carried it all away.
They must both have been nearer sixty than fifty, and showed a quite
extraordinary physical strength and stamina; the five or six young men
who moved us in were staggering and groaning all the way. These old
two did it all without a murmur. Strangely I enjoyed the first two days,
the throwing away of rubbish and the rest – a feeling of movement,
healthy change. But we spent a last night in the empty house, got up

at dawn to sweep the floors, do all the endless last jobs: and that was
horrid. We moved a lot of things to Charlie Greenberg's mill at Farway,
and spent another night there; another visit to Belmont, to go round
with Quicky for his opinion.[1] He was very useful, if pouncing on dry rot
and countless other faults is to be useful. In a way it's bad. We don't
want to leave Dorset, or the coast; so we have to take Belmont. But this
time we got up to the attic rooms and discovered a splendid view down
the coast – one of these little skivvy's rooms, to the south-east, would
be a delight if we could change it to a penthouse.

20 September
Hampstead. Working with Jud on the Ira Levin script, with which I am
now thoroughly bored. The storyline I sent in is the only one I could
be interested in; and now they want all sorts of wild changes. Such
slender reeds, these film people. The least breeze from the latest successful
movie sways them to their damp roots.

   To Charlie Greenberg's in Putney. He now has the mania I once
suffered from: the once austerely contemporary sitting-room is encased
with bad Victorian paintings, every table laden with bronzes – he is junk-
mad, in short. Though with such a chubby-Jewish enthusiasm that it's
fun. One can only like him for it.

   London is hard to get used to. I couldn't live here permanently again.
I think it is less the noise, the overcrowding and the rest, than the pressure on the artist: the constant inrush on the mind of new ideas, new
successes, new mayfly fames. I find all this deeply unsettling.

1 October
Meeting with Tom Maschler. He wants the two endings switched, the
'author' suppressed, from *The FLW*; otherwise only very minor changes.
He remains, as a person, as difficult to like as ever. He gets more and
more El Greco-like in looks; something famished in his eyes. He's much
more the devil than the saint, of course; and deep in him lies a homosexual butch, who has to rape and bugger everything in sight. This desire
to mount above, to be righter than right, to come off best, is comple-
mented by a sort of craving for affection that belongs to the other
homosexual partner, though at the first sign of sentiment the butch in
him cracks the whip. It is very weird, this mixture of suppressed innocence and abruptly black arrogance (the impression he always gives of
not being able to spare you more than a couple of minutes, of having
no time for your arguments – which really is an impression more than
a fact, since he is a sensitive editor under the graceless first force with

[1] 'Quicky' was local builder Cecil Quick, who advised JF on maintenance and
repair work.

which he demands changes). If I oppose him he climbs down with a ludicrous swiftness: 'Oh, I don't know, perhaps you're right . . . OK, don't let's bother.' Everyone maligns him, and he maligns everyone else: Why do I put up with such hopeless agents, such dull accountants; and so on. I think of all the Jews I know he is the most Jewish: the perfect example of the bitter, wandering, cast-out son of Israel. The sad Quixote of English litbiz.

Our relationship may go beyond the literary. He's all set to become a film producer now and he wants to use *The FLW* as his first step in the field – somehow he's managed to spirit the book away from Cape and get it to Karel Reisz, who Tom claims is a 'very close friend'. I admire Reisz, so I play along for the time being; and then all Tom's useful qualities, his force, might make him as good a film man as he is a publisher. But somehow I have to get him to be less suspicious and schizophrenic with me.

2 October

He has offered an advance of £8,000, which he says is the highest Cape have ever given outside the Len Deighton and Ian Fleming thriller class. The papers these days are full of the plight of the novelist (financially); so it seems a little unreal. I can't really believe the book is that good; or will ever earn, in this country, that kind of money back. I've told my parents and Charlie Greenberg, but with a distinct embarrassment.

11 October

To Farway, to Charlie Greenberg's. We (Charlie and I) went to Exeter, to the antique fair, on the Saturday. We make a thoroughly dangerous combination, exacerbating each other's already sufficient mania. But I enjoyed the 'fair' and the sight of all the New Hall china, which has now climbed to six, seven, eight times what I paid for mine a few years ago. I didn't buy any; but a very fine little Prattware jug, a nice miniature, a Regency windharp, two jolly paintings; and a Japanese print at another shop, and two Mogul paintings at another.

17 October

I have been this week alone in the mill at Farway, working on the accursed script. It is one of those plots where nothing will go right, nothing works in naturally, every turning a spiral into an added complication. My only companions are the starlings that roost in the roof and clatter about all night long. Sometimes they seem to put on small nailed boots and march up and down. The old apple-trees have nice birds, too: every day long-tailed tits, marsh tits and treecreepers; the odd buzzard mewing, the old man who comes and hoys the cows in from the field opposite, the old lady with a baritone voice across the road talking to her dog. I walk up the hill a mile or two. It's very fresh and green, this valley, a second growth in everything, full of streams, of beeches grey-stemmed in the sunlight, orange-leaved. I picked a scabious still in flower at the top towards Honiton, where the vegetation goes a little moorlandish; acutely pleasurable, that shaft of another season, another landscape, which some flowers give. This gave chalk downland, marbled whites, blue distances at one's feet – no painting, no symphony, nothing could give it so intensely and completely, in one instant. The scent of some flowers (a sprig of thalictrum – July, watermeadows, punts, beer outside country pubs – I also picked was the same) really constitutes a hidden art.

These walks, on which I see nothing unusual, confirm me my love of this countryside very strongly. I do not want to live anywhere else in the world. I never want to live for more than a few days at a time in London again.

29 October
The Cape party, which we haven't been to for several years. It amuses me that none of the directors there said a word to me, apart from Tom, of course. Michael Howard plainly didn't know who I was, Tony Colwell and Graham Greene[1] didn't 'want to' know who I was. I feel they blame Tom for giving such a high advance; but can't blame him to his face, so blame me to mine. But it may be simply the Englishness of the English; that ineffable reluctance to seem to know. We talked with the Tarns[2] and the Wisemans[3] and Tom's father, who's a nice old Swiss-German, gently amused by his son's success and a little envious of it, since the Nazis forced him to give up his own left-wing house in Berlin in the 1930s. He was angry with me for smoking so much; one gets so used to mocking talk about the dangers of oversmoking, and I liked him for refusing to take it lightly. He's made me cut down a little.

Edna O'Brien was also there. We are very evidently not on her list of knowable people any more. I affronted her by kissing her on the cheek when we met; and I think we affront her, or her life principle, by remaining married; or perhaps she sees me as some kind of dangerous literary rival, personifying a philosophy of permanence against her own steely determination to celebrate the very opposite. She is a treacherous woman, very much the classical siren. I watched her exerting her charms

---

[1] i.e., Graham Carleton Greene, nephew of the novelist and the then managing director of Jonathan Cape.
[2] The poet Nathaniel Tarn and his wife Patricia. Tarn was then director of Cape's poetry imprint Cape-Goliard, which he had founded the year before.
[3] The novelist and former film critic Thomas Wiseman and his wife Malou. Jonathan Cape were about to publish his novel *The Quick and the Dead.*

on the other men there; there is something in their eyes that is very much what must have been in Odysseus' sailors' – say the word, and I'll unbind myself.

Roy's novel, which we have at last bought (*The Nightingales Are Sobbing*); it is an egomaniac's book, of course, each character a thin mask over his own face; and full of a clipped gusto – shades of Ruskin Spear[1] and Gulley Jimson[2] – that is as uncool as can be. A lament for his own lost past, really; and it would have got attention twenty years ago.

31 October

Denys,[3] who has been living in London this last month – he's head of the British Council Language Institute in Portland Place now – and avoiding us like the plague, came to spend an evening drinking with me. He hasn't changed, and soon got, after a half-bottle of whisky, on to the old elegy of his failed ambition; the futility of his present work; the mess of his life. 'All I've ever done is hurt people.' He seemed shocked when I said I knew about his affaire with the French woman in Nigeria. I said, 'But Eliz and Monica are close now, I've had a back-wash of it from them.' He is always distressed to be known for what he is, not as he gives out. 'I know for you I'm poor old Denys, the eternal clown . . .' I told him he was a victim of the Tristan-and-Isolde sickness, he could write, it was only a little finding of time, a little courage – all of which he agreed with; but he loves it, that myth. He has – has always had – a remarkably clear death-wish; it's as plain as stigmata on him now. Not a literal death, of course; but a long lingering over the death of what he might have been. He spoke of having to support Monica and Michael as if it were a kind of crucifix; a responsibility unimaginable to me or any other but his rare class of martyr. 'I'd leave the Council tomorrow if we hadn't got to provide Michael with some kind of stability.' Then he confessed that he had written a few commencing pages of a telly play recently, but 'as soon as I was back in my office on Monday, I had all that pressure of reality on me'. It's rather like some free man saying, I couldn't do it because I had to report to the Tower to be racked. I mean there is something medieval in his determination to be deter-mined by what he hates.

To be a writer it is not enough to jettison what is bad in you; the good also – the good you might have been, or done, in other fields –

---

[1] The portraits of the British painter Ruskin Spear (1911–1990) were notable for an often strong element of caricature.

[2] The bohemian artist in Joyce Cary's trilogy of novels *Herself Surprised, To Be a Pilgrim* and *The Horse's Mouth*.

[3] Denys Sharrocks, whom JF first met in 1952 when they were both teachers at the Anargyrios and Korgialenios School in Spetsai.

has to go too. It is certainly more difficult to get rid of this; and much more important.

Hardy, *Jude the Obscure*. I think this is the most interesting novel the old enigma ever wrote, though a long way from the best. What is lacking from it is an extra dimension of irony – the kind of trick (deliberate use of coincidence) that Pasternak used to bring off *Doctor Zhivago*; and then he lacks the courage of both his private past and his public present. Clearly the book should be subtitled 'The Story of My Love for Tryphena'; and clearly he chickened over Sue, by making her the febrilely unsexual being she is – surely the biggest cockteaser in all Victorian fiction and seriously damaging of the book's structure as a result.[1] Gosse's famous question should really have been: What has fear of his public reputation done to Mr Hardy that he cannot curse Providence *more* under his Wessex skies?[2]

Of course, Hardy had also his pathologically intense need to cover up the past; but I am sure the real truth of the Tryphena affaire is in *Jude*. It points to a passionate (and very un-Sue-like) liaison in the 1867–8 period. The birth of an illegitimate child (the Arabella child in *Jude*, 'Little Father Time') who must have died by the time Hardy wrote the novel in the mid-1890s. Perhaps the suicide in Oxford is the truth . . . or near it.[3] From 1870 on, perhaps earlier, there is a revulsion in Tryphena, a sudden yearning for respectability, a feeling that she has flouted religion, etc . . . on top of whatever family secret may have been involved (hidden in 'the Fawleys must never intermarry', etc.). Arabella

---

[1] In *Jude the Obscure* unhappily married stonemason Jude Fawley separates from his wife Arabella, and leaves his home village for Christminster, where he hopes to enrol in the university. Here he falls in love with his cousin Sue Bridehead who marries schoolteacher Richard Phillotson, but then abandons him to live with Jude. JF's conviction that the novel offered a key to Hardy's hidden romantic past was shared by several biographers. But although the consensus is that after returning to Dorset in the summer of 1867 Hardy did have a romantic relationship with his sixteen-year-old cousin – who like Sue Bridehead would become a teacher – there is no solid evidence as to the exact nature of that relationship, and JF's theory that the two had an illegitimate child together is speculative.

[2] Edmund Gosse's actual question, in a review of the book, had been: 'What has Providence done to Mr Hardy that he should rise up in the arable land of Wessex and shake his fist at his creator?'

[3] After their separation, Jude's wife Arabella goes to live in Australia. Returning to England, she reveals to Jude that there she gave birth to his son. Jude gives a home to the child, who he learns was not christened 'Jude' as he had supposed, but had been given only the nickname 'Little Father Time' because he seemed 'so aged'. He and Sue struggle to look after the strange child in considerable poverty together with their own two children. 'Little Father Time' hangs the two children and himself, leaving a note, 'Done because we are too menny.'

is plainly Emma Lavinia, suitably, though not essentially (contemptuous of the finer Jude, hooking him sensually, and so on) disguised.[1] Phillotson is Charles Gale; I think there must have been some desperate scene in Plymouth between Tryphena and Hardy from which comes Sue's last phase in the novel.[2]

This (the inner true story) is what carries the novel through; what makes Sue, in spite of all the inconsistencies (beyond the intended) in her characterization, so vivid. I'm sure that's why the photograph was burnt; he knew he had her far better by then. She reminds me very much of Sanchia H;[3] precisely that phasal quality, that priestess of Astarte aura, with the genius for luring and receding, shimmering, rainbow-like – unattainable as the rainbow's end. It is really a Jungian novel, the history of an obsession with the rain-virgin, the *princesse lointaine*, and all the rest of that shadowed phylum.

I feel very close to Hardy. All through *Jude* I found myself seeing his technical mistakes; and understanding them almost as if I had written it myself. I feel I know exactly how his mind works, how he creates, not because I have any special knowledge of the objective correlative – what really happened to him in his life – but because I have that same kind of mind, that adoration of personal myth, that ability to use it and transmute it. Sarah in *The FLW* (I had never read *Jude* till this last week) is a form of Sue; and the second 'bitter' ending I have written is really a kind of homage to Hardy – how he would have ended it.[4]

He is to me in prose what Clare is in poetry; in some way that any sane academic critic (who would know far more in all factual ways than I do) would dismiss as mere vanity, I know I am closer to these two than to any but the very closest of the living; I feel almost the sense of a re-incarnation in reverse, of my living in them still, therefore their living

[1] In 1870 Hardy met Emma Lavinia Gifford. They married in 1874. Although the marriage turned out to be unhappy, they remained married until Emma's death in 1912.

[2] In 1877, Tryphena married publican Charles Gale. Settling down in the village of Topsham in Devon, she gave up teaching and had four children. In Hardy's novel, the terrible loss of their children causes Sue and Jude to break up. Sue goes back to live with Richard Phillotson, and Jude goes back to Arabella.

[3] Sanchia Humphries, a student with whom JF had a flirtation when he was a teacher at Ashridge College in the 1950s. See *The Journals*, volume 1, pages 315 ff.

[4] In *The French Lieutenant's Woman* ex-governess Sarah Woodruff has a love affair with aristocrat Charles Smithson, but then disappears, leaving no forwarding address. After travelling abroad, Charles eventually manages to track down Sarah and their baby daughter to the house of the painter Rossetti, for whom Sarah works as a model. In a first ending, Charles and Sarah are happily reunited. But in a second 'bitter' ending, Charles realizes that he cannot win Sarah's unqualified love and leaves her, resolving to depart for America.

still. There is a great poem of Clare's madness ('Song Last Day' – 'There is a day a dreadfull day') that haunts me as if I wrote it myself. I keep on going back to read it *precisely* as one goes back to read an own poem, just written, that one likes.

4 November
Another 'celebrity' party, this time at the Wisemans', to celebrate the publication of Tom Wiseman's novel *The Quick and the Dead*. Edna was there again, and a batch from Tom W's old professional world (he was film critic once on the *Express*): Penelope Mortimer, Milton Shulman. Diana Rigg and her director lover-of-the-moment, Philip Saville. Carl Foreman and Ken Adams, who does the James Bond film sets. Quite what is so unlikeable (unstomachable by Eliz and myself) in these filmbiz people I don't know; it isn't just their egocentricity, their assumption that one must be successful, that today's and tomorrow's fame must be synonymous – the Egyptian quality in show business. Perhaps it is the constant misuse of language; a treachery both conscious (the eagerness to establish links, relationships, futures at the cost of real personal feelings) and unconscious (a pinchbeck vocabulary) that gives a kind of seething, serpentine quality to such congregations: that of a nest or swarm of beings self-adulatory, warming to one another, and yet fanged in every external reality. We stayed on after everyone else had gone, with Rigg and her husband; Milton Shulman holding forth. He has that Canadian Jewish love of being outrageous, a little comical, as talk-monopolizing as a Dr Johnson – his thesis being that individual art has gone for ever, that now only community art (the cinema and TV and pop art in general) remains. It all hurts Tom W, who has a very un-Jewish lack of humour and is easily baited. Shulman (theatre critic of the *Evening Standard* and I suppose third or fourth in 'power' over the London theatre) shocked me more when he said he was bored stiff by the theatre, cared now only for TV criticism. His is precisely the most current evil in English criticism: a state of apathy in which shock (the bizarre, the not-done-before) becomes the only way he can be jabbed into praise. These people (this state of mind) have far too much power.

13 November
Norman[1] ridiculously undercharged me for some books yesterday. I said I must pay more. He said, 'Money doesn't mean anything to me now.' Then he told me how Janey, his fifteen-year-old daughter, had climbed out on the roof behind the shop last July to fetch in her cat; had slipped and fallen and been killed outright. Though I hadn't seen her for years

[1] Francis Norman, whose secondhand bookshop in Heath Street, Hampstead, was a prime source of old books for JF.

– or more than a glimpse of her – it gave me a terrible shock. I didn't know how to say it; one could only have stood in tears. He talked about his wife, who has been a schizophrenic for years, with frequent fugues into the blue – he hasn't seen her since before Janey died, apparently. He said, 'I was Janey's mother as well as her father, I ironed and darned her clothes, cooked for her all those years.' He was very near tears, poor man. I have always felt the greatest affection for him. It seems intolerable that one man should have so much tragedy to bear (he lost his first wife and family in the V-bomb period); and to bear it so quietly. 'The shop keeps me alive, that's all I keep it on for.' I added a pound to the cheque I wrote; but he didn't even look at it, because I think he would give books away now. He is like Lear or Oedipus, well through and past a barrier where one can reach him. A very ancient Greek feel about him: one on whom the Gods have pronounced. But earlier he was joking in his old way, showing me absurd snippets from some Catholic leaflet on the conduct of wives; he's a very brave and honourable old man.

Janey was a very pretty child, very Victorian, with dark grey eyes that seemed almost black, like buttons in a small pink face. The kind of child Martial wrote his finest epigram-epitaph for.

28 November

We were planning to go down to Lyme today. But Eliz is ill with shingles, the doctor won't let her go. So I drive down with Charlie Greenberg, who wants to go to the Honiton sale. He is now a complete monomaniac, blind to everything but paintings. We stop at Salisbury – and a shock there. In one of the shops the dealer says he has a Rossetti at home – not for sale, but he takes us to look at it. It's of a girl, some substitute for Siddall, painted in 1868 with auburn hair and staring out of the frame, a New Woman. It had a strange effect on me; as if there *had* been a Sarah Woodruff, she *had* gone to Rossetti's house, he *had* painted her, and here she was.

1 December

At last to Belmont.

I wander round the empty rooms, trying to make up my mind what needs doing first. Three main problems: the floor over the cellar in the east room is rotting; so is the south-west room, the damp beading almost up to the ceiling; and the central heating. Then a host of minor ones – windows to be knocked in, walled up, the wiring to be seen to, the stables to be saved (they're like one huge sponge at the moment), the garden, the fencing – I draw up endless lists. And enjoy it, the peace and quiet after London, the feel of the house, almost a gratitude that something is going to happen after its ten empty years. It has a kind of female feel, this Belmont, I don't know why; a bit of an old whore, with its splendid façade and all the mess that lies behind the façade rooms.

And as for the garden, it is a whole world – a jungle of bramble, but still with relics of its former grandeur, still some rare old shrubs surviving. The magnolia tree is in full bud; the japonica is coming into flower, some sort of delicate little white ornamental onion also. I hacked my way through to a linhay near the bottom, a nice little building two stories high. We'll make a summerhouse out of that. Discovered another huge pittosporum, a palm-tree, an auracaria, apples. It is a garden full of levels and terraces and lost corners, and seems more like ten acres than its actual one and a bit. I don't mind its state of ruin really. There are so many enjoyable things to do and discover. Like a huge toy.

I wish Eliz were here, though. It seems such a pity not to have the first days' fun together.

8 December

To London, to fetch Eliz and meet Oscar Lewenstein, whom Tom M has 'interested' in *The FLW*. He's a gentle-bright little Jew, very understated, a robin – a dunnock, rather. One sees him slipping quietly through the movie undercopse, getting his ends. The last man, really, at first look, to achieve what he has done in the cinema.[1] He lives in the splendid Gothick house in Belsize Lane.

He is fairly optimistic, seems to see the difficulties on a script-style level well. But where my choice would really be Ken Russell, his is Dick Lester – mainly because the latter is 'easy to finance' and has a firm relationship with Lewenstein. We settle finally for a list of three top choices: Lester, Russell and Lindsay Anderson. Tom has complicated matters by trying to get Freddy Raphael interested as well – but he's cabled back from Jamaica to say that he's interested only if he can direct as well. We can't tell Lewenstein this.

Roger Burford[2] is full of doubts and queries. I begin to see already that my Candidean notion that this – besides getting a better film – would be a simpler way of doing things is absurd.

9 December

We come back by train.

[1] Theatre impresario Oscar Lewenstein (1917–1997) was a founder member of the English Stage Company at the Royal Court. He presented some of the most notable plays of the 1960s, which were at the heart of the British revival in the cinema during that decade – including *A Taste of Honey*, *Billy Liar* and *What the Butler Saw*. He was also a director of Woodfall Film Productions, among many other films producing Tony Richardson's Oscar-winning *Tom Jones* in 1963.

[2] JF's film agent.

The more we uncover the more seems wrong – rotting wood, leaking drains, broken joists, which Quicky and his crew meet with calm and a certain pleasure.

The garden begins to defeat me, so vast the work to be done; and wherever one digs, one digs bulbs. I begin to discover the old paths and walls; a bed of spring irises, clumps of day-lilies, an old cast-iron seat. And everywhere the accursed brambles, I think my most hated plant, though I suppose there's something admirable, as with the sparrow, in such evolutionary tenacity. I've debrambled an old fig-tree; but some animal is killing it off by chewing the bark, the way roe deer do. It can't be roe deer. I suspect rats, though there are no other signs of them. Possibly a rabbit or two survives in the lower jungle.

Meanwhile, Eliz gets better, thank God; and we begin to live a faintly more civilized life.

20 December
Gillon[1] says Little, Brown have offered $125,000 advance; 60/40 on the paperback; and a flat 15 per cent royalty.

Quite good reviews of the film of *The Magus* in *The New York Times* and in *Time* magazine; two bad ones elsewhere. The good ones are absurd, the bad ones correct. I am beginning to feel like not selling film rights again. Paramount still don't like the revised version of *Dr Cook's Garden*; it's 'not near enough to *Rosemary's Baby*, not exciting enough'. Jud rang from California last night to say he was baffled, didn't know where to go; he clearly has as much chance of getting artistic understanding out of the studio as he has of swimming the Pacific to Japan. There's nowhere to go.

15 January 1969
A fortnight or more of the worst depression I have had for some time. I feel full of bile, a kind of smouldering anger against the time. I think in a way it is being British: being of a country that has what is clearly a death-wish, a longing for disaster. Yesterday there was the worst trade gap for months; today it is announced that we are bottom of the EFTA export list; every programme of *24 Hours* has news of some further idiot clash between organized labour and disorganized management. The dissociation between the public and the private view of Britain (and being British) widens and widens; people are looking for some kind of black saviour – a major slump, another war. That will shake us up, they think, everything rotten will be swept away then. It is a bizarre amalgam of hedonism today

---

[1] The literary agent Gillon Aitken, who was then working for JF's agent Anthony Sheil in New York.

and masochism tomorrow – a deliberate running up of bills, a secret delight at the thought of the bailiffs to come hammering on the door.

Part of the depression comes from *The FLW*. The two huge advances it has got have mysteriously devalued it in my eyes. There is one straw in the wind that suggests they were overcalculated: neither British book club is interested in the book. And so I feel myself an impostor – almost, under the new consumer protection act, a criminal, asking an inflated price for a spurious product. Somehow the flop of the movie of *The Magus* (Judith Krist has just pronounced it, fairly enough, as one of the ten worst films of 1968) seems a truer judgement than that of the English-American publishers and agents' quartet of enthusiasm for the new book.

A ridiculous question from one of the American Who's Who compilations that list me: what are my goals in life, and what my contributions? Ridiculous – and yet irritating. One should be able to answer; and then it seems healthy that one can't. I sent back: 'To escape; and to help others escape.'

18 January
Tragedy at the bottom of the garden. We've had two or three days of violent gale and wind, to hurricane force at times. Just before six this evening the catamaran in the harbour broke adrift and to sea. The little lifeboat put out to bring it back; overturned; and one of the men, Robert Jeffard, known as Nimmer, was drowned. We didn't see it happen, but went down at midnight to the Cobb and saw the battered lifeboat being trucked back. It wasn't, alas, a simple story of heroism. Jeffard and Roy Gollop, the fisherman, had a salvage interest in the 'cat'; and rang up the lifeboat secretary to ask if they could use the lifeboat. He foolishly said they could; so they did a stupid thing for a few pounds. We'd been watching the huge seas all day from the house, saying how no one could have lived out there in it. Now the whole of Lyme is angry and wants a scapegoat. But in a way it was a regional tragedy: the traditional greed of the inshore seaman, always on the scrounge, and West Country hatred of seeing a good penny roll down a drain.

31 March
I am forty-three today. And alone (Eliz is fetching Anna down from London), so I can ignore the whole thing. Until two or three years ago I suppose that would have been bravado, a sort of pose; the old Leigh-on-Sea thing, the terror of letting anniversaries, private or public, slip by unnoticed. Now I really do see them all as tribal, neolithic, runestone rubbish. I watched Eisenhower's funeral for a time this evening; that too is neolithic – much nearer painting oneself with red ochre than to the age of Apollo Nine.

16 April
Panther offer £11,000 (plus £1,000 as a film escalator) for *The FLW*. Pan wouldn't go above £8,000. I feel no guilty conscience about leaving them; paperback firms are faceless, and indifferent to the one thing most writers care about: some kind of human contact.

17 April
Anna is accepted at the Exeter College of Art; great relief all round. She irritates me a little by the way she never helps Eliz; but rushes off every day to work at the riding school at Chideock Seatown. But neither of us were gracious eighteen-year-olds; and at least she is admirably equable, un-neurotic about life.

18 April
Literary Guild in the States will take *The FLW* as an autumn choice. Another relief.

24 April
To London, to meet Lindsay Anderson, whom Oscar has interested in the film. He's a curious mixture of aggression and shyness. A huge Cyrano nose that scents for trouble; and sits in all sorts of odd contorted positions, as if to suggest he is at ease, when the reverse is true. I rather favoured making more of the author-figure; but the others didn't like that. The general feeling seems to be that a voice-over commentary on the historical sidelights would be best. It wasn't a very conclusive meeting; Anderson managed to convey the feeling that he was interested, but rather like the toreador in the first rituals of the bullfight: not his time yet. It was decided to approach David Storey to do the script – Anderson has just produced a play of his. Tom and Oscar seemed very pleased – as I will be, if it works. But I now think everything hinges on Storey. If he says yes, we have Anderson; if not . . .

4 May
Storey says he doesn't want to do the script; admires the novel, so Oscar tells me, but finds no male character he can 'relate' to. Oscar says, 'He has this thing about strong men – when he did *Wuthering Heights*, it was all Heathcliff.' So Anderson is havering again.

14 May
We are in the house now – have been so for ten days; and like it. The garden runs amok; it needs six gardeners working all week, not old Board for two days and myself spasmodically. It calls me away all the time. I start one job, remember another, go to do it, see some new flower on

the way. I like it so; and at least the jungle has given us a resident blackcap and whitethroat. A tawny owl comes each night and sits in the magnolia; a bulky black omen. I presume it is Tiberius transmigrated, and comes after the dormice.

12 June

Publication day. This time, thank God, I've been spared the wretched publicity interviews; whether because I asked Tom to spare me them, or because nobody wanted to bother anyway, I don't know . . . and care less. I dislike this time intensely. And haven't even bothered to buy the undelivered papers with reviews. A good one in the *New Statesman*, a bad one in the *Times* – full of misunderstandings, the voice of the literary establishment. But I know now that good or bad they're irrelevant; praise or damnation in this poor sick culture – they alter nothing. Even the harshest reviewer is never the real enemy.

15 June

A fair review in the *Observer*, a silly little piece in the *Sunday Times*, so skimpy it would have been better not written. But I feel some relief that I've been dropped by the vogue-addicted Thomson Organisation; and given a little more credit from the Left. I think this time will be a test of 'name' against 'reviews' – on review form I shouldn't reach the bestselling list.

More reviews. An excellent one in *New Society* – not particularly excellent for me, but in its accuracy. I might have written it myself; which is more than I can say for the best review – publisher-wise – of all in the *Financial Times*. It's very flattering to read, but not really about the book I wrote. The others are all bouquet-and-reservation; damning with faint praise, in fact. Tom Maschler is depressed, thinks they're all mean. I think both he and Ned Bradford overrate me; my commercial value, anyway.

19–21 June

In London, to fetch Anna down. She is ours now, thank goodness; that is, she will go to Exeter next year for her art training and stay here till then.

We at last persuaded Denys to meet us again, one evening. And Ronnie and Betsa came in. Ronnie and Denys took to each other, which pleased me. I suppose it ought to have offended, their being so much more interested in one another than in me; but in a way it gave me a subtler vanity. That two nice, if wayward, men should have such identity. That is, I picked well.

25 June

A strange moment in the stable. It was dusk, I was standing at the foot of the stairs up to the hayloft – the dark stairs and the square rectangle of grey light above. And a sudden very sharp sense of an uncanny fear. I am so totally unsuperstitious, unbelieving in 'psychic' phenomena, that it can't have been anything exterior to me. Yet afterwards it came to me that it was my own ghost. In some bizarre way I was haunting myself. Being dead while I am still alive.

The feel was of something looking down.

I have, have had for some months now, a sort of apathy about existence in me, and it probably sprang from that. It is a kind of constant dwelling on death, and an indifference to the idea; at times, almost a will-lessness, a morbid aboulia. Something has gone wrong with my kidneys or my liver, I don't know which, but I keep passing dark urine and as soon as I work in the garden there's a pain in the small of my back. This started eight or ten weeks ago and I should have gone to the doctor. I feel ill, but not too ill to live the lazy life we lead here. It is as if I wanted to be very ill. A kind of expiation? I don't know.

It is bound up too with the wretched business of the absurd quantity of cigarettes I smoke – still fifty or sixty a day. Ten minutes won from the wretched things is a kind of victory. I try and stop, some mornings; but can never make it last more than an hour, and then smoke twice as fast as before. I can't smell flowers any more and have a permanent smoker's throat. Wake in the night and swear I will stop. It has sapped all sense of power in my own will, really. I can't live, certainly can't write, without nicotine.

27 June

Yesterday I began to plan the novel I called before *The Two Englishmen*. I think I'll call it *Futility* now. I want it to be the two sides of myself, two men, friends who have drifted apart, the outward success and the inward success. But over both of them a sense of failure, of being defeated by their time. In the spirit of my own sickness.

Today I've written a first chapter, set in Los Angeles. But it won't do, the angle's wrong. It is very difficult, this first approach, getting the first chapter right; like searching for a key among a forest of accidentals; a style. I think I must play no tricks this time: something classical, third-person and past tense.

5 July

I am reading de Retz's *Memoirs* at the moment in a 1719 Amsterdam edition I bought recently from Norman (the first edition was 1717).[1] I

---

[1] Cardinal de Retz (1613–1679) was one of the leading figures during the period of civil wars in France that became known as the Fronde (1648–1652). A classic of French seventeenth-century literature, his memoirs provide an eyewitness account of the early years of Louis XIV's reign.

suppose it is ridiculous, with so many modern annotated editions available, to have this *lubie* for original texts. I'm not quite sure if it's just the type, the bibliographical pleasure, or the lack of notes and apparatus; but I derive from such reading something more vivid – sharper in focus. I mean I find myself more present, though understanding less, than with a modernized, 'explained' text. And being there seems to me so much more important than knowing there.

21 July

The moon landing. We watched the box from six in the evening till six the next morning. The landing was beautiful, too good to be true, more exciting than (though strangely similar to) the best fiction on the subject. I am against the whole project on moral and political grounds; but I think it was perhaps an allowable fling, a forgivable last sowing of man's wild oats. It is all, of course, highly sexual – not only in the Virgin Moon context, the rape – but even more in the constant analogy of thrust and ejaculation. But now the party's over; back home, the mess has to be cleared.

15–18 August

To Wales, to spend a weekend with Tom M at his country cottage in the Black Mountains. Tom has a new girlfriend now, called Fay Coventry; a milky, intelligent, quietly self-possessed creature. We hardly saw her, she spent the whole weekend in the kitchen, making jam, cooking, cooking very well, and I think making a web for him to fall into. He zigzags about like a daddy-long-legs half in love with death (marriage to her); and half in love with pleasure (which means just using her). I think he is the most *désinvolté* person I have ever met; though there is something cruel in his airy freedom, a contempt for people who don't make an equal amount for themselves. Something cruel and easily hurt also. We went for a walk in the mountains and I can't stand his restlessness, the feel he gives that one must be getting somewhere. So I suggested he went home and left me to idle on in my own haphazard fashion. He was tired, wanted to go home; but I see it offended him, that I could do without him, that I might have some secret, some pleasure perhaps, from which I was excluding him. Like all Jews, he finds it immensely difficult to take any but a very cursory interest in nature; yet feels he ought to, because he sees the inconsistency in living in such a wild place and not knowing anything about the life of it; and then again, hasn't the patience, must get on.

In the cottage it's all games. He has an insatiable enthusiasm for them: darts, backgammon, ping-pong, carpet bowls. He needs competition as other people need hashish. Which we found enjoyable, over a weekend; and I find absurd, as a way of life.

15 September

A depressing month since I last wrote here. It's partly the weather, I've come to rely on September being fine. Instead, we've had a fortnight of low cloud, first in drought, now in rain. Anna left last week for her art course in Exeter, so we're on our own, in the old familiar mood of Dorset *huis clos.*

Eliz has succumbed to her usual autumn depression; her hatred of the country, our life in it, all life in it. We live where we never wanted to live, we are trapped, everyone we know is poor, yet we sit in this huge, empty house . . . and so on. I feel the waste of the house most. We use the same four rooms, the rest are rooms we pass through occasionally. I think our trouble is our terrible, insatiable boredom; with both of us it has become an almost positive thing, a dominant. I come off better than Eliz, since I can imagine, dream, write my way round it; can treat people I fundamentally dislike as biological specimens. And so on. But everything bores her now. The idea of having people here excites us in advance; then irritates us progressively as their arrival draws near; and they start boring us within minutes when they come. And this is with old friends; so we can't risk having any contact with the Lymers. The only ones we do see occasionally, the old doctor and his wife next door, confirm all we fear. He tells pointless stories at great length. My mind wanders, I smile without knowing what he's been saying, then I say ridiculous things myself to get off on some other subject.

The FLW depresses me, I can't say why. It has been much better reviewed, on the whole, than the other two. But it feels like a stone in a rough sea. One saw it a moment, now it's sunk for ever. All I'm left with is the reviews and three or four letters people wrote; and the feeling that it hasn't sold well at all. It's really all summed up in the total indifference of Lyme itself to the book. Only one person has even mentioned reading it to me; the local paper has passed it by in total silence. There hangs over novel-writing now a sort of twilight – just like today's weather, in fact. No one cares. I don't even care very much myself.

Two more directors have turned the film down. That too seems doomed.

18 September

I gave up smoking five days ago, I think perhaps as a reaction against so much else in my life that seems adrift at the moment. My mantra has been 'Do something else'. I don't miss the physical 'pleasures' – aroma and so on – of tobacco at all. What is agonizing is the cigarette as part of the normal punctuation of life. Not smoking is rather like reading without such punctuation, without indents; that is, it makes getting through the day a tense, totally unrelaxed business. The worst difficulty of all is at the typewriter. For years now I have more or less chainsmoked while writing; using the cigarette to concentrate, keep up the flow. If I am at a loss for a word, a bit of dialogue, I reach for a cigarette. It is so slow now. My mind drifts off continually.

3–11 October

In London, and not enjoying it. Eliz has her usual autumnal depression, and I have the vile nicotine-withdrawal syndrome to cope with. It is not so simple as it seems, doing without it. One's mind seems to stop. I forget things, both physically and mentally, have no certainty that I've done simple sums right – even opening a tin is difficult. It's very strange, the actual direct physical desire to pick up a cigarette and light it has almost gone; but again and again I catch myself half-asleep, purposeless, absent-minded . . . quite blunt, in fact. I both waste time and hate having my wasting of time wasted by anyone else.

Then F[1] has had an optic coronary and lost the sight of his left eye. We drive down to Leigh, where it turns out he's not so bad as he sounds over the phone; that is, he can see quite well out of the remaining eye. We spoil him, take him bits of cheese and champagne bottlets. It is beautiful weather, which always makes us hate having left Lyme.

F's Duchesse d'Angoulême pears were ripe; and the James Grieve from the old tree he bought forty years ago for a shilling. I think probably the best apple-tree in England, its fruit is not like that of any other James Grieve I have ever eaten: but mellower, sweeter, more buttery. The pears, watery and very fragrant, are also beautiful. Quite how he became such a genius with apples and pears I don't know; perhaps it is just the having had endless time to waste in too small a space. I speak of him in the past tense, because I feel he will die this winter. But he is very tenacious, it may not happen. I can't bear to think of a time when I shan't be able to taste that fruit – which sounds selfish. But the best of him has passed into those trees.

Nabokov, *Ada*. He's a wicked old man, a dirty old man; this is more masturbation, delicious old man's dreams of young girls, all drenched in a kind of Watteau-like autumnal mist; and very beautiful, he evokes scenes, moments, moods, long-past hours almost as well as Proust. The weak half of him is the Joycean one, though in a way I think he needs that weak half more than most writers. I mean, his sticky, silly patches glide so smoothly into the better, Proustian scenes. I think the pointlessness of so much of the erudition (which is just having had out-of-the-way hobbies and reading habits) will always keep him off the top of Parnassus; but even if that weren't so, there is something nasty in his

[1] JF's father.

shadows: a narcissism, an onanistic adoration of Nabokov. Almost as if he were Genet – but with none of Genet's frankness.

We couldn't stand London, it was so hot. An afternoon at Kew, very enjoyable. I picked a leaf of the great gingko and put it between the pages at Nabokov's reference to the tree.[1] And the orchid house, an acute half-hour's pleasure. I like particularly the minute orchids that bead like very small pearls along their stems. One has a major new smell – it doesn't remind me of anything in the known range of scents. It is simply a quite new smell, like a new colour.

That evening we went to see *Easy Rider*, a film that's been the rage this summer in the States and now here. Very pretty to look at, but frightening in its emptiness and shallowness. We must have been the two oldest people in the packed cinema – the average age can't have been much over twenty. I felt very foreign. It's the apotheosis, really, of the visual heresy – the actors say nothing, they have made an art of not being able to say. It is hazard, what happens, one drifts, one is happened to, one moves on – and the poor young nits around us evidently thought it was very sad and very profound and very beautiful. I give it prettiness; and nothing else.

I think this is the trap the younger generation today are falling into: they have rejected culture, book culture especially, and they embrace direct experience, doing your thing, finding your own scene and all the rest of the cant phrases – which is good, it may be, which does give them a sharper experiencing of now, a Zen-like piercing of the overlay of reason and culture. What worries me is what happens when they grow up and find they can't live the direct-experience life any more. It'll be too late for the books, the culture, then.

Kenwood, to see my favourite Rembrandt. I stood down by the lake afterwards, under a row of very tall oaks and beeches. The upper branches were full of squirrels, clowning among the green-gold.

16 October

Hardy, *The Well-beloved*. Very bizarre, that he should have spent so much time on such an impossible idea.[2] It was a notion for a poem, I think; but so relevant for his own predicament and tragedy that he could not resist it. In a way some of it so bad, so cursory, so indifferent that the book has a strange power – that is, one senses that the novel is no more than the clumsy shadow of something much more profound going on

---

[1] In Nabokov's novel the character Maria Dourmanoff pastes an example of a 'Golden [gingko] leaf' into a flower album.

[2] *The Well-beloved* tells the story of sculptor Jocelyn Pierston, who, in an ultimately futile search for an ideal of womanhood, falls in love successively with a mother, daughter and grand-daughter.

in the poor man's bold-timid, faithful-adulterous mind. In a way it is an important book. It says more about Hardy than almost any of the great novels, apart from *Jude*. And the narrative thrusts through: that part of the carpentry he never fails.

Two journalists to interview me, for the American publication: a man from the *NY Times*, another from *Time* magazine. I find it more and more difficult to say what I am, what writing means to me; how I answer their questions seems fortuitous – what words happen to be in my mind, what ideas. More and more the other world of the imagination becomes more real; I am not good at re-entering their reality. So many of their questions don't really mean anything to me. What do I think about the break-up of novel form? I think nothing, I write as it comes to me. I try and explain to the *Time* man about novels being like trees, not machines; about the other world, its gates, districts, wandering through it from type to type of novel. But it's all really a *fiction* about myself; even as I talk to him, I think, I'm probably someone else; I probably really am from another planet. If I feel it so often.

1 November

The first reviews (advance proofs) are coming in from the United States. They are all 'raves'. That is, for me, the *mot juste*: there's something faintly hysterical about so much of the tone of American praise; and they mishandle the language so. I can see they're slightly dazzled by the language I use; and that has a cheapening effect on their own praise. I suppose I credit only praise from someone who writes as I do myself. That is, currency problems: their money and my money are not on changing terms, alas.

Not that it isn't nice to be called 'the most brilliant of stars', 'better than Bellow, Roth and Updike', and the rest. I have a sense here, in Lyme, our little Lyme contacts, meetings, conversations, of leading a secret life. A small shadow, a big light. In Lyme I'm the man down the wrong end of the telescope; over there, the giant of the next few weeks. And neither eye knows the other's image.

One reason I dislike the transatlantic froth and lights is that I can't write at the moment. It isn't really a block; just a taking stock, and a nasty feeling that I'm being forced out along a tightrope – I've got to get bigger and better and stranger and God knows what else. I was happy with *Nugae* (the Collioure novel)[1] until the US thing began to swell up. It was small, but made part of the pattern. Now I think I will do the thriller next (publish it next), just to stop this higher-and-higher thing. If you're going to fall, you may as well do it in a way you choose yourself.

[1] See note 1 on page 17.

7 November

To the United States, to promote *The FLW*. Hitherto I have typed an account of the trip as it goes along; this time I jotted notes. And now I'm back at Lyme, so gratefully back at Lyme – a quiet winter's day today, no one by the sea except two women and a pram. The gentleness of life here. I must never be rude about Lyme again. It's like some rare plant, some fortunate ecology; not of the same planet as the unhappy world from which we've just come.

Last shopping in London. Eliz wastes money on clothes she does not want, and I finish *Ada*. I enjoyed it very much; a novelists' novel, as some of Bach is said to be musicians' music. That is, only another writer – to be precise, a writer of the secret-garden kind, like myself – can really understand what it's about. I think I *understand* Nabokov better than any other of his readers – which is not of course to say I know him better in the sense of references, cross-references to other books, but as I understand Clare, Hardy. I am psychologically of the same tribe.

I like especially Nabokov's idea of time as a function of memory rather than space – the present being whatever is present in the mind, the past what is not; so that what is remembered may be closer than what is perceived by the immediate senses.

To Boston, to spend the weekend with Ned Bradford at Marshfield. He meets us at the airport. Everything is all for the best in the best of all possible reviewing worlds. There is a 'rave' in the Sunday *NY Times*; the first print was fifty thousand, and they've just increased it to eighty. I sit in the house at Marshfield and read Richard Boston's 'profile' that goes with the review. It seems like a time for champagne, but we have a simple supper and go to bed at nine.

We sensed from the beginning something wrong about Ned and Pam. I smelt alcohol when I kissed her in welcome; but that first evening seemed normal enough in their severe New England terms. The next morning she was 'ill', and didn't appear; we drove round and about, had snatched meals, which Ned got. Ludicrous, the poverties he imposes on that house: no butter (fear of cholesterol); the milk is '99% guaranteed fat-free' – and tastes it, by God. We go to bed at nine, are expected to be up at seven. Eliz smokes, but we have a feeling that even that is allowed only as a special favour to a bestselling author's wife.

I wake up early, ill-omening crows are cawing outside; three, on the grass, identical in appearance to English crows, but their voices are higher-pitched. A heron, by the pond. I walk in the dark woods, collect sumach and milkweed seeds.

We toured antique shops that day. New England has lost its charm for me. Not that the houses and architecture are any less pretty, but I hadn't noted before the poverty of culture – in all this area, no animals. No cows, no horses, no sheep. No fields. Nobody walking. Nobody working their gardens. Just the quiet endless flow of cars. Everybody going somewhere, but arriving nowhere. They seem to me like people in a dream, quite unaware of how narrow and imprisoned their way of life is. At one antique shop there was a herb garden: a sudden human touch. Thyme, camomile, marigold, mint. An old woman made it.

Pam did not appear that night. The next day we went down to Plymouth to see the Mayflower settlement museum – a series of thatched huts, *cabanes*, supposedly authentic in construction and furnishing; though most of the blanket-chests, bible-boxes and the rest are a hundred years wrong. Girls and willing matrons dressed up in contemporary Puritan rig.

Plymouth Rock. It's marked by a sort of bandstand erection. Near by, a replica of the ship the settlers came in. There's a waxwork of William Bradford, the first governor, Ned's ancestor. I stand behind Ned's two children as they stare at the wax face. There, in the ship, one begins to comprehend what settling really meant – that first terrible winter. Perhaps the trouble was always in the land. They never wanted to come, they never really liked the land. From the beginning they schemed to get away from it, control it, remove themselves from it as much as possible – fear of the land, America.

Ned goes off to phone Pam. She feels better. Suddenly he tells us what it's all about – how she's an alcoholic, she won't stop drinking. He's like his ancestor, a kind of obstinate pioneer: 'I've argued, I've begged her, I've tried to get her to see doctors . . . But God darn it, it's almost as if she *wants* to be the way she is.' It's so 'classic'; and classical, the old battle between puritan and pagan. I had a talk with Pam before we went to bed. She'd had three pints of vodka that day when we arrived. 'Ned wants me to be perfect, he doesn't understand ordinary people, he can do anything he wants. He decides to stop smoking, he stops smoking, he can't understand I'm different.' Then how she was bored, her life was a failure, she wasn't beautiful any more – the sad, trite litany.

It shocked me, I thought too well of them before as exemplars of all that is good in the American character not to be so. I still like Ned. He is that rare thing, an absolutely honest man within his limits; but they are perhaps far more crippling limits than I realized. In a way he is living a totally inauthentic life. I wonder if this is not so among other Americans: that is, the external mess drives them to be overexigent and childishly blind in their own lives.

A bad beginning, a sour beginning.

10 November
The 'tour' begins. All goes well there – every review so far is good, even the daily *NY Times*, which usually disputes the Sunday's judgement. A

third print, bringing the total to 100,000. We do a breakfast TV show. The girl who interviews me hasn't read any of my books. 'They only told me five minutes ago I was doing it.' It's like that throughout – the standard of TV-show interviewing is abysmal. One would do better with tailor's dummies. Harold Robbins is on the same programme; in a green velvet suit, a frilly green shirt, doe-eyes, tanned, quiet-spoken, 'I'm a great admirer of your books.' He seemed to me a reptile, but I mean that in a kinder sense than most literary people in the States would understand: that is, like a basking lizard. He likes sun, high sales, publicity. He offered us his house, his car, his office in Hollywood. The silly little bitch who interviewed me asked me what I thought about writers who exploited sex . . . I saw him talking to Elizabeth beyond the lights, and dodged the question.

Everywhere we went I was congratulated for 'putting down' the 'sex' novelists like Robbins and Suzanne; booksellers kept saying it was so marvellous to 'have a bestseller you can believe in'. Which is all very well, but they still display the books they hate. Robbins is nothing; the sickness is in the society that cannot resist his wares.

Bob Fetridge. I spend the morning meeting Little, Brown people in his office. His nervousness appals me. He seems continually about to squint, his hands shake. When he came with us (on the California leg) we discovered he too was on the way to becoming an alcoholic. The shaking stops on the third Martini.

We flew down to New York in the late afternoon – a glimpse of Manhattan, the hundred towers of pearl . . . We sat around in the hotel for hours, unable to face going out. To face New York. It's partly the wretched central heating, the abominable lassitude it induces; we have a suite with a huge drawing-room and two double bedrooms, two bathrooms, a kitchen – just for the two of us. It seems as unnecessary as Belmont, and a good deal less pleasant.

11 November

I have to get up at six to 'make' the all-important *Today* show. The publicity girl is Lynn Caine, an emaciated 44-year-old Jewess; a face, eyes, out of some Kathy Kollwitz drawing. She believes herself a witch, does palmistry. But I like her, she's intelligent, dry, nobody's fool. She shepherds me, five feet nothing, with the book eternally in hand; I lumber behind. Her use of language is noticeably sharper than the Bostonian; that's nice, too. Later I got out of her that she didn't like Ned, for what sounded good anti-snobbish (anti-Wasp) reasons; but he and she make between them what I like about the States: a seriousness and an astringency.

At the *Today* show I meet a nice red-haired pregnant girl who has come in to have me sign her copy of *The Magus*. Then a silly interview:

a hollow man, a hollow woman, who bicker across me during the commercials and turn on enthusiastic interest like electric light when we're back on camera.

14 November

We met Bob Fetridge at Kennedy and flew to Los Angeles. It is so clearly a city of the damned that I enjoyed it rather better than New York this time. In Manhattan one can still, just, feel that perhaps the inhabitants know what they are doing; here they are quite plainly mad: three-quarters of a million people in one of the prettiest sites and best climates in the world rapidly poisoning themselves to death. The obvious poison is petrol, of course. But the total obliteration of nature, the endless crowding of lot upon lot upon lot, street after street, is equally lethal. There can never have been such a repulsive city. It is almost explosive, the screaming desire it creates for all that it lacks: peace, solitude, silence, fresh air.

We are whisked almost straight away from the Beverly Hills Hotel to a dinner for Los Angeles booksellers. My suit is too hot, I feel ill. The meal has been arranged by some professional Los Angeles gourmet, a Greek homosexual. It's supposed to be Greek, in honour of *The Magus.* I start getting nasty when it turns out there's no ouzo. But they find some retsina, and later even some ouzo; though the food is no more Greek than the Egyptian belly-dancing that passes for Greek in America.

At last we get back to the Beverly Hills Hotel, which we like: its ridiculous banana wallpaper, its staff who actually are what the brochures always promise (friendly), its faint tattiness, feel of so many past glamours and tinsel glories. There's a nice cigarette-girl, Dominique, who reads my books, wants to bring copies for me to sign; and for a moment it's like the other tours with Bob, drunken, exhausting, mad, fun – all that.

15 November

Every night, Bob Fetridge gets stoned. His eyes hood over; each blink takes place in slow motion and sometimes the eyelids stay down for two seconds or more. But he holds his liquor very well. I told him at dinner that I'd seen Peter Ustinov in the lobby; on the strength of having met him a couple of times, Bob called for the telephone and asked him to come down. Rather to my surprise Ustinov agreed. So we had an evening with him. A genial, empty man, bloated and blasé; a little devious, not quite sure if you will buy the carpet he's selling and then again whether he ought to care whether you do or not. A Russian, under the English class mannerisms. A bit of a shambler. Eliz said I looked intimidated; but really it was pleasure at having such a rare specimen under the glasses, and not knowing quite how not to show it. He told some funny stories: about Queen Juliana; and Nabokov, a neighbour in Switzerland.

He mimics beautifully a very precise, too precise Russian speaker of
English, and his snobbisms.

A sad man, like all first-rate comedians.

19 November
We fly up to San Francisco. The pleasure of seeing – we arrived about
five – office-workers streaming home on foot; the scaled-down buildings, even the slow-moving traffic. It is very noticeable, the humanity of
people's faces here. This is still a human, a concerned, an honourable
city. One that knows it is in danger; eyed, after Los Angeles's blindness.

22 November
We are free till evening: the first time we've been alone for so long since
we arrived. We walked down to a gallery. The owner, Hank Baum, has
prints done by some man inspired by *The Magus*. They're pretty unin-
teresting; and I decline buying a set at $475. I like much better the
'light' sculptures Baum has. We had a drink with him afterwards in an
Irish bar, run by a friend of the painter Kitaj's. They damped my ardour
for this city. 'It's provincial,' says Baum; and I feel he knows what he's
talking about.

We went on to Ghirardelli Square, a very pretty and cleverly designed
shopping enclave: extremely successful both in itself and in its siting,
looking out towards Alcatraz and the Golden Gate. The shops stock
goods from all over the world – even a first-class Greek-Turkish grocer's.
A great feeling of all the riches of the Orient (and Occident). Venice.
The shops I liked best mixed antique jewellery from Afghanistan and
South America, African objects, modern Scandinavian, Polish weaves –
really a little magic in such profusion.

That evening, a final party had been arranged for us by Willy
Abrahams of *Atlantic* and Peter Stansky, a Stanford don.[1]

Out to Hillsborough; a nice one-level house, two nice intellectual men,
whom I take to at once, because they're intelligent and sophisticated
and both Anglophile. Suddenly I'm back in Oxford and a land where
nuances of language have meaning.

The guests start arriving. Wallace Stegner, whom I'm supposed to
know all about, but have never heard of: a white-haired man, he killed

[1] A poet, novelist and an editor for Atlantic Monthly Press, William Abrahams
(1919–1998) was also the senior editor and judge of the O'Henry Awards short
story collections, published in the United States annually by Doubleday. In 1968
he and Peter Stansky moved from Boston to live together on the West Coast when
Stansky was made associate professor of history at Stanford. They had co-authored
for Little, Brown *Journey to the Frontier: Two Roads to the Spanish War* (1966) and
would go on to write several more books together.

a young rattlesnake this morning.[1] Jessica Mitford, aristocrat playing at schoolmarm. Yes, she remembered Michael Farrer.[2] 'He's my first cousin, I can only think of him as a little boy.' She tells me he has divorced Constance, and that's a kind of shock: not because it was ever not probable, but because my memory has fixed them forever in a distant summer on that farm.[3] Old Mrs Mitford ('that dreadful, horrible woman' says Jessica) is dead, it seems; and the colonel (also 'dreadful' – '*he* died, thank the lord'). Jessica's husband now is a left-wing lawyer, called Treuhaft. He has a faint, and very inappropriate, resemblance physically to Enoch Powell; he listens grinning to her. He's a real radical, it seems, not just a Mitford eccentric.[4] Then Donald Davie, the English poet, a strangely bitter man, grey and bitter, saying how much better life is in an American university,[5] but seemingly consumed with resentment that he found no niche in English academic life. I don't know why the English are so ungenerous, so crotchety: he seemed to me like some character from a Webster play, so locked in shadows, obscure vendettas, dark currents that it was difficult to grasp what he really felt about anything.

26 November
Our last day, and Willy Abrahams comes to take us out along the coast south a little way. Thank God for homosexuality, I say; I don't mind the bubbling, the malice, the subject-hopping mind, the mania for personal references and name-dropping. I probably couldn't stand them in England, Willy and Peter Stansky; but here they're almost an oasis. The drive is horrid, down a long coast raped by free enterprise; uncontrolled

[1] Wallace Stegner (1909–1993) had a considerable reputation in the United States as a writer of novels set in the American West, and was a campaigner for the preservation of the American wilderness. In 1964 he established the Creative Writing Program at Stanford University and remained a member of the faculty until 1971. His novel *Angle of Repose* would win the Pulitzer prize in 1972.
[2] JF's friend at New College, Oxford. See note 1 on page 22.
[3] After coming down from Oxford, JF spent a few weeks working on Michael Farrer's estate at Cold Brayfield in Buckinghamshire. See *The Journals*, volume 1, pages 38–42.
[4] Jessica Mitford's first husband Esmond Romilly, who had joined the Royal Canadian Air Force at the outbreak of the Second World War, was killed in 1941 during a bombing raid over Nazi Germany. She met Robert Treuhaft while working for the Office of Price Administration in the United States. They married in 1943 and both joined the American Communist Party. In 1948 they settled in Oakland, California, where Treuhaft specialized in trade union and civil rights cases. When they were called before the Un-American Activities Committee in 1953 they took the first amendment and refused to give evidence. Senator Joe McCarthy described Treuhaft as one of the most subversive lawyers in the country.
[5] Davie (1922–1995) was teaching English literature at Stanford.

building. Then over the mountains and back to Hillsborough. Will and Peter are doing a book on Orwell, against Sonia Orwell's wishes. This coming spring they will take a freighter to England to finish the book. I don't know why other writers manage to lead so much more literary lives than mine; where writing is a priority. I am jealous.

The Hillsborough house again. Peter Stansky appears – he teaches Victorian and Modern Britain at Stanford University. He's a little like Isaiah Berlin, an intellectual burbler, with an extraordinary rank triphthong on certain vowels – a horrid, rancid sound. Their ménage amuses us, they're really a jolly couple, and take us both to a ridiculous Italian 'family' restaurant somewhere off Columbus Avenue. Endless courses are thrust at us; no choices allowed. But in a way it's English; not American, anyway. And I enjoyed it better than any other evening there.

At midnight, the plane back to England.

America, I weep for thee.

28 November

Waking up in Hampstead. Outside, it's snowing, it's cold, small, dank England. I went down in the afternoon to Leigh-on-Sea – alone, Eliz couldn't face it; and after a night there, nor could I. Nothing has reality for them now except their own small world. I think it is time we stopped thinking of people existing simultaneously at a given point. In Leigh, as with so many people here in Lyme, most of life is lived as if the year is 1929 – 1939 at most.

Aunt Maggie died, just before I arrived. In a way it has cheered F up, as he has outlived all his siblings now. He remains clear-headed, thank God.

29 November

Waiting at Chalkwell Station for the train back to London. Dusk. I was the only passenger, the room was unheated, snow everywhere, the grey high tide lapping against the sea-wall just below the window. The other end of the world from San Francisco. It is all as Montesquieu said: a matter of climate.

I was groping for some elusive parallel all the time in California: the Egyptian. That explains the feeling of greater decadence there. The USA as a whole is Roman, California is the place where Rome ends up – in the Alexandrine cults, the grandiose delusions and luxuries of decadent Imperial Rome. It (California) is really based on a fear of death. Thanatos, not the egregious Reagan, is the real governor of the state. That is why it is so full of freak religions and philosophies; in headlong pursuit of every sensual enjoyment. They're dying there; and ungraciously.

A curious note in many of the American reviews: a sort of surprise that *The FLW* is both enjoyable and serious, of its kind. I think this is a by-product of the death of religion. The novel – along with other art forms – has to stand in for the sermon. Thus a serious work of art can supposedly be told by its excessive length (or size), dullness, self-preoccupation and so on.

In a happy world, there would be no art. I retreat too often into my imagination. In a happy world, the experience of reality would be enough.

30 November
Back to Lyme, which is warm after London. No snow. The *Cobaea* still in flower, the winter iris in full blossom (twenty flowers in one clump), the artichokes still healthy. I could stand a year of it; alone, no change of climate. Just for the peace, and the sea; the oystercatchers squilling quietly over the Cobb in the night.

4 December
The film of *The Magus* has been offered to the British public in our absence. It got what it deserved: universal damnation, I'm happy to say.

17 December
Also in my absence I was, it seems, awarded some prize newly cooked up by the English Circle of International PEN, whatever that is. I'd like to turn it down, but since Tom Maschler has already been to a dinner and accepted it for me, I can't. I think the whole principle of the literary prize is wrong, in any case. What is so absurd about this one is that I was never told I was 'shortlisted' (and therefore given no chance to say whether I wanted to run the race); I have still not had any communication with or from PEN (the prize was given on November 20th); the total publicity awarded it seems to have been brief paragraphs in the *Guardian* and the *Telegraph*, and so the only legitimate reason for such baubles (publicity for fiction in general) has not been satisfied. Since my fellow shortlisted rivals were Monsarrat, Margaret Lawrence and Robert Liddell, I don't even have the consolation of respecting the vanquished.

Eliz was supposed to go into hospital today to have her varicose veins attended to. But they rang just before we set off to London to say that there was a 'yellow alert', because of the flu epidemic; no bed available for Eliz. We went to London anyway, as I have to see Oscar about the film.

19 December
Oscar, Tom and I sat and made a list of directors, in order of preference: Lindsay Anderson, Tony Richardson, Zeffirelli, Polanski, Peter Brook,

Zinnemann, Lumet, Jack Clayton, Joe Losey. Anderson, it seems, is still not quite firm with his refusal. Richardson, who we thought wouldn't be interested after his Crimea film,[1] is – or may be. I outrage Tom and Oscar by saying I'd like Richardson because he's from Oxford. They kept hopping back to it. Of course, *he's* not an Oxford man. I didn't dare point out that my motives were really Marxist: an Oxford man knows more about English class, accent and alienation than anyone else – given equal talent in other directions. Richardson has apparently driven his ex-wife Vanessa Redgrave to read the book double-quick. He has always been high on my list – and she, if not visually perfect, is so far ahead in every other ability from our other toyed-with names (Sarah Miles, Glenda Jackson) that I pray we get them.

I went on to talk with Dan Rissner at Warner Brothers – they want me to do an original script. Some months ago I thought I saw a story in John Wesley's adventures in Georgia, between 1735–8. Then there is the script I started a year or two ago, on the generation battle (*The Au Pair Girl*). They would pay me to do either, or both. But money has become an embarrassment. I'll do them if I feel like it. An idea I didn't discuss with them is on the death and the maiden theme; only here the maiden would be death. A young man picks up a girl: she is death.

I came back to Lyme, Eliz staying up in town. I can't settle or enjoy anything at the moment. I want to write a piece about the United States – its lack of poetry, the errors in its cultural and social grammar, and so on. And the three scripts, but don't know which. I seem to have an endless capacity for planning these days, which is a function of depression, I think, not the creativity it might seem. Then the Hollywood–England novel, the Robin Hood novel. I want to do them all at the same time.

20 December

I think, too, I begin to want to direct films – it's partly the collapse of Hollywood; the bankruptcy, literal and metaphorical, of the studios there. I mean, there is space now for the film as literature, for the writer as visualizer.

Stopping myself from smoking is still a problem. Curiously, I managed quite well in the States. I don't need cigarettes to combat nervousness or boredom. Where the trouble comes is in writing. I seem to be in a sort of multiple-possibility marsh at the moment. I no sooner write a paragraph than I see improvements. It's as if I wasn't sure what I wanted to say, although I know *exactly* in general terms. It's intensely irritating and time-wasting, draft after draft after draft, in a sort of unimproving

---

[1] *The Charge of the Light Brigade.*

circle, since there always seem to be as many faults in the fifth as in the first attempt. It's like being, however hard one tries, in a state of constant partial error.

Just as the novel is becoming a minority art in our culture as a whole, perhaps it will become, should become, a minority feature in the writer's output. I think the division we make between film and novel may be artificial – like early biologists counting the whale as a fish because it lives in the sea. The real division must be between creators, not arts. What I said about the polystyle in *The Aristos* – this is the logical extension of that, too. If I write in many styles – why stop at the printed page?[1]

I've been reading the miserable *Times Literary Supplement* this last few months. It is like some freak group therapy unit: where the English literary and academic 'establishment' go to pretend to rape one another in the dark.

A travesty of what a country's central journal of literature ought to be.

23 December

Richardson doesn't want to do it; but he wants Redgrave to.

Perhaps it is this, the problem of writing: till a certain age you can say because you don't really know – then one day you know, but you can't really say.

24 December

To Leigh for Christmas. Dan and Hazel and the children are there; the twins have a gravity and solemnity highly pleasing in two-year-olds. Simon, who has the malformed hand, seems the dominant and more stable: yet another proof of the principle of the blessed defect. I suspect that this is where eugenics will always fall down, with human beings; if you always breed for the flawlessly superior, you won't get it – not in human terms.

Reading Wesley's *Journal* (1735–38) for his time in Georgia. He is very English, a do-it-yourself saint. No visions for him, one feels; he would qualify by hard work and drudgery. Only would-be Olympic athletes today show his addiction to routine and self-punishment. He is Protestantism's great athlete, in fact; and I don't mean that as a compliment.

The material for a film is there – for many films, I suspect. Perhaps we should set a new vogue for Wild Easterns; on the same principle, though a century or more earlier, as Wild Westerns.

---

[1] In *The Aristos* (note 10.67) JF wrote: 'What will matter finally is intention; not instrumentation. It will be skill in expressing one's meaning with *styles*, not just in one style carefully selected and developed to signal one's individuality rather than to satisfy the requirements of the subject-matter.'

26 December
Lyme again. NAL have offered $15,000 for the paperback rights to *The Aristos*. That pleases me very much.

20 January 1970
This last three weeks I have been writing on the United States. I call it: *America, I Weep for Thee*. It has cost me my fight with Satan, though. As soon as I was into it, I began to smoke. Now I am back on sixty a day or more. My mind runs so much more freely and inventively. Nicotine is undoubtedly a concentrative drug.

30 January
We shall be No. 1 on the *NY Times* list next week, at last. That makes the grand slam.

9 February
A strange weekend. In Anna's new lodgings in Exeter there is a woman (Pat Conn) with her two small children living on National Assistance. The marriage broke down, the husband's a painter and penniless; so she brought them here for a little treat. The mother is not very attractive, and yet one has to admire her. One guesses some bad petty bourgeois background in London, then a revolt against it, the painter, the flight to the arts and I suppose a general fecklessness in every other direction. Such a victim, and one can't dislike her for that and the plucky way she has faced her situation; but something I did dislike – I think the culture and the cultural assumptions that have formed her. The vanity of unsuccess, the self-preoccupation of Bohemia; something like that in her husband must have steamrollered over her. She's not to blame, yet she is one of those human beings who seem to exude some archetypal sense of evolutionary failure: she'd always have been this, one feels. What I felt about her was precisely what I despise in other humans in their attitude to other forms of life: horror of snakes, bats, spiders and so on. And I didn't like my dislike.

But the strangeness of the weekend was really in her two daughters, Emma aged eight and Sophie aged six. It was a sort of headlong love at first sight between us, Emma attaching herself to me, her little sister to Eliz. A parentlessness in them fusing with our childlessness. In a way, of course, it was slumming: every little sight, every little gift to them came absolutely pure and direct, with an innocence so unadulterated that it took breath and heart away at times. I took them to pick the snowdrops on the bottom slope, in a snatch of sunshine; and though I hate people picking my flowers as a rule, they could have picked the garden clean for all I cared. They made giving the only pleasure that could match their joy in the taking; and then I realized that Emma was in a way the only other person who has seen this garden quite as I see it, which is still with the eyes of my own deprived (in terms of space, wild growth and so on) childhood. Other adults look at the view, aspect, the weeds, the mess, and so on. They can't live in its small corners, its being what it is, now, just as it is. She leapt on the weed-curse, old Jack's nightmare, the marsh burdock, which is in flower; and of course quite rightly. It *is* a pretty flower, a pretty scent. All good children are Zen Buddhists by nature; classifications like weed and garden flower are meaningless to them.

She has a small white-and-pink face, blue-veined at the temples, a strange direct little pair of eyes; *would* sit on my lap, hold my hands, ride on my back, curious little sidles and shy shifts, whose purpose was always to get closer. All seduction. Very gentle with plants, very quick at seeing their correspondences, remembering their names. Something about her haunted me all through the weekend, some parallel – I see now it was Alice Liddell. Alice must have been just such a gay-grave, sensitive-bold, imperious-submissive child; with that same faint hint of sexuality, that same strange ghost of a first-class intelligence. Very interesting to me were the pieces of glass she picked out under the old dump on the edge of Black Ven, the glass smoothed by the sea – how she would reject many that attracted me (that is, a mind conditioned by so much 'classical' art, from Roman glass to 'art' glass of today) and established a counter-aesthetic, say a piece of – at first sight to me – rather horrid multicoloured glass; then I looked at it twice, and learnt to mistrust my own taste.

I couldn't face going to the station with them when they had to catch a train on Sunday night. I knew she would cry all the way; and only my age would prevent my crying with her. I suppose it was childlessness, though I don't – or haven't for years – wanted children, and still don't want children; I just wanted this one child. And I suppose she knew; children like that read minds far better than we suppose. I would like to have given her prosaic mum some money, but Eliz thought we should pay their winter electricity bill and leave it at that. And teaching her; I know exactly how to teach minds like that. On the way home from the beach we came on an oiled guillemot. I explained to her that it would probably die, but I wouldn't kill it, because there was just a chance it would survive. Fifty yards later she made a little poem. 'Some will die and some will suffer,/But it's best to eat your supper.' I suggested better rhymes. She tried them out, but rejected them.

And the innocence of children: to show them what seems paradise to them, then to deprive them of it so brutally. They can't understand, and you understand so well why they can't understand. The younger sister, Sophie, was much more of a little monkey; she'll suffer much less in life. A philosopher, like her mother; and Emma was a poet.

Without any prompting from me, the second morning, she made the
snowdrops she picked into a chain; almost as if she knew that scene
from *Poil de Carotte* – the old man leading the two children across the
meadow – that has always haunted my mind.[1] I photographed her and
her sister wearing it. No man will ever see them quite like that again.
And in a way I don't want the photographs to come out.

And I mustn't forget I owe this strange experience, which touched
me very deeply (but that isn't its only strangeness), to Anna: she too is
a philosopher, and I think a much better one than either Eliz or myself.
All real philosophy is doing; we think and dream too much.

24 February

To London. Eliz goes into hospital tomorrow for her varicose veins operation. We had dinner at the Keats with Ned Bradford. He's over here
doing cloak-and-dagger negotiations for some Russian MS that's just
been smuggled out. Almost at once he was talking about Pam – the day
before he flew they were to have a dinner party, and she was 'smashed'
an hour before the guests arrived; so he rang them up in her hearing
and at last told the public truth. He is like a man who sees the whole
ethos of his life destroyed by lightning and unreason – quite literally
smashed. We discussed the American 'pamphlet'; he wanted to know
what had distressed me so much about the United States. I could have
summed it up in three words: You and Pam. But of course I couldn't
say that; and, alas, I don't know now how good a judge he will be of
the book. If he can't see what has caused her to become an alcoholic,
I can't expect him to see what *I* see wrong in the States.

25 February

Evening with Tom and Fay in their new Vale of Health house. It is very
pretty, very *House and Garden*, very visual; another step on their way to
being Beautiful People. I sensed a slight reversion in Tom to his old
independent self. 'Marriage isn't going to change *my* spots.' Fay looked
white and tired; we guess she is pregnant. And Tom was full of talk
about children, also. I helped them move furniture in the *salon*; where
a massive seventeenth-century court-cupboard, their pride (and a nice
piece in itself), obstinately succeeded in dominating everything else. In
the end it would only go where it blocked two electricity plugs. Never
mind, there it must go. Effect, effect, effect. Now Eliz and I were doing
just this the other day at Belmont, so perhaps I'm just being jealous of

---

[1] *Poil de Carotte* (1931) was a film directed by Julien Duvivier from a Jules Renard
novel. In a lyrical sequence, a little boy and girl pretend that it is their wedding
day. Bedecked in flowers, they process along a river and across a meadow while
a fisherman sings a marriage song for them.

their singlemindedness and sparsity. But I hate more and more this predominance of art in houses; and the lack of a human poetry: mess, objects, nothings that attach. I think Fay will do Tom great good. She gives me dry looks when he says outrageous things; an English resistance movement forms.

27 February
The operation goes well.

9 March
Back with Eliz to Lyme. My heels burn in London at this time of year. And cool only when we head for the south-west.

25 March
At the moment, bogged down with the American piece. It's really the dreadful pile of books to read: Tocqueville and his brood. I could easily write, I feel like it, but 'background' reading bores me most terribly; so I do neither. I think this is some kind of conditioned reflex from my teaching days – a nausea before duty reading; even when it does fundamentally interest me.

And also a lot of work in the garden. We have now got the vegetable patch in order. The daffodils have started.

Oscar has been these last ten days in New York; trying to set up the film – and without success. The problem is not really lack of interest, but lack of direction in the backers. They want to pay for an extension of the option, no more. The whole industry is waiting at the moment to see which way the fickle public cat will jump. What will make money next. The book is still top of the list. Up to a year ago we could have asked for anything we wanted, and got it. Personally, I am quite indifferent. In a way, I should be happier if the film came to nothing, since the book has already come to something like everything.

22 April
Anna has got into Bristol for her graphics course.

24 April
To Wales, for Tom Maschler's wedding to Fay. We drove down with Kasmin, the gallery owner, and Edna O'Brien. Kasmin is small, myopic, smiling; with the characteristic English-Jewish drive and bounce – the predominant type at the wedding, really, since Freddy Raphael, Wesker and various others – Tom himself, of course – were present. I think their characteristic (strongest in Freddy Raphael) is impatience, the wanting to succeed fast, the disgust with any present that is boring. A hatred of wasted time that can become almost a tic; a kind of psychological tremor.

A corollary contempt for other ways of seeing life – the stock English way above all, of course. 'Can't stand this country any more,' says Freddy. 'People won't leave you alone.' And in the car with Edna, who belongs with this group by adoption, it is all names, the network, the most 'in' of now. I think this is why I like Tom Wiseman, who – though he likes names – seems to belong to an older and sager Jewry. Edna was nice to us in the car, but once again seemed disinclined to like us when the journey was over. I don't like this turn-tap use of the Irish charm.

We stayed at Llanthony Abbey, which must rank as the oddest hotel in the country; set hard in the nineteenth century, run by a bizarre ghostly couple who seem quite indifferent to their own or anyone else's comfort – the woman (Mrs Knight) Ibsen-like in her alienation. Apparently always behind the next door, listening and waiting. I saw her one day in the dining-room, alone, sitting in the chair in front of the only electric fire in the whole establishment, her face raised curiously, with eyes closed, like someone in profound pain; waiting for death. The bedrooms all furnished with Victorian things – not artificially, as décor, but simply because they had always been there. Each room petrified in the past. The whole place like that. Ticking grandfather clocks. Silence. Waiting. The first night, when the other people staying there came (Edna and Kasmin were with the swinging side of the party in Hay), it seemed ludicrous and absurd, one long giggle. Tom's father Kurt showed unsuspected talents as a clown, stopping all the clocks, asking the phantom Mrs Knight whether *she* had a nice, warm room. Then Rita Masseron, Tom's mother (divorced from Kurt): a woman like a robin; and as sharp and aggressive as one. She and the old man kept a dry hostility up. Ed Victor from Cape, a fashionable young expatriate. An artist called Tom Taylor and his wife; he works in TV and came to film the wedding 'cape'. Graham Greene and his wife.

We had to go to Hay for the register office wedding the next morning, with Kurt delaying everything by trying to turn his car on the beautiful sward before the ruins; not moving and getting in a strange foreigner-in-England's panic; reversing and revving up – and all the time the car slowly sinking down to its axles. In the end we got him out, with the lawn looking like a tank training ground. Rita: 'We must not tell Tom, we must not tell Tom.' I travelled with the old man, to calm him down. All the way he talked about Edna. 'Why has she left Tom?' (She went last year to Weidenfeld.) I told him what she had told us the day before – it was easier to work with Tony Godwin editorially. But he couldn't understand. I suspect that it was Fay who sent her off; the prospect of a happily married Tom. But I couldn't say that.

The register office, with Fay looking like a Vlach gypsy, pale and composed; and Tom looking foolish. He was nice all through this weekend; slightly abashed. Confetti and rice. Then we all set off for Arnold

Wesker's. He and his wife Dusty did all the catering. He has a farm near by. Champagne and nice East End food – Bloom's food: salt beef and potato-and-onion pancakes. Wesker in a black velvet shirt showing his hairy chest; his hair down to his shoulders. I think he is the most human as well as the most talented of all these Anglo-Jewish writers: the impatience is there, but directed at society, not his own career. Deborah Rogers, Roy's agent; one of several ex-loves on both sides. A dreadful woman from *Encounter*. Doris Lessing, placid-looking, with close-combed hair, more from the thirties than this decade.

After lunch we all went up to Carney. I walked with Freddy and his wife; he seemed in a constant state of anger with life. 'Nobody reads my books.' He'd just seen Antonioni's *Zabriskie Point*. 'Marvellous. All movement. Running up and down hills. Explosions.' All impatience, in short.

Then back eventually to Wesker's for the wedding dinner. I sit next to Deborah Rogers, unable to hear most of what she says. During the speeches she twists the ends of her hair and stares at the tablecloth, not happy. An awful Oxbridge speech by some Trinity young man to toast Fay; embarrassment, Jewish hackles rising. Then Wesker is embarrassing also in his praise for Tom; he wants us all to stand up and say what we think of Tom, as if Fay wasn't there. I feel my English hackles rising. But Doris Lessing says a few quiet words: 'We all know Tom can also be a bastard.' And that saves things. Tom's father hits it just right; and Tom toasts the skeleton at the feast – Fay is five months pregnant. I didn't know then, but apparently Edna and Kasmin had started smoking pot. And all around them. A segregation into squares and smokers. The evening bored me, but then all such evenings bore me.

4 May
April 4th. Slipped at long last. Now second in *Time*. 130,000 copies sold.

9 May
London, to meet Dick Lester, the latest candidate for director. He looks and behaves rather like a distinguished Jewish-Viennese composer of the last century. Mendelssohn, perhaps. The language is hip, of course; and the clothes. But the dandyism, the bald brown head, long sinuous gestures, aggressive-defensive eyes, always testing, probing, doubting you. I could see he dazzles Oscar and he very swiftly dazzled Tom Maschler (who's been against him from the beginning) – in fact he was obviously a little bit what Tom wishes he was. For the first time T sounded faintly ashamed of publishing – a strange tone, almost of apology for being involved in such a square old profession. I think we only have Lester because of the sick situation over financing in the industry at the moment. He was as sour as a Morello cherry (with justification, apparently) about the studios. 'Why don't we go to the banks and get a loan?' Oscar, thank God, has

more sense than that. I think I really don't want him; he's too much of a dark horse. Too much the old Jewish pursuer of his own ambitions. They ride athwart society, culture, and everything else, these men; and ride with it only to suit their own ends. The deeper motive of their hatred of fascism (beyond recent history) is that a rigid closed society restricts personal exploitation. Like the humour, that is something they share with the Anglo-Saxon mentality; we call it 'freedom', and they really haven't got a name for it. But I suspect a historical situation might come about whereby either race could become fascist – indeed just such signs are already apparent both in America and Israel. That is, 'love of freedom' can be simply a camouflage for keeping the field open for personal advantage; and if the personal advantage happens to be suited – and favoured – by political power, the game can be closed for the other side.

10 May
That evening, Tom's party in the new Vale of Health house. I liked it better there, though the same people were present, plus the Amises. I talked some time with Mrs – Elizabeth Jane Howard – a large, Nordic ladylike lady with staring and demanding eyes. In a kind of Austrian peasant dress, white blouse and brown velvet. A seventeenth-century miniature that she turns from time to time; a monogram now, now a child's face. I avoided asking questions about it. I think, though she was full of praise for *The FLW*, that we did not like each other at all.

Difficulties between Tom and Oscar, as the former has modified his previous admiration and the latter thinks an assistant producer is getting more and more of a nuisance. I told Tom that I wasn't prepared to play English Muggins and the if-you-really-love-me game. He was very good about it. I seem never to say kind things about him here. But more and more I think kind things about him. I think he has changed this last year.

The permissive society upon us in London. Jud, it emerged last week, is having an affair with Barbara Kohn. He asked to borrow the flat when we weren't in town. John Kohn has been having his own affaire with Judith Goodman over these last twelve months and now lives apart from B and the children; now wants to come back. Jud is at his best, turning the whole beastly, quasi-incestuous mess into a comedy. B's father, Sam Jaffe, has told her that she has swapped a 'born no-good' (a player with women) for a 'born loser'. At the same time he is pressuring her to take John back; the old Jewish hatred of divorce. Peter Kohn, the fourteen-year-old son, is deep in the Oedipus role. Barbara was tired one lunch: 'If you weren't up half the night screwing with Jud,' says Peter, 'you wouldn't be like this.' Jud has started divorce proceedings with Suzanne. Stephen is to go to boarding-school in Rome. According to Jud, he doesn't care either way about the divorce. 'In three years' time I'm going to be free of both of you. So do what you like.'

Suzanne wants to cite Yael Dayan, Moshe's daughter, as the guilty woman. Jud says that if she does he'll publicize the psychiatric reports about her paranoia. Now he's scared (with justice) that she'll find out about Barbara Kohn.

As Jud says, you can't win. It always catches up with you.

And then Anna's boyfriend Eric reappeared in London. We'd hoped he was going for three years to the Red Sea on a surveying ship. So they sleep in the living-room and we sleep in the bedroom. Roy apparently hates Eric. As a person I rather like him; but he seems to have a Svengali-like effect on Anna. She cried all Monday morning, when he'd disappeared back to Hull. I don't mind their sleeping together at all, even right under our noses. But it irritates me that they play the welfare state so meanly. Anna doesn't work at all, goes in once a week at most to her college. While Eric, as soon as he'd drawn his grant for the term, simply left Exeter. He has no intention of going back, either. Neither of them really deserves 'higher' education. She wants to come back to London next week and have the flat again. We said it was promised to Jud. Eliz feels guilty about that. Me, not.

12 May
Now ABC, who are most interested in the film, declare Dick Lester 'totally unacceptable'.

15 May
Daniel Halpern appears from Tangiers; a nice young American, on the drift. He's been living with Paul Bowles for eighteen months and has started (with Bowles) a new magazine, *Antaeus*, to which I've sent some poems.[1] He has come to tape an interview with me and would obviously stay and stay and I like him; but get rid of him. I was mean in the interview and held forth about how I 'hated' people – as opposed to birds, nature, solitude and the rest. I think I was trying to tell him to stay away from 'famous' elder writers. I suspect Bowles may have told him the same thing.

6 June
A cocktail party at Maisie Forrester's in Ware Lane; the assembled upper middle class (in Lyme terms) of the town. They really are the dullest and most abominably retarded community one can imagine; there is a bizarre air of being besieged about them. A constant harking back to the past: who lived in which house, how long their family has had associations with Lyme. It's how the pecking-order is established. Of course

[1] As well as editing *Antaeus* and writing poetry, Halpern would the following year found in New York the literary publishing house Ecco Press.

they are intensely suspicious of us. We are interlopers – even though most of such people have only lived here a year or two longer.

The one tolerable person is the old actress Maisie herself, her face rouged and made up so that she looks like a stout old geisha, or a distinguished brothel madame. She's good; salty, with style. A credit to the humanizing power of the theatre.

The encounter made Eliz rage against Lyme; I get away by retreating into my ornithological self. I find such people agreeably clear-cut, both specifically and behaviourally.

10–15 June

A call came from Leigh to say that F had suffered a stroke and was on his deathbed. So we got off within the hour and drove up to Leigh, arriving there about seven in the evening. M is suspiciously near enjoying every minute of it; the drama, what happened, what's going to happen. It seems generally agreed that a quick death would be best. According to the doctor it is not a stroke proper, but a critical hardening of arteries and consequent oxygen starvation in the brain. F doesn't recognize us till later, but his pulse is good; and he's clearly not dead yet. We get a night nurse in, a nice brisk Irish woman; and he becomes lucid almost at once. I think he and M have preyed on each other psychologically for so long that this is really the culminating counter-attack. Eliz and I feel wild with rage at her insensitivity – her constantly talking about him as if he wasn't there, her fussing over him that is one per cent solicitude and ninety-nine, needling.

We stayed on for six days, gradually trying to cool the battle area. In a sense, of course, neither is to blame; what has determined them is the wretched little house in the wretched little road – their timidity and refusal to change.

F gradually gets better. I had a long talk with the doctor, who seems to understand the nature of the relationship. 'Yes, I realize they're not on the same wavelength most of the time.' He's briskly indifferent about the prognosis. F may get back to his old self, he may have a worse hardening and 'snuff out'. He thought it would be better if we took them away back to Lyme. So two days ago we did that. The old man survived the journey quite well and seems perked up a little now. And my mother seems a little tamed and chastened. I dread to think of putting them back in that Leigh environment. On the other hand they are conditioned to need it now; he wants to be nagged and deafened, she wants to do it. Physically he is rather like a small child, shuffling in tiny steps from one chair to the next. I've been dressing and undressing him. He always fights wildly when he takes his shirt off or puts it on; weird flailings of the arms.

22 June

An article for *Cosmopolitan* on first ladies. I have been up to my old divagating, wandering games this summer – partly because of all the long-lasting psychological upset of Eliz's operation; she has lost faith in Lyme, in this house, in our way of life, the old relapse. And whereas at Underhill Farm I could cruelly cut myself off in the workroom, here I have to suffer with her: her boredom, emptiness, waiting. But it's as much this inability to be simple and concentrate – the old anxiety, difficulty, of total economic freedom in me. I work spasmodically at the thriller; not because I don't quite enjoy it, but because it seems indefinitely postponable. The same with the book on the United States. Why hurry, why care? In the latter case, to every argument of the one-ought-to-care kind I can put a counter-argument for waiting till the style and content come solid. More and more it is the problem of penetration (ultimately of time, or oblivion) that obsesses me. Not how to get heard today but to remain heard tomorrow. This is bad socialism, and it worries me; that is, the huge backlog of 'pending' work I have amassed worries me. I wrote a short story recently about a bomb incident in New York, got excited about that, involved Jud Kinberg, sent a copy off to Warner for John Calley to look at as a possible film.[1] And then yesterday when Calley rang me from Hollywood I suddenly felt bored with the whole idea (which I don't think he likes much, anyway); with Hollywood and film involvement. And then I think it would do me good to be forced to work, which is why I 'set' myself the *Cosmo* chore in the first place. Then the novel about the mid-Atlantic Englishman (*An Englishman*) begins to loom over everything else, so that all other work seems to stand in its shadow. It has to be tackled next; and I know it's a Himalayan – no little bit of English cliff.

What Calley really wants is to get a lien on the thriller – a first option. Hitchcock has also cabled for a first look. Such approaches make me mulish and indifferent.

3 July

Now Oscar wants to withdraw if I decide to go forward with Pollack[2] and ABC. I have decided to do so; I couldn't tell him, but his wanting to pull out made the decision even firmer. First, I think the novel is damned as source material for films and it cannot be translated – one must always end with some kind of travesty. Second, the movie gets the book read and re-read, and I don't think that it makes any difference if it is 'good' or 'bad' – the 'good' film satiates and one loses as many

---

[1] John Calley, who had joined Warner Brothers the previous year, was Executive Vice President responsible for worldwide production.

[2] The director Sydney Pollack had the year before received an Academy nomination for *They Shoot Horses, Don't They*.

readers that way as one does by the bad film's repellent effect. Third, I am getting very tired of Tom's and Oscar's high standards – especially as they seem to be so anti-American; I don't really share their infallibility as regards artistic sheep and artistic goats. Pollack is a gamble; he may be very bad; but there's at least a chance that he may be very good. All this may add up to a general bad motive, a kind of spite against them and English fastidiousness in general. But I made my 'existentialist' choice some weeks ago; and I shan't renege.

All I've asked is that he should at least do the deal before he backs out; and he's agreed to give Pollack a chance. Meanwhile, it remains to be seen if there is still a deal to negotiate. We haven't heard from ABC for over a month now, though they say they are still 'interested'.

15 July

Not being able to write poetry because you see too much of it every day. All the poetries in this garden; words are like throwing stones at swallows. Both mean and futile.

Anna is now back from Exeter. To Eliz's rage she has got herself a job (part scullery and part barmaid) in the hotel next door. Not that we care a hang socially; but the kid's lack of enterprise worries us. I think it is as much a kind of love for us as the psychological 'laziness' that Elizabeth sees; and we have no right at all to blame Anna for her timidity about new environments. Partly it is that we are such word people, and Anna is so very much not. She is becoming quite sophisticated visually – no time at all for anything not pattern and texture and environmental object; but verbally she expresses herself in a stream of mechanical trivia, like some secondary-school drop-out.

20 July

To London, to find Betsa Payne collapsed, as Ronnie has just left her. Tom and Fay had been down for the weekend here in Lyme, with Elizabeth in one of her copeless and hopeless moods – a kind of Betsa mood, in effect. I took Tom and Fay antique-hunting on the Saturday and E rang Betsa 'for sympathy' – only to be out-trumped all down the line by this greater horror. Apparently Ronnie has been having an affaire for some months with a 26-year-old woman journalist, Celia Haddon of the *Daily Mail*. A few days ago Betsa and he were having dinner together. She happened to say how much better and happier she was feeling; whereupon he announced the truth of his own life. The new woman 'gives him faith in himself', etc., etc. E went round as soon as we arrived, while I sat drinking with Jud; then she came back to have a meal with us; then she and I went back about midnight to Highgate (another friend from the psychiatric hospital had been with Betsa till then) and sat for another four hours going back over – over and over – Ronnie and his life. It seemed clear to me that all this was a function of his sense of failure – a double failure really: both of his Fleet Street ambitions and his own falling short of them. He has failed at something he knows wasn't really worth succeeding at. And this escapade is a long-pending settlement of accounts with all that. B says he blames his journalistic 'bankruptcy' on her; which only proves my theory. And then also his gift is for entertainment, wit, idiosyncrasy (all the things his friend Alan Brien represents in the current Fleet Street); not for diplomatic analysis and the hard-boiled foreign correspondent persona.

We felt, and feel, very sorry for Betsa, much as she has irritated us in the past. She is hanging on in the hope that R will 'choose' her in the end. I somehow can't see much hope of it; and on the face of it, little hope for a single her. Though gradually during this white (or rather, grey) night I sensed a hardness and toughness in her: that perhaps after all she could face her solitude, widowhood, whatever, and more successfully than we had till now suspected.

I feel surrounded, besieged almost, at the moment by female neuroses; they seem all based on a sense of futility – of not getting from life what ought to be got. And I think the main trouble with this generalized feeling of dissatisfaction is that it calls into question the one principle that really can't be denied; that ought to be 'given' and accepted; which is that some effort has to be made to do what you want in life. Blake said it best in the apophthegm about unfulfilled desires.[1] This constant infanticide of the secretly wished is a fatal disease. Of course Elizabeth has carried it to the subtle scholastic point of claiming that she lacks secret wishes even; she is wishless. In a way this gives her a better 'defensive' (if defending oneself from cure is worth the name defence) position. Betsa is more naked.

We did what we could; she must ring us, come and stay with us, whatever she wanted.

22 July

To Podge and Eileen's, at Garsington. A pretty little old cottage, with the usual skilful assemblage of books, gewgaws, pictures, bits of old furniture. Eileen has a sort of genius at picking on objects in a very narrow range: both charming and unpretentious, both well-chosen but careless. She sees the face value of things, which is rare. One suspects she and Podge aren't normally on speaking terms (again), but communicated while we were present. The cause of war now (as before) is Podge's mother P, whom he keeps in a kennel-like garage beside the house – a

---

[1] 'What is it men in women do require / The lineaments of satisfied desire. / What is it women in men do require / The lineaments of gratified desire.' (*MS Note-Book*, p. 99, 'Several Questions Answered'.)

small garage at best, but made like the Black Hole of Calcutta by a bed, chairs, tables, a grand piano, a chest-of-drawers and eighteen thousand cardboard boxes of the old girl's former possessions. I helped Podge move the grand piano round while we were there, which meant shifting this vast pile of debris as well: old saucepans, chipped fish-slices, piles of old clothes, books, plastic whatnots. Eileen wants the old thing put into a home. Podge says, over his dead body. P herself maunders on, lucid one sentence, incomprehensible the next. Eileen stares out of the window. Podge says, 'Don't listen to her.' I think on the whole they treat their dog Robbie better than P. The subject at issue has gone far beyond concern for the aged; well into the realms of Ionesco and the absurd. Eileen is sticking up for the right to be Irish; Podge, for being unhappy. I liked it, as an ambiance; the contrast between the really rather sweet old cottage-and-garden and the sharp antipathies inside. Philemon and Baucis gone very sour; yet somehow refreshingly sour. Like a squirt of lemon on a hot day.

We had promised not to tell them of the Ronnie–Betsa business. But Ronnie had already told Podge. Now Podge said Eileen mustn't be told: 'It would upset her.' But in that situation it's simply that a secret is too invaluable an advantage to be shared.

25 July

Hazel and Dan and the three kids for ten days. Not exactly happy, with Eliz groaning under the workload, Jonathan showing incipient signs of paranoia (over the twins), Hazel driving us mad with her silliness, Dan with his prickles. He carries the children like a crucifix . . .

Betsa was here for the latter part of their stay, faintly like a being in a coma, helping with the housework, sitting silent, brooding. She came down with Ronnie, who went back the same evening. He and I had a talk in the garden. He wants categorically to leave her, he sees no chance of a return; she's ruined his life, she's denied him sex 'for a long time', she's turned him into a male nurse. He went on and on about the joys of his new bachelor, single-room existence, and of the new woman, Celia. She's also separated, very cool, very 'smashing', very indifferent about commitment. 'God, it's so wonderful,' he said, 'their generation. How civilized and undemanding they are.' It seemed to me that he was in full flight from responsibility. He even looked much younger. He thinks he may go to Washington now, but daren't tell Betsa. I asked him why he didn't tell her the truth – had there been any suicide record? It seems she talked about it. But it wasn't that. He can't drop her cold, he still feels responsible to that extent.

Another thing was her psychoanalysis. He was vitriolic about that.

In my turn I couldn't tell Betsa, when he left. I tried to hint that it might take a long time, etc. But she's still in a state of shock. On her last day here she and I walked along the beach fossil-hunting, towards Pinhay. She seemed to enjoy it; at one point I could even hear her singing to herself. It's possible that in a way this will be the better therapy.

20 August

Another round of absurd intrigue over the film of *The FLW*. Oscar's option fell in on the 7th. Since ABC still haven't made up their minds, I gave him an extra month. Now John Calley from Warner has come through with an offer of $20,000 if I will organize a script. A week ago United Artists did exactly the same thing. Tom Maschler has been working on their London man – a gentleman I didn't take to at all. Both are anxious to go behind Oscar's back, of course. Owing to some absurd confusion, Pollack has told Oscar that Warner are interested, when the truth is they are interested only if Oscar is dropped from the proceedings and so don't want him to know they are sniffing around. The situation is now quite watertight: everyone has to lie to everyone else. It needs a Marivaux.

21 August

Tom M rings to say that he has heard unofficially that I have won the W. H. Smith £1,000 prize.

23 August

A sparrowhawk in the garden. The only one I have seen this year.

24 August

F is ill again. Apparently he won't eat, says he 'wants to die'. Poor old devil.

28 August

Lunch with Kenneth Allsop and his wife. They have bought a mill at West Milton, behind Bridport; white doves, water, fake Italian statues and urns; meant to catch the eye, which it does. He's nice enough, though not quite free of that varnish of vanity the medium seems to bestow on its façade men.[1] I didn't really believe his modest desire to be thought of as a writer. Writers don't live in such decors. And can't function behind such a persona as men like Allsop are condemned to wear; eternally genial, shrewd, wise, relaxed. It's not really all their fault,

---

[1] Kenneth Allsop (1920–1973) was a journalist and broadcaster. In the early sixties he was a reporter and interviewer for *Tonight*, the BBC's first evening current affairs programme, and then went on to present its successor, *24 Hours*. He had also written the books *Bootleggers* (1961), about Prohibition, and *Hard Travellin'* (1967), an account of the American hobo.

of course; though Eliz and I treated his desire to meet us (for a possible TV programme) as a joke, it is rather like an invitation to meet royalty of some minor kind – the new chosen élite of the masses, one of their screen-gracious majesties. I think I fear less and less the 'visual-oral' challenge to the print medium – in a way men like Allsop are scape-goats or publicity conductors (like lightning conductors). They are where the public deposits all its least durable love and admiration.

Tom and Malou Wiseman and Boris came to stay for a week. And since Tom knew Allsop in his Fleet Street days, we went over there again to a Sunday party – TV people, the playwright Ann Jellicoe. I liked her, a quirky peasant-faced woman in her thirties, red-brown cheeks and robin eyes. Tom and Malou are like Japanese water flowers, expand in such milieux; only fully come alive there. It's not clear to me why either of them really need analysis, but perhaps it is something to do with their seeming inability to 'relate' to anything but more or less 'celebrated' other people. I sense that Tom gets positively starved among nonenti-ties and nondescripts; faced with someone of name he becomes ponder-ously boring and serious – as if he's at last back on a level where he can operate and use up his frustrated psychic energy.

6 September

To Leigh, where Dan and Hazel have been looking after F – M having resigned the job and refused to nurse him any more. He lies in the back room overlooking the garden, white-grizzled, sunken-cheeked and bleary-eyed, mostly in a kind of sleep coma. Every so often he struggles up and gets in a panic about the bedpan. We went and found a room in a nursing home in Imperial Avenue. It had the sad waiting-room-of-death atmosphere of such places, but the nurse in charge seemed capable. He is far beyond the capacity of this house now; like a small, sick child. He hasn't eaten for ten days, and I don't quite know what's keeping him alive: courage or convention. Not wanting to die or not knowing how to. In his drugged sleeps he comes out with weird answers to questions. He'll have a sherry, thank you. He'll put the fire out. The night nurse called it aural hallucination, but it's obviously a terrible energy of dream still in him. In a sense I think this is keeping him alive – feeding on the past.

7 September

We moved him, in an ambulance, to the nursing home. He was too drugged to realize what was really happening; but the next day when we went in to see him he was like a frantic child: 'Oh, John. John, thank God you've come, you must take me home, I want to die at home, this place is like a prison . . .' and on and on, descending into groans about his leg, the expense, and everything else. We managed to calm him down. Normal, says the nursing home. I would have taken him out, if it were not for M – indeed, almost in spite of M, so determined is she now that he must die quickly. I don't know if this situation is common: so many years' poison, resentment and humiliation come to the boil – or more accurately, to *a* boil in the other sense. M feels only death can lance it. She makes me very male and angry at times – a very black Oedipus – one with reversed roles towards his parents. But a lot keeps emerging – the appalling financial subjection he has kept her under these last ten years or so (when there was no need for it – I've just been through his papers, to discover he has £6,600 on current account and God knows how much more invested); all kinds of ancient Victorian male and female grudges.

Picking his pears and apples. Some of the old trees have been so pruned that the fruit spurs are as brittle as sticks of charcoal.

I was alone with him in his room and he began to mutter in his sleep: an extraordinary poem-like, unpunctuated little paragraph.

'Bobby Charles I sat beside him he was hit in the stomach I said you'll be all right Bobby he said I've seen too many like that too many out in No Man's Land.'

An unwritten fragment from *The Waste Land*. Then a few moments later he opened his eyes and groped round for me. 'You must send me the bill for this. I want to pay the bill.'

I said, 'Yes, all right, I'll send you the bill.'

Of course the real bill is from those years between 1915 and 1918. Among his papers I came on his officer's passbook from the First World War. He went to France in January 1915. I think this is where the terrible restlessness, the blanket-groping, the fear of leaving home, the miserliness (or deep timidity about spending) springs from. That trauma is still as strong as ever. You survive by lying quiet; and you die lying in a nightmare.

8 September

He is suddenly lucid and patient again, almost his old self. Now M is terrified.

This wretched house drives Eliz and myself insane with its crabbed tattiness, its absolute lack of amenity. By chance the woman next door asked us in to look at some antique furniture her dead husband bought years ago. Although she has very little taste, the contrast between her bright, clean and uncluttered house (with its scatter of nice antiques) and this hideous rubbish-dump is very painful. Of course M has no aesthetic sense whatever, but quite why F has so rejected that whole area of life puzzles me. Tucked in among the business papers I came on little scraps of poems, all apparently written during the last year or so.

LOST
The poet has lost his rhyme
And that is the reason why
His cup of verse is dry.
But wait. Stay a while.
Chaste contemplation of your beauty
Will restore wisdom to his mind
(And strength to his legs and eyes)
And once again he'll versify your virtues.

WHAT GOETHE FOUND
I strolled in the wood
For no reason at all
Looking for nothing
That was all.

I saw in the shadow
A little flower shy
Like a shining star
Like a beautiful eye.

I was going to pick it
When it suddenly said –
Am I to be gathered
Just to be dead?

I dug it up
Roots and all
And carried it to the garden wall
By the house on the hill.

And planted it again
In that quiet place.
Now its roots spread
And it again blooms apace.

I suppose the last is a translation from Goethe. What is so sad is the
drive to 'versify' and the miserable notion that verse is something that
rhymes – the ignorance that 'versify' has been a forbidden verb for at
least sixty years. I think he never read any modern verse, as he never
liked modern music, modern art or anything else. Yet underneath all
the total inadequacy of this as poetry is that mysterious drive: all his
life he has scrawled on bits of paper. It is like that hopeless novel he
once made me read; the novel of someone who has never read novels,

even the classics – let alone anything else written since he was born. I feel a sense of gigantic hereditary luck: that I am what he was always so afraid to be that he couldn't make even the faintest effort, beyond writing in secret, to achieve it. He would never admit what he really loved and wanted.

One of the poems I found genuinely sad; sad in its badness, sad because he almost certainly never knew of Milton's agony in the same fire.

RECOMPENSE
How oft when the sun shone
Brightly in my garden
And I looked upon the flowers and ripened fruit
I saw them not.

But now in my darkened world
I sometimes think I see more clearly
the beauty of things
I missed when sight was mine.

Maybe God in his charity
Forgives my one-time negligence
For seeing not what nature gave me
And grants me this
Further gift of seeing in my mind
What once I saw not.

12 September
To London for the afternoon, to discuss the Warner offer and potential script-writers with Tom Maschler and Roger Burford.[1]

F seems to have settled down to the nursing home and an invalid life. He gets no worse – a little better, if anything.

14 September
Back to Lyme.

15 September
A specialist has been to see F. The leg is gangrenous and must come off. Strangely, such things almost make me believe in God again. I have to vent my black rage on something.

---

[1] The Warner Brothers offer for *The French Lieutenant's Woman* was accepted and the playwright David Rudkin commissioned to write a screen adaptation.

16 September

M rings to say he has come through, has even been chatting with the nurses; also that he is much happier. He thought he was sent to the nursing home (he is now in Southend General Hospital) to die – now something is being done. According to the nurses he must have been in great pain with the leg for some time.

19 September

W. H. Smith confirm that I have won the £1,000 prize.

25 September

I go down alone to Leigh. F seems a little weaker; otherwise not much changed. I had hoped that I could leave and we could get back to Lyme; but now the hospital talks of discharging him in ten days' time, which puts M in a panic. Lyme and peace begin to seem remote as the Hesperides. Nobody wants me to be a writer.

28 September

Back to Lyme. Now it's Eliz, arguing and weeping through the whole journey. I despise her, ignore her, etc., etc. I feel my head will burst open. At home we argue into the small hours. Now she wants to sell Belmont. We are to have little houses dotted over the landscape, staying a few months in each: I ought to be able to write anywhere. I listen to her, and think of the garden. The strawberry-tree is in flower. I try to explain I can write here because there is peace here; that I need a known environment, one I feel no drive to get to know and explore, in order to stay cooped up with a book. I can't go into the unknown from the unknown.

17 October

Jud has sold *Zip* to Sidney Glazier. $5,000 for a screenplay.[1] Roger B would be shocked that I sell myself so cheap. Also David Tringham wants to try to do something on the short story called 'The Last Chapter'.[2]

Anna turns up from Bristol with a new boyfriend, Eric having been sent on his way with a flea in his ear. This time it's a Welsh doctor's son,

[1] *Zip* was based on a short story JF had written about a failed writer who bombs a New York cinema in an attempt – as JF had commented of Robert Kennedy's assassin – 'to do something about his nothingness'. See note 1, page 42.
[2] Tringham, who was first assistant director on *The Magus*, had written to JF in May asking him if he had any material available for adaptation. JF suggested 'The Last Chapter', which was unpublished. It is the story of a thriller writer whose fictional characters begin to slip out of his control after he meets a young woman.

indistinguishable in appearance, manners and everything else from a Welsh labourer's son. We feel these boys must put on some sort of mask with us – to see how much they can make us detest them and their uncouthness. Even Anna, it turns out, doesn't really like him – 'but there's no one else'. I feel she's a clipped dove let loose in an aviary of falcons. So plump and gentle and inviting of emotional rape. I'm beginning to wonder whether those old fairy-story kings and their ruthless selection boards for suitors to their daughters' hands weren't right. The Welsh boy would have gone straight into the stomach of his country's symbol, so far as this king is concerned.

18 October
To London, a lovely October day. We went and saw Tom and Fay in the evening, and don't feel all is well there. The baby is nice, very Chinese – Tom hands round photos – 'Now don't you feel she looks Jewish there?' – and Fay grimaces. One never saw a less Jewish nose, and she has her mother's very pretty almond-shaped eyes. Tired eyes now, she looks as if baby-maintenance is killing her on top of all the Tom-maintenance.

19 October
To BBC Lime Grove for a recorded interview with Kenneth Allsop. It starts badly, a central-heating pipe starts ticking, then a microphone boom breaks down. Technicians, producer, Allsop all in a rage. The conversation was bad. I can't project and I can't be simple, especially before such general questions; any one of them would have taken me the whole programme to answer properly.

20–23 October
At Leigh F is weakening; one knows it in a way because he won't admit it, talks more and more about when he will come out. Perhaps it is partly a conscious protection – a spirit of hopelessness hangs over such wards as this. More and more I think the trouble is aesthetic. It's not the nursing that's wrong, but the décor – or rather the absolute lack of it. Why should people *have* to die in long, anonymous rooms – rooms that are in agony themselves because no one has ever looked at them or loved them?

    In London that evening, Ronnie P brought Celia to meet us. We took against her almost at once: a tall, willowy (I don't like willowy women, women you have to describe by that particular word) girl with long blonde hair; faintly Teutonic-looking, a shade fey. I didn't find her attractive and she didn't find us attractive. Over a Chinese dinner down in Soho we suddenly had a row – of all absurd things, over PLR rights. She had all the old Fleet Street contempt for authors, for those who can't 'make an honest living' out of writing. Poor Ronnie tried to umpire the fight; but Eliz joined in, even angrier than I was. At the end, she started muttering: 'Perhaps I was wrong, I do see your point . . .' Peculiar surrendering. There was no need. It was obvious we couldn't stand each other. Withdrawals only made matters worse.

I don't understand Ronnie any more. Betsa at her worst is better than this creature at her best.

24 October
Back to Lyme. I develop a foul cold and in the end I let it send me to bed.

26 October
When I come down, about ten, Eliz says M rang up at eight that morning to say F died at five, just before dawn. Her mother is staying with us and they look at me as if I ought to break down. But I don't feel sad at all, only relieved. I think my views on death were best crystallized by *Mrs Dalloway*;[1] the real death is when you are no longer remembered by a living soul, when it is as if you never existed. I feel I have him still very living and secure in me. That I shan't see him again is like that I shan't read this book again or see this place again or drink this bottle of wine again. It is very bearable. I go back to bed and read all day and don't think about him.

30 October
To Leigh, for F's funeral. I have rotten bronchitis, after the cold; and Eliz is the same. We got to 63 just before the hearse turned up;[2] a white coffin, brass handles. I wonder if they unscrew the latter before the rest goes into the furnace. Eliz and I go with M behind the hearse, in a black Rolls. At the crematorium the Southend Fowleses; Stanley and Eileen; Geoffrey Woolf, the wicked Gertie Fowles's son, a soft, sibilant gent like a well-to-do retired bank manager. An absurd service in a 'contemporary' chapel; outside the window a brick pool with goldfish. A terrible old priest mangling the service, as sincere as a plastic bucket; I suppose he does four an hour all through the day. F would have hated it. I felt bad, one shouldn't have shuffled him off like that; I'd rather have had the full C. of E. ceremonial. Ridiculous, I felt much sadder at poor old

---

In Virginia Woolf's novel, Clarissa Dalloway has a theory of how the 'unseen part of us' can survive after death: 'You were given a sharp, acute, uncomfortable grain – the actual meeting; horribly painful as often as not; yet in absence, in the most unlikely places, it would flower out, open, shed its scent, let you touch, taste, look about you, get the whole feel of it and understanding, after years of lying lost.'

The Fowles family home was at 63 Fillebrooke Avenue, Leigh-on-Sea.

Cameron's cremation at St Godric's.[1] Here, I just wanted to get outside; the wretched dog-collar muttered a sort of sermon of condolence, fixing me with his fish eyes, leaning over our pew.

Outside, and meeting the family. Back to 63, and some drinks; they all got a little drunk. When they'd gone, I went through the bills, six or seven years of bills he'd kept. Talking about him, how ridiculous he was over money. We left at ten, to sleep in London, since Dan and Hazel and the kids were sleeping at Leigh. I'd secretly abstracted his 1914–18 paybook, some poems (those I transcribed earlier), two letters from old Tucker.[2] I think no one at the funeral understood him. I should have given the sermon.

31 October

Back to Lyme. We lit a fire; peace and autumn. I read *Le Grand Meaulnes*, for which I'm doing an introduction. In French, then in English, a new translation by an American called Lowell Bair; which saddens me. It's not that it's inaccurate; but just pedestrian, too literal, uninspired. It's not that my French is better than his; but that my English is. A little of the fault is Alain-Fournier's. There are carelessnesses, clumsy repetitions and over-uses of words in the French text. But in any case that works partly through its sparseness, its simplicity, the readings it evokes between lines – unsaid things that have sometimes to be said in English. I feel sad most of all for Alain-Fournier himself; people cannot understand. He cannot get through, in this form.

7 November

David Tringham comes for the weekend, to talk over the short story. He has just been first assistant on David Lean's *Ryan's Daughter* – then before that Losey's *Figures in a Landscape*, which John Kohn produced. He is something of a mimic and funny about the absurdities of the movie world. Losey's nickname was 'Sitting Bull'; a cameraman who couldn't stand the height they were filming at (in the Sierra Nevada) 'Return Ticket'. Tringham's a nice young man, rather nervous and I suspect too modest to 'make' it. The whole wretched industry is geared to the sacred monster.

He wants to write the script, to which I willingly agreed.

8 November

I began writing a story about a Jesuit priest who loses his sight. It began with the idea of a blind man being seduced. It may come to nothing. I

---

[1] While JF was teaching at St Godric's, he attended the funeral of a fellow teacher, Martin Cameron. See *The Journals*, volume 1, pages 532–4.
[2] J. T. L. Tucker was a relative who had been godfather to JF's father Robert and had helped to run the family tobacco business.

have no plan for it; no idea how long it will be. I see the blindness being the instrument of his discovering the world of sensation, pagan eroticism, humanism, etc.; losing his faith. I like the technical difficulties it already poses, and holds in promise.

13 November
John Calley calling from Hollywood about the film, mentioned in passing that Warner have just bought Simon and Schuster and that he had just asked Tom M to run it. When Tom had demurred, Calley offered to buy Cape as well.

16 November
John, Hooray hooray. *The French Lieutenant's Woman* will be on *The Times* bestseller list next Sunday for the fifty-second week. One solid year. Best to you both.

Ned

23 November
To London again. We drove up. Lying on a damp grass verge near Blandford Forum, an elderly woman with her face covered in blood. A skidded truck, a smashed car. We imagine 'blood-red' much darker than it is. The real thing has an orangeness, a fresh lightness about it that doesn't correspond with the mental correlative.

24 November
Lunch at Strand House with the head and some directors of W. H. Smith: two Tweedledum-and-Tweedledee figures, an Old Etonian called Simon Hornby. And the boss, a man called Troughton. A formal, gentlemen's-club atmosphere: silver and mahogany. We serve ourselves in a private dining-room. Talk of cricket, oysters, collecting postcards. I listen to myself being what nothing real in me is. Such experiences are so remote from literature, let alone the business of being a writer. I feel near to being very rude all through this lunch; and so come on very bland.

I should have refused the prize. I don't believe in prizes; I certainly don't respect W. H. Smith and their attitude to fiction (as evidenced by their novel-buying policy). I think I must give the money away, but I loathe the vanity of the grand public gesture of charity. Also I have no money at the moment. I've just had to pay two large retrospective surtax bills and another even larger one is due on January 1st. It is absurd. I have £100,000 or more in the States; and once again an overdraft on current account here.

Also I'm ill: a constant pain in my left lung and breathlessness. For weeks now I have been fighting the demon nicotine. Absolutely without success. I've no physical strength or energy.

25 November

With Jud. He had just heard that Suzanne tried to kill herself a few days ago in Casablanca. Apparently she slashed her throat and hands. It can't have been too serious, as the hospital discharged her the next day. Now he thinks she's in Paris. Poor man. He is crucified by the inauthenticity of their past existence.

26 November

Home to Lyme alone. London in an opal soup; mist all the way to Yeovil; then clean sunlight. I go back to the story I started on the 8th. I mean it to be a short novel – 80,000 words, not more. But already my proliferating imagination expands it. I know I can't finish it now. I must do the script for Jud, the thriller must be finished, the *Meaulnes* introduction and translation editing waits. I feel vilely unfit; but fertile.

This 'feeling fertile' is very much an awareness of imperfection; a seeing deeper into what one is. It makes many writers unhappy; it had made me unhappy in the past (laurels turned to ashes); but now I like it. It is not destructive, but springlike. A simmering pot. A machine running. A seed germinating.

27 November

I renounce the cigarette; this time I will keep on with cigars.

Eliz has gone off to Birmingham and I am plunged in editing Bair's miserable text. Pure love and homage for Alain-Fournier, really.[1] I'm doing it for nothing; or for everything his generation died for. I'm also reading Jean Loize's extraordinary biography:[2] a book that is like a dream, so closely does it follow Fournier's life. I suppose I write it more than I read it – I see it as I see what I am writing and time doesn't exist. I dread ending it. Fournier's death.[3]

3 December

To London, for the W. H. Smith prize. I loathe the speech, the publicity. Yesterday I had a TV team here all day, a silly young interviewer and four crew, whom I could stand better: that bored cynicism of the working-class professional, the new artisan class of our world. Shot on the Cobb, on Ware Common, down in town; in my study. While they were 'doing'

---

[1] For JF's special attachment to Alain-Fournier, see introduction to *The Journals*, volume 1, pages xv–xvi.

[2] *Alain-Fournier, sa vie et le Grand Meaulnes* (Hachette, 1968).

[3] Alain-Fournier was killed in September 1914 near Verdun, aged only twenty-seven.

the Cobb, an unsavoury character in a long black overcoat came up; sideburns, shifty eyes. He asked what was going on and I shrugged and turned my back. He went and listened, then came back to me and said, 'Are you John Fowles?' I nodded. He held out his hand. 'I'm the mayor.' We had a talk, he isn't really shifty, just a bit of an old Lyme know-all.

Jud. Suzanne killed herself yesterday in Paris. He doesn't know how yet. Poor man, I wanted to be very sorry for him; but he couldn't quite hide his relief and very obviously didn't want to see us. I persuaded him that he must let Stephen's headmaster in Switzerland know; I couldn't bear the idea of the boy picking up the *Herald Tribune* or something and first learning of it there.

4 December

The prize-giving. All literary Fleet Street, looking blasé and dry. The prize was given by Lord Goodman; he's mountainously fat, a sort of cross between Orson Welles and Isaiah Berlin; balding, crinkled hair, voluble. I liked Troughton better; he made a nice, very complimentary and genuine-sounding speech. Then Goodman. Then myself trying to be funny ('Why are you so humourless?' asked the TV interviewer the other day. What a lovely first question, and how I longed to be Evelyn Waugh). Then a bit more serious.

I went off afterwards with Anthony Sheil. We agreed I should sack Julian Bach. Then back home at five, feeling upset and tense. I went back to Loize and Fournier; and soon felt cured.

5 December

Back to Lyme. And more Loize.

6 December

The TV interview with Kenneth Allsop is shown on BBC 1. It made my skin crawl a bit. I am print, not words. And that appalling voice.

16 December

Finished my introduction to *Le Grand Meaulnes*. And wrote the axe-letter to Julian.

29 December

Podge came for a night. Eileen has 'left' him and is living with a friend. He dismisses it with a shrug, a merciful change from all our other broken-marriaged friends. We can't really blame Eileen either, since he is *so* difficult to live with. From the moment he gets up he discusses ideas, opinions, definitions – no wonder they finally gave Socrates his glass of hemlock. One can stand just so much of this furiously intellectual, mental approach to daily life. And he doesn't realize how different a world I live in: that of imagination and composition. The (for a Marxist) poison of our capitalist world is my meat; that is, I agree with most of his diagnoses and attitudes; but agreement or action taken on it is not what I am here for.

7 January 1971
David Tringham for the night, to discuss his script of 'The Last Chapter'. He's converted it quite nicely, more or less straight from the story.

10 January
A sublime day, as warm as late April. What a strange winter this is being, climatically.

A great public smoking panic again. I had mine just before Christmas, resolved never to smoke cigarettes again, but not to try my will-power too far – therefore to change to cigars. Now I am more or less chain-smoking them. It is hopeless. I cannot write or think without nicotine.

12 January
Still with the thriller. But I am supposed to have started the script with Jud – *Zip*. Somehow I keep getting myself in these ridiculous situations. Getting myself in an impossible corner over work.

20 January
Working on the script of *Zip* for a few days and not enjoying it at all. I go back to the thriller.

23 January
A nice young American from London, Dan Crawford. He's running a pub-theatre in Islington and has taken on Brian McDermott's adaptation of *The Collector*. Because of the postal strike, he brought down the revised version by train. I suppose it will do: my indifference as to whether it 'does' or not I couldn't really hide from him. *Zip* came into it: the futility of trying to twist the demands of one form into the requirements of another. I'm not sure this isn't the curse of our age: nobody will let anything remain what it is. Of course many things political and social ought not to remain what they are. But universal change is the death of all poetry – both historically and qualitatively.

4 February
To Budleigh Salterton, to see Eileen, who is staying with her sister there. The husband wears an Old Etonian tie, a face like that of an amiable starved vulture. The sister is an egotist, hears nothing, very far from Eileen. They live in a centrally heated no-man's-house in the Budleigh no-man's-land. Being awake is waiting for meals, according to E. She is

not going back to Podge. How's he getting on? 'Ask him. How should I know? I'm the one who's left him.' She is very skittish and chirpy, a woman reborn.

8 February
The play of *The Collector* opens in London. The reviews are quite good.

15 February
Today I finished revising the thriller – now called *The Device* instead of *Somebody's Got to Do It.* I've enjoyed doing it most of the time, but today it has depressed me. The great spaghetti tangles of plot and motive that have to be unravelled. Perhaps that's why most thrillers are so short: the strain of being realistic on the surface, totally unrealistic down below. Perhaps it is the most tiring of the artificial forms. I crave realism again, now.

16 February
To London, which we did not enjoy. Ronnie and Betsa still circling warily – and wearily, and wearyingly – round each other. Jud in his black pit. Everyone seems depressed, and we are no exceptions.

22 February
Back to Lyme with M – her long-dreaded stay with us. I spend the week in the garden, and E goes mad. M's mindlessness defeats belief: she sees nothing, hears nothing, and will not leave Fillebrooke Avenue and all its zombies alone.

   We saw Ronnie Payne the day before we came back. He seems adamantly determined not to return to Betsa. We took him back 'home' – a horrid little one-room in a court running off Fleet Street. A feeling of emptiness, of hours to kill. Futility. He'd just been with Enoch Powell on his anti-Market trip to France; and was funny about that. Apparently the egregious Enoch had his lectures written out in good French and all went well enough there; it was when he answered questions that the joys began. One answer began '*Quand j'étais dans le cabinet ombre . . .*' – responsible for shady privies, no doubt.

4 March
M departs back to Leigh. I suppose we treat her with appalling unkindness; I won't speak to her at all half the time and Eliz keeps exploding with rage behind her back. If only her narrowness of mind and reference and her stupidity in what she says were simple – could be simply explained; if only she showed the slightest self-awareness. Perhaps we are wrong to interpret this as a kind of knowing malice. We think she must see the real reason for our hints, our silences. But

somehow she doesn't, I suspect. So eternally she tries to drag us down to where she can 'place' and handle us – my childhood, her childhood, Fillebrooke Avenue; and eternally I refuse.

8 March
The postal strike is ended. I have enjoyed every non-delivery of it. And wish it might continue for ever.

24 March
London. And Podge. We go to see the Montherlant play (in French) *La Ville dont le prince est un enfant* – and vote it a sanctimonious and hypocritical bore, for all the raves it has got. I suppose it is the most typical play of the Gaullist period: inherently fascist. Then the next day to see Visconti's *Death in Venice*, a good, solid piece of grand opera, its few faults easily forgiven. Though not by Podge, who has one of his scab-picking moods towards people who are not frank (bloody-spade frank) about homosexuality. He enrages Eliz. The Mann is so clearly about dying, age, time; and only quite irrelevantly about ephebophilia.

The Wanderer, the film of Alain-Fournier's *Le Grand Meaulnes*.[1] A failure for the interesting reason that it was made with love and out of great respect for the text – they try to cram every moment in, every scene. So it comes out choppily and often incomprehensibly; the strange celebration misfires badly. It moved me, though, knowing all the background as well as I do now. And the young man who played Meaulnes had the right face. But finally one sees the book can't be made physical; it works in the subconscious, but not before the camera.

The W interested me particularly because Rudkin's script for *The FLW* has just turned up and makes the same mistake of being overfaithful; much too 'rich'; lacking in rhythm. One of the triumphs of *Death in Venice* is precisely the paucity of dialogue, the predominance of the visual.

3 April
I get very rapidly very sick of London these days. We had to wait till today for Rudkin to turn up – discussions all day down in the Vale of Health with him and Tom. Fairly fruitful on the whole: he gave in much more easily than we anticipated. Then the evening with Jud and his new girlfriend, Monica Mennel. She's the daughter of some South African millionaire; rolling in it. And Jud is suddenly rolling in happiness: a new, optimistic man. I find the girl too clever, too eager to be clever, sensitive, knowing of the world. She's an old girlfriend of Tom Maschler's,

---

[1] Made and released in France under the novel's original title *Le Grand Meaulnes* in 1967, the film was directed by Jean-Gabriel Albicocco and starred Jean Blaise in the title role.

it seems. 'He's crazy, the girl's mad' was his comment when I told him about Jud. But we're glad for Jud, at any rate.

Fay has taken against Hampstead and the house in the Vale of Health, now. I sense Tom has his problems. And I have mine, Eliz having sunk into one of her old hatred-of-Lyme moods. I suppose that at least we have learnt that this has nothing to do with what we feel for each other: we row over some third thing between us, not one at the other. Since Christmas, she has stayed in bed till eleven or twelve every day. Nothing will interest her; or satisfy her. I've dug my heels in, I will not be uprooted and uprooted each time her boredom with herself ('my inadequacies') reaches a climax. She won't read, she won't look at the garden; she won't help me secretarially; all she will do is turn Belmont into her crucifix.

13 April

Tom rings. He has read *The Device*, and obviously doesn't like it, behind a token noise of enthusiasm. He wants it cut by a quarter; it's too complicated. And Eliz at last says what she thinks: which is that she mostly hates it. I feel I ought to feel upset, but don't. In a sense it has in any case given me all the enjoyment I can get from it – in the writing of it; and now I don't care whether it is published or not, I even think of destroying the wretched thing, so little do I care about its future.

20 April

Now Anthony Sheil's opinion on *The Device*. No better than the others. My instinct is more and more to kill the thing.

23 April

A translation of Perrault's *Cinderella* for Tom Maschler. Our life here has recently got so black and sour that it was absurd: like having a picnic on a battlefield.

The battlefield is Eliz and her profound depression – nothing new, but so deep this time that we live outwardly without rows or fighting. She calls it loss of identity, I call it inability to love. I think, though it may be a close thing, that she hates herself more than me. She can't face people now; my cousin Ann Richards and her husband called in the other day at two-thirty in the afternoon. Eliz was still in bed and refused to meet them – I took them in the garden, and she dressed and went out. They must have seen the VW was here when they came and gone when they left.

24 April

Anna came for a day or two before her new term starts. Apparently Roy is also in a state of deep depression – drinking, taking to his bed and the rest. She has had to spend her holidays with them, to try to ease the situation. I feel sorry for the poor child: and thank the genetic miracle that so few of her two parents' self-destructive and endlessly self-concentrated neuroses have been passed on. Liz at least has the courage to put up a front of normality with her. But Anna's not a fool, and must have a long nose for stress by now. For once *The Times* had a good editorial today: about how Anna's generation sees ours. Every word of it seemed right to me. Of course we are historical victims; that doesn't make us any less full of *mauvaise foi*.

I persuaded Eliz to invite the two little girls, Cinderellas both, from Exeter: Emma and Sophie Conn. Strange, they seemed little changed from that memorable first visit. The same attachments: I am Emma's, the younger one clings to Eliz and Anna. Emma is a formidably complex child, I am told very unlovable at home compared with her sister; sulky and 'difficult'. She is very possessive, and knows it; makes me her substitute father one moment, holds me at a distance the next. Curious searching looks: who am I? I mean that question in its full ambiguity. Who am I, who is this man, what is this relationship? She was very aware this time of its ephemerality: a kind of metaphorical pinching herself – I must be grown-up, I must recognize this can't last. On my side the awareness that she is one of those very rare children I should have liked to call my own; and an awareness that her intensity is a function of the real context (our actual very tenuous and remote relationship in any practical sense) and not the totally unreal one of a wish-fulfilment. She's a poem-child, a lyric; but only as long as she doesn't last.

On the Sunday we went to Branscombe beach for a picnic. Emma and I wandered on to the next bay, then up in the cliffs behind, under the weird 'castle' of chalk and flint; and back along a cliff-path tapestried white with sloe in blossom. The long-haired child with her strange oblique eyes, running ahead and turning; the sea, the herring-gulls on their nests on the inland cliff.

And Eliz on the way home, after we had left them with their mother, trying to kill the poem stone dead. 'You and she just cut the rest of us out,' and so on. But a tiny part of that child – tiny, but still a part more than most children have – is pure love and affection; and all I show to her is what I cannot show to Eliz herself or to Anna. Or only very indirectly to Anna; I know something in her doesn't want me to quit the roles we play – two comparatively sane, but different, people in an insane context. She gets through by normalizing. She finds me faintly comic with Emma; and perhaps senses dimly that Emma is also an Anna-substitute.

It struck me at Branscombe also how important the part played by nature is in all this: what an easy environ it is in which to establish proper, that is loving, relationships. I become progressively less interested in identifying natural objects and progressively more deeply involved in natural process – in *Mother* Nature, to use the old term – not really a pathetic fallacy, I think. Emma and I communicated almost purely through her showing me nature, my showing her – the tokens are crabs, sand-eels, flowers, stones, nothings, mere counters. Such things bore Anna, unless they have some immediate visual charm; and Eliz rejects them as she rejects the whole idea of garden and gardening as an aspect of natural process. Spring never fails to reawaken something childlike in me: part of me at Branscombe, a large part of me, was precisely the same age as Emma, nine, ten, whatever she is. And aware, bitterly aware, that I am a vicar who had married an atheist.

22 May
A dismissive 'Second Opinion' on my work by Alan Brien in the *Sunday Times*. I am a glass eye, a maker of soft-centred chocolates, etc. It depresses me, since I can't say 'it is true' or 'it is not true'; value judgements can't be answered, and even worse, can't be forgotten. I can tell myself Brien is a Narcissus, a failed novelist turned shrewd journalistic clown; but it is just one more nail in a coffin that already has enough. There was a ridiculous article in *The Times* the other week: full of factual errors, and not getting who I am at all – but setting me up for cutting down. I shall answer neither piece; I simply don't care any more.

27 May
The Whitsun madness: traffic all night. One casualty was a hedgehog outside our gate. It filled me with anger. I thought it was the larger of the two I give bread and milk to every night. But they were there again.

Tom Wiseman and Malou and Boris came for the weekend; a decision three days ago by Eliz, regretted as soon as it was made. Boris exhausts us, Malou and her chatter exhaust us, Tom has always an air of being out of his element. Eliz has her martyred face, and I put on a show of affability. And we are all bored together: even Boris. Chekhov, without the humour.

Quicky and his men are building a terrace and new steps. They look nice; as with everything else here nowadays, I wonder how much longer I shall enjoy them.

3 June
Eliz to London by herself, after a terrible afternoon of despair. I have a TV interview tomorrow and shall go by train. Her withdrawal from the world is beginning to frighten me. I am the powerless villain in the piece and I simply don't know how to cure her. I am now to blame for leaving the farm; she sees it as some fatal throwing-away of paradise,

having forgotten how much she hated so much of her time there; in fact, has regretted every move we have made since Church Row days. She has become a specialist, aided by her refusal to take an interest in anything outside her own physical and psychological state, in wringing every last drop of misery from all we do or have done to us – a threatened visit by her mother and the two sisters, it assumes end-of-the-world proportions.

The combination of her gloom and my sourness is getting too much. The smell of bile all through the house. I escape it only in the garden. I can't write, I can hardly read. I fiddle with the script for Jud, that's not writing. The irony beneath it all is that I have to cling by my fingernails to a life most people would envy us. Today she said she could live happily only in total isolation – this would never have happened if we stayed at the farm. But it would have. If only she would face up to this capacity for hating the present – that is, *any* present, not just the one that chance has placed her in.

16 August

I went to London to see Boxall. I knew his wife had died unexpectedly in May. He came out with it all at Hampstead; it was suicide and the poor devil has been half-destroyed by the whole thing. She was Czech, very gentle – he kept on repeating it, very gentle, so gentle, she would never hurt people – and had been hit hard by the menopause. They had a family Sunday, perfectly normal, his mother there, the children home for the day from their boarding-schools. When he came home on the Monday evening, he found her dead body in the kitchen. Sleeping-pills. And a note: *Forgive me, darling. Be happy.*

As he said, it effectively destroyed his happiness for a long time to come. He couldn't go back to the house for weeks. By an irony, he put it in her name a year or two ago – 'an accountant caught in one of the first traps he warns his clients about'. He can't stand living there and he can't sell it now without getting a capital gains assessment. He said he'd learnt more about himself in the last two months than in the previous twenty years. 'Half the time I sit wondering what life is supposed to be about.'

And blackbirds – had I noticed how loud the blackbirds had been singing this year? He said there seemed hundreds in the part of Hampstead where they live. 'I can't sleep in the mornings for them, they wake me up at dawn.' It seemed blackbirds were what his wife best remembered about her girlhood in her parents' flat in Prague. He was sure it was the sound of blackbirds that had killed her.

Tom Wiseman's new novel, *The Romantic Englishwoman*, is one of the Booker entries: embarrassing to read, it's so autobiographical, such a thin disguise of Malou and himself. I had dinner with them after my sad afternoon with Boxall; and the Maschlers were there. Then on the

Sunday I took Malou to see Eric Rohmer's film *Claire's Knee* – after the novel (about a writer's wife running away with another writer) it couldn't quite be a normal event. I thought I saw something mournfully determined not to be shocked in Tom's eyes as we left him sitting in Arkwright Road with his mother. Malou, on the other hand, seemed very anxious to seem normal, and equally anxious not to discuss the novel, which she knows I've read. It was comic, really; I realized it was her way of saying the novel isn't true.

Claire's Knee was very fine: as good a film as I've seen for a long time. Marivaux, a touch of Racine: the analysis of feeling. I don't think it would be possible over here – not only our lack of directors and cameramen with that sobriety and delicacy of taste. Simply we have no language on which to base such scripts.

22 August

Wicked (though a future editor might not think so), but I haven't written anything here these last two months. I've had to steal up from behind on any writing. I suppose it is accidie; as much a boredom with others' words as my own. I've read thirty-five books for the Booker Prize (with five more to go) and that has made me very tired of the novel. At least half the entries I would normally have never finished; some even now I couldn't manage – a case of a judge falling asleep in court, I suppose; there are only three or four I feel real enthusiasm of any kind for.

A good summer, a lot of sun until these last two weeks. And Eliz has made one of her miraculous recoveries: a saint of briskness, getting up before eight every morning, dashing about, no complaints. I shouldn't have doubted her resilience earlier this year.

Podge came to see us in July: E walked out after he had hit her over the head with a plastic bowl one evening. As usual he turned it all into a comedy. A great examination of what I had meant by saying in a letter to him that Eliz and I wanted 'to stay neutral' – 'I can't possibly tell you about it all until you elucidate that term.' Apparently Eileen had offered to produce seven witnesses to his cruelty if he contested the divorce action – which he didn't, but those sombre seven and unnamed rats have obviously preyed on him. We assured him we weren't to be counted among them; and were granted the story. Podge was sad late one night: about the waste of his Oxford years. 'When I look back, I see no one I've been friendly with over the last twenty years was ever worth an hour of my time. Their common factor is total inauthenticity.' He has a more practical nightmare, poor man; Eileen is out for her pound of flesh and insists on half the value of the Garsington cottage; he has to find that now. I offered to help, but he thinks 'Wonder Boy' (his American son-in-law) will raise it from his mother.

25 August
By sardine-can, alias Trident, to Nice, for Jud's wedding. He's there to meet us. I feel hot and bad-tempered – Eliz having forced me for some incomprehensible reason to wear a brown suit – and Jud is neurotic and bad-tempered. He bawls out the Hertz car-man because he is five minutes late with the car we are to rent. I feel the trip is predestined to disaster. Jud once again producing a bad film, and knowing it.

3 September
Up at four, and then through the dawn to Nice airport. Back in Lyme after lunch, splendid September weather.

4 September
I started finishing the *Ourika* translation before we went.[1] I see it with 'scholarly' apparatus; and something on the nature of freedom and the part education plays in it.

14 September
The first Booker Prize meeting, in the St James Hotel in Buckingham Gate – a suite. Saul Bellow, in a letter we all vote offensively priggish, has refused to turn up for this one. He has chosen what seems to me the worst book of the lot (which is no vain insult), Robinson's *Goshawk Squadron* – as did Muggeridge.[2]

Philip Toynbee is in baggy pants, tired coat, old-fashioned shirt and tie – very much a man of the thirties, rather dry and excitable and lugubrious and cantankerous.[3] He reminds me of Podge; very swift to be bored and declare himself bored. But we form a kind of alliance,

---

[1] *Ourika*, a short novel by the Duchesse Claire de Duras (1777–1828), was published in Paris with considerable success in 1824. It told the story of a Senegalese girl who is rescued from slavery and brought up by an aristocratic family at the time of the French revolution. In spite of the genuine love she receives from her adoptive family, as a black woman Ourika faces the ordeal of living in a society that has not been so re-forged by its revolution that it can extend the values of *liberté, égalité, fraternité* to her. JF had discovered an original edition of the book in Francis Norman's bookshop many years previously. Impressed by the story and convinced that it had been an unconscious influence while he was writing *The French Lieutenant's Woman*, he decided to translate it and to find a publisher as 'an act of homage to a forgotten writer'.
[2] The journalist and author Malcolm Muggeridge (1903–1990) had started out as one of the Booker judges but was so disappointed by the submissions that he withdrew a few weeks before the date of this diary entry.
[3] Philip Toynbee (1916–1981) was chief reviewer of the *Observer* and had written several novels, perhaps most notably the semi-autobiographical and experimental *Pantaloon* (1961).

and I'm glad he's there. I trust the seriousness of his judgement, which I can't with the other two. John Gross, a shade too happy to be chairman and organizer and general London literary man.[1] Talks too much; and I can see he wishes I wasn't there with my quirkish view of establishment reputations in Eng. Lit. – and probably wishes Toynbee wasn't there with *his* awkward sincerities; but then he's a big fish in the scene he favours, and has to be respected more carefully. Lady Antonia Fraser is a tall blue-stocking with pretty eyes and an over-large chin and a manner a shade too gentle to be true; cultivation of it shows through from time to time. Strong resistance from her when Toynbee and I start trying to bulldoze our horses (B. S. Johnson, Kilroy, Hill) through against hers (Read and the egregious Robinson).

All we did this time was fix four certainties for the shortlist (Richler, Naipaul, Lessing, Taylor) and name six others as possibilities for the last two places. I detected in Gross and A. Fraser a determination to get Naipaul the prize; a certain amount of smooth manipulation was going on.

All this against a background of teeth, my teeth; a stopping Barton made a month ago still hurts, while another broken stump is doing more than hurt. It hurts so much that I start doubting my views on a socialist health service: that wealth shouldn't allow one to jump queues. I dream of some Harley Street man at my beck and call. Meanwhile Barton never has time, is always booked up for weeks ahead. Now I live for the 21st, when my turn comes.

20 September

Final Booker Prize meeting. This time in the Booker boardroom, overlooking the City. I arrive, nursing my tooth, to find Bellow, a little man in a green suit and tie with emerald-green circles. Something oddly Irish about him; a dryness and wryness. He brings me compliments from an admiring friend, adds his own; he wishes to be diplomatic. The others come, we sit to lunch. Bellow declares himself anxious to get it over and done with. A little flurry of British horror at this American brashness. Toynbee suggests perhaps we wait till coffee, in that lovely English voice that is outwardly exquisitely polite and inwardly tells you you are a bloody fool. Dangerous – Bellow has a long nose.

When we do begin, John Gross sounds off about Tom Maschler – who'd already rung me that morning, having sniffed somewhere that we were going to list Naipaul, and said it was 'impossible, ridiculous,

---

[1] A former lecturer in English, John Gross had contributed to various periodicals, including the *Observer* and *Encounter*, and had won the Duff Cooper prize for his book *The Rise and Fall of the Man of Letters* (1969). He would go on to become literary editor of the *New Statesman* (1973) and then editor of the *Times Literary Supplement* (1974–1981).

the book isn't a novel'. It must be stopped if possible.[1] John Gross uses all this very skilfully, Antonia looks gently shocked at such an attempt to defeat the course of justice, Toynbee gets excited and shouts, 'To hell with Tom Maschler', Bellow rallies to the call. Even the PA[2] girl, Marilyn Edwards, weighs in: 'He hadn't even heard of Rule 2d' – about the judges being the final arbiters of eligibility – 'until I told him.' All this accompanied by glances at me, Toynbee puckishly malicious, Gross and Antonia with a certain cautious coolness: I see I'm cast as Maschler's man, they know it will all get back. Even something in Bellow's eyes allows me to guess that he's been nobbled beforehand. From that moment on, Naipaul had it virtually, though we spent another two or three hours haggling and trading. We (Toynbee and I) got the Kilroy on the shortlist, but had to allow the wretched *Goshawk Squadron* its place too. They were then discounted as winners, which left us with Taylor, Richler, Lessing, Naipaul.[3]

Bellow spoke damningly against the Richler: he found it 'vulgar', 'a long way short of Roth's energy', 'I suppose one of a kind I'm partly responsible for and wish I could disinherit'. The treatment of Jewish Canada was 'potato-faced'. If I felt betrayed there (but not too surprised), at least he killed the Taylor also – 'weak and insipid', my own view. It came at last to Lessing and Naipaul, with Toynbee and me for her, Gross and Lady A for Naipaul. Bellow therefore had the casting vote, and it went finally to Naipaul.

It was all a chess game, really. Toynbee and I had stopped Bellow's first choice, *Goshawk Squadron*. Bellow and I had stopped Toynbee's first choice, the Taylor. Bellow and Toynbee had principally stopped my first choice, the Richler. The other two just sat and waited.

After that, Toynbee and I got a little drunk. I must come and see him in Monmouthshire, hadn't it all been fun . . . I liked him best of the others, for all his rogue emotions and cantankerousness. Bellow spoke best: very carefully articulated judgements, apophthegms about novel-writing.

[1] The Booker prize rules stipulated that an eligible entry had to be a 'full-length novel'. The Naipaul entry, *In a Free State*, consisted of two short stories and a novella framed between a prologue and an epilogue drawn from Naipaul's travel journals, all the parts sharing the common themes of exile and liberation. Although the prize was administered by the National Book League, Tom Maschler was an influential figure as the award's founder, having persuaded Booker to set up and finance the annual prize only two years previously.
[2] The Publishers Association.
[3] The final shortlist was: V. S. Naipaul, *In a Free State*; Doris Lessing, *Briefing for a Descent into Hell*; Mordecai Richler, *St Urbain's Horseman*; Derek Robinson, *Goshawk Squadron*; and Elizabeth Taylor, *Mrs Palfrey at the Claremont*.

5 October

Booker Prize turmoil over this intervening period. I wrote to Tom on the 21st, telling him to calm down on the eligibility of the Naipaul. But he wrote a good letter back: he couldn't accept it. We began comparing notes. I think the honest truth is that I drank too much at that second meeting, to keep the wretched tooth quiet. Toynbee was the same – he has some vaguely hinted-at personal problem at the moment, something to do with his wife. And we were bulldozed; and some odd things happened at the end. Bellow's shooting-down of the Richler is oddest – as in his letter of ten days before he had put him equal second with the Lessing. Then Antonia Fraser, when we were doing the final averagings, suddenly announced that she 'disliked the Richler so much that she would hate to see it win' and refused even to put it third on the three writers we were listing – making a nonsense of the averaging. John Gross allowed her to do that. Richler was deprived of only one mark (which would have made no difference); but I didn't like it.

Next Tom persuaded the permanent committee to force Gross to issue a justificatory statement for all the judges to sign.[1] I refused and launched a huge letter to say why not.[2] Then an answer from John Gross; Antonia Fraser weighed in; mollifying answers from me. They deny what my memory recalls of that first meeting. But I'm sure Gross did say he had spoken to Naipaul;[3] and Tom Maschler thinks G told him the same; Marilyn Edwards, who was there for the PA, also believes he said it. Again, I'm sure Fraser said she'd asked Naipaul to drop the two stories. But what can one do? I simply have to take their word; and suspect they're lying in their teeth. From Bellow and Toynbee, silence through all this.

On October 3rd, the permanent committee met to decide what to do. Apparently John Murphy took legal advice and was told the rule about judges' views being final must stand; so now we have formally to vote again. It will depend on Bellow and Toynbee, whom Tom thinks will now change their votes. I don't think they will. Bellow is too smooth to offend the London literary establishment, Toynbee too rogue-critic to care about paltry definitions.

[1] This statement argued that *In a Free State* counted as a novel because it was unified and coherent by theme.

[2] JF explained in his letter that he had declined to sign the statement because he did not think the book met the criterion of 'full-length novel'. Coherence of theme, which could apply to any great book of short stories, was not enough. 'What is lacking is any narrative or character connection.'

[3] To inquire of Naipaul himself whether he considered *In a Free State* to be a novel.

15 October

A letter from Marilyn Edwards at the Publishers Association. Bellow agrees with me and has said no to Naipaul; but the other three have said yes, it seems. The announcement of the shortlist was in today's *Times*. Bellow wrote on the 6th and Marilyn said 'as John Gross will have already told you'. I am now cast as the rogue elephant of Lyme: not to be trusted till the news is out.

20 October

About ten days ago, I started writing *The Englishman* (also called *Futility*), which I have had in mind for so long. I began in Los Angeles, but then suddenly switched back to Ipplepen in the war.[1] I don't know why; where these unexplained intuitions have come from. And how I could re-evoke a wartime harvest in one day's writing. I would have sworn twenty-four hours before that I could remember nothing of all that. The 'here' (Dan) takes shape; and two women (Jenny and Jane). It's two years now since I wrote seriously. The experience is divine, there's no other word for it; exactly like the first week or two of a plant's growth – nothing in the future can ever equal these days. The intense reality, and malleability of reality. I said it in a passage today.

   Now I have to stop work to rewrite the *Zip* script; but I don't really mind. I'm five chapters in, and secure. Landed.

31 October

Podge came last weekend with Cathy and her American husband, John Steinberg – and a load of trouble. Eileen is claiming half his worldly goods now the divorce is over – half the value of the Garsington Cottage, in effect. I have promised to try and lend him the £3,000 or so needed. But his son-in-law is the more present trouble: a remarkably surly young man, the most undomesticated New York Jew I've yet run across – and that's saying something. He refuses to stir a hand. Podge keeps getting us in other rooms and muttering and complaining about him. The lad wants to be a writer, and I suspect the general anti-literary atmosphere P carries with him is a chief cause of offence.

12 November

To Bristol, to celebrate Anna's twenty-first birthday, which was yesterday really. We gave her £100; and she has bought a stereo deck and radio. A bespectacled young man sits on the floor, assembling it; then her new Hungarian boy comes. Anna a little tense throughout. But I remember

---

[1] Ipplepen was the Devon village where JF's family lived during the war. See introduction to *The Journals*, volume 1, pages x-xi.

my own parents' visits to Oxford. How one loathed it, how little there was to say. Anna even adopted my defence then – the glories of the city. It distresses Eliz, the gaps between us. But I think it's largely cultural, not emotional. Perhaps we try and enter their world too much – the awful pop music one mutters appreciatively about, when one really wants, I really want, to tell them to grow up and leave such sweet mindlessness behind.

18 November

Jud and Monica here for two days. Jud and I discussing the *Zip* script. Monica I find increasingly hard to stand. She seems to come out of some antiquated poor-little-rich-girl phase of history: a distressing sense of total inauthenticity. I suppose they must both feel it, as they are both such compulsive over-praisers of everything in sight. This gushing response to even the most trivial things completely devalues any real contact. She turns me into total natural historian: I just observe her. And for Jud's sake: it is all so much less offensive in him; merely his courtesy to her.

21 November

Wasps still eating rotten apples.

22 November

To London, to meet Franklin Schaffner and his producer Lester Goldsmith. Dinner with them, and Tom and Fay Maschler, in some supposedly Greek restaurant off Bond Street. Not a success. Schaffner is grey-haired, one of those directors who might have been US ambassadors; a lot of fencing.[1] I'd have done much better to meet him alone somewhere. But he seems keen to do the picture after he has finished *Papillon*, which starts shooting next spring. He hates the Rudkin script. Lester Goldsmith is a little fat-spider, soft-spoken (yes, Frank, no, Frank) Jew – one of those producers whose financial power is a little hard to believe.

We went the next morning to the preview of *Nicholas and Alexandra*, Schaffner's latest, at the Leicester Square Odeon. Tony Richardson was there, David Niven, Sam Spiegel (who produced) mournfully and impatiently shepherding people about. It's not a great film by any stretch of the imagination; fairly good by David Lean tasteful-epic standards. Whether we 'go' with Schaffner is academic now, really; we have to snatch at a maw of his 'bankability'. Whether Columbia back the film

---

[1] Franklin J. Schaffner (1920–1989) had the year before directed *Patton*. The fact that at the 1971 Academy Awards ceremony the film won seven Oscars, including Best Director and Best Film, would no doubt have contributed to his sense of importance.

depends entirely on whether he convinces them he wants to do it. So the die is cast.

11 December
Bridport. I buy a Neolithic axe, Cornish greenstone, in an antique shop. £4.50.

20 December
Working all day and every day since I last wrote here on the *Ourika* book; it is changing shape, I make it more personal, trying to make it more about myself, evidence for or against myself, that is the 'creative writer' – what I am calling the myth-maker; not evidence for or against my theory of perennial sensibility.[1] A month or two ago a man called Rose, assistant professor of psychiatry at Yale, sent me two papers he had written about the psychoanalytical genesis of *The FLW* and the novel, art, in general. It articulated what I always felt (in spite of some rather absurd evidence he adduces from the text); and now I am binding that in to the ever-lengthening chapter on sensibility.[2]

All this against a deepening crisis again in Eliz, her usual winter horrors of boredom, alienation, angry frustration. It reduces my writing to a kind of bulwark against her depression and all that part of it that I share; and given the self-searching nature of the present material, it's a fragile bulwark. I know academics will pounce on it, tear it to bits; I can see with my rational mind that it is an obsessive illusion that one can approach art-history in such unresearching and personal terms; then that all writing is an attempt to keep reality at bay. Her very active and depressive reality I can't keep at bay sometimes; and this is partly because I am mother-fixed and she is father-fixed. In other words, my writing, my spending long hours away in my room, represents her mother, the intrusive rival in her relationship with her father – as do other women, with whom she always has a confused love–hate relationship. I am failing to please the mother-substitute Eliz represents for me, so I am guilty; and she can only see in me the failed father. We are even typical of our kinds in that she (authoritarian father) rejects all this 'Freudian rubbish'; and I, with qualifications, believe in it.

I have too a lump, a swelling, a constant small pain in the crutch that haunts me. My two closest companions these last few weeks have been death imagined in all its details, and indifference.

---

[1] As a result of his work translating *Ourika*, JF began to write an accompanying essay, called 'Sensibility', which was inspired by its themes.
[2] In his paper, '*The French Lieutenant's Woman*: The Unconscious Significance of a Novel to Its Author', Gilbert Rose argued that the novel was an imaginative record of the author's Oedipal reunion with, and separation from, his mother.

Christmas Day. We walked out along the beach to the beginning of Pinhay Bay; a grey day, still mild. I meant to dig up bee orchids. But the colony there seems to have collapsed into the sea already. I found six or seven young ones in a tipped-up lump of earth, its face almost vertical to the ground. The ones I transplanted to the garden some three years ago have all survived. It is curious how they appear above ground so much earlier than any other orchid outside the *Ophrys* genus.

Boxing Day. Over to the Allsops at West Milton. The usual crowd of indeterminate young people. Kenneth is fighting two battles at the moment: to save Powerstock Common from the Forestry Commission and ban the wretched oil-prospectors from the Bridport area, where they have recently started sniffing round after black gold.

7 February 1972
A blue-winged Quaker parakeet: I picked it up dead in the vegetable garden. Ken Allsop says there was an article recently in the *Western Gazette* suggesting they may have gone wild and be breeding here now.

12 February
Ned Bradford here for the weekend; he seems greyer, more New England than ever, the least likely chief editor in the world. We took him for a tour of the Honiton antiquers, all of whose prices have risen ridiculously this last year – like those for property.

We asked the Allsops over to meet him; they're better on their own. But then who isn't – I think people meet *en masse* to justify their social laziness.

15 February
A strange sexual dream. Fortunately I woke up immediately afterwards and could note some curious things about it. It began with a wild love-making with Anna – I say Anna, but I could recollect no image of Anna's face at all, it was just that I 'knew' it was Anna. I also knew Eliz was in the next bedroom, but this gave no sense of shame or guilt. I just knew she was in the next room. It was also a brightly lit scene and did not corre-spond with realistic sight-perspectives – there were angles that required a 'camera', a third viewpoint. Two quickly succeeding 'shots' of cunnilingus and fellatio were coloured and really 'photographs' of the woman's body, any woman's body; and yet I felt I was in the middle of the actions at the same time. This was followed by coupling and dreaming the whole process of ejaculation (but not ejaculating in fact). I can't recall such dreams not turning 'wet' ever before. The next scene, I was in a car about three or four houses up from 63 Fillebrooke Avenue, on the opposite side. I was naked. Eliz stood naked by the open door, on the pavement. Looking down towards 63 Fillebrooke I realized simultaneously that dawn had

begun and that M was standing in an oval first-floor window, arranging flowers, with a smile on her face. (This oval window has no real correlative, of course.) I became alarmed, in case M saw us. I then saw my father walking towards the front gate, M behind him. Eliz drove off. But for some reason I was not now in the car and had to run along the little side-road above the playing-fields. I looked up the first road leading to the London Road, and could not see the car. I ran on the next . . . and woke up.

The strange thing about this dream was the very clear entry of the triple goddess theme – mother, wife, daughter; the total absence of guilt – even the bit about driving and running away was more like hide-and-seek than anything to do with fear or shame (like the enjoying 'Anna' even though Eliz was in the next room); and its extraordinary aftermath of warm sensuality, a sort of golden physical peace. I see it in terms of Rose's paper – it was obviously based on forgotten but acute infancy pleasures, in which fluidity of identity played an important part; and also connected with the old theory about the psychic relief of the dream experience. What was unusual was not really the dream, but waking up in the middle of it and having it still so vivid.

One last little thing. In the car I was able to duck very easily out of sight of M – as I could do in reality only if I had the body of a small child. Some hide-and-seek game in a pram?

The real Anna, alas, is being far less amenable in real life. She's now elected to drop out of her graphics course. Eliz accuses me of not taking 'a line' with her, but I simply don't know how you exhort people in a trap, which is not even of their own making. Anna really has that mysterious kind of mentality I tried to fictionalize in Sarah Woodruff: she is self-intelligent and academically ungifted. She can't stand the increasingly commercial nature of her course, she doesn't want to go into commercial graphics (which in any case lacks the jobs for all the applicants); she is bored with the endless prospects of study if she takes some other form of art. She has no 'creative' gift; so that leaves only teaching, in effect. Another stress is having to be both student and housewife – she and Nick now live together.

19 March
I've been rewriting *The Device* this last month or so; out of perversity, not conviction. As some kind of test, I don't know. I've also agreed to let Daniel Halpern publish some poems in book form.

28 April
Working all the time on my 'paper' on subsidence in Lyme Regis. Lots of old lore; and photographs. A treasure has indeed been the *Lister Thesaurus*, which is tucked away in the Council offices; a scrapbook compiled by Giulielma Lister and copiously annotated by Wanklyn. Full of good things.

'Miss Coade came to Belmont 1784, was there in 1802, was not there in 1817.'

A French smack of eighty tons was wrecked at Charton Bay on January 1st, 1851. All drowned. Gravestone in churchyard.

The Vicar of Lyme between 1830 and 1870 was Thomas Emilius Frederick Parry Hodges, with an equal detestation of both Calvin and Rome. A New College man (and Fellow). Always known as 'the Doctor'. He 'rarely mixed socially with the gentry of this little town' – only with the county.

1 May

Schaffner, James Goldman[1] and mistress, Lester Goldsmith and Tom Maschler come down from London. I take them out to Underhill Farm and then they insist on going out over the cliffs. So I march them down through the jungle and along Pinhay Warren above the bay, then back to the path. In their dapper clothes. They flop and wallow and fall about, get stung by nettles (what is that goddam plant?) and torn by brambles. It becomes sadistic. I smell an American version of Guy Green in Schaffner – the same insecurity deep down and disinclination to take risks. He plays the percentage game, I suspect. Goldman is bearded and genial, a nice man, but no flair or fire, at first meeting. Little Lester G. is like a small white owl, or toad; says nothing. The only time he sounded in his element was during some interminable call to Los Angeles on some financial matter. That is what is so distressing about these 'international' film people. One feels they are only really at home in a jet, or on a long-distance phone line, or in the latest 'great' restaurant. Most of each of them is always somewhere else. Neither Schaffner nor Goldman would talk about the script at all; or casting. I have a feeling that they have made up their minds already on what they want; and want no argument from Tom or myself. Tom is still optimistic and I feel he is naïve.

2 May

Committed now, anyway. I went up to London and swore the documents with Goldsmith at the American Embassy.

4 July

To Denholm Elliott's house in Camden Town for the read-through of *The Last Chapter*. Elliott I liked, an actor through and through, wry and very funny about his life and profession. The house is agreeably messy

---

[1] The playwright and screenwriter James Goldman (1927–1998) wrote the screenplay for Franklin Schaffner's film *Nicholas and Alexandra* (1971). In 1968 he won an Academy Award for the screenplay of *The Lion in Winter*, which was based on his play.

and informal, none of the monstrous show-business glamour, the contrived décor – though I suppose, in these days, that to stay simple and disordered has to be contrived in a way as well. The girl David Tringham has found is pretty, fine brown eyes, the right background: Susan Penhaligon, she's Cornish. Elliott reads through very well at once, even the girl promises well.

Vodka and tonic, then a long drunken lunch, very delightful, with Elliott pouring out stage stories, David fizzing. Elliott has just had a great success with the new *Hedda* – and in a good TV series he is doing, and is obviously a man who feels on top of the world . . . and we're lucky to get him. Something about actors, a kind of golden dream they can live in, a living in today, none of the neuroses of writers; perhaps it is partly their delight in being able to talk, to tell stories so well. And their formidable malice, of course.

He told a story about the wretchedly sycophantic John Mills, who seems universally detested in the showbiz world.

7 July

To Shepperton, to see the sets for *The Last Chapter* and watch Elliott and Penhaligon walk through their scenes. I hate sets, immediately saw a number of things wrong with the décor; but this is a shoestring production. David getting nervous, Elliott a bit bored; but something began to take shape. The whole atmosphere has been jolly, so different from that of my two 'big' pictures. Shepperton is sad – in its last days, since the land has been sold for building houses. Strange, that glamour of the movie world. The wardrobe mistress and the make-up man fussing round the girl, trying on clothes; the carpenters on the set. It makes living pleasant, and art difficult.

Chabrol's *Le Boucher* that evening – very pretty and stylish, but *pas sérieux*. He's a confectioner, that's all.

14 July

Tom and Fay and their two children here for the weekend. Anna has given up her washing-up job in Bristol and retired here for a week or two. She goes to Italy with Nick later this summer. T and F are their usual fastidious selves – puzzling how the very fastidious never seem to realize how absurd their demandingness is. In this role they deserve a Molière or a Congreve – Sir Thomas and Lady Fay Only-the-very-best. To be fair, they prefer exquisite simplicity to fuss; and I suppose such successful and physically attractive people might have far worse foibles. Hannah is delightful, though already showing Tom's self-will. We're not quite clear why they seem so fond of us at the moment – of Eliz principally. We suspect it's Fay. She was in tears several times over the weekend. Tom is handling her like a very difficult author; but finds it hard to keep it up day and night. He seems more and more obsessed with playing games every spare second he has: badminton, darts – even on the beach it had to be *cailloux*.

22 July

Critique, an American academic magazine; an issue devoted to Barth[1] and me. The three pieces on Fowles depressed me. I have little enough interest in what people think I am, let alone what I was. All books are forms of error. Forgotten is best. I can't forget them, of course. The novel will die not for 'cultural' reasons, but of self-consciousness. The best book I wrote was *Tesserae*, because it was closest to what I remain.[2] But if I published it, it would turn stale on me, like all the rest.

I do not know if it is a curse or a blessing, this total intellectual vacuum in which I live. It struck me while Tom and Fay were here – how serious (or even intelligently humorous) discussion has now disappeared from the life of the successful intelligentsia. I threw out bait once or twice, but it is (I think not just the clumsiness of the angler) regarded as absurd, almost irritating. John Fowles mumbling something obscure again. I suspect that this is a new general feature of English culture – or a marked new aggravation of one always inherent in it. No one writes letters seriously any more, no one talks (as opposed to chatting and gossiping) any more. One can leave all that for the telly one doesn't watch and the books one doesn't read. We had Anna's Nick and two of her other Bristol student friends here two days ago. I'd like to think I intimidate them (that is, I'd rather think that than that they have grown as apathetically mindless as our generation), but whatever it is, only the Hungarian Nick has any real feel of seriousness and intelligence – and he, poor boy, is hampered by his émigré disorientation and lack of factual education.

I can never believe that I do intimidate people, though I had odd proof with Tom when we were alone a moment while they were here. He asked me with a (in him) ludicrous shyness whether I was writing anything. I said no, just an article on cricket for *Sports Illustrated*; and eyed him. That was the only game over the weekend he refused to play: what his erstwhile *protégé* is at.

He also informed me the other day that Booker were very distressed that I hadn't cashed their cheque for the £250 fees I didn't earn (unless as a kind of martyr) over last year's prize. He did at least convince me that I should give it to a charity. I nominated the RSPB. That'll infuriate them, he said delightedly. He doesn't understand me very well.

---

[1] John Barth, the American postmodernist novelist.
[2] Over the years JF would repeatedly revise this autobiographical novel which drew on the period when he was a teacher at St Godric's College in Hampstead. It was called *Tesserae* because it had been constructed as a mosaic of narrative fragments.

Another misunderstanding, from when we were in London. He came in one evening and announced that the Arts Council Literary Committee – of which he is a member – had 'almost certainly' decided to start a new critical review of fiction. I said that what was needed was a magazine for fiction, not reviews of it. No argument developed; I became unspeakable. To try and help fiction by reviewing bad novels more extensively is like improving surgery by more extended coverage of failed operations; what is needed is more opportunity for the surgeons to learn and practise their craft.

27 July
The American novelist Joyce Carol Oates and her husband (Ray Smith). Tom Maschler said 'God help you' when we told him she was coming and we had expected some imperious, devouring wordwoman; instead we got someone painfully diffident and overconscious of the literary pecking order (I rank higher, it seems). I have tried but cannot read her books – they are so long and screwed up to too high a pitch. Curious that such a frail, shy creature should be so different in her art. I rather liked her. Eliz liked them for booking themselves into a miserable pub in Axminster and having a meal at some caff on the front here before calling. Oates kept on saying, 'We don't want to impose, we can't stand imposing . . .' Uriah-Heepish in a British mouth, but refreshing to the overvisited.

28 July
Dan and Hazel and the twins. Alas, they very rapidly exhaust us both physically and psychologically. I feel some sympathy with Dan, who is a born wanderer and dilettante and seems set for another self-granted sabbatical year. I sense it is self-defence, to stop himself from going mad by being trapped by Hazel and the children. Of course we don't discuss things as openly as that, one has to read between the lines. He wants to write sociological history and I think accepts that that entails an ascetic world of poverty. Hazel very obviously doesn't; she simply hasn't shaken off the mores and cultural aims of Fillebrooke Avenue – the safe job, the well-lined nest and all of that. She also doesn't very well conceal her envy of our worldly wealth and infuriates Elizabeth by never saying thanks – a kind of gormless gracelessness that puzzles me. At least F and M were very punctilious about that sort of thing. Hazel is like a small child who both demands to have gifts and then seems to resent them when she gets them. I suppose we are really just an area where she can show her displeasure at Dan's asceticism and I think fairly genuine indifference to money.

30 July

Out with Jonathan and Joanne,[1] lobstering with Quicky; a very fine pale dawn, the Cobb empty (swarming all day), redshank on the beach, small parties of razorbills steaming quietly about. We went along the Undercliff, so beautifully still in its solitude, in the early sun, not a house or other boat in sight. Only the sea, seen close to, is sad: it will never be clean again. We had three lobsters, and ate them that night.

Nature, art, then life as it is lived. All those I live among have the reverse order of priorities.

7 August

Anna rings, to say that Roy has been admitted to a psychiatric hospital – they are going to try ECT – and that Judy has sent off the children for her to look after. He seems to have been getting more and more difficult for a year now; unable to work, eaten by all the old egocentricity. But where it was (or seemed) conscious and deliberate, it is now clearly pathological. Somehow he still wrecks the lives of those around him.

27 August

Podge and Cathy come. Cathy has 'separated' from John Steinberg, he was too demanding and possessive, it seemed. By the end of the weekend I felt some sympathy with him. Endless, endless, endless talking, sitting round the kitchen table and analysing. They exist only in words, Podge playing Socrates, Cathy his most difficult student – distinct signs of baiting him, but then he likes it so much, being shocked. She now has a new man, a Jewish doctor called George, who is married, loves Cathy ('a perfect match', says Podge), can't leave his wife. He kept on talking about Cathy's extreme Marxist-radical 'set'; but they seemed not very distinguishable to us from Anna's hash-smoking and acid-tripping Bristol friends. Interminable talk about marriage, non-marriage, to bear children or not, social responsibility. I sit stunned and dazed through most of it, aware that Cathy has been analysed and interrogated and talked at all through her life into her present not very attractive self. In a sense Eileen, who actually goes and works part-time in a geriatric hospital in Oxford, is the only authentic one. Travelling round the world and loving the socialist countries and living in radical milieux in London somehow seems less socialism than escapism. Nothing is more unreal than constant *talk* about reality. Every so often Cathy slipped away into the flat, where she was sleeping. We found a little pile of stubs outside the window when she left – talk-fuel, or hash. What seems to haunt these (Podge's words) 'acutely sensitive and politically conscious' young people is something

---

[1] Elizabeth's sister.

very like the old romantic idealism. Cathy is just a twentieth-century version of René[1] and wallowing in *Weltschmerz*; longings for a nobler world and a perfect partner. She cried on Sunday because she couldn't write the letter she wanted to the new man in her life. It is romantic idealism, not dialectics, that ruins her generation.

After she went (hitch-hiking alone back to London, mainly to infuriate Podge, so far as I could see), we forced him out for a walk. Under Ware Cliffs I could stand it no more and wandered off, while he discussed contraceptive methods with Eliz. I searched for flint fossils (and found a new large echinoderm, much bigger than Micraster) and kept out of earshot. Not quite – among the endless rhubarb, rhubarb, rhubarb, there kept tolling the word 'responsibility' and its variants. I think only the irresponsible could use it so much.

Still, Podge is *sui generis*. His astringency remains, his liking for the paradox. He is like a sauna-bath or a boxing-lesson. One is grateful afterwards. And in a desert . . .

I am going ahead with the poems for Daniel Halpern, who will publish them in New York next year.

20 September

I have been writing a short story for a week: 'Poor Koko'. Finished it today. And reading some stories by Frank O'Connor, which I haven't read before. At his best, he is very good; quiet and deadly accurate – like the Maupassant of the Normandy stories or the Maugham of Malaysia. The short story requires a very distinct and uniform culture to be successful; requires a primitive culture, in other words, as Maugham had in his convention-bound planters and district officers *and* the native life in the adjoining compounds. The trouble is that the consequent aesthetics of the form involve a distortion of reality: Maugham doesn't write about planters – or their wives – who do not meet disaster. O'Connor doesn't write about Irishmen who escape the consequences of being Irish – or even those who sincerely face up to it. His is an Ireland without Joyce and Beckett and even the less noble kind of exile represented by girls like Edna O'Brien.

27 September

To London. To see *The Last Chapter*, among other purposes, but that never came about – the Boultings have taken a fancy to the thing and are 'polishing' it, while David himself is off on another film. Robert Bolt has also declared renewed interest in doing *The FLW* script – Tom swears he wants to do it, it's merely finding the time.

---

[1] JF is thinking of King René of Provence (1408–1480), who was devoted to the cult of chivalry and organized his court around the ideals of knightly conduct expressed in such legends as Tristan and Iseult or King Arthur's Round Table.

16 October

We take the Allsops out to dinner at Tytherleigh. Ken has grown a silvery-grey moustache, which makes him look like some distinguished diplomat, a sort of cross between Anthony Eden and De Sica. Self-deprecating ('Everyone in West Dorset now hates me') and fastidiously gloomy. We think Betty Allsop, the full horrors of whose long-winded banality of mind have dawned rather gradually on us, must be part of the gloom. He seems to have disappeared from the television scene nowadays; a man facing retirement and obscurity of some kind, and split over it. I try and jolly him up by pointing out my own laziness; but he seems to regard it as a kind of secret recipe he hasn't discovered. I am envied my quietism. But he's a would-be knight, and I'm a would-be peasant.

20 October

Tom and Fay for the weekend, because Robert Bolt is coming – not to do the script, that's certain now, but out of respect for book and author. I had a shock when I opened the door to him, he looked so uncannily like Roy Christy, a likeness that didn't diminish on acquaintance. Anna, who was here too, confirmed it. A Roy who has made it, so can let his good side show – the jolly bluffness, pride in North Country origins and simplicity, all the soul-to-soul stuff. We had a business-type talk before the dinner, what we should do with the script and all that, and he put on a big-time director *persona* that I didn't like. One senses that he is a bit dazzled by his work for Lean, Spiegel and the rest; by his own rise to fame, in fact. He knows he has all the middle-of-the-road virtues, solid craftsman and the rest; but apparently confuses them with what true art is about – in the cinema, at any rate.

Various references to Sarah Miles, his wife – 'Can't even boil an egg, poor girl' – had us all metaphorically sniffing. Though he was nothing but patriotic about her, we sensed that what rumour (and David Tringham) has her to be is true. He claimed she wouldn't come to Lyme because she wants to play Sarah so much – the rest sneered disbelief after he'd gone, but perhaps it was true. Celebrities know what people think, how what they would be and what they are get laid barer and sillier than one evening can counteract.

I liked Bolt better when the Maschlers went to bed. He would sit up and drink and talk – about his father, a secondhand furniture-dealer, Methodism, his life, his money ('I've got £80,000 in the world, including my house' – a figure none of us could believe, but he seemed so anxious to take on my own kind of cryptic colouring). At three a.m. we walked down to the end of the Cobb, at his insistence. A curious and finally rather likeable man.

He has 'given' us one good idea for the script, also: to make the author-figure Charles as well (the same actor).

30 October
Ronnie Payne came in for the day, having spent the weekend at the Hoggs in Charmouth. Nothing was said of Betsa, or Celia. I feel he wants to talk, but can't. We've grown older, and he's stayed put.

10 November
Ken Allsop here all afternoon, he wants to do a piece on me for the *Sunday Times*. He writes a weekly column there now. I've tried to put him off, but I feel sorry for him. He's parted brass rags with the BBC, now *24 Hours* is defunct; one has a sense of a man fighting to keep his world from falling apart. His secret self is deeply rooted in an outmoded view of nature. Somehow he's never shaken off the influence of Williamson, Jefferies, Hudson, all that *galère*;[1] goes purple with his prose much too fast, and his heart. If he is the prodigious womanizer rumour says, it must be out of sentiment, not Don-Juanism. He had to ring up his wife twice while he was with us; very guarded, the tone and overt solicitude. All marriage is between a masochist and a sadist, he said later. I would like to know the true story of *his* heart.

I was gloomy about the novel (in general), having just taken up *The Englishman* again and feeling in fact more free of gloom than for some time past. It was rather like a cat full of cream complaining of starvation to the RSPCA.

12 November
To London.

13 November
At last we saw *The Last Chapter* – with Roy Boulting and various other industry people. I sat next to David and Annette. Not too bad for a first attempt, and I didn't have to put on a mask to say so to David afterwards.

14 November
Over to Tom Adams' flat in Fulham;[2] he has grown a beard, but seems as nervous and high-strung as ever. The flat, in an outwardly horrid sort of Peabody building for the petite bourgeoisie, is very pretty inside, a forest of Victorian and Edwardian bric-a-brac, books, whatnots. He showed us some sketches for a series of paintings he is doing on the theme of Mary Kingsley, the West African explorer – so obviously based

---

[1] Henry Williamson (1895–1977), Richard Jefferies (1848–1887), and Walter Hudson (1841–1922). All three authors wrote novels inspired by their love of nature and country life, and were perhaps best known respectively for *Tarka the Otter* (1927), *Beavis: The Story of a Boy* (1882), and *Green Mansions* (1904).
[2] Tom Adams did the artwork for the Jonathan Cape editions of JF's novels.

on Nolan's famous series on Mrs Fraser.[1] They're very pretty and skilled, but hollow, no real emotion or guts. I think his problem is that he will not accept he has brilliant gifts as a decorator – and none (that is, no originality) as a 'serious' artist. He should have been born in the Belle Époque. But a nice, sincere man, for all that he is self-baffled.

15 November

Arguing with Eliz all afternoon. At least we don't shout at each other now. Her depressions arrive with ominous promptitude once winter starts – her self-boredom, her emptiness, her futility, her lack of identity. Like Tom Adams she lives with a dream of what she can never be. She is a standing argument for longer education; though she complains bitterly about the domestic routine and the 'weight' of Belmont on her back, they are not really the problem at all. It is having to use such activities to fill time that destroys her.

31 December

An exceptionally mild winter, even for here; we've had no frosts yet; even a Portuguese cistus in flower; on Christmas Eve I picked two splendid narcissi. The passion-flowers on my balcony have fruited heavily this year; still orange rugby footballs by the dozen. The birds seem reluctant to eat them, alas. A negative sign of the mildness must be the absence of marsh tits (only one seen so far) and of tawny owls.

7 January 1973

Ken Allsop's article on me in the *Sunday Times*. He is irredeemably romantic; a comic reference to the 'raven-haunted cliffs' round Lyme Regis comes straight out of Emily Brontë. He likens me to a badger pursuing its undergrowth paths; I should have hoped to rate at least a buzzard to his peregrine, but no matter. The boys at Spetsai called me Arkoudi, the Bear – and that is evidently my totem sign. The Bear divagates much these days – once more the novel stopped before Christmas. It worries me day by day, but not deep down. Time is not enough, but neither are books. In so many things now I reap the benefit of a lifetime of magpie knowledge; I am laterally mobile, thank God.

15 January

One dormouse nest, but empty. We have cleared part of the bank above

---

[1] The Australian painter Sir Sydney Nolan (1917–1992) produced a series of historical paintings inspired by the story of Eliza Fraser, who was shipwrecked off the Queensland coast, captured by aborigines and then rescued six weeks later by a convict called John Graham.

the palm-tree this winter, and I'm afraid it must have been dislodged from there.

The *New Statesman* asked me to review novels last summer; and at last have taken up my counter-offer to do country books. The one they sent was worth waiting for: Ladurie's *Times of Feast, Times of Famine*, a remarkable and (unintentionally) poetic account of past climate and how it is detected. Extraordinary, the painstaking ingenuity of the methods used.

29 January

Still freakishly mild. *Schizostylus* in flower, also the first crocus and *I. reticulata.*

I've been back on the novel a week. The meeting with Jane, and then with Anthony. The latter has caused endless trouble, and is still not right. It would have depressed me in the past; but now it is a pleasure to work it up.

30 January

Off on a little Cornish trip. We went by Ipplepen,[1] I wanted to see Dornafield, which I shall use for Daniel's farm. Quite absurd, it was not at all as I remember it, only the old stone doorway; an ugly mess of farm buildings which are all after my time, I think. But how could I have forgotten that to the north the dell is open to the main road and bungalows and other horrors? It was so like the as yet unwritten chapter when Daniel will take Jane back to his harvest field . . .[2] Collapse of stout memory, indeed.

Ipplepen has been hideously built over – it is a dormitory village now for Newton Abbot. We went past Ashleigh (unchanged); but at the top of the lane by the Majors' farm, where a narrow high-banked lane went towards the main road, all is now widened and municipalized. I did not dare go to see the Quarry Field. It isn't just the green-gliding of adolescent memory; the place is debased almost out of recognition by the population problem.

8 February

The galleys for the Ecco Press poems arrive; nice simple typography. I cannot imagine how they will be received; perhaps not at all, just ignored. I should like that best.

A letter from Podge – 'P' (his mother) has died, at long last. He is characteristically incensed that she was given a Christian burial; and will riposte by reading extracts from Camus's *Le Mythe de Sisyphe* at a little

---

[1] See note on page 114.
[2] This chapter never would be written.

commemoration meeting at the Oxford Atheists' Association. Now he thinks he will start a commune at Garsington.

25 March
We've bought Anna, who recently passed her driving test, a Volkswagen Beetle; second-hand, £450. She came today with Nick to collect it. He is in agony, poor boy, waiting to hear if he has got into the RCA for his post-graduate course. It seems to have become like the Ecole Normale in France, so cream of the cream in the students it will take that even to be given an interview is an honour. He brought one or two pieces, little pots encrusted with vaguely pre-Columbian figurines, that he's recently made. They are very impressive, in one so young and culturally lost in other ways.

29 March
First chiffchaffs singing.

30 March
To London for a few days. We saw a Buñuel, *The Discreet Charm of the Bourgeoisie*; as always very seeable, though I prefer him in a darker key.

Dinner with Jud and Monica, who presents us with two silver serviette-rings – what guilty conscience does that symbolize, I wonder? I should be giving the gifts, more and more I have to hide what I think of them. Jud is becoming aggressively vulgarian – out to punish 'pure' art and intellect whenever it raises its ugly head. The usual back-biting of Tom and Fay; how terrible the pieces she writes on restaurants every week in the *Evening Standard* are – 'pretentious bullshit, she's so goddam fastidious'.

Which she is, of course; we joined one of her Michelin-tests at poor old Fagin's Kitchen opposite the flat the next evening. And she slammed it without mercy the following Wednesday; though quite wittily, she writes rather well. But they are forgiven all at the moment, as Alice, the Bat, is in hospital, has some mysterious anaemia that required a blood transfusion last week. Fay suddenly cried during the meal, poor thing; when one puts so much energy and devotion into living in the best of all possible contemporary worlds . . . I'm doing a preface to a new edition of Conan Doyle for Cape – *The Hound of the Baskervilles*. I think he and it need some debunking; nothing the English love better than a writer who dodges all the serious problems of society. Ian Fleming's most solid support came from the right-wing Establishment. What could be safer than violence without reality and sex without a grain of eroticism? Not that Conan Doyle wasn't an almost touchingly nice and briskly concerned English gentleman-cricketer-doctor in his private life. I very much liked an entry from a diary his ten-year-old brother Innes kept when he was sent off to live with Doyle before his marriage: 'This morning after breakfast Arthur went downstairs and began to write a story about a man with three eyes, while I was upstairs inventing a new water-works that will send rokets [*sic*] over the moon in two minutes and they will send small shot at the same distance then it was a quarter past one, I had to go and put on the last potatoes the only six we had in the world.' They were living on a shilling a day at the time.

We hear Nick has been accepted for the RCA. I am delighted for him.

Evelyn Waugh's diaries are being serialized in the *Observer*, which gives everyone the chance to say how nauseating he is. I feel sympathy for him, on the whole. He was nauseated as much as nauseating; and one can forgive such a sharp eye and such a trenchant, pruned style almost anything. It is not the vindictive, deranged social censor that matters so much as the brilliant prose censor of what he observed; a diamond is still a diamond, whatever the mud it lies in. And he doesn't hurt the Left at all; no socialist could damn the Establishment and its fringes more comprehensively. He remains our most serious eccentric; five thousand 'nice' Conan Doyles would not fill his nasty little finger.

11 April

At Crewkerne, going through some old postcards in a junk-shop. Eliz comes in. 'Look who I've just met in the supermarket.' And Jean Shrimpton grinning behind her. On her way back from Cornwall with her latest man; still gangling and giraffe-like, with that angel's face and staring-blue eyes. Her sister is settled and married down. Terry Stamp has become a 'pathetic old bore' – she wasn't catty about him; just how he still thought of himself as a great star. 'He's so sixties still, he's never grown up.' We went and had a cuppa in a caff. Her new man is nice. A nice simple pair.

26 April

The Ipplepen chapters of the novel; the vicar and Nancy. A great pleasure to write.

30 April

A foul, sudden virus some form of flu that came out of nowhere an hour after I got up. Ague and fever and swollen mump glands, a kind of painful bit in the right nostril, a sore mouth, fuzzed head. Very unpleasant. We are due for France on the 7th May.

1 May

The doctor diagnoses the new all-purpose disease: There's-a-lot-of-it-about.

The wretched Nixon climbs down over the Watergate mess.[1] His stale
cliché-ridden voice announces his whole being is a lie at the first sentence.
The Americans have lost all contact with natural judgement; they respect
any dislocated puppet, any clapped-out old ham, above what just says. You
can't just-say there any more; that's the sickness. You have to research,
package and sell; and to off the scene when the customer starts
complaining.

2 May
Each day I read from six a.m. to eight a.m. Today – till midnight. Quentin
Bell's life about Virginia Woolf.[2] It is very nicely done indeed. I suppose
only other writers would question the values of (and current attention
devoted to) the Bloomsbury–Cambridge scene. So much dross in art
and in people got caught up in the real gold . . . Carrington, Partridge,
Clive and Vanessa and all the rest seemed a high price to pay for
Forster's one great novel and VW herself. The only real saint is Leonard.

The Post Office misrendering of VW's cable to her pompous
half-brother on his engagement to a young lady from the aristocracy.
VW's family nickname was 'Goat' and she wrote: SHE IS AN ANGEL
GOAT. It arrived at the castle: SHE IS AN AGED GOAT.

The Bell biography frightens me a little too: my now total isolation
– it was always a remoteness – from that world; from other writers,
literary intelligences. Those letters they were always writing. That need
to meet. I read and read, I write, I think about writing; fire off the odd
letter to some misguided American student. That is all. I am happy,
the experience of reading and making is enough. But it is bad that I
am happy.

11 May
Up again. We have delayed the French trip, I feel weak and feverish
still. In the garden a badger has appeared. It has tunnelled a sett under
the old rubbish pile beside the east end of the lawn. It has also, I suspect,
killed the Morrises' cat, whose corpse I found today. We dare not tell
them. I threw the body into the bottom jungle.

13 May
A Sunday, off to Southampton, as we catch the morning boat tomorrow
morning. We stay at an abominable hotel, the Skyways; all outward
'luxury' and inward lack of service. Dreadful food from a pretentious

---

[1] In a broadcast to the American people on 30 April 1973 President Nixon declared
that he was prepared to take responsibility for the Watergate scandal, although
he denied personal involvement: 'There will be no whitewash at the White House.'
[2] *Virginia Woolf: A Biography*, volume 1 (Hogarth Press, 1972).

'French' menu; in the room, a kettle and sachets of tea and instant coffee; a packaged airline-style breakfast is dumped outside your room – you make your own drink. Despite the high prices, it had a distinctive petit-bourgeois clientele. I suppose they think the slick mechanization (which is really an elimination of the human element) chic. Nice people are all equal, and don't like servants or service; which allows the hotel a wider profit margin. This is a loathsome form of Protestant puritanism.

14 May

The ferry is swarming with school kids, like a cage of excited monkeys. An easy crossing; then Cherbourg, so much nicer to land at than the endless labyrinth of Le Havre; one's out of it in five minutes, and deep in the countryside in ten. It's very sunny suddenly, the hedges green and smiling; hosts of early purple orchids along all the verges. I feel we haven't really come abroad, so familiar and loved it all is. A great colony of green-winged orchids on a common near Lessay; one, a beautiful pale rose sport. We touch the coast again at Port-Bail, an area of sandy lagoons, sparkling blue sea. Our first coffee in a little café, and I buy a map in a newspaper shop – first contact with the French, the 'shock' of their politeness again, the degree of human service *they* are still prepared to give. It is largely a convention, of course, a matter of ritual good-day, thank-you, a liberal hand-out of *monsieur*'s and *madame*'s. But it is based on an assumption of good manners in other people – of *honnêteté*; which we now lack completely.

22 May

A ridiculous article in *Figaro* by some general: it is inadmissible that the army should be laughed at, it is time the nation pulled up its socks. Such nonsense would cause a major scandal at home. But of course this is the other side of the 'obscenity' coin – the freedom that allows me to buy 'pornographic' verse from a respectable bookshop's front window is also the freedom to be much further to the right than we would ever tolerate. *Gaullisme* and *gauloiserie*[1] are products of the same basic phenomenon: do what you will. The Revolution was, or turned out to be, a proclamation of the right to be what one liked. The great centrist country has always been Britain, not France. Our only freedom is to be centrally respectable. That is why England is a morally good country to live in; and France an enjoyable one.

We had intended to stay at Cognac, but all the hotels were full to the attics because of some congress. So we had to rush on to Angoulême, a seemingly endless road; all the hotels on the way similarly full; the

[1] Obscenity, bawdiness.

situation as bad when we got to Angoulême. But luckily the owner of the second hotel I went into was just turning down a room somewhere else over the telephone for two commercial travellers by the desk. I took it. We had to cross to the other side of the city – to find a wretched place on a narrow part of the main Paris–Bordeaux road, heavy trucks thundering past every thirty seconds. The hotel like a *maison de passe*, run by two sleazy-looking females; a bad meal at last. But we slept somehow. I think this has never happened to us before on our French trips; we take the availability of rooms where we want for granted.

23 May

We went up into the old city in the morning, market day, plenty of life. The monotony of French taste over flowers is very striking – the same kinds of geranium and begonia and indoor plants on every one of a dozen or more stalls. The same goes for their gardens, of course. They simply don't realize what they could grow here – all the New Zealand, Australian and South American flora. The prices are wicked, too; bougainvillea at £2.50 a small plant.

On for a 'blow of the eye' at the sources of the Touvre; then to the forest de la Braconne, really the domanial woods of the Rochefoucauld family; very large and beautiful, mainly oak, many flowers and butter-flies.[1] We had lunch on a thyme bank studded with flowering spikes of the little bee-orchid *O. scolopax*. I have got the British flora with me, but identification is very rough-and-ready as far south as this. A very pretty wayside flower here is Meadow Clary, splendid rich blue spires of sickle-shaped flowers. Even the cultivated part of the Angoumois[2] is attractive: meadow after meadow of marguerite and buttercups, lucernes and clovers. Opposite this bank, in a broom-clearing, I found a solitary fly orchid; a longer and darker labellum than the English kind, rather a sinister plant.

We stopped a few minutes at La Rochefoucauld, to see the outside of the château from across the river; a painful thing there, very bizarre, a swift caught on a fish-hook. It had flown up and the gut had tangled round some telephone wires. It must have just happened, for it was still alive, hanging in the sky, frantically fluttering, then still, then struggling again, inexorably impaled by the hook. It was high over the water, impossible to reach; and intensely distressing to see, in some way an apotheosis of the nightmare in which one is ludicrously but fatally

[1] The three springs of the Touvre river, the Dormant, Bouillant and the Lèche, are about 10 kilometres, and the Braconne forest about 20 kilometres, to the east of Angoulême.

[2] The region around Angoulême, approximately co-extensive with the départe-ment of Charente.

trapped and condemned. And in that setting . . . against the towering walls of the castle and birthplace of the great cynic.[1] Medieval torture, unheard screams, agony. I refused to take a photograph of it.

We drove on through the north part of the forest, looked at the Fosse Mobile, a strange dark mouth in the earth, then over gentle country to Chenomet, where from Michelin there seemed to be a nice isolated hotel. It was certainly isolated, but tree-shrouded off-putting; a garden full of peacocks, a total silence. I rang a bell. An elderly queer appeared, very anxious to see us go away. Which we did. Curious, it must be some *nid de tantes*. He gave us a card for the château-hotel at Neuil, so we drove across country to that. One of François I's hunting-boxes, surrounded by moats and huge flowering chestnuts: expensive, as they all are, but this one at least had a welcoming atmosphere and a lack of the usual right-wing snobbism of such places. A stroll by a lake near by; swarms of tadpoles and huge carp leaping in the middle. Then a good meal; and nightingales the only noise outside at night.

We hear of the great Lambton–Jellicoe scandal in England;[2] *Figaro* rubs its hands in sanctimonious glee.

25 May
It is more interesting on the continuing French–English social war in Bordeaux (in a special article). The château-owners are bitter about the great shipping-houses in the city, who seem to carry their Anglomania and sense of high caste to absurd heights. A nice story about a Parisian who gained access to one of their mansions and met a daughter who spoke French with such a thick English accent that he politely switched the conversation to English proper – only to find that she did not speak it at all. This identification of the English with all that is right-wing and snobbish is one of the great lunacies of European culture. At the château de Neuil Eliz and I hid the Union Jack (each table had a flag on a little base) away, which distressed the proprietor. All his other guests liked the flags. He said one English visitor had put it on its side, because 'the Union Jack was done for as long as Harold Wilson was Prime Minister'. I suppose the cultural reason is simply a matter of travel statistics – the fact that most visitors to France have come from the upper classes, from the eighteenth-century milord on. Even today it is not a country that the 'uneducated' visit; no package-tour industry. The appeal of England is therefore to the

---

[1] The seventeenth-century writer of the *Maximes*, François, duc de La Rochefoucauld (1613–1680).

[2] Anthony Lambton, the minister for the RAF, and Lord Jellicoe, the Conservative leader in the House of Lords, both resigned from the government within days of each other after admitting that they had associated with prostitutes.

French right wing, as if England were the right-wing country *par excellence* of Europe; the confusion obviously lies in a misunderstanding of where English centrism and conservatism springs from – the French don't realize it is a part of the Protestant–Puritan ethic, a political answer to private and archetypal notions of sin and duty, and only secondarily to do with monarchy and aristocracy. We have a queen because she fits the structure; they think it is because we adore queens and *ancien régimes.*

28 May

To Chinon, to get some money and buy a set of *pétanque* balls. Then back past La Devinière, Rabelais's birthplace, and into the Fontevraud forest. It's good for orchids. Some huge *P. chlorantha,* two feet or more tall; a number of Monkey Orchids, near the end of their flowering; and one small colony of a yellow-flowered orchid that seems to be *D. incarnata ochroleuca.*

We picnicked in the woods; and a shock. We'd bought the papers in Chinon to read about the call-girl scandal; and then suddenly I am reading an obituary piece on Kenneth Allsop. It doesn't say how he died, we gather the news is a week old or more. I think of that swift on a hook at La Rochefoucauld, wonder if it was the same day. It seemed a presage, even then.

On to Angers, Eliz in tears. It's too big for us, we don't feel in the mood, so we go on, up the Mayenne valley to Château-Gontier; and by some miracle end up at a charming little hotel at Mirvault, just outside the town; the broad river, a mill, a weir, great peace and another excellent meal, lamb's brains and then a brochette of calves' kidneys and salt pork.

30 May

To Cherbourg on the main road, with a little detour at the end for our last taste of the countryside: the little valley of the Saire, very green and peaceful. Then lunch and a walk round Cherbourg, buying the groceries, a bottle of Calvados. A much nicer town than Le Havre. A quiet crossing, a moment of horror at the customs as I realize we are to be searched by a sharp-eyed lady officer – with four boxes full of orchid and other illicit roots to be found. But she seems satisfied with charging duty (£15 on 36 bottles) on the wine. Home to Lyme at one-thirty in the morning.

4 June

We learn a little more about poor Ken Allsop. He died from a four times the lethal dose of barbiturates, but an open verdict was returned at the inquest. It seems clearly a case of suicide; though perhaps done when he was drunk, a little on the spur of the moment. I talked with him just before we left for France, and he seemed very cheerful then. Everyone blames it on the pain his leg gave him,[1] but I suspect something else; money, failure of career as TV star. It was the day after Mandy's birthday, she and Betty had gone up to London for the day and he was alone. He wanted to hurt as he went, I think. Some mystery. Eliz wrote a nice letter to Betty, but Tristan rang to say she was going to London.[2]

13 June

A very pleasant trip down to Plymouth for an interview on Westward TV; two superb blue days, this June has turned magnificent . . . though grim for the garden vegetables.

14 June

We went to the studio at noon to meet Colin Wilson. He appears in a baggy suit and an old blue poloneck sweater, a fisherman's tweed hat; rather tall, he briskly shambles, trails people behind if he walks with them; quite remarkably like an eccentric university don for a working-class outsider. His eyes never seem quite in focus; as if he were one-eyed in both eyes, I don't know why this strange way of putting it came to me. We have lunch in a Chinese restaurant, he talks endlessly, the TV people twig him gently; his erudition, his obsession with murder,[3] his absurdity. He talks about 'second-rate novelists like Hardy and Jane Austen'; fun to be preposterous and watch the fish rise (this one didn't, but the director was outraged). 'No writer who has a philosophy of naive pessimism can possibly be great,' pronounces CW. Then, 'Jane Austen is just a woman's magazine writer.' It's strange, his overweening vanity doesn't offend – it is so childlike. The constant references to his own work and status – delivered so firmly, so *assumed* that his genius cannot be in dispute. During a break in the interview (they've had a job taming his inclination to ask endless questions concealing his own views, but he was very succinct with me) he suddenly said idly: 'I don't really know if I want to be the most famous writer in Western Europe.' There is some very deep fear in him. He cannot seriously believe all he claims himself to be, yet he is intelligent, he must know this is the impression he gives, of a blind vanity; yet finds that easier than a modesty. He is a rare case of someone who lives as if his dreams are true. We left at four, with signed copies of his two latest volumes; goodwill. I am so much what he is not, I think we do not conflict in any normal literary way.

---

[1] Allsop lost a leg to tuberculosis during the Second World War, and continued to battle with the associated pain for the rest of his life.

[2] With his death, Kenneth Allsop left behind his wife, Betty, and three children, Amanda, Tristan and Fabian.

[3] The latest of several books Wilson had written on this subject was *Order of Assassins: The Psychology of Murder* (1972).

4 July

Betty and Mandy Allsop come to tea, an occasion we somewhat dreaded; death obliging some sort of effort towards the formality we avoid like the plague elsewhere in our lives. Eliz went off with Mandy to the kitchen, and Betty launched off at once into the truth about Ken's death. Apparently there was a long letter. He wrote it at 9.45 (it was timed so in the heading) in the morning, after Betty and Mandy had left for London. The daily help was there until one o'clock. Ken then drank a bottle of wine and ate some Blue Vinny; then went to bed and took every pill in sight. She said it was a sweet letter, a beautiful letter; he listed some things he would regret never doing, one of which was 'walking with John Fowles in the Undercliff'. She blamed it all on 'the oil' and all the letters he got from people who needed help over similar problems; Ken's feeling of hopelessness and defeat. It seemed clear that it was really a case of overinvolvement, a kind of fixing of the battle-field against his own chances – as if, because he had 'failed' as a novelist and hated his involvement with the BBC, he decided to make total victory his goal in an area where it cannot be got.

She said she couldn't, still, cry about it. 'I just sat in the kitchen (when she was called home) and wanted to smash the whole place up.' He has left a financial mess behind. The Mill was in his name, so she must now sell that to pay the death duties. He was under-insured, now she'll have to find a job.

In a way his suicide is an example of the dangers of idealism. I always felt he did not really understand nature: that adoration of the purple-prose nature-writers, his obsession with the 'noble' genera of birds – falcons and hawks; his apparent lack of interest in botany and ento-mology. Too much of winged freedom (perhaps because of his own wretched wartime tragedy – crashing on his first solo flight and being grounded for ever because of it); too little hard-headed knowledge. Being a town boy, never having hunted or shot wild animals. He never realized how resilient nature is; how the death of species is part of the system. To me, nature is a sanctuary, a buttress against the possibility of suicide; that there was something profoundly wrong in his attitude is proven by the fact that the pleasure he maintained he got from nature was weaker than his death-wish. The countryside did not fail him; but his false concep-tion of it. There is a theme there; but it would hurt the living too much to use it.

21 July

Anna rings Eliz with the news that Roy is near the end of his tether. I spoke with him on the telephone – for the first time in years – some three weeks ago. He was making his will and (reasonably enough) wanted to know if he could take it that Anna was looked after by us.

He seemed normal enough then, but the threat of a gallstone operation this autumn must have driven him over the edge. Apparently he
has taken to buying 'ghastly' new furniture. Anna found the whole house
changed, in that way. A new car they can't afford. He has developed a
crush on Winston Churchill – photographs on the wall of him. He has
started hitting Judy, smashing things with a hammer – with which he
also threatened Anna. He told her there was the material for a 'certain'
bestseller in the bank – something to do with the inner secrets of football. She must exploit it if he 'goes'. The children had to be evacuated
to a friend's house until Anna arrived – now once again, poor child,
she has the responsibility of them in Bristol. He has gone into the
Charing Cross Hospital, but we don't know whether it is as a gallstone
or a psychiatric patient. It is the paranoiac side of it that frightens me;
with his egomania, he is quite capable of trying to take everyone around
him out of this life.

23 July
An unusual butterfly in the garden – the Ringlet variation *arete*, where
the usually ringed spots are simply obscure dots on the dark brown
background.

   Also a profusion (on the buddleias, at night) of the yellow underwing
group of moths; the dry season has helped, of course.

   The corollary of my conception of fiction (as 'natural', partly unconscious in origin, improvised, etc.) is the mistake: that is, one can think
of two kinds of novel – the one highly polished and corrected, the
other spontaneous (hazardous in the sense that the growth of a wild
plant is) and therefore 'soft'. Precisely the difference between a stone
and a leaf.

29 July
Lunch at the Allsops, to meet their doctor friend and his wife – Mike
Hudson, who practises at Beaminster. A shrewd young couple (he shares
two manias with me, oddly enough – orchids and cricket); too shrewd,
we somehow feel, not to see a little through the Allsop dream with all
its contradictions. He has a little the hard-headed indifference to other
people that is nice, and proper, in doctors being sociable; not much
time for Mandy's sub-spiritualism, the 'presences' she claims she feels.
We feel sorry for Betty, though; as with Betsa Payne, misfortune has
brought out a brave side of her. We went after the lunch to see the
cottage she has just bought in Powerstock – a terrible comedown after
the glories of the mill; once again, the mystery of how Ken could deprive
both himself and his family of such a setting. So much remains hidden
there; something in Betty seems faintly glad a dream was shattered.

   Her cottage at Powerstock is opposite the Jackmans' – he writes on ecology and the rest for the *Sunday Times*; a nice, gentle man.[1] They came back with us and we drank tea in the mill kitchen. Mandy returned with Rodney Legg, the fierce little editor of the *Dorset Magazine* – who is on the memorial fund committee. They had been to see the Frys, who farm the south side of Eggardon; they may sell. Mandy is all emotional and ecstatic, what a nun she would have made in St Teresa's convent; Legg is like a weasel, weasel-eyes, trusts no one and fears no one. He's really formidably well equipped for the role he has assigned himself and his magazine – of attacking anything that attacks Dorset.

8 August

A Silver-washed Fritillary on the flagstones outside the kitchen. It seemed unable to fly, meaningless circles. Until I threw it in the air, then it rose spiralling with great speed and quite extraordinarily high, vertically, two hundred feet or more; then sailed away north-east.

9 August

The twins from Norwich with us for a few days. Eliz goes to London to bring them here. They are very engaging, and totally time-consuming. We spoil them, of course. They have to be interested, a part of us, all day long. Simon is the cleverer with words, more imaginative and more aggressive; Tom is physically and psychologically much more like his mother. For the first time I learnt to see them quite clearly apart. Tom is always a little nervous, wistful, concerned. Apart from their mock-fights their gentleness to each other is very touching; almost biblical in its lack of selfishness.

We took them to Bristol to see the 600th centenary exhibition,[2] really a great tented fair on Durdham Down. A visit to the camera obscura near the Clifton Bridge first; they liked that, and the bridge – then round the endless fair with Nick and Anna. A lot of life, it managed to have some of the feel and atmosphere of one of the great medieval fairs. In the evening a splendid display for little boys in all men – the RHA[3] doing a musical cavalcade, galloping and wheeling gun-teams. Then two hot-air-balloon ascents.

On Sunday to Eggardon, to meet the Allsops and Brian Jackman. Legg wants me to do a 'blurb' on the botany for the memorial campaign pamphlet. But now they've learnt the farmers who own the land want £45,000 for the forty-five acres – all unploughable, worth only a poor keep value. The price is so monstrous they shouldn't pay it even if they could raise it. A sort of mini-Camelot atmosphere prevails, though. 'Was

[1] i.e., Brian Jackman.
[2] To commemorate the date on which the city received its charter.
[3] Royal Horse Artillery.

ever a place,' said the apparently sensible Jackman to me, 'better made
to fit a man?' He is another hawk maniac; constantly raising his glasses
at the distant speck in the sky.

14 August
Eliz takes the twins back to London; very great heat, in the eighties
every day. The twinless peace is beautiful.

15 August
Anna and Nick come from Bristol, to which they have now said goodbye.
They have quietly and informally plighted their troth, it seems. Which
delights us.

16 August
I go to London myself, for Tom Maschler's birthday party. Doris Lessing,
Arnold Wesker, Deborah Rogers, Graham Greene, the Desmond Morrises,
Tom and Fay and ourselves; an elaborate meal and a sort of elaborately
informal politeness. Ramona Morris is a drag, but the others enjoyable,
especially Arnold, several lengths ahead of the rest of us in warmth and
humanity. Lessing says little; seems so prim, then sudden vehement damn's
and bloody's, as if something is suppressed. Arnold has made us one of
his famous strudels, spent all afternoon at it, but Fay has provided an enormous meal first; and eventually it's burnt and only just edible.

18 August
Back to Lyme.
    An unexpected compliment from Tom M at his dinner: that my intro-
duction to the Conan Doyle series was the only one that 'said anything
new'. Not very kind to Graham Greene's father and uncle, who did other
introductions, or Graham himself. It must have been birthday euphoria.[1]

23 August
And the reverse from Anna, via Nick, at dinner here. 'Anna says you're
interested in flowers because you haven't any children,' he suddenly says
out of the blue, in all innocence – how's that for a theory then, John?

---

[1]Jonathan Cape were publishing the Sherlock Holmes stories in a nine-volume series.
JF had written an introduction to *The Hound of the Baskervilles* (see page 129). The
father and uncle of Cape's managing director Graham Carleton Greene were the
broadcaster Sir Hugh Greene, a former director-general of the BBC, and the novelist
Graham Greene. Sir Hugh wrote an introduction to *A Study in Scarlet*, and Graham
to *The Sign of Four*. The other contributors of introductions to the series were Len
Deighton, Eric Ambler, Kingsley Amis, Angus Wilson, Julian Symons and C. P. Snow.

20 September

Anna and Nick have been with us all this late summer. Badminton and *pétanque*. Nick tries to paint. Something in him wants to be more than just a potter. I write the long story, 'The Ebony Tower'. I now see the book: 'The Ebony Tower', 'Poor Koko', 'An Enigma', 'The Cloud', in that order; Pisanello's girl from Mantua on the cover. I've worked very well this summer, I don't know why; since summer usually silences me.

Eliz and I go on playing badminton now Nick and Anna have gone. One dusk two pipistrelle bats come and start diving at the shuttlecocks. They stop and whisk away at about eight feet, apparently the range at which they 'see' the outline on their radar, or register its true size.

Dan Halpern sends me a review of the poems – only the second I have seen. Apparently they have sold some 3,000 of the print of 3,500.

Eliz down in the dumps again, winter coming and the children gone on their separate ways. Nick to the RCA, Anna to Birmingham. She will not live for herself – or for me. Unless she is with people to whom she has to pretend, she makes no effort. She 'forgets everything', she 'can't talk'. Every day she stays in bed till midday or later, she sleeps badly at night. I am to blame, of course. But she is now so dissociated from my writing . . . I *am* to blame, for being what I am. But I don't know what I could be that would satisfy her. Behind all this the wretched Arab-Israeli war has started,[1] as if there weren't enough stupidity and doom inside the house already. I have no sympathy with either side. Alternately I hope Cairo and Damascus will be razed to the ground; and then Israel. All these less-than-nuclear wars simply create the promise of more to come. Only some major catastrophe can end the poison.

13 October

To Leigh, straight from Lyme, to see M. Her usual birdmindedness is somehow heightened by a new hairstyle, which gives her a bizarre air of outmoded frivolity; as if she were once someone she never was in fact. I think she means well by it, though; no more talk about leaving the house for a flat. Now she wants to cut some of the apple-trees down; it's not necessary, except with the old Beauty of Bath tree near the kitchen, but she has some sort of craving for change, for doing things. We had her old TV set changed for colour, to encourage this.

Thousands of Brent geese on the Leigh flats, a very fine sight.

16 October

To Hampstead, to see Boxall. He has bought a house opposite us here, in Vane Close, but now has to sell it because his musical daughter has

---

[1] Syria and Egypt had launched a surprise attack against Israel on the morning of 6 October, Yom Kippur.

come home again and can't find a place for her harpsichords. I feel sorry for him, he seems so tired and colourless, imbued with failure in some way. He took us round the house in Vane Close – a pretentious little jerry-built box, with a bare minimum of furniture. He seemed proudest of a 'real' goose-feather mattress his wife had brought from Czechoslovakia, kept on feeling it and making us feel how soft it was. I think he would like to get beneath it and never wake up again.

He is not much good as an accountant, I suspect. Now he thinks Belmont should be in our joint names, and refuses to believe that we put it in Eliz's only on his advice. 'I can't have told you that.' But he did. It is like the stockbroker he introduced me to last spring and who recommended Rowntree-Mackintosh shares, just before the appalling mess they are in over cocoa advances became public.[1] The shares are now at half the value we paid. I shrug, inside. I think we have had our rich years in that sense, and the prospect of never seeing them again does not worry me at all.

Lunch with Nick at the RCA. He seems to have got himself into precisely the situation I have adumbrated for the girl in 'The Ebony Tower'.[2] He says that in the ceramics department self-expression is dominant; everyone trying to be different, no interest in craft or functional values. He was throwing a bowl one day. 'Oh, Christ,' said another student, 'not Bernard Leach.'[3] His professor, David Queensberry (the Maschlers' friend), is resigning, it seems in something like despair. Nick is shocked by it all; but I think he has the nous to see that his old-fashioned 'difference' pays. An interesting fact he has had from Queensberry (who designs commercial pottery) is that there is enough tableware unsold for at least the next five years. In other words it is a buyers' market. Only striking design sells; there is no basic need.

Though I enjoyed London 'culturally' and seeing friends, the place seems to have got worse since we were last there; a really terrible sense of doom hangs over it – it is faintly like the Middle East War situation, that is, it won't be solved except by a sudden catastrophe. Its deepest horror is that it happens so gradually. The petrol stench and the air get a little worse each month, the parking worse, the cars, the inescapable people. We spent one evening with Denys Sharrocks, who is thinking of giving up his career in the British Council and teaching at a much

---

[1] The share price of the confectionery company slumped after it announced on 12 July 1973 that it had made a loss of £20 million on the cocoa futures market.
[2] In 'The Ebony Tower', Diana, who has become an assistant to the great painter Henry Breasley, explains that she left the prestigious Royal College of Art after only two terms because of the pressure of 'doing what everyone expects'.
[3] The British potter Bernard Leach (1887–1979) was renowned for a functional but elegant style influenced by the Eastern tradition of ceramics.

humbler level in Shropshire. He talked about the absurd irritation, the bloody people who get in the way wherever you are. I felt just that. A constant impatience. It is very largely the car, of course, that causes the problems – and the insane use of road transport for goods. We came out through miserable jams on the way back to Lyme, hundreds of huge trucks around us, and listened to a news item on the wireless – how a commission had decided that road transport must be encouraged, otherwise the 'quality of life' would suffer. It is such a blatant capitalist argument. The only thing that would suffer is speed of delivery and unnecessary proliferation of product.

A city in distress, and to leave it was a great relief – to me. Eliz hated being there and hated coming back to Lyme, in her usual fashion.

31 October
Back to Lyme, to find they have cut down the huge row of macrocarpa that used to dominate our skyline due south. Like a hole knocked through a wall.

In London I translated Marie de France's 'Eliduc', and will put that in *Variations* after 'The Ebony Tower'. It is very good: she had all the gifts in embryo of a fine novelist. She wrote it almost exactly eight hundred years ago, give or take a decade or two. I feel very close to her. One lovely little didactic touch: she twice makes Eliduc send a servant on ahead when he goes to visit Guilliadun. Quite plainly she was telling the gentlemen of Henry II's court that you do *not* barge in on your lady-friends without giving them warning. By chance I saw at the V and A a fourteenth-century belt of the kind Guilliadun must have sent Eliduc (since there is a reference to him fitting it to his waist): it was made of links, with a hook at one end, and the whole longer than was necessary, so that the unused links could swing free.[1]

A letter from Lord Butler asking me to give the Clark Lectures at Cambridge in two years' time. I refuse. And a profile request from the *Sunday Times*. Also refused.

---

[1] A native of Normandy, Marie de France lived during the second half of the twelfth century in England, where she was probably attached to the court of Henry II and Queen Eleanor of Aquitaine. Her *Lais*, of which 'Eliduc' is one, consist of twelve Celtic tales written in Anglo-Norman couplets. The background to 'Eliduc' is as follows. When the knight Eliduc of Brittany learns that he is in disfavour with the king, he decides to go into temporary exile in England, promising his wife Guildelüec that he will remain true to her. In England, he fights as a mercenary for an old king whose daughter, Guilliadun, falls in love with him. She has her page take to Eliduc her belt and gold ring, hoping that the way in which he receives these gifts will offer some sign of whether he loves her in return.

4 November

We go to Weston-super-Mare to visit Steepholm,[1] which the Allsops now think might do for Ken's memorial, Eggardon having been declared impossible. Mandy comes with her fiancé Rodney Legg and a BBC man, John Percival, Jacky Gillott's[2] husband. Assembled also are the members of the Steepholm Trust, who lease the island from the Baroness Wharton, an old bird who's lived in Portugal these last thirty years. We sense they are on hot bricks at this proposed change of landlord. Natural history chat on the boat out; we land on a shingle beach, then up a rusty iron ladder to a path that leads over the cliffs. It is a very bizarre place both ecologically and aesthetically. Ecologically it is dull – the 6,000 pairs of herring-gull that breed here in the summer have driven everything else away except a few cormorants; and the botany is all introduced – privet and elder and nettle and an astounding blanket of alexanders. Virtually no grass. Among all this a whole series of fortifications, from Victorian times on – a dozen or more rusting cannon lying about, weird underground chambers, relics of ammunition railway. Splendid views. A twelfth-century priory in the undergrowth, which the baroness will not allow to be excavated as she believes in not disturbing the dead. There is one habitable house, the old Victorian barracks. Meanwhile we make friends with our guides and begin to realize they are rather less what they outwardly seem, university naturalists and archaeologists, but a band of jealous kids, scared stiff that their playground is about to be wrested away from them. The Allsop party had tea in a Weston hotel afterwards and decided to ditch them – with my encouragement. We devised how to get rid of the gulls; a herd of goats or a few ferrets seems best. The public should be let in, I think, and the place used not for preserving the present ecology, but altering it. A very tempting toy to play with, as well as in.

A bizarre sexual dream. I am lying in bed with Eliz. A girl climbs on top of us and offers me her naked breasts. They are very hard and small. I think (in the dream), like tennis balls. I realize the girl is Evonne Goolagong,[3] I see her face quite clearly.

The explanation. Last night there was a showing on TV of a Norman McLaren cartoon – points of light that grew from a tennis ball.[4] I enjoyed

---

[1] A small island in the Bristol Channel, about five miles off the coast of Weston-super-Mare.

[2] Jacky Gillott (1939–1980) was a novelist and broadcaster on current affairs and the arts.

[3] The Australian tennis-player, who won the French Open and Wimbledon ladies' singles titles in 1971.

[4] Working first for the GPO Film Unit and then the National Film Board of Canada, Norman Mclaren (1914–1987) was an animator of abstract cartoons who pioneered the techique of drawing directly on celluloid.

watching it. Goolagong completely puzzled me for a while. But I also worked yesterday on the 'Eliduc' translation. Very clearly Goolagong is a pun on Guilliadun, the wayward princess at Exeter.

What interests me is the childish absurdity of the thing. The super-ego just being made a fool of. Eliz was cast as Guildelüec, obviously. And my noble romance made a joke of – just as I had Henry do with it in 'The Ebony Tower'.[1] Perhaps that is it.

I am getting the short stories for *Variations* typed out – Ken Allsop's old typist, a Mrs Pitcher from 'under' Eggardon, though she's a Lyme girl by birth.

This November of 1973 will be important in human history – not that the energy crisis now on us was not inevitable sooner or later, but this will be when the dream ended . . . and possibly when the end began. One detects a kind of familiar pleasure in it, the old British *thing*, the need to tighten belts, the 'Dunkirk Spirit' and all the rest. I think the world will not be the same, even if King Feisal softens, even if other resources are found, even if the crisis is one day overcome in all outward ways. It is like a great warning bell.[2]

Doris[3] is with us, has been for weeks. She has shingles, poor old thing, now gastric flu on top of it. Her stupidity drives Eliz mad, though it is inoffensive because it is natural; mainly a product of trying to be 'good', to fit in. We play Monopoly with her – now three-handed whist. I can't stand card games, but whist has something – it is very simple and full of hazard. Agreeable, if one must waste time so.

7 December

A fine badger on the lawn, when I went out to piss after one of our late whist sessions. He sniffed and sniffed in the torchlight, then lumbered quickly off.

12 December

Mrs Pitcher brings in the last of the stories. They please and displease me, often in the same day. It is like having an affaire, then having to make it public. A terrible sense of the pleasure being past. Only the sadness now.

---

[1] Henry tells Eliduc's story, but his narration 'was more reminiscent of a Noël Coward farce than a noble medieval tale of crossed love'.
[2] On 17 October, in the middle of the Yom Kippur war, the Arab members of the Organisation of Petroleum Exporting Countries, led by King Feisal of Saudi Arabia, announced that they would reduce production and place an embargo on the export of oil to Western countries who had supported Israel in the war. Oil prices quadrupled.
[3] Elizabeth's mother.

A half-hour script for David Tringham: *The Girl in Black*. I wrote it in two days.

13 December
National gloom and disaster. Heath announces all the controls needed to meet the fuel crisis.[1] We had a notice saying we shall have no more oil till the end of January. Fortunately the weather is mild at the moment.

17 December
To Bruton to lunch with BBC TV producer John Percival and his novelist wife Jacky Gillott: an odd little house perched up in fields with arms of the town on both sides. They evidently live a life of left-wing community participation blended with conservation; plus dogs and children and horses. She drifts in and out, I sense in some way hostile to me, or jealous. Rodney Legg and Mandy Allsop are also there, it's to discuss the Steepholm project. I wrote a long letter recently to Betty arguing for it, despite all its risks; and am now called to account – will I join the management committee? I say yes.

Against the background of the energy crisis and national disaster, it seems a little like fiddling while Rome burns – or freezes.

We haven't used the central heating for a week or more now; huddle over a log fire, watch the telly till it dies at ten-thirty, then play rummy till midnight. Whist is discarded.

19 December
All day paginating and collating the typescripts of the stories. Anthony's mother is taking them to him from Budleigh to Gloucestershire, where he'll be over Christmas. They too seem redundant at the moment.

25 December
Christmas Day, on our own. We had a walk along to the cress-bed beyond Pinhay Bay, and picked the first cresses. Totally deserted, a very lovely blue and sunlit day. The sun set as we came back to the Cobb, sinking huge into a mist-bank over Torbay; a resplendent deep pink and reluctant orb. We had the cress with our goose.

---

[1] In Britain the fuel crisis caused by the Arab embargo on oil had been aggravated by the decision of the National Union of Miners on 8 November 1973 to work to rule in support of a pay claim. On 13 December the prime minister Edward Heath announced to Parliament that to conserve severely depleted supplies a three-day working week for industry and commerce would be introduced from 31 December.

26 December

All afternoon at Charlie's mill at Farway, drinking. I can only deal with Pat now in an alcoholic haze. We went in the evening to see his converted house at Branscombe. It is very attractive visually, very *Architectural Review*-worthy; but somehow impractical: one tiny bathroom, a warren of minute bedrooms. We had dinner after that at the Mason's Arms. To our delight, C tells Pat to 'stop talking for one minute, if that's possible'. And she did, by God, for at least twenty; but I wonder what price the poor man has to pay later.

29 December

To Steepholm again. Anna and Nick arrived from London (where Roy is ill and difficult again, it seems) two days ago, and we went with them. A bleak day, twenty or so people, environmentalists and journalists and whatnot; plus two men from the Steepholm Trust we propose to oust – Ted Mason and an ornithologist. Rodney Legg and I explored the top of the island – some nice old ruined cottages, and surprisingly 'open' space where the pre-1939 farm fields must have been. Many more herring-gulls than on our last visit; apparently they are, under their huge population thrust, taking up breeding quarters and behaviour with increasing earliness each year. Their wailing and constant moaning seemed to depress the others. I suspect Rodney and I are now the only real enthusiasts. Brian Jackman was there, and his last words, back on the mainland, were that he was 'not convinced'. Fabian Allsop seemed disillusioned as well. I think it was not nearly Romantic and fashionable enough for him.

Small colonies of the Culvert Spider in the old powder magazines.

We left the Maschlers at Lyme. They arrived the previous evening. Fay looks abominably tired and pale.

30 December

An odd day. I took the children down with Tom in the morning, another lovely blue day, to the sand-bar in the Cobb. Hannah insisted on swimming, despite the cold and in the end we undressed her and let her realize by direct experience all is not warm that laps and glitters; curious, her inability to separate sea and swimming. Then Tom and I went off and played *pétanque* for three hours on the glass beach – quite alone. The bowls ran superbly and endlessly on the sands, curlew and oyster-catcher crying, the lovely blue and gold winter day. Lucky males – at home Fay, I learnt later, poured out her marital woes, her tiredness, Tom's exhaustingness, her inability to keep up. We feel sorry for her (having rather forced them to go back to London that evening) and guilty. He *is* the most exhausting man in the world, the most voracious for the best. Playing bowls, darts, a new card game we have fallen for (Black Maria), all that is acceptable with him. But everything else has to be enjoyed under such pressure; the slightest failings (i.e., what is not to his personal taste) are pounced on. Fay has apparently been to a psychiatrist, but it is Tom who needs to go – to have this pathological drive explored. Apparently Fay feels she is ruining their marriage – the psychiatrist advised her, the dolt, to examine her own faults more closely; as well ask someone standing under a waterfall why she feels wet all the time.

1 January 1974

Anthony rings, he's read the book, guarded compliments, he thinks it will do well in the States, here there will be the usual complaints about the wicked readability and the didacticism. He likes the first story best, the intruder story least. And I am left, as usual, not knowing what his real feelings are.

All this provokes Eliz to read them at last. She finishes the first in an ominous silence. Now I wait for Tom's coffin-nail. My dear old trio of hatchet-faced midwives.

4 January

Tom rings, full of nice words for the book. I think he means most or some of them. He wants a new general title, and some rearrangement of story order.

10 January

I finish the article on subsidence in Lyme; give it to the Pitcher to type out.

Our new card game is piquet, which I used to play with my father as a schoolboy. A very great game, far nobler and deeper and more enjoyable than the others we have tried. No better blend of skill and hazard.

Endless gales, three in the last week; one this morning was briefly the most savage for a long time. The branches of the old Italian cypress were bending like trout-rods. I will my trees to survive. And more rain this month already, it seems, than for the whole of January last year. I fear the ironies of existence: that my paper on subsidence will be met by reality at the bottom of the garden.

11 January

The Allsops and John Percival and the boy who will be warden on Steepholm – if it is got – here for a committee meeting. The Friends of the Earth contingent and Brian Jackman have washed their hands of the whole business, so we are down to a distinctly incestuous nucleus – which worries me. I feel Betty and the children still want something instant and romantic; I'm not at all sure they have the stamina Steepholm will need, in the best of circumstances. Percival and Rodney Legg are at least practical and hard-headed by comparison. We draw up a list of

1. John outside Belmont House, c.1968.

2. Elizabeth, John and Anna, Lyme Regis, 1966.

3. *Left to right*: Eileen Porter, Leonora Smith, Elizabeth Fowles, Anna Christy and Fred Porter, c.1966. (*Below*) 4. John in Lyme Regis high street.

5. Ned Bradford and his wife, Pamela, on Cape Cod, c. 1967.

6. Tom Maschler in his office at Jonathan Cape.

7. Belmont House, Lyme Regis.

8. John and Elizabeth at Belmont House.

9. Anna Christy's wedding to Nick Homoky, July 1974, in the garden at Belmont.
In the foreground: Nick Homoky, Roy Christy, John Fowles, Anna Christy, Boris Wiseman,
Elizabeth Fowles, Ian Friend and Fred Porter.

10. John Fowles, Malou
Wiseman and Tom Wiseman
on the beach at Lyme Regis,
1974.

11. On the set of *The French Lieutenant's Woman*: Harold Pinter, John Fowles and Karel Reisz, 1980.

12. At the BAFTAs, 1982. *Left to right:* Jeremy Irons, Antonia Fraser, Elizabeth Fowles, John Fowles, Harold Pinter, Sinead Cusack.

13. John in the garden at Belmont, 1995.

chores and decide the campaign must be launched this spring; I will compose the appeal pamphlet.

16 January
We were due to drive to London, but yet another – the fifth in the last fortnight – massive gale. A pane in the greenhouse roof went, then another as I was trying to block the hole. A lump was also torn out of the perspex roof over the balcony. Due south-west, and the most savage wind yet, enormous driven and whipped drifts of spray over the Cobb. It died down a bit about two o'clock.

But perhaps even these wild gales are preferable to the peace of slow death that seems to have settled over the country. It is all people talk about – and talking seems all they feel able to do. Yesterday the Governor of the Bank of England forecast at least ten years of 'austerity' and I think for once he was not just propagating an Establishment scare. The stalemate between the Government and the miners is only a symptom of a much deeper sickness – though I believe it less a terminal condition than a symptomatic one (in evolutionary terms): a kind of inevitable stage justice-obsessed advanced democracies must go through. Part of me even welcomes it, inasmuch as it shows up the hollow inequity of 'free enterprise' and other capitalist notions. The simple fact is that the British will no longer accept gross inequalities of wealth, but will fight tooth and nail against revolutionary change. It is the triumph of a dream over the will to realize it. We want none of our freedoms, and least of all the freedom to gamble – to stand a chance of becoming much richer than anyone else – diminished; and at the same time we want more equality. This is precisely the dilemma I analysed when I wrote about America: the triumph of self and self-consciousness – which has led to a huge increase in both individual egocentricity and social empathy.

17 January
To London, and straight to Anthony's for dinner from a meeting with him and Boxall. A estimates probable income from the new book in the £80,000–£90,000 area, which seems to me wildly optimistic – and coldly unattainable, in any case. There will be £130,000 or so left in *The FLW* account in Boston when that contract ends two years hence. I sense Boxall gives up, and Anthony feels no writer should have it so lucky. We devise ways of making Ned Bradford cough up more in a new guarantee as a reflection of the interest Little, Brown have on my 'capital'. Absurd; like over-hoarding squirrels.

The dinner was profoundly unhappy – and strange. A had also invited Ronnie Payne and Celia Haddon. Something went wrong between R and myself from the start, and got progressively worse. I had a disturbing sense of a hatred, a rancour, a sourness; a chasm between him and myself – all the old war between Literature and Journalism made alive again. He had an obsessive use of 'boring' and 'little' – which Celia has now learnt off him – that I know I provoked. 'Boring little man', 'boring little film', 'boring little book' – the real attack being on pretension, i.e., anything that is not outrageous and amusing. Celia even produced the extraordinary phrase 'rather a sweet little boring man'.

The attitude is petit bourgeois, the language upper-class – a dreadful conjunction, in other words, of the worst elements of both classes. I see Ronnie is jealous of my 'prestige'; and Celia remains incipiently angry about it. Terrible, I felt our friendship died during the evening; or returned to its starting-point, our mutual distrust and contempt for our public roles at school. He used to irritate me then – for wrong reasons on my part (because he was a junior prefect and notoriously broke rules about smoking and the rest);[1] now I feel less guilty about the irritation. The real affection of the intervening years has become 'boring' and 'little' as well. I am a successful novelist to be got at; and he is Fleet Street.

By an irony I am now – in *Daniel Martin* – at the chapter with Barney Dillon.[2] The temptation is clear, and I must avoid it. *Comprendre . . .*

A much more tangible tragedy was taking place during all this, though we knew nothing of it at the time. Anthony was rather mysteriously absent for twenty minutes on the telephone during the dinner – I thought on literary business. Two days later he told me it was because his sister had died of leukaemia – which gave us a bad jab of guilt, since we had stayed on an hour after Ronnie and Celia left.

21 January
Vale of Health for lunch. Fay is pregnant again. It seems curiously ill-timed, since they are now moving into Karel Reisz's house this summer. Alice is full of health now; Hannah her usual seductive, ebullient little self. I feel sorry for Fay; she is neither physically nor psychologically cast for the Queen Bee role.

Tom and I went for a walk on the Heath alone after lunch, and we came to the pill behind his previous sugar about the book. Neither Graham Greene nor Catherine Storr[3] like 'Behind the Scenes', and want

---

[1] Contemporaries at Bedford School, both JF and Ronnie Payne had been prefects; John was also Head of School. See introduction to *The Journals*, volume 1, pages xi–xii.

[2] The scope in *Daniel Martin* to borrow details from Ronnie Payne's life was considerable. The character Barney Dillon is an Oxford friend of Daniel who has become a Fleet Street journalist. In the chapter 'Hollow Men', Daniel meets Barney Dillon for lunch after discovering that his daughter Caro, who has got a job on Barney's newspaper, is having an affair with him.

[3] A reader for Jonathan Cape.

it removed.[1] My personal digression 'belongs in the blurb or somewhere else – beautifully written though it is' – a number of statements in this form. He must know I see through him when he attaches criticism to other people and benevolent neutrality to himself. 'One person' found the Marie de France translation 'laughably absurd'; but T wouldn't mind if it was tacked on in an appendix. Then we discuss the title. He reminds me how well *The Love Object*[2] sold on title alone.

I think the digression should largely or completely go, so there is no argument there. It belongs with the architect's plans, not the building. 'Eliduc', we'll see. I feel what vitiates these kinds of discussion is best-sellerdom, not proper artistic considerations. T sees me on some kind of fragile minor peak, liable to topple off at any moment if I am not nursed and shepherded. It is by no means all his fault, of course. I sounded sweet reason through all this; and ran through my forest, hidden and watching.

22 January
We took Betsa Payne to see the film *Paper Moon*, by Bogdanovich. Soft-centred, but tolerable. Then dinner afterwards. She has a new lover, an Indian archaeologist; and seems to have come through formidably well. I thought of Celia Haddon at Anthony's, watching her shred her paper serviette and roll the shreds into little balls, chain-smoking my cigarettes, nervous as a white cat – how deep Betsa is beside that shallowness. Deep in another way, since we went home with her and listened to some records, ending with Flagstad[3] and the Liebestod finale from *Tristan and Isolde*. Whereupon B told us that it had been the key element in her moment of madness after the marriage broke up. She had been driving over to her sister Joanna's, down Portland Street (where – I think not a coincidence – we had driven to get to the cinema to see *Paper Moon*) and then suddenly had the total illusion that she had crashed and was crushed beneath the car. On the opposite side of the road she could see Ronnie laughing with Celia. All this was against the Liebestod aria. Something in her still drove on, though her face was streaming with tears – it seemed more because the illusion had been so intense that she took it as a sign of madness than because of its actual content.

Now she told us – it was two in the morning – that this was the first time she had been able to listen to the aria since that incident three years before. I was touched. We see her so little. But her reality, her

---

[1] 'Behind the Scenes' was an essay in which JF attempted to explain the story-telling process.
[2] A novel by Edna O'Brien, which Jonathan Cape published in 1968.
[3] The Norwegian soprano Kirsten Flagstad (1895–1962).

sense of affective and affectionate reality, is far deeper than Ronnie's. Achievement, having it or lacking it, dwarfs the male.

14 February

To Penzance, for our trip to the Scillies. An abominable drive, yet another gale had started, endless rain, floods everywhere. We got to Penzance just before six, and found the Abbey Hotel; and a real find, as we were to discover – lost down a side-street, a very pretty Gothic house full of antiques and threadbare carpets, with a labyrinth of connected buildings and court-yards behind. It is run with inspired eccentricity, a kind of friendly hatred of pretention; the antithesis of everything that is so depressing about the average contemporary hotel – very simple but well-cooked food, no central heating, no service (you just go into the kitchen and ask for what you want); no plastic, nothing but the old and tried. More like a private home.

At seven-fifteen to the station, to meet Tom and Fay from London; then out to a supposed good restaurant, the Tarot; a mistake, the hotel food was much better. Tom and Fay rapidly into their only-the-very-best act, which we had to undergo all the weekend.

15 February

Up at seven-thirty to catch the helicopter. Tom has a friend, Rex Cowan, who descends on the Scillies tomorrow, but who has meanwhile blazed the trail for us.

Down to the boat to Tresco, and big seas on the way across, the same boatmen we had last time. The island has been badly hit by the gales, everything wind-blown and salt-scorched; far less in flower than during our earlier visit last year. The Island Hotel is all that the Abbey is not – poor modern design, poor food, all appearance and no content. It is run by a retired wing-commander and his wife, like an indifferent offi-cers' mess.

Fay retired to her room to rest, while Tom, Eliz and I walked out along the coast west. Magnificent seas; the big waves send up bulleting white cores of water which auger into the wind, then disintegrate and die away into spindrift. The only birds out over the huge combers towards St Helen's were Greater Blackbacks and kittiwakes. Turnstone and a pair of purple sandpiper in the bay.

After lunch, Rex Cowan appeared; a very bizarre character, a compulsive talker and organizer. He was a successful Jewish solicitor in London until some eight or nine years ago; then one day threw it all up, and went in for treasure-hunting instead. His wife does all the historical research; he runs the diving teams. He first found the *Hollandia*, a Dutch East Indiaman, with a huge cargo of silver pieces of eight; last summer he found the *Princess Maria*, still secret. It had on board an African crown for Charles II's wife. Meanwhile, he seems to have taken over the

Scillies, like some film producer *sans* film; he doesn't hear what one says, an endless flow of reminiscence, information, boasting, self-mockery, touchiness (some TV programme described him as 'tiny and pugnacious' – which he is – and he keeps returning to it, the offence, the injustice). We were to see a lot of him, and Fay by the end could hardly speak to him, his monomaniacal ebullience put her in such a rage. I found him finally rather comic and endearing; and no fool.

He insisted on Tom and I going out with him to see the wreck sites off Annet and St Agnes, I think in the hope that we would be profoundly sick. The seas grew very big when we got out in the Sound – the same two boatmen, a little blond-headed, bright-eyed young man called David Stedeford and a huge ginger-bearded man, both from Bryher, the boat riding up the huge sea-slopes and disappearing down in the troughs, Cowan dancing about with the heaves and rolls, teasing the two men ('All he does is get drunk and screw girls'). They gave as good as they got. 'Heard of any new wrecks, David?' 'Not since I met you, Rex.' Great guffaws. Tom began to be not amused by the sea; and I was glad myself when they decided the rollers were too big to go out beyond Annet. We turned back towards St Agnes, then seals began to appear, driven in by the weather, strange brown faces floating down the hillsides of water in our wake. They are incorrigibly curious, it seems. It was too rough to land at St Agnes, so we went back to St Mary's and became the shopping bus for Bryher and Tresco; quiet women, babies, children crowded in the little cabin.

Tea at the hotel, and Eliz and I talked with Cowan; he is very articulate about himself and his obsession, the excitement of the archival research, the patient dogging-down of wrecks, the problems with his divers.

At dinner he suddenly pulled a plastic bag out of his pocket and poured out a pile of pieces of eight; they are large silver coins, rather bigger than the modern crown, very prettily milled with a leaf design. Rex's eyes glitter as he watches us handle them; I think rightly. This is tangible proof of the method in his madness – how satisfactorily it both pays and excites. His two auctions of the *Hollandia* treasure have so far yielded nearly £50,000; there is another auction this spring in Amsterdam, and apparently even that will far from exhaust what has been brought up.

23 February

A lovely morning, very mild and blue, the first truly good weather. I went out alone before breakfast; great calm and innocence, the beginning of time. But very little calm at breakfast and as we prepare to catch the launch back to St Mary's – Fay in a very resentful state indeed, since Rex has rung from St Mary's to say that at long last his divers can get to work and we must come out and watch before we catch the afternoon chopper. We leave her and Eliz on the quay in the charge of one of the divers' wives.

We head out past Annet towards the Bishop's Rock lighthouse, search round for the buoys over the wreck. They haven't been able to dive since mid-December, with all the gales. The commander kits up and goes over and disappears down to the *Hollandia* but not for long – this is a deep wreck, fifteen fathoms, which cuts the time below. He comes up in eight minutes, visibility on the bottom is down to a yard. Then we head out to the line of shark's teeth on the rim of the Scillies. The *Princess Maria* went down just inside – not far from where the Cloudesley Shovell fleet foundered outside.[1] Seals bob up everywhere along the rocks, a young one close beside us. It keeps raising its muzzle and sniffing, for all the world like a dog. Roy, the bearded diver, who goes down longer, this wreck being at six fathoms, has a seal friend who plays with him; 'bites my flippers'.

It is very beautiful on a calm day like this, not a ship or a house in sight, the gentle swell, the reefs, the strings of little islets, the seals bobbing in the scurry of white water beside the rocks. Roy comes up with a lump of 'crud', a mass of debris from the wreck. Two ballast bricks stick out of the mass of sand and oxidized iron, which stains black, like sepia; a sea-anemone, limpets. He reports bad visibility also. Serious diving must wait a few days more.

We go back to St Mary's, lunch in Rex's flat, Fay still unmollified, refusing to eat the meal Rex cooked, fresh plaice (because he fried them in breadcrumbs and served sprouts), and sending Tom out for pasties. We went out and bought some wreck photos from the Gibson shop,[2] then the chopper back to the mainland.

After seeing Tom and Fay off in the train, Rex took us round the local antique shops; he treats Penzance as another part of his 'production' – or kingdom. We saw him off at six, on his way to organize a diving team for yet another wreck, this time off Plymouth; among his luggage was a plastic child's beach-bucket, stuffed with newspaper. Inside, a 1740 wine bottle, still with its contents intact.

Peace at last for us. And a good meal at the hotel, even better now after the inhumanities of the one on Tresco.

Home past the weird china-clay valley north of St Austell, over Bodmin, a brief detour to see Dozmary Pool (a disappointment);[3] then home about seven.

---

[1] In 1707 Admiral Sir Cloudesley Shovell (1650–1707) was returning with his fleet from the Mediterranean to England, when owing to a navigational error his ship and two others were wrecked off the Scillies, with the loss of two thousand lives.
[2] A stationery store that belonged to a family of photographers who had over four generations photographed shipwrecks off the Scillies.
[3] According to legend home to the Lady of the Lake, Dozmary Pool was where King Arthur rowed out to claim his sword Excalibur.

We are getting attached to Cornwall; I to my quarter of blood there, the Celtic strain whose value I am analysing in the new introduction to 'Eliduc' for the book. I bought a book on the language while we were there; its last stronghold was on the Land's End peninsula, in the area we like so much.

25 February
The Collector is on at the St Martin's theatre in the West End, with Marianne Faithfull and Simon Williams. A batch of really bad reviews; fully deserved, by the sound of it.

26 February
The Gibsons' photographs of shipwrecks have hooked Tom. He proposes a book on it; Rex Cowan and I to do the introduction and notes.

4 March
To London, to do the editing of my stories; and decide on the title.

5 March
Tom and I decide on *The Ebony Tower*; all done in ten minutes. I half wanted *The Oriole*, but that was condemned as too *recherché*. Then talk about the shipwreck book – I am to do the introduction in a month, we must get it out by Christmas. Photos are coming from Frank Gibson. A sort of mad rush, which I enjoy.

Satyajit Ray's film *Company Limited*; as always, a dozen streets ahead of anyone else.

6 March
We go to see another film with Fay. Yesterday she went for drinks with the Ogden Stewarts at the top of Frognal. Donald, the famous old script-writer, who is now in his seventies, was in a dressing-gown.[1] He said to Fay, 'Do you want to know the first thing Ella (his wife, Ella Winter) sees every morning?' 'Yes,' said Fay. He opens the dressing-gown; and is naked underneath. Fay said she felt *they* felt one could hardly meet a smart young couple of the 1970s and not hint at an orgy for four.

7 March
Into Cape to see the photographs, with Rex Cowan.

I go back to Lyme on my own, to do the introduction. Eliz stays in Hampstead. All the daffodils coming out, the peace, and writing.

[1] Best known as the script-writer of *The Philadelphia Story*, Donald Ogden Stewart (1894–1980) settled in London after being blacklisted in Hollywood during the McCarthy witch hunts.

14 March

Betty and Mandy Allsop come over. Gradually I am being inched towards being the powerhouse for the Memorial Fund, which is not a role I intend to take. They stayed for hours, waffling on, and irritated me violently. Just as there was so much that was suspect in his attitudes, there is a vile amount in theirs. They are celebrity snobs, if not social ones. I think this does not affect the desirability of buying Steepholm, however. They, and his far from sacred memory, can be quite fairly used for that.

17 March

Down to Penzance by train to meet Rex for the Scillies and seeing what else Frank Gibson can find for us. The Cornish countryside very sober and pretty: all muted greens, browns, purples; sallow and hazel in flower.

Back to Lyme. A good sight on the mudflats opposite to Exmouth – some fifteen wild geese. I think they were whitefronts, but it was too misty to be sure.

25 March

The notes finished, and off to Cape.

The book is to be called *Shipwreck*. Ned Bradford will take it for America, we hope.

I am trying to get the profits from the wreck book to the Kenneth Allsop Fund. It seems fraught with difficulty, giving money away.

13 April

Muriel Arber recently returned my 'paper' on the landslips with a huge apparatus of correction and suggestion.[1] Such punctilious scholarship; she is physically of quite immense ugliness, but has a kind of girlish enthusiasm, a humorous grace of character and liveliness of mind that I like. She came today for the walk I had promised out over Ware Cliffs; and seemed to enjoy it. We saw a kestrel carrying a mouse, found a toad under a stone, a badger who had made one of his sett-holes bang in the middle of the upper path to the farm lane; examined her 'horsts' in Long Mead. The old girl stood by Ware stream and recited a poem she had written there when she was nine.

She came back to tea; and as she went, I remembered to ask her if

---

[1] A teacher and geologist who lived in Cambridge, Muriel Arber (1913–2004) had conducted extensive research into the valleys, cliffs and landslips on the south-west coast of England. A regular visitor to Lyme Regis since the 1920s, she was valued by JF as 'a marvellous and ever-fresh source of information about the old town'.

she was related to my favourite Victorian scholar, Edward Arber – whose texts I used to collect.[1] She is his grand-daughter. That pleased me very much.

The novelist Margaret Forster, Hunter Davies's wife, has come up with a technique for giving copyright away. One donates it before writing a word; then the contract is between publisher and recipient. We'll try that with *Shipwreck*.

20 April

I start on the second draft of the novel previously called *Futility*, then *The English Man*; but think I will call it simply *Daniel Martin*, after the protagonist. It was about halfway finished when I dropped it last time.

25 April

Eliz to London again, to buy a wedding-dress for Anna. She will be away a fortnight. I suppose the price I must pay for peace when she is here; she has been good as gold since her last fugue.

4 May

More nonsense over Steepholm. I had planned to go tomorrow with Peter Rees to live on the island for a few days and clear the paths. But the boatman says it will be too rough. This is with the smallest of breezes at Lyme (which continued all Sunday). We begin to realize there is some spanner in the works there.

6 May

Now news that Baroness Wharton, who was selling us the island, died yesterday in Portugal.

The weather continues abominably cold and dry; today a half-gale in addition. I don't feel well. I suppose I eat too little and smoke too much; I don't really want to eat at all. The silence, the solitude, I work on *Daniel Martin*. One has to brew inside oneself, it is 'creatively' good; and physically destructive.

16 May

Sitting on the bench in the cistus walk, I see an ant crawling up my trouser-leg; then realize it isn't an ant, but a spider – and later, under the microscope, that it is the very rare ant-mimic jumping-spider, *Synageles venator*. Locket and Millidge report it only from 'a few coastal sandhills'

---

[1] Edward Arber (1836–1912) was professor of English at Mason College, Birmingham, and the editor of the series, 'English Reprints', which made the texts of hard-to-find English authors accessible to the general public.

and 'in one Huntingdonshire fen'.[1] Its resemblance to a small black ant is indeed remarkable, and probably it isn't as rare as they say. But I was delighted to discover it.

It's the opening day of the 1200 Festival here,[2] so we went down to the Cobb after supper and watched the firework display that followed the torchlight procession – the latter was more spectacular, they marched down the Cobb and its curve was traced in light. Charlie and Pat Greenberg were also there, complaining the fireworks were let off too slowly; Pat with her usual infuriating need to comment on everything verbally. She is Candida in 'The Cloud', I realized that the other day.[3] I don't know where this typically but not uniquely transatlantic habit comes from: whether it is a symptom of cultural inferiority or just of sheer egocentricity. Much nicer were the slow Devon and Dorset voices around us: personally I liked the way they let off the rockets one at a time. To go for aesthetic effect instead of showing how much money had been spent would have been *very* un-West Country.

19 May

With Anna and Nick, who are here 'tying up' the wedding in July, to Bicton. I stole a *Tibouchina* cutting; the dove-tree in bloom, very pretty.

On the way back, we stopped at the tomato nurseries and I went and bought some; and as I waited for them to be bagged, I heard a wood-lark up the hill – the first for very many years, and acutely moving. I think partly because all it meant to me is incommunicable in ordinary life. I said nothing when I got back to the car, though I could hear the bird still singing, above the traffic. It is all I am trying to return to in *Daniel Martin.*

23 May

To London. Tom has forced me to appear at the Cape sales confer-ence. I do less than well, as always on such occasions. They want some turned speech, wit; all I do is sit down and ask for questions. We went with Fay and Tom to see Chabrol's *Nada* that evening. It is supposed to be more serious than his other work; but turns out to be the usual agreeably stylish nonsense. *Nada* indeed. Afterwards to a *crêperie* in South Molton Street, which Fay is doing for her *Evening Standard* column; Tom at his usual best-demanding worst. *Private Eye* is lampooning the two of them currently – how the disadvantage of being 'done' by Fay

---

[1] G. H. Locket and A. F. Millidge were the authors of *British Spiders* (Ray Society, 2 vols, 1951).

[2] To mark the 1200th anniversary of the founding of Lyme Regis.

[3] In JF's short story, Candida is a rather loud and officious child, who is described as 'always underlining the obvious'.

is the presence of her 'over-excitable' husband. I think he was putting it on for us.

In the evening we went to see the Russian space film, *Solaris*; a much deeper and better picture than *2001*; strangely moving in places, with an impressive slowness and concentration on the humanity, not the gimmickry. A very clear case of socialist humanity winning all hands down over capitalist superficiality: terrible that *2001* should be seen everywhere, and this complex masterpiece nowhere.

25 May

To Darlington, for our visit to Dan and Hazel. He was there to meet us, with two of the kids; a very fine Victorian station – York is another. To Great Ayton, where they live in a rented house in a little terrace; quite a pretty village, a stream running through it, the Cleveland Hills close behind. They took us off almost at once to see the house they have just bought in another street. It is an old shop with a pretty ornamental front, Georgian-looking though the house is Victorian, martins' nests under the eaves. Inside it was less attractive, very run-down, everything to be done, daunting; which we had to hide. Apparently Hazel is far from happy with the move from Norwich, and not sure about the house. There's a kind of aggressive fecklessness about the two of them: the idiocy of having another baby at this time – she's due in three weeks; of taking on a major rehabilitation and move simultaneously with that. The baby, it seems, is her price for being forced to give up her medieval archaeology at Norwich. The place is nicer at the back – it was once a smithy; various old sandstone barns, a long garden.

30 May

Back to London.

That evening we went to Tom and Malou's party, to celebrate the publication – *enfin* – of his book on money.[1] He also has a film of *The Romantic Englishwoman* in prospect, Joe Losey to direct. Apparently (we learnt the next day) they felt the party failed, as not enough media people turned up; but I managed to enjoy it – all the 'circle' was there. The Weskers, Tom and Fay and so on. Also Jud and Monica, who didn't want to see us, I don't really know why. Melvyn Bragg, whom I talked to; Alan Brien and Jill Tweedie, to whom I didn't. I was introduced to Losey ('Hello, where's the food?' Perhaps he knows I think him a sham). Bragg was rather carefully smooth; the television work has done him no good. After we left, David Mercer became very drunk. Apparently he has problems – his last play failed. Arnold is a bit the same, complaining (in his much more self-humorous way) about his failure as a playwright

[1] *The Money Motive: A Study of Obsession*, published by Hutchinson.

in this country; but since he recently had three productions opening in three European capitals, I take that with a pinch of salt. They want too much from reality, theatre men.

11 June

To Steepholm, the BBC are doing a television programme on Betty Allsop. We turned up the previous night and stayed in a hotel, with the producer and writer of the programme, and Betty and Mandy – at BBC expense. Two sharp and cynical young men, of the kind I detest; they have both an inferiority complex about the medium and an aggression – very similar to the Fleet Street attitude. They cling to their cynicism, their Tam ratings, their professionalism; they mocked the *Open Door* series, where amateur groups are allowed to produce their own programmes – their ineptitude and clumsiness. Which one can't deny; but that seems a small price to pay to be relieved of such cocksureness about what people can be allowed to see and *how* they see it. These two also went in for curious little in-joke exchanges, tell-tale lapses into funny accents; I'm not quite sure how far removed this is from staff-officers playing war with cannon-fodder.

The island itself was dominated by thousands of pairs of herring gulls – nests with eggs at every step, and the chicks, which flounder about as helpless as penguins. The vegetation dry, the smell of guano everywhere. Shrubs and grass must be got back. But the essential thing is to see whether the money can be raised; I begin increasingly to doubt that.

1 July

Fay comes with Hannah and the Bat; her next baby is due this autumn. Hannah remains the same extrovert charmer as always; the Bat is more temperamental. Fay is muted, seemingly rather bored – whether with us, the children or herself isn't clear. She said one evening, apparently with some approval, that her father had stopped her going to university because it only unsettles women; but all her unattractive traits now spring from the chasm between her intelligence and her education. She seems either blind or totally apathetic socially and politically; or perhaps the aspect of their life which requires them to mix with so many articulate famous teaches a silence there. And then pregnancy; the archetypal mind-dulling thing.

Tom came on the Saturday, the usual sweep and upheaval, upsetting of the quiet little stew of women and children. He didn't press for games this time, perhaps the passage in 'The Cloud' has registered.[1] We had

---

[1] Tom Maschler provided an inspiration for the character of the restless TV producer Peter, who, JF writes in the story, 'is bored, the way people slump around . . . A ball to chuck around, anything, any outlet for normal energy'.

fun mackerel-fishing with Hannah; then all their home movies after supper – so many celebrated people, they will be collectors' items one day. The World Cup Final. He puts Hannah on the kids' trampoline on Monmouth beach; then must have a go himself. Childlike, his innocence and appetite, at times. It must come from Rita, his mother: at the age of sixty-something, she is having a passionate love-affaire with an Ethiopian younger than her son. Kurt went recently to Arnold Wesker to discuss his bad relations with Tom. Poor old man. I incline more and more to suspect whether he is Tom's father at all.

8 July
We drove to Southampton, to the BBC studios, to record my interview with Robert Robinson. He is bluff, outspoken, professionally *homme moyen* and quick to bully down pretentiousness; but all right, seemingly far less neurotic than most of his media similars. An odious hail-fellow-well-met producer called Hugh Pitt; I took against him on sight; they are the current age's equivalent of Victorian bumbledom and beadledom. Nonentity hiding beneath bossiness. I found the interview (not Robinson's fault, mine and the medium's) second-rate and inexact, but they seemed satisfied.

18 July
All this week, Anna and Nick are here, a constant rush-around for the wedding on Saturday. I play gloom to cheer them up; we laugh a lot, thank goodness. Ordering wine; tidying up, shifting furniture, flowers. The weather is everything it shouldn't be: grey and wet.

20 July
The wedding. I woke up early, still convinced, the light through the curtains, that it was cloudy; but by some miracle, a peerless blue day. Anna in a pretty brown dress with old gold trimmings, a flowery straw hat, a posy of yellow cotton-lavender and white artemisia flowers, with one sprig of marjoram I insisted she put in (having just reviewed Grieve for the NS).[1] Roy appeared to take her to Bridport; trembling terribly, poor man, the old hostile stare, though he tried his best. The close family set off in a kind of speedy cortège, but the traffic was bad, we got to Roper's office only just in time; then a clerk interminably and laboriously writing out details before Roper himself appeared to read the act. It seems an empty farce; like some licence one should be able to buy at the post office.

Then back home, and all the guests arriving: Anna's college friends, Nick's endless relations. Podge appeared with his new lady friend, Hilla,

[1] JF had reviewed a reprint edition of *A Modern Herbal*, by Maud Grieve (Dover, 1971).

who turns out to be a gushing Anglo-Indian lady in black. Podge himself with a beard, looking even more the professional gadfly than ever. The Tringhams. We had all the food and the drinks on the lawn, and it went on all afternoon.

A family dinner at the Tytherleigh Arms. I sat next to Judy; a brave woman, she has so many troubles to face. The terrible thing with Roy is his humourlessness, his grimness; his bouts of silence, then flashes of his old self, when he had to dominate conversation by speaking too loudly, too positively, so that one doesn't really hear what he says but wonders why he is saying it like this. As we were leaving he took me aside, a little speech about how wonderful it was we could finally 'get together like this' – as if it were something other than his own incapacity to forgive that had ever prevented it. I think I have never met him – even our very first meeting, when Eliz had just left him – without this speech. His mind is quite remarkably structured on a pattern of resentment and forgiveness; it's almost an Old Testament thing, like Rebow in *Mehalah*.[1] All sins, confessions, guilts, metaphysical charge sheets; he believes in an angry Jehovah and of course has played it also all his life. He apparently writes no more; and is now 'retired' from his job on what is called an incapacity pension. I said something about hoping that things would improve for him, and got a very sombre stare. 'I'm afraid things aren't going to get better for *me*, John.' I would dearly love to know what dreadful trauma of childhood made him the man he is.

24 July
Another pat from the bitch goddess. Literary Guild will make *The Ebony Tower* their shared main choice for January; a guarantee of $50,000.

21 August
A whole chain of publicity interviews. Last Thursday I had Lorna Sage, who teaches Englit at Norwich, a rather fierce and nervous blue-stocking, a spatter of questions so subtle I kept on not understanding them; smoking even more cigarettes than myself. Then Friday, and the BBC TV people again, Robert Robinson. He interrogated me on the gazebo, very determined to keep me down to size, to provoke, to send me up a little. But I prefer his man-in-the-street commonsensicality to polite oil. Monday, an uncomfortable little man called Mellen, half Australian, half French, twilit, ambiguous sexually and in many other ways, thrusting the microphone almost into my mouth and his own face close behind, leechlike eyes; very odd. Tuesday, Mark Amory from the *Sunday Times*, a cousin of the

---

[1] In *Mehalah* (1880), a novel by Sabine Baring-Gould (1834–1924), Essex land owner Elijah Rebow tries to force a young woman, Mehalah, into marrying him. His unrelenting passion leads to the destruction of both of them.

Knightshayes Amorys; a suited Old Etonian bachelor, with a weird high pitch, almost a squeak, to his voice when he was excited; he gave more a sense of impotence than of homosexuality. I enjoyed the interview with him best; which no doubt means that it will come out in print the worst.

These interviews are all something of a face and imposture, of course. Robinson asked at one point why I wrote so clearly and explained so cumbrously; to which the answer can only be that I write so clearly because I explain so cumbrously. None of them understands the unconscious element in writing; and that 'explaining it' is a very secondary aftermath. Then they expect the arranged answers of a performance; not the conflicting, blurred haphazard of the truth.

On Sunday a meeting of the Ken Allsop Trust. It seems, after all, that we shall get Steepholm.

22 August
For some time now, vein swellings on my left leg that have begun to throb and ache. I went to the doctor this evening. He says varicose veins, a lack of muscle tone, too much sitting about, I must walk at least two miles each day, lose weight, wear a stocking. It depresses me very much; a feel of a condition that is irreversible.

23 August
Eliz away to London, then on to Suffolk with Betsa for some art course. We have been at some sort of nadir of contrariness ever since the wedding. She goes resentfully, because I feel too tired, too deep in the wretched hollow time between proofs and publication, to follow such resentment – against Lyme, the August crowds, my books, the publicity, everything – to its lair. I am to blame, when life is to blame. I longed for the peace of her being gone; her perpetual brooding and mulling; so much that I can't write, which is what I imagined I would do. Just wallow in the silence, in the luxury of not having to find something to say, of having bites to eat when I like. Old Wiscombe brought in a lobster, and I ate that; a bottle of Pouilly Fumé, then listening till three to the Goldberg. Solitude, and insomnia because I did not want to lose it in peopled sleep.

The Oxford chapters in *Daniel Martin*: many problems. With 'Jane' the same kind of thing I had with Sarah Woodruff. Such characters are rather like my litle green whirlers in the butterwort leaf; won't be pinned. One has not only the ordinary problems of dialogue form and tone, but the additional one of the character 'behind' being shifting, fluid, unpredictable. That is, I don't quite know what I want her to be. This polymorphism, this shimmer, is valuable, of course – or potentially so. But if mountaineers climb 'because it is there'; how much more peculiar we are – not only the climbing, but the difficult mountain as well. The temptation is to simplify, to facilitate the slope for oneself. In practice it comes out as the character giving simpler answers or explanations of herself than the whole can afford. It isn't a technical problem. But a psychological one: reifying what is unknown in one's own past – and therefore, present.

26 September

Good reports of *The Ebony Tower* in the American advance reviews – especially in that of *Publishers Weekly*, the most important. My chances are far less here; I expect the same as before, the curate's egg kind of sentence. They aren't improved by an article on me in the *Sunday Times* last weekend; Amory's. My fault: he simply transcribed all the chatty and silly bits off the tape he made.

27 September

The finished LB edition – much nicer than the Cape this time. But with such printing and production problems, comparison is hardly fair.

28 September

A finished copy of *Shipwreck*. Better than I had expected.

3 October

First reviews: the *Times, Telegraph, Guardian, Express* good, the *Mail* bad (I am 'turgid'). Tom Maschler is delighted, anyway, and calls it 'a turning-point for Fowles in England'. I suspect he's seeing too soon a summer from too few swallows. He printed 15,000, is reprinting 5,000 more; which is sheer optimism, in this year of grace. Most of the reviews have mentioned 'Eliduc' favourably, and T has graciously conceded there.

Strangely, this time, publication hasn't stopped me going on with *Daniel Martin*; this hasn't happened before. Circumstances must stop me now, though. We go to London for ten days on the 7th, via Bristol. America in November. And possibly Israel this winter: Jud and Monica Mennel are clearing out of England, for tax reasons. Jud is to teach cinema for a year at Tel Aviv University.

7 October

To Bristol, to George's bookshop, for my signing session; a great pile of books, a whole window to myself, like a monkey in a cage – and not one that people wanted to see, apparently. I think we got rid of seven copies in an hour. Odd, suspicious looks from the customers; only two girls, who each bought two copies, to salve my ego; and a strange young man, who was 'a close friend of your cousin Sally Fowles'. Sally who? He seemed very shocked that I declined the relationship. I must know her, she came from South Africa, and her sister Dorothy was here as well – which only deepened the mystery.

Lunch afterwards with John May, who runs George's; a shrewd and knowledgeable man, with a vaguely pugnacious Somerset accent. The Cape people showed him a proper deference. Then we drove all the way down the M4 to London.

I go out; and buy a nasty review in the *New Statesman*. I am relieved that I have stopped reviewing for them myself.

In the evening, to Chalcot Gardens, for my grand inaugural tour of the house Tom and Fay have bought; the circle's opinion seems to be that they have made a mistake, and I had to feel the same. Not an attractively organized house; and they have made it worse by reinstating the walls that Karel Reisz and Betsy Blair[1] removed and painting the walls a singularly unattractive Pompeian red. All their nice old wooden furniture now looks out of place. They need something much more baroque and formal to carry that kind of colour background. Odd, it feels like an elementary wrong move in chess; and from two masters in shrewd positional self-improvement.

We all went out to darkest Kilburn for a Greek (Cypriot) meal; I enjoyed it, but it made me ill for days afterwards; perhaps because we drank a bottle of retsina each.

Also, this day, an idea for a sci-fi novel; taken in part from Mercier's *L'An 2440*[2] and from my 'contact' with Christopher Priest.[3] I wrote a first few pages: a man rescued from Earth in its last days of self-destruction, called by his new masters, mistresses rather, to account for what went wrong.

15 October

A brief radio interview at the BBC, where I was obliged to give an imitation of an expert on shipwrecks. Then to meet Tom, just back from Frankfurt, to advise him on his new garden. We went off to the Clifton Nurseries in Maida Vale, at breakneck speed, leaving a trail of infuriated other drivers behind us (one screamed 'Fuck you!' to be heard the whole length of Eton Avenue); but T was rather delightfully bewildered by the variety of plants, the slowness of it all. He ought to have been shocked by the prices, too.

He's just been secretly to Switzerland from Frankfurt, fishing for a Noël Coward biography from Coward's onetime boyfriend. And there met the Chaplins and their royal highnesses from Monaco. Charlie is very old, it seems. He was offered a bouquet of flowers in plastic and

[1] Karel Reisz's wife.
[2] In *L'An 2440*, which was published in 1771, Louis-Sébastien Mercier (1740–1814) gave a Utopian vision of life in twenty-fifth-century Paris.
[3] The British science-fiction writer, who had just published his third novel, *Inverted World* (Faber, 1974).

tried to lean forward and do a little bit of 'business' over smelling them; nearly fell over, and had to be taken home. Tom sat next to Princess Grace and discovered I have another fan there. He said Rainier declared he hadn't read *The FLW* and wouldn't; he'd spent too much time watching his wife crying over it. Very peculiar.

Tom rushed back to the office, while I sat about the house with Fay and drew up a list of gardening instructions; a constant *va-et-vient* of nurse, carpenter, telephone ringing, suckling, Hannah clamouring for attention. Not cool at all, and I sense Fay begins to realize it.

Back home for drinks with Anthony Sheil and Lois Wallace, his new sidekick in the States, whom Tom M had warned me I would find 'an arrogant little bitch'. I thought she was mousy, rather than that; the book as product, all shop and selling. Then for a late supper with Tom and Malou; more moaning from Tom, but their patience, kindness, affection are all real qualities.

24 October

A foul cold has descended on both of us. Eliz in bed two days, then me. I read Christopher Priest's novel, *Inverted World*: an interesting sci-fi idea, but again the human relationships were mainly cardboard. I'm not sure the whole genre is not based on a general new cultural inability to 'relate' to other human beings; only to fantasies, ideas, technologies, machines. This may also be why so many serious writers (consciously or unconsciously) avoid it.

Also William Palmer's booklet, *The Fiction of John Fowles* – first of the four promised (or threatened) monographs for this next year. Some of it is wildly unrelated to anything I recognize about my past and present as a writer; especially the influences he imagines for me – Dostoevsky, Conrad, J. S. Mill, Carlyle – the latter two of which I have never read, the first two of which I have little knowledge of or empathy for. Palmer did an academic paper some years ago on analogies between Hardy's *A Pair of Blue Eyes* and *The FLW*. I wrote to him at the time telling him to cool it. No recognition of my doubts in his book, no mention of Fournier; only *his* ideas of me exist.

It frightens me, this cloud of hypotheses; how all the false ones will be repeated by every lazy student of my work.

27 October

We are supposed to be going to New York a week today; both choked with catarrh, weak-feeling. And I haven't heard from Little, Brown or Ned Bradford since September 20th; which angers me. I doubt the wisdom of going now.

Most of the reviews here are in by now; and though I can't complain personally, I do generally. Few are more than a paragraph or two. And running through virtually all of them is a ludicrous misunderstanding, they simply don't know what I'm writing about – all this is betrayed in the story summaries, the shorthand travesties and downright errors of fact. Virtually all fiction now is reviewed on the assumption that it is not worth serious discussion – lack of interest leads to lack of space, leads finally to lack of even the most elementary sort of accuracy. The miracle is that there are still readers who buy books. *The Ebony Tower* is on the bestseller lists. It cannot be thanks to the reviews.

I expect, perhaps forlornly, better of the States. I think I could even welcome nothing but bad reviews there – just as long as they are seriously bad, hostile at length. Enough of these indifferent lying scraps of praise and damnation. They are not worth the paper they are printed on.

All explicable in terms of the visual revolution, of course; but I don't fully understand why the disease is strong in this country. Perhaps it is simply that we impose so many restraints on ourselves in other spheres of life, indulge in so much wordy and puritanical gloom over politics, economics, the state of the nation, that the media apply a ruthless *laissez-faire* to their arts pages. The baseness of the circus is to compensate people for the shortage of the bread.

31 October
To London. We both feel ill, the wretched catarrh and bronchitis. I re-read Valéry's *Monsieur Teste*; a ferociously French classic, and invigorating.

27 November
A really strange coincidence. I learn that last week a Labour MP, John Stonehouse, disappeared mysteriously in Miami. He apparently went swimming, was never seen again; rumours of financial swindling on his part, Mafia involvement. It is the first such case since 1765. It was precisely because the contingency was so unlikely that I chose it for 'The Enigma'.[1]

M seems finally to have sold the house at Leigh, nominally for £14,750, but probably less after the surveyor's report comes through.

28 November
Anna and Nick came over to supper, Anna very distinctly not happy with her teaching and envious of our 'exciting' life. They have decided to leave London as soon as Nick is finished at the RCA.

---

[1] 'The Enigma' begins with the disappearance of an MP called John Marcus Fielding, who was last seen entering the British Museum. Although in JF's story what happened to Fielding remains an enigma, Stonehouse, who had attempted to fake his own death, was found living under a false name in Australia a few weeks later. A British court eventually convicted him of theft, fraud and deception, sentencing him to seven years in prison.

29 November
Back to Lyme; it clouds over, there must have been a lot of rain, but the country is such a relief: its being used, tended, full of birds and beasts, wild and tame; almost toylike, some child's loved plaything after the emptinesses, the nature-indifference, of America. Perhaps the essential disharmony really does lie here – not only because I like to think it does.

An interesting letter from a student, pointing out parallels between *Great Expectations* and *The Magus*. Since I taught the book at St Godric's, and have always liked it best of Dickens' work, she may have something.

2 December
We are having a bad dose of jet-lag. We went to bed at midnight last night, I had an appointment with the dentist for eleven-thirty this morning. We slept through the alarm and woke at one-thirty. I spent the whole of this afternoon reading back through this diary, less out of interest in it than to try to remember how you write.

Tom has sold 17,500 copies of *The Ebony Tower*, he thinks the best sale of short stories since the war. Ned writes to say the book will be on the *NY Times* bestseller list next week. Anthony has heard that of *Time* as well.

8 December
Oldfield, our bookie-historian, drops an article on Jane Austen through the door. He can't write, but he ferrets away with pertinacity; and I think proves beyond doubt that the lady never stayed at Wings when she was here; the main reason being that it wasn't even built.[1] I checked through Wanklyn;[2] the house is not shown on either the 1796 or the 1813 maps; nor in the Marryat–Cruikshank prints of 1819; but it does appear in the 1832/3 Dunster print. It was obviously built in the 1820s – a good two decades after her visits of 1803 and 1804.

A terrible day, yesterday, most of the night, with Eliz. I've managed to catch the cold she had in New Mexico, we cannot settle down, the weather is very November-drear, I feel she is reducing me to the point where we must leave Lyme. I came back so wanting to work, and she makes it impossible: even when she is 'good' her loathing of this house and the town in winter broods over everything. The futility of living here, her boredom, my silence . . . And we live now in a dreadful state of disorganization. I really need another room for books and files, but they litter my study instead. I can sympathize with the menopausal side of it, the trauma of Anna having 'left' her (though I am not sure that is not as much female

[1] Jane Austen visited Lyme Regis in 1803 and 1804. Wings was a large house near the Cobb harbour in Stile Lane. It was demolished in the 1940s.
[2] Cyril Wanklyn's historical guide to the town, *Lyme Regis: A Retrospect* (Hatchards, 1927).

folk-myth as anything actual), the much less mythical martyrdoms of the writer's wife. But I do not know how else we are to live, what can prevent us sinking into the kind of misery that affected Hardy and Emma Lavinia:[1] the dreadful feeding on each other's faults, the slide into a kind of sour apathy, the rage I feel that she will not admit that I live, economically as emotionally, by my imagination, her rage that I cannot see that I have 'reduced' her to a kitchen drudge. I suppose we void something in these vilely stupid sessions of accusation and counter-accusation; but they come so often now, and I begin to find them profoundly disturbing and debilitating – and intolerably endless in prospect, since I think leaving here would do no more than provide a fresh décor. No permanent cure.

But she wakes up as if nothing had been said, almost gay; as if last night were a play about two other people on the television. She travels so much faster through the cloud-and-sunshine of emotions than I do.

20 December
London, we have dinner with Tom and Malou; David Jones, the Royal Shakespeare Company producer, and later his wife Sheila Allen, who is playing in *Cymbeline* currently. Jones is a quick-minded Welshman, one of the few of that race I have felt I could like. Tom goes on endlessly about Arnold Wesker, who is suing the RSC because they refused to put on his play about a newspaper office. They had no legal obligation to, but Arnold is out for blood. Apparently the actors unanimously refused the parts offered; Arnold is going to law on the grounds that they shouldn't be allowed to dictate policy, which hardly seems in accord with his much-publicized views on co-operative art.[2] Jones and I think he is wasting time and money, Tom struggles for some saving principle.

From all of which we are finally saved by Sheila Allen. She has always seemed to me an unnecessarily harsh and strident actress, but it must be her stage persona – or the hazard of casting; a placidly definite woman with bruised eyes and a slightly bulbous nose; energy to spare, of course. She recalled Glenda Jackson and Monica Sharrocks. Her costume for Cymbeline; she can't move in it, can't 'point a line'.

21 December
Shopping for our Christmas in Yorkshire. I buy Dan a book on sixteenth-century Durham, a first of Bagehot's *The English Constitution*

[1] Thomas Hardy's first wife Emma Lavinia Gifford.

[2] In 1960 Wesker supported a resolution at the Trades Union Congress, number 42, which recognized 'the importance of the arts in the life of the community'. He subsequently founded Centre 42, an organization that aimed to make the arts available to a working-class audience. The play that the RSC refused to put on was called *The Journalists*. Wesker sued the company for £25,000 but eventually accepted a settlement.

for £2; a *Diary of Sir Henry Slingsby*, meant for Dan, but which I find too fascinating to relinquish; then Pulman's *The Book of the Axe*, the 1854 edition, and in nearly first-class condition – this for £10. Round Lyme it fetches £30 or more.

23 December

By train to Middlesbrough, a fine clear winter's day, soft green and blue distances, the ploughed browns, up through champaign England.

We changed at Darlington, on to a crowded little train to Middlesbrough, students and workers returning to Teeside; landscapes so polluted, forlorn and ugly that they have almost a beauty. Dan to meet us at Middlesbrough, where we bought some drinks. They have their new house at Great Ayton into shape, or as much shape as their own dislike of order (equals pretension) and the three boys will allow. It has a sort of distinct personality, this house, and the garden; a village character that is pleasant.

Our new niece, Kate; a nice, solid, equable baby, always smiling, grey-blue eyes and brown-blonde hair. She lies on her stomach and 'swims', exactly like an infant seal. The boys seem rather endearingly affectionate towards her, under their boisterousness.

Round to see M, in Marwood Drive, where she moved in a fortnight ago. The atmosphere – and not only because of all the old furniture and nick-nacks – is strikingly similar to that of Fillebrooke Avenue; the same quiet little suburban anonymity and uniformity. But the bungalow is much better for her; better organized, neat and draught-proof. We are pleased with it, and M seems to have a new lease of life.

25 December

Christmas dinner, preceded by the grand present-opening in the old shop turned living-room; the boys tear feverishly at their gifts, their voices high-pitched. Some get tossed aside almost as soon as revealed, others carried round. The baby croons and laughs, all this noise and colour and sound of torn paper.

26 December

A walk over the wet fields east of the village; then back to 'Granny's', where I clear out the garage and its still boxed piles of all the things she ought to have left behind in Leigh.

27 December

Back to London. News came while we were away that Stonehouse, the missing MP, has reappeared in Australia. Today the *Evening Standard* rang up to ask about the coincidence with 'The Enigma'; the first public sign that the coincidence has registered.

3 January 1975
Eliz departs for London.

I don't feel well, I smoke too much to be able to eat, keep absurd hours; but I am safely back on *Daniel Martin*, with the first twenty chapters solid; now moving on into second half. Dialogue flows, future situations float down from nowhere; I spend a lot of time just sitting and listening to all the messages from the unwritten. It is not so much that they are valuable, these messages, when one comes to the point in the writing; but they are like some form of melting, or heating, process, very needed in this book I have so often dropped; one has to make it malleable again; spring its frozen winter.

16 January
Eliz returns.

18 January
A long letter from Jud Kinberg, who departed for Israel without leaving us his address: Monica is pregnant again, he is trying to produce two films with his Tel Aviv University students. He wants us to go there, but I want to write now.

19 January
The Ebony Tower is fifth on the *New York Times* list (sixth week on).

I've managed to get a copy of Philip Magnus's biography of Kitchener – for *Daniel Martin*. I can't for the life of me remember now why I picked on the old boy for Dan's projected film script; but my goodness, how well he suits – or could suit, if I weave this theme in richly enough. A very strange character, Kitchener – so many pre-echoes of T. E. Lawrence, even down to the harshly suppressed homosexuality.

12 February
Daniel Martin. I have now reached Thorncombe. A first dim glimpse of an end.

The Ebony Tower has risen to fourth on the *NY Times* list; they even remarked on the oddity last week. Short stories are not meant to be there.

14 February
I've been sent a very solid biography of Alain-Fournier, for a puff; it's by Robert Gibson, Professor of French at Kent University. So back into all that world again; he has some new facts, or new to me.[1]

---

[1] The book was called *The Quest of Alain-Fournier* (Hamish Hamilton, 1953).

20 February
Drove down through Honiton to Sidmouth, where we had arranged to meet Eileen Porter. Lovely, after all the rhubarb of the preceding twelve hours, to hear her Anglo-Irish precision, love of words, sharpness, absurdity. She is one of those rare people who makes one think twice about one's own common usages; that kestrel quality in the Irish I admire, an astringency. She had a row the other day at an Oxford party with Iris Murdoch, who has taken against the IRA; and described how John Bayley came 'creeping' everywhere after her trying to apologize, under the mistaken impression that Eileen was Olivia Manning. Eileen chortles and chortles, inventing dialogue, prolonging the moment when the poor man is let off the hook and told who she really is.

At tea, when we are home, she suddenly fishes in her handbag and produces a twopenny notebook and reads out a letter from the sixteenth-century Erse, translated by Miles N'Gopaleen. Tongue in her cheek; as always.

Hours of talk about Faith and Elizabeth (Mavor) and Haro and Christopher Tolkien; strange forgotten world, but pleasing. So much of what she says of Oxford confirms what I have already written in *Daniel Martin*.

26 February
The 'Rain' chapter in *Daniel Martin*: it has been difficult, the changing of key – to blend the domestic with the deep past; but it must be so, the first spring of feeling in the man.

27 February
Not for the first time, the filmbiz side of my life tumbles into Restoration comedy. Tom M told me earlier this week that Zinnemann liked *The FLW*, and was strongly interested in doing it; and that, that being so, we could drop Lester Goldsmith and raise the money on Zinnemann's name.[1] But tonight he telephoned to warn me that Lester had decided to have a weekend in Lyme and might call and that I mustn't breathe a word of the Zinnemann interest to him. And if I was too busy, I should refuse to see him. I say, it doesn't matter, Tom and Malou Wiseman are coming for the weekend . . .

Whereupon it emerges that Tom's new novel (which Tom Maschler thinks will sell well) has also just been submitted to Zinnemann – by

---

[1] Fred Zinnemann (1907–1997) had built a reputation as a leading Hollywood director with films such as *High Noon, From Here to Eternity* and *A Man for All Seasons*. His most recent film, *The Day of the Jackal*, had been a considerable box-office success and in 1974 received six BAFTA nominations, including Best Film and Best Director.

Tom himself.[1] Tom Maschler discovered this only on Monday, when
he asked Anthony Sheil (whom I've talked Tom W into leaving
Deborah Rogers for) for a loan of the typescript top copy in order to
photostat it. 'I can't do that,' says Anthony, 'Mr Wiseman wants it for
Fred Zinnemann.' Tom M extracts it, on the promise that he will have
it copied that same day. Meanwhile Zinnemann appears at Cape to
discuss filming *The FLW*; and while they are talking in Tom's office
his secretary brings in the photostatted top copy, which he promptly
sends by special messenger back to Anthony Sheil to send on to Tom
Wiseman to take round to the man sitting six feet away from Tom
Maschler.

Now of course I am faced with sitting at a table with Tom Wiseman
and Lester and having to lie in different ways to both.

Zinnemann himself is coming here with Tom Maschler on Tuesday.

American paperback sales of *The Collector* now total 1,080,000; of *The
Magus*, 970,000.

1 March

With Tom and Malou and Boris into Exeter. We went round the
maritime museum there; then an antiquarian book fair, with plenty of
nice things, but no decent prices. Tom W seems all set for a success at
last, but the poor man is so dependent on some sort of triumph for
survival that I'm not sure if he can ever be satisfied; he says he has to
write a book every two years, and raise £7,000 a year from it; short of
bestsellerdom, a formidable proposition. It's a strain with them in
Exeter, they are so metropolitan and un-English; Tom himself seems
to have at least two senses missing, tone and colour – no interest in
either music or art. He wanders, abstracted, thinking of anything but
what he is looking at.

The Ebony Tower is sixth on the *NY Times* list.

2 March

We went out for a walk on Charmouth Beach, but Tom's Citroën has
something wrong with its suspension, they threaten now to stay over
until Tuesday, and we shall be literally down to the screen scene from
School for Scandal, with Zinnemann arriving at eleven o'clock.

Meanwhile, that evening, Lester Goldsmith appeared with his girlfriend,
a production secretary, Claire Rockcliff, from Wolper Films. He now has
a cherubic crop of curly hair; intends, or so he claims, to emigrate from
California to London; they have spent their weekend fossil-hunting, and

---

[1] Set in Nazi Germany during the Second World War, the novel was called *The
Day Before Sunrise*.

he even tried to take the girl on our expedition through the Undercliff of last time.

I had a little business whisper with him on one side. Somehow he knows Zinnemann is interested; about which I pretended to know nothing; and of course presumed he, Lester, was 'in' on any deal. By an additional twist of madness he has also read Tom W's book, and he said he was interested in that as well, if he could 'figure' a way to raise the six million dollars or so he thinks it 'needs'.

3 March

A dreadful morning as we start trying (at eight o'clock, I keep waking at seven these days) to find a garage to fix the Citroën; there is one at Portesham, behind the Chesil Bank. So Tom limps off in his car there; then Tom Maschler rings, and I have to tell him the Wisemans will probably be here tomorrow and we start working out what to do about that. Then Tom M says he is going to tell Lester today he is out of the Zinnemann deal, which makes me angry; once again I am cast as the nigger in the woodpile – I have him to dinner, then I sack him. Loathsome double-dealing world.

An hour later Tom M rings to say that mercifully Zinnemann has cried off for tomorrow. Now he will come next week. My guess, to crown the absurdity of this weekend, is that he has decided to take Tom Wiseman's novel instead of mine. I hope so, for Tom's sake – I shall in any case have to lie to convince Zinnemann I care a damn either way about *The FLW* being filmed. Writing *Daniel Martin* has cured me of all that. I'm not sure the film world isn't as it is with writing – far more fun in the setting up than in actually making the thing public.

(Afternoon.) Malou and Eliz had gone out to see Betty Allsop, and Tom was staring mournfully out of the window at the sea he dislikes; so I told him about what Tom M had done to 'poor' Lester, and dropped it in casually that it was all because Tom M now thought he saw a deal with Zinnemann. He met that without reaction, which was a reaction, of course. I took Boris out on Ware Cliffs. He drives us mad with his constant need to be amused, but he is a different child out on his own, much more charming and imaginative away from his scatter-brained mother and eternally worrying father. We came back at dusk, and I showed him Venus and the Dog Star, the twinkling and steady difference between a star and a planet. I said nothing lived on Venus. That's where the dinosaurs come from, claimed Boris. We saw a rabbit, he first; he liked that, both seeing it first and seeing it.

4 March

They go, and I ring up Tom Maschler to warn him that Tom W now knows. There is also a letter from John Calley, now president of Warner, saying he would be interested in Lester–Raphael,[1] then suggesting Lean, and finally Zinnemann. Lester G is told he is out of this new deal, and rushes from Roger Burford to Tom Maschler to find out what the hell is going on. Did I know, I can't have known, I was so nice to him on Sunday – whereupon Tom M has the effrontery to tell him he doesn't know what's going on either, but he'll try and find out from me.

6 March

A storm in a tea-cup at Lyme. Recently John Oldfield brought me in the results of his researches into Jane Austen's stay here in 1804; and 1803 as well, possibly. It virtually disproves the myth that she ever stayed at Wings. I rewrote the article for him, and then rang up Chessell, the mayor who is also the museum curator, to see if he knew where the maps and prints we need for the article (which Rodney Legg is to publish in the *Dorset Magazine*) are. But his reaction was icy. Did I know that he himself was publishing a book on the matter? In the end he said he'd see if the museum had the material, but very grudgingly.[2] All last week poor Oldfield tried to get at the wretched things. Then Chessell announced that they could not be photographed because they were being 'overdone'.

We reported this to Rodney, who in his usual pugnacious way fired off letters left, right and centre. This morning Oldfield received a frigid letter from Chessell, arranging a date for the photography. However, Rodney is going to have his pound of flesh: the West Dorset District Council, who finance the museum, have been looking through their files and found that no accounts have been presented under Chessell's curatorship.

It's made us all laugh. Chessell is behaving more and more like a midden bantam, determined no one else shall share his little literary empire. He has a corner now in guidelets and booklets, all of them merely lifted from Roberts and Wanklyn.[3] For all his lack of education, Oldfield is ten times more a genuine local historian.

A fortnight ago the Council voted to erect a plaque on the site of Wings, saying that Austen had lodged there. A letter I wrote pointing out the improbability was headline news in this week's issue of the *Lyme Regis News*. Now Chessell claims he knew this all along, even though he presided over the council meeting of the week before and let the vote go through. He says the matter will be reconsidered.

[1] i.e., film director Richard Lester and writer Freddy Raphael.
[2] The museum was called the Philpot Museum and contained exhibits relating to Lyme's local history and its rich geological heritage.
[3] Twice mayor of Lyme in the mid-nineteenth century, George Roberts was a local historian who wrote a guidebook to the town, *Some Account of Lyme Regis* (J. Shackleford, 1882). For Wanklyn, see note 2 on page 168.

11 March

Fred Zinnemann and Tom Maschler appeared just after midday, having trained down from London. Zinnemann is a slight little man – he's sixty-eight years old – blue-grey eyes in a rather wizened face, a swollen vein on one temple; very polite and deferential, he might be a Jewish watch-mender. It turns out he's a great friend of the director George Stevens, who died earlier this week; as also of Willie Wyler. It was a grey day, but I took them out round the town for an hour. Z seemed pleased, in spite of all the problems; kept on turning to me: would that angle pass as Victorian, would that?

A nice lunch. He told us stories about Gary Cooper in their famous Western, *High Noon* – how as soon as he tried 'to emote', or to act, he was hopeless. Then working with Spencer Tracy, how Z would watch him mumble his way through a scene and fear the worst – and how it all looked ten times better, a fine performance, in the rushes. He told us this when we were discussing a casting for Sarah. The enormous difficulty of finding faces that 'worked' on screen – and how it had nothing to do with stage-acting ability. He cited Robert Stephens, and Olivier, as examples of fine theatre actors who couldn't ferry across.

On Sarah, we discovered that we both had a liking for Gemma Jones in the part, but Z warned that a studio might not wear such an unknown in box-office terms. On the studio, he wasn't against going with Warner but he wanted the picture in the 'right all-over production frame' – that is, not to be edged out by bigger projects; and he thought we might have to settle for Twentieth Century-Fox on those grounds.

An impressive, humane man, and he fills me with hope; though much still remains to dash it.

Not least Tom Maschler's part in all this: before they came, Roger Burford was on the telephone saying that Z had told Christopher Mann[1] that he didn't quite see what Tom's role was to be. Tom M rang back that evening when they got back to London, and I felt I had to warn him of this; which alarmed him, of course. Apparently, on the train both here and back, they had 'talked of nothing else'; and Z was content to see that Tom got an associate producer credit. But I still can't see what he will do once a production starts rolling, and I am frightened of the problems that might arise if Z feels Tom is in his hair – that is, of Tom's using myself to defend an untenable position.

At present he has plenty to do, of course. For a script we, or he, shall go first to Pinter, then to Stoppard.

Roger Burford rang me when I got back to Lyme. Zinnemann is trying to get backing from Warner; but producing himself.

---

[1] Zinnemann's agent.

16 March
The Ebony Tower remains fifth on the *NY Times* list; fourteenth week there.

I suspect the way people perceive time is one of the 'dark' areas of human self-knowledge. Of course we all censor the past, especially the personal past, on psychological grounds – at the dictates of our varying sets of Jungian complexes; and the past is censored for us also in the sense that we are ignorant (or forgetful) of vast areas of it; and finally we are condemned 'metaphysically' to only one angle of approach to it, the backward-looking. One can therefore know the past in any objective sense only by extrapolating it from personal distortion and general ignorance; by the judicious impartiality and prolonged research of the good professional historian. But I think the only way to historianize the personal past is through fiction; that is, by treating one's past self as a fictional situation – as a hypothesis.

All this comes from the way I am making Daniel Martin both 'marry' and diverge from myself. I think he may seem implausible finally (but in a way I don't altogether not want) because of this: too self-obsessed to be a plausible scenario-writer. A defect of the cinema is precisely that the medium makes the quasi-objective, or historian's, approach much the easiest – it may be bad history, but it is essentially objective in nature. In other words, it is very difficult to make a good film about oneself, because no one person can control all the functions that make up a community project. Fiction potentially allows this, of course, and perhaps even more widely than overt literary autobiography – which gives personal complexes too much power.

Similarly we all invent the future, both general and personal. I think the individual difference in time-perception really depends on the extent to which past and future are viewed metaphorically and hypothetically. Perhaps some people see both censored past and hypothetical future in a very direct, credulous way – they believe what they think they see, or imagine, in both directions. Others like myself (all novelists, probably) see their pasts and futures in highly metaphorical terms. They are primary ore, counters in a game, mere raw commodities before processing and refinement and manufacture.

I am not sure one cannot derive the human artefact almost totally from a sense of inadequacy in time-perception; as a kind of *horror vacui* – the vacuum being of ignorance as to what happened and what will happen. This would precede the artefact seen as passport to immortality, conqueror of time, etc. – a highly Renaissance concept. That view misplaces the emphasis on the achieved, the what-has-been-made, the perfect tense; instead of the older centre of what-is-being-made and what-is-making and who-maker, the varieties of present tense.

Society, the spectator and reader, is quite rightly interested only or mainly in the achieved state. It is the maker who must never forget that the having made cannot be severed from the making now; that is, he must be able to sever himself from actual past and future in a way that is probably not typical of most minds. An ability to do this may be very largely what we mean by 'artist'.

18 March
Bitterly cold, though clear, weather now for several days. Water froze outside last night.

22 March
I was down just above the bottom spring, at dusk, a still evening, it is not so cold; but a sudden strange little wind, the bamboos rustling. I look up, and there is a moon caught in the sallow catkins, at just that complex point of light, the sky dying but still blue, the moon a soft luminous white like an oil-lamp, the catkins, yellow with pollen, on their black twigs; a moment the greenest Zen novice would recognize; quite perfect, poised. The strange thing was the wind, as if the moon had breathed to make me look up.

Eliz in London a few days. With *Daniel Martin* I am at last in Egypt. Cairo. He has had his first glimpse of the fate I mean for him. Or I have had the first glimpse of the fate he means for me.

23 March
A thump on the study window, a frantic dashing of wings, a tit squawking for dear life; and I am staring at a fine male sparrowhawk, tawny and slate-blue, perched on the balcony rail just two feet outside the glass door. He caught nothing, except me.

A *TLS* review by Stephen Spender of David Sylvester's conversations with Francis Bacon; it makes me want to spit, Spender is such an inflated Twentieth-Century Establishment gasbag. I think Bacon is very much the same case as Beckett: lovely for comfortable 'intellectuals' to show how deeply *they* feel about the 'deep horrors of the human condition', etc., etc. Both men's work is in fact based on a highly selective cliché about mankind – that is, it is a very narrow view, and not an original one. It is simply conveniently pessimistic, a sort of inversion of Pangloss's philosophy; a cashing-in on a hypothetical worst of all worlds.

My objection is that this is unstatistical; but not that Beckett and Bacon see the world this way, as they have every artist's right to (on the one hand, and on the other very probably little choice in the matter). The Spenders would have the rest of us flawed if we do not see it so as well. Beckett and Bacon have a genius for style, for technique; not for thinking.

26 March
We wake up to snow; not very thick, and it thaws by midday, but it remains, especially after a phenomenally mild winter, vilely cold.

31 March
I am forty-nine; and feel it.

1 April
Denys and Monica come for a day or two. Denys now works at Concord College, and they live during the week in Shrewsbury. He seems much less harassed, a little return of his Spetsai self – diplomatic by nature, not in self-defence.

2 April
John Arlott, the cricket commentator, and his wife Valerie for lunch. He writes on cricket and wine for the *Guardian*; a flush-faced barrel of a man, and drinks heavily in his second field. Rex Cowan and the Gibsons – Arlott did a previous book on them[1] – brought us together. One senses a split man: the orotund Hampshire-bucolic voice, his contempt for the cricket establishment (he takes a typical North Country pro's line on all that) fight his collecting of fine wines and books. He has just written a sort of monograph on Krug champagne; stories about the hermetic snobbery of the family in Rheims, which Arlott evidently admired. Denys smoothed him up nicely. There is a little peasant fierceness in Arlott over guarding the knowledges he has acquired, his punditries. They have to be fed interest, as he has to keep drinking.

We drink altogether too much ourselves these days. I suffer permanently from it, waking up with monotonous regularity at seven with a nauseous stomach.

3 April
Hazel rings from Yorkshire. M has broken a femur in her leg and is in Middlesbrough General Hospital. It has been pinned. Denys and Monica seem vaguely shocked that I do not fly north at once.

4 April
We had lunch with them at Branscombe, then they went on their way. Eliz enjoys such company far more than I do, and I try to suffer it for her. All my reality is in the book, or in the fact that I am prevented from writing it. On the way home we stopped a minute or two beside the Axe,

---

[1] *Island Camera: The Isles of Scilly in the Photography of the Gibson Family*, written in collaboration with Rex Cowan and Frank Gibson and published by David & Charles in 1972.

where some forty or fifty wigeon were whistling and pairing themselves off, fighting and show-diving, almost like dolphins. They seemed like an oasis in the desert of these last few days.

It is not the Sharrocks' fault; perhaps this continuing and vile cold weather, which depresses me far more than rain. I feel the whole garden groaning under it.

A call from Hollywood. A George Schaefer, who wants to do a picture of *The Ebony Tower* – the title story. He talks too fast, especially when he is spelling out his high intentions (he wants to direct himself) on the artistic side. But he insists on French locations and a British cast. He offers $50,000 and 2½ per cent. Hustling, but that side is meaningless to me.

10 April

I go to the BBC, and do a half-hour broadcast recording for the schools programme, on the novel. An actor and actress read extracts; all nice people, but the atmosphere of the civil service. During a coffee break, the producer (Stuart Evans) told me that Gerry Mansell is tipped as the next Director General.[1] I think that sums the place up. It is strangely neutral, staid, castrated, like an elderly eunuch or an old maid; in so many ways, it reflects the deep spirit of the whole country over the last thirty years.

I catch the two o'clock train from King's Cross for Middlesbrough. I got to the General Hospital, where M is, before visiting hours, but they let me in: a clean, spacious ward, with three other women; a long picture window with a view of roofs and the arc-light towers of the football ground. M seems in good spirits, in fact rested and quite pleased with herself. The social worker for the ward told me later that M was 'the youngest 75-year-old she had ever encountered'. She remains also the most tactless, talking in a loud voice, with her three as yet unvisited companions obviously listening wide-eared for every scrap of conversation between us. I told her I thought she must go into a convalescent home as soon as the hospital released her; she swallowed that medicine as meekly as a child. I suspect she is enjoying all this mainly because it relegates her to her own adolescence, with all personal responsibility forbidden. She really looked remarkably well.

---

[1]Gerard Mansell, then the BBC's Managing Director of External Broadcasting, would be appointed Deputy Director General in 1977. He had been a next-door neighbour of JF when he lived in Hampstead during the 1950s. See *The Journals*, volume 1, page 366.

12 April

I went to talk with Fred Zinnemann in his Mount Street office; a rather old-fashioned and unostentatious penthouse. He is his usual gentle and soft-spoken self. He has seen Gemma Jones and Kate Nelligan; both are keen to do the part. He wants Orson Welles to play Mr Freeman. We discuss a fit actor for Charles – perhaps Robert Redford, even though he is so expensive, a million dollars or more (which of course he earns back in box-office receipts). Fred Z rates him third in this faculty for pulling in audiences, after McQueen and Nicholson; then Redford; Paul Newman next. I am anxious about his accent. But it seems Warner positively want it. Fred has already been told to make sure the voices are 'mid-Atlantic'. He says this is an increasing problem – American audiences complained in his last picture (*The Day of the Jackal*) of Edward Fox's voice in the assassin role. This appears to be a new tyranny of the medium; and yet one more death-blow to a native cinema.

Rather to my alarm Fred told me exactly the same stories about Spencer Tracy and Gary Cooper as last time; I do not like such anec-dotage.

Then he wants to start the film with Sarah's past, the shipwreck of the French lieutenant. I foresee difficulties getting a convincing sea, but he dismisses that. They can do miracles in the tank, these days. I don't have the courage to tell him that they can't, or not for this cinema-goer.

13 April

Sunday. We took the little back-line from South End Green to Kew Gardens; very crowded, a lot of London had had the same idea. But pleasurable as always, and I was able to attach some names to plants I grow.

That evening to the Maschlers; Beth was there,[1] though apparently Fay is fed up with her. They managed to convey a sort of mixture of exhaustion and boredom, whether with us or with life I'm not sure; like two inimical sisters at Versailles, perpetually scheming for something else and grander. Before dinner I had a private talk with Tom, who does not like my increasing familiarity with Fred Zinnemann; and won't sit quiet under his $10,000 and rotten 1 per cent. Suddenly he goes into a strange pantomime, dropping his voice and gesturing through the wall at the kitchen, where the women are, as if they might hear. He's in terrible financial trouble, he can't pay off the mortgage, he's had to sell the Chalcot Crescent house 'at a loss' (i.e., not at the boom price of three years ago), he can't borrow any more from his father. Touched by this tale of woe, or perhaps just dumbfounded that

[1] Fay Maschler's sister.

he is keeping it all so secret from Fay, I agree to propose $20,000 and 1 per cent. Even that doesn't really satisfy him – he thinks $25,000 is nearer the mark. It is strange, but he refuses to see that Warner, or whoever backs us, will not pay him for his past work; that it is his future contribution, which he now knows can't include much production work, that is being priced.

Fay did cook us a very nice supper. But there are some dreadful wrong values in this house.

We also heard, before we went to the Maschlers, that M has got to have a new pin in her hip bone. The first is being rejected. This means a new operation.

We returned to Lyme; another huge pile of mail. This endless talk of film business, meeting people I don't really want to meet, vile and endless fussing about nothing. My poor book – everything seems to want to tear me away from it.

16 April
Fred Z rings. For the first time he sounds faintly harassed. He thinks Tom's new demand is absurd; he can't ask for it; and can't speak to him about it for fear of endless argument. So will I please ring Tom (whom he wants to speak to about writers) and make him leave the matter alone? I do that. Tom is mortified, of course. I ring Roger Burford, and amend the prices back to the original figures.

24 April
A cable from Paramount in California. They are backing the film. Then Fred Zinnemann rings. He seems pleased. Apparently we were lucky – they were looking for a serious major project. I am to get $15,000 on signing, $85,000 if Fred is satisfied with the script, $75,000 deferred; all depends on a viable script and Fred's health, in effect. He and I have to pay for Tom, so will put up $5,000 and a ½ per cent each; and I have decided to let him have 10 per cent of the $85,000 as well.

3 May
Curious, on this very eve of our going to France again, two of the orchids I brought back last time and had marked Butterfly, and which flowered as Butterflies last year (poorly), have just opened; and they are Monkeys. That is, I must have put two Monkey Orchid tubers in the pot, which did nothing last year, but have survived into this.

3 June
To London, to meet George Schaefer, who is flying over with his films.

4 June

To old Norman, for books from his latest catalogue. He has not changed, the shop still a shambles, the catalogue impeccable in its scholarship. Most of what I wanted had already been bought by the Bodleian, he said they had taken fifty items this time.

That afternoon to see Roger Burford about all our film problems; the poor man looks increasingly ill. It is like being in Chancery, his endless talking on about the legal side – Dickens would have loved it, but I don't.

We go to the private cinema in Audley Square and meet George Schaefer, a man in his fifties, grey-haired and bespectacled. He seems pleasantly straightforward and reminds us both a little of Ned Bradford. That afternoon we saw his American TV series on Fitzgerald, based on the story 'The Last of the Belles'; impressive performances from every actor and actress he used. On that side Schaefer can't be faulted.[1]

5 June

Two more of Schaefer's TV films: one concerning the Belfast troubles,[2] and very impressive – once again, fine performances from Vivien Merchant (apparently the current secret scandal of London is that her husband, Harold Pinter, is having an affaire with Antonia Fraser) and Jenny Agutter. Then a film of a Rumer Godden novel, *In This House Of Brede*; dreadful Catholic slop about a nunnery, but again with some good acting. So we go to lunch at Scott's, and I tell him we're in business. He seems to lack the visual sense, or poetry, I would like in the best of all possible worlds, but I have confidence now in his general taste and skill with the 'cattle'.

Eliz has a mad desire to see Billy Wilder's *Front Page*, so we go on to see that; very professional, with Matthau and Lemmon in fine form. Then on to supper at Tom and Malou's.

Tom is unconsciously very funny now. Zinnemann and Twentieth Century have taken his novel (if all goes well, for shooting after *The French Lieutenant's Woman*) at a good price, and the book promises on the bestselling side. So the poor man has gained a whole set of new neuroses. How to keep all this sudden wealth? He is for fleeing abroad,

---

[1] Made for TV, *F. Scott Fitzgerald and 'Last of the Belles'* (1974), which drew on Fitzgerald's short story of that name, provided a semi-fictional account of how the author met his wife Zelda while he was stationed with the army in Alabama in 1919. It starred Richard Chamberlain as F. Scott Fitzgerald and Blythe Danner as Zelda.

[2] Called *A War of Children* (1972), the film was about two Belfast families, one Catholic and one Protestant, whose friendship is threatened by the outbreak of sectarian violence.

but Felton, who is advising him, says it is too early – I smile and enjoy it all.

Though Losey's film of *The Romantic Englishwoman* has been well received, Tom is expectably dissatisfied. He had a row with Losey after a press conference at the Cannes Film Festival. Apparently Losey went on and on about himself, in his usual style. Then some impertinent journalist asked why nobody in the film ever consummated the act of love, and Losey said he'd better ask the writer; whereupon Tom said that in the book the love scenes had 'gone through'. On the beach afterwards Losey accused Tom of 'putting him in the shit'. High words followed, ended by Losey smashing a wine bottle on the edge of the table. He then walked away. To Tom's eternal credit he snatched up a glass and threw it at the great sham's back – and got a direct hit on the head. All his female court rushed round in consternation, but Barbara Bray came up to Tom the next day and told him he had been right.[1]

As I've been telling him for years that Losey is a mountain of pretension, I much enjoyed this story. Tom, alas, remains clearly a little alarmed at his own courage. Burnt boats diminish his sense of security.

6 June
Back to Lyme. Anna and Nick arrived in the evening. Her old Beetle is on its last legs, so we are buying her a new one.

A dazzling dry spell, cloudless days; the garden groans.

17 June
A very unexpected telephone call, from 10 Downing Street – will we go to dinner there on the 30th, in honour of the Belgian Prime Minister? I immediately suspect a hoax, and play for time. But it seems genuine. Under Eliz's urging, I ring back later and accept.

18 June
A dreadful night with Eliz. This diary, how I traduce everything, never speak well of her in it, give only my point of view – and Anna and Nick, the terribleness of my relationship with them. I didn't say much to them last time they were here, but I get so tired of always having to make the conversation: my point of view. It's really rooted in my domestic isolation as a writer; never talking of books, writing, anything to do with literature, with anyone; as if I worked on another planet in another planet's profession.

---

[1] Barbara Bray had collaborated with Joseph Losey and Harold Pinter on an unrealized script of Proust's *A la recherche du temps perdu*. She went on to write the screenplay for Losey's 1975 film version of Bertolt Brecht's play *Galileo*.

30 June

To London, for our grand dinner. We went to Moss Bros and I hired a dress suit, and Eliz a black dress.

We drove up in a taxi at twenty to eight, were vetted by the policemen, allowed in: a large and pleasant eighteenth-century house, though it would be nicer without the marble busts of Disraeli and the rest, and the famous photographs of overfamiliar faces up the stairs. I chat with a flunkey on the first-floor landing while Eliz deposits her coat. No, the place isn't air-conditioned, it's all falling down. 'Pity the Yanks won't buy it, if you ask me,' he adds unpatriotically.

We go into an ante-room, shake hands with the Belgian Prime Minister, Tindemans, then Harold and Mary. She has strange, slightly goggled eyes, like fish eyes, a mouth askew, a general air of some new mad queen from *Alice in Wonderland*; doesn't hear, doesn't care, or so one feels. A very different woman from the one we met at Cheltenham a few years ago.

Inside, we chat with Tindemans' press attaché and a rather striking languorous creature, a Czech, we learn later; Mrs Diana Phipps, seemingly squired by Sir George Weidenfeld. He keeps on coming up and whispering things in her ear, one that seems well tuned to the inner world of the Establishment. Then a young MP appears and takes my arm. He is Ray Carter, a Birmingham constituency, loves my books, had to meet me; a jolly young man, bright-eyed and outspoken – and naive. We are joined by Mary Wilson.

'Do you know this man's novels?' says Carter.

'I don't like them,' says Mrs Wilson, very firmly. 'Too rich for me. Too complicated.'

Carter protested, and got snubbed.

'I like Arthur Hailey. He does such fine research and works it in so well. Except his last. There was too much violence. I hate violence in novels.'

Maudling, Callaghan, Speaker Selwyn Lloyd, various other notables.

The sixty of us troop into dinner, Eliz and I on opposite sides of the horseshoe, well below the salt, of course. A room with vulgar gold brocade-papered walls, Corinthian columns; Pitt stares down at us from beyond the head of the table. I sit opposite Jack Clayton, the film director, an amiable enough man, but with slightly mad, unsafe eyes. Between Michael Edwardes, porcine-faced, very self-serious, some kind of battery tycoon, prince of the export trade;[1] and a Mrs Donoughue, who works

---

[1] Michael Edwardes was chairman of the Chloride Group. He had a few months previously been appointed by the Wilson government to join the organizing committee of the National Enterprise Board, a new body set up to bring about the regeneration of British industry.

at Cape. She apparently once wrote to me about a book she intended
on Mary Anning.[1] Her husband, Eliz's partner, is Wilson's tame philosopher, head of his inner think-tank.[2] Though she didn't say, I suspect we
owed the invitation to them. There's some sort of attempt to Camelotize
10 Downing Street going on, it seems; to leaven statesmanship with
'culture'.

'Why did you come?' asks Edwardes.

I say, 'Just sheer curiosity. And you?'

'Pays me to keep on the right side of these people.'

Mrs Donoughue backbites her husband's employers a little. 'They
lack all visual taste. Totally. Harold is completely single-minded. He shuts
out everything else.'

He made a bad speech, Tindemans a better one. Toasts. The food
was quite good, one very fine 1961 Burgundy, though we were given
only one glass of it.

There was a reception afterwards, with many more guests. Edwardes
insisted I met his wife, an unhappy-looking little woman whom he spoke
to and prompted like a child, in spite of her obvious resentment.

'John is like you, he loves gardening.'

'Don't be ridiculous, I'm not interested in gardening at all.'

'But darling, you are . . .'

She grimaced.

Then there was a sudden surge of actors and actresses: Judi Dench
and her husband,[3] Patrick Garland, Michael Crawford; and suddenly it's
more human, no one knowing why they're there, all a giggle. Crawford
puts on accents, plays his TV role of the brick-dropping innocent; claims
he saw Wilson and Callaghan in the ante-room, heads in hands: 'Christ,
what a bloody mess we're in.' Carter brings a slightly drunk Mancunian
up to meet me – I think some newspaper correspondent, but I discover
later its the Minister for Sport.[4] Incoherent talk about abolishing test
matches, the one-day game's the thing, something your working man
can see. Then Weidenfeld breaks in, he's been dying to meet me, we

---

[1] Mary Anning (1799–1847) was a fossil hunter whose important fossil discoveries
near Lyme Regis, where she lived all her life, facilitated major progress in the
new sciences of geology and palaeontology.

[2] Previously a lecturer at the London School of Economics, Bernard Donoughue
– now Lord Donoughue of Ashton – was appointed Senior Policy Advisor to the
prime minister in 1974 and set up 10 Downing Street's Policy Unit.

[3] Actor Michael Williams (1935–2001).

[4] Denis Howell (1923–1998), subsequently Lord Howell, was sports minister from
1964 to 1970 and 1970 to 1979. He was not a Mancunian as JF thought, but from
Birmingham. After serving on Birmingham city council, he was MP for
Birmingham Small Heath between 1961 and 1992, and called a book of memoirs
published in 1990 *Made in Birmingham*.

must have an evening together . . . All the time his eyes twitch and dart round the room behind me, as if, eternal refugee, he can't even concentrate on this flagrant preliminary to a publishing pinch. He is a little mad as well. Then we meet other Tribune MPs around Carter; drunk and rowdy, mocking the surroundings.[1] Eliz talked with Harold about his haircutting problems, while Mary kept drifting past like someone in a bad dream, with glazed eyes. 'Oh God, look out, she's coming,' said Mrs Phipps at one point.

We stayed until it was politely suggested that we should go; and left with the Tribune Young Turks. They went bawling down the stairs, just like a football crowd after the match. Past the photographs of previous prime ministers.

'Hey, you'd look good there, Bill.'

'After you, old boy.'

Guffaws.

A posse of police waited gravely in the hall, where I also waited for Eliz to come down. Mary Wilson swept past, ignoring everyone. 'I've had enough. Where's my car?'

She swept out and was ushered into it. One red-headed young MP stood in the No. 10 doorway. 'Dare anyone to knock on the window. "Anyone seeing you home tonight, dearie?"'

They fell over themselves as the car left. My arm was seized one last time – the only other bearded man there, Illtyd Harrington, the deputy head of the GLC. He was drunk, too. 'Oh, Christ, what a bloody evening. People been mistaking me for you all the time. I'm bloody fed up. Everyone telling me what bloody marvellous books I write. I kept telling them, I'm just a rotten little local politician.'

It was a most bizarre and entertaining evening; and an instructive one in a way. Gibbon would have relished it. The decline and fall of a culture. I think not a soul there took it seriously, except perhaps Wilson and the Belgians. But the haunting figure was Mary Wilson's; she seemed quite clearly to me not in her right mind, something beyond a mere bad mood and evening. Which made her, if not in the usual sense at all, the soul of the party.

1 July

Back to Lyme. The Marsh Helleborines in flower. The terrible drought continues, it is now the worst for fifty years, they say; even my Californian trees, and the New Mexican grasses, are giving up the ghost.

---

[1] Tribune comprised a group of MPs within the Labour Party who advocated left-wing policies.

14 July

To London, to see the Dutch translator of *The Ebony Tower*, a young man called Kellendonk; his youngness, and muttered English, alarm me a little, but he seems to know the language well enough.

15 July

I went to see Fred Zinnemann in the afternoon. He was looking very fit and alert, as affable as ever, if one discounts the rather steely grey-blue eyes. He suggested recently a new ending in the British Museum reading-room, and asked my opinion, and I wrote him a little screed on the pro's and con's – about which he was very complimentary. 'Like being in a Rolls-Royce after a Cortina,' he said, rather unkindly to poor Dennis Potter. He let me glance at Potter's script, which is in long hand, laid out like a TV scenario; but I'm not to read it yet (or Tom Maschler, which is causing trouble).

In the evening, Fay's birthday party.

Fay shows us Tom's birthday card, which ends 'I shall love you always, always, always'; and somehow manages to suggest that he hasn't been loving her enough recently.

16 July

My French translator came in the afternoon; a nervous young woman, *assistante* at some comprehensive, called Annie Saumont. I have just checked her first chapters. Her style seems odd to me, but there are such problems – so many semantic nuances in English, such a free way with syntax, against the constant clamouring for 'logic' and clarity in French. She complains about the work, the poor pay. I feel guilty, having promised Israel at Albin Michel to let her have my revisions of the text . . .

So when she goes, work at it. In the central part whole chapters need changing; but suddenly the story, the idea of the book, catches me again; as well as all the mistakes I made in its telling.[1]

I don't feel well, constant pressure near my heart, I think some kind of indigestion or liver complaint, but it seems like the heart itself complaining – moments of weakness, swimming. The accursed nicotine. I drink far less these days, but need far more exercise. I wrote and wrote till after midnight, re-lost on Spetsai. No true novelist needs opium.

Nicholas was made too gullible on those first visits; and the Conchis side of things too literal. He does not have to believe, nor do they have to want to make him believe as they pretend.

---

[1] Having revisited *The Magus* for the French translation, JF decided to prepare a revised English edition to correct some of these mistakes. It was published by Jonathan Cape in 1977.

17 July

Fay brought the two children round. I like her best on her own, and the two little girls are delicious; they must be the prettiest and most engaging pair in London. We talked about the Weskers, who weren't at the party. Apparently Arnold the other day told Fay that she stood for everything he hates in life; and has been firmly crossed off her list for his pains – with Tom's support, since A is also being unscrupulous over a projected book; Tom's idea, but which he now proposes to put on auction. I know what Arnold means about so many aspects of Tom and Fay's life; but he misses a private, childlike quality about them (forgivable, the missing, in someone who doesn't know them well, but not in him) that may be distressingly amoral, apolitical and all the rest, yet redeems them. I think it is largely envy on his part. Because they are set fiercely for success, pleasure, only-the-very-best; and his secret self wants the degree, if not the kind. It is the fierceness of wanting he won't brook.

18 July

I worked all day on the revision of *The Magus*.

19 July

Back to Lyme. A letter from Schaefer. All goes well on that front. John Hopkins will do the script, S hopes by November.

24 July

Daniel Martin, the final chapter at Aswan, it's very difficult, I do a page or two at a time, then rewrite and rewrite; a kind of knife-edge. It is like groping in the dark; feeling the future of these two evading me; though knowing they are there, very real now. It is a prime sign that characters are 'real' when they grow so difficult; like trying to manipulate two people (or penetrate their privacy) in the actual world.

25 July

Eliz's 'party'; the Maschlers and the Tringhams, and we asked the Hudsons from Beaminster; friends of Anna and Nick's from London and Bristol. A fine day, we ate outside, played badminton, the children went swimming; drank Chablis, Pouilly-Fuissé, Quincy, Muscadet.

28 July

Anna and Nick depart for France. Fay has stayed on with the kids, though it is not a holiday; Hannah is ill, and loses all charm. Tom also is ill in London, some stomach upset. Fay looks exhausted, sits at breakfast quietly weeping one morning, while I quietly thank the gods that I have been spared the all-demandingness of children. The days close with endless meal preparation, which I find almost as draining a process as dealing with the kids at the other end of the day. This has become a territorial thing with Fay, food, and Eliz and I make all the appropriate signs of submission.

F was very sharp about Anna and Nick after they had gone to bed last night – why Anna had picked such an ignorant wet, what was going to happen when she saw through him. Strange, she was almost malevolent. I came to the conclusion it was directed at me, something sceptical she detects in my eyes about her and Tom's parameters of happiness; I was to be told there are grave problems in my own household. I do not like this sour streak in her – curiously paralleled in her palate, she likes only the driest white wines, sniffs at all my flowery nonsenses from the Loire – because it seems to hide an emptiness or lack of any value system outside that of 'style' or 'good taste'. She reminds me often of one side of Jane Austen – and also how Austen would have been delighted to observe her and nail that fault, or lack of moral content. Which doesn't mean that she might not have allowed Fay to be a flawed heroine of the Emma kind; redeemable – but Tom is no Mr Knightley, I'm afraid.

29 July
Tom appeared to drive the car back. He went back by train on Sunday, feeling too ill for the motorway. We took them to Bicton, where they played only-the-very-best down the herbaceous borders, things they might try at Chalcot Crescent; all feasibility sacrificed to display.

He came agog with news of the Fraser–Pinter scandal.[1] Apparently Pinter came down from Antonia's quarters at the marital home after their first night of passion to find the hall of the house thronged with newsmen, come to interview Fraser about some political matter. The most prized sabre-slash is Vivien Merchant's reference to Pinter's lack of shoes since he has decamped. 'But he can always borrow Antonia's. She has very large feet, you know.' According to Ronnie Payne, Fraser has been buying off the scandal-sellers for years.

3 August
I have begun rewriting the central part of *The Magus*. It is humbling – to see how badly one wrote, how messy the plot in places. And enjoyable: fixed situations melt, the characters live again, present new choices.

---

[1] Pinter's then wife, the actress Vivien Merchant, had a few days previously cited Antonia Fraser's name in divorce proceedings against her husband.

5 August

Ronnie Payne appears. He's decided to buy a cottage down here. We hadn't seen him since his helicopter crash in the Gulf, a story he told with his usual humour and sangfroid. We dread a little the thought of his bringing Celia; but there's nothing to be done.

6 August

I managed to squeak a young Tawny Owl into believing me a mouse. It sat perched fifteen feet above my head on a dead branch of the old cedar, oblivious of the torchlight, shifting its head from side to side in a desperate attempt to pinpoint this less than satisfactorily authentic sound; a comic little creature.

I'm replunged in Greece these days, with *The Magus*. It is suddenly and miraculously all present and alive again, the book; and my past; and denying totally my theory that written books die for the writer. I am changing many scenes; Nicholas shall have Lily now, in their sexual finale. I should have seen that was better in the beginning. And her twin sister shall have a slightly larger role.

14 August

A beautiful and rare sight, this evening; no less than 140 large yachts strung across the horizon, line after line of cream triangles against a deep blue sea. It was the beginning of the Fastnet Race; the whole armada tucking into the west.

We, Eliz and I, play badminton every evening now. It does us good; and we play rather well sometimes.

The FLW has sold out in Rumania, the entire edition of 45,650 copies; for which I am to receive some £460, a royalty of one pound per hundred copies, or one penny each. I hope their own writers do better than that.

26 August

Sad news from Eileen Porter. She is in hospital, has had an operation, we suspect cancer; a nice letter from her, about Cathy's moral-Marxist solutions to various publishing dilemmas over her book:[1] 'When will that rotten Irish peasant blood show?'

28 August

M and Doris appear. We met them at Taunton, Doris having joined the Darlington train at Birmingham. As usual, M manages to drive us mad with boredom in the first hour. Her egotism now is pathological. I counted a dozen interventions in conversation one day that all contained

[1] *Fathers and Daughters: Russian Women in Revolution*, published by Virago in 1976.

'I' in one of its declensions. In three seconds she will return the remotest subject to her world at Great Ayton, just as she did with Leigh-on-Sea. I suppose it is all derived from the terrible spoiling she evidently got from Grandfather Richards; all the rest of her life has been a clamour for that sort of attention – with the inevitable result that the more she has egotized the less attention she has received. Eliz and I speculate as to how my father stood it all those years without going mad; I think it accounts for his retreat into philosophy and German lyric verse and the rest – anything for a world she could not touch.

I behave badly towards her, showing my disapproval through silence; but largely without guilt. I stem from her emotionally and in my intense relationship with my own ego, of course; that is, I am genetically her child; his by acquired circumstance. I feel no guilt because her egotism is at least partly wilful and calculated – she is, for instance, in terms of information about what is going on in the world (she reads the *Daily Telegraph* every day and remembers most of it) far less 'stupid' than poor old Doris. But she will not tolerate anyone having escaped infancy – that is, a mental condition she can tyrannize. She must know by now that endless talk about children and domestic matters bores me as much as it bored my father; but very deliberately will talk of nothing else.

2 September
Fred Zinnemann came down for the day with Dougie Slocombe, who is to photograph; Tony Masters the art director; Tom Pevsner, the production manager. The latter two have flown from Canada and Israel, where they are working, so I presume things are becoming serious – not that the cautious 'Mr Zee' will say as much. We wander round the Cobb, while they chew endlessly over set problems and angles.

It's fun at this stage, of course; but I hear the first rumbles of all the machinery going into operation – at this level the art of the cinema is as manoeuvrable as a First World War tank.

Fred's latest fancy as leading lady is Charlotte Rampling, about whom I know nothing. He went into raptures about her sexiness and her face and all the rest, almost as if he was couch-casting: Suzman, Gemma Jones, Kate Nelligan and all the rest seem forgotten. I mistrust old Hollywood directors totally in this area – it's not only that they are prey to last sexual desire, but they hanker endlessly after creating stars *ex nihilo* – the godgame with a vengeance.

3 September
Fred is also playing games in another way. As he gave me the first script pages yesterday, he begged me, not once, but three times, *not* to tell

Tom Maschler, whom he didn't want to read them yet. I rang up Tom yesterday evening after they'd gone to tell him how the day had gone; and dutifully did not mention the script. This afternoon Fred rings up to say he has just sent the pages to Tom and 'felt it would not be fair' not to tell him that I have also been given them.

Tom did not take to all this kindly, but I mollified him. We decide that this was Fred's devious way of making sure he got our reactions individually, without any comparison of notes. More and more I realize that he is fundamentally like Willie Wyler; a ruthless old man at heart. It is simply that he uses a much more sophisticated technique. When I rang him and said I liked the twenty pages, he pretended enormous relief. 'I should have cancelled the project if you weren't satisfied.'

I feel almost tempted to call his bluff – I am pretty sure he would find reasons now to go on notwithstanding. Not that Potter's script isn't promising in its structure; the dialogue sounds largely wrong, but perhaps we stand more chance there of revision.

5 September
We took M on a small tour, through the hills east of Dartmoor.

We climbed through Chagford, the prettiest of the Moor towns, and went over the Moor to Ashburton, then through the old lanes I used to cycle as a boy to Torbryan; had a drink at the Church House Inn, went to see the painted screen in the church there; then up to the Ipplepen council houses to see Queenie Hellyer[1] – a little older now, but still the same old Donald Duck smile. We left M to talk her head off and went into the church – the first time I have been there since the chapters in *Daniel Martin* were written.

The Torbryan church tower. M said, 'Like an owl.' The only three words that pleased me during her stay, since they were exact. This was after we had eaten at the pub, later; and came out under the stars, with the tower a ghostly barn-owl grey in the darkness.

7 September
I finish drafting the rewritten *Magus* chapters.

13 September
The full script of *The FLW* arrives. It isn't perfect, it lacks countless echoes and historical depths in the book, it's basically just the love story; but it is something of a feat of condensation and has a good deal of dramatic strength. Eliz doesn't like it, nor Tom, who from finding the first twenty pages 'terrific' now seems full of gloom. I think the schism is between non-creators and creators. I know Fred is full of

[1] Maid to JF's family when they were staying in Ipplepen during the war.

doubts and anxieties, and it is quite pointless adding to them at this stage by being highly critical; as bad as damning babies at birth. Nine-tenths of the problem is dialogue, anyway. Potter, so astute and accurate in his own contemporary television plays, has an oddly deaf ear at times.

26 September

To London, since Jud Kinberg rang a few days ago from Johannesburg to say he would be in town a few days and wanted to borrow the flat. He's there when I arrive, unchanged: impatient, ebullient, sentimental-cynical. He's been writing a lot of scripts, it seems, and he's here looking for more. Monica and he can't put up with South Africa (where they moved from Israel) much longer, and a return to Los Angeles is forecast for next year.

He has very little good to say of Fred Zinnemann, who worsted Jud and Anthony Quinn in some deal years ago. He's 'devious', 'a killer', etc.

27 September

I gave Jud the script of *The FLW* to read in the morning. It produced an expectable reaction. It was appalling, shit, a failure from beginning to end; no drama, you weren't made to care for anyone – 'care' is his current script word, one must make audiences 'care' for one's charac-ters. As usual, some good ideas came floating amid the abuse.

The afternoon with Tom Maschler at Chalcot Gardens, concerting our own criticisms of the script. It was a relief to be with someone moderate and practical again. I hold, through all this, by my view that Mr Z and an eventual production still remain far from certain.

4 October

Shipwreck has earned some £2,061 for the Kenneth Allsop Trust. Betty A has at last faced up to the false dream of being a Dorset village widow – has bought a maisonette in Fulham, found herself a job, will sell the Powerstock house; all of which relieves our conscience a little.

Rodney, she and I met 'officially' last Sunday. The island has had a very good summer, due almost entirely to Rodney's energy and drive. A peregrine has been there all through September. The sale should come within a few weeks now. It will leave us bankrupt, if not in over-draft, but I think the original decision to go for Steepholm is being proved right.

An interesting number of the *TLS* – full of ideas on, or related to, fiction as an analogue (or metaphor) of actual living. Imagination as a kind of mediating zone between external reality and internal psyche, the relation being not only symbiotic, of course, but quasi-military – the embattled psyche picking its defences, tactics, strategy, etc. Then Bloch and his conception of the future, the inadequacy of present man, the vital importance of all future modes of thought (in which one can include technically past description where it represents an imaginary improvement on the historical past – as it almost invariably does, in one form or another).[1] I like very much this view of the fiction-maker as simply a conscious form of what is unconscious in every mind.

6 October

London. Boxall comes in, to go over the annual accounts. There is some £48,000 in the company accounts at the moment.

7 October

The grand script conference, which turned out a near-disaster. Potter was there when I arrived, cinnamon-haired, freckled, crippled hands, suit and tie, dapper and polite – an impression of ginger and indigo. Fred Z claimed he didn't want to run the discussion, whereupon Potter jumped in and said he felt he must make some general observations. My – or Tom's and my – suggestions had 'cast him into deep dejection'. We had signally failed to understand what he was aiming at. There followed a sermonette on the difference between drama and the novel. I kept my mouth shut, as did Tom after a few minutes of this. It grew more and more peculiar. We must observe 'areas of sovereignty', an ominous phrase he kept using. Then there came a speech defending Fred himself from us wicked tamperers with the Gospel. Discussion of the script would only 'upset' Fred, 'confuse issues'; it was 'counter-productive'. We were left finally very nearly speechless. Fred tried to intimate that he could look after himself, but even there Potter gave the impression that he knew better. Tom tried to get a discussion going on Ernestina's character, since she strikes us, as P has written her, as unnecessarily silly. But P killed that at once: she was 'charming', 'delightful'; we weren't 'reading between the lines'. What little discussing we did achieve was all wrecked on this rock: we weren't reading what P had meant. He did at one point admit that he was 'behaving like a thug', but 'only because I know the approach is right'.

And I forgot, he began all this by saying to me that he had 'until this moment' regarded me as dead and non-existent. It was very clear by the end that he wished me so, also.

P, because of his hands, won't eat in public, so he did disappear just after noon. We managed to get some work done during the rest of the

[1] JF is thinking of the German Marxist philosopher Ernst Bloch (1885–1977), whose Utopian interpretation of history suggested that mankind strove to create ever better and more just conditions of existence.

day. Fred was more amenable, if obstinate, over a number of points; but this was in a reasonable way. Potter was beyond dealing with. Fred kept saying, 'Yes, I'll see it is shot like that, but I won't bring it up with Dennis.' (They are to meet next week to discuss the rewrites.) Somehow he has let the man, or his sad physical condition, brainwash him. It's the first time I've ever heard a director pursue the line that one can't be frank with a script-writer because it might hurt him.

I was offered the Karl Marx role again; and turned it down.

Later that day we went to see *The Night Porter* in Audley Square – Fred had it run for us so that we could see Charlotte Rampling. A very sick film; playing on female bondage and Nazi sadism – the others would have walked out, but I took a sort of natural historical interest in it, since so many wrong values were being trotted out. The girl herself has a very striking face, slightly gaunt, with bruised eyes. I can grasp what Fred sees in her. But there is no evidence that she can act.

On the way out I talked with the manager of the place, who said Fred had been running his 'shots of ponds' a few days before. Ponds? Yes, with all the swans and things, down at Winston Churchill's place (Chartwell). That came as a shock to Tom and myself, since we had attacked the repeated black swan symbol on the script all through the afternoon, and not a murmur from Fred that he had actually done some test-shooting on the theme. He plays his cards ludicrously close to his chest.

All this was on Eliz's fiftieth birthday. We went after the film with Tom and Fay and had dinner at one of her restaurants in Battersea – much talk of the Wisemans and their folly in leaving the country for the next two years.

8 October

Fred Z telephones, full of apologies for yesterday's meeting. 'I'm only a bus-driver,' he said at one point. I said I thought he could promote himself, metaphorically, at least to ship's captain. 'No, no, I am a very modest man. It is simply I must get my bus to its right destination.' He was only half joking. I think he is less modest than acutely afraid of seeming a Hollywood tyrant, like Willie Wyler.

Podge appeared for lunch, from Oxford. Eileen's condition has deteriorated rapidly, she will die any day now. They have moved her to a nursing home, which he offered to pay for, but money was raised elsewhere somehow. He has been visiting her, doing his best to ferry people around, etc. But all this 'kindness' on his part – told with a characteristic blend of detail and dismissiveness – was only described to lead up to the final enormity of Eileen having flown at him a day or two ago. Apparently all the old vitriol was brought out. He's outraged, too, because she summoned a priest. I wouldn't let him pursue this nauseatingly puritanical-Marxist line. If it brought her any comfort . . . Whereupon he backed down, but only to say he had mentioned it to show she was a deeply schizoid woman. How could an ex-member of the Communist Party, etc., etc. He had 'never understood her'.

I mentioned E's little dig at Cathy in her last letter to us – 'When oh when will the rotten Irish peasant blood come out?' – but that was a mistake. Podge thought it 'not funny at all'. But it was obviously affectionate, it was Irish . . . 'I don't agree.' He would not concede E any humanity. 'I don't think it's in the least funny.'

I found his intransigence, venomous in its intensity, sad. It is clear the real struggle is for Cathy's soul. He claimed E had also been 'beastly' to Cathy, who is in Oxford seeing her mother through the last days. And he went on and on about the horror of Eileen's other friends, Faith Tolkien, Elizabeth Mavor, all the rest. Some 'impossible' old woman who came in and talked about her 'tea-parties with Lady Cooch-Behar' – how could E put up with such meaninglessness? Perhaps because she was Irish and other human beings amused her? But he would forgive nothing, understand nothing.

In the afternoon I went to see Fred Z on my own – Tom having departed for the Frankfurt Book Fair. He was all milk and honey. He wanted my help, he wanted me to know everything that was going on. He was much franker, and persuaded me that he wants to make the film (sent me to talk with Tom Pevsner at the end, who had the production schedule laid out upstairs); the obstacles remain the budget and the casting. Paramount are muttering now about the film not being commercial. Fred is still far from sure about Sarah's role – will test Gemma Jones and Rampling, possibly Francesca Annis. Redford has just been given the script, but Fred was obviously fed up with all the indecision there – the hanging on a whim that such castings entail, the absurd money the Redfords now demand – a million dollars minimum, plus a huge percentage. He is thinking of Richard Chamberlain for the part – he has said he is 'very interested'.

Fred also complained once more about Tom's 'aggression'. There has been an argument over whether he can be allowed to see the rushes, and Fred is hurt that Tom won't take no for an answer. I foresee mounting trouble there.

But things seem all right between Fred and myself; and the production schedule, those endless lines of lemon, pink, pale green cardboard – black for the holidays – were better proof than words.

13 October
Podge telephoned. Eileen died on Friday, October 10th. They cremated her and had a 'brief secular service' the same day. I said, 'My God, that's

shuffling them off fast.' He was not amused. 'It seemed the intelligent thing to do. Catherine and Kate (Eileen's sister) had had quite enough.' My own strong feeling was that he was very determined no one should be there to show any nostalgic affection for Eileen; especially people like us, who are supposed to be on his side.

Clearing brambles down the bottom; I broke off after an hour of it, the London life makes me soft, and ate three of the little russets still hanging on the centre tree there. They are delicious now. Sweet tang and almondy aftertaste, pure October.

I have started a rotten habit of waking up very early – never later than eight, usually seven, sometimes before. Permanent indigestion; I drink too much, and smoke far too much. The effects of the former are bad enough to make me stop some days; but those of the latter I suspect are worse, and I never stop that.

26 October
Denys and Monica here; strange, he is now in my world at St Godric's, running the language side of Concord College, for rich little sheikhs' sons. He seems to enjoy it.

A letter from the National Theatre – they want me to adapt Molière's *Dom Juan*, for Peter Hall to direct in 1977. I've read it again in my old 1710 edition: a fine play, but formidable translation problems.

28 October
Anna here for a few days, and Podge for the night. We're not clear why he comes, if it is not to irritate us. He dropped casually into one conversation that Cathy had been raped recently, as if it happens to everyone; some driver she hitched. I have a sharp feeling that he is inventing it, or much exaggerating.

Anna wants to buy a house on a mortgage, in South London; for £9,000, if we will pay the builder's bills. The place apparently needs a fair amount of work.

Two depressing phonecalls from Fred Zinnemann: the Paramount audience-reaction man doesn't like the script, 'you' don't know whose side you're on at the end, the only person you identify with (if you're a nice ordinary American) is Freeman, and so on; at least it seems to have convinced Fred that a new writer is necessary. But he's used up his $150,000 exploratory budget, has to ask more to pay a new pen, so if Paramount want to pull out . . .

11 November
I finished a first quick draft of *Dom Juan* today.

I've greatly enjoyed 'doing' *Dom Juan* during these days in London. In a way, of course, it's rather more a pamphlet than a play, a hand-grenade lobbed into the *cabale des dévots* in revenge for their suppression of *Tartuffe*.[1] It has all the smell of being written at great speed. Molière didn't quite know what he was doing – the lapses from quasi-tragedy into *lazzi* – *commedia dell'arte* buffoonery – that we admire today were almost certainly a product of haste, not conscious genius. Unconscious genius saved the day.

12 November
Back to Lyme, alone; Eliz will go to her mother in Birmingham. I read the great bestseller of this last year or two, Peter Benchley's *Jaws*, on the train. I'm not quite sure which is less convincing, the shark or the human beings. It's like a bad Hemingway imitated by a dwarf; and its success, a terrible indictment of American popular taste.

13 November
Eliz returns unexpectedly, unable to face her mother.

18 November
More anguish from Fred Zinnemann over the film: apparently the Paramount people are over to settle its hash one way or another. Costigan thinks the Potter script 'lacking' – young American audiences won't understand what's going on, Sarah is too mysterious, etc. James Costigan a script-writer. So all depends on whether Paramount are prepared to provide more money. The tests were also disappointing, it seems. Gemma Jones was best, but photographs badly; Nelligan and Annis failed in other ways. Neither of the men was any good.

Now Fred talks of delaying the production, even if it isn't cancelled outright. How he can't work with 'second-class' people (Annis and Nelligan). I tried once again to get him to look at Mirren; with no more success.

A pox on all of it.

20 November
I went back to *Daniel Martin*. To the terrace over the Nile.

23 November
The film is definitely postponed. Paramount are prepared to pay Costigan, but it can't be done in time. They will shoot locations in Lyme next

---

[1] *Tartuffe* was first performed at Versailles in May 1664, then banned after protests from devout Catholics, who rightly perceived Molière's creation of the pious hypocrite Tartuffe to be an attack on them. Molière went on to write *Dom Juan*, which was performed at the Palais-Royal in February 1665. While the play showed toleration of the hero's philandering, blasphemy and atheism, it treated hypocrisy as an unforgivable sin.

September now – if at all. Fred Z kept assuring me that he would pursue the project; but he said 'God bless you' at the end of our call, and it sounded to me like a farewell.

26 November

A disturbing letter from Podge, telling us all about Eileen's death – he has completely forgotten that we have seen him twice since then.

30 November

A Sunday. I wrote the last sentence of *Daniel Martin*. I had meant to end it at Thorncombe, but the final meeting with Jenny went badly; they walked on the Heath, she left him at Kenwood; I left him staring at Rembrandt and whole sight.

They came quite easily, these last four chapters. I've hardly been out, or known the 'real' world exists.

It was begun about Oct 10th, 1972.

3 December

Nick telephones. 'John, I'm afraid I have some very bad news about Anna. She's had an accident.' I saw immediately the worst kind of car-crash, but it seems she caught her hand in a buffer at the jewellery class. Bad enough, a finger was crushed, she was rushed to hospital and had an operation in the small hours; he thinks it can be saved. Eliz came in while we were still talking, from taking her mother to the Birmingham train; then left an hour later herself for London. Apparently Anna is tearful and sick from the anaesthetic. It was curious, we were what must have seemed amused by it – just relief that it was not what Nick had seemed to announce at the beginning.

5 December

Daniel Martin. A formidable pile, it must be six inches or more high. I begin to secure it; the danger at this point is always to lose deeper structure to surface detail. I lay in bed early this morning worrying over what I begin to see is the growing deep fault – the old humanist trap in art, and especially twentieth-century art: the absence of despair in the thorough-going humanist. Who wants to be a lucky man? It is the dilemma of my own life, of course. I have now totally humanized the one potential source of despair in the life Eliz and I have made – the absence of children. For many years now that has seemed more good fortune to me than bad; at worst, mere destiny, to be met stoically. Then it has allowed me to be what I am – green in my special sense of the word, able to switch through my different ages, in a way I suspect the presence of children, the corollary assumption of parenthood and at least the mask of adulthood, forbid. I suspect too that my whole notion of parity of existence, my deep feeling that I co-own the land I inhabit with its birds and plants, the way, I suppose foolish, that I always feel guilt when I disturb nature here in the garden, I seem to trespass, that also lives less easily with the archetypal sense of vertical and chronological descent, authority-in-line, that parenthood sets on one. The lack of that role is my freedom.

The outcome of the novel is a paradigm of what Eliz and I have created as a substitute, of course; the better conclusion to which we have come. Apart from the technical problems, all that last part of the book felt profoundly right; the problems were indeed mainly bound up with not making the coming-together too immediate.

The general problem is that Daniel, being my exteriorized imagination – imagination as substitute for biographical realization – must seem in ordinary terms to have the best of both sexual worlds: both his (or the world's) dream and its reality; its Jenny and its Jane.

It needs one more chapter, which I shall put in after Jane's arrival at Thorncombe, in the night: I shall speak from behind Daniel. I think I take this a little from working on *Dom Juan* – the marvellous anchor that Molière's own tearing-aside of the mask of the Dom provides in the great tirade in the second scene of Act V.[1] The whole play spins round that hub.

8 December

Eliz brings Anna down from the hospital; little the worse for wear, it seems, beyond the bound-up hand. Apparently she (Eliz) had an evening with Nick alone while she was in town; thinks we have been unkind to him, that he has problems with Anna's closed side – her fear of new faces, intellectual challenge, her blankness towards any cultural experience. She is a fiercely domestic child, seemingly hostile towards anything outside her immediate emotional and visual four walls; which suits badly with her taste and sensitivity and common sense in so many things. It worries us a little, how she may develop if this barrier isn't broken. It's partly our fault, since Eliz plays along by indulging this inturned quality in Anna – forcing her to films and plays, making her watch our sort of TV programme really isn't enough – and I play along by watching it all happen. But it's very difficult when we live by a language, or cultural knowledge, that Anna is almost totally innocent of; and with our old guilt still.

I suspect one important factor we can do nothing about in all this is Roy. The other day he was sent to hospital again – he ran out of the Fulham house into the street, calling for help, he knew he was going

[1] In a long speech, which clearly represents Molière's own sentiments, Dom Juan attacks hypocrisy, singling out in particular those who 'make a shield out of religion, and, under its cloak, use their licence to be the most wicked men in the world'.

mad – and it seems this time it may be for good. Anna must know now he had to be left by her mother; but I suspect her hostility to culture and language and ideas derives largely from that relationship. Eliz and I are aspects of him, unconsciously; his ultimate revenge.

11 December
Fred Zinnemann rings. Paramount have agreed to hire James Costigan to do an entirely new script. He's flown to London, and hopes to have it finished by February.

12 December
Tom Maschler, cock-a-hoop again that we remain in business. He told me at the end of the call that Tom Wiseman has just got $400,000 for his American paperback rights. Tom and Malou's predictable (and I suppose not wholly far-fetched) reaction is fear that Boris will now become kidnappable.

I've been for weeks in something of a moral dilemma over whether I should send Tom Wallace at Holt, Rinehart the puff he asked for when he sent me the proof copy; decided not to in the end, since I detest the old-boy network in litbiz, the book doesn't need it and I know it was written to make money – that is, out of Tom's insecurity, not the much deeper personality he showed in *The Quick and the Dead*.

Also a little, I suppose, because I wrote *Daniel Martin*; which I have been re-reading and revising. It will be condemned as an élitist book, I know that; and as wicked in its mocking of pessimism and egalitarianism. Once again no one will understand that its real frame is biological, not cultural or political; during the last stretches I thought several times of *The Man of Feeling*;[1] late eighteenth-century sensibility. I think I must work in a reference somewhere to make that explicit – i.e., that the new classicism to be broken is the romanticism of extreme anti-romanticism, all for the worst in the worst of all possible worlds. It is not sufficient to argue that there is some statistical and historical sense in which that is largely true (mankind is going through a bad patch) and that therefore art must faithfully copy that sense (which in any case I suspect is more an intuitive than a rational appraisal); and even if most should, someone should not.

There's a lot about Jane Austen in the magazines at the moment, provoked by her bicentenary: her work seen as a sustained attack on the excesses of sensibility, as a triumph of 'sense' in her own famous use of it. This seems to me to overlook the fact that the rewards she gives her embodied fragments of 'sense' – Eleanor, Emma, Fanny Price and

---

[1] Written by Henry Mackenzie (1745–1831), *The Man of Feeling* (1771) tells the story of Harley, who in a harsh world lives true to his conscience but fails to find love or to achieve worldly success.

the rest – are in fact highly romantic, and they have all had to undergo sensibility in one form or another to win 'sense'. Her real genius is for distinguishing false, exaggerated feeling from true feeling, not between feeling and reason.

It only occurred to me in the very last chapters, at Palmyra, that the Jane of my creation has a distinguished ancestress. I've always had a special feeling for the name, which must I think derive from Austen. I should dedicate the thing to 'Jane' – and all her avatars.

16 December

A dreadful morning. I've taken no exercise for weeks; wake every day before dawn with indigestion, wind like compressed air; and today spent two hours doubled in pain. Absurd, to be psychologically in high summer with the book, physically the very reverse. Part of the fault is the drug-like state my own fiction produces in me. I forget all time in it sometimes, especially at this stage where everything is infinitely malleable, the characters cooperative now, happy to point out their faults and the solutions. Something like horse-breaking – the day the animal responds at last.

2 January 1976

Eliz brings little Hannah Maschler down for a long weekend; on her own. Fay has a notion we may 'sort out' her problems. The poor child has lost all her old charm, become very spoilt, wilful, difficult; alternating, over the days with us, between mania and depression. Endless phonecalls about what to do, whether to give up and return her home. It seems a bad case of sibling jealousy and general insecurity, stemming from her baby brother.

6 January

Podge appeared, mysteriously, at teatime; would not stop. He was with 'a friend'. 'Where is she?' 'Out in the car park.' 'Oh, for God's sake – go and bring her in.' 'I think not. Not with old friends. It wouldn't be cricket.'

All this with his old Machiavellian smile, enjoying the mystery. If he really wanted us not to know he was two-timing Hille, he shouldn't have come in in the first place. We speculated after he had left – and decided it must be some chit of a girl. He grows very peculiar. I think it is something to do with having to be nice to me because of the money I lent him. It is a fatal way of destroying friendship.

7 January

Eliz back to London with Hannah. And I am left in my solitude.

10 January

The building society have refused Anna and Nick a mortgage – a little bit to our relief, since we're clear that they might imprison themselves if they become property-owners. Anna's hand hasn't healed; she has to have a skin-grafting operation now. I hear all this by telephone; she goes to the Chelsea Hospital this time, where Roy is a psychiatric day-patient. He is very ill, seemingly hopeless.

14 January

This strange life I lead here on my own, so inward it is as if I am drugged. Nicotine kills me, permanent indigestion, malaise. I see no one, speak to no one, except a little to old Jack and Mrs P, when they come in to garden and clean.

15 January

I added one more chapter to *Daniel Martin*, on retreat. I have titled it 'Woods and Words'. I work on the book every day, laboriously fining away.

4 February

I put *Daniel Martin* to sleep for a while, having fitted in most of the odds and ends; and revised a lot, to the end.

11 February

Fred Zinnemann rang, to say the Costigan script is no good, and that Paramount feel they can't put any more money in. He sounded sincerely sad about it, perhaps because he fails to understand how unsurprised I am, and how indifferent. Of course he has also failed throughout to see that the book is too complex for the medium, especially when it has to be put over in two hours.

13 February

I have permanent indigestion these days, a worrying pain in my left side, that seems caused by flatulence. I smoke too much and take far too little exercise – less this winter than ever before. I feel it's pointless to see a doctor – even our now universally mistrusted man at Uplyme – when all he can tell me is that no one who lives as unhealthily as I do, flying in the face of all modern middle-aged survival theory, can expect to feel anything but ill.

16 February

I am 'elected' Fellow of the Royal Society of Literature – if I send a subscription. I looked at some of the names of those elected before me, and declined the honour. If they had asked me ten years ago, perhaps; but I doubt it, even then.

12 March

The Tringhams came for the weekend, and Nick and Anna. David full of the usual horrors of his latest film, under the director Stuart Rosenberg in Barcelona; it was a vehicle for stars. Faye Dunaway taking three hours to do her make-up each day: 'Her face is like the moon, full of craters.' And the dreadful wreck of Orson Welles, hardly able to walk now, cantankerous, forgetting his lines . . .[1]

Nick brought some of his new style of pots, which are black and white, very delicate and finely made. One especially I thought of very high standard. I forgive him all before work like this.

13 March

I met death today. It happened very trivially. We walked out in the late morning along the glass beach. I had had the pain in my side, but then suddenly, among the stones just beyond the rubbish dump – I was with the Tringhams' older child Andrea – I felt very ill, I knew I would faint if I did not sit down. I thought it must be a heart attack. It was less frightening than absurd, that it should happen now, that at any moment I was going to black out; the sun on the water, the others straggling along the beach. I stared at the stones beside me, waiting. It lasted for about a minute. I had a sense of all I have not done and also of the intense livingness of the others, of their being in some way ahead of me. I wasn't 'behind' in actual terms, but it felt like that; seeing people recede and knowing one would never catch them up.

After a while I got up, still feeling very ill; then a few moments later had to sit down again, the same symptoms; then began walking back to Lyme, feeling I would never make it; but was better when we reached the town.

I still felt rotten at dinner – we all went to Branscombe. Couldn't concentrate on anything people said, longed for it to be over.

14 March

We went on Charmouth Beach; no repetition, though the pain will not leave me. Fossils; I found a curious fragment of a kind I cannot place, partly pyritized.

We like the Tringhams. Their children are notably well brought up for these days, and I find Annette's a relief from the English female mind. She has a pleasing way of seeming to expect nothing from life, of being content with whatever she has – or is.

[1] The film was *Voyage of the Damned.*

15 March

I went to see the wretched Anderson, our doctor at Uplyme. Doubly wretched, he had the flu. He didn't examine, but sent me off to have a chest X-ray. I can't have a heart condition, he says. 'I can tell that by just looking at you.'

16 March

Harold Wilson springs his great surprise;[1] and enjoys every moment of it. Much talk about his 'place in history'; I hope it won't be left out that to most of his contemporaries his abiding quality was an irredeemable smugness. He would walk a mile to make you think an inch better of him. He reminds me of a certain kind of woman – always fiddling with his reputation, as they do with their clothes.

22 March

As we were leisurely getting ourselves together, at about midday, for our flight from Heathrow, I rang Air France to check; to discover that my watch had stopped on the one hand, and on the other that the wretched travel agency in Axminster had given us the wrong departure time. The direct plane to Nice was leaving in an hour – impossible for us to catch. We had to switch to one leaving at six, via Paris.

Where we got, at seven, at the Charles de Gaulle airport, my first time there. We were impressed, all the moving walks, satellites, glass tubes, cleanliness – it was like a German Expressionist vision after the plebeian shambles of Heathrow. A fit comment on the two countries: one lives by high rhetoric, the other by masochism.

A Jumbo to Nice, very crowded, but noticeably efficient in its service; and the food excellent for an airline, with *apéritif*, wine and brandy thrown in. A sad, sharp sense of how far England has now fallen behind in the simpler pleasures of existence; in *fashion* of being.

We arrived about nine, in the mild air, walked to the lounge past the yuccas, agaves and palms. Tom, Malou and Boris were there to greet us, a little like exiles at last granted some relief; a babble of news; then back by the *péage*, and up past Mougins, through Grasse, to the Domaine du Blanchissage in the Vallée Verte.

It seems the unexpected has happened. Malou is the happier, her peasant blood has come out; while Tom is lost, out of touch, drinking too much, thoroughly miserable, weighed down by the worries over his present and his next book, despite the almost guaranteed success of the first and impossibility of total failure in the second. They live here against having lent their own house in Arkwright Road to John Collier.[1] He's broke, apparently; but wants, or his wife Harriet wants,

---

[1] His decision to resign as prime minister.

a million dollars for the Blanchissage – a price they could get only from a developer; and John C can't bear to see the place developed. He still pays the gardener, Joseph, £50 a week, out of sentiment.

24 March
Tom is hopeless, as resistant to nature as the hardest granite. But I try to work on Boris; catch him a green frog, and a lizard.

Celebrities for lunch – the film-actor Dirk Bogarde and his 'husband', Tony Forwood; an amiable homosexual pair, still not without a dash of the characteristic malice and sharpness of tongue, but a strong air of stable marriage about them as well. Bogarde is the *pathicus*, the wife; Forwood was married once to the actress Glynis Johns, is a grandfather now. Bogarde has deep anxiety lines on his forehead, pouched creases round his hurt eyes – he is, it seems, very shy of meeting people, of revealing his sexual status, and they live like recluses down here, on the other side of Grasse. Tom and Malou were afraid he would be shocked by our presence; but the lunch went on till four o'clock over a huge pasta Malou had cooked – endless talk of the cinema, of being in exile, of what was wrong with England. Bogarde feels he is a failure, outside one or two films; acts now either for money, or for love and nothing. He starts soon on a film with Resnais, on a David Mercer script. His 'master' is Visconti (who died last week); an emotion he can't suppress every time the name 'Luchino' comes up. He claimed before he came that he couldn't stand children; but was nice to Boris, perhaps a shade too caressing.

25 March
We drove down to Cogolin, between St Maxime and St Tropez, to look at the house Tom and Malou bought there before good fortune struck them down; along the coast from Fréjus, the endless line of villas, agaves, parasol pines, all the ugly detritus of beach-worship. There is something lemming-like in this mad desire to find a place in the sun; cancerous – all that is ugliest about mankind crowding into the same area.

Their house is a tiny little barrack, four floors of one room each, in a village street; almost as if they had selected it on a ghetto principle; no garden, no green. From a roof-terrace one could see the country around, but otherwise they seem to have picked the worst of every world. We realize, sharply now they are part of England, that they are the

---

[1] A writer of mystery stories, John Collier (1901–1980) achieved considerable success in the United States with the publication of his short novel *His Monkey Wife* (1930), and began a second career as a Hollywood script-writer, working on films that included *Sylvia Scarlett*, *The African Queen* and *I am a Camera*. He returned to live in Europe in the 1950s, buying the Domaine du Blanchissage in Grasse in 1955.

victims of the strangest cultural naivety – without any visual taste or ability to avoid general heresies of the silliest kind about what is desirable in living-style.

We went into St Tropez for lunch; the crowds already beginning. We had a pleasant meal in a back-street restaurant, ending with a creamy *tarte tropézienne*; then wandered round the place. Its vulgar chic isn't very far from that of Southend, without the redeeming working-class touch there; but Tom purrs, this is success. He sits beside the port, reading his English newspapers – all he really wants to do, I suspect.

He has no eyes, no sense of smell. Eliz showed him a bunch of violets I had picked, held them under his nose for the fragrance; bizarrely for nearly fifteen seconds, as he droned on about American politics. It appeared as if he quite literally did not see them, though only a few inches from his eyes.

We all make fun of him too much. He is much more like a kind of sensual cripple than anything else; and dimly aware that Malou is reaching a limit in how far she is prepared to indulge his lacks. No normal woman could do it; but she lives from moment to moment, quick mood to mood.

27 March

We went to Vence, to see a house Tom fancies. It is in the north part of the town, another variation on the urban ghetto, a tiny garden, cramped, shadowy, a heavy feel of Spanish-style Catholicism about its owners, a busy traffic road right outside. Eliz makes encouraging noises, but I killed the place for them when we left. They are mad even to consider it.

28 March

Sunday. The superbly cloudless weather continues. Boris took me up to the little canal above the Blanchissage, which runs all round the Vallée Verte on its way to Grasse. It is very pleasant, liquid and limpid, swift-running, though only some eight feet across. And there, along the 'towpath', many more orchids.

At noon we went for drinks to an Ivor O'Brien, an English neighbour a little up the road – some kind of minor industrialist who has put himself into retirement and tax exile, first in Jersey, several years ago. An exceedingly dull, hollow man, yet he fascinated me – the emptinesses, silences, boredoms, *désoeuvrements*, that seemed to hover in the wings of everything he said. There is chat about tax laws, house prices, the 'problems' of this area – all the stale themes of exile.

What is so wrily comic about this situation is that what really drove such people as Ivor to flee England for the tax-haven – the hatred of having 'free enterprise' cramped, of having their hard-earned profits taxed, the Puritan ethos, in short – is precisely what makes them unhappy, or at least painfully unsuited to the proper kind of life in such favoured landscapes as these – the Epicurean-pastoral, that of the dilettante and expert at enjoyably doing nothing. They are geared to making money, routine, contracts, appointments, deals, expansions. They are, in fact, literally rats out of the rat-race – axles without a wheel, spinning, unable to progress or mesh with anything. All they've really exchanged is a selfishness that was exercised in business for one incapable of the only alternative: a wise narcissism.

I wrote all this down in much greater detail, for a story. I might call it 'In Exile' or 'The Lucky Few'.

30 March
To the Bogardes for lunch; an honour they seldom grant, we gather.

They live three or four miles the other side of Grasse, at Châteauneuf; a small farmhouse set in several acres of olive-terrace and woodland – the house exquisitely converted, rather stagy, full of pretty objects and paintings, spotlessly clean, white curtains billowing gently in the breeze. They provided an absurdly plentiful lunch on the terrace – enough to feed three times the seven of us; claim to live very simply, but evidently like a certain expansive carelessness – derived half from the film-world, half from their upper-class pasts. Bogarde keeps up occasional mock flashes of aggression. 'Why don't you go and drown in the pool, Boris?' Then to Eliz, when she cut into the end of a new cheese. 'For God's sake don't take the outer slice, take the next, the bloody stuff costs so much it doesn't matter.'

Again it lasted all afternoon – endless talk of Visconti and *Death in Venice*; how Visconti and Bogarde never once discussed his part, it was all done in silence, by intuition; stories about the beautiful young Swede who played the angel of death, his appalling American accent and rock-and-roll vocabulary, how he was 'fucking his governess silly every night', and almost every other young film-groupie in Venice. Tales of Visconti's boyfriends, Alain Delon and the rest; then of other stars Bogarde has acted with, Vivien Leigh, Judy Garland – the latter's planned and stored-up scenes and tantrums, Vivien Leigh's madnesses, locking herself in lavatories and obsessively washing and cleaning. Glenda Jackson was referred to by B as 'Glenda Sludge' throughout.

I asked him about the failure to develop a serious cinema in Britain. 'Not enough love' – what he had felt for Visconti, what 'literally' everyone around 'Luchino' had felt for him. I didn't think that was quite good enough, so he suggested the crassness of Americans over scripts. I found that more convincing, but the mystery remains.

Bogarde took me off alone just before we left to see his estate; they keep it up all by themselves, all the mowing and flower-growing, the rebuilding of the terrace walls, log-sawing. He seems to have a genuine love of nature; I'd already spotted a new orchid in the grass, and he told me he had transplanted several to save them.

I liked Bogarde in the end; the sensitivity of the wounded hart, behind the mannerisms.

On the way home we looked at two more houses: one suburban, the other on the way to becoming it. Endless argument over them. Poor Tom can't see that 'elegance' here is bound up with space and solitude and living in the country. He was astounded when I told him Bogarde didn't want to leave his garden and olive-terraces, even to make a film with Resnais. 'I'm amazed he said that.'

31 March
My fiftieth birthday. Though I have felt better here, I woke up feeling ill again, with the pain in the area of the spleen. We had breakfast outside, more argy-bargy about how we should spend the day. I've forbidden Eliz to tell them it's my birthday. The hoopoe mocks from the hill opposite and reality recedes through the trees.

3 April
Tom is struck down again by gout, which he has suffered from, in a suspiciously psychosomatic fashion, ever since we came. He hobbles about like a very old man; and got very bad-tempered when no one brought him his breakfast outside. After lunch we went without him on a walk in the hills behind Cabris; and when we came back found all the things still left on the table. In this department he outrages even the poor showing I make; almost as if not stirring a finger – according to Malou he never shops for her, refused the other day even to buy bread when he went to fetch his papers – is a matter of principle; if only she could manage a consistency of outrage herself . . . We went into Grasse first to buy cheese and *saucisson* to take home, and a huge *dorade* for our final supper.

A nice excursion among the huge boulders above Cabris. I found a tiny scorpion for Boris underneath a rock – barely two centimetres long, but an active and menacing little creature for all that. Then I lifted another stone and an adder slid away, very torpid, it could only just have woken, but Boris saw it. I also saw two ravens, almost the only large birds we have seen in this area. Hunting must be to blame – everything large gets exterminated.

6 April
Back to Lyme, and the usual pile of mail. The garden seems hardly to have progressed at all. There's been no rain, which has retarded and prolonged all the flowering.

16 January 1977

The typescript of *Daniel Martin* completed. A young woman recently come
to Lyme, Mary Scriven, has been typing it since the end of November.
And I have been working on it every hour of every day since then. She
has been far the best 'secretary' I have found here: commonsensical
and careful. The length, I make 297,000 words.

17 January

Proofs come of the French edition of *The Magus,* which Annie Saumont
finished in the autumn. Those of the Cape edition come next month;
publication scheduled for May.

Eliz and I went up to town; I straight to Anthony Sheil's, to deliver *Daniel
Martin,* all 1108 typescript pages of it.

   While I was there, Tom Maschler rang: quite extraordinary, since a
week or so ago Christopher Bigsby of the University of East Anglia wrote,
on behalf of himself and Malcolm Bradbury, to suggest they try a TV
adaptation of *The FLW*; which I had come to London to second, but now
Tom announces that the producer of the vogue film of last year, *One
Flew Over the Cuckoo's Nest,* has appeared and declared himself interested.
A Mr Saul Zaentz.

18 January

I went to Tom's office and met Zaentz. An alert, no-nonsense man, in
his fifties; a grey-white beard, shrewd eyes. He's made a fortune in the
world of pop and jazz records; financed the Forman film himself, would
do the same with us. A curious blend of ignorance and positiveness. He
sold himself to us. He'd like Louis Malle to direct, David Mercer possibly
to script.

   Tom on top form; he'd put every agent in the world out of business,
if he took that up.

   Books at Fawkes in Flask Walk. Then to Norman's. His new catalogue
came out a week ago, and the wretched Bodleian had pinched most of
what I wanted. The translation of *Ourika* (also bought at Norman's many
years ago) I have done for Tom Taylor of Texas, with Henry Morris
printing, is well under way. I signed sheets for it recently. I mention
Norman in the introduction, and how even he could no longer give
away minor seventeenth- and eighteenth-century volumes for next to
nothing. And while he was off searching for my books upstairs, I picked
up two French pamphlets, a mid-seventeenth-century *Factum* on a
property squabble between Marie de Bourbon, Princesse de Carignan,
and her sister Marie d'Orléans, Duchess of Nemours; and an *Edit du
Roy* of 1705, poor old Louis trying to claw back money from his self-
created bureaucracy. 'How much?' I asked old Norman when he

returned. 'Oh . . . a pound?' Which made a nonsense of my foreword. I did in the end force him to take a pound each. He's a deeply shy, but a dear old man.

A cable from Ned Bradford in Boston:

> *Daniel Martin* is marvellously convincing and absolutely rich in ideas for readers of all kinds to play with. My quibbles will be minor. Incidentally, I must confess I was inclined to mourn a bit for Jenny, although of course she is going to hack it in her inimitable style. Cheers and best to you both, Ned

Anthony and Tom also seem reasonably well pleased. Tom wants to have it out by next November, so I am trying to get my last break away from the text before the editing.

I awaited these first reactions with far less anxiety than before; not because potential cause is not there, but because it is like a seven-year voyage ended. The sudden lack of onward motion is very like what a sailor feels when he is on land again; the voyage becomes a dream – that is, fiction once more turns fiction; as the reader will see it.

4 February
We went to Chard with Charlie Greenberg, to the weekly antiques market. He has decided to run the shop beneath his Branscombe house himself this summer (last year he let it to a lady dealer he thinks has grossly rooked him); and Eliz is to be brought into partnership, i.e., to do most of the practical organizing. His awful quasi-Dickensian seriousness over the whole matter amuses us, especially as both Eliz and I really know far more about the bric-a-brac side of the trade than he does; but he won't have it, he took Eliz away as soon as we reached the market and proceeded to instruct her, telling her she was not to interrupt. I went off and bought a nice batch of postcards.

Then we all drove back to Branscombe, to examine last year's left-over goods in the shop. The biggest eyesores are Charlie's own paintings, as we both were quick to point out, to his obvious mortification. He kept on telling us what they would fetch at Sotheby's or Christie's, but was unable to explain why they had spent the whole summer in the shop without finding any buyers. He really is a kind of Canadian Pickwick, ludicrously serious about what can only be a hobby.

8 February
Anthony rings to say that Little, Brown will offer a minimum of $250,000 for *Daniel Martin*. I think he felt I lacked sufficient enthusiasm. He doesn't realize how deeply I have quelled that demon.

11 February

And Tom, or Jonathan Cape, proposes a £25,000 advance. On top of everything else Zaentz has written to Roger Burford: he seems to mean business over filming *The FLW*. The deal is a $25,000 option, $75,000 on first day of shooting, $100,000 deferred, and 5 per cent. Half a million dollars in one week. I feel like Midas more exactly than most people could ever realize.

12 February

Eliz has been rushing about all this last week buying her junk for the Branscombe shop. We have been 'off' antiques for a number of years now. It is quite fun to re-enter that world.

9 March

To London, to Cape, to sit with Mike Petty and go through his and Tom's editorial suggestions for *Daniel Martin*; they want some of the passages out where John Fowles emerges too nakedly behind Daniel himself – some six or seven pages in all. Probably rightly; otherwise it was just textual warts to be excised.

Mike Petty is pleasantly sharp, no-nonsense. We had a long lunch in a pub in Charlotte Street, drinking draught Guinness; talking about Tom mainly and the agonies of the copy-editor's existence. Petty wants to 'go upstairs', commission books and all the rest, but Tom usurps all the available space.

One curious thing: the pub where Daniel Martin and Jenny end – he wanted to know if it was the Sir Richard Steele. I said yes, in terms of location,[1] but I'd never been in it. Yet apparently it *is* an actors' pub, the walls are covered in signed photographs. I don't think he believed me when I said again that I'd never been inside it – as indeed I haven't.

Tom came to the flat in the evening to discuss the draft blurb (which as usual I can't stand) and I had a cautious go at him about Mike Petty. A stone wall, of course. He has no idea of pricing books, according to Tom. 'You can't run a publishing business on hope and faith.' I suspect Tom is right; idealists should not be in bookselling.

We went out with him and Fay to a little Greek restaurant – the dinner was offered in gratitude by the owners for one of her puffs. It was rather nice, a middle-aged Cypriot couple who did seem delighted to repay their 'debt'. Tom had a bag of bottles thrust into his arms as we left.

Fay had suddenly sprung on us at the end of the meal that we could all go on to Olga Deterding's party – she owns half Shell, or something absurd. Tom was not at all interested, there was a little spat, then he gave

[1] At 97 Haverstock Hill, Hampstead.

in. So we drove down to Piccadilly and went up in a lift to a penthouse, where the lady lives, overlooking Green Park; a roomful of people, a table with endless bottles, my notion of hell. Some dreadful woman pushed herself upon me, she had once worked in Anthony Sheil's agency, had now set up on her own. I was introduced to the cream of her stable, a young man who did articles for *Harper*'s and *Vogue*; a *petit maître de nos jours*. Our hostess eyed me with disfavour. I saw Anthony Howard of the *New Statesman* there; and gave the magazine another bad mark (I suspect it and I are parted for good now that Claire Tomalin has left and Martin Amis taken over)[1]. I was introduced to Jocelyn Stevens, who mismanages the *Express*; a pink, plastic man.[2] 'Super,' he said, and moved on to where the real power was.

Then, thank God, more familiar faces, Ronnie Payne and Celia – I talked with him for a while, then he did what I did not want, brought Alan Brien up to meet me – author meets character in his as yet unpublished book. I quite enjoyed it, not least because he proved he deserves what I give him in Barney Dillon. He doesn't listen, merely talks, insinuates little jabs. I am 'the great unknown novelist' and so on; no reference is made to his piece in the *Sunday Times* of several years ago. Perhaps he has forgotten, but I suspect not. I put on the smile I gave Nicholas at the end of *The Magus*.

10 March
Roger Burford says Zaentz continues interested. He flies soon to London to tie things up.

Eliz and I went round the West End galleries.

We went on to the new Satyajit Ray film, *The Middle Man*. He grows and grows in stature. It occurred to me, watching it, that he may be like Jane Austen: someone whose true importance doesn't emerge until many years later. His own six-inches of ivory have just that central morality we now see in her; the same accuracy, universality concealed in the remote and small. I made a note for *Daniel Martin* – to cross out Fellini's name, and put Ray's in its place.[3]

22 March
Ten days of doing the last changes and rewrites for *Daniel Martin*. A seemingly endless task, with a manuscript this size. Dealing with the

[1] As literary editor of the magazine.
[2] Jocelyn Stevens was then managing director of Beaverbrook Newspapers.
[3] *Daniel Martin*, p. 307: 'the elusive and eluding nature of the English psyche is profoundly unsympathetic to visual representation; and our baffled inability to make good films about ourselves, or to produce artists of the stature of a Bergman, a Buñuel, a Satyajit Ray, springs very largely from that.'

repetition-rashes: the criminals this time were 'little', 'faintly', and 'silence'. It is difficult to write about the English without them.

23 March

Tom and I went to meet Zaentz, who's flown back to London, in Roger Burford's office. I continue to like him; he manages to be jovial, crisp, amused; and clear what he wants. We think of trying David Mercer for the script. Settle a mutually acceptable clause over directors. He will be in touch.

Back in Lyme this evening, we saw him win all the prizes at the British Film Academy annual award gala.[1] I didn't like him so well being grateful for the gilded *merde*. His friend Milos Forman was also there on the podium. Zaentz has given him *The FLW* to read, but thinks it unlikely that 'Milosz' will fall for the subject. I'd just as soon he didn't, good director though he is. His forte is contemporary wry humour.

24 March

A Canadian publisher, Collins, has offered $50,000 and various other tempting things for *Daniel Martin*. Lois Wallace and Anthony Sheil in America – or Australia, actually, at the moment – are cock-a-hoop. The gathering snowball – all I feel is that I am under it, and it begins an avalanche. Money is ice-cold to my touch; stifling in its descent.

31 March

My fifty-first birthday. Not good, I feel a growing depression; emptiness, staleness, boredom, after the last six months of work on the novel. Now it is dead, a corpse and its attendant vultures. I suppose I need a holiday, but Eliz is totally absorbed in getting the Branscombe shop ready. Anna is here now to help her, Doris comes at the weekend. She and Anna are two faces I see for a few hours each evening. I work in the garden a bit, but do not enjoy it. The garden, yes, still, always; but the work seems meaningless.

The great folly of my life was not having learnt to drive. I have days here when I feel imprisoned. No one comes here, I go nowhere. I can't even share the excitements about the book, since we tacitly exclude all that from our life. And that old, old lack of ever having any intelligent discussion about anything with anyone. My tattle, the Branscombe tattle, book sale telephone-calls with London. Television is a great relief, egotropic, at night. And stumbling my way through some Bach scores I bought recently on the recorder; one I love, I begin to master it a little, the Andante from the Italian Concerto.

---

[1] Zaentz's film *One Flew Over the Cuckoo's Nest* won six BAFTA awards – for Best Film, Actor, Actress, Supporting Actor, Director and Editor.

A call from Lois Wallace in New York. *Daniel Martin* will be the Book of the Month Club's October main choice. A few minutes later Ned Bradford was on the line from Boston, with the same news. I did sound warmer to him, liking him so much better. He said the price was $305,000, the highest they have ever got for a novel; and that they were now hoping for half a million for the paperback rights.

8 April
Good Friday, bad for me. Eliz goes off to Branscombe, where it is the opening day. And I wish I was anywhere in the world but Lyme Regis. I think of ringing up Tom and Malou Wiseman and going down there for a week while Eliz is off on her coach tour with her mother. But we're due in Sweden, a prospect I increasingly dread, to do the British Council lecture tour on the 30th. I stare at the fifty thousand things to be done in the garden, and do none of them. Annotate three eighteenth-century plays I bought recently, and envy their authors the humanity of their world.

16 April
Eliz goes off with Doris on their coach trip to York.

18 April
I've had to have a medical for a new insurance policy; from Fernandez, the doctor in Broad Street. He is thorough, but an odd, vaguely embittered, fossilized man; very cautious and guarded. He interests me a little. Eliz says he has notorious problems with his daughters: Lyme tattle says so, anyway. He examined me three days ago, but did not take to my blood pressure. Or any more again when I went back again today. In careful British-doctor fashion, he did not tell me how much out of true it was.

24 May
Five days of nothing but proofs, proofs, proofs. I had to do the Cape galleys with the American ones. Both dispatched today.

28 May
Eliz depressed, and I too a little. *The Magus* coming out, the impending fuss over *Daniel Martin*; ennui with Lyme, which seems noisier than ever this summer (the accursed power-boats); the absurd and Gadarene rush to celebrate the Royal Jubilee, which seems infinitely remote from anything to do with modern Britain and problems – a hope killed, in fact, since the more ancient-patriotic the nation goes, the more it is lying. The monarchy is like the Church of England; five in a hundred are for it, five against, and the rest don't care; can be cozened either way, one suspects, as in so many other matters. Anyway, we suddenly

decide we need France. I ring up the Wisemans in Grasse; yes, we can come down. It is all settled in ten minutes. We will leave about the 12th and drive down to them by the 20th or so.

4 June

Podge arrives. Nick and Anna, beginning to show her pregnancy, are here. P has at long last decided to show us his mysterious 'friend' of recent years. She is a young lady called Rowena, no beauty, a porcine nose, spectacles, very serious and 'ethical', of course. She works for War on Want and Mary Dines.[1] Cathy is with them, and her blue eyes wrily survey this new relationship. I deduce from silences that she does not really approve. We vote Rowena a very great bore. There is the usual endless talk, gas, about the horrors of the Jubilee, the threat of fascism, etc., etc. No household in Lyme where the words queen, monarchy, jubilee, can have been so frequently spoken over the twelve hours. Cathy, I think, is freeing herself of some of her father's worst manias and mannerisms; there must be some accusation implicit in her fierce defences of feminism. She is buying a house near Parliament Hill now; that would once have been seen as treachery to the cause.

5 June

Ronnie and Celia come over for lunch from Cudworth; renewed anathema poured on the Jubilee; but they, benighted pair, think it is all a joke. We find them much easier to get on with; went down on the beach with them after Podge and the two girls had left, walked along towards Pinhay.

8 June

We watched the Jubilee celebrations in London on the TV; the procession to St Paul's and all the rest of the pretty charade. So many absurd gentlemen dressed up in their ancient finery; pure theatre, and pure cultural hegemony. The oddest person there was the Queen herself; she seemed noticeably alert and sceptical, *watching*; even a ghost of her great namesake. To be fair, she plays the role with authority now; but her aptitude for it is not the question.

I went out yesterday night and saw the beacons on Portland Bill and by Hardy's Monument;[2] that did recall the other Elizabeth more clearly. The orange omens of the Armada.

Publication day for the revised *Magus*. A good review in *The Times* from Richard Holmes.

The then general secretary of War on Want.

A memorial tower in honour of Lord Nelson's flag captain aboard HMS *Victory*, Sir Thomas Masterman Hardy (1769–1839), situated at Blackdown, Dorset, near the village of Portesham where Hardy lived.

Less good news in the evening. Peter Hall rang to say that because of the loss of income caused by the recent Trotskyist strike at the National Theatre, they were faced with a £40,000 deficit, and something had to go. The two Don Juan plays, in fact.[1] 'It's been an agony for me . . . I promise you I will do it one day . . .'

12 June

To Weymouth, for France, a cold grey day. We meant to stay at Domfront, then foolishly drove on and ended at Mayenne, to find it crowded because of some 'tripletting' ceremony with a German and an English town; got ourselves into the Grand Hotel, where we stayed once before; and liked it, and its prices, no better this time. As well we went to Sweden just recently; even France cannot shock us now. In fact, as we were to realize, two things stay quite reasonable by English standards: rooms and meals. The first are even still cheap by English standards; the second give infinitely better value in the £4–£6 range than the same-priced menus at home.

We walked afterwards; the old roses, the screaming swifts, the paved quays. That lovely liberal use of town space in France. And the trite formality, in the little municipal park over the river.

13 June

We stopped at La Flèche, in hot sun at last, though a thunderstorm threatened over Saumur to the south; lunched in the Bois des Pins some miles south, beside a little lake of water-lilies. But it began to rain almost at once, so we retreated to the car. There were two lizard orchids out beside the road; one just out, and with some small spider's web across two of the flowers; the other, still in bud, unwebbed.

South: the hedges are rich, poppies, marguerites, the pale blue starry spires of *Campanulus rapunculus*. Bourgeuil, and across the Loire to Chinon. Then west towards Sainte Maure de Touraine; in a wood by the road, one or two mauve spikes of *Limidora*. Later we took an old green road, the Route de la Fond de Chêne, which we travelled once before; and stopped at a hillside where there were orchids. None of the previous Ladies, but the last of the Flies; and Fragrants and Greater Butterflies. Fritillaries. A tree-pipit.

Soon after this we went down a valley of cornflower meadows, beautiful deep blue washes of the plant.

Then into the Brenne again, straight to the Café de la Gabrière beside

---

[1] JF's version of Molière's play would eventually be staged at the National Theatre in 1981. The other Don Juan production that JF mentions is Christopher Hampton's translation of Ödon von Horvath's *Don Juan Comes Back from the War*. It would be performed at the National Theatre in 1978.

the lake. The whiskered terns, as always; and almost as soon as we
stopped, a marsh harrier dropped on to its nest in the reed-beds opposite. The same heavy, indifferent *patronne* and her little boy Pascal; and
upstairs exactly the same room we had last time, as exiguously furnished
as ever. The dinner was quite good, an excellent Pinot Chardonnay; but
at another table there was a group of telephone engineers on some
jaunt. They turned up in their yellow vans, drank, became increasingly
noisy. One became tipsy and very peculiar, refusing to join the others
inside; starting to fight when they tried to persuade him. Then suddenly
he started wading out into the middle of the *étang*, as if to drown himself.
He was got out, and given dry clothes, and put to sleep in one of the
cars. Noisier and noisier round their table, joshing some girls at the
next, despite the presence of their own young men. It would have
brought violence in any other country in the world; but here was
regarded with a sort of tolerant amusement. All of which amused us,
until we went to bed, and an impromptu disco began downstairs. It was
not only the thumping and racket of the jukebox below, but the fact
that an outside loudspeaker double-relayed the sound just beside our
window. We had an hour of it before someone thought to turn off the
relevant switch; and of course . . . anyone but the English would have
gone down an hour before and asked for it to be turned off. I did
complain the next morning to *madame*. She shrugged, in her usual indifferent way. She is very bizarre. She has made a small art of not living
up to every normal expectation of the hotel-keeper–guest relationship;
which, since it has become so artificial, stereotyped, means she has great
charm. We both like her for seemingly not liking us or anybody else.
Just very rarely she smiles, and almost genuinely. I should like to put
her in a book one day; also because she is a variation of that type of
working-class Frenchwoman who arrives, by sheer independence and
contempt for anything but her own judgement and feelings, at a kind
of aristocracy: what I have always best liked on that side of French society,
and which long predates the Revolution. What I like in Annette
Tringham; and in Eliz, who is an English example of the same thing.

14 June
We went to Mézière to get bread for our lunch, stopped on the way, the
flowers are irresistible. A colony of Lesser Butterflies among the tree
heather, Yellow Rattle, *Linum perenne*, the very pretty *Prunella laciniata*;
stands of tall blue-and-pink bugloss. Then another stop to see black
terns insect-hawking; kites, marsh harriers, a huge though distant sparrowhawk of a bird that must in fact have been a goshawk. Hoopoes
everywhere, and the warblers. We went to our old picnic-place, but had
to eat in the car in heavy rain; the weather is not at all as we had hoped.
The Greenwings and Jersey orchids were over, but where they had

flowered was now a huge colony of Lesser Butterflies, hundreds and hundreds of them.

We drove on past the Château de Bouchet to the Etang de la Mer Rouge. Many Lizard orchids beside the roads; they vary greatly in width of the lip-tongue. Also here the exquisite *Lathyrus nissolia*, most elegant of all the vetches; and the delicate *Althaea hirsuta*.

Then another ornithological treat, a bittern flying over, circling, as if it were lost.

Next I spotted a juniper heathlet, that looked good at a glimpse, and proved so; both butterfly species, Fragrants, and a small colony of Bees (which seem rare here). The latter showed precisely the variation between milky and deep pink sepals I find on the Undercliff at home.

A fine hors d'oeuvres for dinner, and a good Chinon. Eliz spends the evening telling me I am too lucky (to have such lovely days with nature) for the good of my soul.

15 June

South to Peyrat-le-Château,[1] but miserable weather from the afternoon on. We took the upland road round the back of Lake Vassivière; mist, rain, mournfulness. Many dactylorchids in the bogs; in places the landscape, or what one could see of it, was washed pink with them. One fine little daisy near Royère, *Arnica montana*; its yellow heads are so conspicuous among the lower and much smaller plants that it looks like a garden escape. Vassivière, shrouded in mist, seemed more like Norway, fjordland, than Central France. We went to the most old-fashioned-looking of the hotels in Peyrat; an overwelcoming *patronne*, remote from la Gabrière. I had a bath; a black redstart on a roof outside.

16 June

To Sousceyrac.[2] We stopped to see the stained glass at Eymoutiers. Market day, the streets crowded, the old church pleasingly deserted and silent. Then on south, Treignac, Egletons: an unpopulated green countryside, combes, streams, herds of cows with their *vachers* and *vachères*. We had a picnic lunch by a rushing stream in a break of sunshine, and watched two Glanville Fritillaries *in cop*. They were at it for at least half an hour, the male doing little dances and wing-flutterings; during cloud they sat wings closed, side by side, like polite small children.

Tree-pipits and woodlarks. I also saw three red-backed shrike during this day (and more on others). It suddenly grew very hot, Eliz slept beside the road, while I watched one of the shrikes: the field below the telephone wires it sat on was full of corncockle, splendid pink flowers.

[1] A small town in the department of Haute–Vienne in the Limousin.
[2] A town in the department of Lot in the Midi-Pyrénées.

From about this latitude they become not uncommon, all the way down to Provence.

Sousceyrac, where the restaurant has a star; but we chose the wrong, the most expensive, of the various menus. It was too heavy, bloating, and we suspected mainly out of tins. The townlet is odd; one quarter is still medieval, *'pittoresque'* with its shadowed cellars, stairs, swifts and martins screaming everywhere. Elsewhere, an extraordinary collection of closed hotels, cafés, shops, some of them of very great Utrillo-like charm; faded colours, signs, cobwebbed windows, empty rooms choked with debris behind. A beautifully folk-lettered HOTEL DE LA TERRASSE in ochre on tired white plaster, beneath a line of dull green shutters; a dead draper's, AU PETIT PARIS, elegant old windows enshrining nothingness; another extinct hotel, an ancient sign in its window, 'oil cooker for sale'. It had obviously been there for years. The place had a painful air of extreme poverty, depopulation; one wondered how its remaining inhabitants live – certainly in a world remote from that of the general 1977.

17 June

Millau:[1] we went to a Michelin-recommended hotel in a converted château just past the town; were lucky, got the last room, in what was evidently the waiters' wing, but agreeably primitive, an old room with ancient arched windows. The hotel is rather charming: full of relics from some forgotten Victorian prima donna's life; its walls covered in *Campsis* vines, red-shuttered, shady. Before dinner we walked out of the village and up beside a tumbling stream to its source in a grotto; passed no one but an old shepherd with his descending flock – whose *raison d'être* in this area we had at the end of a good dinner, a fine Roquefort. It is an appalling price in the shops here; but then it is, we decided, indisputably the greatest blue cheese the world knows. It leaves Stilton and our own Dorset Blue nowhere.

We strolled to the square below the château afterwards: *pétanque* in full boom, some children looking for a dog, a full café, cars, cries, the deadly seriousness with which they play the game. Their refusal to play it on flat surfaces – in other words, the huge element of pure chance, the intervening bit of grit, the depth of sand over hard surface, plays in winning or losing – is very French. One of the young men here was a fine *tireur*. That does involve pure skill, of course. We watched him knock out a given ball ten times in a row.

18 June

We decided to make it a rest day for Eliz, to stay another night. The day started well, then rain again. We wandered round old Millau, gloomy

---

[1] At the heart of the Grands Causses region in the department of Aveyron, Millau is just north of Roquefort.

under the grey skies: meridional high-housed town streets are for shade in sun, not 'English' weather. We poked round a modern pottery, indifferent stoneware, astronomical prices. A very ordinary teapot was marked at the equivalent of £40. Then round a junk-shop. The old-clothes fad has hit France, Eliz sorted through blouses and nightgowns; I bought one or two nice old postcards of Dover and London in Edwardian times but at alert prices, alas. One admittedly very fine card of an early Tour de France team was marked at £3.

The weather cleared a little, so we went up out of the town on to the Causse Noir; superb views, a marvellous coffered limestone upland; its meadows and clearings like a medieval tapestry, enamelled with flowers. We had lunch on the wall of a ruined farm, in whose interstices grew the little toadflax, *Chaenorhinum minor*. Scarce swallowtails, blues, tortoiseshells, fritillaries . . .

We drove on a few miles to look at the natural city (of weather-worn limestone rocks) of Vieux Montpelier; but on a little rise just before we got there I saw an unmistakable ashen-pink as we passed. A Military . . . and then the finest half-hour of my orchid-hunting life, a kind of secret temple of the family. Within ten feet of the Military I had seen I found colonies of Birdsnest, Flies, Burnts, Bees, Twayblades; and close by, *D. fuchsii*, Lesser Butterflies (some of huge size), Pyramids, Fragrants, Greenwings; then *ensifolia* as well as *damasonium* – thirteen species, all within a hundred yards. I found only three other Militaries, alas. They remain a very scarce plant.

Heaven.

19 June
We set off south again, up and across the huge green expanses of the Causse de Larzac, a Dartmoor without the heather – and like Dartmoor, the site of a continuing battle between military and the ecologists.

We left the main road to visit the village of La Couvertoirade, an old fortified 'base' for the Knights Templar – it is impressively unspoilt, thanks mainly to a band of young communards, arts-and-craftsmen, who have taken the old houses over and now do their potting, weaving and all the rest isolated from the rest of the world; have chosen to make a very positive *non au camp* by re-inhabiting the wilderness. One felt sympathetic and at the same time a little sceptical: whether self-conscious young intellectuals can escape so easily, or the battle really be won by such colonies. There was an elegantly primitive young couple in the little castle on the village walls; one was allowed in for a franc: an array of tasteful peasant furniture, pots, old implements and the rest. On a terrace outside we watched a shepherd in the valley below leading a huge flock across the meadowland; a beautiful tidal murmur of thirty or forty bronze bells carried to us on the light breeze. They live a very pretty exile here, if such it is.

From there back to the main road; through, or over, the spectacular Pas de l'Escalette, the first crag martins; then down into the lowlands. We had lunch under the Pont de Gignac, supposed to be the most beautiful in France.[1] It is very pure and sober, even for the Age of Enlightenment; cream-gold arches over deep green water. Cetti's Warblers scolding from both banks, and a fine butterfly, the Southern White Admiral.

One descends very soon, by this route, into the horrors of twentieth-century civilization – if not also those of the twenty-first. Montpellier first, and an interminable circuit of a ring-road to avoid the centre; then into a French California, factories, hoardings, freeways, down to the sea a few miles away. La-Grande-Motte[2] stands like a white turd: the termite future. An endless stream of traffic, and far more roads than my old Michelin map shows. Our destination was Le Grau du Roi; even remoter this time from my ancient memories of it;[3] and teeming, the road and walks beside the canal one mass of people – working-class people, tat. It was like Southend on an August Bank Holiday; some sardine-boats and *thoniers* still, and terns flying over the water; but even the sea was packed with boats, skiers. It was difficult to believe that this could exist on the same planet as the lovely deserted *causses*, La Couvertoirade that morning.

We finally got ourselves into the Hôtel de la Plage; and had not too bad a meal. The place did seem to regain a quieter ghost of its old self after dinner; all the Sunday day-trippers had gone home. We drove east to have a look at the other new pleasure-dome (or *ville-loisir*) that now defiles this strand: Port Camargue. That proved so extraordinary, so endless, empty, deserted, futuristic, that we quite enjoyed it. Boulevard after boulevard (their central green strips apparently watered by remote control, every so often hidden nozzles would suddenly emit arches of water) fringed by largely uninhabited honeycombs of flats; exotic balconies, entrances, rooflines; constant exhortations to visit *appartements-témoin, marina-maisons-témoin*, which give the effect of a harassed super-realtor stuck with an enormous pup – but apparently not, since everywhere also were new waste lots awaiting development or being developed. Cranes, *bureaux de vente; vues inalienables de la mer.* We got completely lost, found ourselves going in mysterious circles, and expected at any moment to see the figure of M. Tati stooping and tripping his way across the road. It is his territory to a degree that speaks well of his genius. His comedies become reality here.

We stopped at last outside the one café, small oasis of light and life,

[1] Designed by Bertrand Garipuy (1748–1782), the three-arched bridge was built between 1776 and 1810.
[2] A modern coastal development close to Montpellier.
[3] During a long vacation when JF was at Oxford, he had helped to take a yacht up the coast from Collioure near Spain to a winter berth at Le Grau du Roi in the Camargue. See *The Journals*, volume 1, pages xiii–xiv.

the place seemed to possess: an ice-cream parlour. A grandiose menu of very superb confections; every flavour, every liqueur, in every combination, and named and priced with a suitable pretentiousness. But they were good. A group of what sounded like Swiss or Belgians. A bored young wife with her *au pair* and child. The vast silences of the mushroom city all around. Hardly a car passed for the thirty minutes we sat there.

What I find difficult to imagine is the kind of person who would willingly live in such a place, and in France of all countries. The rich and fastidious would avoid it like the plague; the working classes would hate its lack of any central life and animation. It can therefore only be for the petit bourgeoisie, the minor *rentiers*, the brainwashed, cultureless, self-exploited lump of the capitalist system; who fall for every admass lie.

20 June

I got up early, and walked on the beach, pleasantly deserted after yesterday's crowds, a Boudinscape. A few other early strollers, a paper-picker, a mechanical broom at work on the promenade. Terns fishing, gulls – and a sight that surprised me very much, five eider, two moulting drakes and three females, off the mole. But the book says they do come this far south.

We set off back to Aigues-Mortes for a day in the Camargue: within a mile of Grau du Roi, flamingoes feeding on the far side of a brackish lagoon; closer, a Gull-billed Tern among some Sandwich. Little egrets and marsh harriers everywhere from then on. Not far from the Vaccarès we stopped to look at a herd of cattle, and then beyond, some eight or nine hundred yards away, a flutter of long black-and-white wings – a luck I had not expected, a large flock of stilts. Every now and then they flew up, the long red legs trailing. We had a picnic lunch on the edge of a field beside the inland sea; many Fan-tailed Warblers, whose call comes from every roadside in this area.

Then more luck: I walked a little along the road and came on a flock of bee-eaters. They were using a small stand of tamarisk as a perch. Their flight is very beautiful. It has a paper-dart quality, and going into the stiff breeze they arrived once or twice at a point of stationariness in the air. These birds seemed always to start downwind on their hunting flights, then to circle back upwind to the original perch; in descending flight they have a strange ballerina-like uptilting of the beak and head, very charming – something parakeetish about them, and not only in the gorgeous plumage. They were very noisy, a constant *pruit, pruit* – as distinctive in its way as the hoopoe's call.

We went on next to the eastern end of the Camargue: whiskered and black terns, another stilt, eight more bee-eaters on electricity pylon wires. I also found a colony of Lizard orchids, but almost over now.

Back through the rice-fields to Arles, then on the motorway west towards the Alpilles. We struck off up to Maussane, beside hedges and *maquis* sweet with the scent of *Spartium. Cistus salviaefolius* in flower, rosemary, origan. At Maussane we went to the shabby L'Oustalou in the plane-treed square; it's another hotel indifferent to its customers, shabby little rooms. But the meal was excellent, and we drank a Listel Gris de Gris from the vineyards we had passed earlier that day. We seemed surrounded by Germans and Dutch: endless conversations in pidgin French about the menu with the waitresses, endless suspicion about the perfectly good *prix fixe* meals, endless searching the *à la carte* section for something they felt they could trust. They must miss so much. We have met very few British this time; we saw the first other car with a GB plate today in the Camargue. Swedes and Teutons are everywhere.

We drove up afterwards to Les Baux, walked round the place, leant over the parapet and stared down at La Baumanière, where the millionaires eat – and I suppose bestselling novelists would, if they could be bothered. Les Baux is chi-chi now, an eternally empty stage; a Greek amphitheatre used only by barbarians.

21 June
We decided to do the longer route through the Durance valley and over the mountains to Draguignan rather than do it all by motorway. A pleasing region, I would like to have stopped more; a true Mediterranean flora begins. *Catananche,* yellow knapweed, all sorts of interesting wayside flowers. We stopped for lunch near Varages, in a valley of stony meadows and oakwoods. Looking for flowers I came in the middle of one field on an extraordinary caterpillar, three inches long, white and red spectacles on black; the larva of the Spurge Hawk, no less. It was feeding on *Euphorbia,* a very handsome beast. Then in the oakwood beyond I spotted a touch of pink in the deep shade beneath a tree . . . and there was the long-sought *Cephalanthera rubra* – the Red Helleborine.

Later, near Draguignan, we stopped in another wood dense with *E. helleborine.* It varies enormously in colour and lip-shape and size; the prettiest have a great deal of rose and purple in the flower; others almost none.

At last we went through Peymeinade[1] and came to St François; and had trouble finding the Wisemans' new house, the Clos des Sources, which is tucked away up the hill near the school. It is modern, nice and airy, a terrace, a splendid swimming-pool; like California, and a long way from our poor little hotel rooms on the way here. Malou unchanged, all over us, Boris immediately showing off with his diving and swimming. Tom appeared later, back from Cogolin, where they move next week,

---

[1] A small town in the foothills of the Alps about five kilometres south of Grasse.

having decided they can't afford the £1,000 a month they pay for this
house. And they have finally decided to live in the USA; will go in
September, when we are there.

After dinner we coaxed out of them the absurd tragi-comedy that has
been going on with the Colliers down below at the Blanchissage. We
were already warned: the old painter Jo Jones had rung me just before
we left about a 'terrible' letter she had had from John Collier: how
depressed he was, an 'awful' situation that had arisen with his 'tenants'
(the Wisemans). Jo, of course, did not know that we knew them. It is
all financial, it seems, a quite appallingly picayunish quarrel over who
owes money to whom. Tom feels full of guilt, almost despair. Being old
friends, they made no written agreement when they exchanged houses,
the Blanchissage for 44 Arkwright Road; it was just understood that they
would settle ordinary running-cost bills during their exchanged tenan-
cies. But Tom now revealed that he had lent John C £600 a year ago,
and met many of the Collier boy's expenses when he lived with them
in London. John Collier now claims it was no loan, but a mere matter
of 'currency exchange convenience'. Every day a long letter from him
is delivered by hand (not his, but that of some estate agent in
Peymeinade), listing dozens of mythical expenses the Wisemans have
incurred at the Blanchissage: use of firewood, vegetables; and his latest
charge is for 'anti-matter' in the cesspit. He claims the Wisemans have
used up 'valuable space there'; wants to charge them for having put up
a TV aerial in his absence (even though they had it taken down before
he returned). The expense here is to John's 'aesthetic feelings if I had
known you had done such a terrible thing'.

It is clear Tom is in the right, and that John C is not only feckless
with money – he has appalling tax problems – but up to every welshing
trick in the game. Tom and Malou are mortified to the depths of their
green souls, but we made them laugh in the end, and tell us about it.
It really is too absurd to be taken seriously.

We sense they are much more at ease with the rich life now. They
say they have made friends, go about much more. I already sense they
are fools to leave France for America.

22 June
I woke up with a chill; and Tom with yet another six-page typed anathema
from John Collier. This one had been posted three days before – from
a house just four hundred yards away. We laze about the pool while
Boris gets a coaching lesson from the village schoolmaster. *Pas d'application*, says the young man when I ask him how B has got on at school.
They mean to send him to the Lycée Française in New York.

We went off after lunch to look at a house with them; nothing has
changed there. It was at Magnanosc, tucked away just under the

hideously busy main road out of Grasse; a wretched little garden. Yet they mull and mull over it, when anyone normal would have said no at the first glimpse. So we piled back into Tom's new white Mercedes, which he drives at fierce speed down the winding lanes all round Grasse – he claims it's quite safe, because of power steering and 'assisted' brakes (whatever they are), but I do not find it so. We stopped off on the other side of the Vallée Verte to see the De Noailles garden: small, but very pretty with its water and its terraces. Some interesting trees and plants. We arrive home to find yet another letter of commination from John Collier – hand-delivered this time. It plunges Tom and Malou into another bout of despair. We take them out to eat up at Cabris, but they won't be cheered up. We enjoy it, all the same; and the view from the terrace afterwards down to the coast, the frogs' voices and the fireflies.

23 June

Thunder and rain, the bad weather dogs us. An Alpine swift overhead, and a buzzard, Sardinian warblers in the garden. I read a biography of Musset, of the affaire with Sand. He was a schizophrenic, of course; but his indifference to all but his own mind, his own fantasies – especially in the plays – makes him an archetypal writer. A sympathetic man, for all his faults.

Eliz and I went into Grasse with Malou in the afternoon, when the rain had eased. It is being killed by the motor-car, though the old quarters are still attractive. There seem ever more *pieds noirs*, one part is now more like a North African *souk* than France. According to Malou, there is increasing ill-feeling and racial trouble in the town.

We had supper in. Tom showed me their neighbour Ivor's masterwork, or 'paper', on his family's genealogy. He traces it back through Clarendon and English royalty to King Brian of Ireland. It is to be part of his biography of another ancestor, Lady Castlemaine.[1] Tom finds it hilarious.

The evening reminds us of 44 Arkwright Road: a strange feeling these two always manage to give of not owning their own surroundings, of being in an eternal hotel – of course, they *are* in a rented house. It is just that they make all their environments seem rented.

24 June

We went before lunch to Castelmaras, an old village bought up by millionaires, now with fences round it and gate-guards, like Bel-Air; to pick up a millionaire's wife. Her husband founded the Mothercare shop-chain. A plastic lady, I thought: much talk of the logistics of the Wisemans' move to New York, her home city. She did try to suggest to Tom that his notion that he can arrive in mid-September and find an apartment with a garage within close walking distance of the Lycée

[1] The mistress of Charles II.

Française was optimistic. But he will not be budged – he thinks a year in New York, then a year in Hollywood. I told him he was mad, the other evening, to want to live in the latter community, especially when he knew exactly what its evils were. He then proceeded to hold forth, in his manner, on the evils; and is still determined to do it. He cannot give up his fascination for the rich and the famous. I think he is trapped now into the kind of writing that will bring him endless misery: that silly rat-race for ever higher advances, ever greater sales.

I went out with Boris in the afternoon: along the canal, to the old ruined cottage above the Blanchissage. We have decided we must line up with the Wisemans. Boris, as always, much nicer and more amenable on his own. He is a bright child, very imaginative about nature. We fished a dead grass snake out of the water, which pleased him; especially when I suggested he put it in the refrigerator for his mother to find. I think they owe him, his more poetic, malleable side, that little revenge.

That evening two young Antibes socialites came over and we went out to dinner: we were fervently assured we would like them, which made sure we didn't. I can't understand how Tom and Malou, who possess sound geigers in a number of things to do with the heart, are so undiscriminating over people like these two. Bob and Maridou Leitel, both divorced, he is an American novelist, she comes from some old Antibes family, *haute bourgeoisie*, a sharp and acid-tongued young woman. She designs gardens for a chic international clientele along the coast. We went to a restaurant in the village on the way to Cabris. It was run, and the meal served, by a loud-mouthed, cornily familiar *patron*. Maridou spent the last part of the meal composing a written critique of the meal (which was not too bad in fact): full of sarcasms and quite witty, if it had not stunk so much of an eighteenth-century aristocrat court lady's eternal contempt for peasants and *roturiers*. But I had to give her a point when we stood up to leave. She simply passed her critique to him. Fay Maschler would have approved of that.

We sat dranking back at the Clos des Sources into the small hours. Shallow chat: things never taken in the abstract, always reduced to personalities – mainly one's own. This is another prevalent form of reification, in this 'set': think things, not ideas or principles.

Musset: *En vérité, ce siècle est un mauvais moment.*

25 June
We went down to Antibes, to look at the Picasso Museum. It is full of his third-rate work: indifferent paintings, some really bad pottery. There was just one yellow-glazed bird-shape I liked. But it was worthwhile for just one drawing by him, of a she-goat: a magnificent piece of draughtsmanship, the goat almost life-size. There is also a good Marquet landscape there.

We went on, my treat, to see the Jardin Thuret on the Cap,[1] but it was closed. So we visited the lighthouse and climbed and looked down on the cancerous conurbation eating up the greenery all around. But the Sanctuaire, the sailors' chapel beside the light, is delightful: a splendid array of ex-voto ship-models and naive marine paintings donated by saved seamen. One showed a blue, black and white sailing-ship off Madeira, in a storm, with a huge orange-red fireball on one of the masts. It dated from the 1830s, a marvellous combination of science fiction and folk-art.

We went back to Antibes and wandered round the old town; bought Boris his ritual present; an 'action man' for 47 francs (cost of production, 5). He is besotted by these toys, which can be dressed in all sorts of ways. It's curious (if you ignore the fact that the clothes are all military uniforms, with accompanying 'commando' weapons) how close the basic idea is to the little girl's doll; of dressing and undressing and talking to the midget face. I insisted on buying a *charcuterie* dinner for us, to Tom's horror. One must not suggest delicious food is nicer than virtuous obedience to current rules of personal regimen. He wouldn't eat any of it when we got home and stuffed ourselves. In fact we begin, with our lack of famous friends and international set connections, to bore him, poor man.

27 June

We got off for the long drive home about midday, on the Route Napoléon.[2] A last look back above St Vallier, at the coastal plain; then into the mountains. It was an easier drive than we expected, very little traffic over much of it; and ever better landscapes as the Alps grew nearer – that curious feeling of returning a season.

Sisteron. The old town down by the river brings one as close to the Middle Ages as one is likely to get at this remove; endless narrow alleys, stepped streets and the strange *androbes*, or corridor-tunnels, built above them. At night it is like a stage set. We wandered down to the Durance, green, alive and silent; had a brandy in a café, with a row of limestone fossils on the shelf behind us; stared at the little house where Napoleon rested. One had to give the devil his due – the speed with which he covered this ground on his famous march to Grenoble is hardly credible today. At least part of the effect he created, the prestige so rapidly recovered during that week of his life, must have been due to his

[1] A botanical garden founded by Gustave Thuret (1817–1875), which contains many rare plants not native to Europe.

[2] Opened in 1932, the Route Napoléon (D85) follows the route Napoleon took on his march from Cannes to Grenoble, after leaving his exile in Elba on 1 March 1815.

constantly appearing earlier than anyone can have expected: human lightning.[1]

28 June

North again, the mountains with snow now. Eliz was exhausted with the Route Nationale driving, so we drove on into a lonely mountain valley, ringed with majestic grey pinnacles of rock, and stopped at a tiny village and winter ski-resort called Gresse-en-Vercors. Then, having got into the hotel there, straight out for a walk; along a lane between Alpine meadows dense with flowers, sainfoin, blue knapweeds and the commonest flower here, the blue *Geranium montanum.*

A good dinner, then a stroll round the peaceful little village; there is a litter of chalets round the nucleus of old houses, but they seemed all deserted. Each old house had a cowshed beneath its roof; an ancient peasant life. Redstarts and serins singing everywhere, no traffic at all. We took to it very much; and decided to give it another day.

29 June

But did not allow for Alpine weather. We woke to heavy drizzle, and yesterday's splendid landscapes all under mist; so reluctantly decided to leave.

A miserable morning's driving in rain and mist; through Grenoble, then Lyons and up the main drag as far as Mâcon, where we turned off for Cluny; the rain stopped by then, but still grey and wintry. We did the Abbey; put our heads into one or two exhibitions – it is getting too much, this way modern artists and craftsmen congregate round ancient monuments. Something parasitical about it that I do not like.

I had wanted to stay at a one-star restaurant hotel there, but its rooms were full; so we booked a table and found a little rooming-place above a draper's. A very good dinner, worth its star.

30 June

To Bourges, which proved a nightmare of traffic when we got there; in fact we went through it, finding nowhere to park – nearly went on, but I persuaded Eliz to try once again. So we turned back, parked, found a little hotel in a side-street. It is a beautiful, rich old city, I think fit to be put with La Rochelle; but one has to work hard to get behind its outward reality of a traffic- and tourist-ruined one.

[1] Crossing the Alps between Digne and Sisteron with 1200 men, Napoleon arrived in Grenoble in the evening of 7 March 1815. Although he was marching over extremely mountainous terrain, he covered the distance of over 300 kilometres in just six days.

The museum and Jacques Coeur's palace were closed for the day,[1] so we went up to the cathedral. The glass there is, I think, the most beautiful in Europe, taken window by window: the medieval range in the chapels behind the altar are of incomparable depth and intensity of colour. The effect is almost of Bridget Riley and Op Art: the retina is bemused, entranced, one kept on having to look back over one's shoulder. The experience is less aesthetic, in fact, than a direct physical sensation of coloured light. No other glass-makers seem ever to have quite equalled the blues and reds here – the sapphires and rubies.

Some of the later medieval and early Renaissance glass is also of the very highest quality; one or two faces worthy of a Botticelli or a Da Vinci.

1 July

We went to the museum, some good Roman and Romano-Celtic things, a rich, long past; and were about to go away, but the for once friendly ticket attendant insisted we should look upstairs. Fortunately we took his advice, for there we came on an extraordinary collection of early nineteenth-century earthenware: the most exciting work of its kind I have seen for many years. It was apparently all produced by one family, called Talbot. Their gift was a wonderful fantasy and sense of form. They made splendid orthodox bowls, bottles and jugs; but also satirical heads, and finest of all, a range of bottles in female shape, some pretty, one or two wickedly ugly, hook-nosed old viragos and spinsters. Almost the same glaze throughout: a rich ochre-yellow. I wished Nick was with us: the inventiveness would have delighted him; the blend of folk-humour and technical skill.

From that to the palace of Jacques Coeur, with all its Renaissance splendours and humours. An interesting man, I bought an account of his famous trial.[2] He ias obviously a major peculator, a fixer, a usurer; and guilty on most of the charges. Yet one does still get the impression of the beginning of a democrat in him; a contempt for the automatic privileges of birth, which was perhaps his downfall – having the spirit of the nineteenth century five hundred years too soon. The charm and wit of so much of the stone sculpture in the palace is also very humanist; far too large a man, in both good and bad senses of the word, for his age.

We went to the cathedral once more to experience the glass. Then set off across the Sologne; stayed the night beside the Loire. A last stroll by the great river, in the dusk. The calm, lithe water, cries of sandpipers, terns.

[1] Jacques Coeur (c. 1395–1456) was the immensely rich finance minister to Charles VII.

[2] After the death of Charles VII's mistress Agnes Sorel in 1450, Coeur was arrested and accused of poisoning her. Although this charge was soon discredited, he was eventually convicted of a number of other crimes and stripped of his fortune.

2 July

Driving all day, and ending at Vire, where we put up at the hotel by the central *rondpoint*; an old-fashioned place, run by a formidable grey-haired lady, a born headmistress. But her restaurant merits its star. We have stayed there before; and I would happily see her in charge of any school for hotel-keepers – provided our friend from la Gabrière was also on the faculty. The type grows rare in France, rulers of their establishments with a punctilious rod of iron. One more black mark against 'progress'.

3 July

To Le Havre, various stops for last shoppings on the way. We got there early, so had a last little spree in a Sunday-filled restaurant; half a dozen oysters each, a sole.

   Then Weymouth, the green evening run beside the Chesil Bank, and home.

30 July

To London, to see Annie Saumont about the French translation of *The Ebony Tower*. She sent me a book of her own recently, *Enseigne pour une école de monstres*; allusive, linked short stories, told in a breathless, jumping style, like some French Virginia Woolf. An odd girl. My straightforward-ness must seem very dull to her. Her sister is married to an English dentist, she revealed this time.

31 July

Also to see Fay Godwin, with whom I am now contracted to do a book on the Scillies.[1] She looked much older, though the cancer is appar-ently quiescent; a lined face, arctic-green eyes betraying her steely will behind the mild manner. She has become a very good photographer of landscape. She said of one I admired, 'I had to wait three days for that.' Her forte is the elemental, the faintly louring. Stones, skylines, moods; the occasional beautiful semi-abstract surface. There was one of flooded grass in a meadow in a recent book she has illustrated; of the very highest class. Of the Scillies set she has done I felt only a few achieved her previous best standards; but she goes again this autumn. An impressive woman, reputedly very difficult; but I have not seen that side of her yet.

8 August

Dog-days. Nothing here since we went to France on June 12th. I have the usual depression, or aboulia, because of the book. The first finished copy came ten days ago: it is dead, but of course won't be buried yet.

---

[1] Published by Jonathan Cape in 1978, the book would be called *Islands*.

Neither weather nor this particular summer helps. It is grey and warm, and no rain, or only the lightest showers. The whole garden waits, as I do, and I cannot be bothered to do anything in it. Lyme is foul, traffic-jammed, overcrowded, shoddy, its largely working-class holiday-makers ever more dispiriting – both sad in their hopelessness and hopeless in their sad refusal not to demand more from life (or a holiday town) than this. The sea is increasingly crowded with pleasure-craft, power-boats, water-skiers. Lyme is the whole country, the whole world; polluted, over-crowded, largely apathetic, fated to dropping standards in everything.

The BBC have been down two or three times to prepare for an hour's programme about me; a producer called Julia Matheson. They start filming on Wednesday, Melvyn Bragg to do the interviewing. Not a prospect I look forward to; and Eliz even less.

9 August

Bragg and Julia Matheson come, to discuss tomorrow's interview. He is polite, relaxed, perhaps a little too anxious not to abuse his present power as the chief circus-barker of the British literary world – though he is shortly to leave the BBC and to act as the presenter of ITV's *Aquarius*. That is slotted against the BBC's *Match of the Day*, which shows what ITV thinks of culture; but he seems to see it as a challenge.

10 August

The crew of seven moved into the living-room with their lights and para-phernalia, and we did the interview. All went fairly smoothly; Melvyn questions well, sympathetically. He is careful, briefed to his eyebrows. I make up answers as I go along, thinking of all the things that are not being said. The fifty other possible answers.

15 August

A photographer called David Stein was here, for the *Sunday Times*. He mentioned he'd recently been doing Robert Bolt 'near Totnes'. My ears pricked up – where exactly? Littlehempston.

In other words, only four or five miles from where I have set Daniel Martin's retreat.[1] It's a very odd coincidence, and an unfortunate one; by a lesser oddity his new house is the one that Ann Jellicoe here in Lyme thought of buying before she settled for Colway Manor. Although he was no way in my conscious mind during the writing of the book – I took nothing factual or material from what I know of his private life – it had occurred to me once or twice, worrying about whether a literate

---

[1] Daniel Martin's retreat was inspired by Ipplepen, the Devon village where JF had lived with his family during the war (see introduction to *The Journals*, volume 1, pages x–xi). Littlehempston is the first village south of Ipplepen on the Totnes road.

and humanistically inclined screenwriter was plausible, that Bolt was a sort of proof that the type does exist.

Stein said he was still miserable over the wretched and now departed Sarah Miles; described him standing near the Dart, almost in tears. I feel sorry for him. The little bitch must have bewitched him, and almost literally. I will send a copy of the book, and what regrets I can for the tricks life plays on fictions.

16 August

Tom Maschler found out today that Bolt has mercifully only just moved to Littlehempston – six months ago, to be precise. Long after the text was in the works.

18 August

We went over to Litton Cheney, to the Old Rectory, at the invitation of the engraver Reynolds Stone's wife Janet, to meet Iris Murdoch and John Bayley – I am apparently at long last considered respectable by that set, at least. To be fair, they were very kind, and it went jollily and well. John Bayley rushing about, supervising the drinks, stuttering and then fluent, like a demented butler on holiday; he's a professor at St Catherine's now. We talked old names, John Grigg[1] and so on. He told me he proposed Grigg for the wardenship at the recent election,[2] but he was voted out; as was Anthony Quinton.[3] He burbles rather charmingly, head tilted, blocked on certain syllables. Iris M has grown dumpy and stout; a blue dress, coyly amused grey Irish eyes. She is much more an Irish earth-mother now than the Oxford don, a comfortable middle-aged lady. 'Are you religious?' she asks me. We agree we are not. I complain of the emptiness and flatness I feel after finishing a novel. 'I don't feel that. I go madly cleaning out the house and hanging new curtains, or some-thing. Or I pretend to for two or three days.' I said I had become far too expert at doing nothing. 'Oh, but that's a great art.' And she talked about her schooldays and a headmistress who insisted she must always be doing something 'worthwhile'. 'I've always remembered that. Worthwhile.'

26 August

I have got very angry with Little, Brown over these last few weeks, for keeping me so ill-informed over *Daniel Martin*; it broke the other day

---

[1] A fellow-student of JF at New College, John Grigg (1924–2001) became a jour-nalist, broadcaster and author of several political biographies.
[2] i.e., of New College.
[3] The philosopher was then a fellow and tutor of New College.

and I wrote to Arthur Thornhill, telling him something had gone badly wrong at Beacon Street. The first American copies have come; I was, for the first time, not shown the final jacket, or the blurb, which contains one silly factual error, and virtually my address here. I would have suppressed that. Then they have told me nothing of their plans: copy price, print, publicity, all the rest. I am hamstrung because I don't want to hurt Ned Bradford. But things have been getting worse ever since Bob Fetridge left: no catalogues for years, no contact.

One reason, which I know only today (since Lois Wallace sent them), may be that the two pre-publication reviews, the *PW* and the *Kirkus*, were both bad, the *Kirkus* very bad. They came out on July 7th and 14th, so they have been kept from me for over a month now. I try to think what has gone wrong over these last years. They are frightened to tell me their judgement of the book was overoptimistic; I am too grand now to be able to bear such things; I am classed as a bestseller, interested only in sales. Whatever it is, I do not like it. I nearly sent a cable today refusing to do their accursed tour.

The two reviews are not the only bad auguries I have had. The Book of the Month Club puff, by Clifton Fadiman, also arrived today. I found that almost worse than the *Kirkus*, in its plastic hyperbole; and failure to connect with anything the book is truly about.

Mercifully the fifth Test was on, in what has been a sick, bad day; and I could watch Boycott, and an eventful match. He is this summer's delight: a man seemingly as naive as an unripe apple off the field, but a master at the wicket – a great craftsman and technician. He 'leaves' balls more convincingly than most batsmen strike boundaries; it is his mastership of judgement that I like best. How seldom you wonder whether he may have made a wrong choice of stroke or non-stroke.[1]

The BBC send the transcript of the Bragg interview. It reads so absurdly that it is almost funny: so incoherent, lousy, quite literally lousy with you know's and I mean's and I think's. I think my almost total inability to say what I mean must be very much why I write.

As usual I keep rehearsing imaginary interviews from the still-to-come American trip. They are quite useless, indeed inhibiting, in any actual interview 'situation'! But I did come on a distinction yesterday I liked (to a mythical interviewer complaining about the sprawl of *Daniel Martin*): 'Most writers have discovered what they are. I am still discovering what I am.'

---

[1] Geoff Boycott had been recalled to the England team for the 'Ashes' series against Australia after the second test, scoring 88 in the third test at Trent Bridge, and 191 in the fourth test at Headingley. On the day of this diary entry, he scored 39 out of an England innings total of 181. England won the series 3–0.

10 September
To Heathrow, for New York. Our plane is delayed four hours. Some
engineering fault on top of the air controllers' strike: all the world on
endless benches in the departure lounge. Arabs and Asians, Americans,
Babel. We got away in the end in a Jumbo, sitting in the centre aisle in
the tail, wondering why we do not travel the first class we can so easily
afford. But I think it remains better that we do not.

We arrived in New York just after seven, local time. A chauffeur and
limo were there to waft us to the Dorset.

11 September
A clear, funny day; the temperature is 20. We went to the Guggenheim;
circled down the walls of the present exhibition; I liked a little group
of four servants best – a fine green warmth. A very good Klee: *Hat, Lady
and Small Table*. Two couscous in pitta in the museum restaurant, then
we strolled back beside Central Park in the sun, a warm breeze, Sunday
New Yorkers. I feel ill, the accursed varicose veins in my legs and the
'pins and needles' in my left arm are back again after a year's absence.
I eat the wrong food, I drink too much (not very much, but more than
I can take); above all, I smoke too much. It poisons my body, as the
accursed television poisons society: with permission. For several years
now my body is both internally and externally something I should rather
be without. I keep it for the input of the senses, not for any pleasure
in their exercise.

12 September
Interviews, interviews. *Women's Wear Daily* in the morning; Herbert Mitgang
of the *Times* at the Algonquin for lunch; Mel Gussan of the *Times* again
all afternoon. The latter sits for hours, slowly pursuing lines. He didn't
go until six; as last time, I remember. A mild, ruminative man, I like him.

Christopher Lehmann-Haupt's daily review in the *NY Times*. He finds
some of the book 'extremely tedious'; but ends with a kind of upbeat.
It seems a non-selling review to me, but the others find it not too serious
a setback. Eliz thinks it is 'very intelligent'.

We flew to Boston at three. Ned was waiting, looking distracted and
grim; then a few minutes later, on the way to Milton, it came out: what
we believed could not happen again, had. Pam had hit the bottle the
previous weekend, had had to be rushed to New Hampshire to be dried
out. It wasn't us, but his sister (who had been staying with them) that
Pam couldn't stand.

We arrived at Hutchinson Street, its Victorian houses carefully screened
by evergreens one from the other; waited while Ned went in the back to
unlock the front door. A long wait. Then he came out, laconic and hiding
God knows what shocked puritanical horror. Pam was lying upstairs,

'smashed'. She'd somehow got hold of some beer. It was beyond him, he washed his hands of it, the party (for the next weekend) would have to go on without her if she hadn't recovered. So we carried our bags upstairs, through the spotless, antique-decorated rooms; everything polished, dustless, immaculate, as in a museum. We are to have Bill's bathroom. Its walls are hung with strange *fin-de-siècle* landscapes; swooning-classical half-naked women. He's at Harvard now, in his last year. Ned asked him the other day what he would do next: he thinks retirement would make a good career. In reality it will be publishing, it seems.

The other child, Kate, was there, and we all went off to the Ritz-Carlton for an early dinner. Kate is seventeen, now rather handsome in an Edwardian way, though we sense something deeply withdrawn and repressed in her – understandably enough. Ned insists on champagne, we try to cheer him up and he tries to be jolly; but it is like inserting an act from Noël Coward into Ibsen or Strindberg.

We went back to Hutchinson Street, began watching a baseball game; then Pam appeared, just able to walk, just able to speak – a sad alcoholic's fuddle of self-recrimination, sentiment, she did love us, it wasn't us, she couldn't help it, Ned didn't understand. 'Oh it's the boss,' she suddenly said at one point. 'Look at him, he's so *embarrassed.*' The strange and terrible thing is that she does seem more human and more open than her husband or either of her children. Somewhere she knows better what is truly wrong in this house. Its silences, its unusednesses, its repressions, its ferocious New England version of the stiff upper lip – the world reduced to a total faith in free will and relentless condemnation of all human weakness. Ned did indeed behave all through this as if she were not there, pouring out her incoherent apologies and miseries. He showed far more solicitude to the two cats and the dog.

He is of course at least equally to blame, if not in the initial weakness, at least in its continuing. He is, and maintains, the culture in which the bacillus must thrive. The two children apparently take his side.

Pam stumbled and clutched her way back upstairs again, and we eventually got to our room: tears and anger from their bedroom next door. Ned was not going to sleep in the same room as her. Eliz pulled a book from a shelf beside our beds. Out fell a five-dollar bill. Ned told us the next day Pam hides money all over the house. He has stopped the local liquor store selling to her; but she simply rings for a cab and gets the driver to go in.

18 September

We set off about eleven for West Stockbridge. Endless miles down the Massachusetts Turnpike. I felt bad about forcing Ned to do this chore, but I suspect it relaxed him a little. He becomes more communicative, normal, even laughing, away from his own house. I asked at one point during the previous evening whether there wasn't someone among the neighbours on Hutchinson Street who couldn't help during Pam's 'crises'. 'We lead our own lives here,' had said Ned, then added, 'thank God.' I didn't dare suggest that this was American self-sufficiency turned into sheer self-punishment; or ask him to re-read the Norwegian episode in *The Magus*.[1]

But at least it was a deep relief to get into the countryside again, even if it was only to see it hurtling past. A profusion of wild Michaelmas daisies, golden-rod species, milkweed.

We arrived at Stockbridge just before lunch, an old Main Street (it is Norman Rockwell's home-town), pleasant houses, a ramshackle wooden giant of a hotel-inn with a long wooden stoop on the street. It is very crowded, not at all the kind of place I really wanted to be in for the signing; but we grew quite to like it. We had drinks and a sandwich, interrupted by the arrival of the thirty boxes each of 500 tipsheets I have to get through.

Ned left, and I got a taxi to take us up the hill to Naumkeag, a local showplace, the home of the Choate family.[2] It is very American (or indeed British) Edwardian; heavy wood, leather-bound volumes, endless Chinese Export porcelain; one expected a uniformed maid bearing tea at every turn. The guiding girl has curiously watchful eyes, as if she were afraid our party might criticize it – Heaven knows why, since the others found it continuously 'beautiful'. It's very curious, this American inability, which seems to me to grow each time we come here, to discredit what they have been taught to believe. I know I owe a good part of my own success here to it, especially with *Daniel Martin*.

One's English self despises it, this addiction to recipe in so many areas of the culture. It is not at first sight compatible with personal freedom, let alone the intellectual kind. On the other hand I am not sure it doesn't finally conduce to more social freedom – even, para-doxically, a more socialist freedom – more tolerance and balance overall, whatever the costs. Americans generally hope to be pleased where the British rather hope to be disappointed; that is, they accord more right to the present, whether it be the present experience in a museum or show-place or the present work of art in the newly created sense. To the British this makes them brainwashed, undiscriminating,

---

[1] The episode concerned farmer Gustav Nygaard, who looked after his insane brother in the Arctic wilderness.

[2] A large shingle-style mansion with eight acres of landscaped gardens which had belonged to Joseph Hodges Choate (1832–1917), US ambassador to Britain between 1899 and 1905.

far too easily conned by self-advertisement, promotion gimmicks and all the rest; but I think that is largely because we are a more disappointed culture, both historically and in the now. Our answer has been to place personal judgement (intimately bound up with personal disappointment or disapproval) above all communal values. That is why Americans are far politer people in ordinary day-to-day meetings; they may be covering part of what they really feel, but the hiding is done with far less resentment.

What confuses this issue is the far greater degree of actual street violence, the murder rate and all the rest, in the United States; but I think that springs from quite different causes. The suppressed (or increasingly unsuppressed) psychological violence is in fact greater in Britain. It is betrayed in our private lives and opinions; in our public attitudes to political or artistic heresy and 'failure'; in the bitterness of our reviewing, the malice of our satire. We want everyone else and everything else to do badly; Americans, sometimes naively, want the external world to do well.

21 September
It stays cold, in the 50s, after the 60s and 70s of our visit hitherto.

We drove twenty miles or so over to the Shaker Museum at Hancock, far and away the nicest experience of this entire trip.[1] There is a whole strange continent to be discovered behind the one thing everybody knows: Shaker furniture. Some sort of paradoxical divine grace seems to have descended on the sect from very early on: its actual theology, the Mother Ann Lee side of it, may be childish, but even that, its inherent feminism, is proleptic, future-looking. Then there are all the parallels with communism in its purest, pre-Marxist sense; the weird borrowings from medieval monasticism. I kept on thinking of the Cistercians at Hancock; of the aesthetic and life-rule purity in their system. Like them, the Shakers make every other extreme sect in their own religious 'genus' look vulgar.

I wrote down magnificent early quotations.

'Beadings, mouldings and cornices which are merely for fancy may not be made by Believers.'

'All beauty that has not a foundation in use soon grows distasteful, and needs continual replacement with something new.'

And best of all: 'All force has a form.'

[1] The community of Shakers, originally called the United Society of Believers in Christ's Second Appearing, was founded in Manchester, England, in 1747. Their nickname was inspired by their frenzied religious dancing. Led by Ann Lee, in 1774 the Shakers came to New England in order to practise their religious beliefs without persecution. Here they established nineteen different Shaker communities. The Hancock community was founded in 1790.

The fifteen or so buildings that make up the Hancock Museum are a joy, as exciting and revealing an experience as one could have anywhere in the world. One of them, the famous Round Barn, must go on any list of the great buildings of the world. Its brilliant simplicity, its blind devotion to function – and then to find it theatrical as well, a treasure-house of complex angles and structures, as pure-pleasing as a Bach fugue. The paradox strikes one everywhere at Hancock, that the legacy is not the intended – not religious, but artistic. No one will ever treat material and form with such infallible instinct for their inherent nature; in iron as in wood. The Shaker stoves are as elegant as the severest modern sculpture. One of the long tables in the dining-room is so perfectly proportioned that it is almost the Platonic idea of a table – that from which all other tables spring.

Another aspect of their life I was ignorant of was the music, the strange singing and dancing that went on in the meeting-houses. They played a record of some of it in the meeting-house here, the Willow song and 'The Gift to be simple'. It sounds very original: like folk-music, but not quite any folk-music one has heard before. I cannot think how the writers of musicals have not leapt at all the material here.

Sadness everywhere, though, since the enterprise has failed; the Shaker Community is now nearly extinct. One of the attendants told us it is not for lack of young people, who would be happy to join, but because the fact that a Shaker shares in the property of the whole 'order', and that the order's holdings in land, buildings, furniture and the rest are now immensely valuable, makes any candidate suspect: spiritual wealth he may inherit, but worldly wealth he certainly will. So everything is to be museumified, frozen.

The worm in the rose of the Shaker credo must always have lain in their attachment to pure form, which inevitably became attachment to repetition; to ritual, which kills spirit in any religion . . . and art. They invested in something visual and static, which meant death to the music and dancing, ongoing faith. The reason for that in turn obviously lies in the origins of the sect, its revulsion from the injustices and vulgarities of the Church of England and the other established sects of the time. But in a way those other churches left themselves work to be done, things to shed and improve. The Shakers died of their own genius for perfection; of, at their best, very nearly achieving it. They were too good for this world, since evolution itself is mainly fuelled by faults.

Never mind: Hancock remains both rich and moving, a record of one of the strangest of all explorations by the human spirit. And it is better to have no more than a fossil than nothing at all.

22 September 1977

I gulp down Edward Deming Andrews' book on Shaker music;[1] when I should be signing. But first things first.

In the afternoon we went for a walk, down and across a footbridge across the river and up through woodlands to a fire-gazebo called Laura's Tower.

---

[1] *The Gift to be Simple: Songs, Dances and Rituals of the American Shakers* (Dover, 1962).

Part Two

24 September 1980
I have written nothing here between that date above and this. I don't know why, these last few weeks, I feel inclined to start again.

The event of these last few days has been Jacky Gillott's suicide. John Percival came home – he works in London now for the BBC – to her cottage at Pitcombe near Bruton late on Friday night, and found her dead. Earlier this year they sold Prospect House, and set up separate establishments; in London, for John, at Pitcombe for her. We went over with Anna and Tess only three or four weeks ago, for lunch, and stayed all afternoon. Jacky took me up to a little cramped workroom under the roof, her bedroom beside it. She wrote a novel that was published last year, set in a fictional version of Lyme; and strangely and rather emotionally dedicated it to me. It was called *The Head Case*; very disorganized, it didn't work. I doubt if I hid that well enough in a letter thanking her for the dedication. I should have read the signs better. She was the only person, bar someone in the *Spectator*, to give *Daniel Martin* a good review. Even then, though I was grateful, more grateful than for the novel dedication, I sensed the review came less from understanding of the book than my being cast as someone she wanted to be. When we met, nothing was ever said. She was pretty, or had been pretty; a brittle, sexy, faintly raucous persona always. The characteristic deformation of the first generation of women's lib, perhaps the one thing the future will never quite realize about it: the cost, the mask it required. Her suicide makes me certain of what I suspected. There was someone very different behind – ugly, confused, uncertain – all that she didn't sound on TV or radio. Crippled by her good looks, presentation technique, and so on. Being a litbiz personality.

I spoke to John on the telephone last night, Tuesday, but he was still near tears. He talked about 'the agonies she went through over her writing'. And before and after I spoke to him, I had Betty Allsop, who had also rung me as soon as she heard the news, on Saturday, in fact told me it had happened. She sees Ken's death in it, I had all that again, and things I had not known about it. 'Such a beautiful girl, so intelligent, such a waste.' But she misread Jacky even worse than I did when she was alive. Yet she is right in one way, there is a parallel: wanting to be a 'good' writer, famous for writing, not for public personality. She spoke of the cunning of suicides: how Ken had seemed to be through his crisis, how he had embraced her that last morning, when she had had to get up early to go to London, how happy their previous evening had been, a birthday dinner somewhere for Mandy, and so on. How she had later realized his recent peace and apparent settling for his fate in life had been because he was decided on death, and was only waiting for the right opportunity. Her identification now with 'poor John' is ghoulish, but percipient.

When we were there at Pitcombe a few weeks ago I went for a walk with John along the disused railway embankment that faces the cottage. And as we returned we saw Jacky at one of the attic windows. It was warm, she had put on a bikini; having rather bizarrely announced that she had to listen to a programme on Beckett, so retreated to her 'den'. Eliz and Anna sat with Tess in the sun outside. She waved to us, as we came back along the embankment, from her window. I thought then, odd behaviour, a touch pretentious, the bikini especially peculiar, signalling something none of us could read – their sons, the two boys, had gone out, but even so. I think perhaps I was meant to go and listen about Beckett with her, perhaps she really wanted to talk. Crossed lines.

Tess is now nearly three, a very precocious and pretty child, though recently she shows will, thus perversity. To my amazement, so much for genes – not quite fair, perhaps it is Roy – her most striking precocity is linguistic. She spoke very early, and is now far ahead of her age-group. I tease her by mispronouncing words, and she grows very prim and school-marmish. 'John, don't say words wrong.' Then she says the word correctly. Anna is pregnant again, seven months gone. Nick now is established as a leading young potter; and seems to sell as much as he can produce. His latest 'style' is a witty send-up of the traditional teapot; a mental finesse matched by his painstaking craftsmanship in the actual making. We helped them buy a new car recently, and he brought two pots as thanks.

It's been a bad summer, weatherwise: much cloud and rain and cold. I have let the garden relapse here, these last years; not because I have lost faith, or sanctuary, relief in it. It is a part of me now, or a mirror, to a degree I conceal from everyone. That is, I have relapsed myself, grown increasingly bored with 'order', being what people, even Eliz, expect. I know what to look for, at what season, when its secrets come: at the moment, the *Clematis orientalis*, which flowers late this year, but is now a huge plant. The other evening I could smell its fresh-cut apricot perfume five yards away, delicious beyond description. Then last year was a wretched apple year, but this is very good: most of the trees fully laden, though a shade small, and very late in terms of picking. Getting them 'in' has been a great pleasure, I think perhaps why I write here again; the trees are closer to me than most human beings. I understand at last what drove my father, with his. The three D'Arcy Spice trees I grew from pips are all ten to fifteen feet high now; they fruited last year, and better this, though still runtish in the fruit. Only one seems to have come true.

26 September

We went to Jacky's funeral at Bruton. I went by train to Sherborne, and Rodney took me over. Eliz from Bristol, she'd been up in Birmingham to see her mother. A staid ceremony at St Mary's Bruton, the church near full; a curious curate, before the coffin was borne in, waiting in the chancel stalls – he kept glancing heavenwards, then sinking his cheek in his hand, as if in an agony of toothache. 'I am the resurrection, I am the life' in stentorian middle-class tones. We shuffle to our feet. Hymns, a trite C of E eulogy from the Vicar, all about Jacky going to confirmation classes with adolescents. The only moving moment was when John went to read the lesson. He nearly broke down, it was brave of him; and did break down at the burial, with one of his sons, the only really human thing, amid all the social nonsense of the ritual. The grave is over a busy street, lorries and traffic passing, a girl on a horse riding past (apparently by arrangement, it must have been Jacky's horse); and that one terrible, explosive sob.

Tea and buns in the church hall afterwards, but John asked us back to the Pitcombe cottage for drinks, and we stayed on with the family till six. The most touching moment of all was when Eliz and I were leaving and saying the usual things, and John suddenly embraced her, broken again. Then he said, 'I always feel people only wanted to know me because of Jacky.' Which we didn't have to pretend to assure him was never true. We've had him marked as a nice being for several years now; and he has patently borne all this with both feeling and courage. One or the other is common, perhaps, but both . . .

22 October

Eliz took me to see the new flat she has set her heart on, in Regent's Park Road. We are to buy it through the company. I don't really want to leave Hampstead, but the lease there is up next year, and the bank won't renew. The house belongs to Lord Crowther, or his family; dusty, dirty, piles of old books and bad paintings, apparently long empty – we are getting it for £45,000, an 84-year lease. Eliz came on it because Tom and Malou Wiseman have bought the flat upstairs. I feel that the world will have either destroyed itself or abandoned the notion of investment property by 2064 (if not much sooner); and now assess value much more in terms of the potential hassle ownership threatens. But move we must from Hampstead High Street.

We had supper with the children at Tom and Fay's. Their marriage has disintegrated badly over these last three years. He has his mistresses (currently Marina Warner, it seems), she her men; and the children the cost. They had to go out to dinner, and we were left to see the children to bed. They went wild, and in the end we had to leave them – it outrages Eliz – to the care of their new 'nurse', a mournful and mute Filipino woman. It is Hannah who sets the tone. This time she began belabouring me with a buckled belt (which hurt) – it begins as a romp, but then becomes obsessive, an expression of hatred against everything around her. I am Tom's scapegoat, I suppose. Nothing will stop her except the kind of bellow of bad temper Tom himself uses when the children annoy him. Of course this mixture of spoiling and berating has been fatal; intrinsically nice children turned graceless. We were going on to Karel and Betsy Reisz's, only a few houses down Chalcot Gardens, and had to walk up and down a bit in the night street to calm down.[1]

28 October
We drove down to Torquay for the night, to see the last few days' shooting at Kingswear. They have dressed the little station there to be Victorian Exeter and turned a nearby pub into Endicott's Family Hotel. White billows of vapour from the hired steam train, rain, dusk, crowds, the lights of Dartmouth across the river; and it is salving to see the now familiar faces again. Ashton, the art director, worried and self-depreciating as always; Ann Mollo, the set-dresser, Leon Clore gloomy and grumpy (his mask;[2] Eliz and I have decided that his 'bad temper' hides someone much more genial), Karel and Freddie. The sets look good. Meryl was there, flown in by Concorde for just this one day's shooting.

   We all went on the ferry across the river to the Carved Angel at Dartmouth and had a farewell dinner for her: very relaxed, jolly, everyone relieved that the shooting is nearly over. This side of the film business is the nicest: the work done, the closeness built, the joshing. We crossed the river back near midnight, the tide running silently, very mild, a moon gleaming on the water. Jeremy and Meryl embrace – affection, there was nothing off-scene between them. In fact poor Jeremy's marriage with Sinead Cusack temporarily broke up during the shooting. Karel told me he congratulated him one day after a good take of the scene where he has to tell Grogan his life is in a mess. Jeremy said, 'My God, I don't have to act that line.' Then embraces all round, and she gets into her car and goes back through the night to Heathrow for the morning Concorde back to New York.

[1] In 1978, Tom Maschler had persuaded Karel Reisz to direct *The French Lieutenant's Woman* and Harold Pinter to write the screenplay. Although Warner Brothers initially backed the film, they had second thoughts and United Artists financed the production in their place. Shooting began in May 1980.
[2] Leon Clore, who had worked with Reisz on several of his previous films, was the producer.

29 October

We walked round Torquay front and harbour in brilliant sunshine. It truly did feel like the Riviera, some interesting plants grow in the cliff-gardens. An Arbutus brilliant with fruit – as mine never are here, because of the birds.

Over to Kingswear for lunch, where I do a couple of interviews. Then the long set-ups for the station scene; we went off to look at some retired general's house by the river, a very beautiful setting, and poked round a strange old house through the archway at the foot of the road to the ferry, with mimosas and a huge fig-tree in its garden, a warren of empty, haunted rooms.

Our own farewells, then home that evening.

31 October

These last years I never have enough time. The Museum,[1] local history, writing letters – the last I have abandoned all hope with, so many require long answers, and more often than not it is the ones that most deserve an answer that do not get one. I have occasional accesses of fiction-writing, which I enjoy; but at least partly because I do not attach it to the notion of publishing now. What little of a 'literary person' I ever was, I have stopped being now. When I answer literary letters, or do interviews, it seems like someone else – another fiction.

4 November

I stay up until two-thirty, watching, out of some sort of masochism, the egregious Reagan being elected. There is no hope for the Western World, it lies self-betrayed by its own stupidity and greed. I feel closest these days to Benn's wing of the Labour Party (*faute de mieux*); but am convinced capitalist politics has lost all touch with reality (and need) at the given point in history. It is my class that are the traitors, the eternal clerks again, above all Fleet Street and television, the accursed 'media'. I loathe them all, the mediators; lock, stock and barrel. Nine-tenths or more of their ethics is based on self-perpetuation. Karel and Leo[2] started union-bashing during our little dinner-party at Dartmouth. I say nothing, friendship is more important than pointing out the idiocy of demanding that the British Leyland workers behave themselves like decent robots while we sit round the table of the most expensive restaurant in the West of England; 'on the budget' (which is running a million dollars or more over), of course.

---

[1] In January 1978, JF accepted an invitation to become curator of Lyme Regis's Philpot Museum, which housed a large fossil collection and other artefacts related to the town's history.

[2] Leonora Smith, a local friend of the Fowleses.

6 November

In London, to do *Desert Island Discs*; I meet the compère Roy Plomley in the Garrick Club: a strange world for me. Klatches of suited gentlemen; mostly lawyers nowadays, it seems, they outnumber the theatre. Plomley is fastidious, overpolite, I suspect a touch bored; *tout vu, tout lu* and also *tout interviewé*. I go down to fetch some cigarettes from my mackintosh and when I come back to the bar he is talking with a bearded man leaning against the counter end, who looks as if he spends his life there, leaning and watching the rest, a touch outcast; in a blue suit, dressed like a businessman. It is John Osborne. We size each other up warily when introduced, and are not impressed. 'God knows why he comes here,' said Plomley afterwards, as we sat in the dining-room, under the walls of splendid theatrical portraits and scenes. I see Osborne sit at the central common table; he is buttonholed by a bore. They are still at it when we leave.

12 December

Anna had her baby, just before midnight. A boy. Nick and I wanted the Hungarian Bela, as in Bartok, but Anna has put her foot down on that; so he is to be William Bela, called William.

Our evening with Karel and Betsy. From being neutral about him (as a person) before the filming, I have come to like him. He is strangely oriental, Buddha-like, and not only in looks; endlessly patient and optimistic, and funny. We watched the Liverpool–Aberdeen match on the telly, while Betsy and Eliz talked upstairs. He has been offered Malraux's endlessly attempted (at production stage) *La Condition humaine*, and thinks he will do it – his 'last picture', he says. We drink tea upstairs, and talk about Harold and Antonia's wedding, to which we were supposed to go. Harold's script is to be published, I have done a little introduction to it: honest in everything but my inward indifference to seeing my books filmed.

It's not that I didn't enjoy most of the filming at Lyme; or what little watching I did of it. Karel and Betsy and Jeremy Irons rented our old house, Underhill Farm (Meryl Streep stayed at Haye House). Lyme itself made general hay while the sun shone. Financially, the weather was appalling and contrary throughout – except for one day when a little storm blew up (something I had assured Karel wouldn't happen) and they were able to shoot the scene (scheduled for autumn) at the end of the Cobb.

I suspect the only person who didn't enjoy it was Tom Maschler, who was put in charge of publicity, and managed to get everyone's back up in one way or another – even the equable Meryl's, when she had to sacrifice one of her rare free days to implement one of his coups. She walked out on a session with Snowdon, he took so long making up his mind. I had to take Snowdon round all the locations: not a very impressive human being, though he is polite and interested – I ended by feeling a little sorry for him, his limp, the way he is endlessly stared at and photographed himself, poor devil. Some stupid woman stood in his path with an idiot smile and demanded to know how his children were, why he hadn't brought them to Lyme. 'I sincerely hope they're working hard in class,' says Snowdon, looking at his watch. One can't blame royalty, it's the high proportion of morons among their subjects who make them what they are.

Great precautions were taken to see that no one knew about the past and modern aspects of Harold's script, though one paper leaked it.[1] Even the crew seemed a bit puzzled. There was a nice story from Freddie Francis, the lighting man, after they had shot one of the modern rehearsal scenes, in which Jeremy and Meryl have a misunderstanding. It went well. Later that evening Freddie saw one of the grips in town. 'Everything OK, then?' says Freddie. 'Except that scene this afternoon,' says the grip. 'I mean it's really bloody marvellous, innit? They're supposed to be stars, supposed to have been working together for three weeks now. And all they can do is start spatting on camera.'

Another story went round on the first day of shooting. One of the electricians said to his mate, 'Who are those two geezers over there?'

'Wake up. That's the bloke who wrote the book and the script-writer.'

'Well, I realized the bearded git was a writer. That other one looks like a secondhand car salesman.'

Harold does dress with some sharpness, and never informally.

We got to like him, too, once we had adjusted to his neuroses. He has to drink a lot, but is very funny once he is relaxed; beautifully phrased anecdotes, rehearsed and timed, I suspect, but none the worse for that. Tom and I went off into the backlands of the Marshwood Vale one evening and had dinner with him and Antonia. She fell asleep at the table afterwards, apparently a common habit, and Harold told us of their first night of love, when the decision to start the celebrated affair was taken. He decided to do it in style, and that there could be no better way to express the depth of his feeling than by reading her some of his poems. Antonia arrives, sits in an armchair, Harold reads his carefully selected poems with the most painstaking attention to tone and phrasing and effect. After a few minutes he looks up. Antonia is fast asleep.

She and I have buried our Booker Prize hatchet.[2] We talk seventeenth-century history now. All Tom could think of, afterwards, was how she had been *his* mistress once, also.

Two other stories about Harold. There was trouble with the proposal scene, and one day Karel rang me up to see if I could help – he felt it was too curt and quick. 'Harold says he'll do anything, but he simply can't write a happy scene.'

[1] In the film Meryl Streep and Jeremy Irons play two actors Anna and Mike who act the roles of Sarah and Charles in the film within the film.

[2] See pages 110–13.

When he came with Karel for a first reconnaissance, we went down to walk on the Cobb. We climbed up on to the Upper Walk, I was beside Harold. After four or five steps he cast an apprehensive look down at the sea, all of fifteen feet below, and raised a distinctly Romantic hand towards his brow: 'John, I'm terribly sorry, but I just can't stand this.' I thought for a moment he meant trailing around after Karel and Freddie while they discussed angles and lighting. But no, he turned and went back to the Lower Walk and strolled beside us down there. It was the height. When we went to the Undercliff, he walked a little way down to my location for the meeting; but then again turned back, the rough going was too much. (But not for Karel, they did eventually spend a huge amount of production money to build a staircase and cable-slings for the brutes and camera down to the ilex-grove.)

Harold is at heart a dandy, I think; whence his acute sense of linguistic style and, less obviously, his truly bizarre social mask. He and Antonia stayed, when they were here, with some titled couple who have a house near Broadwinsor. In all small things he behaves like an Old Etonian: the voice, the mannerisms, everything else. Only his indifference to things rural and nature in general is Jewish still; and perhaps his obsessive neatness sartorially. There's a tiny echo of Mr Jorrocks about him: of a town fish eternally out of water.[1] And a much stronger one of Byron and Chateaubriand, of someone imposing a lifestyle on all around him – a despairing world-view from the middle of an agreeable, upper-class, active, 'famous' life. Of course he lacks the society-flouting panache and physical courage of the two great Romantics, the satanic touch; but perhaps his running off with Antonia is a sign that it is there. I suspect the role he acts is designed to quell it, also; and the neuroses, the drinking, to demonstrate the black heart beneath the bland exterior.

The one thing he failed to bring off in the first draft was the final scene, when Charles and Sarah meet again (in Victorian terms); I think because he couldn't face the need for emotion. He didn't argue at all when I rewrote the scene to put some of that back and read it to Karel and him in a session we had – all this side of things was done without any trouble or bad feeling, in a spirit of friendship and co-operation that must be rare in the cinema. There were one or two squabbles in the production office, but (thanks to Karel) this good spirit went all through the crew.

Lyme also was on the whole good; half the town got parts in the end as extras (luckily we lie outside the area where London professional extras have to be hired). There was some bad blood among the shopkeepers when the money was shared out for 'disturbance of business' and the rest, but that was not the unit's fault, just immemorial Lyme. One

---

[1] Known as the sporting cockney grocer, Jorrocks was a comic character created by R. S. Surtees (1805–1864) for the *New Sporting Magazine*.

gentleman tried to get compensation for *not* having his shop on camera.

Both Karel and Meryl were nervous as cats about my seeing anything, and we saw very few rushes, so I cannot tell about the end result. I suspect it will be a brave effort; and not quite hang together. We shall see.

1 March 1981

I have no will for this. I jot down things to record; then find no time, no inclination; no ego, really. Just as I turn down the lectures, talks, meetings, conferences I seem more and more to get asked to. I have two coming up (talks), one for the British Council in Paris, another at the National Theatre, where they are at long last putting on *Dom Juan* in April. I would rather do neither. I hate all of it in prospect; it changes nothing, or makes it even worse. I feel I should be depressed; but it is a kind of fatalistic numbness, the way old trees have dead branches, and yet go on living. My dead branch is the creative (and sexual) side. It is not just Eliz, nothing stirs me in that latter way any more. She has just had another bad bout of what she calls 'winter depression'; and I know I am nine parts of it – the way we live. The tenth part has been the wretched new flat in Regent's Park, which she has decided is a mistake; and from being all optimism and excitement and energy about it before Christmas has been exactly the reverse ever since. We went up a week or two ago and I forced her to set things in motion. It's not as terrible as all that, it just lacks the life and sympathetic side of Hampstead Village; and far less convenient for shops, tubes, all the rest. I can even enjoy it, in a way; the problems, the having to start from scratch; sweeping and washing the place one day.

I also met Peter Gill at the National, who is to direct *Dom Juan*. I can't have said one word to his two hundred, a quite endless and rather comic monologue about what sort of director he was, how he felt about the play, and so on, and so on.

I was a little disappointed, if I am honest. Everyone says how good he is – or was, at the Riverside. I can believe he does work well with actors, as reputed; but *Dom Juan* needs a touch of sparkle and showmanship, actor-managerishness, as well as the delicate entente with the cast and the ensemble philosophy. The Turgenev has since got mixed reviews; but perhaps that won't hurt us.[1]

Anyway, I am glad it is going on; for dear old Molière's sake as much as mine.

7 March

We saw the final version of the film, at long last, with a nervous Karel,

---

[1] Previously the founder director of the Riverside Studios, Peter Gill became an Associate Director of the National Theatre in 1980. His first production there, Turgenev's *A Month in the Country*, had opened on 19 February.

Betsy and Tom. If I was being very cruel and objective, and marking
Oxbridge style, I would give it a beta plus; I think my main quarrel
would be over the cutting, too sharp for my taste, not enough time to
linger. There have been some losses; one scene Karel has excised is the
rather important final one with Grogan; which has upset (in a mild,
friendly way) Harold. But Karel insists it was below par, Jeremy gave one
of his few bad performances – it was all his (Karel's) fault. Another is
the scene with the prostitute – 'it seemed superfluous'.

But even beta plus – and everyone else except Eliz and I wants to
mark it much higher – is far better than the wretched gammas and
deltas I have had to suffer before. Fine performances from Jeremy and
Meryl, some of the Undercliff photography beautiful; and many, if not
quite all, of the jumps out of past into present work well. I knew before
we went that the reality must be a little of a shock, and in part a deception, in the French sense also – just like the final text of a book. But
we have grown to like and admire Karel – and Betsy – very much over
the long period of preparation and filming. We are in many ways closer
to them in philosophy and lifestyle than we are, say, to Tom and Fay; I
had no trouble in saying gratitude to Karel. I feel it. It is only the suspicious old peasant in me that doubts good news. And even he would
concede that the whole making of the thing was, internally, within the
unit, quite extraordinarily peaceful and unfraught; a model of how such
things should be done, in a communal art.

1 July
We set off for the conference on time at Bellagio.[1] We decided finally
to drive it, Eliz to drive it, via Weymouth and Cherbourg.

2 July
To Sancerre. We drove across the Sologne without stopping, a little bit
of an agony to the botanist in me. What I want on such journeys (to
stop at every promising flower site we pass) and what is feasible are
incompatible with clock-time; a matter not to be raised at the conference. We did stop a moment when we passed through Nançay, to pay
brief homage at Alain-Fournier's shop again.[2] It is undergoing building
alterations, no windows. Inside the empty front room, the old shop,
nothing but a step-ladder, with a swallow perched on top; an occupant
Fournier himself would surely have accepted in lieu of his own ghosts.

---

[1] JF had been invited by the International Society for the Study of Time to attend
its conference at the Rockefeller Foundation's Study and Conference Center at
Bellagio on Lake Como.
[2] Alain-Fournier used to spend his summer holidays with his uncle who owned
the shop. He would draw on his memory of it in *Le Grand Meaulnes*.

3 July

Across the central valley, via Chalons, to Lons-le-Saulnier; thence to an isolated little hotel at Chatillon, in a beautiful upland chalk-flora country; splendid ancient meadows, more flowers than anything else.

5 July

Italy; the roads deteriorate once one has crossed the border. I had intended to go via Locarno and Lugano, Italian Switzerland, but we missed the turning and went on through Domodossola and ended up at Intra on Lake Maggiore. Alas. Oily water, a dense heat, a town packed with holiday-makers. We book into a hotel near the ferry we must take the next morning, the Hotel-Intra; eat a poor dinner there, then two huge ice-creams at a café, stroll beside the lake to a Communist fair, an endless operatic speech from an eloquent comrade.

6 July

And are woken at seven-thirty the next morning by a flustered face. 'Come quick, come quick, your car is kaput!' Eliz had parked it the night before at one end of a parking row in front of the hotel. We supposed someone had smashed into it, endless horror. But it seemed intact, when I had hastily pulled on some clothes and gone down. It wasn't. The fixed side-window smashed, all our suitcases emptied, in chaos inside. We were not the only victims: two other cars near by had been broken into in the same way. One had had its radio ripped out, which we were spared. But both our cameras were stolen (Eliz's she had bought only the week before), my old Zeiss binoculars; a wind-jacket of Eliz's, a bag. It was strange, after the first shock. I felt only a sort of relief, that it was nothing worse; that so much else that might have been stolen, or happened, wasn't and hadn't. Little sympathy from the accursed hotel; it seems only fools leave suitcases, or anything else, in cars these days. Which did not explain why they had not warned us. Detectives appeared, and gave a cursory look-round. Then I cleared up.

Later we went to the police-station, and made a report to a dry little French-speaking woman clerk. No chance of recovery, nothing to be done. It happened '*chaque jour, chaque nuit*'; car-robbery is a major industry now.

Nothing to be done; so we left and took the ferry across the lake to Varese, then to Como, and finally, along a hideously narrow cliff road, to Bellagio.

Into the Hotel du Lac, where Elizabeth is to stay, with the other wives. Then I take myself off in a taxi, with luggage, to the Villa Serbelloni. It is a long ochre building perched above the town, in a park of sixty acres or so, once grandiosely landscaped and alleyed, now in rather a run-down, dilapidated state (the grounds). Inside, one enters the United States; all is smoothly run, comfortable, conventional, jacket-and-tie for dinner. I have a pleasant room looking back down the lake to Como, and share a bathroom with Jean Michon, a Dutch psychologist.

At five, our first meeting in the conference room, a huge oval table, fifteen or sixteen of us, mainly American. I sit between Thornton, a Cape Town professor of anthropology, though American by birth; and Sivin, a leading American sinologist, and polymath, who seems as expert in chemistry and physics as in his own present field. Beyond him, Sir John Eccles, the brain expert and Nobel prize-winner; and Wheeler, said to be America's leading theoretical physicist, friend and student of Einstein.

Julius Fraser, founder of the ISST, and George Ford, make some bumbling introductory remarks. Fraser is Hungarian by birth, an unstoppable talker; and tried throughout to sell his own theory of time to the sceptical rest of them. It seems he is tolerated because of his organizing powers, the Society is his idea, and so on; while he craves to be accepted on a scientific par with the others. He is not very good at listening. Ford is a Dickens expert, and goes on rather like a Dickens character; endlessly amiable and much more at home in the drinking part of the day than the work one.

We disperse, to reassemble for drinks at seven, as every evening. I stare from my room across the lake – last speckles of sunlight swim and glint in a strange slow motion, randomly, yet as if artificially so, like light sculptures, on the grey surface of the water opposite, by Cadenabbia[1] – and wonder why I am here. At dinner I sit next to Jürgen Aschoff, the biological clock expert from one of the Max Planck Institutes; he speaks a good, but crusty and challenging, English. I decide (quite wrongly, it was to turn out) that I do not like him. He demanded to know why I had done such and such in *Daniel Martin* and *The Magus*; then refused to discuss his own work. 'I follow a very narrow path.' Aschoff was not the only first wrong assessment I made.

I did not at first realize that science is becoming diffident; that a certain amount of envy underlay what I took as compliments *de circonstance* about my own work, and art in general. After dinner we are allowed a liqueur or port, then beer. I am not the only one who resents having to dress up. Sebeok, the famous linguistics man,[2] complains: 'I never wear a coat and tie, this is ridiculous.' But protocol at the Rockefeller Foundation is intimidatingly well specified, and no one dares break it.

7 July
I wake early and walk in the grounds along a precipice path, huge plunges to the jade lake below.

---

[1] A resort on Lake Como.
[2] i.e., Thomas A. Sebeok (1920–2001), who was Professor Emeritus of Anthropology, Linguistics and Semiotics at Indiana University.

Our first serious session. Fraser rattles away in his blend of Central European and American English, about Umwelts and mesomorphs, not at all very comprehensibly to me. Then Lawrence. I jot.

'Time is an abstraction from the temporality of events. 1905 and Einstein proves the primacy of events – time and space are thus epiphenomena. Consciousness is separate from reality, but observer consciousness is vital, a precondition of time. S and T are aspects of experience, not a part of it. All mechanical models are anthropomorphic. Physical law is cause-finding, therefore making a machine. T zero ('the beginning'), is it a particle or an event? Organism is a better model. Evolutionary theory is mechanistic, searching for organic plateaux. Prior consciousness constitutes present ones.'

Lawrence is a philosopher, a man I took a dislike to too. Besides our conference, there are various more permanent guests here, research scholars staying for a month or more, with their wives. To one of the latter, who inquired his field, Lawrence replied that he was the most famous philosopher in America – and not in fun, it seems. The lady quite rightly took umbrage. A self-important man, with two voices – one with the boys, another when playing professor. A general fault here – academy and the analytic remained rampant throughout, in papers and public discussions. Eliz found his wife the nicest of the other wives; a sick woman, and we suspect her husband does not help.

We decided by the end of the conference that most of the other 'visiting scholars' were little better than a bunch of free-loaders. Much fun was made of an Indian gentleman doing work on 'the Indian influence on T. S. Eliot'; and of a dreadful Australian working on 'Australian–American relations in the 1980s'. '. . . in the 1980s' was voted a stroke of genius. An unctuous young modern Tory, Professor Gelber, this Australian: the only one I have ever met who had not a trace of the accent. Then there was a Robert Lewis, a distinctly pompous composer from Johns Hopkins. The ones I liked best were the Vorenbergs, he is just become dean of the Harvard Law School; they at least treated it all as partly a joke.

John Wheeler, the physicist, a nice old man, and I thought his paper the best, conspicuously clear; only to discover at the end that the other physicists present thought the exact reverse. It was the same old stuff trotted out again, stale pabulum for laymen. Sir John Eccles came in for the same criticism. They ought to have been attacked, it seems. The latter now travels from conference to seminar, and back again, preaching his gospel that there is more in the mind, and brain, than science can allow for. Wheeler was blamed also for omitting his strangest area of research, apparently beyond any but mathematical description; and in which (if I have it right) the possibility exists that consciousness creates not only the present, but the past. In some way we inhabit a cosmos whose past is presently created to suit us – the most apt, the most convenient. 'Time is what prevents everything happening at once.'

I talked with Wheeler afterwards – these chats and conversations between sessions were often as rewarding as the papers themselves. He said he admired Niels Bohr more than Einstein. He tended to judge people by their wives. Einstein's was 'unfortunate'; Bohr's 'a queen'. But Bohr was also a greater team man, a gatherer of other intellects; Einstein a brilliant individualist. Wheeler is a bit of a grave elderly gentleman, with flashes of puckish humour; he would pass visually as a butler of the old school, more gentleman than his master. He takes copious notes throughout, like a model student, in a fat notebook. I noticed he had pasted in a group photograph we had taken of us, with all the names inscribed beneath; I managed to lose mine.

The other 'character' was Sir John Eccles. His voice slips rather touchingly into a trace of his old Australian accent at moments. He mutters and grumbles throughout, which did not please the American majority at all. It is bizarre how conforming and etiquette-conscious (I think the result of a multiracial society) the Americans are; so studiously polite, in most cases. Eliz reports the same of the wives. And how money-worried, that everything shall be fairly shared. At our final dinner in town, Goldman paid more than his share in the bill. There were quite insanely prolonged exchanges of 1,000 lire notes and coins (i.e., about 50 pence) afterwards. I wanted to hand him the 15,000 lire he was 'owed' by the rest of us, and have done with it; but knew that would have shocked the American soul.

It is stormy that evening; thunder and lightning. I talk with Haber, a historian, and one of the true humanists here; an attractively prickly and sceptical man, beneath his quietness. Then horrify everyone by declaring for Benn and socialism in Britain. Ford is shocked, he has met Thatcher, 'such a doll of a woman'. I like the Dutchman Michon, too; he manages to be both serious and jolly. Huge thunder in the night: it is cooler, but if anything, heavier.

There was a lecture by the other Nobel prize-winner, Eigen, this day, too; but over my head – and almost everyone else's, it later turned out. His field is the evolution of molecules, but his graphs and equations were beyond us.

8 July

I cried off that afternoon and went to Lecco with Eliz, to have our broken window mended. The VW garage could not replace the window they sold us and sent us off to a neighbouring *carozzeria*; where I suspected the worst as regards charges. But not all in Italy is dishonest. The garage-owner charged us only just over £5 and refitting meant total disassembly of the door, nearly an hour's hard work. Intolerably hot again. I really hate this climate.

I sat next to Mendilow at dinner; a dry old Jewish literary man, who started the English faculty at the Hebrew University of Jerusalem; an expert on the Romantics. He made a lengthy humanist point yesterday. The scientists listened in polite boredom. It is absurd how we who are not scientists let them set the register of discourse and tone of discussion. Not a word, so far, about any practical or sociological aspect of all this high-flown talk. We sit in an ochre tower, if not an ivory or ebony one. From time to time I hear the voices through the window that drift from the town below. Our conference-room is hung with tapestries, which move and shift every so often, in the occasional currents of air. A woman's head in one of them amuses me, as she seems to watch the corner of the table where I sit, slyly. My muse, I suspect. In the library next door is an even better personification, the Villa's great and secret treasure, a Leonardo faience bust of Ginevra[1] – at least they hope it is by Leonardo. It is good enough to be, a lovely thing; a little battered, in greyish-white glaze, both subtle and peasant in quality; echoes of Rodin and Maillol.

I set old Mendilow a trap at dinner; which of the nine muses would he appoint for fiction? In the end he decided on the one that I have, without my prompting: Erato.[2]

9 July

Eccles on the brain.

First sense of time in art, Epic of Gilgamesh, 2600 BC. Homer.

Time slows in emergencies, such as car accidents (Michon disputed this afterwards, evidently on sound research grounds – the recollected seeming slowness is an effect of retro-active recall, not something that actually happens). Sound reaches cortex in 7/10 milliseconds; touch in 15/20; reaction about 250 millisecs, but then there is another gap before the brain stimulus becomes conscious, of 250/500 millisecs. I.e., neuronal adequacy must be achieved before the stimulus + reaction can be consciously perceived. Consciousness has to take place in time.

At the end Eccles suddenly branched off into religion, via the indecipherable enigmas and complexities of the brain. Apparently he has become a Catholic; but this was put in quasi-scientific terms, as a hypothesis that might account for various anomalies in the brain/consciousness relationship. He posits something further than the 'computer' and the stimuli it computes, i.e., an immortal soul.

Haber, on history.

1780–1860 marked the change from the assumption of a timeless system of perfectibility, all going to a terminus, a circular system.

---

[1] i.e., Ginevra de Benci, the subject of one of Leonardo da Vinci's most celebrated paintings.
[2] Erato is the muse of lyric poetry.

History was historicized, an imperialization process. Hegel historicized philosophy. Old history seen as illustration of something else, theology, philosophy, etc., i.e., phenomena can't be explained 'inside' history. Then the belief that time must explain something, and so historical method. Twentieth-century revolt against this imperializing process. All new methodology imperializes.

Ideal history = continuity of events. If everything had survived, no history. This is happening since 1940, because too much has survived.

Rowell, on timelessness in music. He gave this lecture full of nervous smiles, as if knowing he was selling a dead duck; some of his examples were all right, others of the outdated post-modernist avant-garde. John Eccles grumbled throughout, the others restlessly attempted polite faces.

Odds and ends: children don't realize they can die until they are 4/5 years old.

I asked John Eccles why memory deteriorates. He says it does not, it is retrieval that is faulty, the indexing apparatus. He solves this by elaborately cross-indexing everything he needs, by filing on paper. I could not really believe this, the notion that we forget nothing; but simply grow worse at finding where it is stored.

Man: What will happen to me when I die?

Quantum physicist: What will happen to you when I die?

Eiger: Molecular evolution requires us to die after two or three generations. We cannot escape the DNA system.

Only one fossil survives of 2/300,000 living specimens.

The wives, who are growing mutinous at being so excluded from the deliberations, are allowed to the Villa for dinner. Aschoff embarrasses me by bringing some of my books for me to sign; then we go off with him and his wife, who proves jollily eccentric, forthright to a hair-raising degree, down to Bellagio and drink. She hints that he is too fond of girls; they mock and tease and torment each other continually. She is a great reader, not the fool she sometimes sounds. He accuses her of being an alcoholic when she joins Eliz in drinking a Calvados. There is a mystery just inside the hotel, visible through the window from where we sit on the terrace: a girl who has been working there all day, rather pretty. Aschoff stands so much speculation, then leaps up and goes inside. I see him smile, bow, sit, engage in conversation; and after a while he stands, kisses the girl's hand, and comes back to us. She is doing some translating for the next conference. I liked this. So un-English; you wonder, so ask. We left Eliz and Philippina, and drove back to the Villa.

He was more than a little drunk, though we had drunk a very little; and took me to the Tower, where his room is, a long way from the Villa itself.

I say, 'Well, I'll say goodnight and walk back now.'

'Oh my God, what am I doing? How can I do such a thing? I know very well you live at the Villa. How can I do such a thing?' And back we get in the car. On the way up he says, 'For years I believed science was all. Now, this last ten years, I see it is not enough. It is not enough.' An endearing man. I liked him very much by the end. His frankness, his life, *élan*.

10 July

Steven Goldman: an archetypal Jewish intellect. I thought of him as the rabbi, he wore a yarmulke all the time. Very incisive, demanding, sceptical of everyone else, and cutting when he wanted. A formidably learned lecture, dazzling in its reading, its knowledge of many sciences. It seemed to boil down to yet another denunciation of nineteenth-century historicism; time as dynamic backdrop, history as 'where we are' causatively. The physicist David Park was supposed to sum up the conference, in the last session; but seemed to me to say little, beyond that 'now' is not denotable. Both science and humanism are 'in the mud'. In the final discussion Sivin was at long last allowed his say on China.

I made a little speech myself after Sivin, declaring that he had convinced me that I was a Chinaman. Then telling them they were a bunch of schoolmasters, treating time as some unruly child, a boy they would belt if they could ever catch him in a corner; while I treasured his mystery and unruliness; that most of the pleasures and piquancy of life came from them. With respect to Sir John, that I would commit suicide if I thought a thinking, conscious part of my mind might survive physical death; that the transience and ephemerality of life were beautiful things, life was meaningless without them. And so on. They gave me a little clap at the end. Fraser said afterwards, 'That was your meeting.'

I could have said much more, especially on one thing I mentioned, the artist's need to synthesize, faced with their adamantly analytic approach (and vocabulary); and on the quite extraordinary absence of any practical sociological discussion, and the importance of death, if one discusses time in any practical way. Time and death are indissolubly bound for the ordinary human being, what I called the 'voices down below in the town' in my little speech; a literal sound to which all present had seemed to me singularly deaf. The only person who mentioned death was in fact Jacob Arlow, the psychoanalyst, an otherwise rather silent member of the group. He at least was obviously pleased by what I said, and scribbled me two notes.

I was not the only bolshie in that last discussion. Wheeler made some pronouncement about science having to retain an inner citadel of belief in objective truth and objective history. 'All history is subjective,' suddenly bellowed Frank Haber, and for a minute or two angry humanism at last had its say. I discovered afterwards that I had also given Wheeler a dig. I suggested to him during my speech that black holes in our general knowledge might be a good thing. Apparently he had used exactly the same image himself talking with some of the others the evening before at dinner, though in terms of ignorance that had to be cleared.

That evening we all went to a dinner in a fish restaurant just outside Bellagio. It soon began to pour with rain and there was a spectacular thunderstorm; increasing gusts of wind, like the immortal scene in René Clair's *À Nous la Liberté*. In the end we had to retreat indoors, in chaos; and return to the hotel in pouring rain still. Then a last session of some of us, outside the Hotel du Lac, drinking beer. Various pent-up malices appeared. Wheeler and Eccles: 'Senior citizens, one can't attack them,' says Goldman. General complaint about Eccles' title: 'Those goddam English titles, why are we always so respectful to them?' They think Wheeler is probably a 'nuker' – an advocate of nuclear weapons.

Nuclear extinction was another matter not mentioned once; its effect on the overvaluing of now, the overanxiety to achieve (painfully evident in a number of the papers, the need to impress one's fellow-scientists), the lust for instant reward in career, private life, pleasure. Which leads to a demand for a present world full of active, transforming, 'boundary' situations – in historically a present world that makes such a demand increasingly difficult and irrational, for reasons of overpopulation, economic recession and all the rest of it. Like all professions, the academic dreams of a quantum-field world full of potential free play and laissez-faire, an ideal projection of the world that is the case.

News came during our sessions of the riots in Britain; perhaps the deepest comment on what went on in our ochre tower at the Villa.[1] Superior intellects remain common ones, or selfish ones, in terms of social relations; this is the one thing a 'common' (uneducated) man would have grasped, if he had been present. This is not to suggest the pursuit of higher knowledge is not a sufficient, indeed vital, end in itself; but that single ends must always be suspect. As Sivin said of the Chinese, science without ethics is no science. The sickness of contemporary human society seems to me more and more clear: physically it is overpopulation, spiritually it is self-conscious greed, that is, obsession with reward *now* – almost a kind of impatience, now that all the old bulwarks of patience are demolished. That is, there is a flagrant need to discuss popular notions or concepts of time. The irony is that just at the period when scientists seem more and more sceptical of the idea of linear, directional, 'historical' time, ordinary humanity falls more and more under its power.

Eccles took me gently to task afterwards for rejecting the notion of an afterlife. 'Wait till you are my age,' he said (he is seventy-eight). I said I had seen that softening take place in my own father; but I ought to have said that 'waiting until you are my age' was precisely the problem,

---

[1] On 3 July a police arrest sparked off several days of riots in Toxteth, Liverpool. Five hundred people were arrested and at least seventy buildings destroyed.

socially. A *nostalgie de la vie* may be all right in art; it is when it is projected forwards that the damage comes.

11 July

We ferried across the lake and went to Lugano, then on the autoroute north into Switzerland and the St Gotthard Pass. We met an appalling southward jam, ten miles or more long, just south of Airolo, on the upward climb; on our northward side of the road, almost nothing. But we stopped at a tiny hamlet, another Gasthaus, before the higher mountain. A walk up the slope before supper. Some lovely alpine plants, archetypal deer-coloured cattle, each with its bronze bell and attendant cowherd. I was looking for a vanilla orchid; but Eliz spotted one first, another new species for me. The crowded flowers are a very dark purple indeed, and make the plant conspicuous at a distance. A nice steak-and-chips supper; we feel kinder to safe, simple Switzerland after our experience at Intra.

12 July

More cloudy, and Eliz goes through an hour of hell. The modern road was closed for some reason and she had to drive up the old paved St Gotthard route, endless hairpins, all in mist, which grew denser at the top. Where we managed to lose our way. I had thought of buying a postcard at our Gasthaus, showing the pass under snow, for a joke. Suddenly we were in the middle of nowhere, with banks of *névé* on one side, an icy lake on the other. We managed to retrace our steps and find the Lucerne road we had missed; and the modern road was open on the northern descent, into rain and grey skies. Lucerne, and on; leaving the autoroute at Solothurn, then up to the French border at Biel.

A sunlit evening, once we are past the border at Col des Roches, a much easier pass than the one we came by. Via Morteau, and down the pretty valley of the Doubs to Montbenoît; where the hotel I picked from Michelin evidently thinks I am slightly mad to think they might have a room that has not been booked. I belatedly remember that it is the weekend of July 14th. We go to an *auberge* in the village; the *patronne* has no rooms there either, but thinks she may place us *chez un habitant*, at a farm. I have visions of something very primitive, but beggars can't choose. We appear at the place; a gentleman is waiting, speaks to me in English. The only thing farm-like about his house is its exterior. Inside it turns out to have been converted in amazing good taste (for provincial France).

13 July

Indecision, we cannot decide whether to stay where we are till the 14th, or to risk going on; the Meuniers say everything locally will be full. I go down to the car to look at the maps; having done so, lock and slam the door; and a second later, shades of Eccles, become conscious of staring through the glass at the keys on the dashboard ledge. I can't believe I have been so stupid – it is something Eliz warns me about every day; almost cry with vexation. In the end I go and ask Meunier for help. No Volkswagen garage in the area; no other garage he rings is open, no one works today. But in the end, with a couple of young friends staying there, he manages to force a bit of wire over the top of the window, loop it over the safety-lock and raise it. At least that makes a decision for us.

Salins for the night. We stopped early; an old coaching-hotel, rather picturesquely unchanged, though the food was very poor. We do a tour of the old salt-works, for which the town is, or was, famous; huge salt-pans (to evaporate the water raised from naturally salt springs underground); then a descent to the underground galleries where the springs were hidden. An old water-wheel there drives a very primitive pump still. The shaft from wheel to pump is too long to run unsupported and is propped by old timber rockers, which sway in time, like ancient and very slow pendulums. Then we watched a local tennis competition, a rather good young left-hander with a bizarre inability to serve, two or three double faults per game. After dinner there was a parade, more Tati-like than patriotic, with a ghastly assembly of pink-jacketed and tight-bottomed drum-majorettes, *à l'américaine*. Their ages ran from eighteen to what looked like four. All done very seriously. *Pétards*,[1] country boys looking for trouble; though none seems to have come. A notice at the *hôtel de ville* expressly forbade their use, but they were being let off everywhere, even under the gendarmes' noses.

14 July

We drove to Arbois nearby, to buy some of the wine. It looks a plump little town, much better-to-do than Salins. Wine merchants everywhere; but Arbois is to be drunk old, not young, and there seemed very little of earlier than 1979. We bought six bottles at the Cooperative Vinicole, then six more at another grower's, who had 1976. We were served by the grower himself, who told us about the *vin jaune* and *vin de paille*, the really venerated wines of the region, and expensive to match. He said good years of the ordinary white improved for twenty or thirty years, though the 1976 was now drinkable. We bought also a bottle of *macvin*, the *pineau*-like aperitif they have begun to make also.

Across country to the Dijon motorway, along that to the main Paris–South one, where Paris-bound traffic is heavy; so off it at Pouilly-en-Auxois, and to Saulieu, on the old N6.

---

[1] Bangers.

15 July

Across the Morvan, then over the Loire, and across the northern Sologne. We stopped for a moment beside a cornfield two or three years fallow, a marvellous display of old arable weeds, among them an exquisite little annual with a soft violet-purple flower, whose identification defeated me; like an *Anagallis*, but between the blue and red varieties of that. A Great Grey Shrike corpse, killed by some car, beside the road.

We ended that night near Olivet, on a branch of the Loire, the rumble of Orléans only a mile or two away. In a weird modern hotel, only recently built, and evidently designed to catch the style-conscious international businessman. Like countless American and British hotels of its kind, but somehow absurd in France – one could not imagine anyone of taste and sensitivity there going within a mile of the place. We dined in a sort of bar, where one paid 70 francs for a choice, and come again, of thirty hors d'oeuvres, a main dish and dessert, and unlimited wine (a watery red Touraine): a system I have never run across in France. I think it will not work. The lady of the French family next to us went back for more hors d'oeuvres, but only to feed the sausages and slices of *Andouille de Vire*[1] to her dog. Afterwards we went for a pleasant walk in a sort of Venice beside the branches of the Loire; some nice old riverside houses, peace, a moon on the tranquil water as we came back. There is no river quite like this in Europe: the way it seems to instil quiet and dignity on all it touches, even in its backwaters.

16 July

To Thury-Harcourt, just south of Caen, where there is a one-star restaurant. A chi-chi hotel, then an excellent meal in a nearly empty restaurant; only one other table was occupied. The main dish was a *jambonneau* of duck in cider sauce, accompanied by roast slices of some old dessert apple, a good combination.

17 July

To Cherbourg, and last shopping. The Sealink ferry back abominably crowded, tired and dirty; it was difficult even to find a seat. Children, coach parties. Muzak and drunken singing, the usual ultimate revenge of the Puritans on the British. Then an endless wait to get off the boat at Weymouth. The Customs were being difficult. Home at last to Lyme. The milometer for the trip at 1,700 miles, exactly.

26 October

This is not a happy year. For weeks and weeks now I have woken up depressed, then gradually daytime 'normality' rescues me a little. It is

---

[1] A kind of tripe sausage from Normandy.

partly the film and all its attendant publicity, career like a millstone round my neck; partly the way Eliz and I drift apart, without hatred or rows, by some process the reverse of osmosis. Her withdrawal is (outwardly) a matter of her hate for this house, for Lyme, for my 'drugs' (local history, old books, nature, etc.) – all that I use to escape the present. Mine is not only from her, but from most of my contemporaries – from all in them that welcomes things like the new 'centre' party, the SDP.[1] But it's more biological than political, a deep feeling that it is the selfishness of middle-class liberals that will finally end the human race. For years I have hid my feelings here from friends, half out of laziness, a quarter from never being able to argue on such matters face to face, a last quarter out of friend-ship – not being able to value truth above that. I nearly burst out against Ronnie Payne one day this summer; and against Karel only last month, at his supper-table, when he said that at least Reagan kept the Russians in check (he has joined the SDP recently). Tom Maschler, also. Most of them seem to me biologically *blind*, there is no other word for it. Their lives, their views, their judgements, are all dictated by a deep longing to maintain the social and political status quo – that is, a world where 'we' and our friends still maintain our absurdly privileged status. Which is of course maintained and propagated, 'down' from the élite, by all our media. All our 'serious' newspapers, the television channels, everything else (including the literary establishment) spread the same manure (you too can be a top person), or cultural hegemony. I sometimes feel I would welcome a Russian invasion tomorrow, if it could take place without too much destruction and blood-shed. To be poor again, and have to struggle, against something better than the insane pressures of a bestselling novelist, the poison of fan mail. When I came back here two days ago it took me three hours to go through all the letters; almost all felt like leeches.

The film has been almost universally praised by the yellow press (some-times for absurdly chauvinistic reasons, as in the *Evening Standard* and the *Daily Mail*), and damned by the more egghead, on both sides of the Atlantic. We all went to the premiere at the Haymarket Odeon ten days ago, I sat between Karel and Meryl. A very silent audience, as if puzzled; most puzzled when it ended, a very odd silence. This is apparently quite common. I liked it a little better this second time round, though still feel it fails – and where it matters most, alas. It looks very good, but is somewhere empty at the heart, perhaps reflecting a fault in the book. The American critics, Sarris, Kael and the rest, have suggested this. Meanwhile it has done very well at the first-run box-offices, beating *Star*

---

[1] At the beginning of the year four prominent Labour MPs, David Owen, Shirley Williams, Bill Rodgers and Roy Jenkins, broke away from a Party they perceived to be increasingly extreme, and, announcing their plans 'to break the mould of British politics', formed the Social Democratic Party.

Wars in Los Angeles for receipts, breaking the record at the Haymarket Odeon. The Turners here in Lyme told me a story about an old lady who came out (our cinema has got an early release) and said, "'Tis lovely, I didn't understand a word of it. But 'tis lovely.' Others in Lyme are apparently less kind; and deeply offended that their faces, as extras, have been cut, or are seen so remotely and briefly.

Mercifully I wasn't here for the Lyme showing, but in London, in our new Regent's Park Road flat. We, or rather Eliz, moved into it in late August. I, or rather the abominable 'John Fowles', dominate our lives so much than I thought it best to stay away; and she seems more reconciled to it, and its improvement on Hampstead, and enjoying the whole process. But then a bronchial cold, then telephoning me one day to say she was waiting for an ambulance, she had just had a suspected heart attack; which nearly gave me one. Joanne[1] went to look after her over the weekend, and another attack, another visit to hospital. But the doctor this second time told Joanne the heart was sound as a bell, it was all 'psychosomatic stress', hysteria in less clinical language, and I am to blame. I go to London, I try to be kind, but feel leaving this house and town for ever is something I can't face – even though being alone here so much this last three months has, God knows, convinced me I can't live alone here, on purely domestic and practical grounds. I eat nothing, I drink and smoke too much, I feel myself surrounded by a kind of shattered First World War landscape, unable to move. What tenuous relations we formerly had with people like the Hudsons lost; doomed. I keep thinking I must buy a car and learn to drive, at last; find someone to housekeep for me, I don't know.

Before this, I did manage to get Mary Scriven for a week, and she typed out *Mantissa*, though I knew it wasn't really ready; and the mood it tries to present is totally contrary to everything I feel. It is about a pathology (and also a spirit of the age – against it, that is). I can imagine how Eliz will hate it, and countless others. I also cannot see publishing 'fiction' again except in terms of punishment of one kind or another – both public and private. The former I can bear, the latter less and less. We went to Yorkshire last weekend, and I feel a kind of leper, an outcast – a piece of luggage Eliz has to carry round with her; just as I feel at Bristol, in fact, though curiously least of all with Nick.

In some odd way, perhaps because of his own growing success as potter, and also his likeable way of taking things at face value, I sense he understands, or begins to understand, A half-hour with him in his little studio, listening to him talk about new pottery ideas he was working on, was so nice after my leper feeling in Yorkshire; and that Eliz and Anna so often give me. Just somebody who makes things talking about

---

[1] Elizabeth's younger sister.

the problems of making things; with everyone else I have *made* things, and that is how they see me. Past, and guilty; not present and innocent. At least Nick understands it is all risk, doubt, not being sure at all; and that is always where one is, in real terms.

15 May 1982
Corrected proofs of *Mantissa* sent back to Boston. LB offered $250,000 for it, which I regard as absurdly over-much (and so do NAL, who have refused to go above $75,000 for the paperback rights), but in view of all they have made from me over the years . . . Tom at Cape also gave too much, £40,000. All this against the ironic background of Anna and Nick wanting a new house at Bristol, and my not being able to find a way to buy it for them – or find the £20,000 or so they need as second mortgage through the company. We are grasshoppers; have never saved or invested. Even Boxall can't believe I have no stocks and shares, no nest-egg hidden away somewhere. They have at last hopes of a house at £54,000. We are going to try to fiddle a personal mortgage from me to them towards that total.

A strange phenomenon. I captured a worker bumble-bee in the greenhouse, in order to release it; then noticed a weird excrescent growth on the clypeus, just between the eyes. A tiny mushroom-like colony, some two or three millimetres long: whitish stalks capped by greyish heads – like minute stinkhorn fungi. Under the microscope these heads revealed themselves as bilobal, strangely like cerebella, that is, creased and folded. I thought at first they were flower anthers, detachable and adhesive like those of the bee orchid family. But I don't know of anything in flower at the moment with such anthers (and no pollen was visible). So far as I could see, also, the stalks grew from small 'carbuncles' in the chitin. The bee itself was obviously sick, able to buzz and walk, but not to fly. I can find no reference to fungoid parasites in Free and Butler's book on the family. The appearance of the poor creature, with this bizarre and seemingly lethal little bouquet projecting forward from its face, was somehow festive, like a Rio carnival woman. I tried to remove the 'bouquet' by needle-point, but it was too firmly fixed.

22 December
Mantissa has done not too badly, despite very bad reviews from all the intellectual critics; only Malcolm Bradbury and David Lodge were faintly kind, of that ilk here – we form a faint sort of school, I suppose. David Burnett's little illustrated edition of the history of Lyme came out a month ago.[1] I am quite pleased with that. I like his tremendous energy. He was here yesterday, on the road, since he is a one-man operation,

---

[1] The book, called *A Short History of Lyme Regis*, was written by JF for David Burnett's publishing company, the Dovecote Press.

his own editor, warehouseman, rep, everything. And cock-a-hoop, as he has since November sold £21,000 of this first four-book Dorset series. Ray Roberts[1] was here recently and I introduced them (LB are taking 2,500 of the history, the same as ours bar a paper jacket and different TP); and now David hopes to be a LB author on his own literary side.

The *FLW* film failed with both the Oscar and English Academy awards. We went to the latter and sat with Harold and Antonia, and the Ironses; a sour evening. Leon Clore was drunk by the end of it and started shouting 'cheat' and 'con' when *Chariots of Fire* won the Best Film title (as it did later in Hollywood). Awful gloom at our table from Jeremy and Harold, while the rest of us rather enjoyed the vulgarity of it all. Harold smiled only once during the endless comedy spiels between the awards, when old Arthur Lowe did an impeccably timed routine. He looked across at me with a grin and little nod of the head, clowning himself: that one passes, yes? The rest didn't, for him; and he just drank.

Lorenzaccio went into rehearsal at the National Theatre a week or two ago.[2] Michael Bogdanov (nicknamed 'Bodger') directs. He is an engagingly untroubled fellow, chubby and workmanlike, a cricket enthusiast; just the sort of man one would like as one's plumber – and a pleasant change from the overnervous Peter Gill, in my book. I again cut the play savagely for him; so much that I finally had to put three or four pages back, at his request. He is pleasant and jolly when we meet; but out of his sight, I am evidently out of his mind – that is, I hear nothing of what is going on.

I do Marivaux – *Le Jeu* – next for them. My choice, and I have persuaded them to let me set it in England, and seventy years later (about 1800–1810, say). I want to escape the decor that has hung the word *marivaudage* round the poor man's neck ever since – i.e., Watteau, the Italian comedy and all of that. It promises to be a fiend to do well, not least because I like M so much.

I went last week to see David Puttnam, who made *Chariots of Fire*, and is the current off-white hope of the British cinema. For months John Mortimer and Rob Knights have been trying to persuade Granada to put up money for a TV film of *The Ebony Tower*;[3] and a month ago finally persuaded Olivier to do the Breasley part. Granada offered, but meanly. Now Anthony Andrews the actor, who played with Jeremy in *Brideshead Revisited*, has pushed Puttnam into getting involved. So I am in the usual dilemma. Knights thinks Olivier will be in his last year as an actor next summer; 'with

[1] JF's new editor at Little, Brown; Ned Bradford had died in 1979.
[2] JF translated and adapted Alfred de Musset's play, which had never before been performed in English.
[3] The British director Robert Knights had directed Mortimer's original TV play *Rumpole of the Bailey* for the BBC's 'Play for Today' in 1975, and worked again with the writer when the long-running TV series of the same name began in 1978.

luck you can get two hours a day (shooting time) out of him now'. I should rather see a feature film made; but am loath to lose Olivier, and Mortimer.

Puttnam is fluent, vaguely ferret-like, frank for his world; but it is the frankness (over past failings, future promises) that success can afford. He is installed in a mews just beyond the Science Museum – part of him is rather engagingly like a barrow-boy made good, prepared to be generous. Another part, I suspect, could be as ruthless as ever. Tom M says Karel says no serious director would go within a continent of him; but I smell a whiff of sour grapes there. P proposes a five million budget (cheap these days); Granada far less (the Granada chief is David Plowright, O's brother-in-law), though O's fee would come from 'outside' – whatever that means. He might work for Puttnam, but would want much more. P does not want to have to take on other people's packages, etc. I see every chance of nothing happening, in the end.

23 March 1983
The *Lorenzaccio* first night was on the 15th, a week ago. This was after endless – and panicky – previews. I went to the first, which was appallingly slow, with all the scene changes. Peter Hall was there, and told Michael he must simplify and cut. I'd been to quite a lot of rehearsals before this – and got very fond of both Michael and the company. They really worked like dogs, and he drove them abominably hard – impossibly hard, if he didn't have them all behind him. Endless discussions. 'What wouldn't I give for a dozen old rep hams,' he said one day. The old hands, the Bryants and Hensons, can do the Romantic stuff; the young ones, not. Michael and his assistant, Alan Cohen, claim it is because they no longer have the provincial training, learning how to vamp out such parts at short notice. They agonize too much over 'feeling' their roles, and the rest. Also TV, which kills the art of projecting; with its eternal close-ups of faces. Some of them remained agonizingly erratic right up to the end; especially Greg Hicks' wife Fanny (Frances Viner), though mercifully she was much better on the first night. She and Greg are bewilderingly inconsistent. He would do something perfectly one day; then seem to forget it all by the next. He would talk about it to me, how it must go with how he feels, he has to experiment, every performance is a crisis, and so on. But he is a fine young actor. We should have been lost without him, and the power and edge he developed by the end.

A not so pleasant experience. I agreed to do an interview about *Lorenzaccio* with the magazine *Time Out,* in the person of one Richard Rayner. So between rehearsals one day, the nice publicity girl at the National, Nickie Moody, takes me upstairs to her office, and we do the interview. An amiable and eager young man, who doesn't seem very interested in the play. Lunch, an hour of chat. When he's gone, I tell Nickie that I mistrust such easy sessions. Fortunately; since the article is vicious, slightly beyond even my experienced belief – evidently pre-determined, and the actually meeting face-to-face was only fodder for it. Every line is written to hurt, with a full use of 1930s fascist techniques. I have bottle-glass spectacles, I wear a quilted jacket because I am at heart a country squire, and so on. I predict a successful career for Mr Rayner.

We went to the Peter Blake exhibition at the Tate, a conflict between great technical skill – some really fine watercolours and passages of oil-paint – and cultural 'softness'. He falls for his age, and its 'pop' aspects. Great artists have always denied their ages, or in some way gone, or foreseen, beyond them. One is left here with many very pretty images and pictures, and a skin-deep philosophy – a standard bourgeois one, in effect. Look, I like wrestlers, pop singers, found objects and collages, and I have great taste, I am a fine colourist and draughtsman. I am also a slave of what has happened. This attachment to pretty image that I sense also in Hockney – is an oblique sentimentality, characteristic in this kind of contemporary art; not sentimental outwardly, of course, and often the very reverse in overt subject-matter; but alienated from lasting values. It purveys no more than *chic*, at its worst.

Gandhi.[1] A triumph of subject-matter over treatment.

Another interview, with Sarah Benton, just elected deputy editor of the *New Statesman*, though this is for the *New Socialist*. A bespectacled young woman, acutely earnest over feminism, so much so that I feel like a chemical solution faced with a piece of litmus paper. I sensed that all my answers, or reactions, were wrong. She rather endearingly found, once arrived, that the cassettes she had bought for her tape-recorder were not in her bag. She had evidently left them on the shop counter. I did not dare suggest that this was endearing. I found her proof I am old, and a new generation has emerged. She'd been very recently to Greenham Common – with which, of course, she was generally in complete sympathy – but was angry that the things hung on the camp perimeter wire, the baby socks, the nappies, and so on, were also the main symbols of historical feminine subjection.[2] Her suspicion of, almost hostility to, my notion that men and women might need each other, seemed to me both sad and chilling. There must be strange blank spaces in the maps of such militant lives.

24 March
Something both curiously puritanical and faintly wistful in the generation to which she and Rayner belong – the young intellectuals; as if they both despise and envy us for being born before 1939, for having been

[1] Richard Attenborough's film of Gandhi's life won eight Oscars at the 1983 Academy Awards, including Best Picture.
[2] After it was announced that America would store cruise missiles at the Greenham Common airbase, in 1981 a group of female activists set up the Greenham Common Women's Peace Camp to protest against nuclear weapons.

successful (in my case), for not agreeing over everything with them. I notice it equally in a recent *Granta* magazine anthology of promising young British writers, headed by the voguishly bitter (if not actually sick) Martin Amis, who makes his father seem like a warm-hearted humanist by comparison. Nausea, in the Sartrean sense, seems far from dead; and a decided cold shoulder turned on any humanist view of life – tolerance, generosity, any classical observer role for the writer. There is a marked shift away from common reader–writer assumptions into a generally waspish personal hatred of all that is not similarly waspish. A literary century gone very sour.

A reading rehearsal with Greg and Michael Bryant. Bryant, they say, is very 'committed' to the left. He is an odd little figure with his white hair and beard, and linguistic violence; full of four-letter words. (Greg says he has a headache. Bryant: 'You shouldn't spend so much time fucking Fanny.') He counts as the 'leader' of the company, a position he holds by being infinitely the most powerful actor, also the lower-deck lawyer and rebel. They laugh at him, as they do at Michael [Bogdanov]; and equally respect him. On the job, even at half-power, he dominates them – gets rehearsals back on keel when the younger ones start falling apart. It's largely in his fine voice, that buried fierceness. He doesn't like his part as Filippo Strozzi. Michael and I discuss something about it, and he cuts in: 'I know, I'm just a fucking old stooge.' Another time: 'Don't be fooled by this bloody Bulgarian, Christ knows why we work for him – what do they call you now, Bodger?' And Michael has to produce a recent cutting and read it out. He is referred to as 'the podgy Wunderkind of the British theatre'. They all laughing, not least Michael himself. Alan Cohen is 'the Scottish Semite'. Bryant has a very unusual fulminant quality – on stage it needs something to explode against, and Filippo, alas, gives him nothing. But Michael says he is the best ensemble company man in Britain – as well as being his one first-order actor, of course. He frightened me a little; something about that always repressed violence in his voice. Which is mine also, that I bury.

The Ebony Tower. David Puttnam never came through with a serious offer, and a month ago I dropped him and forced Janet[1] to go back to Granada, since Olivier remains willing. But since then they have been dragging their feet, too. Today Rob Knights and John Mortimer came to the flat, and we discussed script problems. Olivier is worried about the bad language (I kept thinking at the National how well Michael Bryant could have done the part) and also that he doesn't have a good enough last scene. I said I found that slightly absurd. 'He's a very ordinary man,' says Mortimer, 'who just happens to be a great actor.' He

---

[1] Janet Fillingham, who worked with JF's agent Anthony Sheil.

says he will give him a little last scene as a placebo. John M revealed he had studied art at Oxford – 'painting naked ladies standing by radiators'. He is an amiable, faintly pawky sixty-year-old, more like a worldly don than a barrister; Rob Knights is boyish, eager. He'd spent the day directing Emlyn Williams in one of JM's *Rumpole* series: 'Extraordinary. He actually remembered his lines today.' I hope I am right to elect for Olivier: this sudden renaissance of geriatric actors. I did ask Michael one day if Bryant might be available, but I didn't want to steal him, etc. He said he couldn't be spared this year, but next – 'he'd love it'. I may regret that.

The Granada contracts came through today. Also for a TV film of 'Poor Koko'.

17 June

Monica Kinberg telephoned, from London, en route for Israel. It felt as from another planet, in a time sense; someone 'dead'. She is doing a PhD at UCLA. Jud is unhappy, distressed by his world. She says he is 'failing upwards'. A phrase I could use of myself.

John Mortimer's script came through. It is middling – in places muddling – good. He has changed relationships somewhat, to please Olivier; and Granada, who want an American as David, 'for the sale'. Almost all Breasley's blue language is dropped. But it is reasonably faithful, and craftsmanlike. Jon Voigt is seemingly interested. They have found a location, Plessac, near Confolens; not as I saw the *manoir*, but I suppose it will pass for Brittany. Curiously, only three weeks ago, when we were in France, we came to a fork, two possible roads from La Rochefoucauld on our way north. On one I did notice forest and some lakes five miles away, and would have gone that way; but we were short of time and I took the other road. The area we 'missed' is the one now chosen. I can remember hesitating; but as I regularly cheat a little with Eliz (take slightly longer roads if they look more attractive or quieter), and we were trying to make ground that day, I picked a *Nationale*.

4 July

Something strange, and nasty. Last year a voluble, neurotic woman appeared at Belmont, claiming that Warner had cheated her out of the star role in *The FLW* – that she *was* Sarah Woodruff, and so on.

I came back on Monday from London to find a huge rambling letter from her, an incoherent tale of show-business paranoia, famous people who had let her down, stolen her scripts, not cast her, and the rest. On Tuesday she is suddenly at the door again – I was just in the middle of writing Rebecca's dream in *A Maggot* – and demanding attention. I won't let her in, all this is at the door – she was a greater actress than Redgrave ten years ago, everyone knew; she was the most beautiful woman in the world, everyone also knew; she was a superb writer – then that being 'cheated' out of Meryl Streep's part had forced her to become a street prostitute in America. She says all this with a hypnotically self-convinced blue stare, like a gipsy door-seller, as if she dares you to believe refusing the white heather will not bring a curse on you. I am as cold as ice, I can't help her; and suddenly it all ends in violent screams. I'm like all Englishmen, I hate women. She walked away shouting, 'Shit. Lousy shit!' at the top of her voice, and a distinct threat that I hadn't heard the end of her.

Very disturbing, this violent anger. I locked all the doors, and fully expected her back again; but did not see her. Then two days later I went down to the Museum with Ann Jellicoe's assistant, to give her something needed for next year's play. And she said she'd given a lift in her car to an extraordinary woman, the day before – to Dorchester. And she had done nothing but talk of me. I felt relieved, at least that 'Contessa Veronica' (as she calls herself) was going back to London.

Yesterday (Sunday) I go to Wincanton for a KAMT[1] meeting. After it's over Rodney and Colin drive me to Sherborne station, for the train home. As we get out of the car, we see a woman standing at the station entrance, talking to a taxi-man. It is her again – a coincidence so far-fetched that it frightens me. Fortunately Colin and Rod shielded me, while I began to feel I could not risk going on the same train, if she *was* coming back to Axminster. Then she started to walk slowly away from the station, and past where we stood. Colin thought she did recognize me, but she walked on. She dresses in a fur-coat, with peculiar harem-type scarlet trousers, tight at the ankle. She has a *femme fatale* quality that is really sinister: the conviction of her own madness.

10 July

Eliz has been in Crete this last fortnight, with Anna and the children. By an irony it has been a long heat-wave here, almost Mediterranean in its warmth. Life intolerable without all the doors open; a strange change after the wretched weather earlier this year. I don't really like it, the heat; and pray for the thunderstorms that threaten every day, yet never actually happen. Lyme slips into its ugly high-season self; endless crowds, cars, noise, vulgarity.

I had meant to write, while Eliz was away; have done some, but not enough (*A Maggot*). So much fills my life, and has for several years. I have lost all single-mindedness, and days slip by as petals fall from the roses: over before they begin. The war between the pagan and the puritan in me grows far worse with age. I meant to write yesterday, but spent all day doing the Stile House deeds. Ronnie and Celia came in

[1] The Kenneth Allsop Memorial Trust.

the evening and I took them to the Mariners for dinner. Mary Feather-
stone's endless chatter, which they take to better than I do: Ronnie plays
his jovial, funny self, Celia shows spurts of enthusiasm, as if this at last
is something she can 'relate' to. They are middle, central people; I live
at extremes I realize they can hardly imagine – in tiniest details (as in
the deeds), and more and more *sub specie aeternitatis,*[1] a long way from
what is socially around me and *now*. All that comes sounds like the
spoiling, distracting voices behind the mist.

There was something terminal about the recent election: socialism
died in it.[2] It was a triumph of this same middle, everything from
poujadism[3] at one wing to ineffective 'liberalism' at the other. The new
class dominates: the one risen from below to join the old middle class,
though much more for its old selfishness than for its finer virtues. Half-
education is its main symptom; like half-accent, in voice. Life is to be
faced with the ethos of so much modern commerce and business: to be
worsted and exploited – by conning others to consume, one may
consume better oneself. It is oppressing, this blind new class, because
it is so conspicuously self-brainwashed.

The Labour Party *débâcle* was symptomatic of this. It should have split
into its left and right wings, and campaigned separately. The 'broad
church' talk is nonsense. The left wing would have suffered this time
round, but gained in the future. Both wings should have fought for
proportional representation: opposing that is the worst folly of all. It all
comes from a national and archetypal terror of *not* compromising, *not*
middling and muddling one's way through. There is even something
symptomatic in the fact that the one firm leader and power-manipu-
lator on the scene (that the 'scene' has allowed to be so, of course) is
so popular because she aims and thinks backwards; in British terms, is
safe. Nothing can change, under Thatcher. All may stagnate, all may
wait – and no one will see.

14 July

I am made DLitt, *honoris causa*, at Exeter. I don't really know why I
accepted it, against general principle over such things. Perhaps because
Exeter is the university of the South-West. It turned out there was some
puzzlement there as to why I had taken it, also. My name was apparently
proposed by a scientist, an expert on sea-urchins, not anyone from the
department of English; I liked that.

It was appallingly hot, and I read my speech to congregation in shirt-

---

[1] 'under the aspect of eternity'.
[2] On 9 June Margaret Thatcher's Conservative government was returned to power
by a landslide.
[3] See note 1 on page 25.

sleeves under the robes: mainly to remind the graduates that you have to unlearn university. A pleasant enough occasion, once the silly medieval ceremony, with its doffing and bobbing, was over. I was taken to a party in the English Department afterwards. Morale is low, with all the cuts; and there was talk of my becoming a visiting fellow. The root problem, I felt, is a terrible and long-rooted inferiority complex, partly the usual thing vis-à-vis Oxbridge, partly because the West Country is what it is culturally, a Conservative desert.

21 July

To Cambridge, for the British Council seminar run by Malcolm Bradbury at Trinity. The hot weather continues, we got there on a perfect summer day. Cambridge looked like heaven – or like an Ackermann print, as George Steiner remarked. He came to the discussion Tom Maschler and I led; and to everyone's amazement, said nothing. Margaret Drabble and her new husband Michael Holroyd were also there. I went through it all in a kind of numb depression, watching it all happen to someone else. I find it harder and harder to pretend I am either a serious or a successful writer. I've been reading Culler's book, *On Deconstruction*;[1] feel deconstructed myself, or in need of it. All contradicts in my life nowadays; old values dissolve, old selves bear no relation to what I am.

Malcolm gives up the seminar after next year. I am reading his latest book, *Rates of Exchange*, which I like as an exercise in style – its prolonged sermon on the hopelessness of communication in this international academic world. The seminar showed only too well where he took his raw material from. He is a nice man, he reminds me a little of Denys Sharrocks; one can't imagine him losing his temper, or ever being unreasonable, with even the most flagrant fools. This is a little what is missing from *Rates of Exchange* – venom and anger, something to destroy its premises. He creates only too thoroughly the feeling that double talk rules all. Every atom in the world at a tangent to the rest.

Margaret Drabble is her usual forthright self. I mentioned feeling guilty over Arnold Wesker – not having read a book by a friend (Appignanesi) he has asked me to puff. 'Oh, good God, he sent me that. I just threw it in the wastepaper-basket. He's absolutely no right to do such things, it's very wrong of him. I just won't take it from him. You don't do things like that to your friends.' She only reads the good reviews of herself; the rest go likewise into the dustbin, it seems.

---

[1] Jonathan Culler, *On Deconstruction: Theory and Criticism after Structuralism* (Cornell University Press, 1983).

25 July

M arrives from Great Ayton, with Jonathan as escort. Eliz went to Taunton to fetch them. Just before they came Eileen telephoned from Kent to say that Uncle Stanley had died at five that afternoon. He has had a rapid cancer, and was unconscious at the end. M takes it well, luckily she was prepared – she spoke to Jane a few days ago, and knew death was very near.[1] Her imperviousness to any but her own voice is now almost total. I am given up as a bad job, and she either interrupts the moment I open my mouth or behaves as if I hadn't spoken in the first place; poor Jonathan suffers a little the same way, I notice, by some kind of contamination.

29 July

To Wingham, near Canterbury, for Uncle Stanley's funeral. All the old Alleyn Court and Westcliff/Thorpe Bay crowd are there. An atrociously hot day; the middle-class ritual.

6 August

To London. The hot weather holds, corn being cut in Wiltshire. We had supper with the Wisemans, over from France for Tom Maschler's fiftieth birthday party. Boris is a grown young man. He smokes in secret with us, away from his parents' eyes.

7 August

Tom's birthday. We give him three bottles of 1963 port and a dozen Beychevelle, for the future, when the 1982 vintage is bottled and brought to London. Champagne in the garden, a kind of replay of the wedding in Wales: Doris Lessing, Arnold, Desmond Morris, Sidney Bernstein, the Wisemans, Ed Victor, etc. I talked most with Morris. He is hooked now on archaeology, the Neolithic mind; a cascade of ideas, reminiscences; an intellectual egotist, but rather a pleasant one. He claims carp-watching (he has installed a pool of the things outside his studio in the Woodstock Road, *à la japonaise*) is his answer to nicotine and writing problems. Stories of a racehorse he has bought, of his attachment to Avebury – he was born near by; contempt for archaeologists, their narrowmindedness and lack of imagination. We find we agree on much, and went on talking during the dinner and after, indoors. Arnold made a remarkable speech (it took him three days to write, he said), really rather dramatic, since it kept teetering on the edge of being brutally frank about all Tom's failings, but was generous in the end. Fay looked as if she did not like it one bit, but it succeeded in its odd sour-sweet way. I

---

[1] A teacher at Alleyn Court school in Westcliff near Leigh-on-Sea, Stanley Richards (1905–1983) was the younger brother of JF's mother. Eileen was his wife and Jane his daughter. See *The Journals*, volume 1, page x.

sat between Deborah Rogers, the agent, now married, and Frank Giles'
daughter Sarah, Tom's current flame – who came with us to the first
night of *Lorenzaccio*, and who I managed on this occasion six months
later not to recognize; which cannot have impressed her much.

A kind of absurdity floated over it all, given that everyone knows the
marriage is split wide open. Tom goes off to France alone with Hannah
in a few days; Fay with Beth and the other two children to Greece. Tom
is apparently bored with life and publishing – going through the same
'middle-aged crisis' as most of the men there. Arnold, who sat next to
Eliz, apparently wonders if it was all worth it; Desmond Morris reputedly has marriage problems, Tom W and I are hardly happier. It shows
most in Tom, the birthday boy. He has just pulled off a minor coup
again in his role as my film agent, having harried John Calley at Warner
into renewing the *Daniel Martin* option for $27,500 but seems already
bored by it, a victim of his own skill as haggler. He is become a modern
King Midas, in effect.

9 August

One thing Desmond M and I agreed on – our inability to 'join' in such
Stone Age occasions as the one where we were talking – I had just cited
Uncle Stanley's funeral. He said, 'That's why I find all this (Arnold's
speech) so touching. I wish I could be part of it.' I found that curious
– wishing to re-enter the womb.

Something Arnold said in his speech: 'I start with a 100 per cent
regard for anyone I meet. That puts me in a situation where I can only
lose.' He meant it partly as a joke, of course; yet it is deeply true of him.
True of the Wisemans also – always trying to think the best of people,
which I both like in them and sometimes find irritating, sheer
Panglossism. Malou thinks Fay is wicked to have fought with Tom over
playing hostess to endless writers. 'It is her duty, he must entertain,' etc.
i.e., Tom is not to blame for demanding this. The fact that he demands
intolerably too much of everything in life – not only of Fay – is sublimely
ignored. I'd call this kind of idealism a distinctly Jewish trait, did not
Tom himself so handsomely refute it, by in general thinking the worst
of everyone. He has to be won from contempt, whereas they are gradually forced into it by reality. Something must have scorched this Jewish
trait out of Tom very young; but the effect – his seeming the exact opposite of, say, Arnold – is only superficial, of course. Like all opposites,
they are closer to each other than anything in-between.

11 August

Last night of *Lorenzaccio*. Rather sad, afterwards, in the bar, as it's a major
change-over night – many of the cast leaving. A strong feeling of the
transience of the actor's life. There were various complaints about NT

policy in general, mainly attached to Peter Hall, who's been away doing the *Ring*, and now wants to be director at Glyndebourne also. 'No one ever sees him,' etc.

Our Hampstead oculist: he says my right eye has 'floating opacities', I must see an eye man about it. They are little misty specks, greynesses. The eye aches a little, permanently. Possibly a minor haemorrhage, he says, behind the retina. It has deteriorated optically, also.

Tom Stoppard's *The Real Thing*. Clever, as always; and untouching, thought it would be other. Noël Coward seems to me his theatrical father; he is very chic. We went partly to see Roger Rees, who is to play David in *The Ebony Tower*.

14 August

Back to Lyme, with Doris, who is to move to the Abbeyfield Home at Colyton.

My relations with the abominable novelist and public figure grow worse and worse; two days ago Simon Loveday sent me the typescript of his book on me to read.[1] It is quite well written and in many ways extremely shrewd; a structuralist, partly deconstructionist account of all my faults – mainly to do with my hiding from myself the fact that I am a romancer (in Northrop Frye's sense), not a realist.[2] Short shrift is given to all claims as thinker or socialist. All my virtue lies in being able to tell a tale.

I cannot object to it intellectually (some of my 'crimes' I long ago confessed to myself) or morally, of course. To publish is to ask for such treatment. But something here and there in the tone seems to me gratuitously diminishing and sneering, coldly reifying. This no doubt is how I look from the outside to the post-war generation, 'Fowles' for students – some one to be dissected, and awarded a beta query. Dissected, since I am (in everything but a token courtesy of tense) dead, without feelings and without future. Symptomatic is the way things I said twenty years ago are produced as evidence for now.

This morning Bert Winter showed me an advertisement for a Manchester University course: 'Is John Fowles a great novelist or not?' It becomes absurd. The real question is whether John Fowles is still alive or not. Even to me he feels more and more a fiction of the past.

14 September

To David and Sarah Burnett's, at Stanbridge, to meet William Golding and his wife. David Cecil was also there, and Jeremy Hinchcliffe, a young

[1] *The Romances of John Fowles* (Macmillan, 1984).
[2] In his book the *Anatomy of Criticism*, Northrop Frye explained: 'The romancer does not attempt to create "real people" so much as stylized figures which expand into psychological archetypes.'

weaver turned potter. I liked Golding, who looks older than we realized – and is also sager and calmer than I realized, rather a sweet old man, with little sign of the demon I attach to his books (like most of us, for that matter). He has a finely modelled mouth and eyes, a white beard, faintly nautical in cut; but reminded me most of an intellectual Elizabethan bishop or scholar – a face out of the humanist past, really. We fence compliments to each other, a little awkwardly, I suppose both sensing long noses and formidable prejudices, while Cecil babbles away on the other side of the table in the tiny cottage. He seems quite unchanged from my own New College days.[1] He is doing a book for and with David B, on Dorset country-houses. A characteristic anecdote about his first meeting with Virginia Woolf, where she announced to the room that 'Now Lord David will tell us a story' – and how he blundered into an account of a novel he had been reading, realized it was not impressing and lamely said the story was perhaps better read than told. 'Yes, it does sound better read,' said VW.

To Golding's wife Ann I did not take; a woman with the face of a petulant doll, and a rather aggressive determination to have her say on everything. At one point she threatened, like Cecil, to launch into a story. 'Don't,' said her husband, very crisply. One knew too much about her, by the end.

He is finishing a novel about a novelist and an analyst of his work;[2] to appear next September. I envied him that. They live at Broadchalke.

6 October

They announce that Golding has won the Nobel. I am pleased; far rather he than Greene.

The Museum goes to rack and ruin, or rather its curator does; we have actually made a good profit this year. I can't keep up with all the research. I should resign, and would, if there were anyone to take my place.

14 November

To London again, for the day, to see Rob Knights' TV film of *The Ebony Tower*. We had lunch with him at Beak's, a new smart restaurant, with John Mortimer and his wife and daughter and the Granada producer; Harold Pinter, Glenda Jackson, Albert Finney and other theatrical luminaries at the next table. Mortimer is writing a novel. He says he is tired of the Bar, and a case he now has in Singapore will be his last. I quite like him – it would be hard to do anything else – but in a way mistrust

[1] Lord David Cecil (1902–1986) was a fellow of New College when JF was a student there and had also been Goldsmiths' professor of English literature at Oxford between 1948 and 1969. He lived in the Dorset village of Cranborne close to Cranborne Manor, where he had passed much of his childhood.
[2] *The Paper Men* (Faber, 1984).

such well-fitting men, known by everyone, trusted by everyone, endlessly genial and urbane; like a well-made *pâté* or chocolate.

The film, still only in rough-out, is better than I hoped; with Olivier's present faults well hidden,[1] and good performances from the girls. Mortimer and I argued afterwards to have all the flashbacks removed; and I wished there had been more lingering shots in places, longer perspectives. Rob's fault is rather like Karel's, a hatred of not getting on with it; I suggested the 'message' at the end didn't get home enough, and he is going to try to rejig that – David's defeat. But the whole could have been far worse.

11 February 1984

Tom and Viv. A play at the Royal Court about Eliot's first marriage, and his less than decent behaviour towards Vivienne Haigh-Wood.[2] Well presented and acted, though it is such a sardine-tin of a theatre. Eliot was almost as bad as Hardy, though one feels he was the more conditioned in some ways; that Hardy could have behaved differently. 'Writer destroys wife' may be nearly inevitable; but what is most unpleasant is the attempt to cover up – destroying the documentation (as Hardy did) or keeping it locked away (as the Eliot estate still does). The thing the play leaves out is the fact that Eliot was a great poet, despite his wrong principles and selfishness in human terms. It is symptomatic how this sort of thing, exhibiting the private flaws in 'great' writers, becomes so popular these days; no writer can survive such examination (the way the repair of the initial loss was bodged in private). Are they lesser writers because of all this dragging-out of their dirty linen and meanness? I think they must be, or will one day be so seen; they cannot get off completely on the pleasure or aesthetic principle.

8 December 1985

I have just passed the most unhappy six months of my life; so it has felt, and feels; so it is. It is nothing to do with *A Maggot*, which came out in September, first in America, then here. It had a very mixed reception, as usual, but has been on both bestseller lists. I went through all the publicity, all of that, as in a bad dream, a sea-mist. The people unreal, and myself ('John Fowles') most unreal of all. My sense of personal identity has completely disintegrated, I feel like an actor in a play he despises, or several actors, in a series of roles that are largely meaningless; the author, the museum curator, all the rest.

---

[1] Olivier had been suffering from ill-health for several years.

[2] Eliot married Vivienne Haigh-Wood in 1915. After struggling to cope with her frequent illnesses and depressions, he separated from her in 1933 and ostracized her over several years. On the advice of doctors he had her committed to a mental asylum in 1938, where she died in 1947.

It began indirectly with the break-up of Anna's marriage, which has been taking place all this year; all is now at divorce stage, its death. I can't write its details yet, but its effect has been catastrophic on Eliz and myself. Our own marriage is now in a state as bad, and we live in daily misery, constantly rowing and quarrelling; and that too I must leave for the moment; but our trying to help Anna is the blind, or equally miserable and broken, leading the blind. Anna and Eliz both increasingly blame Nick for *that* marriage's faults. He is apparently deep in his ostrich mood, head buried in a black resentment that Anna has filed for divorce; refusing even to see his own solicitor about it. Clearly he wishes that what is happening was not; as if by calling life a nightmare, its reality can be dismissed. I feel for him, from my own nightmare. You know you have cancer, head in the sand; or less metaphorically – both he and I will bear unhappiness at home if we are allowed to follow our respective arts, to pot and to write. If that becomes impossible, as it is now, we are done for; we become unforgivable male chauvinists, totally selfish, to be damned, cursed, irrefutably blamed. All this is, I suspect, carried on at a fairly primitive, largely inarticulate level between Nick and Anna; Eliz and I are locked in a far profounder battle. I am not claiming the male side is right; a large part of my present depression is not knowing, or simply feeling that one is the slave of history – the latest chapter of Adam versus Eve.

Poor Philip Larkin died a few days ago. Handsomely our finest versifier and 'slogan'-maker since the war, our purest poet; and our most typical, in historical terms. Yet also our greatest depresser and putterdown, a modern avatar of the Puritan spirit, for all his lack of Christianity or belief in God. There was unadulterated in him what was only half felt in all my generation; nothing matters (except perhaps a transient skill with words) and nothing redeems. There is a fine poem by him printed in an obituary in the *Sunday Times* today;[1] a naked *Timor mortis conturbat me*, without consolation felt or offered. A fine poem, yet so cryptoromantically black it offended me somewhere, deep down; that so effective a voice should serve such a personal mood, or style of thought. There is a line between great and brilliantly effective poetry, over which he must hover always. He denies too much; and such pessimists are always deeply attractive to the muddling majority, incapable of the real thing.

Desmond Donovan. He was (apparently still is) professor of geology at Univ. Coll., London. Took on the running of Wells Museum a few years ago; but gave that up, and is now 'attached' to Bristol University; a great authority on the 'head-foots', or cephalopods. He spent two days at the

[1] 'Aubade', which had first appeared in the *Times Literary Supplement* in 1977. See note on page 378.

Museum, going through our collection; a rather shy monomaniac, but a true scholar-specialist. I deeply envy his knowledge; but am (and was always) incapable of attaining it, of the years of concentration it needs; all I could do with him was play the ignoramus, the blind cripple following his guided tour.

12–13 December

Jo Chaplin[1] came over. I like her, but Eliz doesn't (E is in Bristol at the moment). She is a kind of unhibernating dormouse, a squirrel for nuts of information; and enormously 'useful' in sending me Lymiana. The trouble, as with Donovan, is that I am not a writer to such people. In many ways I enjoy suppressing all that side in me in such contexts; playing the very amateur and inefficient museum curator; but feel sometimes an abyss between us. They chug along on rails; and I rove far more than they can imagine.

16 December

To London. An agonized call from Anna almost as soon as we got there. She had gone to have a night in Bournemouth with her lover, Richard. But there they had a call from his wife, Sue, to say she knew what he was doing, and if he did not get back to Bristol at once she would change the locks on their house doors, never speak to him again, etc. Richard drives himself and Anna back to Bristol, in a white panic, and there is a major scene, which the outraged wife dominates (Anna is there). Richard proves, as Eliz and I suspect him, a man of straw. He eats humble pie throughout, denies Anna, must at all costs placate Sue; and Anna is destroyed. Which many suggest, as she deserves; but Sue, it seems, as they both know, has had many affairs of her own. Her crowning coup is to tell Anna that she discovered they were in Bournemouth through Nick, who telephoned her and told her so. Anna ran out and spent the night at the Crosses, who run the Boyce Avenue gallery. She has been foolishly romantic, of course, over Richard. But this seems punishment enough – to watch R crawling to the sadistic-sounding Sue, and then to learn she owes it to a venomous bit of 'sneaking' on Nick's part. I think they are all in hell, all sadists or masochists. Mankind, and womankind, has not advanced in this since Neolithic times.

18 December

We went to see Tom Maschler in the evening with Regina,[2] at his new post-separation flat; he had a nervous breakdown at the end of this year, apparently acute, a profound depression. Regina apparently stuck

[1] A Dorset local historian and archaeologist.
[2] Regina Kulinicz, a film publicist.

by him, and nursed him through it. Tom has bought 22 Belsize Park Gardens and installed himself in the *sous-les-toits* flat; too much of a barn and with weirdly few windows, nor do we like the colours. He says he is recovered, but he has changed; is much thinner, quieter, the sobered invalid. I felt something it has always been difficult to feel for him – sorry. There are still flashes of his old self, but he is much more a shadow of it. This flat has a European 'bourgeois' feel about it, a prison for a bourgeois mind, somehow; at least their Chalcot Gardens house had a kind of easy openness in its 'feel', whatever private horrors it concealed.

19 December
We came back from London, picking up the car at Axminster; but something odd even before we got out here. The front room curtains were drawn closed. I go to unlock the front door; no good, the inside latch is up. I went around the house. No sign of a break-in, no ladder. At last, doing it more carefully, I see the bedroom door on to the balcony: it is open; and that, finally, is how I get in myself.

We were burgled in September, when in the USA; and now again, and much more thoroughly. They had seemingly been through everything, every room (my study door was forced open), every drawer. I called the police, and we spent the next two hours with them. The Benjamin Martin Gregorian[1] is gone; all my trade tokens; all Eliz's remaining jewellery; the little French silk-suspension clock we had for years; all current stamps; a box of cutlery; Eliz's camera; my pocket-calculator; a chocolate ice-cream from the flat refrigerator, its paper left on the floor.

My first reaction is at its seeming senselessness, amateurishness at how much was *not* stolen: no pottery, no books, no paintings, nothing of what an antique-aware burglar must have gone for. Eliz is in despair, it seems most at the idea of some stranger having been through everything. We both share a contempt of worldly possessions in the usual sense. The police must think us an odd couple – the one (me) so unconcerned, the other (Eliz) renouncing all ownership and putting all the blame on Lyme and our living here.

27 December
A non-Christmas, for us. We had no dinner, but bacon and eggs. We are mercifully in peace together, both too depressed to be anything else; zombies. We have sent no cards, telephone no one; but sit slumped before the box. We hate the world. Anna comes on Boxing Day (Nick has insisted on taking the children off to Manchester alone). She cheers

---

[1] An eighteenth-century telescope.

us up a little; she is so even-tempered one finds it hard to believe in the reality of her own trauma; and as eager as ever to make the best of life and to find it enjoyable. Richard rings her every morning; it seems he is forgiven, after being unforgivable only a few days ago. Eliz and I say nothing, but think much.

There is an aspect of Anna I don't like and that I attribute obscurely as much to her infrequent contacts with the Maschlers, Fay and Tom, as to her far closer ones with us. I mean their old only-the-very-best selves, adept at the best food, the best experience, and to hell not only with money and common sense, but with any common philosophy of self-regulation, putting up with what one has. Her scorn with the way we eat now Eliz has given up anything but simple cooking, the way we don't lead a 'smart' and exciting life in terms of winter holidays and so on, is painfully near the surface. All contemporary Western culture (especially its urban variety) is on her side, *Carpe diem*; so I can't really blame her for that (nor the intrinsic boredom of the life children and her husband have forced her to lead these last years); yet something nags. Perhaps it is simply that this is the battle (basically of life values) between Eliz and myself. When we row she snarls about the dollars I keep in dollar account (nearly a million now); as if it is me, not the wretched tax laws, that keeps them there. My own notion, that we give ourselves more than enough for rational people to live on, is anathema. We have more, so we must spend more. I think Eliz lives far more nowadays for and through Anna, and the children, than through anything in our own life; and in that, I retain some sympathy for Nick. He and I both pay now for what happened thirty years ago.

Quite often now, I feel Eliz has acquired a second youth, she is twenty years younger than me, not six months older. Because of her passionate empathy with Anna, there has grown a kind of generation gap between us; and everything I believe in has become impossibly *vieux jeu*, irrelevant and irritating. M telephoned today, the first of 1986, and irritated me wildly over Anna – endless thinly veiled Victorian precepts about 'modern' divorce, or her notion of modern. The same situation, in reverse.

9 January 1986
In London, to do a programme in the flat with Nicholas Humphrey for Channel 4.[1] I read his book *Consciousness Regained* recently, and liked it; though he is too quick, too eager, oddly slapdash for all his intelligence. He reminds me of Freddy Raphael, without the scorpion tail.

---

[1] The programme was part of a six-part series called *The Inner Eye*, in which experimental psychologist Nicholas Humphrey investigated the development of human consciousness.

13 January

Back to Lyme alone. A strange incident on the train. I was alone in a first-class compartment. Just after Andover a boy of twenty-one or so came in; a faintly cherubic face, but queasy eyes; a blouse over a jumper, grey cords, sneakers, cocky in a vague way. He said he was going to Honiton; but money 'I definitely had on the platform at Andover' had disappeared, and now he couldn't pay his fare. Would I lend him a pound? He had cigarettes to sell in exchange. I didn't believe him, but gave him a pound. He pressed a packet of cigarettes on me. 'Go on. Take them. Please.' I waved my hand: no thanks. 'Oh. You sure? OK, then. Thanks.' And he disappeared.

About half an hour later he was back at the door of the compartment, with a can of McEwen's beer in his hand. 'Can I come in? I'm lonely, I want to talk with someone.' He was in and sitting opposite me before I had said anything. 'You sure I'm not bothering you? Do you mind?' He took a swig of his beer and offered me a cigarette, which I declined. He had a marvellous pair of liar's eyes, constantly shifting; then suddenly sincere, faintly quizzical, as if he knew I neither liked him nor trusted him.

I asked him where he came from. He lived at Honiton, with his grandparents, he was unemployed. He wanted to be a pop-singer, but he was going to make a fortune first. How? 'Jeweller's in Kensington High Street. Me and Dean'll get half a million out of that. Simple.' Who's Dean? 'My friend. He's at Portland Prison, stupid, did a job locally. Well, down at Exmouth actually.' He shrugged, then went on. 'Stupid. You have to do one big job, then get out. Then you're set up for life. This jeweller's, I already done it for a thousand. Just snatched a tray and ran. Hypodermic darts, that's what I'll use. Get in, put them all out for six hours, I'd never use violence, just put them out. I'd test the darts on myself first. Get someone to shoot me with one, right? I'd never use violence. Simple, the police don't know me. Do it, then run. They'd never catch me.' Was he allowing enough for the fence's rake-off? 'Sure. I know a fence, he's an old friend. He did the (some name I didn't catch) job years ago. He'd give us two-fifty thousand. Simple.' Where would he go? 'Somewhere like Mexico. Or Canada. Could you lend me another quid for a beer?' It seemed cheap at the price, so I gave him another pound, and off he went again; and offered me 30p change when he returned. 'I'm a bastard. Both ways. Real and the other. My father was in the Army at Honiton. Full of Army, Honiton.'

All this was interspersed with attempts to find out who I was; where he got nowhere. 'You puzzle me,' he said, 'you really puzzle me.' A pretty girl got on at Sherborne. 'That's a cocky one.' How did he know? 'Easy, way she walks, can't you see?' She walked down the corridor outside. He shouted, 'Hi, baby!' She flashed a smile over her shoulder. 'See? I told you.'

He swigged his new beer. 'You like music?'

'Pop?'

'Not pop, rock 'n' roll. That's my music.'

For what must have been half an hour then he continued singing, staring at me with a sudden intensity; old Beatles songs, others by people I'd never heard of, getting louder and louder. At one point he broke off. 'I'm boring you, aren't I? You don't like this, do you? I can see you don't, the way you look.' But he went on singing. I got up to get off at Axminster, dreading he might follow. But he asked for one of my Gauloises, and shook hands three times. 'Are you going to wish me well?' I said, 'For the singing, but not the other thing.'

I didn't take him seriously, except as a psychopathic liar and embryo con-man; and a touch of the sadist about him. I think he was most baffled by my not being shocked and outraged; and something in him was evil, like a leech, desperate to cling. I felt tempted to say I'd just been twice-burgled myself, but couldn't; he was very contemptuous of all the Honiton boys who 'did' local jobs. 'Daft. Stupid. You do one big job and set yourself up for life abroad. Obvious it's best.' How did his friend in Portland Prison, Dean, feel now he was caught? 'Says he's going straight from now on. He won't, I can talk him into the jeweller's. I mean, it's done for, this country. Two-fifty grand abroad, you can do what you like. I tried to get into the Navy, they turned me down, I failed the test.'

I told all this to old Eddie Arnott, whose taxi I caught outside Axminster station. He was shocked. 'They need the birch, that lot.' I suggested that that didn't help, but longer sentences might. He told me then about being coshed and robbed, when he lived in London; a story I had heard before.

28 January

Fernandez, my new doctor here, says my blood pressure is higher than before; and reads the riot act over exercise, not smoking, diet, all the rest. Not as coldly as when he was my insurance examiner, but resignedly, as if I am an idiot; for which I cannot blame him at all. He puts me on Adalat.

31 January

Out of nowhere, a story: or perhaps vaguely from Gracq's *Le Rivage des Syrtes* and Eliz's determination to get me to Crete next month (which I look forward to). A journey through a huge, flat, marshy garrigue-like sort of landscape to a coastal town. A mysterious central character. It is all vague notions, moods. An arrival in a hotel, two women playing tennis. Vaguely ahead (not yet written) an old woman in a lonely sea cottage; irises; folk-musicians; a seduction; a cold anti-hero, no normal views or opinions. I really don't know what it wants to be; yet its very fluidity pleases. And oh yes, this strange country is somehow fiction itself, behind its oddly distinct exterior, in my imagination. That notion appeared within a page or two of the writing. This is a visit 'to where fiction happens, rather than life' – something like that.[1]

Anna and the children are here. She is still at Bayswater Road, but we exchange tomorrow over the Arlington Villas flat at Clifton. I am paying £46,000 for it (out of my own money, Boxall decided trying to buy it through the company was too tricky). I am still not at all clear what we shall have to charge Anna to avoid tax problems. She will not really be able to pay anything (earn anything, that is), so the situation is dark. My 'wealth' is quite beyond me; what I can and can't do with it, on the right side of the tax laws.

12 February
Walking on the Cobb 'sands' and to the Museum to 'see the dinosaurs' with William. It is a freezing cold day, with a bitter south-east wind off the sea. Not that that disturbs him at all, he is all for digging castles and rock-pooling. Our dinosaurs have no interest for him; he wants models of the large land ones, of course – and only because he knows they are large and powerful, somehow nicely terrifying, because they are, yet aren't really, rather like spacemen and film-stars. He obviously thought our ichthyosaurs on the wall – and the one in the cellar – were just poor models. I tried to explain they were real, and very old, and had once lived here; totally in vain, of course. It is rather touching, this inability in children to conceive of the past, death, all of that.

18 March
The Museum on top of me, as usual at this time of year. We have to open early, Easter being precocious this year; and I shall not be here, because of Crete. Nor Tom Gilbert, the only other trustee I can rely on. On top of everything else Peter Langham wants all his fossils on loan back, as he now has the Coombe Street chapel, which will leave appalling 'gaps'. The garden is hopelessly unlooked-after. It wakes slowly now from the appalling winter; while I go to sleep under the wretched blood-pressure pills. In a way I accept fairly tranquilly now that I can't cope with life – it is too much, or too demanding, beyond one man, or this man.

Eliz is angry with Anna again. She has moved into the new Clifton flat, away from Nick (whose father died a fortnight ago); but it seems it is not proving the paradise it promised, with a noisy neighbour upstairs, security problems, endless other ones. Nick has said he is too poor to pay any maintenance this month (the divorce is still not through). Eliz is fed up that Anna is so dependent on us, that we have to buy 'everything'

---

[1] These are JF's first notes for *In Hellugalia*, a novel about an imagined place called Hellugalia.

for her. When she was Anna's age, etc., etc. I defend Anna, who I think is simply being *her* age. Our (Eliz's and my) generation had no notion of 'rights' that Anna's takes more or less for granted: that their own tastes and feelings as regards work are paramount (Anna won't go back to what she is trained for, art teaching), that they are owed support just by being (from state or parents, like us), that we are responsible for the messes they get themselves into (which of course we are, in part). What I think Anna's generation has lost is the notion of fighting, or battling, against the conditions of life; of taking, as Eliz and I did, work we disliked just to get enough money to live through every week – that working-class spirit (half guts, half bloody-mindedness) that is such a sterling part of Eliz's chacter. Anna complains, her mother used to fight, in similar circumstances. We were lucky in one way; at least some sort of work was always findable. There is now a dreadful ambiance of hopelessness in Britain: political remonstrance like Thatcher's, we must pull our socks up, work harder and export more, becomes increasingly empty rhetoric. The country sinks, sinks, and poor Anna is a sad echo of it. Capitalism will fail because it flaunts everywhere ideals, hopes, dreams; and in this country provides miscrably few of the means to attain them. The country gets poorer; and everyone wants to be richer.

25 March
To Crete. We went by car to Gatwick, at one-thirty a.m., for the early flight: Anna and the children, Eliz and myself. An unpleasant flight, on a crowded package-tour charter. We arrived at Heraklion soon after midday, but in a pleasant 60° and sunlight; with the snows of Psiloritis gleaming white in the distance,[1] over the mess – there is no other word – of the town. It must be one of the least attractive in Greece, but the whole of Crete seems to have fallen into the hands of totally tasteless and unscrupulous exploiters and developers. Nowhere is there any sign of planning: everywhere the horrors of reinforced concrete, mainly only half-complete, because funds have run out. Crete remains the most beautiful island in the Mediterranean; and one has sympathy with its natives cashing in after so many centuries of oppression and poverty; but the whole enrages every decent human (and socialist) instinct. Man disgusts.

We head east through avenues of mimosa (I think *cyanophylla*), and through the sun-lovers' paradise (everyone else's hell) of villas and hotels. One does not begin to rediscover the old Crete until beyond the gorge at Selinari. Limenas Chersonisou and Mallia are for the idiot quasi-rich of Europe. There are large plastic-covered greenhouses. Apparently the new favoured crop of the area is the banana. Oranges

[1] Situated in central Crete, Psiloritis is, at 2,456 metres, the highest mountain on the island.

and lemons out of doors, and loquat ripening; hibiscus and bougainvillea. The sea blue and empty, the occasional herring-gull. By the back of Agios Nicholaos, past Gournia, and then to the right and south, through olive-groves, down to Ierapetra, and from there along the south coast, noticeably less green than the north, to Makrygialos,[1] the 'long beach', where our apartments are. Here the plastic green-houses, mainly devoted to cucumbers, become monstrous in their frequency – and their destruction. It leaves an appalling flotsam-and-jetsam all over the countryside, when they are demolished by gales. Nothing is less civic-minded than the new Cretan, and no contrast more striking than the eager greed with which they try to cash in on the new tourist crop and the indifference they show to public order and clean-liness. The dominant tourists now are Swedish and German: how they view the ubiquitous *pagaille* along the coast, God only knows.

I write all this disparagingly, and did not change my mind. Satan has struck this beautiful land, and would turn it into a new Costa Brava, but to be fair it is confined to the coast. Despisers of the beach-and-sun life like me can rejoice; our Greece remains untouched, or largely untouched, only a short distance inland. And nothing can totally diminish the shock of the warmth and colour, the fertility, the jumping straight from English March to June and July, in heat and plant-growing terms.

We have one small flat, Anna and the kids another behind us. Water is heated by the sun. Electricity is expensive here, and almost all recent houses seem to have their solar panels on the roof. We walk opposite, bright sunshine but a cold sea wind, to a Roman villa ruin on a little headland opposite the flats. A great tit calls, unrecognizably by home standards. There are pipits and wheatears. The wild pink gladiolus that we have at Lyme, but paler and more delicate here – it is ubiquitous, like the all-invasive *Oxalis pes-caprae*, or Bermuda buttercup. On the point a small pink cistus in bloom and some white anemones, presumably *coronaria*. A very pretty rosy *Echium*, the *diffusum* that grows in Crete and eastward. But the most charming flower is a tiny blue iris, with flowers only an inch across, and only an inch or two tall; also widespread here. It is *Iris sisyrhynchium*, and has the curious habit of not opening its flowers till the afternoon. Of a morning one can see only bare earth where the afternoon before there were countless exquisite little blue eyes.

26 March
I walked alone to a little Minoan site just behind the main road. Goldfinches and chaffinches seem common here, occasional linnets. There are many warblers, mainly Sardinian. I saw later one Rüppell's; and heard another several times with an exceptionally fine song, I suspect

---

[1] The region of Makrygialos lies in the south-eastern corner of Crete.

the Orphean. But flowers interest me generally more than birds, as I grow older. A dominant one here, beside the Bermuda buttercup, is *Chrysanthemum coronarium var. discolor* – *martolouloudia* in Greek; one of those plants, like the English celandine, one would prize if it were rare, and tends to dismiss because it is everywhere. The two asphodels are on the site, *lutea* and *microcarpus*, also very common (and that I grow in Lyme). The site itself is dull, like most excavated Minoan sites; I remember their great charm used to be the wild flowers that grew on them; but all seemed poisoned now, probably for good archaeological reasons, but poor ones in every other way.

In the afternoon we walked a little way behind the town. A foreign woman invites me to look in one of the cucumber greenhouses. She seemed not enamoured of it. They apparently become abominably hot from now on; and are prey to all sorts of fungal disease. She says they have to spray at least five times during the growing season. The children were hot and tired, so Anna and Eliz walked back while I explored a little goyal with rows of terraces like Aztec courts. I dug up some of the *Iris sisyrinchium* since they were in their hundreds; they have fibre-coated bulbs about four to five inches deep. Rosemary also grew on these terraces, which I explored because they seemed a sun-trap; but I did not then realize how far ahead the Cretan season is.

27 March

I set out to walk to the mountain behind Makrygialos, by the track that led from where I was yesterday, up a long hillside. I saw a number of Clouded Yellows, a swallowtail or two also; the wall butterfly and various blues. In a denser glade in the pine-forest I came on a large three-foot orchid, or what was left of it; one of the last flowers was in good enough state to recognize – *Barlia*, the giant orchis. I mounted up and up until the road to Agios Stephanos, which zigzags up under the first cliffs. Up in them I heard a blue rock-thrush singing, and later saw one. They are very wary, suspicious birds. I climbed up to a great cleft in the cliffs; from beside it a steep paved track mounted in zigs and zags. An eagle came over, dark wings, white belly, Bonelli's eagle; the only other birds of prey here seem to be kestrels and buzzards. It is already lonely up here, despite ugly plagues of the coastal greenhouses and dim noise from Makrygialos far below.

I came again on the Agios Stephanos road at the top of the track, but soon branched off on yet another track to the right along the mountainside. I had a lunch of scraps where I came on yet another new orchid, *O. italica*, like a fancy, flossy *O. simia*; more ragged-looking and open. That too seems not uncommon in the area. Then on the path in the same place, I found a really delicious new *Ophrys*, the sawfly orchid *tenthredinifera*; which wins my vote as the most attractive (with *cretica*) of the genus that I saw here. Its combination of yellow and a lion colour, a sort

of camel beige, rich brown, and the pink upper petals and sepals, is 'original'; one has not seen such colours in combination before. David Hockney
would like it. I climbed up from the path at this point to the first terrace
above, and discovered some cyclamen in flower on the way; very delicate
little pure white blooms. I wandered on up the mountain and came out
of nowhere on a splendid little area for all the above orchids, and *cretica*.

This last is the graphically best designed *Ophrys* here; its black and
white 'faces' are surprisingly vivid as they stand out of the low scrub and
garrigue. Among them was a beautiful little green-banded fritillary. It
was the only one I saw in Crete. The orchids crop up like this; perhaps
for some way nothing, then a sporadic colony, almost as if designed to
delight the hunter; most pleasantly, frequent enough, but never too
common. This had been the first long walk over such rough country I
had done for some time, and I decided I had to give up reaching the
top, and think of getting back. Walking on the scree on steep slopes is
tiring, and painful; one slips and reaches out for the nearest support –
which up here is as often as not thorny broom, and worse than gorse
to grasp in haste. I did it several times before I learnt to slip and fall
rather than grab. On the last slope before I circled back down towards
the Agios Stephanos road there were many sawflies growing sporadically
on a very barren slope, among the yellow asphodels.

A long walk back to Makrygialos by the same mule-track. I was very
tired by the end, but felt returned to the Greece I have always loved. It
cannot be surpassed in such weather, at such a season, before the
garrigue is burnt dry.

28 March
We hire a car, but before we go I am given a birthday present, a Minolta
'automatic' camera; a little in advance, but so I can use it.

Anna drives us to Lithines, on the road to Sitia. It is a little cloudy
and misty. We walk briefly round the village, but the wind is cold; and
no sun returns us to England in a way we do not want. We cross the
island over to Sitia, a remarkably Arab-looking town as one approaches.
But it is the local 'capital' and offers all those things that are beyond
Makrygialos, like good grocers and cake-shops. We indulge those a little
then have a good fish lunch of *barbounia* and *dorade* (they call it snapper
here) in sunshine beside the sea. I did not attempt to get up what little
modern Greek I once had, and it isn't really necessary. All Cretans seem
to know some English now, or German. As time went on I began to
resent this: both the constantly being taken for German and the assumption on the Cretan side that their English must be the language used.
But I quite liked Sitia. It is far from becoming another Heraklion yet;
if not by choice, at least by circumstance.

We returned home with our goodies: *kourabiedes* and other cakes, a very sweet quince compote, honey; and had supper 'in'. Most evenings we go to one of the local tavernas.

29 March

To Heraklion, stopping on the way at a beach where Eliz and Anna stayed a year or two ago. Unfortunately it begins to rain; and Crete cannot deal with rain, either in its buildings or its roads. One feels that in all of that it is being crashed and bulldozed into the twentieth century. Our destination was the museum at Heraklion, where we duly arrived. It is the centre for the Minoan finds, although it is sadly inferior as a museum in many ways: appalling labelling and general display. The one thing that redeems it is the miracle of the pottery and the rest that is there. The Minoans may have been inferior to us in knowledge; in everything else one has a very sharp sense of a superior civilization. No doubt it was for the few, and slave-based, but the general, if cursory, feeling is of a people living in intelligent harmony with nature – everything modern Crete is not, in fact. I had seen it all before, or much of it, thirty years ago; this time the Agia Triada beaker, of harvesters, pleased me very much again, as I seem to remember it did before. There is something profoundly bucolic and human about it, a kind of smiling joyousness that belongs more to the Renaissance than anything else; a total antithesis, for instance, to the art of ancient Egypt. If all Minoan art had to be destroyed, and only one object saved, I would choose this.

We set out for Phaistos,[1] soon in rain and mist. We stopped at Mircs, and took two rooms in a hotel, seemingly the town's best, though poor in every other way. This valley is evidently lush and rich, but Mires has the usual one-horse, makeshift feel. A forest of wires at roof level, no apparent comforts. We ended in a pizzeria for dinner, where the TV was running – such adjuncts to civilization are in all the tavernas now. There was an absurd right-wing American film showing, about revolution in Central America, full of gratuitous cruelty and sadism, and B (or Z) actors. Five-year-old William took avidly to this unexpected treat; and so did the son of the proprietor, of the same age. Both little boys watched with an enthralled fixity that was profoundly sad; the Greek boy with his mouth open, beyond salvation – but so did most of the adults present. There were one or two American hippies, and we met more the next day; Metala on the coast seems the attraction, not Phaistos.

I ordered everyone to pray when we went to bed, for a fine tomorrow. It had stopped raining, but was still very cloudy, and I was certain it would remain so.

---

[1] The second largest Minoan city, Phaistos was built on a hill in the valley of Messara, near the south coast of central Crete.

30 March

But by a miracle I woke early to a cloudless dawn, with Psiloritis to the north, and its snow. We were soon on the road and, by another miracle, the first at Phaistos. It still floats in mid-air above its plain, with the snow-capped mountain to the north, its Fujiyama; still one of the great sites of high civilization. I remember it when it was plant-covered; now it is bare, somehow deodorized. At least we saw it alone for half an hour; but then the crowds began, buses full of them. We had breakfast in the café overlooking the site, where I stayed with Eliz and Roy years ago; and wasn't very happy, if I remember.

From there we went over the low chalk hills to Agia Triada. That too is plant-poisoned and wired-in, only a sere shadow of how I remember it, though the ghost of water, the once close sea, still haunts the place. We stop a mile or two back towards Phaistos, and Anna and I wander off photographing flowers and the rest; only to be attacked, on a hillside where I find orchids, by a particularly aggressive kind of bee. They flew straight into one's hair. I was stung on the scalp, then on an eyelid; then Anna had one entangled in her own hair, which I tried in vain to find. I think it was some kind of mason bee; but a very angry creature. We left the *italica* unphotographed. Crested larks, and a woodlark, it seems a not uncommon bird in Crete. A strangely oblivious rock partridge, *A. graeca*, in the road soon after; just like its Minoan painting.

We had an enjoyable lunch in a taverna at Kapariana, lamb cutlets and calamari. The jovial proprietor thought I was German, as years ago (and much more menacingly) two Cretans did. On the TV there is a long folk-music festival, dancing and *lyra*-playing, but it is difficult to hear because of a noisy party of farmers in a back corner of the room. They offered us wine, and meant no harm, and it was an enjoyable hour. Anna's good looks get us attention; this is another 'Italian' aspect of the new Crete I don't much like – that all foreign women are prey of a sort, to be taken if they will. And I found something sad in the televised folk-music and the tourist-consciousness. I remembered stumbling on my *mandinades*[1] 'competition' in the Lassithi years ago: the simplicity, the fortuitousness of that, and this faintly artificial scene.

A long drive back to Makrygialos. I am allowed a few minutes at Gournia, which is very working-class Minoan, dense back-to-backs, so to speak; a long way from the regal splendour of Phaistos.

31 March

My birthday. I walked on the road inland behind our apartments. It led in very few minutes to what I came to think of as the 'happy valley', a truly delicious area of olive-groves that transmuted into pine-groves,

---

[1] Improvised rhymed couplets of fifteen-syllable lines.

along an old river-bed. It was rich in orchids and other plants, and I grew very fond of it.

In the afternoon we drove to see Voila near Chandras,[1] a deserted Byzantine village on a hill-cliff, vaguely reminiscent of Monemvasia, with several acres of ruins, and on its south-west side an elegant Turkish fountain. Water like this is always pleasant in Greece. Here too grew the very attractive *Euphorbia acanthothamnos* in yellow-green domes, an architectural plant on rocky hillsides; and a primitive one. The ruined town also had much *Vicia hybrida* and some plants of a very handsome kind of *Arum italicum*, I think not the species, but perhaps a cultivar of it, very large yellow spathes. *Ophrys lutea* was everywhere, and some *saccata*; also in the cliff above the town a very small purple orchis, I suspect *anatolica*. I went into the church, which has a good pair of old icons. Here a woodlark sang, as in all happy places. I wandered a little east of the ruins, and found another Turkish fountain. A very green, happy-feeling little place.

On the way back we stopped for a few minutes at the Venetian mansion at Etia; still an elegant echo of Renaissance Italy, for all its largely ruined state.

1 April

I went to the 'happy valley' again, pursuing the orchids and other plants. One that grows everywhere is *Salvia triloba*; intensely aromatic, and with pale violet-lilac flowers. Almost the characteristic flower of this valley, and the area in general. I grew very fond of it, and have brought some seedlings back. I see a hoopoe among the pine-trees briefly. They seem silent at this season, and this was the only one I saw. I walked further up the valley to a deserted hamlet or farm, above terraces littered with shards, but I think all 'recent'. Some of the rooms still retained fragments of roofing. It is laid on canes across old olive-stems, and consists of a foot or so of beaten earth – a 'turf' ceiling in effect, though the summer heat no doubt killed all plant life. Some of the rough ashlar walls had every chink stuffed with chards, making an attractive pattern. The door jambs and arches are of stone, and well masoned in primitive fashion. I liked this farm overlooking the valley; it cries out for restoration.

I then went further up the valley. The mule-track mounts through the pines, many of which grow out of the rock. It is very beautiful: aromatic peace, no tourists, no coastal horror, that unforgettable silence of the old 'wild' Greece. It sounds paradoxical, but one can almost 'hear' it, though it has no sound; something living beyond all sound. I sat under an olive, with a goldfinch singing near by; time was not.

Alas, Eliz is ill. She thinks she caught a chill yesterday at Voila. She and Anna go a little bit mad with all this sudden heat. The locals, especially

[1] A town near the eastern end of the island.

the old women, still wear far more clothes than we northerners; and it is a treacherous climate – more for gods than humans, at this time of year, and especially on the beach, where Eliz and Anna spend their days; hot enough to sunbathe naked, and chill enough in a minute to make one search for something warmer to wear. It really needs those old-fashioned warnings in the Victorian Baedekers.

I took William off for a walk in the evening, down to the beach west of here. This one is without sand, pebbly, many nice fragments of marble, especially a green kind. I try to teach him to play ducks-and-drakes, but he gets bored when he cannot do it. Later he wants to throw stones from the little cliff behind, and goes dangerously near the edge. He seems physically fearless in things like this, to the point of foolhardiness, as he was when he was just a toddler, charging blindly down paths and towards drops. I prefer him now to his sister, who is becoming rather a fastidious young lady; very fussy over what she will eat, or won't, who hates 'walks' and veers bewilderingly between being someone twice her age, and someone half it. I think Anna and Eliz indulge their whims and moods a shade too much, but it is partly a 'guilt' of breaking the home, that they are now 'fatherless' in practical terms, partly the place. It makes me feel a wilful child myself, and a lonely one, obsessed by things the 'adults' cannot understand. I cannot interest any of them in my wild Greece; nor be interested in the endless discussion of which taverna we shall try, and all the rest. We now favour one called Anesis, or 'Ease'; where the owner (or his wife) does at least cook fish, and there is a better (more traditional) class of Cretan music. Anna is obsessed by food: salad, fish, all the rest of it. In this Eliz and I kowtow. I had dinner with Anna alone this evening, among the Swedes. Everyone gets a little drunk, as usual. I feel fit again, in body: only the wretched veins in my left leg nag.

2 April
Eliz still not well. I set off up the 'happy valley' to the mountains, up a mule-track beside the endless black snakes of the irrigation pipes. Higher up water gushes here and there from the track-sides. All these ancient tracks are in disrepair, paved for a few yards here, disintegrated into rubble there. I felt tired and stopped for my 'lunch' (an orange and a sesame stick) on a hill before the mountain cliff. A ruined old mill sat in the col between two of its rocky outcrops; and in the olive-terraces below were fine colonies of *iricolor* and *sphegodes*. I had decided the mountain was too much for me that day, but somehow struggled up to the cliff-cleft and ladder-track beside it; then somehow up that also. I wanted to see *tenthredinifera* again, and it seems not to exist at the lower levels. Eventually I came to a crest and saw across an olive-orchard a road leading to the summit. It was still quite cloudless, and although it was getting late, I couldn't resist it. The road led, in a mile or so, rich in irises and

anemones, to two *kalyvia*, small stone huts on the summit, with its magnificent view down on the coast and backwards on the higher uplands and
mountains inland, with the two villages Agios Stephanos and Pefki. There
was a high wind, but the sky was quite cloudless, very pure. To the west
the mountains towards the sun were deep blue in shadow, with here and
there shafts of light pouring over the peaks and ridges, like something
from a Palmer or a Martin, a Blake-like effect; celestial light, but not
apocalyptic. I noticed this several evenings: this blue-grey shadow of these
western mountains out of the sun, and the light still pouring over.

I had got about halfway back, when a man mending one of the pipes
offered me a lift. He knew a better road than the one I was on, and his
pick-up was near by. So I went with him. These pick-ups, seemingly all
Japanese, have taken over from the old three-wheeled *mechani*. We establish who I am – I say I am a teacher – but my Greek is too rusty now
to converse across a table, let alone in a bouncing truck. We stop somewhere else for more pipe-mending. He comes from Ierapetra, it seems.
In the end he drops me close to the apartments, and the first thing I
see is Denys and Monica Sharrocks. They came to Crete just after us,
to Plaka near Elounda, and have driven over.

We had the evening with them. Denys as always, the perfect diplomat,
his Greek still quite fluent, eager to establish relationships with anyone
prepared to listen. His obsession with this is strange to me now, that he
still seems blind to what I think of as the wild Greece, and cares only for
how well he gets on with the natives, their hospitality, bonhomie and all
the rest. The new Crete makes me regard all that with cynicism, at the least
without the old romanticism; so I see Denys a little as a Dr Pangloss. Yet I
still like him, and the way he goes on in his polished ambassadorial way.

3 April
They stay the night in one of the village tavernas. We are shocked to
hear Denys picked up an Athenian businessman after they left us the
night before and had six *raki* with him. That is carrying urbanity too
far. I read *Le Grand Meaulnes* most of the next day, for an OUP introduction I am supposed to be doing. Eliz still not well. In the evening a
walk with Anna and the children to the 'happy valley'; not a success,
they hate it, William demanding to be carried, Tess in a sulk. All they
want are things to play with, above all adult attention. I am unreasonable to expect more, I know; but we return defeated. We have supper
'in', and talk about Roy when the children are in bed. Anna thinks now,
having avoided him for years, that she should find out which London
hospital he is in, and take the children to see him. I think she should;
I would not deprive him of that, poor devil. He still haunts us all, despite
the years; the nearest we have been to Satan, although he was his own
greatest victim, self-devilled.

4 April

I walk to the east, the unappetizing length of Makrygialos. Its eastern end is dominated by the Scandinavian Sunwing hotel, a large complex and great burner of electricity at night; and various European-built or -occupied villas. It also has a Tahiti-umbrella'd sun-beach, discreetly out of view of the road. What the native Cretans make of all this nakedness is one thing that did make me regret my lost Greek: I should have liked to find out. This place is in fact a little bit like Lyme in the late eighteenth century: many old beliefs are being overridden.

I headed towards the monastery at Moni Kapsa,[1] but soon struck inland across the estuarial valleys. They are very bleak and eroded here, far less rich than even the bleakest mountains behind. I headed for a mountain road that comes down the opposite mountainside from Perivolakia and Pezoulas, a red streak we had seen on our drive to Sitia; and came, just short of it, on a little westward-facing cottage-farm, deserted, like so many these days. A series of roofless rooms, in one of which a stonechat was apparently nesting. Like the great tits, they are quite common here, but with an un-British voice and behaviour. This one showed an odd hovering flight, scolding the while. It is clear the low garrigue scrub doesn't really suit them as a perching place – not high enough – and they tend to fly between whatever taller trees are available, the carobs in such places as this. The rooms had the usual hearths, and recesses in the walls like aumbries, these latter usually made, or framed, with fitting masoned slabs. I presume the function was religious, to hold lamps or icons. One room had the remains of a dome-shaped kiln, made of countless shards, I think too grand for an ordinary oven, so I dubbed this the potter's cottage. None of the shards were anything but recent, none glazed. The earth here is *terra rossa*.

To one side was a spring, with two stone tanks leading to a stone bowl, full of very young tadpoles, faced with imminent death by the drying sun. I caught as many as I could in a plastic bag and transferred them back to the spring. While I was there, and earlier on my walk to the place, I heard ravens far above; and by good luck found them in the little Pentax glasses. They were very high indeed, on one occasion flying from the eastern mountains towards the Psiloritis range, on the other returning. One imagines their lives very insecure here, and persecuted. The common crow in the area is the hooded. I saw no carrion crows, nor jays or magpies. I liked this place, which also had my other 'favourite' bird, singing beautifully in the cliff-slopes behind: the woodlark.

I walked north along the road; again that heavenly peace that one can hear; few orchids, but Sardinian warblers and stonechats, and the woodlarks. A buzzard came over, and from the top of the cliffs the bells

---

[1] About ten kilometres along the coast to the east of Makrygialos.

of a flock of goats. I saw the goatherd stand for a moment, on the skyline. It was a relief to see him, to know that some Cretans still live their old solitary lives, can still walk, not eternally drive in their Japanese pick-ups. I had to strike back to Makrygialos, and forsook this road with sorrow. It was beautifully lonely.

Its only blot, in fact, were lengths of wire-fence here and there, which I met again as I went down the hill. I passed through a gate in one such, not realizing until much lower down the slope that I had walked into a 'sack' or trap – that I had either to climb back or negotiate the fence. That may sound easy, but where I would cross was on a steep slope, and it was six feet tall, with the upper strands cut so that they were as sharp as barbed wire; and no foothold possible in the wire itself. It took me a very cross twenty minutes to get over, by building a small tower of rocks, bending back the barbs, and then taking a sort of desperate half-vault from the top of my tower. My old blue trousers were torn, but I made it finally and got down to a river-bed; which still had some water, and chains of frogs' eggs.

From there on I was able to use bulldozers' paths, for all this area seemed to have been smitten by that dreadful machine, with red owner-ship marks on every prominent stone. It had the sinister feel of the very early days of a housing estate; an area damned by developers, though there was no house or sign of any other activity. As so often here, damnation hangs in the air as soon as one starts approaching the coast, a sort of Californianization pending and imminent. So much for the peace of my mountain-road behind. But that far side of the valley was very beautiful. I shall not forget it.

5 April
We had lunch by the sea. A strong wind, a glassy blue sea, and an almost Pacific surf. I spent the afternoon in the 'happy valley'. Supper at Anesis, with *barbounia*. I never liked them before, and do no more now. It is one of the great overpraised delicacies of the fish world. We listen to the Cretan music, and I get a touch drunk, as usual, unable to hear what Eliz and Anna are saying. I live in my days here, not the evenings.

6 April
We have hired a car for another day, to get to Zakros,[1] which I think would be only a long day's walk as the crow flies, but by car requires a huge detour via Sitia. The children are sick; so much winding up and down hillsides. William recovers in ten seconds, with a disarming rapidity. Soon after we get to Zacros, the inland village. I ask if there are restaurants at the lower village, where the site is. 'Of course, three or four.'

[1] The site of an important Minoan port town at the eastern end of the island.

So we press on. For three or four miles the road is excellent, but then suddenly it turns into stone. The scenery here is very barren, rocky, but grand; we wound down the cliff road, over immense falls of land until Kato Zacros came into sight, just behind a shingle bay with a few houses and other parked cars. It is a mysterious site, somehow lost, without reason: why would the Minoans have wanted a palace and great depot in this forgotten corner of the island? Knossos, Phaistos, Gournia, Mallia make sense; but this, except for its making a good landfall from Egypt, stands unexplained. Yet in many ways it is the most spectacular of the sites, in this hugely barren landscape. We got down to the beach and chose a taverna, and had a good lunch by the beach. The site itself is much more open than the others. There was no one to guard it, spoil-heaps lying about, a feeling of excavation being far from finished. The lower levels were flooded, water between the stumps of walls; a pair of grey wagtails, frogs; steps, roadways still paved, the usual ceremonial plazas and columns. The buildings go up the hill and away to the north-west. I should have been happy to spend a day there, but clouds had begun gathering out of the north, and it started to spot with rain.

We drove back to Palaikastro under grey skies and drizzle, and then took the road due north to Vai. This north-eastern 'prong' of Crete is very bleak and bare indeed, vaguely reminiscent of Dartmoor or Salisbury Plain; a military training area 'feel' about it. Vai beach itself, with its famous colony of *Phoenix theophrasti*,[1] is rather disappointing, but perhaps in part because of the rain. The palms are rather boring, and don't suit the landscape, however anomalous their appearance here. We had a coffee in a sort of beach caff – it does not deserve the name of taverna. For once there do seem to be fairly stern conservation laws for the precious palms, and an area closed off to the public. A mile behind the beach we saw two large nurseries for the plant, well out of range of fire, its great summer danger.

We returned by the western road, over the highlands to a famous monastery, Moni Toplou. Ravens. Moni Toplou is quite imposing. We stopped by the ruin of an old windmill outside, then made a brief visit inside to see the icons. The inner courtyard is pleasant, more Spanish (or Turkish) in its feel than Greek. An old monk shows us the icons. They are accompanied by a table of tourist postcards and booklets; outside the main building, a mason's yard, an icon shop. Like all such places, it has a vaguely commercial air now. It must have been something to visit in the old days, by horse- or muleback, in its upland wilderness.

Anna drives fast back to Makrygialos, and we go to the taverna Fantasia. Anna has attracted a lover, a darkly Byronic young fisherman who has been to England and speaks the language not badly. His interest in her, and

---

[1] A variety of palm-tree that grows only in Crete.

indifference to us, is naked. I get very bored and we drink pointlessly, myself in silence, since Eliz and Anna treat me, or so it seems, increasingly as an old man they barely tolerate. I listen in silence to the endless Cretan music above, or behind, the endless Swedish and German chatter. Anna makes a date with her young man, for when she has got the children in bed. Eliz is angry with her, and worried; and this otherwise interesting and worthwhile day finishes in an all-night row on the usual theme. My indifference, everything's indifference, all the rest on that barren road. I am very happy here, living in my own way, even living their way on the Costa Brava side of life. I don't say what I feel about that, that the human side of the 'beach life' is as bad as one beach near Sitia we passed earlier that day, an unimaginable pile of plastic rubbish from end to end. Nor do I mind Anna having a brief fling with her handsome Lothario.

But peace at last.

7 April

Our last full day. I go off in the afternoon to the 'happy valley', where a bulldozer is working in the cliff just west of the ruined farm, making new terraces, with a terrible droning and grinding of stone. The wretched yellow monsters are the curse of Greece. Development here is plainly hideously underfinanced, as all the half-finished, still empty buildings show. There are going to be terrible disputes when the limited stock of water is at issue between the farmers and the tourist interest; or if the grand banana scheme fails. The Cretans have no sense of even the most elementary public order and cleanliness. The dirt and rubbish outside many of the lived-in cottages at Makrygialos recalls traditional Ireland. Squalor is the only word one can use; yet the older villages and towns appear reasonably clean and tidy. The older Makrygialos was scattered behind, in the hills, it seems; only the tiny port was used. One can't really blame the natives, faced with an unexpected bonanza. But this is a little like the old tragedy of the goat, indiscriminate grazing, all over Greece. Sane control would defeat much better and more sophisticated governments than the country has ever had. God knows Crete needs opening up in communications terms; but not in this hopelessly piecemeal and haphazard way: each man for himself. The trouble is also the island's extreme beauty; it encourages the belief that this or that small part of it can be ruined and ravished, and the whole not affected. My own feeling is that much of the rape is the responsibility of Northern Europe; to what extent this is by direct finance, I don't know. It is certainly psychologically so.

I mounted straight up very steep terraces behind the ruined farm, a difficult scramble in places. I feel my age, and sweat. At the top a very attractive plateau, with thyme and oregan dominant, then olive-orchards. After a while the pine-trees take over and I came on a stone road through them, leading towards Agios Stephanos, along the side of a splendidly

cliffed hill. It is very pleasant here, faintly Swiss, with the wind in the pines
and views down into the valley. Once again I sat on a stone beside the
road, and felt the peace: 'feeling' is the word, it is a physical thing, inherent
in a place, a time. A buzzard came circling over and made a long swoop
down the valley over the trees before mounting again. I have seen them
do this several times these last days, staying high in the thermals and then
doing these breathtakingly fast (so fast they could not check for hunting?)
dives and swoops to tree level for half a mile or so before mounting again.
I saw none take anything, if that was the purpose. This buzzard, like all
the rest I saw, appeared to be of the common kind, exactly like those at
home. But my great ornithological treat of this day was still to come.

I followed the road back, along the brink of the valley that lies to the
west of my 'happy' one. That too looked attractive. There is a village or
hamlet, Tsikalaria, where it enters the plain. The road I was on evidently
descended to that finally, but I struck off eastward down a chalk combe
to rejoin the happy valley.

At the bottom, just above a collection of beehives, I glimpsed a white
bird, which fortunately flew across my path, then settled again on a
bush-top, leaving me in that best evening position for bird-watching,
i.e., 'in the sun'. It was a woodchat shrike, which I recall seeing once
or twice on Spetsai, though never so well as here, and over such a long
time. It is white and black, with an exquisite chestnut-red cap and a
black mask, round eyes and beak. It flew down to one of the *Ebenus*,
and picked almost lazily at some of the heads in flower, which attract
beetles, flopping from branch to branch. A most beautiful and aloof
little bird, and seemingly not to be frightened away when I approached
to within some thirty yards of it. We spent nearly half an hour in each
other's company, and in the end I left it where it was, in its 'restaurant'.

A last look at the orchids in the happy valley.

8 April
The bus came to pick us up for Heraklion soon after nine a.m. Yet again,
a beautiful and particularly clear day, cloudless. I enjoyed our three-
hour ride. I have learnt and recalled so much in this last fortnight. It
has been both a going-back thirty years or more and a very present
experience. The old Crete has gone, but not in a natural history sense.
In that it still remains a very rich cornucopia; and although I did not
like Makrygialos in itself, I became very attached to its hinterland, very
close to the 'garden' of my happy valley. A question that came to me
many times was why I have denied myself this for so long, the experience of it; when I could so easily have afforded it, and all the rest. Yet
I think there is in a way a kind of peasant wisdom in it: it could not
have come with such a delicious sense of newness, freshness, if I had
been back more often. We were lucky, too, in striking the climax of the

Cretan spring in flower terms. The early orchids were effectively over by the last week of March; and all those in flower visibly wilted during our stay. Summer was at the threshold, where we were; most of the *Ophrys* at their last unopened bud.

The flight was pleasanter in the return, in sunlight until we came to the North Adriatic; but from then on things progressively worsened. Gatwick was under cloud and drizzle; and it was bitterly cold. Our taxi back to Lyme was waiting, but England seems a country in an Arctic limbo. Still unemerged from this killing winter; all grey, dun, sere, not a leaf or flower; at Belmont, a frozen house, the endless mail.

12 April

I am still in Crete, and haven't yet been able to face the Museum, ordinary life. The garden, thank goodness, is awakening, with daffodils and violets out, the *Osmanthus* and *Osmaronia*, Eliz's camellia at the bottom, my own *scolopax* putting out their flowering buds, the peonies all in bud. The weather is fairly sunny, but the cold keen.

10 April

Anna's divorce case was heard in Bristol. Nick apparently appeared, but said little. The question of maintenance was left unsettled. They had lunch together afterwards, but Nick was as vague as ever about his future plans.

7 May

Poor Tom Gilbert died yesterday in an Exeter hospital. He caught jaundice after a Channel Island holiday while we were in Crete, and ten days ago was rushed to hospital in Exeter; had a major operation, and apparently never recovered, has been in a coma ever since. It is a loss to me, I grew to like his quiet efficiency, his lack of fuss, over the years, his 'pagan' love of wine, France, his distrust of enthusiasms, including my own passing disgusts for the Museum and all that it entails. He was a Roman, of the humble, vanished sort; a quiet pillar of the Republic. Even his leaving is characteristically brisk, and without fuss.

Hazel has been here with Kate these last days, Anna and the children also. Tess and Kate seemed to hit it off, with the latter cast rather in the role of country cousin, despite her greater age. Tess became rather alarmingly manic on the last day, and was ill the next morning. She alarms me a little, and that the women who rule this household, her grandmother and mother, treat it all as rather endearing and amusing. Eliz says I don't begin to understand her; she is a bright child, with an evident gift for words and a love of make-believe, acting and mimicking, but I think she needs more checking than she ever gets.

Eliz herself is in bed today with one of her bronchitic colds; like Tess she throws herself into these weekends with a kind of manic energy, and pays for it when they are over. I am to blame for wasting time with dead people (both at the Museum and in writing fiction), she proclaims her love for living ones. That I can't deny, but we never discuss these things quietly (or even faintly) rationally.

Behind all this, when Hazel was here, the shadow of M's health. She had a bad attack of septicaemia recently and has had to be in hospital at Middlesbrough, with all the onus of looking after her on Hazel and Dan's shoulders. Apparently she moans endlessly to Hazel, that she wishes the doctors would let her die, etc. I know I am blamed for not rushing to her bedside, although Hazel has kept assuring us it is not necessary. I am counted incomprehensibly callous and unfeeling, and must be in their eyes. They still believe in the conventional middle-class values and pieties, all good sons dance attendance on their aged mothers. They also imagine all sorts of things of 'John Fowles' the 'well-known writer' that I abhor. I was on TV the other night in the Humphrey programme *The Inner Eye*; such a fuss about making sure the children watched it, I nearly lost my temper at this foolish adulation of 'being on TV'. It is the same thing with death and dying; they cannot credit people who do not believe in it in all the normal social senses; or see attachment to it as a Neolithic hang-over. The *Inner Eye* series has in fact been quite good, though it has received very little notice – too clever, too cold to be acceptable, I suspect; and requiring the serious discussion of things no one today (post-Chernobyl, death is closer than you think) really wants to discuss.

Hazel has gone back, to see M back home. We think she is best there (rather than a 'home' in the other sense), with someone to look after her, whom Dan has found. Death seems all around us at the moment.

The Chernobyl disaster.[1] It evokes a kind of dull-ox rage: that it happened, that the Russians mishandled it so badly, that officialdom in the West is so anxious to score; that one can do nothing about it, and could have done nothing, *pre facto*. According to the *Guardian* today the damage may get appallingly worse. Whether man is fundamentally evil or fundamentally stupid, there is the question. He seems both.

Eliz in a foul mood last night; she had read what I wrote here the other day. Endless charges and accusations against me, some of which, perhaps most of which, are justified. I hear it all in silence, beyond attempting any defence or argument. Her voice always rises into a violence beyond mine. I ignore family and human contact, I do nothing

[1] On 26 April 1986 powerful chemical explosions blew off the top of reactor number four at the Chernobyl nuclear power plant in the Ukraine. Thirty-one people were killed immediately and large areas of Belarus and the Ukraine were contaminated by radio-active material. The first Soviet news report of the disaster was made only two days later. The reaction to the accident and the cover-up helped to usher in Gorbachev's perestroika and glasnost reforms.

in terms of household work, I live in an ivory tower, I am interested only in the dead, etc., etc. It is true in a way: that increasingly I loathe most of modern life and its ways, its endless, unstoppable violence.

Endless kerfuffle over the Friends, which poor Tom ran a little bit in defiance of the rules. I have got Albert Brown to take over from him; and he has expectably found many things wrong – no AGMs, etc. Albert is all brisk no-nonsense, suspicious of our soft ways in Lyme, I suspect. He told me today he is thinking of writing, not news I hear gladly. He has written a soft-porn (his own description) story, and so on. My attitude to him is typical of North–South relations in England, perhaps. I like his no-nonsense, his briskness, his taking on all the photographic jobs at the Museum; and feel he has no real understanding of what Lyme is about in historical terms – its moments of pride, its rottennesses and corruption, all the rest of it. I think also he must hate all I stand for; and then some. That is, I am in possession; but hated.

27 May

To Yorkshire, to do my duty by M; her birthday is near.

As usual, endless talk of herself and her world, none of us or ours. We sit there transfixed by her endless babble, looking for excuses to leave almost as soon as we have arrived, to be able to retreat to Hazel's. All hope now lies in her getting an old people's bungalow on one of the local estates; she can't face another winter at 62 Marwood Drive. The lack is of people to talk about herself to, really. I think hell lies very near to that end of a road in Great Ayton, which no traffic ever passes, no stranger, no face one does not know. It has in fact a strangely theatrical quality, six or seven little boxes facing each other and spying on each other – not from malice, perhaps, but out of sheer boredom. It is a sort of English suburban variation of *Huis Clos*; inherent in the very notion of the suburb, too many houses on too small plots, but particularly acute here. The effect is claustral. I am intermittently reading *Thérèse Raquin* at the moment, a novel almost comic in its self-seriousness, its inturned heaviness. Marwood Drive reminds one that it does have a deep metaphorical truth, however remote a Paris city passage might seem from this.[1] The field behind the bungalow is a mass of cadmium-yellow; a crop of rape in flower. Oddly like a Van Gogh reproduction, so intense in colour it is not real. (The oil is apparently used in margarine, and the crop fetches more than barley or corn at the moment, whence its popularity.)

M's birthday, the next day: an incredible number of birthday cards,

---

[1] In Emile Zola's novel, Thérèse Raquin endures the tedium of a loveless marriage to her sick and feeble cousin Camille. They live in a shabby apartment on the 'narrow and dark' Passage du Pont Neuf in Paris.

good wishes and calling wishers with flowers. She was born in 1899. We
take her to lunch at a pub in Great Broughton, and late in the afternoon escape to Rievaulx.[1] Its atmosphere is strangely like that at the
very similar abbey of Hambye, in the south of the Manche in Normandy;
very encombed, warm, fertile. We went later a little south to the meadows
under Ashberry Hill; and there caught the bird's eye primroses just
coming into bloom, a beautiful sight. The fragile little flowers, the
meadow with its clear stream, the silence of the surrounding woods. I
live more and more now for such moments. A few early purples, but far
fewer than I recall when we came before.

4 June
The accursed Adalat pills are slowly flattening me. I have no strength,
mental or physical, no will. Garden, Museum, my literary life, all go to
pot. I also forget everything. It is rather like dying, I often think it must
be dying – not unpleasant in the sense that it is a gentle decline, or
incline. One of the troubles between Eliz and myself is the death of any
sexual wish or potency in me, which began a year or so ago. This is very
different (to me) from the death of love. I need her more, I value her
more; and not at all only for cupboard reasons, because she does so
much to keep our life going. For me that has changed not only our
relationship, but countless others as well. Conscious erection is beyond
me; very occasionally I wake up and find I have an erection, which sinks
as soon as I am conscious of it. I do not think of women as sexual objects
any more; what faint interest I feel in them in that way is much more
'nostalgic' than present; 'I would have fancied her once', with the
emphasis very much on the once. It is like that ancient sense of having
played cricket that still keeps me watching it sometimes on TV; a kind
of physical empathy with what present players feel, against the total
death of any notion that I might still play.

22 June
To London. Eliz went up a day or two before, to say goodbye to Tom
and Malou. 'Madame' downstairs is leaving, and Tom is anxious we
should buy her flat and the freehold: we to move downstairs, they to
buy our flat and extend their maisonette. We really do not like the idea,
and feel it is part of Tom's 'ghetto' mentality – he must own where he
lives, etc.

23 June
We went to view a new flat in Albert Terrace, which we can see from
our present one. It is like a ship, *sous les toits*, rather as we began in

[1] A ruined twelfth-century Cistercian abbey near Helmsley, North Yorkshire.

Church Row; nice views in one way over Primrose Hill, the other down towards the City. There is a horrid new brick block next door, but otherwise it seemed well-planned, and in good state. £165,000, for a 90-year lease.

We went back and discussed with a Madame Lefevre, the wife of the owner and the architect of the flat, and her son, who now occupies it.

Next day, we decided to go for it. This is a boom period for property-selling, and not a good time for selling dollars; not a wise financial time for such transactions. But there it is, and we want it.

16 August

To Edinburgh, from Taunton. A long journey, in rotten coaches, though the last of it, through Cumbria and south Scotland, has fine scenery. Much of it was depressing; the feel of a decaying economy, a dying society, unrenewable. Scotland seems lively and active, by comparison. Waverley Station is abominably crowded, an enormous queue for taxis. We get finally to the Roxburgh Hotel, where we are booked, in Charlotte Square; and have a depressingly dull and expensive meal there.

In the morning I met at the hotel James Bustard from the Scottish Arts Council. He wants me to do an interview with Andy Goldsworthy, the 'nature' artist; to which I have agreed, mainly in the hope of understanding better what he thinks he is at. I like some of his work; and another part of it, not. In the evening we met some of the 'Meet the Author' people, why we are here. I hate very much such occasions; the endless gossip and chit-chat, talk of authors and books I barely know the name of, and haven't read.

Afterwards to dinner with Tom Maschler and Regina, who apparently spent all yesterday combing Edinburgh to find the best restaurant. This turned out to be one in Leith, run by the comedian Ronnie Corbett's brother; which did not endear it to me, but the fish food was quite good.

18 August

We met the other members of our literary afternoon. I was next to Douglas Dunn, whom I rather liked, a bluff, brisk Scotsman. Edna O'Brien turned up late; in black, like a merry widow, wondering *sotto voce* to us why she'd bothered to come. I heard the beginning of her reading, in that rich Irish voice. She reads as well as any of us, I think; but I still don't like reading, or the present enthusiasm for it.

Tom and I did our own bit, with Tom being a good shade too enthusiastic about his own part in *The FLW*. At least this gives me a chance to be cooler and more sceptical about the supposed blessings of being filmified. All this in a ball-room next to the Roxburgh, packed out, and with foul acoustics. Tom had a row beforehand with the leading

Edinburgh bookseller James Thin because he had supplied only paper-backs, no hardbacks. I hate having to sign the former for book-loving reasons (I loathe that soft paper); Tom for book-selling ones. We hope to persuade the Meet the Author people to transfer their custom to a splendid new Waterstone's in George Street – just round the corner from the Roxburgh. It seems there is little hope. Fine is on the Meet the Author committee.

The four of us went to a Chinese restaurant down in Leith afterwards; the beginnings of an argument over my disgraceful contempt for the movies (or my involvement with them), but Tom calmed down before an acceptable meal.

To Great Ayton, an enjoyable train run along the Northumbrian coast and down to Newcastle. Here and there one is over the sea; gannets and fulmars glide below. This was much more enjoyable than Great Ayton, in fact. We both felt ill-at-ease there, unwanted despite appearances.

19 August

With M to Redcar, to see a home she wants to move into. It is a lapsed rectory in the middle of the town, just before the front. We took her into it, where she talked endlessly in the hall; then Eliz and I were given a tour by the proprietress. Such places are always depressing, but this partic-ularly so. It was raining, and we went outside to look at what is intended to be her room, in a still unbuilt wing. Puddles, breeze blocks, a mournful outlook. But we had all agreed beforehand to say nothing but good of it, for M's sake. My feeling was that she really liked it because of the resem-blance to Leigh-on-Sea and the wretched road at Great Ayton, i.e., its depressingly suburban ambience. Hazel took us later to another soon-to-be home, much nearer there. A not unpleasant house, in a very pleasant situation on a hillside, with a nice view. This was to be run by an Indian doctor. Dan liked it (as I did) but the doctor and the 'trees' have made M declare firmly against. All this is absurd. She is fatally conditioned by her past, and one cannot change her; so must lie about what one feels.

28 August

Lecture at the NFT. Malcolm Bradbury interviewed me, then questions. Unfortunately Tom Maschler was there, determined to be in on it behind the scenes. He tends to monopolize all conversation, and whomever he thinks most important; and irritates us – exploits us, we feel. He seems to be on a permanent high, nowadays, his least attractive self, as if he must impress Regina. We had dinner all together afterwards, with Tony Smith, the NFT director.

Back in Lyme. Eliz is in one of her bad-tempered ostrich moods: not wanting anything to do with all that has to be done, now we have decided to move. I come back to find the usual appalling pile of mail. Once again, time is on top of me. I feel I can't go on with the Museum, it is all too much. I enjoy the archival side still, even the geological one; but can never do it properly (either of them).

19 September

To the Faber party and dinner for William Golding. The party was at Faber's, a roomful of literary London. There was something rather nicely humble and withdrawn about WG himself, who doesn't like London, or such fuss as this, I fancy. We went and sat with Ann G, who was giving (as Eliz said) a passable imitation of the Queen Mother; rather grande-damish in a way neither of us like. We are invited to the new home in Cornwall. I score a blackish mark by saying I would not come for *them*, but to see the exotic shrubs in their new five-acre garden; the lady is not quick when she is being teased. A niece of WG, a brother. The latter described himself as 'a minor academic'. We talked also with Melvyn Bragg and Hermione Lee, literary power at such gatherings; but I quite like both of them.

A coach was brought to take everyone to Brown's Hotel, where the dinner was. Peter Townshend, Craig Raine, the celebrity directors of Faber; other celebrities. Champagne there, then the dinner.

We talked afterwards with Ian McEwan, who now lives in Oxford, and his wife. I've met him before nominally, but we've not really spoken. I liked them. Goodbye to WG, who had stayed very sober throughout. I was right to compare him to a Tudor bishop. He has a kind of abstracted quality from this present world, that I very much like.

8 October

Leo Smith and her daughter Sarah come (Eliz is in Bristol). Sarah goes to India to collect some kind of Calcutta art. She is a chic liberal, I'm afraid, paying for her long thraldom in the advertising world. Leo got a little bit drunk. I like seeing her occasionally. They went to see Kathleen Hale in Oxfordshire recently, and Leo was shocked over how bitter she was towards the Carringtons.[1] Hale is now in her nineties, and I suggested this was simply a way very old people show they are still alert and alive. 'Do you really think so, John? That never occurred to me. Oh God, how awful old age is. I dread the day when I get old like that. I hate the thought.' On that at least we could agree.

I was partly glad to see them because I'd had an awful day. The very real loss of Mary Scriven (in August) grows larger all the time, or drives me madder, in the colloquial sense. She recommended a friend from

---

[1] Leo's friends Noel and Catharine Carrington. A publisher, Noel was the brother of the Bloomsbury painter Dora Carrington. His wife Catharine had been a comtemporary of Kathleen Hale, the celebrated author of the *Orlando* books, at the Slade School of Art.

Ryall, one Heather Britchford – a nice little woman, in the Lyme sense, but hopeless. She can't spell, she misses out words, she is snail-slow because her shorthand isn't good. I have to correct her every letter massively. I told her yesterday that I thought it would be best if she left and we 'forgot' it; but she was evidently upset; and has just rung to say she has had a 'sleepless' night, but perhaps it would be best if she accepted my judgement, etc. I hate firing people. But how does one tell them they are no good because they are stupid? All of which has left me realizing how much I have lost in Mary. A paragon *post mortem.*

20 October
A fierce day, with showers and dazzling patches of blue sky. We went over to Seaton, and coming back stopped by the Axe. The gulls are gathered, and the wigeon returned. But it was the behaviour of the gulls and crows on the wing that interested me, flying in from the shore to the east. They seemed possessed of a kind of mad joy in the wind and azure, engaging in wild spirals down to the estuary, a kind of lunatic ecstasy in commanding and playing with the near gale-force west wind. It really was much more than a tactic to reach their feeding-ground on the estuary, but a kind of exaltation, a game or a dance. The same with the crows. I also caught in the glasses a buzzard among them, with half-folded wings, almost hovering in the eye of the wind. A very beautiful sight. It was lighter-coloured than most, and the black ends of the wing-tips much more conspicuous than usual, as they were contracted together by the wing-position. A marvellous sense of tension, controlled power. It let itself be turned and blew away eastwards, in the end. This was at several thousand feet, yet there was another buzzard far higher still above it. A strange sense of universal avian exultation in this wind and empyrean sky. The tide was ebbing and it was not particularly cold.

25 October
Foul murder. When I came down this morning there was a small sea of feathers on the terrace, beside the Coade gatepost. I took William out to look at it. A steel-blue and russet bird flew, flashed away from the ivy behind the gatepost: a male sparrowhawk. Below, the remains of the collared turtle-dove that had been its breakfast. A pair of the doves have been with us for some time, and one was growing quite tame, compared with its usual nervous self. Nature red in tooth and claw, and the sparrowhawks grow rarer every year or the number of times I see them; but this upset me.

10 November
I paid the remainder (of £156,700) for the Albert Terrace flat, plus £1,500 for the cooker and clothes-washer, and share of the management

company. We went to London. All the following week, Eliz in a state of despair. The flat is too small, she has turned totally against it; and Fay and Malou are the same; while I less and less want to leave 48A Regent's Park Road. It has its disadvantages, but they seem small compared to those of Albert Terrace. Fay telephones – she thinks Eliz is intolerably depressed, we must renege. 'We women are like that.' The following Monday I made embarrassing phonecalls to Sully at Cameron Markby and Boxall in Alderney. We are legally entitled to cancel the sale of 48A. The company can bear all the financial muddle that will ensue, and write it off as a bad investment, if we can resell Albert Terrace early next year. So we have made the decision. We feel great relief, and are left with the mystery of why we have been such bloody fools. We shall pay for it, of course. The intending buyer of 48A is understandably upset, poor man; we were due to conclude at the end of the month. He telephoned the agent and offered more money if we'd change our minds; but of course we wouldn't. We opened champagne that evening and asked Tom and Malou down, to celebrate our *not* leaving.

7 December

Bad days. I developed a rotten cold in London, and it passed to Eliz, and now sits on both our chests. We feel old, old, our ages. We came back here to Lyme last Sunday. Our respective doctors gave us antibiotics, but they seem to make us both worse, or feeling worse.

Peter Benson, *The Levels*. (The Cobb Road basket-maker.) Constable have sent a proof. He has cleaned it up, and I enjoyed re-reading it. Some of it remains naive, but it has a nice green sharpness still, like a young Sauvignon. The naivety is cunning in places – dismissing the flashes of beauty, which heightens them; while the sourness is really to do with a much older battle between the rural and the urban – the bile of the defeated. Like a glass of green cider, not Sauvignon.

Voices in the garden. I half-hide in one of the bamboo-clumps. Down the path beside the Cobb Road march two young gentlemen, age about five each. I challenge them: 'What are you doing here?' All such previous encounters have resulted in immediate panic-stricken flight. But these two stand smiling. 'We're going for a walk.' Then one asks, 'Is it your garden?' The other, 'Are you the famous writer?' Already winded by this engaging frankness, I make them take me to where they got in, over a fence a little higher up the path, from the Cobb Road. They have masked it a little with bamboos. 'It's to hide it from Albert and the other boys, we don't want them to know.' 'It's the best garden in Lyme, this,' one of them confided, 'a wizard place.' They were so open that I was their victim. I explained it was a wild garden, badgers lived there, other boys spoilt plants, and so on. They liked the idea of that, they certainly weren't on the mysterious Albert's side. 'He's always in here. There are hundreds

of places you can get in if you want,' confided one, as if we must both
be anxious to stop this. They then asked if they could do work for me.
I said, 'Well, not today'; and gently suggested they left by the path beside
the house. Absurd, they were so innocent and enjoying their adventure
and secret place that one could no more have been harsh with them
than with a pair of robins. I even forgot to take their names. It is not
in me these days to be a proper landowner.

7 January 1987

First blackcap, a male. It was with a female bullfinch, across a puddle
of water, on the terrace, a curious juxtaposition. The weather has turned
cold and frosty.

Anna was here with the children last weekend. Their energy and noise
put us off, the endless priority Anna gives them: where they are, they
must rule – in conversation (which they make impossible), in what we
do, everything. I am in any case almost off my head with all that has to
be done, the increasing chaos of my life, all the letters that have to be
written. A bad stomach on top of all; Eliz hates the cold weather, wants
to do nothing but sleep. Anna is cross with us for not plunging immediately into a holiday in Crete, next Easter; our not being young and
keen for it. We both feel badly beaten by life, at the moment. Highly
suspicious of it.

18 January

An appalling cold spell, this last week, and this already bad winter much
worse. It was the coldest I have ever known it here, and snowed on
Wednesday the 14th, or was it the day before? Mist and misery. Then it
began to thaw a very little. One of our pipes burst in the roof on the
15th, soaking our bathroom and the books below in the living-room.
Then, when we had begun to dry things out, the next day, the pipe
below the old dark-room in the flat also burst; soaked all the old junk
we keep there.

Then on Friday I began to develop a cold. Eliz reads all day, putting
herself beyond reality. I very genuinely wish I were dead. Life has been
such a mess this last five weeks it seems incredible; it is, but is not to
be believed.

All this against an intolerable backlog of work. The annual museum
report to be done. Countless letters to answer. Annie's translation of *A
Maggot* to be read – she wanted it back a fortnight ago. For three whole
days last week I was mopping, drying, trying to save soaked things.
Somehow I have managed to get the Andy Goldsworthy thing done.
(That has been another minor disaster – his 'tape', which I sent to Mary
to transcribe, never arrived – lost or pinched in the post.) I have no
energy, I see no light.

26 January
To Parnham House,[1] in search of Andy Goldsworthy, who telephoned the
other day to say he would unexpectedly be there. We go in and find the
owner and his wife, Mr and Mrs Makepeace, through a room of elegant
furniture (his own) to their private den. I suppose my long-seated dislike
of his local eminence, the city tycoon (in art terms) impressing the local
bumpkins, is irrational. He is soft-spoken, they are nice enough, though
somehow the Strodes, and all *they* stood for in the seventeenth century,
still vaguely inhabit the place.[2] Andy is out at Hooke, it seems, so we drive
on up there. There is still a lot of snow in the colder lanes, and fields. We
meet him and his wife Judith; he is in blue dungarees, faintly squirrel-like,
a feeling of energy and will, as I expected. We walk down the drive a little,
past the circles of wood, or grandiose (compared to his usual scale and
style) entrance to Makepeace's Hooke Park.[3] Andy is only doing some last
jobs to it, mainly fitting in two curved barricades, or weighting their ends
with lead, in place of the standard square ones they have, to his disapproval, fitted. We walk down as far as Makepeace's house or Scandinavian
cabin, that is to be a reception/sales place when the park is opened. We
are both cold, have the wretched bronchial colds. Andy is disappointed
with the interview; he wanted more of me, something more like the bit in
Land. 'All that bit about hating photography . . . I hate photography. We
all hate photography.'[4] I try to explain the problems: the word-length, the
time-limit, and the important thing being to get *him* across, not me. It
seems now the table-book will end up at his gallery in London. He really
wants someone to do a book on him, I suspect; but I haven't the energy
to get anyone moving on that at the moment. It was an overcast day, very
drab and grey. 'Marvellous weather,' he said; and burst out with how happy
he is at his new home at Penpont in Scotland, with the recent cold weather.
Marvellous ice, too, it seems. I am a bit put back by all this young enthusiasm, but still like him, and his ideas. He has the vitality of someone not
quite in this world; not our sort of person, at the moment. We both feel
much older than the world. Yet I would like to know him better.

[1] A sixteenth-century manor near Beaminster in West Dorset. It was bought in
1976 by the craftsman John Makepeace, who turned it into a school for furniture.
[2] During the seventeenth century – and since long before – the house had belonged
to the Strode family, who had supported the Parliamentary side during the Civil
War and backed the Duke of Monmouth in his failed uprising against James II.
[3] John Makepeace was establishing a school for woodland studies in this ancient
forest, with buildings made out of sustainable materials.
[4] In a long introductory essay to Fay Godwin's book of landscape photographs
(published by Heinemann in 1985), JF provided an appreciation of the photographer's artistry, but also, with characteristic outspokenness, explained the severe
limitations of photography for anyone with a true love of nature: 'For me there
is no substitute with landscape for being there in reality.'

A copy of a new book on me (*Critical Essays on John Fowles.* G. K. Hall and Co) arrives. Its general tone is much kinder than before. My arrival in academe-worthy literature is accepted. What none of them seems fully to realize is the remove between a writer's books and his life; the extent to which, with this writer at any rate, the ideas, the characters, the stories are like toys one has played with; or arranged, in the way that Andy G arranges his bits of nature. That is, the lack of intrinsic faith one has in them separately. The awful seriousness of academics on writers, their belief that we must believe in everything we say as heavily as peasant Catholics in *their* creed. This is the influence of philosophy, I suspect. Humour and irony forbidden. One is not allowed an amateur love of the game – to enjoy it, but to find in it all a hint of a joke, when taken so professional-seriously.

10 February
I am wretchedly ill; whatever I had in January has not cleared up. We live in misery, not wanting to go out, not wanting to see anyone or be seen by anyone. I have lost track of all the letters I should have written, all the things I should have done. Some foul virus, I presume. I dither endlessly, without will of any kind. Old books haunt me. Urquhart's pamphlets in the Edinburgh edition of 1774 (which I bought in 1963, but have never really read). He is half madman, half joker, his extraordinary English very enjoyable. Who now can play with the language as he could?[1]

17 February
I go down town, feeling awful. It is a complete lack of both will and energy. I think of doing things, never do. Fernandez put me back on the high blood pressure pills the other day. They seem to vegetablize me. I drink a cup of coffee with Liz-Anne Bawden in her back-room at the Portland. She is the only town councillor with any energy, right ideas. At the moment she is fighting for the old town mill; to force the WDDC[2] to preserve it, as opposed to selling it to the richest developer (she thinks it would fetch at least £175,000 in that market). I hear her bright gabble. I answer with difficulty, all seems infinitely remote. I think, 'She thinks I am taking an interest' – or not. I drift away mentally. All takes place on another planet. I buy two tins of fruit, a malt loaf, I don't really know why. I can hardly get up the hill home.

[1] A Royalist who was imprisoned in the Tower of London in 1651 and went into exile abroad, Sir Thomas Urquhart (1611–1660) was a translator of Rabelais and the author of a number of treatises on various subjects, including mathematics and linguistics.
[2] West Dorset District Council.

24 February

A row over a letter. Some National Park officer wrote and asked if I would do a short piece about curlews – a park in Northumberland. I wrote and said yes, if it is short. Eliz is furious that I didn't turn it down on sight, I have too much to do, etc., etc. I rewrite the letter, turning it down on sight. I would like to have done it, curlews having been to me what they are – still are to me. What is at issue is that I must cut severely down on everything that once interested me, that I believed in. It is an impossible situation. Not by bread alone – I feel I kill myself, whether I go on, whether I stop.

1–8 March

In London. I still feel ill, far from normal.

Malou persuaded me to see a specialist at the Royal Free, a Dr Owen Epstein, who looks faintly like a rabbi. But a nice man. Apparently other doctors go to him with their illnesses. He could find nothing certain, but I spent a morning there taking tests. He thinks thyroid gland deficiency is one possibility; another is that I have something called post-viral infection. Apparently its nickname is the 'Royal Free disease' – after a mysterious plague of it there a few years ago, which was never tracked down. It follows clearer infections by virus – general malaise, depression, etc. My blood pressure is too high. He put me on a gentler pill.

17 March

To London again, for Epstein's report. It is good, except for the high blood pressure (at 200/90) and hyperuricaemia, which may bring consequences – no glandular imbalance. He wants me on a new pill, Enalapril, 5 mg. I am to have a course of that before we go to Greece. A sensible chap, I feel confidence in him. He thinks the mysterious post-viral infection may have happened.

Anthony Burgess, *Little Wilson and Big God*. It doesn't work as a major literary autobiography, but is enjoyable. Most writers must read it with envy: such painstaking recall, such polymathic knowledge. Why is he not a greater poet than he is, indeed a greater novelist? He writes too much, a feeling of too much knowledge; sexual knowledge in particular. I don't think his delight in this, prolixity, is just English or pseudo-puritan baiting; or the dislike of it shown by some reviewers, a reverse effect. It's a sort of muddled moral view on his part: the boasting about his Catholicism, his refusing to divorce, doesn't go well with all the promiscuity, the sleeping (both he and his wife) with anyone in sight. The Protestants are right to mistrust the Catholics; all his fine metaphysics, his Pelagianism and the rest, don't hide that he is a man in a mess, very confused, a drunken priest *à la* Greene. But the memory, and the learning, are good; a very enjoyable read. He has all it takes to make a good second-rate novelist; and lacks all it takes for a first-rate one; perhaps above all lacks faults, defects, blind spots. It is a mistake when fine minds wear a mask of plebeian coarseness to excuse themselves; even truth can't pardon that. It may be true, but he should have hidden more of it – and to hell with 'democracy', 'truth', all else that he might claim to justify the book. In short it lacks what art dictates, which is, among other things, silence.

Although nine years older than me, Burgess was demobilized about the same time. He is good on the London literary world of that time, the late 1940s; that only very, very faintly brushed my own life; Dylan Thomas, its kept-alive loucheness. I don't remember that time with any happiness; feeling eternally unsophisticated, naif, imprisoned in the past; austerity (in far more than material things) everywhere. 1939–1950 was a bad, bad time to be young; whether his youth or mine. It was not just the stupidity of those in power (in any sphere); it was the helpless stupidity of those without it, us young.

31 March

I am sixty-one, and feel every year of it. We went to look at a house, Jessoppe House in East Street – a pleasant Queen Anne house, with older back, including a weird brick tower, apparently put up by a captain of Napoleonic times, so that he could watch shipping at West Bay; but decided against, by exterior alone. Then out to see another near Beaminster, Wantsley Barn. We didn't mean to 'view', but the wife of the owner saw us outside and invited us in. It's a seventeenth-century barn, converted – and very well, much to Eliz's taste; on a south slope facing a green hillside and combe I have noticed and liked for some years back, with Stoke Abbot over the hill. The garden nothing, it is hardly begun; a cow-shed horror just behind, but the whole of that side of the barn is blind. From its windows one sees only the green slopes opposite. A fine view, if untouched. Eliz bubbles with it. From there on to Haselbury Plunknett House; but it seems overlooked and very run-down. From there to Crewkerne, and back via the Tytherleigh Arms, under new management. We like the look and feel of the barn. There is a room for me, and for the children. The pair living in it now, and who converted it, want to go and live in Greece; another recommendation.

1 April

We see the barn again tomorrow.

2 April

In pouring rain, and very cold, so perhaps not proper to judge. We called in on the Hudsons afterwards. I sense they think we are slightly mad, especially to take on a place without a garden. The next day Eliz telephoned:

we were ready to offer the suggested figure, £165,000. But as I suspected, he is really hoping for more than that; he would bear it in mind, etc., etc.; but felt he must remain open for the time being. So nothing can be decided. I sense Eliz's enthusiasm is so all-pervasive that it makes her a touch blind; my case is rather more that if we must move, I would as soon move here as anywhere. The enormous upheaval of leaving Belmont, we have not really as yet begun to face up to that, even in mind alone.

3 April
The Museum opened. In a rather slack way, by usual standards. More and more I leave things to Albert Brown. I still cannot imagine how he will respond to my saying I am going; but he is the only one who can take over.

24 May
Mike and Ann Hudson's joint fiftieth birthday party. It was nice, if the weather cold. I cannot really manage such occasions now. My speech, what little there is of it, gets confused, I think I must be the dullest person there; I am happiest being nothing, doing nothing, thinking nothing. Last week Eliz cajoled me into going to see an acupuncturist at Exeter. Sheila Tozer, it seems Welsh, despite her name and now living in Devon. A sensible young creature, I liked her. She went over everything, then put some needles in – a very painless process. She doubted if they would 'work' this first time; but I did feel better the next two days. Something, or auto-suggestion? The Enalapril, to the 20 mg dosage of which I have kept since the beginning of May, has not worked. She took the wretched pressure, and it was 190.

We gave up Wantsley Barn, after visiting it with Anna, who very sensibly argued Eliz out of it. This gave me a great relief. Eliz is still determined to move and we have seen one or two other places, but liked none except one at Netherbury (Brook House), which Eliz fell for, but I rejected. It reminded me vaguely of 63 Fillebrooke Avenue, and I thought the garden cramped beside a mill-leat. The old mill was also next to it to the north, which did look attractive. But that is not for sale. It was the thought of living in the one house, and knowing that other, more desirable, was close by. Visiting these houses is interesting and amusing for human reasons: how other people live, think, lie, are.

We had the men from Humbert's agency here the other day. They valued Belmont at £275,000–£325,000, despite the chaos of my beloved garden. We have told them we do not want to put it on the market now, just to know what we can expect. London money is coming south-west – plenty are happy to buy their second homes at that sort of price, given the ones in London. It is not so much the thought of moving that horrifies me: but that of having to give up any idea of writing for another year or more. Today I wrote a little mock-scientific bit on the poisonous spider of Hellugalia, based (rather unkindly and absurdly) on poor *Pisaurus mirabilis*, of which I am very fond here in the garden. I have decided H needs such a beast; and think also I will give it a vegetarian dinosaur like Scelidosaurus.

25 May

I finished Golding's new one: *Close Quarters*. Both the *Observer* and the *Independent* asked me to review it, but I turned both down. I am glad now, because I would not know what to say. It is the second of his proposed *Rites of Passage* trilogy. Enjoyable to read, as he so often is; but rather rough-shod and inconclusive, unless I have misunderstood something. The hero is a quasi-comic weakling, very self-involved; some of the language distinctly wild, a parody of Regency and the Napoleonic navy jargon; sometimes disarming, at others alarming. He sounds like a whale or porpoise at times; i.e., one can't follow him. And he rampages like a playful seal, at others, in terms of narrative and deeper meaning. My guess is that it is meant to be some sort of half-humorous entr'acte in the trilogy. The journey to Australia, the journey through life. But it smells of salt, for all the strangenesses.

2 June

I was reading about at bed, some de near one across at 1 a.m. A bay learning about bat night finding oneself at distance at pary in the large.

6 June

I am absolutely buggered, in misery. I don't know what is happening to me, my whole mind is in chaos. When Eliz left, Fernandez decided we must go on to a stronger dose, 30 mg. I tried to write about a bat who came into the bedroom on the night of the second; couldn't as above, can hardly manage now. I went on to 10 mg on Thursday, 20 mg on Friday. I can't sleep, I go to bed at two or three a.m., then sleep like a log, but must wake at seven, seven-thirty or eight none the less. Sometimes I seem more or less all right, at others very bad. On Thursday Ken Gollop came in to discuss becoming a trustee. All right. On Friday I was watching a Kirk Douglas film till near three o'clock. This morning I woke up with a headache, totally incapable of understanding letters, near mad, as if the wretched pills have had an effect out of nowhere, a day late, it is appalling. I can't face the simplest thing, sums, answering banal letters. I lose them incomprehensibly. There was a postcard from Lesbos from Eliz. She does not know how desperate I feel. I don't want to eat, I can't face anyone, I don't know what is happening to me. I have taken to smoking too many cigars and cigarettes. Patches of lucidity, then into waking darkness. It was possible for a few days, now not. I can't think what I am doing.

14 June

I have put myself back on 20 mg. Even that throws me badly, though not to the degree it was on the 6th. Eliz is back in London from Lesbos, where I now wish I had gone. I have not been able to do any of the things I had in mind. I still haven't been able to record the holiday in Greece, at Tolon, April 10–25th. It is a kind of longing to be like everyone else, not to record. I drift through every day here with only half my mind functioning – now and again I summon up the energy to do something for an hour or two in the garden, or down at the Museum; but mostly I just exist. Sometimes I quite enjoy existing, being the pair of eyes in the garden; the way it ticks over. This stops flowering, this starts. The great tits in the Coade Stone box nest have flown.

A letter from *Antaeus* (Dan Halpern) asking for an extract from any diary/journal I may keep. It spurred me a little. I have almost given this up these last weeks. The trouble is, after such onsets of laziness (though to make of it some kind of duty seems to me equally repulsive), that there is so much to catch up. In a sense I turn into a vegetable when I abandon this. That does not mean I am unhappy. I am like the garden, I sleep, exist unseen. It has been a nice summer, on the whole, very quiet and enjoyable. I have not written, and I have not worried. Now I must try to recall some of these last six weeks.

10 August

Coastline, a Greenpeace book. I contributed a little bit on the South-West coast, rather crabbed and unforgiving of the way mankind is slowly ruining it. A first advance copy turned up this morning. A nice production; but I feel it unconsciously falls between two stools. So many of the photographs and writers' texts make the coast all look and sound rather attractive; and don't emphasize enough how at risk it all is through man's stupidity. Like telling a woman with cancer she is beautiful; photographing what is still beautiful in her too much.

14 September

Poor old Doris died this evening, at about half past eight. We had returned from the trip north on the 9th. Eliz brought her here on the 11th, Friday. She passed a bad night and Eliz took her over to see her doctor, Coope, at Seaton. She was obviously weak, and complained of poor breathing and pain in her chest; yet seemed to recover over the weekend. She watched a film on TV with us on the Sunday afternoon, a comedy by the Boultings on the Church of England; laughed a little at it, went to sleep in it. Eliz had gone in the morning for her usual coffee morning with Maureen down town, while I 'watched' Doris – looked in to see she was all right. Eliz was a little late back, we wondered about that. We had chicken for dinner. Doris joked a bit about not being allowed any wine.

On Monday morning she was obviously in distress and far from well. There followed the usual rather desperate calls for a doctor. Coope was away till the afternoon. Eliz rang Bowles' surgery for her own doctor, Vinny; Vinny was on holiday, Bowles wouldn't be in till ten-thirty. In the end I rang my own lot. Llewellen came, Fernandez' new young Welsh partner. He was briskly efficient, just as we were beginning to despair of the NHS. She had had a heart attack and her lungs were full of water, a condition he said was familiar and sometimes called 'drowning in bed'. She must go to hospital at once, the little local one in Cobb Pound Road, just round the corner. He organized an ambulance. He warned us it was serious, but we weren't seriously alarmed, as she had had these attacks before.

Meanwhile I had to go down for the Museum quarterly meeting, one I particularly didn't want to miss, since we were electing Ken Gollop as a trustee and there were various other things to decide. I came back to find the ambulance had come and she was in hospital, to have some morphine and oxygen. Eliz went over about four, as Llewellen was coming in again. When I looked in a little later, she was asleep in the private room they had given her, and I went away. Later Eliz was also there again, but finally came back about eight. Doris was so 'drugged' she too took the sister's advice and left. Then the sister telephoned at about half past eight: Doris was dying, we must hurry there if we wanted to see her alive, there was nothing to be done. We were in the middle of finishing the chicken. We went over, to be met in the corridor outside the room by the sister. It was all over. We went into the room. Eliz broke down. The sister left us. Death is so brutally simple, so naked. Doris lay with her mouth gaping open; the sunken underjaw, that eternal expression of death, unchanged since medieval times, since the first man. It is so final, so stark, so cutting through all the modern euphemism that surrounds the event: a sudden inrush of the reality of nature, its absoluteness and inevitability. Eliz said, 'Oh, Doris, Doris, what shall I do without you?' Tears. She wouldn't touch her. I rearranged her hands a little. They were cold, yet still slightly warm. Finally I persuaded her to leave. I kissed Doris's hand, as Eliz could not.*

In all outward ways it was a 'merciful' death – quick and sudden, without great pain. Such deaths are kind to the dying, the dead person; unkind to those who survive. Its swiftness took, has taken, poor Eliz completely off balance. She will not go into the flat – I write this on the 17th – from which they took Doris in the ambulance. I ask if I can go and clear the room: no, no, she will do it, must do it. She is full of anger, accusations, resentment against me, against everything. Endless hours on the telephone, with Leo, Anna, Hazel, Joanne. Guilt, at first

---

* I touched her hands. I fondled her hands. You see nothing. You feel nothing. All you see is how *you* see. [This comment was added to JF's journal by Elizabeth.]

that she was not there when Doris actually died, then about everything. I suspect the sister made that last call when she had in fact already died, it was simply her way of breaking the news; as indeed was what the doctor said on that Monday morning: that there was little hope, although of course one only hears what little he can offer.

I am no use, I am totally unfeeling. She talks endlessly these days of the past, of life in Birmingham in her childhood, her grandmother Annie, her father's elder stepbrother in theatre management, Percy, the way her parents brought her up, so haphazardly and carelessly in their way, before Joanne came into the world. I listen to her talking endlessly to the others, her women friends and relations. It is all I, I, I; never a we. I do not exist, and she must arrange everything, decide everything. The psychiatrist in me doesn't mind; this is her road through the trauma. She stands always on the brink of a row, but I won't let her push us into one. She curses the poor little local hospital, quite unfairly. They did all they could. We must seem hopelessly far apart, Eliz and I; yet I think we are close. What she cannot stand is my lack of emotion, what she calls 'feeling'.

She was going back this evening to when she started teacher training; how she ought to have switched to the theatre, one of her tutors told her she should do so. This is what has been happening since Monday. She is putting herself in a dramatic situation, an Ibsen tragedy, a sort of process of self-heroinery. It is her defence against reality. I keep saying when she goes back over the past, 'Write it down, write it down.' And she says, 'It doesn't matter, it really doesn't matter.' I suggest it does matter, but in some way this breaks the myth. She wants to be the great actress, not the playwright.

Wednesday. A surprise – a little mourning bouquet from Nick. That touched us. Apparently he and Anna had had, at long last, something of a reconciliation that previous afternoon.

Thursday. A photographer, Grahame Wood, came to do a photo for *The Times*, to help promote the *Coastline* book for Greenpeace. Another machine-gun or shotgun merchant – if you take enough shots, one's bound to be all right – who had me down on the end of the Cobb. Two nice things. I said when we got there that there was usually a cormorant drying its wings on the beacon at the end of the seaward wall. We had only been there a few minutes when suddenly there was. I refused to smile throughout. The pollution of nature isn't a laughing matter, or smiling one. A little later a little tern flew over and I watched it for a few moments through the glasses. Just west of the Cobb it dived: that sudden oblique slit into the water, it was beautiful, as beautiful, in its way, as poor Doris's dead body lying on the bed – the acme of life, as her corpse had been of death. It reconciled me to Mr Wood and his eternally clicking Nikon.

Eliz does not understand this: the naturalist's view of life. For her it is bound up with hobbies, private manias, esoteric knowledge, unfeelingness, cold objectivity. The diving tern was I suppose what a devout Catholic feels when he or she confesses. I dislike such religious parallels intensely. I cannot bear the thought of leaving this house and garden because in it I live in nature. I am conscious of every bird-call, every sound; to live without them is like living without grace. That is why I find it so difficult to talk or write of such things: in common language they become proof to Elizabethans of the very opposite of what they really are.

Doris. Her father was William John Culm, son of John Culm, who had married Ellen, née Beardmore. John Culm was an ivory worker. William was born at Birmingham, 14 April 1873, and married Annie Tadwell, aged twenty, at St George's, Sheffield, 11 March 1899. William's profession then is given as silversmith, his father John's as 'Bone Turner'. Annie's father was Alfred Tadwell, cutler. Eliz thinks that of the three sisters, Flo and Doris were born in Sheffield, Ede in Birmingham. Her affection goes to her grandmother Annie, who began 'in service' in the Sheffield area. Grandfather William had a shaving-brush factory in Birmingham (badger hair), also a brewery and alehouse/pub. He was considered something of a wastrel, too fond of the horses and betting, drank too much. Annie was the solid rock around which the household revolved. Eliz remembers the stove around which the house revolved. She was a good cook, made a little money in later years from laundering and sewing. Eliz was often left in her care in the thirties.

Doris's husband, Edgar Whitton, was in the First World War. His mother died when he was abroad during it. This seems to have marked him for life, a fear and dislike of 'abroad'. He was long a theatre electrician in his elder stepbrother Percy's theatre management enterprise. He seems to have had a love–hate relationship with him; was very upset when Percy died, something Eliz never quite understood. Edgar stopped her going to Czechoslovakia after the war, when she was nineteen, and later discouraged the idea of her going into the theatre. Even before that he had refused to allow her to be evacuated, despite the horrors of the blitzes on Coventry and Birmingham. This seems to have come clearly from his mother dying while he was in Flanders; he was distraught when he was not allowed compassionate leave and was sent to the glasshouse for it, it seems.

Doris was equable and naive, the latter sometimes to the point that made us behave badly and brusquely to her. Eliz makes her seem a bit feckless as a young mother. She never understood her two very different daughters. There was one of the bitter, recriminating rows between her and Joanne a few years ago that are typical of too claustrophobic families – more like a lovers' tiff than anything else, or jealousy. In a sense, though she was really the mother, she was more like the youngest sister in her last years. Where she had an older quality was in her patient endurance of all that happened to her in life; she hated 'causing a fuss', to the very end. I was really much fonder of her than my own mother, who so unerringly strikes the wrong note in any contact and has lived all her life in the terrible fix that grandfather John Richards set her in – absurdly class-ridden and overprotected, an egomaniac to boot. That Doris never was.

8 October

Old Arthur Morris next door, whose shouts and groans in the garden we have had to put up with this last year or so, died a few days ago. We went to his funeral today, at Uplyme. A large congregation of the local middle classes and *bien-pensants* of Lyme. He had been nearly mad for several years. An old GP and staunch Christian. Mary, his wife, I believe once one of his surgery nurses, is 'dotty' in Lyme terms, well-meaning to the point of blindness. She helps in the Museum. He was in his nineties, she much younger. We are glad for her to be released from him, and a little frightened. What will she do now, Sisyphus without the rock? The funeral service was weird, it seemed to us so remote it might have been in the Easter Islands. I analysed some of the hymns, and the 'oration', as it was going on. How *can* one believe all this?

23 October

The land of Lower Ware valley, and the cliffs, was put on sale by auction at the end of last month, and I've been very busy prodding Ron Arnold, the ex-colonel from the LR Society,[1] into getting the National Trust to buy it. This has involved two meetings with Bedford and Ann Attwood, the owners – who live in Maisie Forrest's old house, Lower Ware. They were hardly helpful in the first one, but climbed down a little in the second, when Arnold and I were with the NT people. He would sell before auction at £38,000. We've been on tenterhooks all last week to know if the NT would take the plunge – it had to be finally decided by their regional committee, who met this morning. Afternoon: they will buy.

That still leaves us – the town, the LR Society – to raise some of the money, so all that has had to be organized, as both Arnold and I shall be away through most of November, the time the 'fund' is to run. I have promised to make sure the yield to the NT is at least £10,000.

I like Arnold. He has had a stroke, but was involved in public planning inquiries elsewhere before. Alas, the LR Society live at rather a painful distance from the realities of Lyme, and are not popular, as A knows. The tasteful and concerned middle class, opposed to the trading fanatics, like Cindy Langham, and indeed most of the Chamber of Commerce. But we have got Mike Hartley, our greengrocer and this year's head of the latter, to back our appeal; along with the mayor, Denis Applebee, who sits as usual swaying on the fence.

---

[1] The Lyme Regis Society.

I love that piece of land, and especially the final meadow of it on the cliffs before the county boundary, and was determined the NT should have it. Whence this anomalous sortie into local politics.

14 November
This diary becomes like my life, absurdly fragmented, far more retrospective in its recording than present. I still have not done with the trip North in late August and early September; I have just been in Holland and France (from the 1st to the 6th). I thought I might catch up – now I have to be back in France on the 20th for the Pivot TV programme *Apostrophes*,[1] read the works of the other writers on it. Oxford is sending me all the material for the dramatization of the 1860 debate I've agreed to do – all fascinating stuff.[2] In Lyme they are busy collecting our eventual offering to the NT for the Ware Cliffs land – the figure stands at about £8,000, so I hope we shall eventually raise something like £15,000. Countless other things beset me; like annual accounts. Yet strangely I am not depressed and worried as I was earlier in the year. Somehow I no longer worry about being rushed along in the current of time. In an odd way it is joyous, the clutching at this or that branch or rock, yet being tumbled on, always hopelessly 'behind'; as invigorating as a real mountain torrent; becoming indifferent to what one loses, each day and moment.

18 November
Too much happens to me, I never have the time to record it. Increasingly I doubt if it is worth recording. In a way it is partly the insidious shadow of death, like the cramming of too much into the last days of a holiday. And partly my contempt for what I have long hated about the snapshot, the amateur's photograph – that secret desire to have it recorded that one was somewhere, some place, some time: *bref*, that one was.

[1] Created and hosted by former journalist Bernard Pivot, *Apostrophes* was an influential literary discussion programme. It was broadcast on Antenne 2 between 1975 and 1990.
[2] The debate JF refers to took place at a meeting of the British Association for the Advancement of Science in the Oxford Museum on 30 June 1860. Bishop Samuel Wilberforce and naturalist Professor Thomas Huxley were disputing the theory of evolution, which Charles Darwin had outlined in the *Origin of Species* the year before. Robert FitzRoy (1805–1865), who had been captain of the five-year HMS *Beagle* expedition during which Darwin first developed his ideas, happened to be present at the debate. A believer in God, he felt betrayed by Darwin's theory and angrily intervened. Brandishing his Bible at Huxley, he shouted, 'Here is the truth – in here!'

19 November

I left Lyme for Paris. Eliz would not come, which I thought quite right, as she hates these litbiz events, and shares the general Anglo-American myth of what holidays in Paris ought to be – that is, not in a place where you simply do business, what has to be done. Her inability to speak French, her sad and very English neurosis about the look, *le look* in the French sense (what people think of her), that endless ancient English working-class suspicion of 'them', having to pretend she's what she isn't (as if everyone doesn't today play *that* game) – all this, alas, bars her, or she bars herself.

I read Sabato's *The Tunnel* on the train up, Tom M's new passion. Unfortunately you have to read it 'through' the translation, which is pedestrian, to say the least.[1] But I quite liked it, through the mist.

At three, to Heathrow, with an engaging young Greek taxi-driver. His family comes from Piraeus, he was here to study marketing, but has given it up, it was 'devouring' him, now he prefers to drive for a living. He still misses Greece, he would not settle in London for all his life. A nice young man, and a very clear victim of the illusions of our age who is in process of seeing through them. I arrived at the wrong terminal, and had a frantic rush across Heathrow to the right one; my own fault, for not having checked it first with Air France.

Nina Salter[2] was waiting for me at Charles de Gaulle, and took me off to La Closerie de Lilas, where we had a nice dinner among all the famous ghosts – Verlaine, Apollinaire, Lenin, Modigliani, Hemingway, Picasso, Uncle Tom Cobleigh and all. She reminds me more and more of a character from Louisa M. Alcott, the Edwardian tomboy at heart, appallingly ignorant of this corrupt old city/nation – not quite, since she was under Bob Gottlieb in New York at Knopf, and clearly venerates him. She learnt her own forthright schoolgirl-correct French at Nice as a girl; and shows a blankness of much of the rest of it I find touching. I had some small and delicious Belons, and a *perdreau aux chanterelles*, delicious also; she took some less interesting oysters and salmon. She does not like game, she says; that apparently dates back to an occasion some ten years ago, when it was too high; and I'd have sworn she had never eaten oysters before. She rather closely watched what I did, before she started on hers. I teased her a little over her fear of partridge. We shared a *marquise* at the end, a touch of parsimonious economy on her

[1] First published in 1948, Ernesto Sabato's short novel, which was set in Perón's Argentina, was regarded as a contemporary classic in the Spanish-speaking world. As Jonathan Cape were about to publish an English translation, Tom Maschler had written to JF to ask if he would consider reviewing it.

[2] JF's editor at Paris publishing house Albin Michel, which was bringing out a French translation of *A Maggot* (*La Créature*).

side that I liked. Then walked down the Boulevard Montparnasse in light rain, among the fallen leaves. Very clearly she wants a man, and an affaire; but it would never be me. She is too Jamesian, the eager young American wanting to learn from wicked old Europe.

I slept really badly, not till four or so at L'Abbaye. I think the waiter at the Lilas, disgusted by all our havering over the meal, Nina doubting one moment, impervious the next, gave me real coffee, not the decaffeinated I asked for.

20 November

I had a Belgian journalist at the hotel, then strolled out to the Luco – the Jardin du Luxembourg. The relief, very real, of being among trees again, among family, even though they are only chestnuts. Strange, the conkers on the ground, and the screaming, playing children, who ignore them. They grow chrysanthemums rather nicely here, trailing from the urns round the *bassin*. Everything shut, it is winter. Some tennis-players. I walked out past the Senate, back along the rue de Vaugirard. I have had my eye on a secondhand bookshop here, Le Pont Traversé, run by an old man in whom I scent faintly a Francis Norman; buy some Pauverts,[1] a pretty little edition of *Ubu Roi*, I think of 1916. The Pauverts were *Le Concile d'Amour*, Panizza's mad outburst of atheism,[2] some political texts by Constant,[3] Paulhan's letter to the directors of the Resistance,[4] Théophile de Viau's pieces when he was in prison in the early sixteenth century.[5] I am a catholic, though with a small c, it is clear. After lunch, a snatched sandwich in a bar, a young photographer, who wanted to take me at once back to the Luxembourg. I quite liked him. He is Norwegian by birth, long in France, now bilingual. We talked about that, Norway, and his theory of photographing. I tried to describe Fay Godwin and hers. He is a machine-gunner, not her type at all. A good, well, a rave review from *Le Nouvel Observateur*, and also Bassouls' photos, wait for me at the hotel. These are the ones she did of me at the Trocadéro cemetery. Quite nice.

I try and read some of the books I'm supposed to read for the Pivot

---

[1] Books published by the small literary publisher Jean-Jacques Pauvert.
[2] The German writer Oskar Panizza (1853–1921) was sentenced to imprisonment for blasphemy after the publication of his satirical play, in which God invents syphilis to punish humanity.
[3] The Swiss political philosopher Benjamin Constant (1767–1830).
[4] An eminent literary figure in France, Jean Paulhan (1884–1968) had been a member of the Resistance during the war. In 1952 he published a pamphlet, *Lettre aux directeurs de la résistance*, in which he attacked the arbitrary judgements against, and blacklisting of, writers perceived to be collaborators during the Occupation.
[5] The acknowledged leader of the free-thinkers known as the Libertins, the poet de Viau (1591–1626) was in 1625 imprisoned for blasphemy in the Conciergerie, where he wrote several pamphlets in his defence.

programme this evening, but the Pauverts win. At seven Nina comes to fetch me for the TV thing. We got to the Palais-Athénée in the Avenue de Montaigne, near the studio. There we meet Annie and Michèle Gaillard, the publicity woman, and go down to the English Bar. Annie is her usual shy self, watching life both timidly and drily. She is a long way from the media-mad Paris publishing world. We are joined by Michèle's husband, who is the sales chief of the much larger Gallimard. Such marriages, between husbands and wives in different houses, are apparently common here. I ask what they do about 'house' secrets. Nina is sure that they tell them, but keep quiet. I am politely disbelieving.

We go over to the studio. Many people, enough to drive any British studio manager mad. It is apparently a much sought-after honour to be in the studio with Pivot. I meet the great man himself, who has some vague resemblance to Tony Hancock, the other writers; go and get made-up. Pivot appears briefly. Have I ever done TV in French before? No, I haven't. Not to worry. He is off.

I've been supposed to read the work of the others this last ten days, since I was here earlier. Jorge Semprun, the novelist and script-writer, *Netchaïev est de retour*, a novel a bit too close, if I am honest, to a slam-bang thriller of the American kind, although its main theme has to do with the perversion into terrorism of the extreme-left part of French youth post-war, and I found that interesting. Semprun has long left the Communist Party, it seems, but had a long record of being fully involved in the Franco days. I liked him, he is grey-haired, rather like an old-style trade-union man, solid, but fairly uncompromising over his principles (and the follies of old-style Communism). Huyghe, a young man, sociology professor, who has put out a book called *La Soft Idéologie* – how all the old ideals have gone, everything nowadays is compromise, obedience to the market economy, TV culture, all the rest. I didn't really like it, but they warned me before that Pivot can't stand back-biting and needling among his guests, so perhaps it was as well that when we came to discuss the books, Pivot left me out on this one. I would have complained about the Franglais, all the Yank-based argot. The Norwegian told me of a recent review of it: '*Le Livre-choc qui fait toc*' – the shock-book which flops – which sounded to me about right.

The other writers were Mario Vargas Llosa, a good-looking man who rattles out French with a strong Spanish accent, rather boyish. His new novel is a sort of Peruvian Simenon, but I liked his *Aunt Julia and the Scriptwriter* of a few years ago, and could say my bit about the huge overall effect of the South American novel – Borges, Marquez, the rest of them. The last was Michel Serres, a French philosopher, quite an old man, whose *L'Hermaphrodite*, a literary 'meditation' based on Balzac's *Sarrazine*, I really liked. He knows his history and has thought a lot about writing. His was the only one I would like to read in tranquillity – a gentle old man, faintly like an Oxbridge professor. I did my little bit, then we had to sit and watch a funny finale, Pivot playing the clown in a mock commercial book programme. This was because it was some anniversary of *Apostrophes*, which had to be celebrated afterwards – champagne, an absurd chocolate bust of Pivot, many press people, all the rest. Snatches of conversation with people. I told Nina I had done badly. No, no, I had done very well. I had made some remark about liking women, being a feminist. That was super. I remember old Attwood a few weeks ago saying he had kept the Ware Cliffs fields well fertilized, the expression of suppressed horror on the Nat. Trust people's faces. I was the same, and could see Eliz's sarcastic sneer.

From all this we went off to somewhere near the Palais Royal, to a private supper given by Mario VL's publicity lady, another smart career woman, very BCBG (*bon chic, bon genre*) as they say – a yuppie in her way, if not socially higher, since her husband, a quiet man in computers whom I rather liked, is in fact a Russian aristocrat (his French ancestors emigrated there at the Revolution). So, although it was past midnight, we sat down to eat, after some more champagne – another long chit-chat. Mario's wife was there, a plump and rather silly little South American, two other publishing men, Michèle and Nina – very boring. I would have much rather had an hour alone with Vargas Llosa, who obviously rather enjoyed it all. He has something rather nicely humorous and boy-scoutish about him, both indifferent and eager. He is not very serious about politics, it seems; more simply feels he has to do his bit for his country. He knows Sabato a little. S was once quite important in science.[1] He has stopped writing now, paints only, mainly imaginary portraits. VL thinks he was brave in the past, in the Perón and Galtieri times. He tells a story, small gales of laughter at himself, about the Berlin Film Festival. He was on the panel, Liv Ullmann was president, a mercilessly conscientious judge. Everything had to be watched, discussed, examined by the most serious standards. One day they watched a boring film *qui durait douze, treize, eternellement des heures*. Mario was ill, in a fever, and tried to excuse himself. The stern Ullmann fetched a doctor, made him give Mario an injection – and Mario had to watch on. His face as he tells this grows as lugubrious as that of Fernandel, his wife screams with laughter. That was the best part of the supper.

We finally got to bed about three o'clock.

21 November
I strolled to St Sulpice, a lovely morning, sunshine, mild, Paris at its nicest. I tell everyone I hate cities, including Paris; and felt for an hour or two what a fibber I was. God knows I do hate cities, but the area had

---

[1] Sabato had been a lecturer in physics until he lost his post because of his opposition to the Perón regime.

all its charm that morning. I went into a specialist bookshop for maritime things; but no, they had nothing on smuggling between France and England. The proprietor seemed almost shocked that there might be anything. *'Non, monsieur, j'ai très certainement rien de ce genre.'* My own *Shipwreck* was on top of his window display. There is a much finer bookshop lower down, and I browsed there for a while; bought two books on La Vendée. By Loïc du Rostu, one;[1] the other a reprint of the 'father of Communism' Babeuf's famous reproach to the Thermidorians over La Vendée.[2] This has a good introduction by Secher putting the case for the more recent theory in France that the suppression of the revolt by the Revolution was really a pure case of genocide.

I buy a jar of cherry jam – *griottes* – and another of quince. It is terrible, I cannot be bothered with presents. It is not meanness, I really want to drift, to browse in bookshops all day, indulge this rare affection for the French Great Wen. I should have telephoned Nina, but decided against even that. At twelve caught a taxi for the airport. The driver played pop music all the way. I picked up a magazine lying in the back, called *New York*, though it was French. That came from Huyghe's world. One cannot call such stuff pornographic, it is so accepted nowadays. I wonder how women can allow themselves to be photographed in such ways. I mentioned it to Tom and Malou when I saw them that evening. 'It's nothing,' says Malou, 'they are paid very well.' *Ça, c'est malouter un mal.* Pretend it doesn't exist because it's natural.

At Charles de Gaulle a band of English, who had been on some construction job in France; all men, all haw-hawing together, hideous; and for whom the girls in the wretched *New York* are photographed, or their pudenda. The human race also disgusts me.

London, grey, colder. I go out and shop when I have unpacked; go rather mad, having rejected all the French shops in Paris that morning, with their far more delectable displays. Buy Roquefort, Parma ham, Bresaola and so on, the latter to give Malou for dinner that evening; chat with the young man in the Italian shop in Regent's Park Road, whom I like.

Dinner with them upstairs. Tom is his usual heavy self, pontificating, Boris guarded, as always, Malou *maloutante*. They are all agog to hear my report on Bernard Pivot, lap up all the gossip about him. I say I think he is a skilled presenter, but his position is unhealthy perhaps for literature as a whole – he has, or has got, too much power. Every word from him will sell hundreds, thousands, of copies. 'We're going

---

[1] *Histoire extérieure et maritime des guerres de Vendée* (Jean Huguet, 1987).
[2] This 'reproach', which François-Noël Babeuf (1760–1797) published in 1794, was called *La Guerre du Vendée et le système de dépopulation.* It was reprinted in 1987 by the publisher Tallandier with an introduction by Reynald Secher.

to print three dozen more copies,' Nina drily remarked to me after the programme. I think he is also a man who knows he has power – and knows equally he must seem to throw it away. In his manner during the programme, he is the iron hand in the velvet glove. Certainly has a fast and sensitive nose for what is growing boring, for what his audiences want to hear. The informal way the programme is run, its *désinvolture*, makes him also seem pleasantly disengaged from it when he wants.

I stayed on very late and watched Visconti's *Obsessione* with Malou. Tom went off to bed, he had 'seen it before'. A good film, in a way very French, one almost felt it needed Gabin; *Hôtel du Nord*, *Quai des Brumes*, Carné, all of that. I enjoyed it, even with Malou malouing.

22 November

I go out and buy the *Observer*. I find papers now intolerable in their size, their consumer madness, the world poor Huyghe was trying to get at. There is apparently another rival book to his just out, by a Gilles Lipovetsky, *L'Empire de l'éphémère*, which is for this world of choice, of consumption, and so on – it is not for him the defeat of serious thought, but part of a splendid liberating present, fundamentally optimistic, great for the individual. I read Secher's introduction to the La Vendée book: its savage indictment of the Convention and its henchmen and generals. The use of gas in theory at least, of ovens, the *noyades*,[1] all the rest, Labiche de Reignefort's grim accounts of the prison-ships and hospitals.[2] I have always had it in mind to tackle this as a novel, feel even more so inclined at the moment: some innocent young Englishman from Pitt's England – obviously he must speak French, who goes there as an 'agent' say in 1793 or 4, becomes involved.

19 December

Our lives are in a complete mess, both individually and between ourselves. An awful evening last night: there is a total barrier between us, and between us and the rest of the world (we approach Christmas in a state of mutual boredom, disinterest and bad temper, getting in the household things, sending the cards, having to put on some sort of 'show', since Anna and the kids are coming), between me and what I would like to be: someone who can actually write. Eliz says my constant busyness is my own fault. I obsessively take on too much. Guilty. She in return hates this house, Lyme, the way we live; totally despises my writing.

[1] Drownings.
[2] Himself a survivor of incarceration aboard a prison-ship, Labiche de Reignefort wrote an eyewitness description of what he had witnessed.

An absurd background motif of these last weeks is that *A Maggot* (*La Créature*) is getting good reviews in France – the best I have ever had there, in fact. If only they knew how I actually lived, in what mess, despair, bloody-mindedness.

A theme haunts me at the moment, concerning La Vendée, which I derive in part from a long curiosity over its historical 'absurdity', its very real horrors during the 1793 genocide phase, the figures of the absurd royal sons (to become Louis XVIII and Charles X), the duplicity of the English, the self-seeking corruption and vanity of the *émigrés* in general.[1] It is a very rich field for the novel. Somehow I see something that centres around the figure of a Royal Navy lieutenant, sent by Pitt or Grenville to watch Artois (to be Charles X) during the absurd landings in 1795 at the islands of Houat and Yeu.[2] Something between the Navy man's contempt for this fool who thinks he ought to be king and a hopeless love for his mistress, Madame de Polastron (who accompanied Artois, it seems). A contrast between English bluntness and innocence, marred by doubts as to what either side (English and Vendée rebels) is really playing at, spiced by his angry sexual attraction towards the lady and her wit and frivolity. I.e., French elegance and values against the eternally naif English ones. All this in 1795, September to November. I would like to introduce the cunning-enduring Charette, too. This mainly I draw from the Anglophobe but knowledgeable Loïc du Rostu's book, *Histoire extérieure et maritime des guerres de Vendée* (Jean Huguet, 1987). Curses, it lacks an index.

25 December

A lovely winter day, not quite credible at this time of year. It is sad for me. 1987 has been a rotten year, I have so much work, it is absurd. Anna

---

[1] In March 1793 the inhabitants of the Vendée refused to accept conscription into the army of the new French Republic and rose up in rebellion. In May the rebel army took the towns of Thoars, Parthenay and Fontenay, and then, crossing the Loire, the city of Angers. But after failing to receive help from the English, it was heavily defeated at Cholet in October. By the end of the year the insurrection was put down and Republican forces sent to the Vendée with instructions to exact heavy reprisals.

[2] In 1795 one of the leaders of the Vendée uprising, François Charette, reached an agreement with England to land *émigré* royalist forces in Brittany. The landing was thwarted, but none the less Charette planned to receive the younger brother of Louis XVI, the comte d'Artois, back in France with a view to engineering a restoration of royal authority. The comte d'Artois landed on the island of Yeu off the coast of Brittany in October, but soon returned to England, judging the situation on the French mainland to be too risky.

and the children are here, driving us both slightly mad, and very guilty. I don't blame Anna, who has to be both father and mother to them both. The egocentricity, wilfulness, of modern children is terrifying; refusing anything they don't, or think they don't, like. I want to be alone, Eliz (faced with their reality) wants to be alone. I have an hour in the garden, as usual a merciful relief, although that too brings guilt, it is so neglected now.

28 December
A truly terrible Christmas, I hope never to have another like it. On top of everything else the cold I had before has turned to bronchitis. We are both totally without energy, without hope or any drive, as if in a Black Ven[1] quagmire. The children upset us both with their noise, their endless small squabbling; they are altricial, painfully so; always on the grab, merciless to all else. Anna only slightly less so. She and Eliz had an argument last night but two.

31 December
Last day of this wretched year; by an irony, an exceptionally mild and fine one, not winter at all. I went to see Llewellen, Fernandez is off; a pleasantly quick, brisk young man. He gives me antibiotics, Vibramycin, for this rotten bronchitis the pre-Christmas cold has developed into. I gave up last night, those weird shivers were on me, awful cold, though no fever. I walked out of doors when I got home. Strange, two Painted Ladies in the sunlight; basking, one was taking honey from one of the *Patasites.* They seemed almost perfect, new from the chrysalis. A bumble-bee, some drone-flies. An absurdly mild day.

I walk round the garden. Endless clearing up to do, that normally I should enjoy. But this mild spell has hastened everything too early, almost as if setting everything up for the guillotine of frost. Eliz has sinus, we lead half-lives. Lol today said he had never been to a doctor since coming to Lyme;[2] I envied him that record. I feel sometimes I have the energy, if I had only the health, and the will. The dollar falls and falls. I divagate in the French Revolution. It seems very much the only revolution; every attitude, every dishonesty, every human folly and brutality.

Anthony Barnett, *Soviet Freedom.* They sent me proofs of this just before Christmas. A sharp radical's look at Russia, and all that has gone wrong with it since Lenin. I enjoyed it, but the final conclusion must be

---

[1] An area of landslip between Lyme Regis and Charmouth known for its mudflows and quicksands.
[2] 'Lol' was the nickname for JF's gardner, Lawrence Kitchen.

pessimistic: all that poor Gorbachev has still to defeat. I gave it a puff, as intelligent liberalism. The worst follies of Russia were all reproduced in the French Revolution.

10 January 1988

I am such a lazy writer; next door to a non-writer. Constantly nowadays a sense that I have no time; this reduces me to silence, a kind of fatalism; thinking about what I ought to do, which means in effect that I never do anything. A vague short-story idea that I have had for weeks – very simple, a figure that stands on the lawn at night, by moonlight, below here in effect. No explanation, or many, that come to nothing; it cannot be reached by reason. I think sometimes of beginning to write it, but don't. It comes vaguely from *The Turn of the Screw*; also from that poem I wrote years ago: 'On the Upper Terrace', 1969; the reproachful, watching figure.[1]

The Polastron/La Vendée idea. I have a notion this should quite deliberately reject the 'sound research' notion of the novel: that is, be created from the imagination, frankly admit it is not history, a dream of what might have happened, very roughly.

14 January

Upset at the Cobb, in the middle of the night; countless flares, the lifeboat crawling round outside the harbour. It seems some young man, drunk of course, tried to swim round the outside. They picked up his body the next day. The Cobb is like an old cat; half-asleep, but with its paw ready to flash out if a foolish mouse mocks it too close.

20 January

One of our sad, seemingly eternal rows, that hop from thing to thing until Eliz finds one that can stick, or be used for beating me with, a stick for a stick. I went off about ten, down to the Cobb. It is very mild still for late January, and a very low tide. Oystercatchers in the harbour, and one of the construction men still at work, with a Komatsu crane, repiling the boulders inside the Outer Pier. Above, a fiercely starlit night, Orion and Sirius. I watched him for a while, and then walked a little on the sand inside the harbour. They are clearing the hedge just west of the house, beside Cobb Road. I suppose it had to be done, but it loses us a valuable screen, when the grockles come.

---

[1] In 'On the Upper Terrace', published in *Poems* (Ecco Press, 1973), JF describes a figure 'standing there/white in the dusk/the windless dusk/standing above me/white and silent/in the dead dusk'.

7 February

A week has gone, and I've done nothing, can do nothing, about the 1860 debate for the BA. It is absurd that Durant twisted my arm into doing it at such short notice.[1] He has sent me the bare bones; but why were not acknowledged experts like Stephen J. Gould and Adrian Desmond approached to begin with? Or if they were, why did they turn it down? My half-baked ideas keep on turning on me; I ought not to be attempting this, I ought to have refused Durant when he came down here. It is partly a scientific thing. I see the importance of the 1860 debate; but to treat it non-scientifically, as I must, before the BA especially, is madness. When I think of how long Darwin himself took to come out with his theory, it is blasphemy. I feel like poor old FitzRoy in reverse, able only to wave the Bible (though of science itself, this time), while the 'audience' itself demands that I ask a proper question. My whole body revolts against the demand; my whole soul, inasmuch as it is scientific, rebels. I know I must tell Durant I can't do it. I am wretchedly ill also, in physical terms; unable to write. This is a nightmare – being talked into something one cannot do, one ought not to do, one must not do.

Crows' parliaments. There have been several recently, in this mild weather. I have an idea they are partly part of a process in which parents drive away last year's (the 1987) brood, tell them in effect that they have to grow up. Clear off, in effect. There are two kinds of caw; one at a slower rhythm than the other. The dry throat-rattle, rather raven-like, seems an essential part of the proceedings, although comparatively muted. It sinks musically, towards the bass. Is it female, or non-breeding? Territorial caws, lowest and at the slower rhythm, seem well-marked. There is chasing away also, I think of the younger by the older birds. Somehow they need to congregate (1) to announce that territory, the need to breed again, trumps the original 'last year' parental instinct with its 'responsibility' and apparent altruism; (2) to ritualize the disconnection and driving away. Perhaps it is best to conduct this communally, to show the 'young' that all parents behave in the same way. There have been at least three such 'parliaments' (of 10–15 birds) this last week. One this morning, another yesterday, one only a few days ago. They are very noisy, and last about half an hour or less. A mystery in nature. I am fond of it. It excites the magpies also. They were chattering and challenging the one this morning, without joining in, out of some kind of corvid sympathy. Their 'parliament' gatherings seem to take place earlier.

---

[1] John Durant, who had edited a book on *Darwinism and Divinity*, was a tutor in the biological sciences in the Department of External Studies at Oxford University.

8 February

To London. David Attenborough, 'Mr Nature', was at Axminster, and we travelled to London with him. He had been down at Lyme to see Peter Langham,[1] in connection with a series of programmes on fossils. A kind of fever of energy, which I find frightening, menacing, in my present totally energiless state. He is alternately serious and frivolous. Isn't life terrible, isn't it a joke? He is well briefed on everything, of course; a happy man with his work, his position, his endless trips round the world. According to Ray Roberts (who is in town at the moment, and we discovered he had had dinner with Attenborough at Richmond last week), he lives in great harmony with his wife, who runs his life for him in most practical ways, letter-answering, dealing with would-be interviewers, all the rest. It's not that I dislike him; perhaps simply jealous that his life seems so well-organized, so smoothly run, he himself so full of ebullience, ability to cope; perfect order compared to my illness and lack of organization.

We say goodbye at Waterloo, very casually. He, I suspect, thankful to be rid of us; we, slightly dazzled by such a happy energy.

Regent's Park. We go to Tom and Malou for supper. They too have an energy in their way, a tolerance of life as she is. They are kind to be so welcoming to such a pair of old grudgers as we are now. Suspicious of everything, and without any ability, as a pair, to deal with it. Everything, these days, throws us into gloom. We are at the very pole of all Darwin 'offered', in terms of challenge beneath the first shock; a mechanism one must learn to ride, at least in theory. To be the fittest, to survive. I somehow still want to survive, that is, to regain health. Suicide has no attraction; but have not the least idea how to survive. We had a Museum meeting this morning, and I said I must give it up by the end of the year (1988). That is, gave them a year to find someone else. Albert Brown again indicated no. I tried to inject some of my own gloom (not wholly irrational) about the Museum and its future into them. But the spirit of Lyme is used to the lamentations of Job. One talks and talks, and wraps them in a blanket. Something will turn up. That is almost the *devise* of Lyme.

Tom Wolfe, *The Bonfire of the Vanities*. It is the current bestseller of New York, and looks as if it will be so here also. A huge book, it is hardly a novel, not a serious novel; but I rather suspect a skilful case of running with the hounds *and* the hares; that is, sitting on the fence. Good journalism, in his style, satirizing every foible of 'Taste' in dress and behaviour; both the goodies and the baddies are equally damned, both Park Avenue and its faults, and the Bronx and its. In a way it is almost a French eighteenth-century account, as told by an urbane and deeply cynical moralist, a La Bruyère or a La Rochefoucauld. Suspect everyone and their motives; or 'the entire system is wrong, but I am above it'. I

[1] A fossil-collector based in Charmouth.

rather admired that by the end of the six hundred or so pages no one has come well out of it. Its blackness and pessimism remain, last. Its form is of a kind of whodunnit, a police thriller; rather superficial, to carry the weight it has to bear. It becomes readable by the astute sharpness of the observation. A sharp eye above it all; not a great novelist's. No sympathy for the underdogs, either in the story or in the society it conveys. If one finally feels a ghost of sympathy for anyone, it is for the Park Avenue victim, the vain and lying fool Sherman McCoy. Ordinary ('normal', in terms of the common dream) America lies crucified; justifiably, in the old Marxist terms, but the motives of the crucifiers are equally contemptible. So in the end one is left with a kind of old-fashioned Christian pity for him: that such a rotten man should have such a rotten crucifixion. A shade too chic and smart, in short; what that, or indeed now this, culture may admire, of course.

In the afternoon we had gone to see the accountants, Boxall and the new man, Speller, in the Aldwych. Polite chat, no more. I apologize for the lateness and awfulness of the 86/7 papers. I can't really explain how terrible I have been, both physically and psychologically, this last six months. All that is waved away: they're sure all will be well. I feel like Tom Wolfe's 'hero' *in parvo*. A feckless ne'er-do-well and do-nothing. I do not care what becomes of us, that is the difference. Or I cannot care: it is all too much.

11 February
To Cape to sign TPs for the peculiar Pieraccini in Finland. I can hardly do it, I am so bored by such petty fiddling, nor can I even write my name consistently. 'John Fowles, 1988'. This is how writers are killed. All this in Graham Greene's office. I saw Tom briefly. He wants me to see his own specialist, although Tom (Wiseman) does not think much of him. It seems he is (so Tom W says) a well-known showbiz doctor, most famous for having treated Elizabeth Taylor for her drink problems; very expensive, and a smoker and drinker himself. The Ws think I should see someone else they know, a lady neurologist in Harley Street. I would as soon see Epstein again, at New End; and am at the stage where all seems hopeless. What is the good?

13–14 February
A Saturday and Sunday. I was foolish, stayed up to read the Saturday night, then went to bed about three, and slept like a log. At some point in that oblivion I must have had a stroke. I had stayed up to read the end of Gittings' life of Keats,[1] those terrible last weeks in Rome. That was an irony. At any rate, when I tried to stand up as usual on the 14th, the Sunday morning, I couldn't. It was as if it, the leg, was drunk, though

[1] Robert Gittings, *John Keats* (Little, Brown, 1968).

the rest of me was sober; no sense of balance, unable to walk straight, all the rest. It was something like the pins and needles one sometimes gets from sleeping too heavily, in too stiff a position; but I had no pins and needles. They call Malou and Tom's doctor, a Dr McGregor, he comes. He puts me through various exercises. I have had a stroke, it is slight, I am lucky it has not affected more of the right side. He wants me as a casualty to the Royal Free in Pond Street, overlooking the Keats/Brawne house, Wentworth Place. It is technically a 'transient ischaemic episode', it seems.

It seems absurd at first: no pain or great discomfort, only this inability to balance, to control my right leg. An ambulance takes me to the Royal Free, where I am seen by a shy and serious young man, a Dr Rose. I am to go temporarily to the McLaggan Ward. Then I feel numbed with horror; like leaving a mountainous and beloved island, with all its valleys and slopes, seeing it recede for ever. The folly of life, its bitter futility, its remorseless Darwinian nature, the non-survival of the non-fittest. Not being able to experience any more. One wants to groan in pain at the senselessness of it, that one cannot escape *what is. Tenthredinifera*, I should never see it again in the mountains in Crete. I don't know why I kept thinking of this in particular.

The first two or three days of this limbo-hell were superbly fine, it is the mildest of all recent winters. Sunshine, clear skies, out there. The ward looks down on South End Green and over the houses to the southern half of the Heath and Highgate. The appalling hospital routine takes over; the waking at half past five or six, the taking of blood-pressure, the nurses; outside, the pigeons and crows, the pigeons bizarrely close-far; only three feet, through the glass, yet three miles, for what good it does. The Royal Free is like a great tower, dissociated in some strange quasi-medieval, quasi-mythical way (despite all its science) from reality. The man in the next bed – this is really an ear, nose and throat ward – has an operation. He works in Trusthouse Forte's head office. An Austrian, 'out' most of the time. Other people drift in and out; a young man for a wisdom-tooth operation, a black man for some kind of dialysis. I have a CAT-scan, a not very pleasant experience, vaguely claustrophobic in impression, though not in nature. I am shown one of my cerebellum sections. It is bizarrely fenestrated, like so many dead roots of a tree, the *lacunae* in my brain; the loss of memory I have talked vaguely of for some time now is not imaginary.

17 February
Sawyer, the Registrar, a Nigerian 'white' or half-caste, who evidently has a sense of humour, brisk and authoritative, and the preoccupied Rose see me. They want to move me upstairs to another ward, the Crawshaw.

Tom, Malou and Eliz appear. I long for their coming, then when they have come don't know what to say. Their chatter seems unreal. I long for Eliz especially, just to hold her hand. The horror of all that has happened these last days, one can hardly even speak of it, only live it, the experience of it. This at least I am certain of, I need her, as a child needs its mother, but also in a metaphysical way that has been missing from our life these last years.

It all follows from the cold truth that Darwin and Huxley brought into the world: that nothing, certainly not some consoling outward religion, redeems, compensates objectively. At the end of the day there is no hazard for the individual: all dies, all passes. The only hazard is far less, in comparatively what kind of life, or passage, the individual has; whether he or she dies young or old, what quality, what external circumstance, the passage has; like Keats, with a genius, a light, or like the great majority, with effectively nothing. Eliz is my not nothing. I am very aware of it, here. This is not an intellectual thing, however badly I put it; but a fragile reality, a kind of last bit of wood to a drowning sailor; it throws the lesser hazard, the chance of the passage, good or bad, totally to the fore.

Eliz has telephoned Durant, or his secretary, at Oxford, to say I can't do the 1860 debate for the BA. I had really given up that idea before this last attack; Durant's demand last year was absurd, when people like Stephen Jay Gould or Desmond (and no doubt thousands of others whose names I do not even know) were about, or could have been about, with a little forethought. Some kind of cowardice, I see in retrospect, in silence itself; not wanting to walk through a minefield, with the eyes of one's colleagues on one. Let some other poor flesh try to blunder through.

Doubt of one's own mind. I try to look at the *Guardian* crossword every day: it is incomprehensible to me, most of the time, from another world. Books the same; they seem not real, strangely incomplete. My mind jangles, like a shaken kaleidoscope. One cannot recall what association the fragments or bits have.

I went up, to another ward, the Crawshaw, only two or three below the top of the tower, with a fine view to the south, down across London, immense. A mile south, I can see the gold dome of the mosque in Regent's Park; a patch of green that might be Primrose Hill. Closer, Belsize Park, the register office where we were married. I remember there was a crematorium behind, I suppose where the Royal Free is now. Rose comes in about one. Some neurologist is to see me, a brain man. They are checking on diabetes; I may have the maturity-onset variety, it seems.

The staff sisters and their underlings, the trainee nurses. Some ward assistants are helots, black, barely literate, but pleasantly jolly, human. Their chatter irritates me, alas, especially in this new ward. The total banality of visitors, also in the old one, a kind of parody of Britishness, the retrieved nothings people exchange. The need to kill silence, killing in itself.

There are two old men in the new ward: one a would-be gay old dog, ex-RAF, he is in his eighties, always joshing the nurses, faintly immoral propositions. 'I'd like to see you in a Chinese dress, green. And silk stockings, sheer silk, not nylon.' He can barely walk, poor old devil. I begin by disliking him, as I suppose I would have in pre-stroke life; but prefer him in the ward to the other person, an overprecise member of the in-between classes, very positive about all the things he does; his occasional marches round the corridors of the ward, his washing, his eating. He speaks in an authoritative way to his dowdy wife when she visits; a little dictator in his own home, one suspects. But oily and subservient with the old RAF man, who is clearly of a higher class. They are both pro-Thatcher, and read the *Express*. The RAF man *knows* about life; the other agrees.

The patient beside me is strange, a Jewish religious maniac, so possessed by praying and ritual, it seems, that he can barely eat. He is a private patient of Epstein's. He draws the curtains round his part of the ward, he does not like being nursed by women. At first there is nothing but Yiddish voices, he has friends of a like persuasion in his 'tent'. Every so often they break into singing, some part of the service in Hebrew, elaborate melismata, fragments of chanted melody. I rather like that, a whiff of the desert, of something exotic. The boy's name is Isaac Feihen. Later, when his guests have left, I see him faintly through the walls of the tent, praying, praying, as if the wall-light is his Jehovah. Every so often he breaks into his religious melodies in a kind of *mezza voce*, snatches of them. He is very pale, unhealthily so. The RAF man loathes him, he warned us as soon as we appeared. Religious meetings, it was mad; and for some reason the boy came and went as he pleased. I read his 'notes' the next day, when he was moved to another room. He was to be treated with great care, all his religious obsessions tolerated. The mutter behind curtains, very indrawn, involved.

London, dark grey and rose, gold and pale blue. Far to the south, the planes landing at Heathrow. Pigeons pouting. What is terrible is the being isolated, cut off, from the outside. A bunch of anemones that Eliz brought. My eyes cling to them. I say little to the two other old men.

I wear a label on my wrist: 'J. Fowles, 42885.' All your outside conforms, your inside screams.

Anna and the children appeared yesterday, when I was in McLaggan. The children are bored, poor things, William especially. Nick is probably going to Baltimore next year. I try to say something to Anna about it. But she seems indifferent, as always. 'He does so little for the children, anyway.' I think Tess can live better with it, certainly she can sympathize more with her mother. The situation malforms William worse. To him, the invalid I am is a bore; in Tess, I sense a ghost of sympathy. Eliz says that they don't want to go out in London; it is in a sense their revenge on poor Anna, for not giving them a 'proper' home and father in Bristol. I think of that awful last Christmas we had at Lyme with horror.

Dr Wilson, the neurologist. He thinks the attack did not come out of the blue, it has had a long history, been quietly signalling for a long time. I am conscious of using the wrong words as I talk; of having lost the right ones; ridiculous, a sense of having been at least a fair shot in the past, now a hopeless one. Eliz tries to explain my liking for 'wild' landscapes, for botany, Greece, France, all the rest. He seems doubtful as to whether I shall be able to do that again. A nice man, in a two-edged way. You feel he is being nice, then you wonder what he is hiding.

An article in the *Guardian*, about installing the new printing process. 'If war was hell, progress runs a pretty close second.' I wrote this down; it seemed very significant.

Familiar streets. Downshire Hill, Fleet Road, which can be seen from the other side of the ward; which on the whole I prefer, in spite of my life-long bias to the south-west. The only good view of it, to the north, is from a room reserved for smokers and TV viewing. I go in sometimes for the view, that is all. It should be so kept for all the patients, that is, for the view – I feel. Not for the TV, by morons and for morons – to be honest, for the working classes, for this is 'their' room, its view, compared to that of the accursed screen, non-existent. Curious, too, how the unspoken (and spoken) ethos of the endless chat shows, quiz programmes and the rest somehow pervades the hospital. It is of democratic tolerance; we have to understand one another, so let us all use the same sort of *lingua franca*, seem to live by the same standards, believe the same things, all the rest. Part of me approves of that; yet in a way it seems a dodging of scientific, the Darwinian, truth. Someone must shout, must scream no.

They have moved a speechless old man into the Jewish maniac's bed. It seems he was once in the fight game, he can only communicate now by grunts and notepad. He is fed by drip. A wife and daughter come and see him. They manage to laugh at him sometimes, he wants to live. Last night he had some sort of attack, the nursing staff around him. They seem quick and calm, even when there is a minor panic. It is strange, this keeping alive, this obstinacy both in patient and nurses. And touching, a sort of eternal, touching futility.

Sawyer, the Registrar, and Rose came to see me. My blood-pressure is not sufficiently down, they want me to stay another two days. I see also a dietician. My sugar balance is wrong. She brings a chart, a sort of final revenge of the puritans on the hedonists. A final 'greying' of life, and farewell to the 'glamour' of normality. No oil even in salad dressing; no sugar, of course, no puddings, pastries or sweets. Fruit, fruit, fruit. I must try to lose about a stone – that is, from the present 13 stone, 2 pounds (82.3 kg). Eliz is tired. It is still fine outside, but colder. I am depressed when she goes. I want to cry, like a child.

19 February

Friday. I lost all sense of time during this stay in the Royal Free, can remember clearly no sequence in which events happened; very often, even what was said to me. Today Sawyer decided I could go home to 48A, though he wants to see me again on the 29th. I wait impatiently for Eliz to come. Anna and the kids went back to Bristol this morning. Somehow we get a taxi back; it is a kind of heaven, to be out of that grey tower, to be back in normality, whatever its faults. I was endlessly pacing about the ward at the end, waiting for her, in the corridor outside the ward, where the stairs were, a kind of meeting-place with another ward and the medical school. I cannot walk straight unless I concentrate; if I look away for some reason I lose both balance and direction. Sometimes my step seems hardly affected; at others I am as if drunk.

I am grateful to the Royal Free, I suppose in a sense 'our' hospital in London, where Eliz went in the old days for her operations; overlooking Keats Grove, the hill of Hampstead; Mike Hudson's hospital also. At the end I asked Sawyer, the Registrar, where he came from. He was born here, but the negroid part of his face is from Nigeria. A quick, intelligent man; something of the black part of him makes him relaxed, faintly indulgent, one suspects amused: what fools these wholly-whites are, with all their ancient prejudices. Look, at last they begin to realize they need me.

It changes all my life, not least the giving up of tobacco; I think even more of that glimpse of the cerebellum in the CAT-scan; its holes and lacunae. I am lucky it was not worse, the stroke; but perhaps with writers, all such changes affect more. The very nature of our profession demands a more particular balance than with most. Balance, in all senses, is what I lack at the moment. Pity for the sick and ill (not just myself), I have gained that. It is typical of this ruthless society that it does not really care about such things, witness the present row over financing the NHS in general. I feel softer than ever about the blacks; tolerant of them and their faults, their loquacity, even when it irritates.

20 February

A long walk over Regent's Park, at least to the duck-pond by the Inner Circle. The ducks are so beautiful, the geese, a moorhen. Even the footballers are beautiful, all natural movement. I walk not too badly, if I concentrate. As soon as I look aside, I start veering.

23 February
Tuesday. To Hampstead. I buy a long green overcoat; with a hat, £152, from John Lidington's, the old shop by the Tube. The man in the shop thinks Hampstead is going to the dogs; Camden 'persecutes' old-fashioned shopkeepers like him with their rates and rents because it has become such a shopping and food magnet for North London trade. 'They all come here nowadays for the restaurants.' I had just been in the new bookshop in the High Street, Waterstone's. Would it affect trade for Ian Norrie's, the High Hill shop down the hill? Obviously it would, I thought. I told the man we had known Hampstead and indeed his shop since the 1950s; and the moan then was the disappearance of the working-class from the village. That was when the boutiquification began, the modern rot.

24 February
Back to Hampstead and the Royal Free, this time to visit Keats' (or rather Brown's) house.[1] It is quite a good small museum; carries many whiffs and echoes. It is in financial trouble, now it is in care of Camden. Where the library now stands was once the vegetable plot. Only the old mulberry in the garden, fallen and propped up, predates Keats. The plum-tree beside the house, where he is supposed to have heard the nightingale, is a substitute. So much else is changed, altered, substituted; somehow more alive in the verse, in Gittings. One can live a past reality so much closer in books, biography, in the verse itself, than through a so much changed present attempt to recall it, a museum. The cramped overcrowdedness of Wentworth Place in the beginning, when K and Fanny Brawne lived there; its freedom and greenness, the field behind running down to the cottages and pond at the foot of Pond Street; so long all endless houses, this area. Such 'progress' is a nightmare, a very bad evolutionary joke; quite grotesque. I enjoyed this afternoon; in one way so close to Keats, in another, so infinitely far; all irreparably gone, all changed.

25 February
To the Royal Free again, to see the physiotherapist. She gives me no exercise, I have lost my finer sense of balance, my 'head-righting' ability; that is, not losing balance when I look aside, as I do. This was apparently a fairly late evolutionary gain in primates; 'before', they had to look straight ahead to stay in balance.

---

[1] Although it became known as 'Keats' House', Wentworth Place actually belonged to Keats' friend Charles Armitage Brown.

26 February

I wake up early, depressed. I read Mattingly's *Spanish Armada*,[1] which I am enjoying, partly because one can get lost in it. After lunch I walk out over Primrose Hill, alone; not only on the paths, across the grass also. It is green, but largely natureless. A missel-thrush, on the hill itself. Magpies. Flocks of starlings. Something terrible in the way everything but grass has gone. I crave the wild.

27 February

Caryle Steen comes in in the afternoon. My BP reading is 140/80. She has holidayed in Uplyme; a nice, sympathetic woman. She sits and watches me, I recover normal speech with her a little.

I find it difficult to write, even to sign my own name; that is different from the mistakes I make here, typing.

28 February

M rings, from Redcar. Incoherence on both sides. She hasn't been told about the stroke, I have to lie, triviality, I hate it. I suppose she is in a sense, traditionally, the person to whom one needs to pour out everything, the mother confessor. But now even speaking to her is distasteful; she has never been able to hear, of course. And I am crippled by guilt that I tolerate this old barrier, silence and indifference, between us. It is the final cruelty of the Darwinian system. Its silence, inherent in its transience.

Afternoon. We go with Malou to Kenwood, her usual kind, chirruping, babbling self. Years since I walked there, over the southern part of the Heath. A faint ghost lies over it all, of a rural, country-house past, of a once rich nature. A kestrel flashed past, chased through the trees by crows; Malou did not see it. That too was typical: even what little's left of the past is not seen. Nature is dead, nature dies.

We ended back at South End Green, from which we started. I stumble along, behind the two women. In everything now I feel I stumble. They do their best, are tolerant, solicitous. But everywhere I feel isolated and rejected, in health, by the rest of mankind; left behind. This sense of being jettisoned, found wanting, a design failure, is ubiquitous. I almost see it, in people's faces. Look, I am fit, I am normal, I am not like you. We are not you. Individuality is the curse of mankind; being separate. I was allowed a cake, some kind of apple danish, as an indulgence and a treat. The hospital looms over us, where we are in the cake-and-coffee place.

29 February

Monday, I go to the clinic to see Sawyer. A depressing experience, the

[1] Garrett Mattingly, *The Defeat of the Spanish Armada* (Jonathan Cape, 1959).

waiting, from nine-thirty to eleven; the queues of the sick and ill, a harassed mother with two unhappy children, whose mewling really epitomized everything for us adults. We don't, any of us, want to be here, in this situation. In the end I see Sawyer with Eliz. My BP remains down, I can go to Lyme, which increasingly worries me, whatever is going on there. But I must come back to London, to have an X-ray about the prostate problem, the cloud that overhangs everything. That is for ten-thirty on the 21st March.

1 March

What is going on at Lyme – there is an article in the *Independent* this morning, about the lifeboathouse at Lyme; on the side of the objectors, of course. I have missed all that, they will not care. Another also about Andy Goldsworthy, which says of him what I have felt from the beginning: that he is different from the merely 'smart' art world, though that is where the article would place and embroil him. Has genuinely his own thing; his own view of life. In that, truly walks alone.

Yesterday evening, panic and gloom about Anna, which spoils Eliz. Tess is ill, has been sick all day. Is it something serious, or a virus at the school? Eliz blames me, I did not relate properly to T when she came to the hospital and needed encouragement, I do not understand her, I am too absorbed in myself, etc., etc. From there to what I had done with Fay years ago when we were alone at Lyme, the ridiculous ghost of that old possibility of adultery, in which, God knows, there is no more truth than as in most ghosts. One may have dreamed of possibilities, eventualities, alternatives at the *time*. In that sense there was perhaps on my side betrayal, but that is of the body, the animal in the zoo; but in all physical senses, none. Such plunges into the submarine horrors of the past are typical of Eliz at the moment. I see it in her eyes: 'Have I really time for this wreck?' I must stay sane. We had seen Fay on the way back from the hospital, in her little house just north of England's Lane; she is compact, well-organized, tolerant of others, but it seems determined not to be too affected by them; slightly cool and distant, as she always was. I like her style, her take-it-or-leave-it manner of pleasing public taste in her cookery writing: she tastes of lemon-juice. There are worse flavours.

Dostoevsky, *Crime and Punishment*. I bought this on impulse in the High Hill Bookshop. How depressing, that first chapter. Someone plunging downwards, inevitably.[1]

---

[1] On a hot July evening a penniless, solitary and desperate Raskolnikov slips out of his garret room, taking care to avoid his landlady. Nervous and on edge, he walks along plotting some unspecified crime. He reaches the house of the old woman Alyona Ivanovna, where he pawns a watch. Then overwhelmed by confusion, he leaves again shocked that he should be in such a nervous state that he could contemplate killing her. The chapter ends with him drowning his sorrows in a tavern.

2 March

Home to Lyme. We caught the 3.10, crowded, somehow a landscape of the dead; I have never been through it before, it seems nothing to me.

We can't get through the door at Belmont, so many letters, endless letters. There is mail for a year in the short time we have been away. It disgusts me, I cannot even face it, Eliz goes through it. We have two small fillet steaks I had bought that morning in the Regent's Park Road. Some wine, I keep to some of that in the evening. The nicest part of the day is putting my arms round Eliz. I could not stand the thought of us sleeping apart any more, as we did here before we left and even in the little bedroom at 48A. A great need for being mothered, for feeling someone physically; miserable cipher though I am, sexually. This is the purest kind of love in a way, needing another presence, anything to kill the isolation.

By some miracle, the house was not burgled while we were away. I cannot believe such luck – that at least its past, my past, our past, still survives.

3 March

The garden, I stagger and wobble around it. Some early daffodils are out; the Osage, at the bottom, the camellia in full bloom, the single rose, some twenty flowers out. The *Clematis balearica* is also heavily in flower, its crimson speckled blooms clustering the top branches of the myrtle, like paper moths. Female skimmia in flower, the male coming; some oxlip, *Anemone blanda*. The Lenten roses are fine this year. Growth, the season already into its stride.

In the afternoon I walked over Ware Cliffs to the county boundary; that too was nice; some rabbits darting into the brambles. I feel I am dying, this is a last walk, I am glad we bought the land for the town. I meet Jean Wellings taking her dog for its walk; the man who has moved into the Orchard, Dobson's Cottage, is not pleasing her. Her dog ran into the cottage garden the other day; and came back minus its collar, obviously removed by the man; a senseless bit of resentment. She thinks she will go back and ask for it. Jim Moss and Sheila. I do not want to talk to them; they will despise me for having had the attack. Correct people do not have attacks, do not die. I hide behind a furze-bush and let them pass. But I liked the way the land was being 'used'.

5 March

To the Axe. Eliz goes on to Seaton to shop; I walk along the shore. Flocks of wigeon on the west side. I enjoy the walking, but a bad tooth, the Royal Free prostate X-ray hanging over me. Life seems hardly worth living. The misery of being allowed to eat nothing one wants. I feel hungry always.

Anna came in the afternoon, minus children. I feel absurdly grateful to her, close to her, though of course she comes for Eliz. For her normality.

9 March

Eliz feels ill, she has a pain in her side, she may have caught something from Anna. We are a couple of wrecks. To Sidmouth, where we ate some sandwiches on the front. It rained, drizzled. I walked east on the cliff towards Salcombe Mouth, to where the National Trust land starts. Formidable places there for suicide, vertical from the cliff-tops to the beach. I am miserable, but still not tempted. Alexanders grow all along the path. I chewed a leaf-stem, bitter stuff.

Eliz in despair when we get back, because Albert Brown wants to come round. *Faute de mieux*, I depend on him to look after the Museum. Yesterday I met Liz-Anne Bawden down town, and told her of the attack, the mess we were in. Later that day she rang to ask if she could take over, rather to my surprise. In a way it is a relief; anyone rather than Richard Fox, one awful proposal – or Albert even, whom I just can't trust. That is what he wanted to see me about this evening. He'd been thinking perhaps it would be better if he took over the curatorship for a while, and Liz-Anne later. In short he doesn't want to give up his own chance at it. He admits he can't really be interested, but I can see he doesn't like the idea of Liz-Anne 'sneaking in' ahead of him; knows too I depend on him at the moment, to keep things going. A miserable situation.

10 March

A lovely day, sunlit, clear skies, a truly Greek day. Poor Eliz feels lousy, and I also with my own pain, in the left side. I bask in the warmth in the garden, and feel done for; one can't, at such a season and perfect day of it, imagine anything wrong. Everything is wrong. The irony that all the spring flowers should be blooming now. It should be endless midwinter.

11 March

A Friday, I think. Terrible, I cannot remember days, when anything happened. I think Jean Wellings came, letters. I know about mid-afternoon I was bored by it, I had to go out, and couldn't, till she left about five; and then walked out over Ware Cliffs, and along the lane to Underhill Farm, up behind. A grey dusk, somehow peaceful, rabbits in the field, in front of the Orchard. No one about. I wandered through the trees, along the little ridge, to Chimney Rock. A large tree has come down on the slope just below; there is a 'staircase' there now, a wooden bridge over to where the Underhill Farm spring is collected. Golden saxifrage in the damp hollows, as always. I sit, in a kind of quiet despair, semi-suicidal. The greyness, the dusk, the absolute lack of colour, I do not want to leave it, or lose it: the melancholy man in the woods. In the end I walk home, when it is near dark.

Eliz waits, in a temper that I have not told her where I was, am. She is right to be in a temper. I was lost in some desire for oblivion. People playing with suicide should not play with those they depend on. I know it when I go to bed, and she not, she goes off to her old room in front; and I live in hell, unable to sleep, drowned in the worst *affres*[1] of solitude.

I need her, so badly, and so without any right to need her. A terrible weekend. She is hurt, and ill, herself. My only happiness is at night, beside her. Non-sexual, of course; just her being there.

15 March

We drove out, a cold, blustery day, to Lambert's Castle;[2] couldn't stand it, it was too cold, deserted except for one or two dog-maniacs. The dark, bare woods, the Neolithic turf; how it has all changed from the past, to this mere dog-walking place. I was caught myself, my bowels had to be emptied. I went to a furze-brake to the east, trampled by the bullocks they run here at this time of year, the cold wind. Every two or three days I shit like this, a large load, no diarrhoea. I have a semi-permanent pain on my left side, at about the lowest rib. Ludicrous, defecating on the blasted heath. It was almost as ludicrous as the scenes in the Commons, over the Budget speech, which we sat and listened to when we got back to the car. Lawson being mercilessly pro-Tory, helping the already rich, the successful succeed even more;[3] Labour impotently howling, breaking up the session. I'm worried now about my own financial situation, obviously, I suppose I count 'just' as one of the rich who is being helped. I had very sharply the feeling of precarious displacement; of some reality in this cold and windy place, some last disappearing remnant, in the bare beeches, the torn fragments of distant crows' and seagulls' wings in the wind, the blown leaves, of a saner and safer world and society. It was the wind of those voices at Westminster that was disturbing, all the wind of the outer world tormenting the dead leaves of this, its insane purge.

17 March

Haircuts, down the road. The fat girl we both rather like, Debbie, simple, but rather endearing. She lodges with her boyfriend lower down Pound Street; her mother left her father, who remarried, apparently doesn't care about her. She feels embattled, alone. A story about her flickers vaguely through my mind.

19 March

A grey day, like yesterday, one of eternal rain. We had to pack up to go to London, the prostate X-ray at the Royal Free on Monday. I did a

---

[1] Torments.
[2] An Iron Age hillfort about six miles away from Lyme Regis.
[3] The Chancellor of the Exchequer Nigel Lawson cut the highest rate of income tax to from 60 to 40 per cent and reduced the basic tax rate to 25 per cent.

tormented, feverish circuit of the garden before we went. Eliz said, as
if it is the last time you will see it. It is not that: the torment of so much
needing to be done on it. Old Lol has not appeared this week, I think
I must change to Peter Benson just down the road. Lol is largely useless,
poor chap. Everything just coming into spring flower; the camellia
ending, the viburnum and *Osmanthus* just starting, all the bulbs, the
violets. Eliz talks of us going to Crete, on the spur of the moment. She
takes our new passports, 'just in case'.

   This ten days here has been bitter-sweet, for me: a memory of all I
thought I should never see again, when first in hospital; memories of
what I treasure and like at Lyme, Underhill Farm and behind it, the
Ware Cliff fields. Then the chaotic mess my life here is in, the Museum,
all the rest. The old gloom about leaving again: we shall be burgled.
And poor Eliz is not happy here, as always; complains of the shops, the
eternal poverty of resources in Lyme. She looks forward to returning to
London, while I dread it.

   A bad journey on the 3 p.m.; it is re-routed through Westbury and
Warminster, through strange country, somehow intolerably pinched,
flowerless and birdless, destitute, wet and winter-barren. We get to
Waterloo half an hour late only, but with the detritus of some football
crowd (red and white caps and scarves), blundering, noisy, shouting
lungs, somehow like tanks, obstreperously blind. London at its ugliest.

   Dinner with Malou and Tom, dear blind-kind souls upstairs; as
relieving as ever, and as infuriating. They leave for France next
Thursday, which both relieves us in one way and alarms us in another,
the absence of that dull, but comforting presence. We are too fastidious, too critical of them. It is the 'smart' world that condemns them,
not their reality. Boris is there with some young American at London
University, one Keith. He wears an absurd woman's ear-ring in one ear;
none of us adults quite knows what it means – neither about him, nor
about Boris, whether he has gone, or is going, gay. Tom thinks he is
simply 'lazy' about girls; can't be bothered to pursue them, or put up
with their ways; so he is tempted to the homosexual world (so his theory
goes) simply by lack of energy. Malou and he are worried by it.

   They had dinner with Dirk Bogarde recently. He lives now in London,
off Kensington Church Street, in a house he bought for some £500,000,
it seems. His friend Tony is dying of cancer, and Dirk has retired here
to look after him. He too has apparently just had a stroke. We speak
of them as of venerable, time-sanctified queers; nothing like these
present young mysteries in the family, Boris and Keith. Keith looks rather
alarmingly like a girl, not unnatural, with his pearl ear-drop. Tom thinks
he must ask the obvious question of Boris. Apparently he has already
banned the idea of letting B bring Keith to France.

21 March

Last night I had my purge, which worked without too much discomfort. Then today to the Royal Free at ten-thirty, where they did the X-ray. A brisk technician. He made me go and urinate twice, the kidney and bladder dye couldn't work without this. Having fasted most of yesterday, and this morning, I was cold. Lying on my back in the X-ray room, the shabby panels of the ceiling. It is boring, chilling; one is nothing, simply meat, a link in a process. The miracle is that any humanity, anything beyond the process, remains. Too many people, too much to do. Of course the staff must seem indifferent, must seem in a metaphysical sense not to care. Pretending to care, but ultimately not really caring, that is the truth of hospitals. Not that I blame the Royal Free at all. It is inevitable. The staff cope with other human beings at risk, not themselves; they can only do it if they don't really care.

24 March

A bad, bad day, I wish I had not lived it. Tom and Malou and Boris left for France early, and we got up to see them off. I feel appalling sadness, I could burst into tears – and feel envy, too, that they are going on holiday. Absurd, that so much about them annoys us when we know them in the flat above; and now we feel bereft, nowhere to turn. The silence above is terrible, a death. I tried to write a letter to Friend, the Baker, Rooke accountant; impossible, it is so muddled. I am ill, curse it, wretchedly constipated, the pain in my left side. About midday I went out alone, Eliz stayed in waiting for a window-cleaner, who never turned up. It was windy, bright, very March-like, the sort of weather I like as a rule; I walked up Primrose Hill, feeling savagely depressed.

After lunch it turned grey, cold, threatening to rain. We went to the Zoo. Eliz went, bravely, she hates such blustery days. The Zoo is sad these days, and in grey weather like this. It seems to be mainly children and teenagers who go; as if it is not fitting for adults. We stride about, keeping mainly indoors, in the aquarium, to the 'moonlight' house where they keep the small mammals out of their circadian rhythm; in the insect house, which I remember from fifty years ago. Its cruelty, for the mammals, is what strikes one: their various cage neuroses; the jerboas springing monotonously against the glass, even the endlessly circling, pointlessly darting fish. Hell haunts so many cages, once one starts translating them into human terms; that we should condemn so many other species to look like this, half-live like this.

A swarm of locusts in the insect house. The meerkats, the slow loris, the sloth. We wandered back in a spitting drizzle, and then down the Regent's Park Road, miserable, miserable.

Tom Maschler telephoned, at one point. He meant to be kind, but he too feels gone, departed. He is sorry Graham Greene has been sacked; but 'he couldn't take it, there was only three-quarters of a job left for him'.[1]

25 March

I force myself to write a little idea I have for a story, based on the hair-dressing girl at Lyme, Debbie. I had this idea the other day; about human communication. Her murder, but that to be thrown away; not the point, the point being the cruelty and misery of her life, or as I imagine it. As I feel in general, the awful gaps between human beings, our inability to 'feel' across them, to sympathize and empathize. It does not go well, my typing is such a blundering progress these days; yet faintly better than I thought before I began. Some small ideas come.

After lunch we walked round Regent's Park, round the pond, and the southern half. A pair of Great Crested Grebe are nesting on the pond, poor things. In neurotic misery, keeping the countless duck and geese off their 'home'. The heronry has several pairs in station, oppo-site the Holm, on their island. The park has a peculiar distinct human population; old men, rather mournful; people with children, there for duty; couples, that is, lovers, for the partial isolation. There are of course more typical people there: the joggers, and athletes, today (a Sunday) the games-players. The may was in first flower today, some kiosks open that have been shut before. *Iris reticulata* in Queen Mary's Garden, crown imperial in bud. I feel affection for all this: it is some sort of miracle of history that there is a Regent's Park; as some terrible failing, cruelty, of history, or so it seems to us, that I am condemned to seeing, enjoying it now. London penetrates it everywhere, despite the herons, the grebes, the long-tailed tits, the missel-thrushes (calling high in a tree just opposite the heronry island, today); yet somehow it survives, even today, and condoles, however faintly. One cannot imagine, nor bear the thought of, a London, a world, without it.

The endless bread, mostly white, thrown to the ducks. The flight of the ducks, like memories of a lost world. I shall write of this. The Nash terraces, the old men on benches. A little Chinese girl was happily throwing handfuls of rice; the grebe was furious with too closely approaching ducks, its beak half open as it hissed in fury.

28 March

To the Royal Free, to see Dr Sawyer concerning the X-ray. I have an enlarged prostate, my bladder isn't emptying properly. He thinks it is a benign hypostasis, not malign, but they can't tell until they operate. He thinks I should have it done at some period this summer.

[1] Greene resigned after Random House, which had recently bought Jonathan Cape, appointed someone over him to run the company.

30 March

We went back to Lyme, which seems more and more merely a change of scene for the slow nightmare. Eliz hates it, I find some sort of relief.

31 March

My birthday, a non-day. Anna brought a present when she came on the 1st. Lear's *Cretan Journal,* his pretty landscape sketches from Western Crete in 1865. Reading it is a kind of doubly bitter sadness; that all this is so gone, in terms of history; so gone for me now, too. One dislikes even L's anger and grumpy grousing against Crete during that spring of long ago; all those flowers and birds that he could not really see. Poor M sent me something also, some soap and shampoo. She has had a poor winter in the Redcar home. I dare not think of all that; the son in worse state than the mother.

15 April

A phonecall from Dan in the evening. They have been on holiday in Turkish Cyprus. He had bad news. Poor Jonathan flew to Israel again recently, to try and find work. There he had some sort of psychological collapse; was medicated and somehow flown home. The English doctors think some kind of schizophrenia, complicated by sexual problems. Dan says it is his third breakdown of this kind; there was something at York quite recently. Tom had apparently to go and rescue him from some sort of fugue; then before that, when he was at school. In Israel he apparently had his passport stolen, poor chap. The awful ghosts of Alan and Dick, and Bobby, poor Peggy's brother, rise and haunt me; bad genes, sick destinies.[1] Dan sounds choked, embarrassed. Eliz thinks it has been his fault, and Hazel's also, her mixture of placid softness that springs in part from her foolish Leigh-on-Sea need to conform and respect the wrong values, in part from that old peasant stock in the Fowles that I have always vaguely dreaded, as well as respected; the ability to suffer through generations; not to fight life, but just to endure it, fecklessly. Here and there, as with Hazel, to *want* better, but even to allow that to mislead one, to chase false ideals. Not that Eliz feels that we have anything to boast about, in view of Anna, the mess she makes of her life. I sometimes think of some great test for all the world, of the fitness of each to live or survive; the Fowleses would not pass it. They make me feel helpless; as I do myself, since I am part of them.

[1] The example of these relatives offered some grounds for the conviction that the more usual fate of a Fowles was to live an unsung and insignificant life. Alan was the half-brother of JF's father. An asthmatic and physically weak, he lived with his mother and then his brother Dick. JF's cousin Bobby was sent with his brother Frank to a children's home, after both their parents died. Eventually he settled in South Africa, where he spent the rest of his life living with his sister Peggy.

Dan has inflicted on Jonathan his own life-pattern, inflicted on him by his Indian resident-magistrate father; always in the shadow of a career-brilliant elder brother, poor Dan, as Jonathan in the shadow of the twins and of Katie. He is somehow non-existent because so unwanted; in my shadow also a little, perhaps, poor devil. They have kept Tom back from art college, to help. Simon is seemingly of less use, Tom has the goodness and kindness. Eliz spoke with him yesterday. He does his best. I would like to write to Jonathan, but T thinks it useless, he is locked away in his own world of misery and drugs.

If only I could think, and write; even this sad event seems to happen in another world, to other people.

Joan Walker was talking yesterday (Saturday the 16th) of being depersonalized, of not feeling really who you are. On top of this, the Royal Free wrote yesterday. I am to meet the consultant urologist, Kaisary, on May 25th, to see about the prostate operation. No France, no Greece, alas. Greece flowers now; it is already too late.

Not feeling who you really, actually are: like being a spectator at your own demise. Of course what happens is intensely personal, but it seems not, as in a dream happening to someone else, as in fiction. I suppose this is in a sense a sort of consolation: that one can see one's own life, however miserable, as a novel; as not truly real, even when it is happening.

And the Fowles. There are many rabbits this year, I see them at the edge of fields, mildly browsing, inoffensive, timid. That is Fowles. Not what Darwin called for.

17 April
A Sunday, the weather is in a dreadful grey sea-misty phase, as heavy and oppressive as lead. It depresses us terribly. This morning Janet Fillingham rang from Anthony Sheil. The BBC have refused to take up the *Daniel Martin* option. There is a nasty little piece in the *Sunday Times* about it. 'Many critics found it unreadable, now it has proved unfilmable.' Apparently it was the new drama supremo, Yentob, who decided to drop it. It does not surprise me, really, it seems they were costing production at around the six million mark. I just feel numb and hurt, hopelessly wounded. They decide, I suffer. Apparently they tried to telephone me about it last week, and couldn't get through.

18 April
I spent most of grey, dreary today reading old diaries of 1963; trivial and foolish they seem now. Except for the accounts of Greece and America, here and there. I had promised that on the US, the beginning of the film production of *The Collector* in Hollywood, to Dan Halpern and *Antaeus* in New York; gone with the wind, of course. I can find only the original, not the 'edited' version I made once. All in it will be dead

by the time it could be published, as the original stands. Why did one write like this – truthfully, but unpublishably, in libel terms?

19 April

Mist, fog, it seems eternally. We went to Whitford, opposite Musbury. A dull village, the mistless weather there listless, the dull waiting of spring. We walked up on the Shute Road, under a railway bridge, then a little up an old care-lane to Shute House. Eliz, it seems inevitably, in a bad mood, in a temper with me and my dullness, my uselessness. I can't blame her, who wouldn't be? A heron by the weir of rocks at Whitford Bridge; close, yet difficult to see. In breeding plumage, very fine. Some swallows also. We had a M & S stuffed chicken that night, and I dosed myself with Quiet Life. My misery is intolerable. I hate myself.

21 April

To Honiton. We went to see Charlie's gallery, pretentiously called 'Honiton Fine Arts', in the west of the town opposite the Dominoes restaurant. His old neighbour and Eliz's partner in the antiques days, Yvonne, sits in there, a tiny house C has 'converted' into a gallery, and full of absurdly over-valued (in aesthetic terms) and overpriced (in commercial ones) pictures and watercolours. Yvonne is cynical about it; no customers have come in, she sits there wasting her time. We chat, but can't offer much better hope. It is all poor Charlie still scrabbling after his dream of being an accomplished art-dealer; and rather pathetic. One can't succeed with little hand-written notices saying this is a 'nice painting' or a 'skilled watercolour'; useless telling one's would-be customers what you hope they'll think.

We drove up the Chard road, the A30, and then off down the Stockland one, and then got lost in the upper Yarty country, to Eliz's despair. My fault, I no longer seem to have my old directional and map-reading ability. We end at Case Bridge, for what it is worth; a nice stretch of purling river, but nowhere to walk, so we go on down to the Beckford Bridge, and start walking south down the left bank. Not propitious, yet it became a strangely soothing, water-meadow walk, under the shadow of the farms high up the hills to the east. That rare thing, a faintly magic place, haunted by a past. We drove back over the lane that runs past the three farms above, and comes finally out at Castle Hill in Axminster. Odd, that little corner of country; locked away.

One needs some phrase for these last niches, memories, of a simpler past; I find them infinitely touching now, I suppose partly because I mourn my own past, the collapse of the world I was brought up in, that I loved, still love where it is not quite crushed, as in parts of France and Greece. It is like being in some slow flood of death, everywhere the death of the old world. To be sure it was always blind, foolish, greedy for its human part. Simply in the past it could not destroy itself; now it does. Armageddon is not nuclear war, but self-strangulation, the pressure of a hopelessly overpopulated world, even here in England, on itself.

22 April
With Leo, to Sidmouth. We took her afterwards to Dunscombe Cliffs, between Salcombe Mouth and Weston, the woods partly hiding the endless caravanville they have there. Then back to Branscombe; supper at the Masons' Arms. It is a rich man's pub now, where executives bring girlfriends, that sort of thing; gentrified like the village itself. Leo lives still in a dying world, and thinks only of her little garden at Axmouth. I took her a *Viola rosea* this morning. It and seedlings flower well east of the lawn here, in the shade of the old 'cedar'. She gardens well still; we find her alternately maddening in her absent-minded way and sympathetic.

23 April
Saturday. We went to Clapton Court gardens near Crewkerne, but had picked the wrong day. It was not open, though we wandered up near the house and garden centre: closed, closed. A small boy raced round on a bicycle, some radio blaring, ignoring us. We went back through Drimpton to Broadwindsor then west of it on the Birdsmoorgate road, to where the ridge-track up Lewesdon begins. Bluebells just beginning, many patches of wood-sorrel. A strangely deserted area, not a soul about, over and above the sheep-pastures to the north and south, eventually into the beech woods and bracken. From the north-east a strong, cold breeze, but down the south-western slope, in the sunshine, warm. Where we lay and rested on the dry bracken, high above the green Marshwood Vale. The whortle-berry bushes in flower, fat little blood-and-water bells. Some bumbles, a wasp, were busy on them. A cuckoo and one or two swallows, but otherwise this high beech-tree and bracken-common world is birdless. We wandered on until we came on the path down to the road that skirts the south side, and runs through very pleasant combe-y, swelling hillsides. The England of Nash paintings, dimly beyond that, of Palmer. That is, so isolated it is haunted still, not real, somehow still waiting. Space, bosom-curves, springs, greenness. Lovely almond whiffs of gorse in bloom. Beyond Brimley Copse farm the lane curves into the hill, beautifully deserted. In one field two little groups of grazing roe deer, three in each; in another, a solitary deer, standing alert and suspicious in its very centre, then trotting up to a furze-brake just before the trees start. It stands a few moments, watching us. Such wildness, such isolation still, that today no one passes here. From there we come past the nice-looking old farmhouse at Wall, half-hidden even at this time of year in its trees. It intrigues us a little; what lucky recluse lives there? Then finally up the steep little hill over the ridge of Lewesdon, to where we left the car. This long walk exhausted us, but pleased me deeply. I did not want it to end. Eliz is brave. The up

hills exhaust her, but she manages. Somehow good temper returns, to both of us, on them. But these excursions are not walks of discovery in any proper sense; much more of reconstituting loss, both in terms of cultural history and our own lives. How lovely this land can be, on such a peaceful, manless, sunlit spring evening; and how it is going, going, no one shall know and feel it as we do.

A lovely evening walk, I was exhausted when we finally got home; then could not sleep, that kind of hell.

24 April

Anna rang. She got back to Bristol yesterday. She has been on Spetsai and Hydra, it seems; bad weather up to the last day, it seems also. I tell her of our walk yesterday. I cannot express it. She is full of Greece still, of all this country lacks.

That is another horror now; no one can see England any more, they are dazzled, blinded to the beauty of such landscapes as Lewesdon and its southern slopes by abroad, the public myth of abroad. Here I too have sinned, God knows. To long for 'abroad', when this paradise is only a few miles' drive away. We are mad.

27 April

With Muriel Arber, for the day. Devon Books produced her *Lyme Landscape* earlier this week, it seems to me quite well, and she does not seem unpleased by it. We took her for lunch at the Bovey House Hotel, now under new management. The old order of things, or rooms, is changed. I found it vaguely stifling, boring. Rain. We went on to Sidmouth, where Eliz had promised to search for Muriel's godmother's grave. We at last find a huge cemetery, it looks impossibly full of the dead. I go to a man mowing, and surprise, he is helpful, he will go and look in the book if I can supply some details. Ethel Sargent, spinster, died 1918. He disappears, then comes back with this book, and jollies us to the north. It won't be here, this is unconsecrated ground; something oddly cosy and chatty about him, almost as if all these ancient corpses were still alive, and his pets. Some of the graves have iron stickers, vaguely like the tee-number markers on some golf-courses. Suddenly, at a cross-park of amelanchiers, is Ethel Sargent's grave. It announces she was a botanist, it seems one of those first scientific ones; who had worked with Muriel's own mother. Muriel is happy and pleased we have found the grave. I find the whole experience deeply morbid in a gentle way, and futile. All this careful attention both once and still paid by the living to the dead; a most powerful sense of the sheer uselessness of it all, of its rather pathetic vanity. I tip the young man with the grave book a pound. He at any rate was eager and kind to us delvers among the dead.

We were back in Sidmouth by five, only to find all the tea-places shut; absurd, as if there were some law: 'No one shall serve tea in this town after five o'clock.' But Eliz persisted, eventually we got tea and biscuits in the lounge of the Riviera Hotel. We chatted till seven, then went home, a golden evening at last. Muriel's quiet common sense relaxes finally. She wore a black beret, was dressed, as always, like some elderly Girl Guide, austerely practical, stout shoes, woollen stockings, a fat grey canvas bag in which she carries her camera and other impedimenta. She is a brave old soul, nearly in her eighties now; a very distinct character, both literally and in the collo-quial sense. Twelve years ago, in 1976, she had cancer of the breast.

Joan Walker's expression 'bud-haze'. Muriel wonders if it is a proper word, or her invention. It makes sense especially at this time of year; the beeches, half-bare, yet veiled in their own leaf-mist.

28 April
A bad, bad day; a fine one, hazy-fine, in itself. I slept rottenly, it seems not at all, which becomes 'as usual'. Peter Benson comes and does some digging in the garden, which runs more than ever out of control. April is slithery and syncopated, so fast over, with all the flowers rushing out, the birds rushing in. It is ended almost before it begins; overgrowth rules. The *Cantua buxifolia* I bought at Forde, which was full of buds, has grown miser-ably, all the buds have dropped off, and many of the leaves. I feel exactly the same; feeble and ill, like a sick plant. Letters came from Speller, at lunchtime post. I owe some £70,000 on corporation tax, it seems, possibly some £23,000 more, this is for the tax year ended April 1986. Awful; I should go to London to see him about all this mess. Cannot face it.

29 April
I took more of the Quiet Life pills, mercifully slept well. The mayor, Dennis Applebee, came to discuss the Museum. He is like a great ball of cotton-wool, poor man; a spreader of oil, a clumsy diplomat. He too wants to have the curatorship decided 'democratically', he will try to manoeuvre the May 9th meeting so, and avoid alienating Albert.

We rushed from him out to Seaton to do some shopping; maddening (bank holiday madness) crowds in the shops, the weather has changed, it rained in the night, it is cold. Rather frantic rushing round Seaton, the worse alternative to hell.

Then back to Lyme by one to meet Anthony Sheil. He comes down this weekend to stay with his sister and her husband at Yeovil, or East Coker. We lunch at the Alexandra. He is sympathetic and gentle as always. I try and convey what a mess I'm in financially, how much the foolish virgin. We buy some wine, and he takes it back up the hill for us; then comes out for a walk, along to Underhill Farm; the grey day, a cold wind in the sycamores, the farm seemingly more ruinous than ever.

A cat watches from the window in the hut beside the house, in the room where I wrote *The FLW*. No humans.

Home. He has a quick cup of tea. We agree we are both very fond of him. Find him endearing, that he ambles like some eccentric knight, some weird Irish Don Quixote, through life. Awful sadness, when he goes; I keep wanting, on such occasions, to embrace him with tears in my eyes, emotion, emotion; and of course let him go dry-faced and unemotionally. How one regrets the English dryness on occasion; that of course one can't sob, moan, be tearful.

30 April

Denys and Monica drove down from Shropshire, arriving about four. They will stay only the night. I am fond of them, of course, but they can't realize this horror. We have salmon, drink too much wine. For the first time I feel envious of Denys, his calm, quiet life, his going next month to Italy to inspect some school in Brindisi; even Monica's independently going on teaching, supporting herself. Eliz is a worry for me in that she can help neither us nor herself there; cope with my financial collapse, our collapse. Money is even less real to her than it is to me; either there, or not. We are suddenly aware of this, that we are, after years of always 'having enough', nearly broke, in a mess.

1 May

We walked out to Underhill Farm, as we did with Anthony on Friday. It crumbles, is empty; two cats. Monica and Eliz remember our time at Pembridge Crescent; Monica was staying there when Eliz and I had some row, I left London early and alone to come back to Lyme, to Underhill Farm. I cannot remember it; even worse I can't remember Pembridge Crescent, the flat. I strain: nothing. It is a total blank. Apparently I eventually let Cathy Porter take it from us; I can't even remember that. It appals me that Eliz and Monica remember; and I, nothing.

They leave again, about four; absurd iron in their resolution; and leaving us feeling bereft, at a terrible loss. Denys had made us laugh, in the old way, his being bereft at the lambs going to market for slaughter, near Clun. We are his lambs now, though neither they nor ourselves realize it. We envy them Michael also, now a town-planner in Hong Kong, it seems comfortably established in terms of salary and so on, disappointing them only in not marrying and having grandchildren. We groan a little about Anna and her ended marriage, her inability to earn. We say we wish she would try again with Nick, but know that it is a lost hope. It is like some perverse fate, it seems life will never be kind to Anna, nor she kind to life. I see the Sharrocks thinking she must be well off because I am well off. Little do they realize.

3 May

About four, I make Eliz drive us to the Charmouth Forest, off the Crewkerne Road beyond Hunter's Lodge. It is grey there, it seems to amass cloud. We plod, it seems endlessly, down the foresters' unmade roads, out into the open country south-west of it all; then march all the way back. Bizarre, this corner of country; how totally isolated and conifer-remote, somehow dead and as if from the heart of some huge continent. Eliz hates such country, in such weather. Yet I feel very close to her. It is somehow symbolic; our isolation, our plodding on for what seems miles. I suggest we go and have dinner at Hunter's Lodge on the way back; which we do. Wretched place though it is. Yet I happily stuff myself with some pie and overcooked vegetables, a pint and a half of beer; happy that we finish doing this normal thing of years ago after that strange solitary march together.

Life carries us backwards in some strange way; to want to taste what is now lost.

4 May

Reed and two other men come to replace the central-heating boiler, as arranged; but seem puzzled by it all, the piping system, why we have never heated the water off it, but off the Aga. I explain it is because of this draughty old house, we decided at the beginning not to control the heating thermostatically, or use it to heat water, because of potential fuel bills and expense. The two men stare at me, it seems not understanding; as if I am a fool. I feel the same with Peter Benson, who comes to help in the garden. He helped me tie the honeysuckle to the balcony rail this morning. It is just about to flower, I won't hack it off. Peter goes off next week to collect yet another novel prize he has won in London. I don't envy him that at all; just re-experience it all vicariously: success – or rather 'success', unreality in quotes.

Eliz wrote a letter of semi-despair to Boxall today, about the financial mess we are in, my inability to cope; and I, by the same post, one to Boxall's replacement, Speller, saying more or less the same.

The obstinate regularity, the fearsome, fixed determination, of nature: how it must go on, must continue, whatever the observer's mood. I've noticed it lately with the thrushes and blackbirds singing. The sort of thing, in an ordinary human context, that would make one say: 'Oh, for God's sake shut up, stop it!' It is sweet, the exuberance, the fecundity that remains; but somehow seems bitter and inexorable also, this season.

5 May

We went to Higher Westwater Farm again, beyond Axminster. Our impression of last time was not false; some aura of the past hangs over it, some benign remoteness. A man raking the garden. It seems he is the farmer, has been there for thirty years. We presume he will be cultured; but rather pleasantly he has a broad East Devon accent. He says the house has eight bedrooms. It was once also a mill. Someone else has the fishing rights, but hardly uses them now. He sees few fish this year. I had been looking up the stretch near the farm just before: few rises, though plenty of mayfly. A pleasant, quiet man, in his ruined paradise.

We went on from there, up the hill and on to Beckford Bridge, then on to Stockland and the restaurant-pub there. I enjoyed this outing, both the Higher Westwater part of it and the pub at Stockland. Life at the moment is a switchback; so abruptly up today, down tomorrow.

6 May

Down tomorrow, a perfect May day; not a cloud its whole length, yet we are miserable. Eliz gives up sometimes, collapses under the general gloom, that awful drive-to-compare that haunts poor Anna also: that others are happier, she ought to be happier, life is not fair, a brooding discontentment. Everything is 'bloody', 'fucking'; she will not try. This mood descends after that reasonably contented evening at Higher Westwater; blackness after a golden evening light, sad though my green-winged orchids made it.

8 May

To Ronnie and Celia's, at Cudworth. His friend Ron Hall and wife Christine (who runs the *Sunday Times* Travel Section) were staying. He was one of Harry Evans' 'men' in the old days, and is now the London editor of the Evans glossy in New York, *Traveller*. An amiable walrus or bear of a man; he hopes for a job on the *Independent*. The world of easy money and word processors, foreign travel, cushy jobs. He lives in Pond Street behind the Roebuck. I just about hold my own, but feel fatally separated from this world, kind though Ronnie and Celia are, or tolerant of us.

11 May

With Leo, to West Milton, to see a former farm there, for sale. Court Farm. It looks rather as if someone started reconstruction, then gave up. Fields up the hill behind, but invisible; various old buildings. One likes the idea of taking it in hand, but oh, the money it would need, the energy.

12–13 May

Bad, tetchy day for both of us. Anna rang in the evening; she has been to London to see Roy, poor man, now in some wretched hospital in SE London after a heart by-pass operation; they have put in a pace-maker. She is depressed by the hospital, by his dying, the fact that Adam, her half-brother, is mysteriously ill with some infection caught in Africa, now lies in bed and won't be reconciled with his father. Judy, Roy's second wife, has bad arthritis; even the active cousin and family support, Keith, is in trouble financially with his new restaurant. It seems a cursed family, almost Atreid as victims of an implacable destiny, though so much more banal. Roy has flashes of his old self, it seems, but it isn't clear how much he registers of reality, of his old world. Anna is upset, of course, and Eliz in sympathy; poor Roy, dying alone in London; the lonely mess of most people's ends. We can neither of us sleep. I have to take three of the vegetarian sleeping pills most evenings nowadays. But not sleeping well seems nothing to the horror of other lives; one remembers the Roys of this world as they were, at their egomaniacal, selfish and self-deluded worst. But Eliz can imagine how they are now, alone and lost. We walk a tightrope over hell.

13 May

Leo comes over from Axmouth, to look at the old police station, in Coombe Street, coming up for auction. We go with her. It is the little brick building, rather pompously and meanly crammed on its narrow site. Cramped rooms. Absurdly, what the estate-agent called a 'bell-tower', hidden at the back of the house, above a little stone-paved corridor with two police cells; heavy doors, peepholes. Somehow touching, their comparative innocence of so many years ago. A cramped and derelict little garden, another houselet, behind. We suspect Leo's daughter will be attracted, but feel it is totally unsuitable. The cells are the nicest part.

15 May

With Leo again. This time she offers us a picnic, then to some gardens near Crewkerne, Hinton St George.

An enjoyable day, though Leo rather cooed over the plants and how lovely everything else was; she sees only what pleases her, in some vague and slightly eighteenth-century Church of England way, snobbish but benevolent; how nice that is, how pretty. She is precisely the sort of person for whom this hideously overcrowded and money-obsessed world was *not* created. And quite remarkably unsour and unenvious; that is what I like about her and I envy. That she can so enjoy what little she has, indeed like a good old-fashioned Anglican. That 'village' contentment, love of established order, of modest or demure good looks, this was a day from the past, of pride in one's garden.

19 May

A walk beyond Monkton Wyld. I walk a little in front of Eliz on the uphills, which she has to take slowly; awful, I turn and see her trailing behind, and could weep. Not that these country walks do not please me; our solitude, their solitude, the way such landscapes still live, faintly survive, beside the vulgar, common bustle of ordinary life. I long to plunge more into them than we ever can. Eliz goes through them a little against her nature, and certainly against her condition: suspicious of all shadow, all damp, all difficulty of passage.

22 May

I garden all afternoon in the silence, sun and wind. The garden defeats me; what does one do? We think the house might make £300,000 now; but the most miserable places now in Lyme fetch up to £200,000. None of them begin to equal Belmont. I do not want to leave this area, for all its faults in town terms; petty politicking Lyme, hellish Seaton.

23 May

To London. That long south-western approach, from Basingstoke on, confirms me in my hatred of the Great Wen; the endless suburbia, over-crowding, antheap of it. Only a sick race on a sick planet could not see the folly the human race has led itself into, the city mania, the way need for money and economic success has perverted every decent value. In London you see it also, a kind of fixed look, half-avaricious, half-determined, in the people going home from the office; of the trapped in a certain way of life.

24 May

Malou. She has come back alone, leaving Tom in France, to look after Boris. To us he sounds a spoilt nightmare; he has been living with friends, including the ear-ringed Keith, in the flat, and apparently drinking Tom dry. He had a row with the Irish Mary, who blew him up one day for his sloppiness and laziness, like any good puritan-Catholic Irishwoman. Poor Malou, she tries to find all sorts of excuses for him, the mess he leaves, his now not working, his seeming lack of interest in girls, tries to excuse his never doing any laundry, all the rest. We fear the worst of him, and for him. Eliz thinks it is like Dan and Jonathan, Boris's relations with Tom, his father. Tom doesn't really care. He worries, but lets Malou bear the practical brunt of it.

She tells us Tom Maschler is ill, or so the Wisemans think. He is in France, it seems, in a kind of exile we cannot believe wished, wanted, from his old friends. Malou says they were burgled in the Belsize Park Gardens house; and have cancelled their purchase of Peggy Ashcroft's old house, in Hampstead.

25 May

Rather a futile visit to the Royal Free, to see Kaisary, the Egyptian urologist; a rather dapper little man. He asks questions about what diffi-

culties I have in urinating; how often, what pressure, and so on. He slips
a finger up my anus, and briefly feels. He can't tell, it seems, about
doing the prostate, he wants another X-ray to check flow-rate; brisk,
non-committal. 'I will see you again.' I am a plumbing problem. We go
down to the X-ray department. I make a date for June 21st, two o'clock;
with Kaisary again for 6 July, one-forty. Irritating, the futility of it all;
that he will decide nothing now. It wastes the summer.

We call in on Fay on the way home. She is not there, but in France.
Alice Maschler is there, lost in her exams, at the awkward age, shy, full
of problems. Eliz compliments her on her legs. 'They're another of my
problems.'

Notes for a story, perhaps 'Birds' or 'Wings' or 'Three Wise Men', three
men who go regularly to Regent's Park, who sit there. Each part of the
Park is stained by the part of London contiguous to it, that is, the lake
in the south-west is very different to this northern part. We walked there
today, a bad day, Eliz in a foul mood, I didn't sleep well, the wretched
pain in my left side increases. Eliz is angry that I want to go back to Lyme.
Our life here is misery, we know no one any more. Malou, energetic and
maloutante, disturbs us with her busyness, all the people she knows. Without
meaning it, she taunts us with her normality. Eliz dreads her talk of our
going down to Spéracedes; and I too a little, though where or how else
can we expect to be invited? The summer slips past and I have an awful
fear neither of us shall ever see another. We are scuppered. I took stale
bread today to feed the ducks as we walked around the lake; even that,
the feeding, and the flowers, the trees and green landscape, however
paltry, is a sort of consolation. We did the same walk yesterday, Sunday;
Eliz groans that I make her do it again. It is the choice of countrysides I
miss from Lyme, having always here to return to the same one, Regent's
Park. A strange day, today; rain, rain, but then in the afternoon splinters
of blue sky, lakes of sun in the clouds, succeeded yet again by rain.

The bean-trees by the south entrance to the Inner Circle were in first
flower yesterday. Children and mothers, lovers, old people. The park
selects, chooses.

2 June
Back to Lyme.

17 June
Terrible, the endless drifting. I answer no letters, read no books.
Occasionally I 'fiddle' in the garden. Ray sent me Marquez's latest, *Love
in the Time of Cholera*; can't get on with it; they've just sent Brian Aldiss's
Forgotten Life; unsavably beta, second-class. He is trying to do what
Ballard did, but can't, poor man. He is in writing terms virtuous and
industrious, like a good shopkeeper's clerk. He means well, like so many

writers. But good writing is not about meaning well. In a sense all would-be writers, all of us, mean well; and perhaps that 'meaning well' is the great disadvantage. It is when we become most pedestrian, plodding, without poetry. Aldiss has the face of a well-meaning vicar. Benevolent, innocent, trusting, conscientious; yet his fiction never sounds quite true, even when evidently based on personal recollection.

29 June
To Exeter, to judge the Peninsula Prize. Fay Weldon and the others there; not the TSB man, though they are funding the prize. I had thought nothing worth winning, but Fay was enthusiastic about *Keeping Faith*, by Steve May of Bristol; which I had found sharp and quite funny in its way, and at least by a writer, not a mere copier of someone else. It is the staleness of people's minds that these competitions reveal. They read 112 this year, as opposed to last year's 190. We didn't discuss for very long, since both Fay and I liked *Keeping Faith* and didn't like most of the rest. I'd really have withheld the prize; but the head man at Devon Books killed that idea at the beginning, and Fay seems to feel that if money is being handed out, then one must seize it. There is something in this, perhaps – that one should help writers if one can. May reminded me a little of Peter Benson, who helps in the garden (and wrote *The Levels* last year); sharp and egalitarian, and faintly hopeless and cynical.

5 July
To London, for the Royal Free tomorrow. I don't want to leave Lyme, to leave the way we now drift through life.

6 July
To the Royal Free. I am supposed to see Kaisary; but he does not appear. Instead, some young intern with a nasal voice. I cannot understand most of what he says. He explains what he thinks is wrong. I tell him about the sexual mal-, or non-, functioning, since he says the only drawback of the prostate extirpation is sexual, some minor loss of semen. I explain I have had no semen for several years. I am sent off to have another testosterone blood-test. He thinks Kaisary will want to operate in two months' time. I am dissatisfied for the first time with the Royal Free. It is not good enough that I am not told all this by Kaisary himself. The young inarticulate had to learn from me what Kaisary had said when I couldn't produce any urine last time. Eliz is fed up, and I too.

We walked down to Belsize Park and went to the Screen on the Hill, to see *A Handful of Dust*, the new Waugh film. It is better than I expected, though too stylish and shallow; it is what today's people like, of course. So elegant, the Mad Twenties. There is not a shadow of serious society or history, of anything but either the very rich or the very feckless. An interesting new actress plays the adulterous wife.[1] The only two 'stars', Guinness and Anjelica Huston, are both bad, miscast.

8 July
Back to Lyme. We leave 48A without regret, during the redecoration. Malou and the new madam downstairs chose a terracotta colour we neither of us like. It is too purply-pink, like some kind of jam. A mistake.

9 July
To Buckland St Mary, for a drink with Bob Robinson, the TV compère, and Ronnie and Celia. He is not changed, a rather too confidently solid, genial man around an emptiness; he is to conduct a series on Dickens. I don't mind him, but dislike his wife, we feel an overassertive anchor; better Celia, burbling on about her garden series. I tell Bob R I don't like Dickens, as indeed I don't; but can't really explain why, in this present muddled state.

14 July
Rain, the year turns, becomes too heavy, too grey and green. There is a weird pair of herring gulls on the roof, absurdly territorial and posses-sive. They watch for me like a pair of stormtroopers, or Stuka bombers, wail, and descend as soon as I can be swooped on; I have their beaks if they can manage it. Insane dives of frightened rage, and they squirt droppings. I thought they must be breeding on the roof and went up there today. They attacked me as soon as I appeared, and even though I could see not a sign of eggs or young. I climbed back into the skylight after a time, but they continued their diving at my face behind glass. This has not happened in previous years; a strange experience.

Peter Benson's new novel, which I think Constable have taken. I do genuinely wish him well, and wish this were better. It is called *A Lesser Dependency*; politically about the British ousting natives (to please the Americans and give them a base) – Diego Garcia in the Chagos archi-pelago. Rather feckless drifting natives. The trouble is that this back-ground is not at all well presented. What is better is the offhand, oblique way his native family is presented. Peter can write, at his best with great economy; but doesn't really know what he is doing, or rather what he can, and can't, do.

We, or rather Eliz, are on a Waugh thing at the moment, following the TV trilogy on him, on BBC2. He remains a very good writer, and a nearly impossible man; Frances Donaldson's book,[2] which Eliz picked up the other day secondhand in Sidmouth, makes it clear what a

---

[1] The character Brenda Last was played by Kristin Scott Thomas.
[2] *Evelyn Waugh: Portrait of a Country Neighbour* (Weidenfeld & Nicolson, 1967).

tightrope he walked, between, for example, finding life absurd yet insisting on conforming; or using his own self-amusement to end his own boredom. He was a black absurdist whose greatest absurdism was his own life: his Catholicism, his cruelty, his snobbism, they are so many misty panes over seeing him. Perhaps the mistake is thinking that the 'dirty window' hides someone perfect. Our age's admiration for him is really part of its general one for style (as opposed to content); the prose equivalent of 'smart' photography, effective design. This does not mean Waugh is not a good writer; but he benefits in addition from a major change in human values.

Waugh is one of those writers who best symbolizes this great moral rift in human, or at least European, history. It began in Victorian times, both because of the writers, like Lear and Carroll, who turned 'serious' content on its head, and because of the constant thousands, exactly opposite, who showed continued respect for the moral and the serious. These latter very largely bored mankind. People like Waugh, Wodehouse and Firbank amuse them. In a way they represent a convenient excuse not to take life seriously. It is all a joke: so laugh; or because it *can* be made into a joke, a sneer or a snigger, life must be devalued. It is of course an intensely selective view of life, so sits well in the consumer societies of Europe and America. Being witty and rude, and a considerable stylist, like Waugh, is a little as everyone would like to be (or 'fun' to read about, if not to be). The old notion, that his views may be wrong, disappears. Since they are 'fun', their wrongness hardly matters.

24 July
Anna and the kids run down for the day. She brings her new *inamorato* or boyfriend, the Brazilian-born architect Charles Glass, who has found her some art work in his Bristol practice, sketching in the trees and gardens in elevations and perspectives. A nice polite young man, we liked him. His grandfather was some quite well-known missionary in Brazil, apparently wrote some books on it; his father also, who married a Portuguese. This Charles is bilingual, having lived in Rio till the age of eighteen; English now flawless. He and Anna go with the kids to Portugal soon for a holiday. He's married, has two youngish children of his own. About that he said nothing, but interestingly blamed his missionary father for having retired to Southport and condemned his mother to this climate. She is a manic-depressive, poor thing. Anna rates him as very good with the children, Tess and William; the latter needs checking all the time, but of course it is unreasonable to expect him to to play the father this early in the relationship. I felt him, on a little walk we did to Underhill Farm, a little too anxious to please them, to curry their favour, and perhaps Anna's as well. But these are early days, and we liked him otherwise.

25 July

I was doing a bit of gardening with a new hook. In full accord with my new physical clumsiness, which infuriates me, I sliced across the knuckles of my left hand; a flap of skin, blood. I covered it in antiseptic, plaster. Eliz is right to curse my stupidity. I curse it myself.

Agnes, old Jack Board's wife, rang. We saw them only last week, in Axminster, and I thought how hale and hearty, bluff and forthright as always, he looked; how I really must tape-record him, now I had more time; and how rich and dialectal his voice was, although I can remember not thinking it particularly so when he worked here. But now, after this general stamping-out of dialect, it seemed rich. Agnes had rung to say the poor old man had died, that day, it seems suddenly. He was born in 1903; it is in a way as if the century had died, a whole vanished way of life.

3 August

Jack's funeral, in Axminster Church. Hymns, prayers, a little speech about him from the vicar. We neither sing nor join in any prayers. Funerals are the most Darwinian of all occasions for me; demonstrations of the final futility of it all, once the life is over. They brought the coffin and hearse up just as we approached the church, at the traffic lights there; which was where we had last seen and spoken to Jack, the week before. We do not use the living as we should; that is what we mourn, not the person. Our own futility.

We hear that poor old Lol or Loll died at Pilsden the other day, it seems unexpectedly – a heart attack? I'm glad I am not superstitious; with old Jack's death also only last week. I went through some of his clothes only the other day, Loll's. I think he slept in our stable some of the time. There were changes of clothing, many old razors, a down-and-out's miserable collection of belongings, including some Christmas cards. His name was Lawrence Kitchen, sometimes he was called 'Lonk', not Loll. He had relatives in Rotherham; references to 'the pit'.

I threw all his gear away; but feel a guilt over him, at not having worried more about his dereliction, which had a kind of additional feck-lessness about it; that is, he did not care what he was become since he left the mines in Yorkshire, it was said because his wife had left him. A sad speck of humanity. Why did we not care? The world grows somehow bare of all its old virtues.

8 August

What I wrote of Waugh, on the 19th August. I finished *A Handful of Dust* today, also Donaldson's book on the writer. What strikes one favourably today is Waugh's economy, his lack of excess in everything, except perhaps the absurd. Donaldson speaks of his 'preference for the absurd over the heroic' and of his being unable to communicate with any but his own very small world; any but those able to consider themselves as the upper class, 'loose and conglomerate', as she puts it. Perhaps the final irony is that he hardly belonged to it himself except by wanting to believe he did; and yet so strongly defined it and its eccentricity. What is good about *A Handful* is how much it leaves out. He had, among other things, all the exquisite taste and flair of the good antique dealer. It is also all a supreme example of English meiosis: overstating by understating.

Denys and Monica came in the afternoon, from Shropshire. I like to see them, and Eliz adores it. For me it is sad with old friends, after the stroke. They seem to escape, like someone walking faster, dwindling ahead; whereas for Eliz the need is to keep up, to be with them. They tease me a little, my hearing isn't always brilliant; I put it on slightly for them. It is partly physical, in the ears; and I think also partly psychological, being so often bored – or deeply disinterested – in what people are saying.

How much escapes. I meant to write down an anecdote I saw (I think) in one of the Somerset books I bought recently in Taunton for the McCullin photographs intro.[1] It concerned a master of foxhounds calling to a yokel outside a pub. He wanted two whiskies fetched. The yokel, thinking one must be as a reward for himself, did so. It was a cold day. The MFH took both whiskies. Not a drop passed his lips. He poured one down one boot, and then the other down the other. This Waugh-like story much pleased me.

I posted the McCullin piece today. It encourages me a little, perhaps I can still write in a fashion. Eliz helped me cut some bad bits out; seldom to be faulted, her instincts here.

1 September

Torn weather, sun and shower-clouds. The last of the grockles are still here, to our rage. Eliz is permanently disgruntled, or angry; I drift on the rush of time, like a piece of helpless flotsam; it is less drifting than rushing down, as on a mountain torrent. This afternoon we went to Charmouth in a bad mood and set out east down the beach; a rough sea, a dirty, litter-filled beach. We walk beyond the people, then on, it is at least a relief to be clear of the litter, though even here there are nasty washes of the plastic litter and the rest where the tide permits. I was looking for the steps up to St Gabriel's, but it seems they have gone. Eliz more and more fed up with this 'pointless' walking, she thought the tide threatened; it didn't, but it was quite a walk. It horrified me that we walked so in silence, like two creatures in their separate limbos;

[1] Tom Maschler had invited JF to write an introduction to a book of photographs by Don McCullin on the countryside that surrounded the photographer's Somerset house.

I usually ahead, she behind; oblivious of fossils, anything else, plodding endlessly over the shingle and strange 'hards' that here and there underlie it where the pyrites leach out. Then all the way back to Charmouth, into the wind. It began to rain, and soaked our clothes; a bitter walk, so absolutely without affection.

2 September

We hear from Ann Hudson that Betty Allsop crashed on the way home from staying with them the other day. She came here last week, infuriating us by arriving late for tea on the day we were going into Exeter; so late, I insisted we left. She had finally come for the tea the next day. She is very woolly-minded, ravelled in her own self, her children, and so on. We pitied her, and were glad we were not she, at the same time. It is by others' sickness that one judges one's own (comparative only) health. The car is a write-off, it seems; and she has broken her ribs.

Phonecall from Lois Wallace in the USA. It angers Eliz, and myself, that she is worried about retaining the agency of me there; wheedles, vaguely nags, across three thousand miles. I am a soldier without weapons, not worth the despoiling.

Anna telephoned; I liked the look of a road near hers when we were in Bristol the other day. Now she has heard that a house is for sale in it. We are to go and see it.

11 September

To Bristol. There is a lot of chicory beside the motorway, beyond Bridgwater; pretty, that lettuce-blue. Later, teasel everywhere. We got off on this trip in the usual flurry; to my rage I could not find the usual Levels and Moors map; terrible, these leaving flusters. We got there in time for lunch, which Anna gave us. We walked round to the Buckingham Road house. It is owned by a solicitor, with a large family; not a bad-sized garden, for Bristol, but we did not like it. That being endlessly overlooked; a cramped, dark basement. Nor did I like the decor, pictures and so on, much; not of course that that would matter if we are serious. But we are not. The solicitor thinks he will ask £365,000; in this area the boom apparently still soars into the empyrean. From there we walked across the Clifton Bridge and up North Road, to the Botanic Garden, which I had noticed was having an open day as we drove in.

Very enjoyable, it is a surprisingly good little garden with many plants, and many for sale, and good greenhouses; a fine selection of insectivorous plants. Too many to take in on such a short visit, but I must think of joining it. We walked back across the bridge. They were climbing at the Bristol end, on what Charles, who claims he was once a mountaineer, says is a severe pitch. As always I could not see why anyone should ever climb for pleasure. Heights I like, but the huge risks on virtually sheer cliffs like these – one slip, and one is done for. The place here is of course very public, you are almost climbing with them; I wondered if that was not part of it, the pleasures of risking your life so under public scrutiny.

They had a very pretty clump of *V. spicata*, the Avon Gorge rarity, in flower at the Botanic Garden; I might just climb a bit for them, but not otherwise.

We took them to Parks for supper. We are getting a little more used to Charles, but he is one of these very dapper young men, of small, well-organized lives, that escape us. We see he does the children good, since he is very patient and forbearing with them; teaches Tess the guitar, my old one, and so on. Apparently he did his thesis on Ruskin; but Eliz says he seems almost totally ignorant of him as a human being; had seemingly never heard of Effie,[1] and so on. We realize that he is far more foreign than he at first seems; really does not think in an English way, for all his cultural knowledge and having lived here so many years. He knows more than Nick, yet is of the same kind, and we wonder what it is in these foreign young men that obviously holds a deep attraction for Anna; or what it is in their English equivalents that repels her. We speculate about Charles's wife, who we think must have browbeaten him, worn the trousers. She does not want a divorce, it seems. He is, we guess, being something now that really he is not; not, on that side of his life, being gentle and caring.

Tom Maschler telephoned. He is back now in London, 'feeling much better'. He says he is pleased with the little McCullin introduction, 'just what I expected'. I ask him if he feels any nearer knowing what has been wrong with him this last year or so. He is sure it is not Fay; he doesn't know, perhaps it was his father's death, 'though I said I didn't care a damn and I really didn't'; perhaps it was selling Cape. He and Regina have sold the Ashcroft house in Frognal. He realized it was going to cost – the buying and the alterations – a million and a half; the house in France is very beautiful, now they are going to buy a maisonette or apartment in London.

15 September

With Leo and Sarah to Hatch Court, at Hatch Beauchamp, on the way to Taunton. We went first to Winsham, where Sarah wanted to look at a house. Hatch Court is faintly disappointing. Not a disagreeable building or setting, the interior with the staircase really rather nice; but neither we nor Sarah took to the various ladies-cum-guides, it seemed one in every room, between whom we were passed.

---

[1] Ruskin's wife, who left him eventually to marry the painter John Millais.

19 September

Peter Benson was born in 1956; he is thirty-two years old. He comes to help in the garden every Wednesday; last week he said he must now charge £4 an hour, so I pay him some £15–£16 for his usual stint here. He brought two short stories he has had published in recent collections today. I like him, both as a writer and a human being. His quickness and obliqueness. They are a different breed from us, I mean my generation. Knopf sent me Harold Brodkey's stories the other day. He is rather the same. I feel slightly that they are speaking a different language; the unsettling thing is that it is the same.

The moon hangs low over the sea, this is Indian summer weather, warm and greyish. The herring-gulls clamour at sea, it is sprat and spratting time. I feel a vague recrudescence of energy.

22 September

I tried today to think of the right word to describe the brilliance of the moon. It justifies all the usual old poetic clichés; gold, silver, all the rest. It is very faintly yellow or yellowish, much more so where its light reflects in the sea, which is truly golden. I think the truth lies in Ruskin's remark about the sky not showing blue colour, but blue *light*. The moon is not a colour, but a light; lambent, not gold or silver in reality.

David Sylvester, in a TV programme on Henry Moore. The distinction between beers and doers. The beers become what they are principally by being born what and where they are; the upper-class landed nobleman is the typical beer, or royalty. The doers are the artists, etc.; anyone who makes his position and importance in the world fundamentally by his own actions, though of course sheer hazard, or luck, must play its part. Perhaps women have always tended to be beers, not doers. Man will have encouraged that, since it leaves more space for him to be a doer.

Kaisary, the urologist at the Royal Free. So much for my absurd old sticking to a belief in the NHS. He was on the telephone to Eliz today. He has lost his ward at the Royal Free; in any case there is such a waiting-list he can only take the emergency (cancerous) prostate cases at the moment. He recommends a private clinic and operation. He thought it would cost some £2,000 'or more' for someone going private like me. Tom Maschler, when I said I still had faith in the NHS managing to get the operation done, told me I was insane. Not Tom being just his cynical old self, or his millionaire new one; everyone else would agree. No one can understand that I am not insured; past fecklessness.

Zilli Sternfeld sent me Frederick W. Case's *Orchids of the Western Great Lakes Region*, a very fascinating incitement to my ancient orchidomania; a lovely book. It is kind of her, after so many years and past gifts, and I feel bad about my last letter to her this past summer, thanking her for another of her contributions to the Museum and being gloomy both about the Museum's future and myself. I almost put her off sending anything more.[1]

30 September

A very fine day, even better than yesterday. Mercifully Leo rang and asked if we would walk on Beer Head, the only way to answer such a day. Superbly clear and warm. The *Spiranthes* still showed in the little field, no longer in flower, but with plump little seedpods. The gulls and jackdaws, the chalk cliffs, the space. We walked as far as where the hill drops to Branscombe. It was very warm, the thorn-trees red with berries this year. I took a camera and, for the first time in years, some photographs. On the way back along the flint road, a creamy cloud in the far east, over the Chesil, threw a lovely opalescence, pearly, over the very calm blue sea.

We joked a little about how good God had been to us, or more precisely, the skyscape, this day. It was very striking when we drove over to Axmouth at lunchtime; how exceptionally well arranged and ordered the sky was, all the way to Dartmoor; neat little fluffy-fleecy clouds, neither too large nor too small, as far as the eye could see. As if there were a God who was a shepherd, and insisted that his cloud-flock keep to strict rules, as in some eighteenth-century pastoral-classical painting.

6 October

Back in London, for the prostate operation. It was absurd, in this morning's post, at Lyme, for there was a letter saying I had a bed at the Royal Free – this, after we had arranged everything to be done privately at Kaisary's private hospital. Perhaps by luck Hazel telephoned, and more or less said the money didn't matter, we should go ahead with Bryanston Square. The Royal Free bed is 'if available'. It still annoys me that Kaisary did not let us know this was about to happen, and that I shall have to pay £2,500–£3,000 for the privilege of the private treatment. This upset us, and we left in a panic, catching the one o'clock train, I felt with countless things undone. We are the very antithesis of well-planned and 'organized'. I write a frantic card to Zilli Sternfeld, desperately dashed off. More and more these days I write what I know is bad – bad in both ways, firstly in not saying what I mean and believe, secondly in a more literary sense, in the words and grammar. I had written a much better

[1] Zilli Sternfeld was a keen gardener and admirer of JF's work who lived in Toledo, Ohio. After a visit to Lyme, she fell in love with the town and over twenty years kept up a correspondence with JF. She made regular donations to the Lyme Regis Philpot Museum, but insisted that she should remain 'an anonymous donor'. After her death in 1999 at the age of eighty-six, with her family's permission the Museum acknowledged her as a generous and valued benefactor.

letter to Zilli in my mind, in the garden, only the afternoon before; but in reality that never got written. It is the fleeting immediacy of this imaginary letter-composing that baffles me; at the typewriter I forget totally what I was going to say. All such writing is on water, the shimmering water on a running stream.

A windy day, but sunshine; the country up to London fresh-looking, green and tranquil. London as foreign and off-putting as usual. The way cities endlessly compartmentalize, divide into little boxes. I can understand people wanting to come to London; but only as travellers, to visit more or less quickly; that people should wish to live here, that is incredible. I find its inhabitants subtly changed nowadays; somehow colder, more concerned for nothing but themselves, as if foreign, on their guard.

The house at 48A, which we haven't seen after its redecoration this summer, shocks us a little. It is less Malou's longed-for terracotta than some coarse shade of raspberry sorbet, not a success at all; now unhandsomely the most vulgar house in this quietly mercantile row. Even Mrs Marks, our rather Golders-Greeny new landlady, is disappointed. We agree we were all foolish to succumb to Malou *maloutante*, being swayed by some notion she had of what would or might look fine in the south of France or Italy.

7 October

Eliz's birthday, what a wretched day for it to be; as usual I give her nothing but flowers and a card, since I dare not prejudge her taste, and we are in one of our usual we-are-absurdly-overcluttered states – why do we own so much, why can we never rid ourselves of more? I bath, we go to the Fitzroy Nuffield Hospital in Bryanston Square soon after half past one. This is the world of the Power; more like a discreet luxury hotel (or a *maison close?*) somehow than a hospital. A dreadful and boring afternoon in a private room at the back of the third floor; the sky a luxury blue, with honey-and-cream clouds outside. It seems that many other of the rooms on this floor are empty. I am angry they have made me come so unnecessarily early, though everything else seems unexceptionable, if private comfort and luxury can seem that, in this age. Eliz books for the new *Tempest*, with Max von Sydow. I try to settle to Stephen Jay Gould's *Time's Arrow, Time's Circle*. We treat all this lightly, despite a slight 'shadow under the knife' feeling. This afternoon seemed to me full of the uselessness of its own waiting, of the futility of it all, and the cost. The weight of so many things I might say to poor Eliz, but dare not, cannot. 'This is how the world ends . . .' it is not even with a whimper, but with near silence and stock phrases. The anaesthetist, a Dr Higgs, and Kaisary come in and explain what they hope to do. It involves a catheter up the penis, then some kind of 'mincing machine' to remove the offending prostate, which I shall be slowly pissing out over the next two weeks. All I should suffer will be discomfort. I bought myself a present, on happy impulse, yesterday; the new edition of Eliot's

Letters, and read that this 'final' evening.

8 October

A Saturday, a sunny day. I am woken at six-thirty, have a shower and don a backless gown; then am wheeled down to the mezzanine floor. I remember nothing more. Kaisary in heavy tweeds is leaning over me. It is a grey day now. I feel a small pain, there is a catheter up my prick, draining pipes; some for liquid introduced, draining and washing, the other for getting rid of the urine. Fine, says the nurse, it is like *vin rosé*; i.e., I was pissing blood, the prostate débris, in an appropriate way. I drowse through most of that day, half read, try to do the *Guardian* cross-word, as Eliz and I now do every day (not the full one, now usually beyond me, but the quick one, absurdly easy), but cannot. It is like some very old age; intelligence flying to the horizon, only flickers. I think I rang Eliz.

9 October

Reading Eliot. It is very enjoyable, lighter and more humorous-American than I expected. Pound thunders and flashes. TSE's endless solicitude about his mother, evidently in part guilt that he had left her transatlantic world. It reminds me of my own useless relationship. I decide I must write to M in Redcar (and do so the next day). I've never really decoded or deciphered what I feel about Eliot. He has always been, of course, 'my' poet, the only one whose words, as with Shakespeare and the Bible, I remember, a kind of patron saint. The great slogan-maker, I said once, as if he were the gifted copywriter of some advertising agency. By that I meant simply to acknowledge his poetic power, and yet also to dissociate myself from him in many other socio-cultural ways, that religiose side of him he generally kept hidden (these letters run only up to 1922, the appearance of *The Waste Land*). Reading him, and of him, is pleasant, inasmuch as the religious side can't affect me. It is like having a patron saint, yet remaining a firm atheist; admiring some beautiful flower, but knowing it is inherently very poisonous yet that this poison cannot touch one. Pleasantly torn between great liking and secret loathing. This is just as I feel about Larkin, of whom I must very soon also write.

11 October

The catheter tube got disconnected in the night, and the runaway pipe leaked. But the catheter itself came out today. Anna, who came up from Bristol on the 9th to sleep with Eliz, and Eliz, came in, Anna on her way home. I have a bad pain in the foot, which Kaisary thinks may be gout. A specialist is to look at it tomorrow. I claim it can't be gout, I can feel something is dislocated. We shall see.

12 October

I manage to sleep without pills, and have a bath. A Mr Churchill-Davidson from Harley Street looks in and feels my foot, not very interestedly; I must have X-rays and blood-tests. He is rather plummy, yet short-tongued; the sort of doctor who makes one wonder how much he will cost almost before he opens his mouth. He also thinks it may be gout, but 'we'll soon know'. I go off downstairs and have a series of X-rays.

Churchill-D. comes in again. I have a badly arthritic joint in my right foot. He puts me on pills, and I am to see him *chez lui* next Tuesday.

It's a cloudy day, rain. Eliz is here, half-asleep, lying on the bed. She has hardly left, towards six, when Tom Maschler appears, so little changed, so much his old self it is difficult to believe he has been ill. He is very ebullient, at his most only-the-very-best-like. They have sold the Ashcroft house, they have sold the one in France, which it now emerges was not really the very best; not nearly old or prestigious enough to satisfy them. Now they have found a seventeenth-century *bastide*, 'only ten minutes from Apt', in seventy acres. They will move there in December. It is perfect, of course; he will live spells of months there when he retires, he says. He goes with Regina to Paris this weekend, as it's their anniversary, sort of.

I am glad to see Tom; he is still like a gust of fresh air, he has the old impresario *panache* and sweep, blowing all objection aside, a naked will, whatever it is that has made him so successful with women. Yet somehow his verve and *pétillant* seems that of cheap champagne; he survives, but he has coarsened. To be swallowed, not savoured.

13 October

Home, I walk a little on Primrose Hill and down the Village. We have coffee at our usual Polish café; the sharp individuality of all I see, even the most banal things: thorn-trees, dead leaves, pigeons, a girl in an absurd coat, apparently lifted straight from a Miró painting, who was wandering about the street.

14 October

An autumn dusk, mild as down, the evening lights gleaming softly. I climbed Primrose Hill. A young man met a very pretty Indian girl there, it seemed by some arrangement, it was what Hardy would have called a tryst. They were very shy and very close to each other. Not that I felt in any way jealous or envious; just the memory of what it felt like to be in love, of what I lacked now, any sexual instinct. I went down into Regent's Park Village, to see if I could buy the new collected Larkin; it is out, but hadn't come in. There is a good review of it in the *Guardian* this morning; Germaine Greer blaming him for his negativity, how his virtue lay in all his statements of failure – which have made him the most typical English poet of this century, the closest to the national zeitgeist. A patron saint I would rather not have, though must, for his excellence as poet. Never mind, for all the sere and the summer's end, both literally and metaphorically, I enjoyed this October walk.

I read the faintly ridiculous, but painstaking Robert Critchfield's account of modern Britain. It was first published in the *Economist* of 21 Feb 1987. Rather gloomy reading for an Englishman, inevitably, as there is so much about the sinking of the sinking island. Difficult not to feel what I have felt all my rather wiser life, that we are historioculturally done for; hopelessly moribund, compared to the USA. Their faith in progress, advance; our deep 'faith' in failure, or seeing some virtue in it. They see themselves always transcending history, 'breaking' it both as one breaks a code and breaks a horse; we are always its 'victims', the mere effects of what it was, caused not causing. Strange this should come when I have been reading and thinking a lot of Eliot and Larkin, our two outstanding poets of this century. It is what set Pound to his thunder-flashing (hatred of England) and drew Eliot himself to England as opposed to New England. In a way TSE must have realized England was in a tragic state, that is, its mood suited him so much better than foolish Gilded America. He smelt a good tragedy, in short. In a dreadful way this applies to England still today. It can smell its own tragedy and bizarrely finds that more interesting than all the cheap attempts – above all Thatcher's – to resolve it. Critchfield mentions somewhere that our train services are terrible: true, but we like it that way; that arrival on time is always slightly a matter of chance, that the service is not as fast as it might be. It allows us to opt out of progress, an inclination which really does suit our zeitgeist. We adore being able to retreat into the past, as into a comfortable sofa. This is also bound up with the two concepts of time in Gould's book, i.e., as straight-flying and as cyclical.[1] Outwardly we may seem to believe in the first; our deep spirit dwells in the second.

This tells me much of my own interest in the past and concern for nature. Nature now becomes the past, in the sense of the what-is-going rather that what-is-gone. In that sense it is my church, where I retreat, a very cyclical church (like all churches). This is why so much in modern life (and modern London) alienates me, why I have such doubts about the political left; that is, my token 'socialism' of the last twenty or thirty years is abraded by the endless pressure of common 'taste' and the common 'thinking' (themselves largely formed by Eliot and Larkin)

---

[1] A study of the history of geology, *Time's Arrow, Time's Cycle* distinguished between straight-flying time, which manifested itself in a progressive sequence of one-off events, and cyclical time, in which phenomena occurred repeatedly according to immanent laws.

that socialism is in itself bad, greed and avarice 'naturally' good. Like so many others I retreat to the cyclical, not least because it is more comfortable; that is, to the consolations of history in all its forms. This is what I was groping towards in thinking of a book I should call *My Gardens*, which would describe gardens both wild and artificial, nature as much as the cultivated, and slide on also to include books. *Gardens*, in short, in the most metaphorical sense. All that is a retreat into the cyclical, of course; also into a great deal of what Critchfield suggests is absurd about England, why it 'falls behind'. This is also why the loss of nature, our favourite armchair, is so terrible to us. Our hatred of Thatcher is that Britain is not leading the war against its disparities. Her solution to the general problem of decline is not credible; we are a historically 'defeated' nation in economic and manufacturing terms, washed out. All this talk of 'wets' and 'wimps', this attempt to bolster or sergeant-major us into a more 'positive' frame of mind, is futile. It goes with the old concept of men as cannon-fodder, of its being possible to understand humanity through mere statistics. We cannot be changed into something we are not, as if by shaking a cat you could turn it into a dog.

This may not make England unpleasant to live in for the time being; we are a train off its tracks now, running wild.

17 October

The 'indomitable spirit of mediocrity' – TSE's phrase from *The Cocktail Party*. I think of this for Lady Dee;[1] slowly her figure dominates Hellugalia, though I can still count that only a project. Eliot sobers. It was both too far and too little 'fetched' as I conceived it. Imagining a new nature and natural history, and a new history, for a country, is fine. I suspect trying to introduce some spy-thriller, James-Bondish element, the women he sees playing tennis, was wrong; too artificial. His own sexual involvement. But the imaginary country itself, Hellugalia, has some reality in my mind now, and Lady Dee herself.

18 October

To Harley Street, and Churchill-Davidson, at the top floor of a plush house. They are enormous, some of these medical palaces, the whole area stinks of money. He gives me back the X-rays. I have a 'moth-eaten' (his word) joint in the right foot, it may be touched with gout. I must come in 4–6 weeks and have a blood test for uric acid.

---

[1] In JF's sketches for *In Hellugalia*, Lady Dee was an old woman who recounts her adventures during a civil war in the imaginary country of Hellugalia, where she had been wife of the English ambassador.

19 October

The actor Robert Stephens, whom we see quite often these days in the 'village', the Primrose Hill end of Regent's Park Road. He is usually more or less drunk. I called old Jack Board a kind of walking definition of 'hale' just before he died. Stephens, poor man, is equally so of the word 'raddled'; always as if he has just emerged from some dreadful *bas-fonds*, the lowest underworld of human experience.

I went to buy Larkin's *Collected Poems* at six, from the Primrose Hill Bookshop; we went on, armed with flowers, to have dinner with Tom Maschler and Regina – and straight into the kind of world Larkin so loathed; for they weren't alone, as we had expected, but with a quite awful American publisher and his lady colleague – Roger Straus of Farrar, Straus, and Pat somebody, whose position, except that she circled close to his flame, wasn't clear. They had been staying at the Connaught, after Frankfurt. He brought out the naked worst in Tom. Endless talk of deals, money, names, publishing gossip. Everything is ground to mush in such mouths, as in some homogenizer. Straus has that awful conversation-dominating voice some Americans command, which insists one hear them out. Everyone is churned down to the same level; the writers them-selves mean nothing, only what deals were done over their work. Straus aired a suspicion that T. S. Eliot was a closet homosexual, which Tom gleefully sprang to support: he'd always wondered also. What irritated us both most was the way Tom was so anxious both to stimulate and to compete in this world.

The meal and wine were excellent, of course. Yes, they had to have somewhere larger in France, weren't they lucky to have found it? The *bastide* near Apt would allow them to employ a *gardien* and wife to look after things. It then emerged that they are leaving Belsize Park Gardens and moving to Belgravia, Eaton Square. They were burgled in Belsize last year; even just this very last 'anniversary' weekend in Paris, in a hotel. Tom says it doesn't matter, the hotel was insured, anyway. What has struck them, I think, is the inane fecklessness of the very rich. Silly talk between the men, how it is impossible to find a 'decent' apartment in Manhattan under a million dollars, in London under three-quarters of a million pounds. I wish I were a Grosz,[1] and could etch such prof-iteering millionaire-pigs. This was a very depressing evening – the loss of two people almost like a drowning, except that, bloated, they are floating into a stratosphere, where there is no air.

Sinister, how the rich and powerful try and pour oil so heavily over troubled waters, that is, other people's envy. 'We're human and ordinary,

---

[1] The German writer and painter George Grosz (1893–1959), whose work offered a savage caricature of German society after the First World War.

like everyone else'; that is precisely what they are not, of course. Jews like Tom and Straus make it so desperately difficult, after evenings like this, not to be anti-Semitic.

Larkin. The power of 'Aubade', of 1977; and 'The Old Fools', of 1973. This ('Aubade') is what I felt when I was doing the Darwin thing at the beginning of this year: the reality of nothingness, the futility of so much we try to obscure that reality by.[1]

Larkin's genius is in saying what people would like to say, to declare what they truly feel; it creates a kind of nakedness, like that in the final oven before the holocaust. 'This is what you really are.'

Hell is a suburban single room, having nothing else to read but Larkin.

20–21 October

>TWO JEWISH PUBLISHERS
>Deals, deals, endless great names, called all
>By the first, of course, as in infant school;
>They knew them well, these millionaire crows,
>These jackal masters – though of what they wrote,
>Of who they were at heart, of thoughts and values,
>Of how they turned idea and phrase
>And what they mean to us guileless goys,
>Nix. Literature, schmiterature, don't give us that.
>We are back to the real, my friends:
>Hawked carpets on the beach at Haifa.
>Dollars, dollars, feel the pile, all is money.
>If it were not a holocaust, it might be funny.

My malicious and anti-Semite contribution to the other evening. They asked for it.

21 October

Ray Roberts came for dinner. He arrived here in England only yesterday. Unchanged, we liked his normality after the horrors of Tom and Roger Straus the other evening. He thinks the New York Graphic Society, the Little, Brown associate, have bought the McCullin book. He laughed when I told Straus's story of LB being sold a few years ago. 'He couldn't

---

[1] 'Aubade' articulated the poet's intimations of death: 'I work all day, and get-half drunk at night. / Waking at four to soundless dark, I stare. / In time the curtain edges will grow light. / Till I see what's always there: / Unresting death, a whole day nearer now.' 'The Old Fools', about being old, appeared in Larkin's collection *High Windows*.

have afforded it. Everything in New York is always for sale.' It seems LB are now thinking of expanding, and among their possible future buys are Farrar, Straus and Giroux. Straus is a Guggenheim, it seems; very rich. Ray's mother was killed in a rather miserable-sounding crash with an oil-truck during this last year; he and his two brothers and two sisters are suing because the oil company wants to pay very little – the death of a woman seventy-seven years old, no longer salary-earning, rates very little. He says wrily that the death-and-funeral did not bring them together, he and his siblings. There is some rift there, we presume over his homosexuality. Ray is a little like a neutered tabby, very reliably safe and unchanging, careful not to flash his claws at anyone – an excellent pet. That sounds condescending, but I do not mean it so, between would-be tabbies and would-be tigers, I much prefer the first. We enjoyed our evening with Ray, the stroll down to Odette's (a nice dinner, I had partridge, we drank a white, then a red, Sancerre).

22 October
Back to Lyme. It fills me with a kind of relief, Eliz with gloom. One always returns, these days, in the expectation of having been burgled. This time not. A mass of mail. The water-tanks have been overflowing, but that soon stops as we use them again.

Curiously the yellow clematis, *orientalis*, has completely ended its flowering while we have been away. It was crowded with buds when we left; now not a flower. Not so the passion-flower, that still has many blooms out.

25 October
I walked over Ware Cliffs, a grey mild day, despite a brisk breeze from the south. But just before dusk a flame-orange sky for quarter of an hour, little tufts of cloud lit up intensely, as in some forge furnace.

26 October
Tom Maschler telephoned. He has seen Don McCullin; they have decided 'Open Skies' is to be the title, rejecting both mine, 'Winterset', and Tom's 'Another Country'. I preferred an alternative Don suggested, 'On the Edge'. But I don't really trust Tom any more. The last thing the book answers to is 'Open Skies'; that is, Tom has funked what it is really about, Don's uneasiness.

28 October
Another fine, sunlit day, very genial and mild. Peter came. He says this weather worries him, it is too fine, some effect of the ozone-layer horror. I know what he means. I enjoy it, but it vaguely worries me also.

30 October
Sunday, a completely cloudless day, though it is colder; but a near perfect autumn day. And yes, too perfect. Absurdly, it worries.

3 November
The weather has turned colder, winter is suddenly here. I have a bad stomach, diarrhoea, I can't eat or drink, which is a misery. I still walk about down town, or work in the garden, in a physically weird way, half blunderingly, never sure of my balance. I feel it very sharply when with other people, as today in Taunton; how sure and adept they are in their movements, how quick and firm, where I sway and rock. I have to think when I move; they just move.

We got off late, and I started to wash out the fridge in the flat, breaking a jar – all this to Eliz's annoyance. She has wretched eyesight problems these days, can see nothing close to, such as labels when she is shopping; nor, in domestic terms, the countless small things a 'housewife' needs to see, the dirt in the refrigerator, and so on. At some point I dug out the old brown envelope in which I keep the seventeenth-century pamphlet facsimile reprints I bought at Helmsley in Yorkshire some years ago; and get lost in one of them. *A certain Relation of the Hog-faced Gentlewoman called Mistris Tannakin Skinker*, originally printed in London, 1640; which must have been a year a little like this one now three and a half centuries later; ominous, with all sorts of contagions and strange 'prodigies' in the air. This stayed with me all day, that wonderful secrecy we bibliomanes have, like a miser's knowledge of his hoard. No one else here will have this book, or may go home from dull old Taunton like me to read it. It is what I feel even more strongly with *Le Faut-Mourir*. It is not in the least the owning its probable rarity; but that so few others will know it even exists. I read now also a Dutch-pirated (*chez Jean Malherbe à Amsterdam, 1702*) *Mémoires de Mme La Marquise de Frêne*. She sounds a foolish, also sharp and greedy, lady. It seems I have read it before, but cannot recall doing so. Such books are my orchard. I begin to like wandering in it again.

9 November
Bush is elected president. He is clearly a yes-man, a mere cipher. It is pathetic that this and Dukakis are all that American democracy can throw up. I wanted, inasmuch as I wanted anything, the Greek to win; anything promised better than Bush and his ridiculous 'vice', Quayle. Bush shows the terrifying weakness of the American system; of amoral, if not positively immoral, men bickering and finagling for power over a stupid electorate. The faces of some of the people supporting these men: they express an idiot-simple enthusiasm, a smug happiness at being swayed, that is like a disease. What is so conspicuously absent among

common Americans is any European scepticism or suspicion of power-seekers; and so conspicuously present, the lethal innocence of the culturally poor. The fact that there is a class of intellectuals well above and beyond all this proves nothing. They allow the USA to be content with itself; and nothing to change. The foolishness, the lack of culture, the imaginative poverty (of the majority) rules.

Why are so many humans unattractive or ugly? I thought this in Taunton the other day; how they are 99 per cent ugly on sight. Why are we so taken up with the exceptions?

16 November
Rick Gekoski, from London, the book-dealer. He is an American who came to Oxford, and taught at Warwick University later. A big, bearded man and Jewish, he reminded me faintly of someone from the Hollywood cinema world. A certain amount of 'big' talk, valuable stuff he hashad through his hands. Tomorrow he is to have tea with Graham Greene, who it seems has some very rare signed Nabokov for sale, etc. Difficult to have too much contact with this world without a feeling of nausea.

Anyway, I sold RG various signed copies and 'likely' proofs of other people's novels; he also took many of the wretched foreign-language copies that clutter the front room (and drive Eliz mad); also the MS of the piece I wrote on Golding, for which he offered £500. The whole came to £1,644. I quite liked him, as people in that world go. They are much closer to publishing than to writing; but I found RG closer to Jud Kinberg than to Tom Maschler, also – that is, fundamentally sympathetic with his salt and cynicism well dominant over the trader self; not someone you are endlessly plunging into phases of intense dislike with. It is always the state of the moon with Tom; whether you feel close and friendly, or circling at an immense distance in the arctic cold of space.

20 November
Ray Roberts rang during this last week from New York, to ask if Little, Brown (or its owner Time-Life) could buy me a word-processor. I begin to feel I have to face this, though I still think it must damage one's writing. All those years of having spelling and grammar drilled into one – it may be partly resentment at so much seemingly wasted effort, but to transfer it all to machine, the knowledge and the rules, worries me. This must bring an impoverishment to the writer, that he will no longer be able to spell and to write grammatically by instinct; and as for word-processors with 'built-in' thesauruses, that is giving one's land – or more exactly, one's imagination – away. The writer must suffer.

I went and saw Frank Lestner, our local 'computer' man, who was helpful – not in the least a salesman. He thought I should ask as many writer-users as possible for their advice. We went to Ronnie and Celia's for supper last night. They both have Macintoshes, but their main use is for journalism, of course. I don't really think Ronnie can write very well, and Celia seems mainly driven by her neuroses (that she must earn, always be 'on' some book besides the newspaper and magazine pieces). They are strongly 'for' their machines, of course; and I suppose my own worries and disinclinations must strike them as highly theological. Quantity dictates their view; quality ought to dictate mine. They were very kind yesterday evening; yet I felt a long way away, psychologically or temperamentally.

23 November

An intense moon last night, bathing all around the house not in a greater reality in any normal visual sense, but in a more imaginative one, a more poetic one. The garden seems curiously alive; figures must stand, ghosts must walk. I think this is why strong moonlight is so closely associated with the supernatural; it somehow breeds potentiality, its viewer becomes more novelist, more poet, however mundane and anti-sentimental his or her normal nature. A curious *waiting* presence about it, like a tree that must burst into bud.

This morning also nice, a benignly clear sunlit day to begin with, making all, Black Ven, the beach at Charmouth, parklike, augustly pastoral.

We caught the three o'clock to London; jostling, overcrowded, in a hurry, as usual.

24 November

To see Kaisary, at 6 Devonshire Place. His waiting-room is full of what look like Egyptian villagers. They surround him when he appears, shaking his hand, like eighteenth-century suppliants fawning round some rich man. One is suddenly in the Middle East, not staid old London. This visit was mainly to discuss the sexual situation, my impotence. Eliz thinks we should leave it alone, the thought of our ever 'having sex' together again alarms her; all that, for me, also feels a country for ever lost. It is odd, since I do not feel totally deprived of sexual feeling, say in looking at women casually encountered in public. I can see Eliz remains attractive for her age, vaguely physical attractions in other women I know, or see in photographs. But the mechanics of sex – only some vague Neanderthal (very primitive) instinct makes it possible even to contemplate that; Kaisary, nice little man though he is, makes it doubly impossible. He said the first thing to discover was whether I could not get an erection because of failure in blood supply. That meant seeing if I had sub-erections when asleep, which would involve sticking little rings of perforated blue paper round my penis, and seeing where they tore, if they tore. This was too absurd, I think we should both have

laughed in other circumstances. My testosterone count was low, it
seemed, but not totally lacking. It was up to me. He sent us away to
think it over. If I do nothing it will cause no harm, he says; though in
some way (some lingering folk-belief, perhaps) I feel it must, psychologically. Eliz treats this, in bad moods, as all my own fault, my indifference, my not having wanted to think about it when – say five years
ago – there was still time to do something. (When the nifedipine pills
I now take every day had not yet had their deadening effect.) It is a
castration, in effect; in a sense it separates me from the rest of
humankind, or their common experience. But being a novelist was
already a castration of a kind. In some way it puts one into another
world, a distant future. All this is like the moonlight the other night;
casts strange shadows and lights on the familiar. I haven't really absorbed
its implications as yet.

26 November

To Ayckbourn's new play, *Henceforward* . . . ; at the Vaudeville in the
Strand. It was amusing, even funny, during the first half or act; but
becomes less so in the second, a working-off of bile against many aspects
of modern life, the incipient fascism, the young, our general surrender
to the electronic machine. With which one can hardly disagree, in this
year of disgrace. But something about Ayckbourn displeases, some vogu-
ishness, some slickness; it is somehow haunted by the ghost of classical
comedy, or rather, not, showing an absence of its spirit; that is, something is missing. It is all finally a touch synthetic, artificial.

29 November

I bought Johnson's *Rasselas* in a new OUP edition. Strange, how enjoyable
it is to read. I must have read it before, but cannot remember a thing
about it. I bless this total oblivion that descends on my reading in the
past, and so allows me to read as if for the first time; yes, in a way I wish
I could see what I thought of it before, if I bothered to note it here.
That would be the ordered, the Johnsonian reality; not this seeming to
enjoy an eighteenth-century masterpiece so freshly.[1]

What I felt immediately is that *Rasselas* gives me a great clue, or
guide, as to how to write the Hellugalia novel; that no more needs to
'conform' to Albania, or the Balkans, to whatever vague real model I
had in mind, than *Rasselas* did, or does, to Ethiopia. 'Research' in the

---

[1] In *The History of Rasselas, Prince of Abyssinia* (1759), Rasselas leaves the Happy
Valley of his birth with his sister Nekayah and the poet Imlac to travel in Egypt,
where he seeks the happiest mode of living. Having tested several options that
include the hermit's life, the scholar's life and family life, he concludes that life
is 'everywhere a state in which much is to be endured, and little to be enjoyed'.

usual novelist's sense, making sure your text tries to reflect some reality, is simply Johnson's 'star-knowledge', largely irrelevant beside his true, or self-knowledge.

I am reading this 'between' or 'among' a proof novel that Tom M has sent, Lindsay Clarke's *The Chymical Wedding*. I am enjoying it, perhaps because my own work, both *The Magus* and *The FLW*, feels as if it lies behind it. It is not always quite successful, but I have found it very enjoyable on the whole, well-rooted in the past, and rich in echoes. A considerable new writer.

30 November

I finish Lindsay Clarke's novel. I wonder if he is not a clergyman himself, he seems so eager to be concerned about 'deep' things. It is written in places, in words and phrases more than in paragraphs, to a high level, but in the end it disappointed me. It is all too sensitive, and becomes a sight too narcissistic, its actors all taking themselves too seriously. The overemotion of the Victorian characters seems absurd today. It is all finally too involuted and mystical, the characters seem in a dull rain. But it promised well, for all its preciousness, and has a number of felicities. Serious matter.

2 December

In the evening with Malou to see *Distant Voices, Still Lives*, perhaps the most praised English film of recent months (director, Terence Davies);[1] which disappointed us. It is truthful in an anthropological sense, as the observation notes on a particular tribe, the working classes in the 1930s and 1940s; but is of artistic pleasure only in its surface truthfulness. Too much of a heavy, slow-panning camera, and far too much reliance on the popular, half-American music of the time. The characters seem capable of expressing themselves only through this derivative music, the pub singsong, and so on. What is not clear is to what extent it is a nostalgic harking-back to the 'people', the back-to-back life of mid-century; how much we are expected to look back on all that with some sort of regret and longing. In Eliz's and my case, it was much more with revulsion. We (she especially) had to live through it and don't want to be reminded, especially if we are being told to remember it all with affection. I suppose the film might have been intended as concealed satire, but all the evidence is not. I don't wonder it was not given the prize at the recent Berlin festival. This is why the British are neither understood nor loved in Europe. Why are they so proud of their inability to enjoy life, their lack of *joie de vivre*, of their culturelessness both in

---

[1] Presented through vignettes of memory, the film evokes the experience of a working-class family in Liverpool during the 1940s and 1950s.

'peasant' and bourgeois terms; of their having been steam-rollered first by the Puritan ethos and then by the Industrial Revolution? Flattened, then homogenized. This is perhaps why they are shown (in the film) so resorting to American music; though ersatz, it represented a kind of escape into arrow-time from cyclical time, into the present and future as opposed to the past.

The way most of Britain lived through most of this century was miserable; no amount of family sentiment, nostalgia, political sympathy with the working class, and all the rest, can hide that. All that literal and metaphorical cramping, mental and cultural, social and architectural – the war in a way was a blessing, in that it allowed us, as a nation, to glimpse an uncramped life. An irony, that we saw it as a fight against fascism, of a brave little free country struggling against hideously 'tied' ones. We were, and are, perhaps the most tied of all.

5 December

Churchill-Davidson, who says I have too much uric acid, i.e., gout. His bill is for £110.

6 December

Back to Lyme. A crowded train till Salisbury. Nobody has broken in, mercifully. Tonight was the Museum 'reception', to thank the volunteers, which I had forgotten; and the train was late, in any case, so I did not go.

9 December

Eliz in a foul temper. These things burst out over the normally smooth skin of how we are like eczema; poison pustules over everything. I am forgiven nothing. I know I am gloomy about life, I suspect the worst of everything, I dress badly, I am in a thoroughly bad state physically and psychologically; I know myself, and feel myself, a mess. Poor Jonathan has had a relapse in Yorkshire, it seems. I mention watching a bit of the film *Equus* last night; I am trodden into the ground. I never saw the play like Eliz. I watch the Russian earthquake on the news.[1] Trodden again: the Russians knew it was coming, they could have warned people to evacuate. I won't believe this, it makes them worse than Stalin. I am hopeless, she says, always hours behind on the news; that on TV is 'sentimental', worse than the cheap press. I am like some dog she tortures; what I was as a writer, nothing; the money I earned us, and which we still live on, nothing; my 'interests', nothing. We had the

[1] On 7 December a massive earthquake struck the Soviet republic of Armenia. Four major towns were severely damaged and, according to initial Soviet estimates, 55,000 people lost their lives.

beginnings of all this in London, over the Ayckbourn; which I dared to find, though amusing enough, not a great comedy, by the standards of Wilde and Congreve. I am hated for that. My only peace is sometimes in bed, when I feel her sleeping beside me, some sense of togetherness. She talked tonight of not being able to live any more with me. She cannot stand Lyme, the shops, everything I say and think. I dread the idea of living apart, but she forces this on us, almost as one throws vitriol. All tolerance and goodwill, let alone love, die.

10 December

An exceptionally fine day. I worked for an hour down the bottom, in the very mild sunshine, near the woodcock orchids, showing green in the leaf-litter. As always nowadays I am swamped with the number of things I would like to do in the garden. It drowns me, overwhelms me, my behindness.

I must stress the double nature of man for the Common Ground anthology about trees – the fact that we all have two selves: one, that awful superior being, self-promoted, left us by the wrong side of so many religions – man in God's image, appointed the steward of nature, and so on; the other, much less perceptible and greener, closer to nature, sensing some sort of harmony with it – as I am, on mornings like this.[1] It occurred to me, so much happier than in any other 'world' or circumstances, so much more at one with the non-human world. I have always been 'for' conservation, the protection of nature and all the rest of it – at least since my twenties, when the killing phase was over; but feel this was indeed an intellectual thing. Now it is more like realizing one truly belongs to the other side; that one has always somehow been on the wrong one. I suppose, as many Frenchmen must have realized in the war – not just that they were against the Nazis in principle, so coldly neutral, but that they could not bear their presence, must fight to rid their world of it – join the Resistance. A final revulsion against something one has long disapproved of; now hates. That, in the sunshine, over the blue sea.

13 December

Eliz leaves for London, to go alone to the Cape party; from Taunton, the terrible crash two days ago at Clapham Junction has blocked our usual line.[2] I didn't want her to go; now is like being a small boy again,

---

[1] JF was writing a foreword for *Trees Be Company*, an anthology of poems edited by Angela King and Sue Clifford (Bristol Classical Press, 1989), and sponsored by the charity Common Ground, which sought to encourage people's involvement in local landscapes, habitats and cultures.

[2] Thirty-five people were killed and many injured after a collision on the morning of 12 December involving three trains.

a child, unable to face the solitude, the loneliness. I despise myself, I even despise myself for not going, for not being tempted by the glitter, the names, the publishing brouhaha. All I can think of is that I shan't, wouldn't hear half of what was said; that I am too much of a literary wreck, a ghoul, to want to meet anyone, or imagine they should want to meet me. She is worried about leaving me alone; but what I fear is psychological, not physical. I stay partly to get the brief introduction to the trees anthology written; that causes me endless unease, quavers of doubt and indecision. I can write after a fashion here, indeed writing this, or keeping it, is my sole consolation these days. But anything more considered – I could not face other writers because I should be so envious. To command words, it is the impossible.

We sit and do the crossword, as every day, before she goes. I want to burst into tears, I think not so much in fear of what might happen to her, of the 'danger' of going to London; but in frustration and self-anger at this state I am in. Eliz would not call it love, now I am impotent. I lie beside her at nights, in a kind of numb despair, that we are condemned to this. She blames me now, for not seeing a change in our lives was essential; not seeing that her, our, life in this large house is impossible.

I went out for a walk as she left, just before dusk; over Ware Cliffs and the circle round by Ware Lane. There was a razor-bright new moon in a part-windswept sky. The rocky beach, black stones, yellow-opalescent water, a heron motionlessly silhouetted, the cries of invisible curlew down there; it is very bleak, cold though it was not, in terms of temperature, cold at all. I met, alone, at the stile to the Underhill Farm lane, Helen Yool, the chairman of the Lyme Regis Society; a dry, rather austere woman. Chit-chat. Solitary people, on solitary walks at dusk. Then home, to a very silent house.

14 December

In the *Guardian* today, a touching article about real poverty in Glasgow. One cannot think how people stand it, not being able to allow oneself or family the kind of luxury even the normal person of these days would think not luxury at all, but necessity. 'One cannot think' is wrong; one can – one cannot bear to think of such meek, if grudging, acceptance.

A copy of the psychoanalytical journal *American Imago*, vol. 45, of last spring. An article by Julius Rowan Raper on *The Magus*; which I rather liked. At least it senses what I was trying to do – that its ends lay more in psychotherapy, mending the modern soul, than literature. He makes some shrewd comments, not least on where it was inadequate. Much mention of a Heinz Kohut, a name unknown to me;[1] of the *grandiose*

---

[1] Heinz Kohut (1913–1981) was a leading post-Freudian psychoanalyst who conceptualized the psychology of the self.

self erected by most of us (and Nicholas) to counter low self-esteem. Lily
disabuses (my 'disintoxicates') Nicholas too severely and abruptly – this
was not offering 'an optimal process of frustration', as he (or the patient)
needs. I go about all day in a sort of glow of renewed confidence. *The
Magus* did mean something; it is declared. This little surge of, or in, my
own grandiose self is absurd. But there it is. Kohut sounds interesting.
I must try to read him.

Eliz comes back – with the beginnings of a cold, as I feared, though
she could hardly have caught it in London. The evening was a success,
it seemed. Tom Wiseman got drunk. Tom Maschler was there. Eliz
spoke to Clive James, Brookner, the new hopeful Lindsay Clarke, who
is apparently about fifty, with a broken marriage behind him. He worked
for a time in Norwich, in the same technical college as Dan, oddly
enough. The 'Lindsay' was some mistake of his mother's, he used to
be known as Vic. Many others, of course. That world does not tempt
me one bit.

I forgot. Yesterday during that grim walk, I thought of a theme for a
story. It began: 'This afternoon I decided to kill myself.' Curious, though
I wrote, later that evening, only a page, the merest sketch of a possible
beginning, how consoling it was; in short, that despite the miserable
day, I did not want to kill myself; that literature, writing, would always
be my escape. Strangely apposite the essay on *The Magus* should arrive
the next morning.

16 December

We've had to saw down a middle-aged holm oak in the front, as it's
pushing out the wall. I hate having to do it. Quicky would console me:
'Useless, it's full of sap, that timber. Weed, that's what the forestry call
it.' Fools.

To Honiton, which feels very alive after this unsuccessful little town.
We went over Farway Common; the gorse well in flower this year. We
bought a little: a shawl for my mother, a piece of Dior costume jewellery
for Eliz; some fish, some wine. Hideously too much traffic, on the way
back; each slow van or lorry trails ten or more cars. Eliz feels ill, as if
'sickening', throughout. For the five hundredth time it is absurd that I
cannot drive.

19 December

Eliz in a terrible temper all day. Her cold, which I feel growing in me
also. I went down the road to see about new glasses, and chose black
frames I know she will hate. I have failed to keep the deadline for the
trees anthology foreword. All endeavour becomes pointless. Her illness
and despair are like bad apples; they corrupt all around them. She was

cursing our eternal clothes problem here this morning: that we have more than we can store – which is true, but *we* have more because she owns three-quarters or more of them, and won't jettison any. Always to accept, to buy, to want them; and never to arrange to keep them. Never to be content with what she has, ever discontented.

In a way it has all to do with something I dislike intensely in this 1980s culture: the preoccupation with style, *le Look*. All that old tatty, duffel-coated indifference to such things, to one's clothes, to what one ate, that being happy just to get by – it is unthinkable, these days. An article in the *Guardian* today suggests all men need two suits – life gets shallower and shallower in the attempt to force people to be more respectable. 'Respectability' in this sense has nothing to do with any real values, culturally or ethically. Ethics are nothing when being ethical becomes a matter of looks.

24 December

To Bristol, a very watercoloury morning, limpid, aqueous, like driving through a Cotman. Not much traffic, either on the way or in Bristol. We go and buy some wine at the Clifton Oddbins, then later to the hotel where we stay: the Glenroy in Victoria Square, just opposite Lansdowne Place. It is a pleasant room, overlooking the old cemetery of St Andrew's, the blitzed – and vanished – Clifton church. Something about this view, over a plain little back-garden and minor side-road, on to the yews and gravestones, greatly pleased me.

25 December

Christmas Day. We went round for the present-opening. Anna cooked two pheasant for the dinner; and then, when it was early night, we all went for a walk. Eliz and I had already done one earlier, while the dinner was cooking. Bristol is nice at this time, almost without cars or people, in a way a ghost city; what it once was, or Clifton was, is acutely strong, and makes one realize how much has been generally lost by the wretched motor-car, by overpopulation. Too many people, that is the great curse; curiously echoed in our St Andrew's cemetery, very powerful with its silent screaming, its remember-me, remember-me. So much effort was put into the graveyards of the well-circumstanced like this: effort of orna-ment, of religious texts, of well-phrased hope; army officers, naval offi-cers. In one place we went through a gate in the railings that line the main walk, which is a sort of birdcage walk. By day pigeons, goldcrests, blackbirds, a squirrel; it is an excellent nature sanctuary, also. A tasseled *Garrya* grows at the north-east corner. The tombs seem mainly of the late Victorian period, from the 1850s on. In the evening we walked round the Polygon, and back through this 'dead' cemetery; perhaps it is especially nice because there is now the church and it is so derelict, brambles and ivy everywhere, dark grey and dark green, the speechless words of inscriptions; for they begin now to erode away, to become illegible. It asks for some ghost story here; but not merely to frighten, to 'play' on the supernatural; much stranger, something of the futility of it all, at least of the hopes the dead, or their friends and descendants, now long dead themselves, so vainly sent into the future. A curious place, tenderly foolish in an outwardly macabre sort of way; in reality rather poetic, the very present nature there today so much more still-living than all those old bones, corpses, Victorian hopes. It all seems a huge Victorian madness, all these worthy attempts by the well-to-do merchants and distinguished men of so long ago to survive; like some weird cavalry charge, of a totally static and very heavy brigade, thundering mutely into nothingness; such a mania for appearance, for doing the done thing, dying in the right way.

Suicide story: why it is not real. The 'I' sees another suicide, so gives up his own.

The cemetery, no, the *graveyard*. Like some huge merchant venture, so typical of the old Bristol, that failed totally; and that the modern city, and its inhabitants, cherish a past folly, consider it an amenity. The more normal ruthless drive in our own age would seize on the space, the site, and 'utilize' that. Perhaps the 'I' is an architect, on a first prospecting visit.

27 December
Back to Lyme.

30 December
To Axmouth for lunch, in the pub opposite the church; where we came on John and Jean Loveridge. He looks and behaves more and more like a heavy and port-sozzled eighteenth-century squire. They start next year a new preparatory school at St Godric's in Hampstead, it seems, having diminished the foreign students' branch. John himself has become obsessed by painting, now wants to publish a book on it. How is he to do it? I promise an introduction to Anthony Sheil. We heard recently from Leo that the Bindon estate proposes a by-pass around the village, which must take them to the west of the present road – on John's land, of course. I secretly fear it, for the potential damage to the river and its bird life. They seemingly (the Bindon estate) propose to pay for this by development building along the line of the new road. The son, it seems, now runs both the college in London and the Bindon estate. I can't feel John himself, for all his Tory crotchets, mania for Elizabeth I and Churchill and all the rest, would be a threat. Something in his very unreal and protected life means well (or would not support true development evil); but his son – I fear for Axmouth. That stretch of water is too tempting

for the exploiters; with a dam across the river, where the present Trevelyan bridge is, the prospect would be hideous. It could not endure in peace.

All this came with the arrival that morning of a (for once) formidably good number of *Time* magazine, dated the 2nd of January. It is devoted to the manifold threats to the endangered earth. It says nothing new, but makes it clear overpopulation is the main threat. This is what I was already saying in my draft to the Common Ground introduction: the Devil is too many people. John L, Sir John, says there is enough food in the world to feed everyone; he is angry a trade war threatens with the USA, affecting agricultural products, he believes in free trade, etc. So silly, sitting there like a swollen mouse in his squirearchical comfort and mouthing all his Panglossian optimisms. 'I live in great comfort in my Elizabethan manor up there, why is the rest of the world not like me?'

1 January 1989
Lyme is a town of burnt-out cases. Poor Doris Winter reminds me of this, and the widow Helen Yool, who runs the LR Society; both somehow reproachfully mournful. It is reflected everywhere in this town of retired people, left like some detritus after a high tide, stranded above reach of further water. People whose personal high tides have all passed; from whom everything that life made enjoyable has receded. They are all people of the day after, never of the day itself.

The gulls hanging in the air (grey cloud, a steady western stream), quartering and patrolling. They are at their most vaguely ominous, like this, most like pterodactyls. Only too fit emblems for the *Time* article. I struggle on to get the Common Ground foreword completed. They can pay no money, so Eliz feels it is a waste of time.

4 January
I meet Doris Winter down town. How is Bert, I ask brightly. He is dead, he had been cremated at Exeter only that morning. Did she think it was, on the whole, what they call 'a blessing' here in Lyme? Yes, she supposed it was. I had, through the usual fog of polite surprise and condolence, a sharp sense of the real bitterness of loss. We are of the age now when one automatically casts oneself I think less as the real loser, the person who has died, than as the one losing, the suddenly partnerless. I felt sorrier for poor Doris than I could express; one's total futility before that so well imagined and now empty house.

JF, in the garden: 'Sorry, I've forgotten its Latin name.' Peter Benson: 'Doesn't matter. I don't expect it (the yellow buddleia I was referring to) knows it either.' I like this occasional plebeian sharpness in him.

5 January
Liz-Anne seems to have done nothing about the Museum. In many ways
I like her relaxed and take-it-coolly way of being curator. I went down
to the Museum for the first time since Christmas today; the usual chaos.
I fear she will be caught by time.

6 January
The Common Ground foreword. At last, today, I post it off.

12 January
To Exeter, about three. A strange day, one of those whose 'feel', whose
light, makes all that is now seem mean, fallen inadequate. There was a
'gracious' clear sky, all late sunlight, a few white-tipped clouds, honey-
coloured, very peaceful, in the distance. And all the fields like
eighteenth-century parkland, calm and Augustan. I tried to think of a
painter who 'caught' this feeling – Corot, I suppose, in the Italian days.
There is a varnish of very pleasing light over all; which both hides present
ugliness and somehow makes it – by recalling so many days not like this
– more obvious. It is like some very real memory of a lost golden age,
both sweet and bitter. The biblical imagery, of the fallen, of paradise
lost, is very strong. I remember this feeling from Greece, it is not religious in that sense. Simply that certain days and their lights bring acute
remembrance of past delight, both personal (that is, in one's own lifetime) and imaginary (long before one lived).

14 January
A pleasant surprise, by the post; from Knopf, a proof of Sybille Bedford's
Jigsaw, an autobiographical novel, with the background truth, or the
parts missing, of and from *The Legacy*, which we read and enjoyed last
year. Something casual, grammatically light and informal, about the way
she writes pleases me very much; a kind of deft watercolourist of the
1920s kind.

   Also *Granta* 25. I did not like a clever story by Martin Amis; a little
too much pleasure in describing the slick and sleazy side of the world,
of screwing his heel in the face of England. He makes his characters
nasty, but almost as if he can use them as an excuse, if anyone accuses
him – nasty people in a nasty world, what more can you expect?
Something sour in him, as of battery acid.

   That 'green and golden' day we had the other day going to Exeter,
its powerful sense of our having 'fallen' from a more pleasant world or
state. Is not this in part a characteristic of England, because of our
climate and geography? There is a good passage by Bedford in *Jigsaw*,
about the endless sun and heat of the Midi. One can hardly dream of
more perfect climates and landscapes than that. Even that can satiate,

drop one into that peculiar state of discontent we used to call the Aegean blues on Spetsai, a *cafard* that came from being in a too perfect world by the standards of our northern dreams. That is, suddenly we were granted the weather, the light, the superb climate; we then had to imagine all sorts of other things we lacked – fame and fulfilment, women. By 'we', I mean Denys and myself.

22 January

A very fine day. I work in the garden; or fiddle, I cannot call it work. Eliz spends endless hours, after her usual little coffee-klatch down town, reading the newspaper, the wretched *Sunday Times*; as she spent many hours yesterday reading the *Spectator*. This town bores her, as does this half-life we lead. It appals me that I seem unable to answer letters, to do anything, that I drift so. She does not help, share any interest. We talk about books, about what has been on TV. We are happy only in bed, in that ancient warmth. She would not come to bed the other day. As always I could not sleep. I ought not to love her; but I do, hopelessly. We are become parts of each other, both victims, almost totally dependent. The only blessing in our not going to London is that we escape colds and bad chests, all that horror. We may suffocate here mentally, but not physically and literally.

27 January

Yesterday morning *Omni* magazine, of which I had never heard when they approached me a week ago, through Anthony, telephone from New York to interview me about London, its future; some girl, Marion Long. It was absurd. I never could talk well, and even less in this mind-struck state. I should have insisted we did it, as a queries-and-answers thing, by mail. I had already jotted some down, their questions having arrived by fax; but could not get them across by telephone.

31 January

We cannot decide to face London; but think in the end that we will do so tomorrow. It is partly that we manage to survive here, despite Liz's hatred of the place, at its awful winter worst at the moment; though in its weather this winter has been kind. We have played a lot of Scrabble this last week or so; a foolish game, fundamentally, but it keeps us amused. I 'win', usually. Poor Eliz feels ill and weak most of the time; will drive out when we have to, but never just to walk or have exercise. I do not like never going out with her as companion. What comfort we have is being in bed together, the animal closeness; despite the death of sex in me.

We went this evening for our supper at the dreadful Hunter's Lodge pub, as sometimes we do. We despise the food there, but not quite so much as elsewhere. Tonight, not a soul else to eat there. We have overcooked roast beef and vegetables, a tired, tired meal; and a poor bottle of Rioja. When I went to order that last at the bar, round the corner from the absurdly named 'Mr Toby's Pantry', where one eats – the very name, some ad man's invention, supposedly redolent of rubicund cheer, irritates us, as well name an undertaker's parlour a 'centre of contentment' – there is a line of men, drinking their beer. They do not make room. I ask for the wine-list (itself a bad joke); their heads swivel, they eye me bleakly and suspiciously: who's this then, with the posh accent? I see their wives at home, gawping at the telly, perhaps happy to have something like this to keep the men out of the house, wagging their gloomy provincial tails at the bar; all waiting, one feels, to prove they can talk and show off. They now, at long last, are free of the dreadful class gag. I think this is where I must start *In Hellugalia*: in the heart of the appalling banality of provincial England.

1 February
To London, and another form of hell. How I hate it, its overcrowdedness; too many, too many, too many. We had supper with Malou and Tom – and I feel them quite blind to how much we have changed, how different are our values now; or how much the same, as they always were, are theirs. It is like bumping into a tree, or a boulder, in the darkness.

2 February
An indistinguishable cry, a handbell crying. I look out of the flat window. It is a rag-and-bone man, or some sort of last ghost of one, wheeling a hand-trolley, very fast, as if he knows he will have no trade in this plush area. I have not seen one here for years, shall I ever see one again? It is sad, a passage; yet who could mourn that society, the modern world, has no further place for them?

Paul Sayer, *The Comforts of Madness*. This has just won the Whitbread Prize, the judges having clashed on the Rushdie and something by A. N. Wilson; which I can't mind, as I dislike them both. The Sayer is so grim, hopeless, I suppose minimalist, such a paring-down of the human situation that it is really absurdist in its gloom. The 'hero', a mental deficient, sets Sayer a problem; he is too shrewd, since he is the 'I' narrator, and puts it all into words. His bloody-minded withdrawal into himself is credible in reality; but not that he could analyse it and write about it. But the atmosphere of total futility and gloom is some kind of achievement.

The poems not written, insights not recorded, savourous or beautiful moments not fixed, 'set' as one sets butterflies, treasured things not kept; all fluid, melting, vanishing in flux.

We went to see Speller, for the 87/88 accounts. Speller gabbles figures, alternatives, possibilities. I am not to worry. I sit there, worrying. He wants me to increase the pension-fund premium. Already I feel that largely futile. We shall not live to enjoy it. It is just another of those maws into which money has to be poured. We do not discuss the possibility of my writing something else. It is all how to make do with what JRF Ltd already has.

We walked through to the Lumière in St Martin's Lane afterwards, and saw Mike Leigh's *High Hopes,* which I liked. It is much better than Terence Davies's *Distant Voices, Still Lives;* partly uses an old technique of caricature, that of Gillray and Cruikshank (gross exaggeration), partly that of Dickens. The dreadful sister-in-law and her husband, the equally awful young yuppie neighbours, are not meant to be realistic. One senses, in Leigh, a Marxist who has got wise to himself.

14 February

Rushdie fuss.[1] Eliz in a paranoiac state, that I might support him. This is a clear moral choice. From what I have heard of him, I do not like him. I haven't read the book that has so upset Islam. But I must be on his side against the mad mullahs of Iran. Everyone falls over themselves to avoid the truth: that most Muslims are very primitive people and can't be treated as sophisticated ones. If you endlessly prod a tiger, of course its claws will flash out. And all this forces us, on behalf of the principle, to volunteer to be martyrs. Absurd.

Golding, *Fire Down Below.* The *Independent* want me to review this by March 15th, a week before in effect. Eight hundred words. I enjoy it, and its bluff and breezy, jaunty style, even its happy ending, which cocks an implicit snook at the post-modernist novel. Much more in the style of Marryat than Conrad; or perhaps, in its grotesqueries of behaviour and description, nearer Swift than both. He disclaims the *Odyssey,* but perhaps it is nearer than he thinks.

18 February

Charles and Anna and the children have come. Their standards, expectations, needs, upset us. Eliz in a panic that she can't get enough food in, Anna evidently not happy that she has to bring some from Bristol. Tess has passed her exam for entrance to the Colston school; we must pay fees.

19 February

To Axmouth and Seaton with Leo, to look at some lodge, of a house called Wessiter, in one of the densely built-up areas of the town. It was a run-down remnant of an old carriage-entrance, with the beginning of

[1] On 14 February 1989 Ayatollah Khomeini announced that Muslims had a duty to kill Salman Rushdie because he had blasphemed Islam in his novel *The Satanic Verses.*

a drive, lined by chestnuts, down to the main house (North Wessiter
Lodge in Marlpits Rd). It must once have been quite a spacious Edwardian
estate; now endlessly fragmented into bungalows and houselets. Leo was
excited by it; we, secretly depressed. Outside, after we had poked round
it, a dim forgotten croaking high above; and there, three black specks
cannoning and caramboling towards the north: ravens, the first I have
heard here for many years.

Back to Leo's for tea in her little conservatory, full of flowers, *Iris
reticulata* in bloom in the pots outside. I forgive her much for being
such a good little gardener; her silliness (today she was singing the
praises of Islam, which she has some odd idea is meek and gentle, like
some mild variation of Christianity) irritates Eliz very often. I think
wrongly. As well hate a sheep for its foolishness.

25 February
Rain all day. We had asked Ronnie and Celia for supper; but they rang
at seven to say they had only got as far as Windwhistle, and then turned
back. Eliz drinks too much, a miserable evening, as we float adrift on
all our limpings, failures and shortcomings – nobody loves us; I'm selfish,
have no sense of humour, etc., etc. We both suffer from reading too
much about other writers, that is, live in envy of them – John Mortimer
in some hotel in Morocco, writing a novel; what we read of Chatwin;
even Rushdie's celebrity, always their life seems far more glamorous,
rich. And ours, at any rate, terribly dull and unrewarding. We are the
ones ruled by unhappiness, like bad weather. In one way I was glad to
be spared Ronnie. He has been in Italy and on the Canadian St Pierre
and Miquelon Islands for the *Telegraph Magazine*; another lucky person.

28 February
Another book I bought years ago. Bishop Joseph Hall's *Satires* and *Hard
Measure*. This is a Chiswick-Whittingham edition of 1824, with a 1925
bookplate I suspect may be by Rex Whistler. I like their sinewy and often
obscure nature; and the passage in *Hard Measure* about the Puritans'
desecration of Norwich Cathedral: 'Lord, what work was here . . .' etc.
He was ejected, poor fellow; a reasonable man, though a sarcast, in a
time without reason, the mobs ruled by imams and mullahs, exactly as
in Iran today.[1] They are precisely this distance, 340 years, behind us.

[1] The Bishop of Norwich Joseph Hall (1574–1676) was one of thirteen bishops
imprisoned by Parliament for several months in 1642. After his release on bail,
he returned to his diocese. But in 1647 the cathedral was desecrated by a Puritan
mob and he was driven out from the Bishop's Palace. In considerable poverty, he
retired to the nearby village of Heigham, where he spent the rest of his life writing
and preaching.

Reading it, and the Norwich Puritans' folly, made me send off my signature and a cheque in defence of Rushdie to the Society of Authors. BBC2 asked me to go to London for a programme about him this last week; apparently everyone was asked. Ian McEwan spoke for English authors; we hear his life is threatened now. Steiner also spoke, saying he found Rushdie unreadable, but must defend him against the wretched Khomeini. I agreed with almost every word he said. The issue is not whether R is a fine writer or not.

5 March
M's letter:

Feb 6th
The Old Vicarage
Redcar

Dear John –
I don't know how far I will get with this – it's my first attempt to write for many weeks. My eyes are so weak to see anything close to me, I am now registered as visually handicapped & to receive various aids – I have already had talking books & cassettes but so far not been able to use them until the Blind assoc. send someone to help me. Life is so empty to sit and do nothing & one feels useless. I know it takes time to adjust & accept. I have had a lot of nasal-catarrhal trouble since Christmas so life is not very happy. I was so pleased to have your letter & so hoped to be able to answer it. I carry it about in my bag – it makes me feel at least in contact. I am so happy for you to be able to get back to more normal life and interests. The garden must give you a great interest. It is so close to nature & life.

I am sorry not to have written to thank Eliz for the beautiful 'Poncho', a comfort by day & night too.

March 1st. I wrote this a few weeks ago – I can't reread it so will add a little (blindly). As usual I have had several weeks with the old chest trouble and congestion, made more difficult and depressing with the diminishing sight. I am feeling better and getting back to a more normal life. Do <u>wish</u> you would phone & hear your news. I get so desperately sad at the thought of never seeing you both again & anxieties about you – and if everything is progressing well.

(another page, then) I wish my mind was less active – I would just settle down and not bother – I find the blindness <u>so</u> frustrating . . .

And so on, poor woman. There must be some special final bottom circle of modern hell for sons who don't care for their mothers. She finds it hard to write now, and barely punctuates; but still spells not badly. I note that, and think how brutal I am to note it; as I am to leave all the care of her to Hazel and Dan. We just about manage to look after our wretched selves these days; the thought of a journey to Redcar, and the expense, dowses the gutting candle of my energy like a bottle of water. We went to Honiton on Friday, March 3rd. I was supposed to be in Bristol for the opening of their fossil saurian exhibition that evening, but could not face it. Ordinary people with their appetites and energies, however mild, confuse us; as foreigners confuse you by speaking some strange language. Eliz wanted to buy herself some clothes, but could find nothing, or cared for nothing she saw. She 'doesn't know who she is' any more, has lost identity. I feel the same. We cling to each other in this tumultuously rushing, grasping, wanting world, unable to do either of those last two things.

7 March

A wretched sickness hits me; quite literal, I can't stop being sick. And also a crippling dizziness. I seem to keep swaying, lurching, bouncing to the right. We get Fernandez; he is in a state, having just had to deal with a builder fallen from a ladder and has little time for me. He thinks some middle-ear upset, gives me pills, rushes off.

I dreamed last night, or the one before. This is rare now. I suppose I must dream, but never remember. But this was a pleasant green farm, lying in a wild valley or combe; nothing of the farm about it, in reality, but wild countryside. Some weird composite was there, half Jud Kinberg, half Charlie Greenberg. They were somehow worried about a boy or son that had disappeared.

I manage to get off a review of the new Golding. I regret, having pronounced it farce in the farce-or-tragedy context, that I had not added, 'though of a quasi-divine kind'. I still, as I always have, like him and his writing, but the oddly jaunty gusto of this huge novel is faintly off-putting; that he feels so capable of it, when I feel the very reverse. This dizziness is worrying: but I don't feel mentally incapacitated, or worse than I was.

Dwindling down. I need some such expression, the being able to concentrate on the small, the ordinary, the banal. The retreat into that, and ignoring the large. I live like that.

A new book from Katherine Tarbox in America, *The Art of John Fowles*, Univ. of Georgia Press. Tarbox comes from Maine, in effect. Slightly sour and priggish, in the usual academic manner; school-marmery. But good and fairly thorough on the whole, especially on *A Maggot*.

24 March

Yesterday Jean Wellings typed out my draft of the beginning of *In Hellugalia*. His hatred of the village and area in which I have put his father: Bransford, by which I mean Colyford, one of those villages behind Seaton. This is the first serious attempt at writing for nearly, if not over, a year. Too much hatred of this now-and-here. But it is deeply relieving, to discover that I can still write.

Eliz is in a poor state, very cross-tempered, totally indifferent to what I am doing. She wouldn't come to bed this awful night of the 24th; she didn't feel like sleeping, why should she bother, she didn't sleep, why should I worry? This total indifference to what she is, and what I am, is chilling. If I say this house is in a terrible mess, and mainly because you have let it get that way, her only answer is that who cares, she hates it anyway, as she hates the garden, the town; and behind all, she hates us and the way we live. I try and write this beginning of the novel; and feel immediately I have to slip back several steps. She destroys whatever warmth I feel from the Tarbox book; whatever warmth I get from the garden.

25 March

Sarah Smith drove us to Abbotsbury with Leo and her other daughter, Charlotte. The camellias are out, I bought a *nigre*, a dark red one, a Chapeau de Napoléon moss rose and another called Blairii. A grey cold day, mist descends as we come back.

Something I need to insert in *In Hellugalia*: that the world now is innumerable and ordinary – too many people, too many interested in nothing, or only in spending and gaining more money for spending. The 'commonification' of the world. Absurd that the long dreamt-of and long-desired improvement of the human condition, the partial coming-to-be of its Utopias, should result in this tasteless proliferation.

3 April

We went to supper at the Tytherleigh Arms. Eliz reminds me it is our anniversary; I think April 2, 1957. We are married for thirty-two years. We never remember it, or celebrate it, or at least I don't. What does it mean, beyond the obvious, that so many do?

4 April

Bitterly cold weather, north winds. We shiver.

16 April

A dead, grey day. I walked just beyond Underhill Farm, to the fern-covered common (bluebells, at this time of year). There is a well-worn path south across it, but it leads only to the relic of an old beech-marked hedge; not down further south to Horseman's Ground, as I remember. Strange, how little I seem to have been down here, these past years. I am not steady on my feet, in balancing, but can manage. I carry Quicky's roebuck-horn-tipped stick. I walk westwards trying to find another path down, but fail. It seems no one ever comes here now. Ferns will cover all in a month or two. The main Undercliff path is muddy and near impassable, at least for those here for pleasure. Irritating for tourists, fine for nature. I know which side I am on.

21 April

I went back to the fern-and-bluebell common just beyond Underhill Farm. I scrambled in the woods a little further west, and tried to get down to the Horseman's Ground cleft, along which I used so often to walk; but had to give up. I am poor, near useless these days, at negotiating scrub, especially when it is on very broken ground, as here. I stood at the bottom of one steep slope coming back, and realized my balance just wouldn't let me tackle it; an awful feeling of impotence. Not that I might not have managed it, on hands and knees, clinging to stems, and so on; but being put off by the struggle, the effort, when I remembered the past; how I once knew this land, and its roughness, so well, and negotiated it so easily; and now can't.

Peter says the path beaten across the common is by the Primal Scream people, whose centre seems to be in Charmouth. They have their meetings there sometimes. His rather incoherent account of their goings-on puzzles me; they apparently believe they can get in touch with the holy men of the past (*their* holy men) in such wild surroundings. I find that not unattractive, partly because I had a faintly similar experience on this abortive walk, which ended with me on a little bluff, seeing the cleft to Pinhay Warren far below; perhaps only 2–300 yards below, but impossible. While I was there, in the scrub, I felt how lonely, yet how clean, pure, it was – and not just an unmarred, hostile solitude, but one for which I felt an old affection. The trees (just coming into leaf) I knew so well, the plants of the ground cover; mercury, pendulous reed, violets, bluebells, primroses. It is not frightening in the least, this loneliness, this feeling that no one ever comes here; like meeting old friends, or family, after many years in another world. Another common ground plant at this time of year is wood spurge. I think it likes the broken ground.

21 May

Strange weather, very hot, the kind of weather most people mechanically term beautiful; but actually too cloudless, powder-grey. The moon at night, orange. It is all somehow ominous and menacing. It brings out the people and the cars, all life turns coarser and more vulgar. The primrose and double white lilacs in flower; and the old pink cabbage (Charles de Mills) just coming. We went over to Celia and Ronnie's for lunch; nice, that rural peace. I telephoned M this morning. She remembers when she was young no one had holidays, I must put up with the grockles, just as I must sell this house, get rid of the garden – all things I can't imagine doing.

We go to Crete on Tuesday; endless anxiety and worry about that, it is absurd. I feel quite incapable of writing, don't write endless letters I should. Peter produced his new novel the other day. I quite liked it for its quickness, its light bubbling on; I told him he was like a pond-skater. It is set in Charmouth, or just behind. Light and empty, we think 'very eighties'.

I am useless, all sharpness and precise will gone. I seem capable of finishing nothing. I potter in the garden. It is near three o'clock in the morning, the sea quietly seething, the moon tawny, the old honeysuckle richly scented, the occasional faint chink of blocks down at the Cobb.

9 June

Awful, I woke in the night, deep in some dream, that we had stopped off with Anna and the others in some sort of youth hostel – that it was full of sleeping people, I had no light, no knowledge of where I was, I must piss. I found my way out of the room where I was, eventually down some stairs into another room. I imagined it full of sleeping people, gave up, went back upstairs; could hold out no longer, pissed eventually in a recess, praying no one asleep should hear. And strictly only then realized I was doing it in a corner of our own dressing-room, that I had just been down and up our own stairs, that our own bathroom was beside the bed from which I had risen. One cannot believe one's unconscious was so stunned by sleep that one did not realize this. The feel that these mysterious rooms were full of sleeping people was overwhelmingly real, I was totally 'duped'.

21 June

Rick Gekoski, whom Golding savaged in the *Paper Men* (as Rick),[1] drove here from London, to take us to meet Graham Greene's son Francis, about whom he was slightly mysterious. But it turns out, to our surprise, that he lives at Ashe House, near Axminster. Its name is not announced outside now, and there is no longer a living 'museum' of fowl, as in the old days.[2] It seems they have been there for some twelve years, and have evidently managed to keep quiet about the relationship with Graham. The old house, with its little chapel standing separate, has been done up, a shade bizarrely, that is austerely: walls largely without pictures, a staircase without a rail, a general bareness. The lawns widely planted

[1] In the *Paper Men* Rick L. Tucker is an American academic who will stop at nothing to become the biographer of famous English novelist Wilfred Barclay.
[2] Ashe House in the village of Musbury was a sixteenth-century manor which had belonged to the Drake family until the end of the eighteenth century.

with young trees. There are some windows and doors from Newenham Abbey, a fishpond fed by a stream, Warlake.

They came over the grass to meet us. A thin bearded man in his forties, who reminded me alternately of Anthony Sheil and D. H. Lawrence (or as one supposes him from photographs); a rather bubbly, eager woman. They seem to know no one here, to be very 'retired and private' people. He talks fast and quite incisively, a touch of impatience. He has been living in Carolina, learning to fly some new kind of plane professionally. Having to fly by commercial line to France is boring. A slightly impatient tone, one suspects he cannot suffer fools, that he is wounded in some way, and not only for being the son of who he is. It seems no children nor local acquaintances. But we (nor Rick) know nothing of them, not even who he is or what he does. Rick thinks something to do with computers; though he seems intellectual, well read. She seems easier; but both rather frightened at the idea of giving anything away. We go after lunch to where the collection of Graham Greene's detective books are, in a little room, not much more than a large cupboard, off where we had drinks. Rick behaves like the Jewish book-dealer he is. Greene, who had apparently read the entire collection, is faintly disdainful. I pick one or two from the shelves: they lure a little, as always, and some of the illustrations are amusing. I have already said that Victorian detective fiction, this collection's theme, does not interest me at all; but we vaguely discuss what I might write. Francis thinks something light and amusing, it is up to me.

We go outside, I ask to see the Newenham bits and pieces; most so is perhaps a small cellar door led down to by a little ramp. Then we walk over to the chapel; it is unused, though still presumably consecrated in its original Catholic form, from before the Dissolution. A piscina, bits of glass. He says the Drakes were fierce Protestants, in such a way that suggests he himself is Catholic; but it seems indifferent, since the chapel is obviously deserted now, left with its open window for the martins. One feels she, and perhaps he, are passionately for nature.

She had already had something like a spat with Rick, who had been attacking Wordsworth heavily for not writing more of the ugly side of nature (we had been talking of the trouble they have with mink, which Francis has to trap); and she attacked him. One feels they fiercely defend their little island, six acres, at Ashe. We chatted by their cottage. A terrible silage dump, black plastic weighed down by car-tyres, lies just over the wall. They say they are persecuted by wind, but it seems, silage apart, a pleasant place. Just somehow soulless, with this aloof and well-bred couple. We drank a spritzy Swiss white wine at lunch, a present from his sister there. Liz had heard there was such a daughter, but neither of us, a son.

*

We drove home, discussing them. I can't believe they much like Rick who remains much too American-Jewish for us English, a blend of faint respect and sudden bursts of iconoclasm, as over Wordsworth. He says he has no interest in the country or nature, only in art and the city. Rushdie has let him have two stories to print, under his own imprint, but (though they are printed) he now fears to issue them, for his wife's and children's sakes. R still lived in London, it seems, but is splitting from his wife, Marianne Wiggins. His son, at school somewhere in England, has not been touched, which somehow diminishes the fabled fury of Islam. Rick himself remains a typical East European Jew, well soaked in the USA. He was obviously angry with 'Bill' (Golding) for having mocked him, but had made it up as one senses any proper Jew would, bending with the way of the wind, or the business and money pressure.

He took away two boxfuls of foreign editions of my own work; for which he gives me nothing. But Eliz – and I also in a way – am delighted to see the back of them.

28 June

The Peninsula Prize horror upon us. They have sent six shortlisted, and four or five others. I plod through them, even though with most one knows within ten pages that they are no good. There is a reciprocally plodding, pedestrian quality with most that is suffocating: that they are written by people under a delusion, and blind to themselves. They make Eliz angry, myself hopeless, in a way the opposite, encouraged: however half-wounded I am, I could not write as dully and wrongly as this. Of those shortlisted, there seems to me only one potential winner: *The Goosefoot*; faintly Woolf-like, Bloomsburyish. Spelling is bad, but he or she has some notion of getting delicate moods, climates, across.

Korsakoff's psychosis – total loss of present memory (though memory of remote childhood may remain), inability to recall the now. And how people customarily fill the gaps with fiction. S. S. Korsakoff, Russian neurologist, 1854–1900.

2 July

The other syndrome I seem to have is Ménière's: or lack of balance. Since coming back from Crete, I have been in a mysterious state of poor health; most obviously, constipated and energiless. I thought partly due to the June heat-wave, but it continues. My balance seems very poor again, my energy – ability to answer letters or do anything else – nil. I feel 'a wreck', in the common phrase. Eliz by some miracle, though also complaining of many things, seems rather better. I irritate her over countless things, from 'bad breath' to 'speaking in an affected voice'; perhaps above all in still having some interest in this town, which she now 'hates' comprehensively.

I don't blame her for this last; some bad change has overtaken Lyme. It is a typical victim of overpopulation elsewhere: far too expected to answer the demands of both too many people and too many cars. It can't, and doesn't. The latest fuss is over a scheme for altering the front and beach (and improving the shingle-flow 'across' the town). Some research group at Wallingford has come up with a scheme that the WDDC[1] approve – and the town seems to oppose almost en bloc. For all I know the scheme may have reason – Liz-Anne seems to think so – but there is a feel about it once again of something imposed from outside, cooked up by 'experts' in their general fields but with little knowledge of past history here. People who have that last (like myself) wonder why the old system of scouring shingle from Monmouth Beach and leading it through the Cobb has been rejected. The usual arm-flapping horror at the thought of damaging 'old Lyme' (of which most haven't the faintest notion) can be discounted; but not the grockle-catering lobby, so determined not to harm any means by which they can be 'milked'.

I've had nothing to do with all this. For me it's a part of the rise of the old 'peasant' or working-class element, of the notion that they are 'free' and must take charge. Their economic freedom is true, but not that they are fit yet to take charge. Middle-class Lyme, of the nineteenth century, is moribund beyond redemption – the newcomers, or better newrisers, have to acquire some of their virtues. That will take two generations at least, I suspect – at least fifty years.

3 July
To Exeter, Hennock Road and Devon Books, for the Peninsula Prize judging. Fay Weldon is late, having missed a train. She is the usual rather blowsy woman, trying somehow not to be what one feels she ought; not a landlady in a bar, but an intellectual one. She has developed a specially quiet, faintly sibilant whisper of a voice (which I frequently can't hear) almost as a way of killing off any notion that she is really more aggressive.

It is all rather a futile occasion, with the two Simons at Devon Books preoccupied by finding 'saleable' fiction, never mind its artistic worth; Fay, something that suits her views on feminism and the rest; I clinging to some no doubt long-past notion of good writing, the ability to portray things like mood-climates. I find Fay a sloppy writer, I suppose really a vulgar one, despite her popularity; I suspect she knows it. So the oversimple *If Greedy, Wait* won: and my overhurried, entered-in-haste *The Goosefoot* got its consolation prize.

We stopped at the Otter Inn coming back, just before Honiton. Swallows and martins over the river, very low in all this heat, and the drought; beyond the trees and water, the endless drone of the traffic. The

[1] West Dorset District Council.

world, and England, dies of the car. I have never known the insidious pressure of people, always too many people so with us, and stifling us. Superb weather, and we both feel absurdly ill. The real, the practical world has escaped us, and now wreaks its revenge; like some once faithful servant in a rebellion, it now leads the sacking mob.

10 July

Dreadful days, I don't know what I am doing – or more accurately, even what I'm not doing – half the time. I feel ill, or permanently weak, and unable to do anything about it. I did go to see the new doctor, Fernandez's replacement, the other day. His name is Robinson. He seemed brisk, though he was late into surgery, having had a 'crisis'. I cannot even explain properly all that seems wrong. The trouble is that I manage to stagger on, though I feel so weak. Poor Eliz, the same; we drown ourselves in Wimbledon, in its small sensations and sometimes barely suppressed violence. I suspect that it is still at heart a war substitute, underneath all the other glosses the commentators pander to: violence described as 'genius', cruelty as 'brilliance', and so on. Enjoyable to watch losers being beaten when one is not, in any real terms, in the war.

I can't answer letters, keep any sort of business, or contact with the world, going. In literary terms I feel completely forgotten, or dead. *In Hellugalia* I still have ideas for; but more often than not, don't even jot them down. I can't even read with any pleasure, it seems a waste of time. Jim Baker in California telephoned the other day: the *Paris Review* editor wanted something urgently for the article he has got them to take and which we have been making by post over these last years.[1] I managed to do that and get it off; a last little flare of vanity. I lie awake and 'contemplate' the mess our lives have got into. I got up at six today, thinking I might find the energy to answer some letters. But I didn't. It is all too much.

11 July

Kazuo Ishiguro, *The Remains of the Day*. I liked this, one of those novels that are victories of a carefully restrained mood. In a way very English, not giving way to the emotions; in another, in aesthetic tone, very Japanese. As the novel in general seems to get more strident and more vulgar (in pursuit of money, quite certainly not of literature), this book's wise restraint is both refreshing and effective.

More and more as I write – I nearly wrote 'write' – I want to put words into quotes, that is, to suggest I'm using them ironically or not in any straight and normal sense. Language seems a cripple, a broken walking-stick. Not a step without stumbling.

[1] An interview between Jim Baker and JF, which appeared in the summer 1989 issue of *The Paris Review* (issue no. 111).

Part of novel-writing (and drama), and practically all of current journalism, is pandering to the worst side of man; in other words, whoring.
This is nothing new, but it seems increasingly prevalent. Ishiguro's severe
restraint – not a kiss in the whole book, hardly a tear – is remarkable.
It is almost like a page of blank paper.

16 July
Strange weather, with which we cannot cope: very fine and hot, a repetition of the June heat-wave. The gardens – all gardens – near dead of
thirst; and we near dead of lack of will, inability to do anything. It
becomes sinister; why this now seeming eternal fine weather, endless
sun and blue skies?

The Revolution celebrations in Paris during this last week. Thatcher
has made an idiot of herself; one may argue over the extent of the French
contribution to 'democracy', human rights and all the rest of it, but not
that her sour intervention was not colossally ill-timed. It is somehow
typically English to be so grudging at the height of the celebrations.[1]

Yesterday I went down to be photographed for *The Times* with the
grand mover and members of COBB[2] on the North Wall; they have set
up against the WDDC plans for the Cobb and beach, and are hoping
to drive them to a public inquiry. I am with them inasmuch as I don't
understand the WDDC proposal, joining the North Wall to land, erecting
three huge rock barriers just south of the beach, all at a price of eleven
million; or don't understand why that is chosen and the old method,
getting the shingle through the Cobb from Monmouth Beach, is not at
least evaluated and tested.

Eliz thinks I am stupid to take part, they are 'just using me'. I think
I should, though I've taken no part in the conflict so far. Lyme is, as so
often in the past, being pushed and rattled into a decision in which it
has had no part, and more time is needed.

Fay Weldon rang in the morning. Salman Rushdie was coming to supper
in the evening, would we go? Yet another very hot, fine day. We normally
would have said no, but the chance of meeting Rushdie again, his notori-
ety during this last year – we went.

She lives in an old farmhouse, Larkbarrow, at East Compton just west
of Shepton Mallet, in a kind of rather blowsy, expansive mess – like
herself, in fact. Her husband Ron, the junk-dealer we used to know from

[1] In Paris for the bicentenary celebrations and an economic summit of the G7
leaders, the British prime minister observed to the French media that 'human
rights did not start in France' and that the French Revolution was not nearly as
important a historical event as Magna Carta.
[2] Committee Opposing Beach Breakwaters.

Regent's Park Road, now a painter, was there; some New Zealand woman or girl apparently helping; several bodyguards (Rushdie has four, it seems, one pair to relieve another, found for him by the police). Bearded rather bushily, in a half Victorian sort of way, balding, heavily bespectacled, was Rushdie himself.

I didn't really feel very differently about him from the last time we met, at Groucho's: that he wants to be quick, incisive and witty, but isn't quite so, that he has a fierce underlying vanity. Ghastly though it is, one feels that in a way he enjoys this new role of being the anathema of Islam, Khomeini's proscribed and condemned victim, all the rest of it. He was most interesting about the early days, after the Iranian death-sentence: how he had first heard of it from some BBC radio person; how hordes of TV and film people had then besieged his house; how he had first taken refuge with his agent, Gillon Aitken, yet none of the hundreds of news-hounds tracking him had guessed that; then gone to sleep in some neighbouring flat or room his wife Marianne Wiggins had rented to write in.

Scotland Yard and the security people had then intervened. He had nothing but praise (peppered with amusement, how amusingly varied the policemen he came into contact with were – one was gay, another Marxist, another a qualified geologist, and so on) for the way the government had defended him. He professed to hate everything to do with the Thatcher government, but couldn't fault them there; even though he was what he was, Iran had been attacking Britain, they aggravated the national horror of beastly foreigners, so he had to be protected.

When he had to go home much later, about one (wherever 'home' is, it seems it is out of London), his armed bodyguards, who had either been lounging about in the warm air outside or watching TV upstairs, appeared, armed.

He isn't afraid of attacks from fanatics, thinks the bodyguards can take care of that; attacks from trained terrorists, someone like the Abu Nidal group, greedy also for the execution money and the prestige, are dangerous. He was a friend of Bruce Chatwin, and went to his funeral service soon after all this happened. A *Daily Telegraph* man there approached him demanding a taped interview. When R tried to get rid of him the man said, 'You can't talk to me like that. I'm from the *Daily Telegraph*, and I went to a public school.' Gillon apparently saved Rushdie with a curt 'Fuck off!' to the wretched *Telegraph* man. This story wasn't quite credible to me – that the reporter could have been such an idiot, Rushdie self-shown as so ineptly persecuted by foolish Conservatives. He keeps throwing in little pats on the back to himself.

There was talk with Fay of the advertising agency they had both belonged to in the past. He tells a story of how he had persuaded Groucho Marx to do some London ad for small cigars; then another on how he had hit on well-known slogans for Aero chocolate because his agency boss had stammered. In a way this small talk was revealing of both him and Fay; they rather suggested that their copywriting days lie behind their later success with the novel – that they have both been taught to 'sell' things. Fay is subtler in how she goes about it, but poor Rushdie, I suspect, feels nakedly obliged to sell himself still.

He feels he's been misunderstood, would like to do another novel about that; he records what is happening to him now through his virtual imprisonment. He feels deprived; no public theatre, cinema, all the rest. He thinks his wife and son are not in danger, because Islam is above taking revenge on him through them. He says his sisters in Pakistan, when he was younger, disliked the Islamic attitude to women; they chose their own husbands. He was the only one for whom a bride was arranged – 'a beautiful girl . . . unfortunately it never came off'.

So he says, trying to be ruefully dry, contemptuous, *macho* and wise all at the same time. That is the poor man's fault. Part of him does know Britain and the British backwards, especially the ad-agency and literary worlds; and indeed this makes him rather like a Jew of the Tom Maschler and Freddy Raphael kind, permanently eager to get on, yet somehow grudging that he is not better recognized; never quite able to bring all his knowledge together, as Conrad did, never to be altogether English. He somehow both wants to be taken as English; and yet free to be a foreigner, and to criticize; both to be loved and admired by us, but to stand apart.

He fascinated the New Zealand girl with his imitations of the differences between Australian and NZ accents. Apparently he had an affair with a Strine girl there many years ago.

All this may seem unkind, and perhaps almost everything may be forgiven someone under menace of death. He makes a fortune on the bestseller lists, but has of course lost all kinds of personal freedom. The book comes out in France this next week. I wished to say how sorry I was over his predicament, but felt none the less that it was in part invited. I did ask him how he had felt about Steiner's reaction (which in reality reflected my own); but he said it had, and did still, hurt. 'It hadn't helped.'

It interested us that Fay had asked us and (or so it seemed) no one else. I am so used to seeing myself as mentally and intellectually crippled and *passé* – a little as Eliz sees me – I can't imagine anyone should want my presence. We didn't start the long drive home, under a low, yellow moon and along moth-studded roads, until two in the morning.

Le Duc de Lauzun: *embastillement.* Another nice word for a peculiar process I met today was *dépanthéonisé*. This was in Goudemetz's *Judgement and Execution of Louis XVI* (London, 1794).[1] Though I opened the Goudemetz by chance, there is a strange parallel with Rushdie – that is, a condemnation that shocked Europe, though R's has not yet been carried out. And just as today one rather condescends to, and pities, Louis, the hunting locksmith, I'm afraid that's what I secretly feel about Rushdie – somehow he does not add up to what one might count a worthy victim, that is, he doesn't quite deserve what has happened. One is in the absurd position of pitying him because it has and doubting it because he isn't a better writer.

22 July

I finished reading Alan Hollinghurst's *The Swimming Pool Library*, a clever homosexual novel, which I quite liked as writing; but as everything else, disliked. He makes homosexual passion seem the crudest and most violent form of libido; and his 'fucking' is especially repulsive, rather as if he must show some queers can outdo orthodox love-making (a euphemism, it is ejaculation). A psychologist from Durham University, Mark Bevan, wrote last week thanking me for *The Magus*, then complaining that I'd offered 'no solution'; that is, that men are still dominated by their sexuality and cause endless problems because they can't control it. He wants men to be more in love with themselves, to be homosexual without being 'queer'. I write back saying the lager louts go down to the beach here, and come back drunk, no wiser: that is, they learn nothing from their sex experiences, such as they are, and nothing of women. They must first get the 'fucking' out of the way. Hollinghurst's is no solution; and in one way he cheats, mentioning but glossing over so much of the filth, the fellatio and anus-licking. They do not deserve the savage punishment society has so often and for so long given them, yet they are perverted, he can't hide that. They have in larger part the erotic crudity of so many men's relations with women. 'Look, we're very like you normals.' But they aren't, except in violence.

24 July

To Axmouth, to meet Catharine Carrington, who's staying with Leo. Her husband Noel, the 'famous' Carrington's brother, died recently.[2] It seems she was born at Walberswick, I think it was the house where Rennie Mackintosh stayed. A sere, quiet woman, in her eighties. She must be, with Frances Partridge, one of the last survivors of that

---

[1] Goudemetz's account of Louis paints a portrait of a shy, indecisive figure who felt much more comfortable hunting or working in his locksmith's workshop than discharging the responsibilities of state.

[2] The 'famous' Carrington is Bloomsbury painter Dora Carrington (1893–1932).

Bloomsbury world. She remembers staying in Crete, at Canea, in some house belonging to John Craxton, the painter. She's a painter herself of sorts, it seems. One's instinct is to machine-gun her with questions; not done, of course. One that would intrigue me is whether she now feels that all the Bloomsbury past was a kind of being on stage – perhaps not so much then, but as seen in retrospect, now it is so reminisced about. In a way the whole set must have especially suited this century, their plays and drama forming a *lingua franca* the spectators can communicate through.

It's Lifeboat Week, the usual noise; and the usual half-educated, half-cultured public announcer; one feels he loves it – that people must listen to him and his awful banalities.

Perhaps I – and many others – have been novelists because we could not stand saying the truth. We always needed to escape from what is, the world as it appears to us; to invent other worlds. The world that is is too cold and cruel to bear; and above all we ourselves (I myself) that are are also a lot too cold and cruel. We create the surfaces of the mirrors we see ourselves in, or how we hope others will see us: that is, distorting surfaces. We are hopelessly remote both from true reflection and from what religion and moral thought say we should be; in effect, exiled by ourselves from ourselves.

25 July

I read the Hydraulics Research report, from Wallingford, that has caused so much fuss here. It seems somehow about some other element, situation and place – not the sea at Lyme; and curiously as if written by someone else, who has never been in Lyme; has merely heard of it.

26 July

Perhaps I should 'issue' what fragments I have, of short stories and novels; as we know of past cultures through fragments, shards, through their archaeology. One tries to make some kind of virtue of their incompleteness. I might call it *Tesserae* or *Fragments*.

I thought of this on a walk to beyond and behind Underhill Farm, one of the rare ones I have done these days, so weak I feel. There was a Painted Lady on the path by the county boundary, small in size, a near perfect imago, the prettiest thing I saw, I suspect that there was in Lyme. Anna is here, and the children. She cooks for us, a great relief. The children aren't, alas, or especially not William, such a strident little boy. We took them to the car park yesterday afternoon to see the Red Arrows (it's the best place to watch their aerobatics, too many trees in the garden). Curious how coolly he watches it, almost as if he's a young prince and it's his due. Tess is mercifully more bored by such noise and 'showing off'. We sat beside a father with younger children; as the planes roared in, he told them they were being attacked. Brief screams and expressions of pleasure. The man, the victim of speed and power; the children, being indoctrinated.

I sent this to Jonathon Porritt, at the Friends of the Earth, yesterday. Eliz thought it was 'mad' – which it is a little, but I feel it – a growing hatred of mankind and his selfish muddle-headedness.

For Jonathon Porritt, Friends of the Earth.
My unhappiness is not over this Dorset I inhabit, nor indeed over anywhere else in particular; but above all over how blindly and selfishly our species goes on living everywhere, seemingly stuck between suicide and senility. Crystal-clear what is wrong, and equally clear that as a species we cannot face doing anything about it. We are now far too many, beyond restraint, and multiplying like an uncontrolled virus.

My thoughts are of all the animals, plants, birds, insects we poison out of this world; and how they have been a chief consolation and delight of my six decades of life. Such a loss may hardly seem to matter; I grow old, I shall soon be gone. What does matter is that for the majority, the younger, loss now becomes the rule. It is like some insane fiat: 'Nature will shortly cease to exist. It is henceforth strictly forbidden to mean anything to anyone.' It won't quite happen so, of course. Such a situation will creep slowly upon us and our confused intelligences, stuffed with conflicting values and notions. But then one day the death of nature will be unopposably real, irreversible. There will be no more green.

So I felt this burning summer, here in North Europe, of 1989. In form I might belong to humankind; in reality I seemed one of a ravenous self-destroying horde of rats. I am glad there is no god. If there were I cannot imagine that we rampant, myopic and insatiably self-centred creatures should be allowed to survive a single day more.

John Fowles

27 July
I went to the new doctor, Barry Robinson, to have the result of a hip X-ray I had a week or so ago. It seems I have osteoarthritis in both hips. I 'shouldn't be on my feet', according to Robinson, I must see the Dorchester specialist. He showed me the corroded joints, the lack of lining to the acetabula. I cannot really understand it, because the pain still seems to be as of a muscular strain, in the groin, not a bone thing. But something is indeed wrong, complicated by the lack of balance.

29 July

I've been reading *Le Duc du Lauzun*. It's by some descendant, the Count of Gontaut Biron, a faintly absurd royalist and chauvinist; yet somehow one of these books one can live in, or through. Perhaps most of all when one is a novelist. I was with him today in Senegal in 1779; then in the American War of Independence in 1780 and 1781 (he was at Yorktown, even supped with the enemy, Cornwallis, the evening before he surrendered). Lauzun was a kind of Byron; rather that than just a Don Juan or Casanova: obviously handsome and headstrong, aristocratic litter for the Dantons and Robespierres. One can guess why he was hated by one party at court; and yet now, at this remove, his life seems bravely active and interesting.[1]

He was a standing insult to all who were unrich and unprivileged, also to all who were merely dull or malicious or conventional in his own milieux.

30 July

A sad and unpleasant day. I'd played *pétanque* with William the evening before, and he'd thrown one into where the Japanese juniper, the noisette rose, the clematis and bramble grow in a tangle over the lawn. It took me an hour or more to get it out. William watches a while, but does not care. He's a classic case of *jemenfoutisme*, that is, believes only in his own 'I want' and cares not a damn about what trouble he causes. It irritates Eliz that he behaves like this and is indulged in it by Anna, who seems to find him endlessly endearing and amusing, or at any rate tolerable. That is not what I and Eliz feel; and equally deeply, that we can say nothing.

After lunch Anna drove us all to Devenish Pitts, a farm in the combe opposite Farway. I left them at the top, and walked a little among the heather and ling that border the conifer plantations. The moor there is burnt a pale ochre; beside the road a rich crop of dewberries; some whortleberries in the plantation, but I could see none with fruit. Then down the steep hill to the riding farm, where Eliz waits in a field with William (he's decided he does not like riding). It is outwardly a not unpleasant combe of meadow and woods, though very dry; but strangely few birds and butterflies as I went down, it seems the world already dying, near dead. William slashes at thistles with a stick, obsessively,

---

[1] Armand Louis de Gontaut, the duc de Lauzun and later duc de Biron (1747–1793), led the French forces against the English during the American War of Independence. Returning to France, he supported the revolution and commanded an army that fought against the Vendée rebels in 1793. But accused of undue leniency, he was put on trial and condemned to death by a revolutionary tribunal. He was guillotined on 31 December 1793.

torturing the peace. He claims he had deadheaded some four hundred. There is some link in my mind between this thirsty, dying landscape and his idiotic slashing with his stick. I walk down to the riding farm, a weird beehive of girls, some very little, not a man in sight, all horse-mad; a six-year-old staggers under a huge saddle she is carrying for some ride, yet can hardly lift. Teenage girls pass, riding, leading horses, disappearing into boxes, preoccupied and determined looks on their faces. I found this whole feminine world peculiar, secret, mysterious under all its obvious outward and petty mysteries.

When we got home, Charles was on the telephone from Kuwait (where he's been doing plans for some entertainment centre scheme, his absence is why Anna's been here); he has managed to get a flight this evening, he'll be back in Bristol tomorrow. Anna seizes on it like a thirsty nomad on an oasis, and proposes she leave after supper, after a lightning pack. She doesn't dare ask Eliz to look after the children (Eliz is out buying milk); I suggest she might take Tess alone, but Anna goes to where the children are slumped watching television, the sadly idiot habit they have from Bristol (it starts the moment they get up here, their gawping at the wretched breakfast TV we never watch); then comes back and says Tess wants to be there to greet Charles. We are suspicious of this on reflection; that perhaps she can't bear the thought of William's greed allowed to exploit *Charles* alone. So all that comes to nothing.

We take them to supper at the Tytherleigh, where William behaves particularly badly, half-finishing his food, lying slumped in his seat or, when she allows him, over Anna's lap. He is like a little boy of four or five. Eliz is furious that Anna lets him conduct himself so gracelessly, I am as always silent. Perhaps she is signalling that she cannot cope, but we have the awful feeling that she does not care, in her present besotted situation.

They go. The children (again as usual) neither say goodbye nor kiss me, but slump in the car. Eliz and I agree on what a little monster he is, with all the makings of a crook and con man, a Felix Krull to be; and how she feels they come here purely to milk her, to extract what money they can – especially William.

But then, after a few whiskies, she plunges into endless gloom and bitterness; the gloom she feels over them, the guilt, the horror that half of whatever money we leave will go to them – that familiar iron-toothed mantrap of the guilt caused by her leaving Anna to Roy's untender mercies in the beginning, our total inability to incorporate her smoothly into our lives, and, on the other side, by our anger that they are such 'difficult' children. My total non-being, non-existence, as an individual, as any sort of step-grandfather, as a human being with tastes and interests, is chilling – not only to me (not that my vanity or egocentricity matters), but I suspect to anyone else who might know the reality of the situation: that this 'well-known' novelist should allow such a situation to develop, like a caterpillar being eaten up by ichneumon eggs. We support Anna by letting her live rent-free in the Bristol flat (we are now expected also to give it to her – and the tax to be paid on its capital value, some £100,000); also by the allowance to her of £230 per month, and the annual director's fees (£4,053 on 27.2.89). And feel that for that all we get in return is her contempt and impatience. I do like her briskness and organizedness over many domestic things, but feel she has swallowed the modern myth, or illusion: if you have the money, you can have no problems. You need a smaller house, fine, sell the one you have (and all you've accumulated over the years). All life can be controlled and fixed over the telephone.

We differ by having other values. Eliz now mourns (over some old photos they were looking at) the evanescence of life, that so much is already past and gone, and that what we have now will mean nothing or little to them – this awful hollowness of having and owning, the falling into oblivion and desuetude of so much one liked and loved, is of course a cliché of humanity; but still hard to bear.

I think part, perhaps a large part, of our trouble is our feeling of emptiness, of having lost all sense of personal value; that we have no children between us, that Anna and her children seem not to care (far less through personal thoughtlessness or maliciousness than through the climate of this culture) only aggravates matters, does not cause them.

She went off to sleep on her own, I on mine. I read Lauzun in the small hours – the misery of those last months of his life, his impossible command in La Vendée, his sense of futility and despair. We are also at Niort, knowing things are badly wrong. We are not understood, nor understand.[1]

4 August

I have increasing trouble with my words; it is a kind of ankylosis in expressing the thoughts, a seeming impotence of conception, I can't erect notions into syllables, denote them.

5 August

After Lauzun, I started to read Saint-Pavin (1600–1670), whom I bought years ago in the 1861 Techener edition. He was a *libertin*, a shade insipid now, but pleasantly neat and unclassical. As pleasant as a real and simple

---

[1] At Niort on 1 July 1793, Lauzun, who was extremely ill and the object of mounting criticism, resigned as the general in charge of the Republican army fighting the Vendée rebels. The response of the revolution's new National Convention was to commission a report that severely criticized his conduct and to relieve him of his command.

seventeenth-century garden, not the grand classical one imagination sees behind the term.

6 August

I ring M for the first time in many weeks. Risible if it were not so sad. She does not understand what I say sometimes, so endless repetitions. Kuwait. Kuwait. Kuwait. Torn. Torn. Torn. (Where Charles is, how the children take the divorce.) Poor Jonathan has gone off on one of his fugues. I say we shall come at some point this month, but the poor old thing seems resigned to how far away we are, to all the difficulties.

7 August

All socialism can seem a bad joke: all the sacrifice, the fierceness, the incorruptibility of the twenties and thirties, and later, into my own life; and now the vulgarity, illiteracy, prolixity of the very class for whom all the endeavour was in aid, the 'working class'. I met two people who live here today, complaining of the filth of this holiday influx, the smell of the Cobb (fish and chip papers), the lack of rubbish bins. One described a German couple going down Cobb Road, in despair that there was nowhere to deposit things they wanted to throw away. So many of us fought, or at least supported, the 'good' fight; and now, this horror.

It must seem odd, this way I plunge into French, such past worlds. I see a parallel with the garden. I need to get lost in it, as I do in them. Saint-Pavin's concision and precision, that is what I lack these days; and poor Lauzun – or Biron as he by then was – at Niort: his handwriting deteriorated badly, became smaller and crabbed. I know that, what horrors, both physical and psychological, cause it.

Sometimes, in these hopelessly overcrowded grockle-ridden months, that individuality seems the great curse of mankind: that man's tastes, interests and proclivities have to be satisfied – and so foully complicate and muddy existence. If only we were fully arbitered and controlled – by nature, not man; as indeed much of nature is.

9 August

We went on to shop in Hell, alias Seaton. Where I bought a bottle of Punt e Mes and then directly after, in the greengrocer's, dropped it from the bag on to a stone floor. The stench of its sweet alcohol. I was in a numb rage. We went on to Axminster, and I passed next to the shop where I usually buy Punt e Mes and saw a row of them. It was almost a pleasure *not* to replace the broken bottle.

Eliz also in a temper, in her cork mood, sinking all through the day, but then bobbing up the next morning. Her resentment over Anna and the kids all coagulates around me; in her fury that there are no better places in this area to shop or eat, she resembles the Anna she professes to be angry over. Her demands for some better situation, in effect for a dream-world, are as unreasonable. I can only bow my head, and let the wind howl.

26 August
The wretched 'incipient' gout in my right foot has returned. I went to see Becker of Charmouth today (doing duty for Robinson) and he gave me Naprosyn, which seems to stop it.

27 August
To Bristol, en route for the North. We got into the Glenroy. The children cycled round to meet us, and William promptly lost all the contents of a packet of Maltesers Eliz gave him, then groaned and whinged: he must have more. His gracelessness gets worse, and my bad temper, that neither Anna nor they seem to see us any other than cows to be milked. We went – with her half-sister, Roy's child Rachel, pleasantly simple and down-to-earth by comparison – to a pizza house, a bill for £40. Anna and Charles were just back from their week in Minorca. They seem to breed soppiness, everything is for the best in whatever they do; or so it seems to Eliz and myself. It is an effect of their having been off alone together. I noticed Anna being rather absurdly indulgent to William (who clearly needed a no or a reprimand when he wanted to do something) and also slipping glances at Charles. She is less to blame than we feel, I think. Something in her does not want to assume the role of Nicholas, and so she seems to us to be bringing them up badly; but also she dares not alienate the soft and soppy Charles by seeming too strict.

29 August
To Great Ayton, or rather Darlington, through all that old carthorse, or millwheel, of industrial England: Birmingham, Sheffield, Rotherham, Leeds. It is sad, so worn out – like my mind, full of voids, grey patches, the fenestrations of uselessness; so many desolate brick-strewn areas, weed-covered waste lots. The neat, well-farmed country from York on is almost a relief: and strange that that ancient industry, agriculture, should have entered the twentieth century so much better than the manufacturing one. Not without cost, of course. There is an atrocious reduction of the wild, yet nothing to compare with the appalling disfigurements of factory industry. As always it is a shock to have to remember so much of the population comes from this world. Over all dwells the ghost of some small, cramped terrace house or back-to-back, set in some vista of endless roofs. So does the huge majority of England live; no wonder the cramped soul dominates so much of our social life.

The twins are at home, beginning to be intellectuals. Jonathan has disappeared on one of his schizophrenic fugues to London, from York, where he's supposed to be hostelled. This time he's ended in some hospital, suffering from sore feet. They have horror stories of his erratic, haphazard behaviour – and whose fault was it, whose family was corrupt, whose behaviour responsible. He is to see a psychiatrist tomorrow, but they have little hope of his being 'sectioned' (kept in hospital). He is at least not violent, but the indifference of the state medical service towards cases like his is terrifying. Even if one could find private medical help, he has to be supported to live within reach of it. They cannot face him here, nor have they room. He's totally irresponsible, or careless, over all money; and throws himself on society by being dishonest. Dan has had to disclaim responsibility. I feel they are at the end of their tether with him, and live in a limbo between Laing's old theory (that schizophrenics reveal the faults in society and the parental upbringing) and that of Psasz (if that's how you spell it),[1] where chemical or genetic imbalance – totally beyond parental control – is to blame. Dan and Hazel tend towards the latter (as I do myself, though I can't, or didn't in the past, believe Dan's brisk schoolmasterishness and common sense have helped). Jonathan sounds like a highly feckless and intemperate girl, not a boy – or man, as he is now. Their latest theory is that he is playing some sort of joke on them with his religious, quasi-Buddhist illusions, his cheating railway fares, his undressing in public, all the rest of it. How he behaves sounds incomprehensible by normal standards, but this reaction of theirs seems to follow the old human recipe of attributing all such mental sickness to malice and bad taste. The poor things just cannot believe he is not responsible, therefore blameable.

30 August

To Redcar, to fetch M to Ayton Hall for tea. The restaurant is hideously decorated with cheap plates; had paintings everywhere. The tea is futile, largely made *ad hoc* by one of the waiters. M, now ninety, goes on in her old way, as if nothing in life, or certainly in our lives, has changed. She complains she has no one to talk to. That's plainly her great need now her eyesight is going. It all pours out, her complaints, her views of life, her endless news of relatives and other people of whom we know nothing. She reduces me almost at once to near silence. Being with her is all duty; a platitudinous mutter. I envy Dan his brisk and polite way of dealing with her, though he got out of being at that dreadful tea.

That evening to a pizza place in Middlesbrough. The twins at least are full of the books they are reading, new ideas, and all the rest. I can't hear all they say, but they are infinitely rare in my life these days: I am

---

[1] JF is thinking of the American psychiatrist Thomas Szasz.

or was a writer, I might have something to say. To everyone else I was never a writer, and never have anything to say.

1 September

Back to Bristol. We caught a 13.30 from Darlington, where Hazel took us; and Anna met us again at Bristol. William has had a cycling accident and broken his watch. I start reading Brenda Maddox's *Nora Joyce* on the train; and enjoy it. I suffered, it seems like everyone else, from the usual misconception about Nora: that she was a near-illiterate skivvy-cum-laundress. She comes very fresh from these pages, alive and living, and Joyce too, all that strange chain of qualities and complexes that made him what he was, a quite certain genius with words – not least as Nora spoke and sometimes wrote them. She reminds me, with her flair for appearance, clothes, her quirkiness, her underlying constancy, of Eliz. Joyce is in many ways devious and unreliable, a 'bastard', yet redeemed, now it's all over, by the splendid books.

2 September

We sleep at the Glenroy, in a sort of garden-flat room. Then a morning of chaos, shopping with Anna. She wants us to see some new frigidaire-freezer, then to buy shoes for Tess (over which Eliz has already spent hours in vain up north) and a new watch for William. Meanwhile we have to go to Marks & Spencer for food to take back to Lyme. We shall all meet at a coffee-bar when that is done – to which we duly go, then wait, and wait – on a balcony overlooking the ground floor of John Lewis's, a slow seethe of shoppers, buying, choosing, fingering, buying. It is insanely irritating that we have to spend the morning like this. We think it may be some sort of revenge on Anna's side: that we won't buy Tess's shoes or William's watch, so let us stew. Eventually they return and we have to buy very expensive chocolates (he'd faint if he had less) for Charles's birthday tomorrow. We are all in barbarically bad tempers. They sit and have lunch, we watch. This is so we can say goodbye to Tess, who goes with a friend to swim. As usual she goes without saying goodbye to me, no word of thanks for the trip north, nor for the paying of her school fees, which I had done before we went out. I see all young people as sponges nowadays, simply expecting money; but even the twins and Katie thank me for the small uncle's tip I gave them, as Hazel for the money. What angers me about Anna and her children is their fierce uncouthness and gracelessness over these things. It makes even Eliz angry at times, but she blames it on me: I'm not nice enough. But that is to expect me to behave as softly and sentimentally towards them as Charles and Anna do themselves – though for different reasons – and to indulge all their already far too indulged faults.

I suppose in a way I judge them as I would my own children, if I had any.* But I 'stole' Anna's mother from her, and she can't forgive. I have no rights, and reason has no place in it.

6 September
I went down town and spotted a farm on sale beneath Lambert's Castle, Bridewell Farm. Leo was here for tea, and later we rang the agents and arranged to view; someone called Bamberger, evidently quite well connected. The farm is down a long lane just opposite where we usually park for Lambert's Castle; one comes finally out of a long tunnel of bushes at a very lost and remote cottage, hardly a farm. This is very much an acid area, though the owner claims there is a colony of green-winged orchids just north of the house; many marsh orchids in the fields just south of it that slope up to the beech-woods of the castle.

He marched us round the six-acre field he sells with the house; nice overgrown hedges, great silence and peace; then round the orchard beside the house, overgrown and wild, but with true magic still. The wife says it reminds her of how I described Coëtminais in *The Ebony Tower* – they know who I am, it seems. I agree, as to its lostness and remoteness. We go round the house. It seems more like a yacht, very small, but not unpleasing. Flycatchers, which apparently bred on one of the walls of the house, perch and flit about the roof. Some nice eighteenth and early nineteenth-century knicknacks and paintings; naval figures, ambassadors, prim Regency or earlier ladies – I suspect German or Austrian. The Bambergers were nice to show us round, and we liked them; but I smelt some mystery: that they were leaving such an idyllically 'lost' place after only two years of living there. It was a very clear, sunlit evening, perfect for it, for enhancing every charm it had; yet I could imagine it under cloud and rain, or in cold. It was not for us in our state of health, with Eliz's dislike of solitude (this was worse even than Underhill Farm), with my absurd (so it seemed there) inability to drive.

So it seemed easy to say no; yet really it was saying no to one's own past, to what one once was, to living lost in nature. Even if I was fit, I could not cope with it. Terrible, to know such a large part of one's old hopes, wishes and dreams had to be denied; that one must reject what one's youth and middle age would have loved. Eliz mocked when we left: there'd be nowhere, in that small house, for all our 'possessions'

---

*You did not. Did not want. And can't imagine. You were and always will be dead about the living reality of children. Tot up sums. Now. You might have done this years ago *if* you had wanted children. [Added to JF's journal by Elizabeth. Her subsequent comments in the journal are likewise included as asterisked footnotes.]

– my pots and pictures, books, and so on.* That was true. Age has caught us totally unprepared, unarmed. This was sad: driving up to the road, and knowing it was not for us – the very opposite of most such 'visits', not disappointing in itself, but in knowing this dream was no longer habitable. It was a visit to ourselves, really; and what we have become rejected what we were.

Letter from Tom Maschler. He has an aneurysm of the aorta, and has to have an operation.

8 September
Not sent. Eliz thought too 'moany':

7 September 1989

Dear Tom,
Sorry to hear the news about the aneurysm operation – I do hope the operation will pass off smoothly, and you'll soon be on your feet again. I've presumed you've been at the new house in France. We've really been out of London and even further out of the book world, this last summer. I won't pretend life has been idyllic or even pleasant, because it hasn't. England seems impossibly overcrowded – cars, cars, cars (power-boats also on this coast, curse them) and equally endless people. We have developed a bitter dislike of the New England, and its population, and I'm afraid that more and more I think like a conservative, though I still claim to loathe Thatcher; I indeed do, but this huge increase and social rise of the half-educated and cash-mad is my real *bête noire* . . . the trend in our culture on which she has simply ridden to the top.

I do still dicker about with writing, but writing proper it isn't. There are past things I suppose a 'real' writer would get out and have retyped (past MSS and so on) and submitted to you – but somehow I don't feel I should be contaminating paper if not fully fit mentally. I *feel* I can still judge books, but am not sure; so must put up with the waiting-room. Not having earned anything for nearly two years now has also 'altered my prospects'. All those happy-go-lucky years – the money never seeming quite real – are gone. I'm not a pauper, but learning to curse my past lack of financial acumen.

---

*Pots, pictures, I mocked. There is nowhere to go. We are crippled with possessions. In which we have no pleasure. It began in London. Sale auctions. Bond St. Collecting. I mocked then.

We've had no news of Tom and Malou, and hope the long-awaited book isn't causing trouble – how the Americans have received it. We do think of you all, Tom, but really feel we no longer belong in your respective (the other Tom and yourself) high-powered worlds.

Two people have recently written books about me, so I don't feel quite forgotten; but the books seem sometimes about a person who is dead; somehow not me. I become a bit of an old cynic about books, and authors, by no means excepting J. Fowles. I've read Ishiguro with some pleasure this last month or so, but alas am not getting on with Julian Barnes's latest. I realize I'm a hopeless narratophile, lost when I don't have a story to get lost in; and that is what I miss in him, clever chap though he is and though I so liked *Flaubert's Parrot*.

How did the Lindsay Clarke do? And whither the old Cape? I wish we could have a quiet meeting one day, and a talk!

Eliz sends regards; and ours to Regina. Sorry to think of you leaving Belsize Park; but then all life disintegrates, or so it seems, these days.

Yours,
John

9 September
Nora Joyce. The difficulties of their life after the success of *Ulysses*: his having teeth out to improve his eyesight, his divine (or diabolic) insouciance over how he got money, i.e., that the world (or Sylvia Beach, or rich Americans) owed it to him.

10 September
A curious 'waking' illusion. I must have been dreaming that we had returned to Belmont to meet my father, who was ill; but he had not been there (this was all in the presumed dream). I woke and got up in reality. But then almost at once heard stertorous breathing from the dressing-room. I turned to Eliz, still asleep in reality, and fiercely whispered 'He's here' or 'He's come' – or words to that effect. A few steps towards the dressing-room, and consciousness burst out: that of course he wasn't there, it was all some trick of the mind, indeed like that insane escapade of earlier this (now last!) summer, when I sought desperately for somewhere to urinate in this supposedly unknown house supposedly full of unknown people. In fact, these days, I never consciously dream, or wake, except in this bizarre fashion, with clear evidence that I've dreamed.

In the afternoon we went to Bridport: strange (as we so rarely go there nowadays) how it seemed full of life and passable shops, almost Parisian – or how drab, cramped and 'closed' Lyme seemed. Eliz hates it, and every interest I take in it. She is testy these days. I carry heavy bags through the town – our shopping – and feel myself like some poor old carthorse flogged by a peasant. I don't mind, she drives us everywhere. But wish Lyme was not so petty and miserable.

I met Helen Yool yesterday, on the advisory committee over all the sea-defence and sewage fuss, which the hostile referendum has forced the WDDC to appoint. She seeks my name for some new national publicity. In truth the whole thing exhausts me. The WDDC did, I suspect, try initially to ride roughshod over the town's feelings and experience, but the way it has all shattered into fragmentary opinions, a sort of madness of would-be democracy, like a shattered mirror . . .

20 September
To dither, dithering, is the exact word to describe my state; or so I thought today. But it comes from didder, with more of the sense 'to tremble or to quiver'; related to dadder and dodder. I don't tremble, but feel mentally and psychologically frail and ineffective. I thought the other day of being some object in a stream or torrent, against which many things bumped – or it bumped against many things.

Unarresting and unarrestible.

21 September
Sarah Burnett rang in the morning. Would we go over to Stanbridge that evening to have supper with Elizabeth Frink, who was also coming? We were suspicious, such a mad late invitation. I was worried, for Eliz's driving – or hatred of it; but then, after a second call to her, we went, leaving about six-fifteen, getting there at eight, after one or two of the usual angry spats about the right road.

The Burnett house looking relaxed and expansive, Sarah it seems as burbly and inconsequent as ever, and David as bluff. He somehow always seems vaguely *déclassé*, or *dépaysé*, as if he is some young aristocrat down on his luck, but bravely struggling up again. But perhaps that is just the effect of the success of his publishing and Sarah's wool-jumper and dyeing business. They have now had a swimming-pool erected in the garden. David claims he needs it for the exercise of his bad back, but it feels a little like conspicuous consumption – doing what the well-to-do in such an area seem always to demand or claim for them-selves. At any rate, a feeling of a new wealth and comfort, of deciding to stay where they are. We must envy them that, though feel happy for them both, and that they have overcome the horror of the brain tumour operation. Eliz thought there was a new sobriety about her, under the froth.

Frink and her husband came soon after (meanwhile I had felt Sarah's skull, at her invitation, for the trepan scars), and we were more normal.

Frink is white-haired and middle-aged, in her sixties, pleasantly bluff and direct, faintly, but only faintly, mannish; perhaps only in her no-nonsense aspect. I sense a pleasing absence of vanity of any little kind. The husband is more curious, a fat, rubicund little man, vaguely horsy, it seems the son of a Hungarian countess (who turned lady's maid when she had to emigrate). Frink tolerated him, as if he amused her. He apparently has charge of her business affairs. They live at, or near, Bulbarrow.

22 September

We spent the night there, a little holiday for us, cramped though it is. I remember how large we are here in Lyme, in terms of moving about; how little ordinary houses are. A nice breakfast, talk, sunshine. We look at the swimming-pool, the garden – the *Campsis* I gave them years ago is now fat and floribund. David gives me back some side-shoots of the artichoke I gave him, also years ago. They are on rich alluvial soil, all grows well here. At last we go off, feeling we have overstayed our welcome – not from their feeling, they are kindness itself, but from that stock notion of 'good' behaviour we all live by, or under.

They create something, get somewhere, and are – or seem – content. Eliz and I are never content with what we have; want always to have something else, be something else. I would stop struggling now; Eliz never.*

1 October

An evening at the Museum, for the Listers. Mary Sybil Octavia has given Slopes Farm to the Woodland Trust, some eleven acres of what would otherwise have been prime development land, worth several million pounds. She couldn't come, but her sister Elizabeth Pryor (from the Lister-Palgrave marriage) was there and one of her daughters, also Sybil; also her son Richard. Around them the Mayor, Town Clerk, chief executive of the WDDC, engineer, various 'personalities' on that foolish ladder of local government; and the patient Listers, playing aristocracy of a kind – and one I like, since their superiority lies in their sense of public duty and their morality.

Suddenly Eliz, when I got home, and later that evening, was furious she hadn't been invited – which only that morning I'd made plain

---

*We create nothing. We never move on, we remain static. They totally rebuild & enlarge a tiny cottage. We live in a dead dying house & garden now too large & unnecessary for us. It had a life once. Now it is gone. You never saw when I suggested it happening. Contentment is nothing to do with it.

You pile up, surround yourself with meaningless objects. Letters dated 1985 on top of the pile of boxes. What do you mean you would stop struggling? Me never.

she had, but presumed, such is her scorn and hatred of Lyme, that she would reject.* In a sensible world she would have come as I did, out of amusement and curiosity; she would have liked Sybil, the local bigwiggery. The Listers were everything the eternal working classes are or were not; to lump them in with all she hates about Lyme is foolish.

7 October

To Sidmouth, with Leo. It was Eliz's birthday, her sixty-fourth; it wasn't a success, she was very depressed at the end of the day, when we were home – and quite rightly blamed me for not even buying her a bunch of flowers. Birthdays mean nothing to me, but I've no right to think they mean nothing for anyone else. For years I've asked her to buy something for herself – it is like my not driving. I am a pig. One begins by ignoring many conventions, in part to establish what one is; then realizes finally one is self-marooned, self-damned. Either one defends what one is (why one depises birthdays, conventional celebrations, all the rest) or one is martyred by it – one's own Guy Fawkes.

She went off to bed on her own, and I read *Huxley*.**

13 October

Dreadful days, quite literally. That is, one is obscurely full of a sense of dread. I think of it as *les affres*, not quite in its proper sense: what causes the general use of *affreux*, all that is shocking, rather than 'throes' or 'pangs'; *effroi*. The feeling that the world is running out of control, certainly that our health is. Eliz reads and reads, stays up half the night, I try feebly to copy her. We are not physically ill, but I feel we ought to be; or to be more precise, I know my body is wrong, not functioning properly, and sense myself waiting for something worse to strike. Like someone waiting for a military attack, an air-raid, in a kind of ominous stillness. I finished *Huxley* a night or two ago, partly discontented with him, his being surrounded by friends, knowing (or so it seems) everyone and everything, his sweet reason, his dying quietly, also with sweet reasonableness. In a way he constructed his own universe, his own reli-

---

*You did *not* make it plain at all. In a sensible world you would have asked me to come. You assume my rejection. Your silence is rejection. Always you presume. Always you say nothing. But presume.

**Yes, and you spent that day establishing what you are. It wasn't only the non-flowers, it was your 'establishing'. And my not even existing. Even if I spoke of Huxley, which I had read previously, you shout over as if your opinion – at that point unrealized. I was discounted, criticized, put down. You performed on a book you hadn't even read.

gion (though *sans* religion), to die comfortably in. He rationalized death. I die angrily, not understanding. More and more it seems eternally futile.

I cleared up for a few minutes at dusk in the garden. The holly-leaved *Osmanthus* perfuses its orange scent in the calm, mild air. A huge full moon floats in the east, a luminous white. I think of writing this, an hour later, still under the brilliant moon in my study window. Why am I so much less happy than for many years, than since – I can't remember, perhaps ever?

17 October

To London, for the first time since last April. All seems dully strange, known, but as dead; bizarrely revisited. Above all it is devitalized, I suppose some effect of the libido having gone, a desexualization of everything, less in any obvious sense than a mysterious one. There is nothing normally sexual about fields and hedgerows, but even they, this fine October day, seem grey. That is it, a greyness, as in black and white photography, compared to colour. One can see the autumn colours, but all is grey.

I feared the worst – *les affres* – for the London flat, here where I write. But it seemed untouched, just six months empty, its very unchangedness somehow vaguely sinister.

18 October

And beautiful, it is a peerless October day, not a cloud, as mild as summer. We rearranged the bedroom, cleared away dust, I washed the bathroom, in the morning. It exhausted Eliz. Her usual complaints, about how old and worn everything is. I see it with some affection. She says it was all bought when we were broke, must therefore be worthless. This is the foolish Western, bourgeois *and* capitalist view; not just that money can buy everything, but that one ought, somehow, to devote oneself to buying.*

In the afternoon I walked over Regent's Park, to the lake and the heronry. The *Eriobotrya* (loquat) where I cross the road is in flower, the mimosa round the corner in St Mark's Square budding heavily. Weather as mild and Mediterranean as this throws all normal seasons out of gear. There seemed many shovellers on the lake, and all the other duck; the wigeon and eider and exotics. A heron stands on one leg on his

---

*You did not see or understand that I bought and put that flat in order once. You had nothing much to do with it. What affection do you have about anything domestic? You are the bourgeois capitalist. You list prices. You notice foreign girls among the grebes. And all is pleasingly pastoral. Was it ever such.

nest-site, the grebe nose anxiously about, the shoveller up-end, and dibble. Foreign girls lie on the grassy banks over the water. It is pleasingly pastoral.

20 October

I read Bruce Chatwin's *Utz*. It's neatly done. His lightly worn learning, his knowledge of Meissen and middle Europe, are agreeably austere; but the whole somehow cold, unfeeling, in a sense as if by a man already dead (as he nearly was). He was too dazzled by his knowledge to see that he hadn't yet found humanity.

24 October

To Tom and Regina Maschler's new flat in 42 Eaton Place. It is on the ground floor, and in the basement a subterranean patio. It reminded me of nothing so much as a well-appointed tomb, more Roman than Etruscan. It has been expensively refurbished. Tom seems more or less to have given up with Cape, though still officially chairman. They have put in a plastic tube to bypass the suspect aorta. He says he is depressed and bored, but looks forward to seeing their grand new property in France, of which they have possession at Christmas. I can't imagine why he has let her talk him into this present grand property – it is surrounded by embassies and Belgravian façades, the high wall of prestige at every corner. He laughs, how easy it is to get service, things on appro from antique-dealers, etc., at an address like that. A flash of his old Jewish contempt (and adoration) for prestige and class. And how nice it was that most of the other tenants in the house had country-house properties and estates, so left them alone through most of summer; very *ancien régime*, such silly boasting.

25 October

I make Eliz, who is both ill and increasingly tetchy, go and see Caryle Steen at the Kentish Town Health Centre, in Bartholomew Road.* It is an august, classical day, blue and gold, very mild and genial, as well as noble. An awful taxi-ride, crawling through a traffic jam, continuous from Camden Town. The Health Centre in a once (or so one feels) passable

---

*You do not *make* me. I telephone. I make my own choice. I decide how I shall proceed on my day – who to see. You have not even a notion of who to phone or how to arrange to see a doctor in London. You are inept. But imagine yourself all powerful. After a doctor I feel I need to see an intelligent female – Fay Maschler. You walk with your feeling of freedom in a park. And criticize people for not living in the country. You do not live in the country. You potter about your garden and a seaside town. Open fields. Country. A tourist trail.

area of superior artisan houses; but now under the usual pressure of too many people – and too poorly educated. Benches in the forecourt are bound by heavy chains and padlocks to the railings. Around them, a little sea of beer-can and Coke-can tags. I can't think how people stand living in the horrors and overcrowding of the modern city, in such unfree worlds of repression; and felt it when I walked home (Eliz went to tea with Fay Maschler). Indeed had to go out over the Park, which at least has some space, some feeling of freedom with the golden setting sun and in Queen Mary's Garden, where I finally wandered.

27 October
We return to Lyme, in a sort of bad-tempered panic. Anna may come to Lyme tomorrow.* Eliz in a foul querulous temper because of her antibiotics. A crowded train, even people standing in the first-class corridors, no seats. The carriage windows filthy and, it turned out, without interior lights. This coincides with the resignation of Lawson, the feeling that the already rotten and hypocritical Tory government has now fallen into an even worse state. Apparently Tess had written a letter to Mrs Thatcher telling her she is a fascist; a sardine's nose butts a ship's bottom. I had feared the black climax of the day would be the arriving home, what had happened during all the storms while we were in London. But fate spared us that worst; another gale is blowing up, but no obvious bad leaks or tiles off.

15 November
Longwalls, the house next to Sid Abbey,** which we looked at a year or two ago. It was built in 1939, a miserable house, with 'nice' – that is, rather ghastly, limited owners.

Moore Hall, at Sidbury. This lies just behind the church, running down to the river. Two cottages run into one by some farmer. It is lived in by a New Zealand woman; a rather engaging mess, one feels she drags parts of her past life behind her; too much so, chrysalis debris clinging to the imago. A huge old basset-hound, a Japanese painting of persimmons. An alder grows from the river at the garden foot. We suspect draughts, on top of the mess.

We enjoy these house visits – or this one, if not that before. I cannot

---

*Eliz feels bloody ill. But deals with packing up one house, bags, etc. Sorting out food, clothes that need taking – washing – leaving. I leave one house – ill – but have to think of the next. Neither has life till I inject it. You imagine it. But it does not.

**Sid Abbey which *you* rejected. *We* did not. *We* did not have that option. You. I am not a 'we'.

imagine why we should move, except to answer Eliz's hatred of this house and town. The vendors, or showers, are curious: one feels nicer than normal, and reluctantly. It's a British bourgeois oddity: this embarrassment at having to sell.

17 November
Down the bottom, clearing the bamboos. There are enormous quanti-ties and they make a fierce fire; a strong west wind leaps up the slope, hungry. Peter would break and burn all, but I think I should save some. Somehow they should be given away, or sold for charity. It hurts simply to destroy. That old demon, Public Duty, at its capitalized worst. It leaves Eliz very cold;* and I, lukewarm.

20 November
Roses du Temps Passé, a catalogue of old roses from near Stafford. Leo grows some of these, and I follow this world, though hardly take part in it. In some other world, I should like to. It is one of those little booklets that lets one glimpse what one lacks, and will never have. I daydream of women like this sometimes, of women I shall never know and never 'have'; so of these charming and romantic old roses.

21 November
I scrabble after fragments, in terms of the novel; jot down faint ideas. Always I shall set to with it tomorrow, or next week. Even the intro-duction to Rattenbury I had Jean Wellings type out last week – it is still there, uncorrected and unread.[1] And all else I have timidly tried this last year. I can't imagine *doing* anything; only that I shall continue to imagine.

Eliz is not well, and can't help. I irritate her, everything about me annoys her, all connections with the town, with nature, with writing, all I once was. I love her with a kind of hopelessness; that she will ever understand what interests me, and how destructive to both of us is her resentment of everything in Lyme and my life. Her boredom with it all is flagrant. I understand where that graceless impatience in the children – whatever bars them from what they want – comes from.**

I broke off and went for a walk over Ware Cliffs, to Underhill Farm. It is terrible, the way we drift apart, not understanding what each other

---

*How do you know it leaves Eliz very cold. Did you ask?

**You understand nothing of graceless impatience in children. You know nothing about children. You are theory and non-life. Pretend 'Nature' is all.

[1] John Rattenbury (1778–1844) was a Devon smuggler from Beer. JF had been invited to write an introduction to a reprint of Rattenbury's *Memoirs of a Smuggler* (1837).

is (for she could say as much of me). That word I coined in *The Aristos*, noscentric – we make a mockery of it.

The house really seems dilapidated now; ivy clambers over the eastern end, everywhere cracks shiver up and down the walls, the old lavatory next to the greenhouse in the garden crumbles.

26 November
A crystal-clear day, quite cloudless except on the horizon, at dusk.
    Eliz gets drunk on a bottle of Bourbon we bought in Bridport on Saturday. All the old miseries, guilt over Anna, resentment over me, pour out. It erupted in all she has scrawled here; so much for which I am not forgiven. I feel she has closed against all I am, with all my faults; like a house with closed shutters, uninhabited. At one point in our row I foolishly said, like brandishing a red rag before a bull, she earned no money. Screams of rage about the money she had earned when she worked at the Medical Research Council in Hampstead, and so on. I was objecting to her use of 'my money' (when it is really our money, and truly earned from books), as if I have no right even to mention or think of it.

29 November
She doesn't care what happens, she doesn't want to live any more, and so on. All this excoriates.

4 December
We have invited ourselves to Tom and Malou's at Spéracedes for Christmas.

5 December
The rather prim physiotherapist, for hip exercises. She says I should swim. I walked into the Undercliff in the afternoon, as far as the ponds towards Pinhay. This dry, cold weather suits the path. Not a soul, nor anything there except for the occasional bumbarrel and roosting black-bird. I find this total solitude not frightening at all; but almost familiar. I prune a little with the secateurs on the path. A strange querulous yapping up the hill towards Ware Farm as I return, near enough night that the light of the half-moon casts shadows. I think, a vixen. I suppose it's something I can walk these two or three miles without much trouble; and can somehow still feel so one with this green desert; almost as if it is mine. I understand why Sarah Woodruff went there in a way I never did when I wrote the book.

6 December
Bruce Chatwin died of Aids, according to a newspaper a week ago. See what I felt about *Utz*, on October 20th. That sad, underlying cold was

homosexual, it seems. Something seems tainted, that he did not admit it. The homosexuals may argue, but not being normal in that way seems sadly to mean that the cold and lifeless will somehow always creep through, as rancidity through milk.

Why have I not turned to poetry? What keeps me in exile?

15 December

There are no lights on the Cobb tonight. There was a savage storm last night, and the electricity cable was broken. We went down earlier with Leo Smith and Minnie. The Monmouth Beach shingle broke massively through the neck of the causeway and has deposited a pile in the harbour, I reckoned at least fifty yards long, and bellying out some thirty yards.

17 December

To Exeter, the winter landscapes rather beautiful, a ghost of Corot, full of a limpid clarity, exquisitely delineated. We meet Charlie Greenberg by chance in Honiton, fiddling with his gallery. His paintings seem to me, as before, absurdly priced. He says he has sold none for four weeks now; but does not care, it is his hobby. One feels him more content at moving in the grand art-dealing world, at sounding an expert, than at anything so vulgar as making money. He has still very little taste, poor man; that is, all beauty in painting lies in what it might fetch, not what it is. He irritates us both a little, though we feel affection for him – how frequent it is that this happens, one feels the affection, but not the liking!

Exeter full of that underlying intentness of shoppers, passers, at this season; they seem faintly panic-stricken, as if they must buy, they must enjoy. We went to a new book-store, Dillons, though really there for clothes. They are beyond me, I do not care what I wear; then worry that I have nothing! Eliz does care, also finds she has nothing. She is difficult these days, like a bad-tempered, frightened cat, so quick to the spitting and the claws. We nag and accuse each other every day, then get over it; yet it's always latent. I sound angry in defence, sometimes before she even speaks.

18 December

Eliz drinks three-quarters of a bottle of sherry, in anger at me, in sympathy with Anna, who is depressed about Charles, Life, everything. All her old guilt returns; and her anger at that is indiscriminate.

19 December

A fine morning. Thrushes are singing. Quicky comes in to mend the slates on the roof, blown off in the gale. I walk round. The mimosa is heavily in bud, not so far behind that we are to see in France the next week.

To London. I start James, *The Awkward Age*, under a very grey sky. We go to the Lemonia and drink two bottles of retsina, though we have to be awake at seven-fifteen. We go in a kind of despair, almost unable to believe that some catastrophe doesn't await us.

20 December

We get early to Heathrow for our flight to Nice. We feel it wrong to be going; to be running away, and we shall be surely punished by the flu epidemic currently at Lyme. Every day waking up without the dread choking of the lungs seems some quasi-miraculous extension of grace before execution. The private taxi gets us there, a dry but dank day. Heathrow at this season is like some *cloaca maxima*, choked with people all intent on their various personal ends. We have to wait an hour, then off. The civilizedness of Air France is a pleasant surprise, or a memory. The English no longer behave like this; a kind of veneer that this is a fascist state, and you are the master-class. This goes with the other side of the French character, from the Revolution, that all men are equal, even if some are richer than others. Altogether, for all its unfairnesses, I think this makes for a better society than the British, who have had to pay for never having been through the 1789 upset with all its horrors (and virtues). The French live happily in two contradictions: that all men are equal, and that all men are free to make themselves richer than their contemporaries. The British have never been able to live with this paradox: that is what makes their archetypally Puritan selves so constantly grouse and feel uncomfortable, and why they can never enjoy what pleasure life has, but must always show they are unsatisfied and ill at ease.

Nice, the neatly barbered palm-trees outside the airport, the warm air. Malou. It is nice to see her and her *maloutisme* after so many months, but by the end she was exhausting us, Eliz especially. She seems to live on an almost permanent 'high', some excessive thyroid activity. She lives on her nerves, clatter, clatter, clatter, and ours also. But at this point we are grateful she has invited us and her busyness takes over. It is like dropping into a mountain torrent, being carried away by it. Only, after a day or two, one starts wondering where one is being rushed, hurtled pell-mell, like this.

I go off with Tom and we walk on some lane from Spéracedes towards Cabris; a mild grey evening, the lights of the plain softly twinkling below. He has to revise his thriller for the American publisher, and they have now hired a flat in the Place de Vosges at Paris. He strides faster than I am used. We talk of Rushdie. I feel I ought to say how grateful we are to be here, like poor relations; yet also feel I'm supposed to be a more 'important' writer despite my mentally limp and wounded state. It seems he can hardly realize I am any different from when we first knew each other.

21–22 December

Days disintegrate, flow into one another. We go with Malou one day so she can attend her lecture course, on Plato, at Nice or Palmtreeville. Fine at this time of year, their pinnate fronds bursting in elegant spumes, like black fireworks, against the light.

The generally birdless skies here are a tragedy, which few realize. In the garden the *Ophrys* (*fusca*) are fatly and greenly in leaf on the third terrace down. I mark them with olive twigs, as I do those up by the front of the house (I suspect of a different species). There also the first narcissi are just about to open their white petals: delicious. They did so on Christmas Day, and I knelt every day to smell that entrancing perfume.

Each day a blue sky, quite extraordinarily mild – we breakfasted and lunched out of doors almost always. It finally honours the reputation of this little *coin* under Cabris. The sea past Cannes golden in the sun. Scabious, wild pink and many other plants still in bloom. We watch the TV every night, the death-agonies of the Ceauşescu regime in Rumania; and one night Terry Gilliam's *Brazil*, an imitation of Orwell's *1984* – and also of *Metropolis*. The lights of Cabris high above shine through the little windows beside the fire, outdoing the constellations. I walked up there on the lane west with Boris and Malou one afternoon; a lovely smell of oak-leaves and pines.

28 December

We pack. It is fine again, after yesterday's hiccough. The white narcissi are now all out. Malou takes us into Grasse, *maloutante* worse than ever, dashing here, dashing there, changing her mind. Tom in his room, endlessly working. This marvellous spell of weather has been such a pleasure. I am grateful to them for that; their faults and foibles seem small beside it, for me dissolve into nothing beside the warmth and the light. I feel I should fall on my knees in gratitude that they have borne with us, that we've been permitted to foist ourselves on them. And of course, don't.

I buy a Calvados and a Suze, Eliz her cigarettes. The plane is not full, and I rather enjoy the meal and little bottle of champagne. But at Heathrow, no valise. They think it will have gone to Frankfurt. 'That's usually what happens when things go adrift at Nice.' In anger, a need to mortify ourselves, we catch an airport bus to Baker Street. We end sitting sourly in a pub in Gloucester Road, drinking bitter.

29 December

A cold, dank, grey reality. The death of light is the hardest to suffer. I fetch some milk. The road is full of playing-cards, wildly scattered all over the street.

The suitcase comes, about midday. No explanation.

31 December

To lunch with Fay and Mary Coventry, her mother. Her new lover Owen, a sociologist at one of the polytechnics, was there. He reminded me of John Kohn, a tall, both sharp and easy, very American American; not like him, in that he seemed left-wing, critical of England and its establishment, and anti-monarchical. She tossed together her usual fine little lunch for us; an excellent Sancerre and champagne.

2 January 1990

Back to Lyme. We catch a bus back from Axminster station, there being no taxis; and have to walk, lugging our bags and valise, from the Mariners to Belmont. There seems nothing changed, to our surprise and relief. The *Urginea* has grown longer leaves. I repotted it just before we left.

3 January

The poverty of this town, of provincial England, is a shock, after La Vallière and that southern corner of France. Even a little village like Peymeinade seems incredibly luxurious by comparison. Here is like somewhere from the Gulag Archipelago.

8 January

A very unclouded, mild day, like those we had in France. The birds I see, longtails, a nuthatch, even magpies and crows, have the unreality of illustration, unnaturally beautiful. We went to Axminster in the afternoon, and came back via Musbury; a splendid sunset, the sky washed with pink, some sombre brownish purple, with very delicate cloud, vermiculated, like sandbank ripples, standing high where the sky is clear, very pale blue and a light-filled green.

Eliz felt ill, and was grumpy, all day long. It distresses me that she never takes a step into the garden, and misses all this, the winter-sweet, the lovely weather, the way Lyme acquires a pale almost Piero-like quality and light on such days.

11 January

Another excoriating spat with Eliz; her bad temper, hatred of everything to do with me, reduces me to silence. It is partly her anger at England, and Lyme, after France; which I share. This truly is a wretched country. (I think Lady Dee should understand this through food. The misery the eternally puritan English condemn themselves to.) But to blame it on me, or that we live here, that I tolerate this 'miserable' town, still have some interest in it . . .

She went off alone to Axminster to shop, which she said was 'boring and miserable'. I went for a walk over Ware Cliffs, then up the steps to Chimney Rock, bramble- and ivy-shrouded. The Cobb, visible at times of the year like this (normally the top branches of one of the huge old ashes on the slope block the view), half-coiled like a fat grey serpent – it is at its best from this angle, still a strangely man-made thing poking out from the woods and fields. What a shock it must have been centuries ago, to see it projecting there, like a space-machine out of wildness.

At the top I went over the stile to the field west, and on for two fields more, filled with Allhusen's sheep. I looked for Jones' Chair, but could not see it, despite the bare trees. Patches of warm amber and golden mist over the sea down towards Torbay, until I came to near Pinhay. There is a bad dump of old sacks and cans in the first field after the one with the Chimney Rock upper path. In that field, two ewes with their lambs. I held out my hand, or finger, to one. Eager, febrile sucking; it was quite unafraid, the rasping of weak little teeth. It still touches, the innocence of lambs; their engaging greed.

13 January
Another very mild day, blue-skied. We could have eaten out-of-doors as we did in France if Eliz had not been feeling ill. She went to the doctor, Becker, who diagnosed spondylosis. We sleep, these days, in different rooms. She claims her pain and insomnia will wake me; but not knowing her beside me wakes me even worse. The thrushes and blackbirds singing in the garden: they suddenly seemed far sadder than usual, yet more intensely poetic. I had been getting a huge old pine stem up from beside the path down to the bottom terrace, and suddenly this seemed close to these avian voices. Who had planted that long-vanished tree? All those, long dead, who must have known it. Is it heard by those dead as it is by the living? All of me says no. It isn't that I suddenly believe in the possibility of an after-life; just some strange delicate sense of the wistful sadness of birdsong; of being dead so long, and not hearing it. The acute reality it must have had for so many pasts. Yet they can't have heard it quite as we do now, so stripped of past illusions and myths, so standing against doom. More a harbinger of that than symbol of sweet hope.

18 January
Another very fine day. Eliz in pain with her spondylosis and constipation. We went yesterday to Sidmouth to look at a new bed. They can't promise

one before a month. Today, when she tried to get a doctor's appointment, not before Monday. The weather may be superb, but the way society runs, not. It frays at the edges, badly.

23 January

I turned down the Vice-chancellor of East Anglia today, who offered an honorary doctorate. I suppose I owe the offer to Malcolm Bradbury. But alas, the salesman has taken over literature: that is, sales values – which is like the Midas touch. Everything or anything that might increase public success contaminates; from the money obtained to the academic honour.

I had an idea I'd have counted exciting in the past – of telling *In Hellugalia* as much by footnotes as by main text; the one expanding the other, contradicting it, confusing it. Not so much contradicting the main story, as countering it; like two contrasting melodies in symphonic music.

27 January

Washing a tiny dead spider down the sink. It wasn't even 'worth' looking at – long dead, perhaps some linyphid. But as I did it, I thought suddenly, acutely and vividly, of the human parallel; of being washed into oblivion down a sink. I think evolution must count nothing of memory, of being remembered, important feature though it is in our lives. It would have been nothing in that minute shrivelled cadaver. Can we imagine being man without memory, even the most primitive recalling powers, let alone the highly sophisticated manner of it (as in great art) we humans now exhibit? But what would 'evolution' care of it? Nothing.

I was in Axminster shopping yesterday with Eliz, and we were briefly parked in the Square. As we went round it to come home, a woman in the doorway by the bus-stop. I did not even look at her, or see her properly. I couldn't describe her accurately, indeed in any way at all, even if my life depended on it. Yet I went home with a sort of consolation; that I still had the power to describe her if I wanted; that is, to *use her in fiction*; which isn't at all to describe her in a police sense, literally or photographically. It is that I could still 'use' the world, though I've written no fiction properly these last two years.

Today I tried to say this; that I can 'fictionalize'. I failed miserably; and yet not quite so. That I knew I failed was a kind of proof.

29 January

Foul winds. They drive poor Eliz mad. I went out this afternoon in driving rain, down to the Cobb; savage gusts of wind, that particular blend of livid grey-white sea, black-silhouetted trees and angry wind that

Tom Adams caught so well in the flypapers for *The FLW*. The shingle comes over the causeway again. I stopped out of the wind in that corner by the end of the Cobb hamlet. Twenty or thirty wagtails on that filthy beach in the lee. Neat and dapper little birds, rather frivolous, rejected in such weather. Out at sea a razorbill or guillemot flies into the teeth of the wind, then lands (curious we have no word for coming down on water) in the lee of the North Wall. Misery. The world is galed out of existence.

2 February

The surgeon specialist, Mr Jeffery, sees Eliz at Martinstown. Eliz feels she can't drive, Peter takes us over. I'd rather I paid him to take us over than a taxi. It is a straggly village, in a shallow combe bottom. Peter and I go and look at the church while she waits. It is rather dull, one from which first the Puritans, then the Victorian restorers, took all charm. I think of the lovely old painted churches along the Loire; mutilated ghosts here. Two pillars on which once stood saints' statues; the arcade of a Norman quadrangular font, in whose arches figures would once have stood. A mournful churchyard in the dusk.

Jeffery can find nothing certain; she must have a barium meal X-ray on the 9th. We come home, then one of those idiotic and vindictive spats that are a sad feature of our life these days. Everything I do irritates her, everything she says irritates me. This is a bad time for both of us, I see no point in bitter resentment and almost willed misunderstanding. We should cling, and aim at some sort of common sense. Instead we fling apart, and make bad worse.

3 February

Eliz in pain all the time. It is not clear if it is the back or the bowels. She sleeps poorly and intermittently; eats almost nothing, reads nothing, takes no exercise. She remains eternally querulous, on the brink of complaining, near despair. We walked briefly over the car park, she can't face going downhill, because of the punishing walk back. We eat scraps of food. Yet she has moments of self-concern, even of a sort of humour and excitement about life, with other people. It is as if I am the cause. She keeps some at least of her old interest in books and writers; yet cannot bear any sign of that literary side of life in me, the occasional letters and academic things. This is our worst winter.

8 February

Eliz preparing for her barium-meal X-ray tomorrow. In despair last night. This afternoon we walked over the car park. The weather has suddenly turned mild after the wind and rain; the daffodils and camellias are out. There is the awful feeling that we only just survive; that if I fall ill – no friends, nothing between us and disaster. The sea is still lumpy after the storm, but the coast of Lyme Bay benign. She manages twice round the car park.

11 February

Anna down for the day. She cooked us a chicken, one of the few hot meals I've enjoyed in this bad time. Eliz is a grizzleguts, repelling all good will – or the good will one wants to feel. This illness drives her into a *noli-me-tangere* state. Or, that all offends her. My domestic clumsiness infuriates her. The barium meal X-ray and enema did not satisfy the radiologist. We shall hear next week. The trouble, to me, is the bewildering symptoms: first, of some back problem; second of something intestinal – she claims to have been in agony all this last week (I write on the 15th); and lastly, of the chest, the old emphysema problem. We have to go to Exeter to see yet another specialist, about this last, next week. Peter has driven us twice to Dorchester; now I'm getting Brian Hayball, Julie the hairdresser's husband, to take us. Being ill is expensive.

17 February

I walked out past Underhill Farm yesterday; and today have twinges of gout, for my pains. The crow I saw some weeks ago, seemingly a first-year bird, is definitely a partial albino; some odd very pale brown, like weak milky coffee, primaries. There are cracks in the road just beyond Clitden – only a half-inch or so across, but ominous.

19 February

Vini took a blood test yesterday. Low potassium levels, and a poor platelet count. He took another test this morning. The potassium seems better, but the platelets dangerously low. She has had severe nose-bleeding all morning, he thinks a result of the blood-clotting powers, or rather the loss of them, in the platelets. He thinks she should go now into the Royal Devon, and have a transfusion, and proper investigation from a haematologist.

20 February

Peter took us in to see Siddorn, the chest specialist, in Exeter. He was shocked by Eliz's appearance, and bullied the Wonford into finding a hospital bed, where we took her. And eventually left her, getting back to Lyme about four. Anna and the children had already arrived from Bristol.

21 February

Black Day. Tess was ill in the night, Anna up with her. We get Leo Smith to come over to sit with Tess; then off to Exeter. Eliz lying wan and sickly in bed. They have given her a blood transfusion. Siddorn asks to see me.

A Chinese-looking houseman stops me: he says the news is bad and goes and fetches in Siddorn, who takes me into a waiting-room. They took a bone-marrow sample yesterday to try to discover why the platelet count is so low. It was riddled with cancer. They do not know the primary source outside the marrow; perhaps the stomach. At worst she could have a fortnight to live. He agrees I should get another opinion, and will arrange for it. The future: I say I should like her, if die she must, back in Lyme; that I want to tell her the truth. He agrees that I should in a day or two, when all the investigations have taken place; and Lyme, if proper nursing can be arranged. I want to cry, and cannot; for hours on the 'dangerous' brink of bursting into tears. I go back to her, keep touching her poor, pasty body with its blood speckling round the ankles, its phlebitic-looking purple patches on the legs. Her grey eyes watch me, already (I feel, and Siddorn also guesses so) half-suspecting something terrible is wrong. I keep patting her wrist and leg, I want to sob, but can't, with William there, and Anna still not knowing. We walk into the city to Clare's restaurant, where I went yesterday with Peter. I am silent, stunned, like some boxer knocked out, though still on his feet. It is a beautiful sunny spring day; crocuses, daffodils. Everything without colour, flavour, any reality. The impotence already seemed half a death; this, far worse. We go back to the hospital, and leave her. I ask if she would like some champagne splits, as she jokingly said the other day that she would. Am I mad? What would she want with champagne in the public ward of a hospital like that? She is shrewd enough to know I wouldn't have brought that up unless I were hiding bad news from her.

We drive back to Lyme in the lovely afternoon, along the coast road. Anna wants to know. I say, '*Pas devant les enfants*', with William listening in the back. But he begins feeling car-sick as we go over Haldon. We stop in the car park. And then at last, as he is busy throwing stones in a muddy puddle, I tell Anna. Who cries, we cling together. I had smelt just before the lovely warm scent of a gorse bush. That is the agony, constant: that my other half will never know. It does not exist, if she will never know. This beautiful afternoon, these calm green vistas; a kestrel, a crow with a nesting twig in its beak, a thousand things. Even though, when she was here, and for a long time now, she had no interest in such matters; or at least it had to be unusual for me to break through my reluctance to stimulate her out of indifference.

Such days, one dies also. I cursed God, to Siddorn; who said, wise man, that that was not much good. I said I agreed, and was really a Darwinian. That there was no 'God', so cursing him had no point.

22 February
We go in again, and I see Siddorn a second time; also the oncologist, on whom I had insisted, for a second opinion. He is an East African Indian,

dry, a touch on his dignity, called Amin. He can offer no help, and is against surgery and the usual therapies. The cancer is probably in the liver. Siddorn thinks I must tell her now. She has developed jaundice. So Anna and I are put with her in another waiting-room. I break down, Anna sobs. Eliz herself is the most normal. 'I can't believe it, I can't believe it, this isn't real, it's not happening.' We get her back to bed, then walk out in the sunshine round the north of the hospital, Clifton Hill, in the end back to the city centre; go to Boots, buy some orange-juice and sandwiches, then sit on the edge of the rockery in Princesshay, like very poor tourists. It seems madness, everything is madness. I walk back alone to the hospital, where eventually they return. Children are a kind of cumbersome and appalling irrelevance on occasions like this: that you cannot tell them what has happened, that they have to have their little egos pleased. I sense that Tess realizes that something awful has happened, but William (or so it seems) has not. We stop in the breeze and sunshine on Woodbury Common, as yesterday, and they fly some kite they have made, Tess more intelligently than William. Who plays his silly-buggers self, constantly crashing it, attempting to seem the master of it. Home, in a sort of nightmare. It can't be true, it can't have happened.

Last night I had rung Denys and Monica; and sobbed, I was incoherent. The awful choking realization of what has happened. It takes one's breath away.

23 February

I go in alone. She is asleep, terrible deep breaths, the wretched stomach heaving. I sit beside her, resting my hand on her two, crossed on her stomach. They have moved her bed into another branch of the Hurst ward; awful chattering old people. She grimaces when she wakes, not realizing how long she has slept; and how awful the place is. Just before I left Lyme with Brian Hayball, Siddorn had rung, saying that they think her form of cancer is amenable to chemotherapy, and they want to try that. It can sometimes 'respond' and allow months of remission, though fatal relapses may occur at the end of it and there are unpleasant side-effects. This therapy must be done at Exeter. I take it as at least a real glimmer of hope, though he warns it may cause nausea and hair-loss, among other things. But then, while I am there beside her, the little Chinese houseman comes in and explains they are now not so sure of the identification of the tumour, apparently usually associated with the lungs (the liver being a secondary infection). It mimics another form, violently antipathetic to the treatment. Science, science, science.

24 February

We went to the Heavitree to bring her home. Anna travelled in the ambulance with her. Siddorn was in the ward with her when we got there. They have started the chemotherapy, though without much hope. She is riddled with 'secondary' cancer, it seems.

Lady Dee. Her companion must die like this, not as I have it in the draft: the numbing horror of the reality seems worse than the worst Gestapo callousness and cruelty, or whatever I gave her.

26 February
I drift, hopeless and useless, through the days. Anna has taken over all the nursing, has taken command, in effect. I have woken in the night sometimes, thinking this has been a nightmare; and now I am awake I will remember it doesn't exist. Then truly wake: the nightmare is the reality. The awful fictional imagination also plagues me. I foresee a thousand things about after she is dead – my mind somehow leaps that Becher's Brook as if it does not, shall not, exist. I find it impossible to talk to her when I am in our room; or only the stupidest trite nothings. Never about what is the reality of the situation, even what people must suppose is its reality: that all one's thoughts must be on death, the not being any more. Perhaps some mercy keeps us tongue-tied, mute. 'I can't talk, I can't talk.' She has flashes of her old humour, pawky dryness, piercing a sort of numbness, still as if she doesn't quite realize what has happened.

Anna is a great consolation and an excellent practical nurse. I think of all Eliz's ancient guilt and worry over her, my own occasional cynicism and anger over what Anna does or has done, the wretched coldness between the children and me. I have judged her by the absurd standards of the well-to-do middle classes, Oxbridge; everything she does these days disproves that. She carries so little of the bad seed in both Eliz and Roy.

Somehow she is a regaining of balance in evolution, a not conforming with immediate expectation.

1 March
Death, death, death. I cannot believe it. Anna slept with her last night, she was in pain, I went to the hospital to get a stronger shot of diamorphine. Soon after the little nurse Nimmi came, and decided to put her on a morphine pump. A fine March day, sunshine. She begins what I think of as the breathing of the dying; in a sort of coma, head thrown back, mouth wide open, erratic gasping swallows of air. That sucking of air is heartbreaking, terrible. I still feel I am experiencing *my* loss, not truly living here. We mistake sickness and death, the passing anxiety of the first, the gigantic enormity of the last. I feel that second close, that she is struggling literally for life. Somehow this kind of death wears the face of the plump little East African Indian nurse Nimmi; I doubt what she is doing. Feeding her constant morphine: that is, I suspect they are

deliberately putting her to sleep; yet must allow it. Mike Hudson comes to take me to lunch down at the Alexandra. We sit next to Alec Britton and Kellaway, talking about geology. Mike makes me talk about myself. He imagines Denys was her husband. I talk, in the end we return.

She lies with open mouth, still stertorously breathing; an awful cadaverous look about her. Denys and Monica arrive from Shropshire. I telephoned them yesterday evening. We cannot take them up, though Monica goes and kisses her; but she now neither hears nor recognizes anyone. Just lies there, mouth agape, with that awful wheezing breath. Later about five, I sit alone with her for an hour, trying to wake her for a moment by pressing her hand, damping her face. I watch the trawlers coming in, on a livid grey-green sea, every tiny detail clear. A huge tanker passes on the horizon. Mike told me he had had a patient who survived four months like this, on a morphine pump. I put the radio on. She makes a strange sound, half like a groan, but does not respond when I kiss her, I press her hand, fuss with her nightgown and bedclothes. I wish it were over, yet I dread its being over. I went downstairs about seven in the evening, and Denys went up to keep the vigil. But he soon came down, saying he did not like the shallowness of her breathing. Anna and I went up. There were no more great sighs of the breathing, a fatal stillness. I looked for any sign, Anna tried to find her pulse. Then we both started to sob.

It is the bitter speed and tiger-spring suddenness of it all that is so savagely incredible. She has gone in just ten days from Siddorn's first announcement to me. Some insane hope – it seems in retrospect more like an idiocy – believed it was indeed not real, that at some point she would smile, sit up, I don't know – anything but not let it end here. The absolute end of everything. Only that morning she had made some of her little jokes. 'What a fuss.' 'What a nuisance I am.' I must go now and help Anna sort out some trousers in the flat. Now her flesh grows cold, I realize she is gone for ever. It is the enormity, the stupendous enormity, of death; one may read about it, imagine it, think it – but all are hopelessly trivial beside this reality. My poor Eliz there, dead. I make a strange noise, half sob, half growl of rage. What did she say? 'This isn't real, this isn't real, it's not happening to me.'

All is changed.

2 March

Anna has just been comforting me in the kitchen, I started crying as I wrote this; that overpowering knowledge that she will never be here again. Our life seemed incomplete. Anna is glad her suffering is over, she had 'never been the same' over this last year. Which is true. I think of her endless tetchiness and bad temper, only a small fraction of which I have written about here – yet still the enormity of what has now happened. She will never be here again. It is as simple to write as it is impossible to believe.

I cut a lock of her hair, of that fine ashy blonde, the day after she died, before they took the body away; and stole a coloured thread of Anna's embroidery bits to bind it, that was lying on the round table we brought up when she came back, to die, from Exeter.

All that was wrong, this last year, or years, disappears.

Anna took the children back to Bristol yesterday evening. I have passed my first night alone. Of revenants I have no fear; I should be so lucky, that she should return. I watched the television in the evening; at one moment nodded off – my sleep routine is quite changed, I live under Kalms, I wake each day at six-thirty or seven – and waking with a start did what I always used to, glanced across to see if Eliz had noticed, since my dozing before the television always annoyed her. Fully awake, I know she isn't there; but less than that awakeness, I forget. This and countless other tiny things are the agony: that Anna lives 'differently' in the kitchen – pots, knives, spoons, plates are not in quite the same places. I cannot mind, obviously, when she is so helpful; but it disturbs my soul, that the old order, that compromise by which we lived – her yearning for cleanliness and order fighting with her apathy, her profound suspicion-belief that nothing matters. That last was somehow at the root of her working-classness, that is, she used her instinctive knowledge of that, almost a folk-knowledge (which brings it near the 'wisdom' of some sages), to give the underlying purpose and point to her nose for the pretentious and the posing. Her dream, always for more simplicity. She never forgave it in me, and usually even less in anyone else.

3 March

My watch stopped last night. It needed a new battery. A beautiful early spring day. I went with Charles, who was here, to Richards' watchshop, to get a new battery. Banal chit-chat; which relieves, and maddens. Why is the whole world not choking with sobs?

5 March

Anna rang from Bristol. *The Times* has got the announcement wrong. Elizabeth Sowles died, not Fowles. They will put it correctly tomorrow.

I telephone my mother in Redcar; Hazel had already told her. She is upset, poor old thing; and sounds, with her slurred speech, completely sozzled on whisky – equally poor old thing. Tom Maschler also rings. I am to go to France when they open their house.

When did Eliz write this? The girlchild is Anna. I think this was many years ago. It turned up among her papers this morning.

eating an orange in front of the fire
watching its peel caught up in flame

I remember charcoal
oranges
Greek winter sun and a girlchild's name

I didn't know then that
alone
alone
is always the same

eating an orange in front of a fire
I watch the peel in the flame.

I am reminded of charcoal
oranges
and greek winter sun

it was a sadder happier time

Index